Quite Ready to be Sent Somewhere: The Civil War Letters of Aldace Freeman Walker

Edited by Tom Ledoux

Contact Tom Ledoux, the editor, at webmaster@vermontcivilwar.org.

Printed in Victoria, Canada

National Library of Canada Cataloguing in Publication

Walker, Aldace F. (Aldace Freeman), 1842-1901
Quite ready to be sent somewhere : the Civil War letters of Aldace Freeman Walker / edited by Thomas J. Ledoux.
Includes bibliographical references and index.
ISBN 1-55369-394-9
1. Walker, Aldace F. (Aldace Freeman), 1842-1901--Correspondence.
2. United States--History--Civil War, 1861-1865--Artillery operations.
3. United States--History--Civil War, 1861-1865--Campaigns.
4. United States. Army. Vermont Brigade, 1st (1861-1865)--Biography.
5. United States--History--Civil War, 1861-1865--Personal narratives.
6. United States. Army--Officers--Correspondence.
I. Ledoux, Thomas J., 1950- II. Title.
E467.1W15A4 2002 973.7'81 C2002-901562

TRAFFORD

This book was published *on-demand* in cooperation with Trafford Publishing.
On-demand publishing is a unique process and service of making a book available for retail sale to the public taking advantage of on-demand manufacturing and Internet marketing.
On-demand publishing includes promotions, retail sales, manufacturing, order fulfilment, accounting and collecting royalties on behalf of the author.

Suite 6E, 2333 Government St., Victoria, B.C. V8T 4P4, CANADA
Phone 250-383-6864 Toll-free 1-888-232-4444 (Canada & US)
Fax 250-383-6804 E-mail sales@trafford.com
Web site www.trafford.com TRAFFORD PUBLISHING IS A DIVISION OF TRAFFORD HOLDINGS LTD.
Trafford Catalogue #02-0207 www.trafford.com/robots/02-0207.html

10 9 8 7 6 5 4 3

In Memory of Mrs. Rhoda Walker Teagle.

Contents

Preface

The "Vermont in the Civil War" Internet project (www.vermontcivilwar.org) is a grassroots attempt to document the Green Mountain State's participation in the War of Rebellion. Its amazing growth and continued success since its inception in early 1996 has been the direct result of hundreds of descendants, private collectors, re-enactors and amateur historians who have been willing to share their personal or professional collections of memorabilia with others. Among the first to contribute to the project was Mary "Muffy" Moore, who sent a copy of "The Vermont Brigade in the Shenandoah Valley" written by her great-grandfather, Aldace Walker, who served in the First Artillery, Eleventh Vermont Volunteers. A few months later Muffy asked if the project would like to use his Civil War letters. I already had a few dozen letters, from a number of other contributors, but was more than happy to accept a few more. I just was not ready for what we were about to get!

Initially Muffy just sent us a list of the dates and locations of the letters, all 288 of them! An older transcript of the letters, single-spaced on legal-sized paper, had filled 305 pages. Her son-in-law, Dave Robinson, had retranscribed the letters from the original transcript, and compared them with the original letters, held by Muffy's mother, the late Mrs. Rhoda Walker Teagle, of Woodstock, Vermont, Aldace's granddaughter.

I was extremely pleased, to say the least, but when I started to read them, I found myself in a serious quandary. The letters were far too valuable to put on the website as it existed at the time. I felt they needed to be formally published! After a lot of deliberation and procrastination on both sides, the family and I agreed that the letters needed to be published. In keeping with the grassroots spirit of the project, all profits from the sale of the publication of these letters will be contributed to battlefield restoration.

This is the first non-Internet publishing effort by "Vermont in the Civil War."

In order to focus on Aldace Walker's letters to his family I have omitted a few letters to the editor of various Vermont newspapers that were included with the original letters and included in the original transcript. (These letters have been published on the website).

I standardized the spelling of place names Walker used inconsistently (Opequon vice Opequan, etc.). Where surnames are at variance with published rosters, I left Walker's spelling in the text, but endnotes use the spellings from therosters, e.g., Walker used Salisbury, the rosters spell it Salsbury; Walker used Fullam, the rosters spell it Fullham, etc. Finally, in order to meet the strictures of modern publishing, a few paragraphs, salutations and closings have been merged, or separated, but no wording has intentionally been changed.

All names, dates, ranks and units listed for Vermont soldiers in the endnotes are from Peck's Revised Roster, the 1864-1866 Adjutant General's Reports, and the Adjutant General's Burial Indexes, unless otherwise indicated.

Acknowledgements

My greatest debt is to the late Mrs. Rhoda Walker Teagle, who preserved her grandfather's letters and was willing to share them, as well as other material that helped put this project together. My biggest regret is that we did not complete this project prior to her passing last fall. I'm also especially grateful to her daughter, Muffy, for sharing the letters, photographs and the family genealogical information. Thanks also to David Robinson, Muffy's son-in-law, for his fastidious transcription of Aldace's letters.

Thanks to Don Wickman and Jim Fuller, for pre-reading the manuscript. Thanks to Don, also, for copies of Aldace's service record, for putting me on the track of the picture of Walker in uniform and for additional documentary support.

Ed Italo's impressive collection of 1st Vermont Brigade materials provided the photographs of some of the soldiers Walker mentions in his letters. Nick Picerno shared information on Kimball Union Academy and its Civil War veterans, including the school's general catalog to help identify Walker's KUA classmates, and a rare photograph of Aldace Walker in uniform.

Thanks also to Tony O'Connor, Vermont Civil War Enterprises, for reprinting many of Vermont's Civil War books originally published in the 1800s, which are difficult to find and expensive in their original editions. They aided greatly in my research. I am also grateful to National Park Service Guide Ron Harvey Jr., who shared his knowledge of Fort Stevens and the other forts in the defenses of Washington.

Tyler Resch at the Bennington Museum, Hans Raum, at the Starr Library at Middlebury College and Paul Carnahan at the Vermont Historical Society, provided unique materials from their respective archives and support and guidance on where materials existed.

I am also indebted to Drs. Benjamin Franklin Cooling III, Ed Hagerty, Barry Shollenberger and Charles White, graduate program instructors at American Military University, Manassas, Virginia; their wise counsel and instruction on the deeper subjects of the Civil War made it easier for me to decipher some of Aldace's comments and references.

Finally, my thanks to my step-daughter, Wendi Florio, who created the basic design for the cover. The background text is from Walker's "The Vermont Brigade in the Shenandoah Valley, 1864," impressions she got from reading his letters, and Walt Whitman's "As toilsome I wander'd," originally published in 1865 in "Drum Taps," and later one of the twelve poems in "Leaves of Grass."

While all of the above contributed greatly to this effort, all errors of print, interpretation, ommission and grammar are mine alone.

Introduction

They came from 216 towns, from every county, from every corner of their beloved Green Mountain State. They came from Canada, Massachusetts, Maine, and New Hampshire. They came more than 1,300 strong, and added an additional 1,000 to their ranks over the next three years, making their regiment the largest organization contributed to the war effort by the state of Vermont, with an aggregate of 2,320 men. They lost 73 men killed in action, another 79 who died of wounds. They lost 210 to disease, 175 who died in Confederate prisons, and two who died in accidents. And, regrettably, 124 deserted. These were the men of the First Artillery, Eleventh Regiment Vermont Volunteers.[1]

But the "Heavies," as they came to be known, have been pretty much ignored since the war. In the backwaters on the northern side of the Defenses of Washington during the first part of the war; few paid much attention to them. Later, attached to the First Vermont Brigade, they are rarely mentioned as a part of that unit, except by one of their own,[2] even though they participated in and suffered through all of the major actions the brigade witnessed in the last year of the war, from Spotsylvania to Appomattox. It is well past time to rectify this serious omission, and Aldace Walker's letters are one giant step in that direction.

Aldace Freeman Walker, eldest son of Congregational minister, the Reverend Aldace and Mary Ann Baker Walker, was born in West Rutland, Vermont, on May 11, 1842. His ancestry has been traced back to Samuel Walker, who arrived in the Massachusetts Bay colony sometime prior to 1643. The family moved to Connecticut, and finally settled in Vermont around 1800.

Educated in local Rutland schools, Aldace followed in his father's footsteps, attending Kimball Union Academy,[3] in Meriden, New Hampshire.[4] Following his graduation from KUA in 1858, Aldace Walker entered Middlebury College at the age of 16, the youngest member of his class. He participated in sports; he enjoyed singing and was a member of the school's quintet club; he was a devout Christian, and a member of the Philadelphian Society, a religious organization that had been part of campus life since 1804.[5]

In 1901, President Ezra Brainerd of Middlebury College, who had been two years behind Walker at the college, remembered him as

> The best scholar in a class of 21 men, many of whom have attained to distinction in professional life . . . [h]e was not a laborious student, one who had to drudge over his books, but he mastered his lessons quickly and easily, displaying even at that early age the alertness of mind and the rapidity of forming judgments that characterized his subsequent professional career.[6]

But that professional career would have to wait. The Civil War interfered, and like many other young Vermonters of his time, Walker was eager to get involved.

He had apparently tried to enter the service for almost year before graduating, and had actually enlisted, been commissioned as a First Lieutenant in the Eleventh Infantry and was drilling his company at the time of his graduation as valedictorian of the Middlebury College class of 1862.[7]

> On commencement day, when he was to graduate . . . he was still in camp. . . . The graduating exercises went forward until all the class had spoken, except Walker, who had not yet appeared. The president called for music. All eyes were turned toward the door, fearful lest the exercises should close without the farewell addresses from the young soldier. At the last moment, he entered the church in his new uniform and with quick strides stepped upon the platform. The cheers and enthusiasm of that large audience were unbounded. The oration and the farewells were spoken in an earnest and impressive manner never to be forgotten by those who heard him, and the thoughtful student, after his four years of college, stepped at once into the arena of active life and began that career of public service which has made his name known and honored throughout the land.[8]

Walker was commissioned First Lieutenant, Company B, on August 13, 1862, the same day he graduated from Middlebury College, and mustered into the United States service on September 3rd at Camp Bradley, in Brattleboro, Vermont. In his first extant letter, he claims "life here is somewhat monotonous, and it would be rather hard to invent material for a very long daily letter," but he managed quite nicely over the next three years. In fact, historian Benjamin Franklin Cooling III, who has written several books on the defenses of Washington and Jubal Early's 1864 raid, indicates Walker's letters were the best "account of the 'life and times' of junior officers in the wartime defenses of Washington."[9] In this editor's humble opinion, Walker did not do so badly chronicling the regiment's active combat period either!

Before the regiment was officially sworn into Federal service, Walker was occasionally Senior Lieutenant of Guard. He had to make sure that "the posts are right, the orders understood and executed, the prisoners kept in order, the various reliefs fed, and order maintained generally throughout the camp,"[10] a fairly strenuous task for a young lad just out of college. But he seemed to think he was well-fitted to be a leader of men, telling his father he found that he had "considerable scold in me, as I found out when I blew the company up last night for turning out in a dilatory manner for dress parade. At the next roll call we were the first company through."[11]

The daily humdrum of camp life in Vermont continued until September 1, 1862, when the unit was officially mustered in as the Eleventh Vermont Infantry Regiment. One week later, the regiment entrained for Washington, arrived four days later, and settled into their new home, Fort Lincoln,[12] on September 11th. The regiment was here to fight, and they thought they might have an early introduction to some active campaigning:

> We found a great deal of excitement in Philadelphia and Baltimore about Jackson, and with good reason. Fort Lincoln is on the railroad (or near it) to Baltimore, about four or five miles out of the city. It is the center (headquarters) of a string of earthworks, some dozen, seven miles in extent, under command of Col. Gibson of a Pa. Regiment. There is a regiment or so, I suppose, in camp near each, and the line is quite strong. It is really the advance now, for there are strong expectations that Jackson will turn up on the railroad near Bladensburg, two or three miles from here, within reach of three of the posts, and if he presses toward the city from this direction, he will go within half a mile of us. So there is a possibility of something to do.[13]

But nothing came of it, and the regiment settled down in its new digs, and started "constructing rifle pits and ... building a fort."[14]

Walker kept his father, mother and sister Mary[15] fully informed of his activities with long, informative letters, almost invariably twice a week while he was stationed in the Defenses of Washington, between September 1862 and mid-May 1864. From comments in his letters, he also maintained a voluminous correspondence with many other friends and relatives. He talks of the officers and men in his regiment, and friends or classmates in other regiments as well, most of the Vermont regiments in the field at the time and a number of other states' regiments. Major topics of concern in his letters are religion, the weather, food and the status of promotions for the officers in the regiment. He discusses all of the significant battles and general officers on both sides of the conflict, and many less significant ones as well. He has decided opinions on most of them. Some reflect his youthful naiveté, but others foretell the wisdom he exhibited in later public life.

When Captain James T. Hyde, Company C, resigned in mid-November 1862, Walker was promoted to Captain, effective November 30, and joined that company, albeit rather reluctantly, feeling that the company was "a set of hard tickets, and troublesome to manage," but he was pleased with the honor bestowed on him.[16]

The infantry regiment was converted to a Heavy Artillery Regiment in December, gradually expanded to twelve companies (or batteries) with 150 men each, and remained in the defenses of Washington until mid-May 1864.[17]

Walker commanded Battery C until July 11, 1863, when he transferred to Battery D. In mid-May, 1864, Ulysses S. Grant's plans for an overland campaign required significantly more troops, and "quite ready to be sent somewhere," Walker was granted his wish. After twenty months of digging rifle-pits, forts and other buildings, maintaining the ever-present paper trail required of an army, watching out for his troops, sitting on court martial proceedings and enjoying the social benefits of being in and around Washington, Aldace and his comrades set off for the war.

The regiment joined the First Vermont Brigade at the end of the battle of Spotsylvania, staying with the brigade, in the Sixth Corps, until the end of the war. Walker was promoted to Major on June 28, 1864. Brevetted Lieutenant Colonel April 20, 1865 for "distinguished gallantry in the several engagements in the Shenandoah Valley," he was formally promoted to that rank May 23, 1865 and mustered out with his regiment on June 24, 1865.[18]

After his regiment joined the First Vermont Brigade in the Sixth Corps, he was often forced to break his twice-weekly writing routine, but his letters continued to be frequent, informative and enlightening. Aldace's rendering of his first time under fire, south of the North Anna mid-May 1864, was factual, but somewhat tongue-in-cheek:

> I changed the videttes about six in the morning, and just as Capt. Loomis and I had reached the end of the line, we were fired on seven times in succession by sharpshooters, while we stood still expecting that they would stop to load presently. We were not hit, though some shots passed between us - poor marksmen, I think. They did not accelerate our departure in the least.[19]

He would, however, witness some of the bloodiest battles of the last year of the war, and consistently provided his parents with detailed reporting on what was happening.

As the war wound down, Walker found himself, with the rest of the Army of the Potomac, before Petersburg. Commenting on his endless fatigue duties in early January 1865, he jokingly told his father that he would be qualified to "boss a marble quarry" when he got home.[20] But his post war life would be far more challenging. Obituaries and funeral notices appearing in Butte (Montana), Chicago, Denver, Los Angeles, New York, Philadelphia, San Francisco, San Jose (California) and Vermont newspapers attested to the national influence of his substantial career as a lawyer, commissioner of the Interstate Commerce Commission and finally president of the Atchison, Topeka and Santa Fe Railroad. He was also active in post-war fraternal organizations, including the Vermont Officers' Reunion Society, the Grand Army of the Republic and the Military Order of the Loyal Legion of the United States.

Aldace's son, New York lawyer Roberts Walker, related his father's life and career in an article submitted for the National Cyclopedia of American Biography in February 1916. His final draft of the article is included as the final chapter.

Aldace mentions more than 100 general officers, more than 80% of them Union, as he relates his news of and reactions to the progress of the war, and he usually has rather decided opinions of them. While most of his interest and writings lies with the men of his companies and fellow officers in the other companies and the field and staff of the 11th Vermont, he mentions more than 200 soldiers in his and other Vermont regiments, classmates from Middlebury College and Kimball Union Academy, as well as friends, relatives and visitors, as well as the Congressional contingent from Vermont.

In addition to keeping the family abreast of his military and social affairs, Walker kept busy with official record keeping, but found quite a bit of free time on his hands. Walker was an insatiable reader. He occasionally complained about not having enough to read, and welcomed almost anything his parents would be willing to send him, except perhaps the classics, which he was "not familiar enough to enjoy without a dictionary or a pony." [21] He regularly read newspapers from Vermont, Baltimore, Boston, New York, Philadelphia, Washington and occasionally a Richmond paper.[22] He devoured every monthly copy of Atlantic magazine he received. He read "Les Miserables," Shakespeare, especially MacBeth, "Bivouac and the Battlefield," a book by his brigade's Commissary, a Captain Noyes, Charles the Bold, Blackstone's Commentaries on Law, "Peculiar," a novel, Loomis' "Trigonometry," Hugh Miller's "Essays," Bulwer's novels,[23] Fanny Kemble's book on plantation life, books on tactics and military law and others.

In addition to reading, Walker has an unusual fascination with pianos. In October, 1862, he discovers a "beautiful Chickering" at the Blair house, played by the Postmaster General's daughter. Walker was more taken with the piano than the girl. When his father apparently talked about getting a new piano, Aldace goes on at some length on the various brands available, including Steinway, Worcester, Edwards and Nims. He favors the Chickering, " a splendid, superb, best, piano," but recommends the Nims, because he wants "mellow instead of brilliant,' and wants to play "the Portuguese Hymn," not "O, Hail Us!" Eventually he sent home $100 to help pay for the piano.[24]

There are several other stories and incidents, notably Elias Howe, Jr., and Vermont's Rebel Heroine, but we'll leave it for the reader to discover and enjoy these and others for themselves.

----

1 Theodore S. Peck, Adjt. Gen., Revised Roster of Vermont Volunteers and Lists of Vermonters Who Served in the Army and Navy of the United States During the War of the Rebellion, 1861-66. (Watchman Publishing, Montpelier, Vt., 1892), 409-455. Hereinafter referred to as RR.

2 Aldace Walker, The Vermont Brigade in the Shenandoah Valley, (Free Press Association, Burlington, Vt., 1869).

3 Kimball Union Academy, named for Daniel Kimball, of Meriden N.H., was established by a council of the Churches of New England in 1813 "to assist in the education of poor and pious young men for the Gospel ministry." It became co-educational in 1839. General Catalogue of Kimball Union Academy, Meriden, N.H., 1813-1930, (Dartmouth Press, Hanover, N.H.), v-vi. Hereinafter referred to as KUACat.

4 Aldace Walker, Sr., (1812-1878), KUA 1833, DC 1837, ATS 1840. KUACat, 10.

5 "Col. Walker's Funeral," Rutland Herald, Tuesday morning, April 16, 1901.

6 Ibid.

7 Walter Hill Crockett, Vermont, the Green Mountain State, (Century History Company, New York, 1921), 374-5.

8 "Col. Walker's Funeral."

9 Benjamin Franklin Cooling III, Symbol, Sword and Shield: Defending Washington During the Civil War, (White Mane Publishing Company, Shippensburg, Pa., 1991), 175.

10 Aldace Walker, at Camp Bradley, letter to his father, August 24, 1862.

11 Ibid. August 26, 1862.

12 See Appendix A for details on the forts around Washington, D.C.

13 Col. A. A. Gibson, a regular army officer in the U.S. Artillery, assumed command of the 112th Penna. Infantry, redesignated the 2nd Penna. Heavy Artillery. Benjamin Franklin Cooling III and Walton H. Owen II, Mr. Lincoln's Forts: A Guide to the Civil War Defenses of Washington, (White Mane Publishing, Shippensburg, Pa., 1988), 176-7.

14 Private, later Lieut., Nelson Newton Glazier (1838-1922) to his parents, September 17, 1862. Letters of Nelson Newton Glazier, 1862-1864, available from http://vermontcivilwar.org/1bgd/11/nng1.shtml; Internet.

15 Mary Manning Walker, Aldace's sister, turned 11-years-old November 18, 1862. Family genealogical materials provided by Mary French Moore.

16 Walker, at Fort Massachusetts, November 23, 1862.

17 RR, 409 passim.

18 Ibid.; Walker, Fort Saratoga, D.C., to his father, 8 May 1864.

19 Walker, May 24, 1864.

20 Ibid. January 1, 1865.

21 Letter from Fort Massachusetts, 18 March 1863. According to the Oxford Shorter English Dictionary, a pony is U.S. slang, which originated in 1832, for a school of college 'crib.'

22. Among other papers, Walker read the Rutland Herald, Middlebury Register, Vermont Chronicle, the New York Herald, Times and Tribune, Philadelphia Inquirer and religious periodicals. No attempt has been made to differ-entiate between the Rutland Herald and the New York Herald, except parenthetically on occasion.

23. Edward George Bulwer-Lytton (1803-1873), a British novelist and poet, best known for his opening line in the 1830 novel Paul Clifford, "It was a dark and stormy night..." The Edward George Bulwer-Lytton Homepage, available at http://www.cadenhead.org/book/homepage24/examples/Stormy/eddie.html; Internet.

24 Walker, to his father, 26 October 1862; Ibid, 19 July 1863; Ibid., 28 July 1863.

Aldace Freeman WALKER
1842-1901
(Picerno Collection)

1.
Initial Training
Camp Bradley, Brattleboro, Vermont

Camp Bradley,[1]
August 21, 1862

Dear Father:

Our life here is somewhat monotonous, and I would be rather hard to invent material for a very long daily letter. We are now settled and at rest in our new camp. It is more favorably situated than the old one, and more comfortable in every respect. We officers have larger tents, and I have just got mine nicely floored and a table in it. I have no chairs as yet and find the trunk very convenient. When I get a home here I shall be most happy to entertain company. I have sent to Prof. Parker[2] for my mattress, and it came by express today. I expect to enjoy it while here, and then I can send it home.

I had a sick turn last night - ate a hearty supper at the hotel, and contrived to throw it up mostly in the course of the night. Such an operation won't hurt me in the long run, however. A great many in camp are suffering from dysentery; I have had a touch of it, but not enough to prostrate me materially. Everyone attributes the trouble to the coffee we have had, but as I have not drunk any I am rather incredulous.[3]

I guess I have received all your letters - had one tonight. I don't want the shawl at all. The Bible I would have liked, though we have a Testament in the tent. I have drawn a blanket and overcoat, and with a couple of other coats can pass the cold nights capitally. Last night was warm however, and tonight bids fair to be so. The Captain went home this afternoon to stay until Monday or Tuesday, leaving me at the helm. I took the company out at dress-parade this evening successfully, and shall soon get the hang of things in good shape. The great trouble is the incessant application for passes and furloughs. I hate to refuse, and can generally shove the responsibility on to a superior officer. I shall be much relieved when we are brought into the stricter harness of soldier life three hundred miles from home.

Our company has just been examined by Dr. Phelps.[4] Six or eight were thrown out, but we have still an overplus. Young Hitchcock of Pittsford, a Norwich cadet,[5] entered upon his duties as drill-master for the company today. We have three daily company drills and a parade at sunset to hear the orders for the morrow. I went to the village depot today, by invitation, to meet Miss Emma Allen[6] of Middlebury passing through, and went to South Vernon with her, returning in an hour. Had a pleasant ride. I have no means of knowing how long we shall remain here. We shall probably be mustered in some time next week and then paid off. I anticipate a fort-night longer at least, though the Capt.[7] has been so long getting off, and the 2nd Lieut.[8] is ahead of me, that my visit at home must be narrow. I don't expect to get there, if I come at all, before a week from next Sunday. I suppose this will find you at Wallingford. What time does the first train leave Rutland for W[allingford]. in the morning? I got my two dollars a day from Gen. Washburn[9] today - forty-four in all. I have got a loose blouse made here, as the other officers are doing, for $5.50. Our swords, etc. will come tomorrow. Am going to fencing as soon as possible.

I don't know as I told you that we have three surgeons with the regiment, and the 10th also.[10] Our third one has just reported. He is Ed. Porter[11] of Cornwall - a man who has been one once and who examined me when I enlisted - a good fellow. Our Quartermaster's supplies come in slowly. Nobody is to blame, I suppose. There is an immense call for army goods just now.

Direct to Lieut. Aldace F. Walker,

Co. B, 11th Vt. Vols.,

Brattleboro, Vermont

Guard Tent, Camp Bradley,
Sunday Evening, 9 o'clock.

Dear Father:

I am in a fair way to forget all days of the week for all that I see. I was put on senior Lieut. of guard from eight this morning for twenty-four hours, and have been hard at work all the time since. I have 130 men in my guard in three reliefs, and have to see that the posts are right, the orders understood and executed, the prisoners kept in order, the various reliefs fed, and order maintained generally throughout the camp. There is enough to do, but the work is not so hard after all as what I have had for two days past since the Captain has been gone. I have had the whole charge. Smith is not worth much for help. I have issued to the whole company their allowance of shoes, shirts, rubber blankets, haversacks and drawers, marched the company to the village for guns, and other stuff of the same sort I have done too numerous to mention.

I have been called away, and it is now nearly ten. I may be able to write three minutes without interruption. Torrey Farr,[12] an orderly in the 10th, came from Thetford yesterday, and brought me a letter and some goodies from Aunt Molly. I expect Capt. Hunsdon back tomorrow, though his leave runs till Tuesday. Smith is going tomorrow to settle his recruiting accounts, and I shall be alone. I am good for it, however. The boys help me very willingly. I expected, or foresaw, this press of work, and went to the hotel and had a good sleep last night, the first time I have seen a bed since I have been here. I feel very well now and hope I shall remain so. We shall be mustered in Wednesday or Thursday. I hope and mean to be in Wallingford on Friday or Saturday. Is there a morning train from Rutland to Wallingford? If so, I shall perhaps come that way.

We had a service on the ground today. Haynes[13] and the 10th came over here to hold service, and Bogart[14] made arrangements for a supply also. The Col. supposed that Haynes was his supply, and both men came in front of the regiments to preach at the same time. They compromised, however. Haynes prayed, and the other man, a Methodist, preached. A little, faint attempt at singing completed the services.

This is rather hard work, making out a letter by inches, and I shan't go much further. We officers have to go to the village twice a day to drill; it makes us quite a journey.

Good night.

Aldace.

Camp Bradley,
August 26, 1862

Dear Father:

I wrote you Sunday eve. while on guard duty - have not heard since. The trains failed to connect at Bellows Falls today, throwing back our mails and various passengers. Our Capt. was to come by the train. Our 2nd Lieut. went Monday morning, and was to return - but I am still alone. I slept a little Sunday night, and was relieved at nine Monday. Smith had gone before I reached my tent, and I was left with the whole responsibility. I worked well Monday, slept huge Monday night, though I had to turn out at roll-call at five. I slept till 5:30, and then had to see the company out on drill, and slept again till seven. Felt capitally this morning. Have been down town twice today to attend officers' drill - a regular institution - and managed things generally on the ground.

We have a drill-master - young Hitchcock of Pittsford - who drills the company three times a day, so I am relieved from responsibility in that line, farther than seeing the company out. The regiment is improving wonderfully in drill. We have several Norwich boys here, and every company has a drill-master. We all have guns. The officers' squad is at work on the manual, and I learned how to load a gun today. It is a different operation to load to kill a rebel, from loading to shoot squirrels. I passed surgeon's inspection today, all straight. It is very hot here. I am writing at 8 p.m. in my shirt and pants, and hot at that; and by the way, these shirts are splendid - I don't mean to ever wear anything else. Our staff officers are not all announced, but I like the appearance of things at present very much. Ripley has resigned.

There are a good many sick in the regiment. We had nine excused from duty today, though only one in the hospital. I see Mr. Tyler occasionally. He has invited me to take a meal at his house, and I mean to do so if I ever get in a situation where I can get away for a couple of hours. I can learn nothing definite concerning the time of mustering in - indications seem to point towards Thursday, though I am of little faith that is will be as early as that date. I am bound for home if I can get away, though we may be ordered out of the State at once. I am nearly ready, I think. I mean to get a sole-leather valise, from $6 to $9, and take one trunk between us three commissioned officers, in the hope of being able to keep the valises at all times.

We are on the eve of stirring movements. At first I had some difficulty in obtaining news, but henceforth I am to have a Boston Journal left at my tent at 11:30 a.m. for three cents a number, and am reconciled. I am in capital health and spirits. Smith got real homesick, but I am not troubled that way, nor any other just now. I have not had much time to write of late - am afraid my correspondents will think I am negligent - but must write if I expect to hear, and the postman is the source of my greatest pleasure now. Thomas[15] is occupying my tent with me, now I am alone. It is far more comfortable than his quarters, and I enjoy his quiet company. He is 3rd Sergeant, acting as company clerk. I have got considerable scold in me, as I found out when I blew the company up last night for turning out in a dilatory manner for dress-parade. At the next roll-call we were the first company through. Our regiment has a surplus of 75. Very truly,

Aldace F. Walker

I can send a line by Mr. Chatterton.[16] The Capt. has returned, but he is officer of the day today and I am not relieved of any responsibility. I am at work on our company allotment rolls today, and it will take all day. Will write more soon. Meanwhile, we shall (so I heard Gen. Washburn tell Col. Warner[17]) be inspected on Saturday and mustered in Monday, and I imagine we shall leave the State the last of the week. It is very doubtful if we can get home, and I wish you would come down Monday. We shall be paid off Tuesday or Wednesday, and I have some hope that I shall be able to return with you for a day or two or so. In fact, there is a probability of this. Still, if you can, please come down - by the early train if not too tired - and we can visit some and consult some. I remain well and happy.

A. F. Walker

Camp Bradley,
Thursday Eve., August 28, 1862.

Dear Father:

I saw Smith Chatterton this afternoon, and sent a note written in a great hurry by him. I don't know whether you received it or not, and will write a little more. I am not relieved of much care as yet by the Captain's coming back, as he has been or is officer of the day, in charge of the whole camp, and I am left alone with the company. The Capt. of Co. A has been promoted to Major, (a Dartmouth graduate[18]), and it leaves us the ranking company. I don't know whether we shall change our "letter" or not. Our acting Major Benton has been promoted to Lt. Col. - a capital officer.[19] Our Col. Warner is doing very well. Our Adjutant is a fellow by the name of Burrows,[20] a green at the business - has a capital clerk, Glazier, from Amherst College.[21] The Surgeons are good - two of them from Addison Co.[22] Carleton, Quartermaster, is a Montpelier merchant.[23]

I have been at work today with the allotment rolls - have worked ever since dinner, and have got through with 41 names, at 9:30. Shall have another siege at it tomorrow. The company is signing very liberally. I have signed fifty dollars a month to the State Treasury. Can send it to you if you wish to use it, or can invest it to more advantage than 5 percent. Usually the boys send to their families. I had charge of the company this p.m. during our first battalion or regimental drill. My platoon did very well indeed. We drilled until a thunder storm sent us to our tents, and then the boys were unfortunate. It was the first rain we have had, and the tents were hardly prepared for it. Some got a good deal of water into them.

I thought that I would rest last night after the Captain came back, and so went down town and went to bed. I slept very sound and nice till 7 o'clock; got up and bathed and had a good breakfast. But I caught a little cold some way. It was rather queer, but I expect to get over it in a night or two in my tent. I will repeat what I wrote this morning - that we shall be mustered in on Monday. I tried to get home today, but we must stay to Inspection on Saturday. We shall be paid off as soon as possible, and then away I suppose, for it is expected that other regiments will be on at once to occupy this ground. As I said, there is only a probability of my getting home. If you can get a 22 inch sole-leather valise for less than $10, you may I guess; for I shall want one, and can save it without much doubt. If Clark[24] can get me a Colt for $15 or even $18, I reckon I had better have it. My outfit is quite expensive, but I may as well go in comfortable shape if I am to have $1200 a year. I hope you will not get all worn out in moving.

Write often.

Lt. Aldace F. Walker

Camp Bradley,
Monday Morning (1 September)

Dear Mother:

I expect now to be with you before this letter reaches you or rather the same day. I think I will get off at E. Wallingford, Tuesday p.m., though it is so uncertain as yet that I hate to make the appointment. If it is a pleasant day, however, I guess Father may ride over, and not be disappointed if I don't get along so soon - always supposing that you got my last little note and that he don't come down today. I think we shall be mustered in today. I worked most all day yesterday on our pay-rolls. We had a service by Bogart at 4. He did very fairly. And then the company had to sign the rolls. I am well and busy.

Yours truly,

Aldace F. Walker

Brattleboro,
Saturday P.M. (6 September)

Dear Father:

The 10th have just gone - were announced to get away at 12 and left at one. We have orders to strike tents at 5 tomorrow and leave town at 10. We go by boat from New Haven direct to Jersey City, and thence on at once to Washington. I am very well now. Am waiting at an office down town for Gen. Washburn with a deserter, whom we wish sworn in. He has not received anything yet, and is unwilling to muster, but will I presume.

Evening. I have worked terribly today, but am all right now. We shall be ready to leave in good order. Are to take three days' rations and shall have a pleasant journey, I think. Gen. Washburn took my deserter to Major Austine,[25] the mustering officer. He refused to take the oath, and the Gen. ordered a court martial and [had] him put in irons. The fellow was frightened and mustered in. He had got to Canada, but was enticed back. I am officer of the guard for tomorrow - shall have charge of the train, and don't like the job, but must put it through. I can't write much - am lucky to have a chance to send a line from here. You must write soon, and direct to Washington. I will write every chance. I have no chance to see any friends at New York, and don't expect to; shall go round the city in the night. Katie Child went to New York with Willard today.[26] Harley and Charley[27] went on with Joy, to return in a day or so. I may see them at the city somewhere.

In haste,

Aldace F. Walker,

Lt. Co. B, 11th Rgt. Vt. Vols

----

1 Named after William C. Bradley, a former U.S. Representative from Vermont.

2 William Henry Parker, Middlebury College Professor of Mathematics and Natural Philosophy, 1848-1881. Duane L. Robinson, General Catalogue of Middlebury College, (Middlebury College, 1950), xl.

3 Nelson N. Glazier opined a "change of diet, lying on the ground, etc. have brought it on probaly [sic] in a great measure" in a letter to his family, August 29, 1862. Letters of Nelson Newton Glazier, 1862-1864, courtesy of Connie Snyder. Accessed 1/19/2002, available from http://vermontcivilwar.org/1bgd/11/nng2.shtml; Internet.

4 Dr. Edward E. Phelps, Chief of Brattleboro Army Hospital. Norwich University (NU) 1823. Robert G. Poirier, By the Blood of our Alumni: Norwich University Citizen-Soldiers in the Army of the Potomac, (Savas Publishing, Mason City, Iowa., 1999), 312.

5 Cadet Elisha P. Hitchcock. NU 1864. Poirier, 303.

6 A hometown acquaintance, possibly the daughter of Deacon Allen.

7 Capt., later Col., Charles Hunsdon, Shoreham. RR.

8 Lieut. Charles E. Smith, St. Johnsbury, resigned 7/25/1863. RR.

9 Vermont Adjutant and Inspector Gen. Peter T. Washburn, Woodstock, formerly Lieut. Col., 1st Vt. Infantry. RR.

10 The 10th Vt. Infantry mustered into U.S. service at Brattleboro on September 1, and would depart for Washington, D.C. on the 6th, the day before the 11th Vt. Infantry started. Frederick H. Dyer, *A Compendium of the War of the Rebellion, (Morningside, Dayton, Ohio, 1979 reprint) 3:1653.*

11 Dr. Edward O. Porter, Cornwall, Assistant Surgeon; resigned mid-January 1865. RR.

12 Sergt., later Lieut., Edward P. Farr, Thetford, Co. G, 10th Vt. Infantry. RR.

13 Chaplain Edwin P. Haynes, Wallingford. 10th Vt. Infantry. RR.

14 Chaplain William E. Bogart, Weybridge, a Methodist, resigned at the end of November. He was not replaced until April, when Rev. Arthur Little, a Congregationalist from Ludlow assumed the position. RR; George Grenville Benedict, Vermont in the Civil War, (Free Press Association, Burlington, 1888), 2:344, 349.

15 Sergt., later Lieut., Cyrus Thomas, Weybridge, Co. B. Middlebury College (M.C.) 1864. Robinson, 134-191. RR.

16 Apparently an acquaintance from home.

17 Col. James Meech Warner (1836-1897), Middlebury. Kimball Union Academy (KUA) 1854; attended Middlebury College 1854-5; U.S. Military Academy (USMA) 1860. Lieut., U.S.A., 1860-1. Robinson, 134-191; KUACat, 40.

18 Maj., later Lieut. Col., George E. Chamberlin, St. Johnsbury. MWIA 8/21/1864, died 8/22/1864. RR.

19 Lieut. Col. Reuben C. Benton, Hyde Park. Resigned 6/21/1864. RR.

20 Lieut., later Capt., Hunt W. Burrows, Vernon. RR.

21 Private, later Lieut., Nelson Newton Glazier, Stratton, Co. G. RR.

22 Charles W. B. Kidder, Vergennes and Edward O. Porter, Cornwall. RR.

23 Quartermaster, later Lieut., Alfred L. Carleton, Montpelier. RR.

24 A hometown merchant?

25 Maj. William Austine, U.S. Army, mustered in most, if not all, the Vermont regiments organized at Brattleboro.

26 From the context of later letters, Katie Child (Mrs. Edward Ashley Walker) and Willard Child are probably cousins of Walker's. His paternal grandmother was Chloe Child. Willard was Assistant Surgeon and Surgeon, 1st, 4th and 10th Vt. Infantry regiments, mentioned later. E. M. Haynes, A History of the Tenth Regiment, Vt. Vols. (Tuttle Company, Rutland, 1894), 399-402, provides additional details.

27 Harley G. Sheldon, Rutland, served in the 1st Vt. Infantry and later in the 14th Vt. Infantry. RR. Charley Sheldon was a fairly regular correspondent of Aldace's, and visited frequently with Harley, of the 14th Vt., and John Sheldon, of the 10th. John and Harley, both of Rutland, were 21 and 19, respectively, when they joined the 1st Vt. in 1861; Washburn, 1864, Appendix D, pp. 17-18. John Sheldon's father was Charles Sheldon. Haynes, 235-238 contains a biographical sketch and photograph of John.

President
Abraham Lincoln
(Italo Collection)

2.
Arriving at the Seat of War

Fort Lincoln, Washington, D.C.
September to October 1862

Fort Lincoln,[1]
Thursday, 11 A.M. [11 September]

Dear Parents:

This is the first chance I have had since we left Brattleboro to write a word. We have been continually on the move, and are not settled fairly even yet. I have not had any writing material with me, or I might possibly have written on the cars, though not with much profit. Since we left the cars we have seen nothing but a continual tote, and no peace. I am well yet, however, though somewhat tired. The regiment has done first rate, and is still plucky. We left Brattleboro, as we expected, Sunday morning, about ten. Went on nicely to Springfield, and there we found a house across the track, and a road had to be built around it. Detained us some two hours, which the good people of Springfield improved by introducing all the liquor possible into the cars. I was officer of the guard and emptied several canteens myself, and we kept all out we could; and no trouble, serious, arose from the run.

We got to New Haven about six, and embarked in an hour on the steamer Continental - a splendid boat, one of the best running. I met Emma Allen in the boat house at New Haven. Saw none of our relatives there. The Col. complimented me much on my work through the day, and I did work hard to keep the boys on the train and everything straight. Morning found us in Jersey City. We got in about three, had breakfast, and got away by eight. I went across to the city, thinking I should go to Hoboken; but was afraid I should not have time, and came back. Pretty soon Uncle and Aunt[2] came to Jersey City, and I had quite a visit. There was a Mass. Regiment came from Pittsfield down the Hudson in the Oregon, which got away just after us, and met an accident on the way. A train ran into them and killed three, injuring many. A New York regiment which got here just behind us broke down near Annapolis Junction, nearly killing a Capt. and injuring others. We had a safe and very pleasant trip on the whole. We spent from one to seven p.m. in Philadelphia. Peaches were freely distributed through the cars before we crossed the ferry, and the regiment was fed, as all are, in the city - and very well too. From here the boys had freight cars to ride in, which we did not like so well of course. Our Co., however, had passenger cars to Baltimore, because there were not enough cattle cars to go around.

We left Philadelphia about 7 p.m. and were twelve hours going to Baltimore, 90 miles. I slept some through the night and felt well in the morning. Had to march a mile and a half in both Philadelphia. and Baltimore, and it was hot in Philadelphia. We had breakfast in Baltimore and came on very slowly, reaching Washington about six Tuesday afternoon. There was a supper ready, and we camped down in barracks close by the depot

- that is, in big sheds where every man could have a chance at the floor. I slept soundly however, and lived well at a restaurant near by the Capitol. Had supper and breakfast there. After breakfast yesterday we had orders to leave for an encampment on Capitol Hill - about a mile and a half off. We reached a good place, and were ordered off; we got to another, formed a line and were staking out a camp, when we were ordered to report to Fort Lincoln. We went another mile so as to be out of the way, and stopped to rest. Some meat and bread that we brought from Brattleboro were issued, and that was the last we had till eight this morning, when we had some salt beef and hard crackers, not enough to go around. After our dinner we started off. Marched to the depot again, and then out on the Bladensburg road to our camp. We marched some four miles, and found ourselves half a mile from the place where we started, and had four miles more to go then. It was very hot when we started, but rained presently, and we got wet and dirty. Our position on the line has been changed by the promotion of the Capt. of Co. A and we are now at the head of the column, a place where we can march much easier. We came very slowly. The men were heavily loaded with knapsacks, guns, haversacks, canteens, boxes, belts, overcoats, blankets, &c., but kept along bravely, and turned at last after dark into an open field, dropped on the ground and went to sleep. My valise came along and I changed my stockings. My waiter had kept my shawl, with slippers done up in it, with him, and I found much comfort from the pumps and slept in the shawl. Much of the rest of the baggage is yet at the depot. My calf boots made my feet sore at Brattleboro, and I put on the others as I came away. They are not fairly broke in yet, and my feet are a little sore, but pretty well on the whole.

Our quartermaster has some stores for us at Washington, but had 17 wild mules that never were halter broke issued to him, and can't get them harnessed without four men to each mule. When our rations get here we shall know it I suppose. This morning we laid out camp and pitched tents. It is now raining hard, but we are comparatively comfortable. I received no damage sleeping on the lee side of a fence - not even stiff in the morning. We found a great deal of excitement in Philadelphia and Baltimore about Jackson,[3] and with good reason. Fort Lincoln is on the railroad (or near it) to Baltimore, about four or five miles out of the city. It is the center (headquarters) of a string of earthworks, some dozen, seven miles in extent, under command of Col. Gibson of a Pa. regiment. There is a regiment or so, I suppose, in camp near each, and the line is quite strong. It is really the advance now, for there are strong expectations that Jackson will turn up on the railroad near Bladensburg, two or three miles from here, within reach of three of the posts, and if he presses toward the city from this direction, he will go within half a mile of us. So there is a possibility of something to do. The 9th Vt. are off toward Harper's Ferry. The Cavalry is over the river near Alexandria. Our first work will be to dig, or help dig, a chain of rifle pits connecting these forts, though we hear 500 negroes will be here soon. We have just heard that the 10th, which we have not seen, has marched 2000 rebel prisoners into Washington; whether we ever hear of it again I doubt. I am glad we are out of the city, and we are in a very pleasant place. Will write more in a day or two.

A. F. Walker

I sent money to Middlebury to pay all my bills. Have money enough for the present.

Direct to Co. B, 11th Vt. Vols., Washington.

Fort Lincoln,
September 16, 1862

Dear Father:

I received your second letter tonight. Am still well and all right. We have got out of the trenches, but more work is provided for us. We now go to work at an earthwork, and more rifle pits I guess, so far away that the men will have to carry their dinners. I wish we could drill, and the Col. grumbles a good deal, but there is nothing to be done but to fall in and keep picking. I am to be officer of the guard tomorrow - rather hard now as the sentinels have all to be instructed in the duties of active service; but I shall be off the next day, and mean to see the country some in this vicinity. I remember distinctly writing you (in my long pencil letter, I think) that I had paid my Middlebury debts and had money enough for present use. It will be rather expensive living here - butter is 50¢ a pound, eggs 30¢ a dozen, etc.; still I mean to live comfortable as long as I can, for the time may come when I can no longer. We have officers schools now in the tactics, reciting every evening to the Colonel. Some of the officers are dull enough I assure you. We are getting monotonous in our life now.

The recent victory of McClellan[4] has relieved our apprehension of an attack, and we expect now orders to leave at any moment. We should like well to stay here a month or two or three, and may. I never was in a place where I knew so little of what was coming, and where I cared so much less. I think the regiment as a whole is well officered. There are a good many fine men as captains, and three or four capital first lieutenants. There are some complete ninnies also, and growing more so every day. It did me good to see one of them make a fool of himself at guard-mounting this morning. There is the most made of this of anything in the service; it must be done just so and with a long ceremony. The Col. has taken it in hand and it is improving. Don't know but I shall appear as green as any of them tomorrow, but think not. Monday the officers had a drill, and I had command of the whole regiment in the rifle pits. It was quite a job for me to boss, but it was all right. I have received no letters except from you, and one from Henry. Have you ordered the [Rutland] Herald for me? I did not receive it last week.

The nights are very warm here; we hardly want anything over us. Still, the days are very comfortable. We have had no rain except showers, though a storm is threatening now. We heard the firing in the battle of Sunday, and some on Monday morning. When the news reached us, the companies were formed and the news announced. Hats went up, I tell you. I get your letters in about three days. This will do very well for mail matter. Please keep sending them. The 10th we hear has been ordered up the Potomac on a long march. The 9th is under Gen. White,[5] in trouble at Harper's Ferry. We have the easiest time of all, and are thankful for it. When times will change we don't know. The Cav. boys come this way occasionally. I have seen no acquaintance but Grid. Perkins.[6] They have had rather a rough time. No rest for nine days and nights except what they could get on the ground with the halters tied to their wrists; and no food for the horses except what they picked up thus in the night. I think I told you that Higley[7] is Adjutant. The tattoo just beats for roll-call.

Aldace F. Walker

Fort Lincoln,
Sept. 20, 1862

Dear Father:

I have written once or twice this week, but a letter received from you just now puts me in the writing mood. I thought by the last letter I got that you had heard from me once then from here, but it seems not. Letters are long enough on the way - this one, four days; but then if we write once in so often, they will come steadily, and that is the essential. Myself and Lt. Goodrich, or rather G. and I, have just come in from a drill among the sergeants. The Major has charge of the squad, and the drill now is that of skirmishers. The movements are all on double quick, and the exercise is interesting, though tiresome. We have little drill now - an hour before breakfast is all - so improvement is slow. The Col. is much troubled that we spend all our time in the trenches, and when we are called to the field shall have so little preparation. The regiment is among rifle pits some five miles from here, where they have to carry their dinner and spend the day. It is a hard days work, though of few hours. We go out at 7:30 and get back by five. Our Co., however, has not as yet been outside the reach of a warm dinner - being at work upon an earthwork for eight guns, some two miles from here.

We are getting so as to live quite comfortably. Have quite a kit of tools, stove, toaster, pans, pails and kettles, in our mess. The boys, Capt. and Lt., have given me $5 each to provide till the $15 is gone; so we have fresh meat often and eggs, butter, cheese, chickens, potatoes, soft bread and toast, as we wish, and live high while we may. I am gaining flesh, and feel capitally. We are afraid now of the equinoctial storm. Have had very pleasant weather so far, but it now threatens a storm. We are much better protected and ditched around our tents than when we first came, and shall be ready, I think, for a spell of weather. Yesterday I bossed our Co. all day in the trenches. The day before I came off guard in the morning, and was at liberty all the rest of the day. The guard duty is somewhat different from that at Brattleboro. The detail is not so large, but the duties must be more strictly performed, and on the whole the work is as great - especially the night work, when we have a countersign out, and the new men must be instructed in their duties. Tell Mary the countersign for the night was "Nerva."[8] It is the same through all the grand army. We are still in constant expectation of a move.

The defeat of McClellan would have involved an attack upon our line of defense. His victory probably involves another advance into Virginia from this direction, so we are liable to be called away. A regiment that came to this vicinity the same day that we did has been relieved and sent away, and we may follow. The 10th has left tents and everything almost at Alexandria, and gone up the Potomac. The 9th, we hear will have a chance to fight without violating their parole - against the Indians in Minnesota. I don't envy them their position, nor their Commander - Pope,[9] whom the Cavalry boys cordially detest. Day before yesterday I went with Lt. Foot[10] to Bladensburg, some two miles away. The village is terribly run down, and looks most emphatically Southern. The houses are shabby and mean, the negroes are plenty, though the majority have skedaddled, the bridges are rotted away, and the teams drive through the river. There are some fine places, however, and we called at one. Were received hospitably, and treated to peaches. Had a pleasant visit with the lady of the house, and a pleasant afternoon generally. Shall go again without doubt.

We officers have had the question of rank agitating us somewhat. The companies were arranged arbitrarily by Gen. Washburn - ours coming in second, though organized fourth. However, the lieutenants expected to follow the rank of the captains of course. The Lt. of A had been promoted, leaving me senior. Goodrich of Castleton (Fairhaven Co. C) was next. The Col. gave orders for a roster of lieutenants according to date of commissions to report to Col. Gibson, who had asked a roster with the ranks. He, Col. Warner, imagined that this was the only way he could legally do. Goodrich and I blew some - in a gentle way, of course - but the Col. could see no other way than to follow the "Regulation" and the dates of commission. So it went in so, but was promptly returned by Col. Gibson, who did not "care for the date of commission - the Department had ordered volunteer regiments to rank according to order of muster," and so the Col., very sheepishly, I thought, told me that I remained first, as I had been acting. He said that he was best satisfied to have it so, as far as persons went; and I reckon spoke the truth, for the senior lieutenant by his arrangements was a fool, who could not act as adjutant better than a stick, and I have had that to do several times. This Goodrich is one of the best fellows in the regiment. The officers, I reckon, did not know of the change contemplated, except us, and we were bound to have our dues if we could. The Col. had promised to leave it to Gen. Washburn, if Gibson had not amended.

I am ready to hear often. Shall mean to write twice a week. Have not heard from anyone but you, save one forwarded from Brattleboro, and have received no papers. Am very anxious to get some Vermont news. Please write all you can, as I seem in a strange land. Think of me as contented, and always remembering my friends with much love. I have written many letters, and shall get replies presently.

Aldace F. Walker

Camp near Fort Lincoln, D.C.,
Sept. 24, 1862

Dear Father:

Some way or other I receive very little mail matter in this region - a Rutland Herald today being my first installment this week. I have heard once from Aunt Minerva, with the [New York] Tribune's account of McClellan's great fight, which I was very glad to see. The papers from Washington and Baltimore reach us regularly and early - the W. at six and the B. at seven; but they are very unsatisfactory, and a New York paper is a great treat. My letters seem to be peculiarly unfortunate in time spent on the way, but I expect the gate will be raised sometime and the flood come. The Herald I was very glad to see. I have been away from our fatigue duty today, and in fact all this week, at work upon our company books. It is quite a chore to start the accounts, clothing, etc., correctly; but I am getting to be quite a book-keeper, and like it much better than ditching.

Our regiment is still at work, though I suppose it is almost through - in fact, would finish this afternoon if it was not raining. This is the first rain we have had in the day time since we came here, I believe, and it is very gentle now. We fear, however, that it is setting in for a long pull, as we have not had our equinoctial storm yet. The clouds look light, however. Since we have been at work, the regiment have dug several miles of rifle pits; have built a battery, or rather earthwork for eight guns; and have been of late at work upon a military road, which is nearly finished; and then Col. Gibson says we may commence drill. I understand that it is the intention of our officers to be very thorough with us if we ever get at it, and am glad of it. Eight hours a day, however, will give us quite a pull. We are gaining a very good reputation around here - so much so that Col. Gibson is straining every nerve to keep us in his brigade on this line of defences, and the probabilities now are that this disposition will be made of us. He says that he wants his men to be in contact with such a regiment, that the duty will be light, and the time for drill plenty; and we think it all very good, though we should like to get into the field after a month or so drilling, or the 11th won't have much of a name in history. Still, this is principally surmising. The appearance now is that we shall remain in this place some time; tomorrow it may change. We shall be very glad to stay here a while, as we are most pleasantly situated.

I have never been in better health - have not had a touch of dysentery since I have been in camp here - eat heartily - feel well - and am well enough contented. We have things arranged now so that we live as well as we do or should at home. Get fresh meat when we want from the city markets and at reasonable prices - bread very nice - butter, good but dear - eggs, ditto. Then we have coffee, of course, twice a day - potatoes at $1.50 a bushel, rice, beans, salt pork and beef, etc. - too numerous to mention. We can find no fault with the cooking - have a stove, pots, pans and kettles, and things generally clean and neat. Have been living on fresh pork steak today at 12¢ a pound, with other things to go with it of course. I am commissary for the mess. Can't tell how much it will cost, as we have been getting tools, etc. It will be somewhat expensive, of course, but we may be put on to short rations, and we need not scrimp now. I have some money yet - say $15. Shall probably want more before pay day.

We had the honor of officiating in dress parade last night before Hon. Wm. H. Seward,[11] Lord Cavendish, and one or two other English sprigs of nobility, including an officer in the English army. They complimented the Col. very highly concerning the regiment; the officer said our appearance far surpassed that of a British regiment he just saw arrive in Canada. Seward drove up behind the Col. and spoke to him three times, but he never answered or moved a muscle to see who it was till the conclusion of the parade, when he turned and saluted. I like our officers very much. Their principles are not of the highest cast, though the Col., Lt. Col. and Major, always attend the meetings on the Sabbath; but I like the men, and think they mean to do the best they can. Some of the line officers I don't like at all, but this I should expect.

Last Sunday Bogart had a service at 11 a.m. A Methodist Pennsylvania chaplain preached - well enough. A church, or body rather, was organized in the afternoon. I did not join, though I meant to, as they finished taking names before I was aware. I was rather glad I did not, however, as they proceeded at once to the administration of the sacrament, kneeling of course, and the clergymen passing around talking continually in a manner that seemed impious to me, or at least entirely destroyed the solemnity of the occasion. The prayer meetings I attend often, but have not participated in. I am willing any one should know where I stand, and presume they do - my acquaintances, at least - as the adjutant, a rough fellow, and one whom I very little like, asked me the other day if I had intended to enter the ministry.

Our Company stands well in the regiment. Our Captain is conceded everywhere to be the best, and my situation seems in every way as pleasant as could be expected. If we stay here our position is safe enough if we take decent care of our health. I have bathed every week so far, and am intending to keep it up. I find the mattress a great advantage. Smith has a buffalo, and between us we have no trouble in keeping comfortable. We fear, and expect, that if we spend the winter here we shall be divided - a company or two to a fort. This will break up the unity of the regiment, which is great now, and hope to find our winter quarters further south. Please write as long and fully as possible. Any items of course will interest me, though Wallingford news is not West Rutland. You may here from there occasionally. I find my slippers a very great convenience here; shall get some more when these are used up. I have got my oration of the chaplain, and return it. Please put it with my other papers, as I showed. Have you received my "Will" from Kellogg?

Truly,

Aldace F. Walker

Camp near Fort Lincoln,
Sunday Eve., 10 o'clock

Dear Father:

I received a letter from you on Friday, after I had sent one, which I hope you have received before now. We remain in the same place. The men are at work now digging rifle pits to connect our line of forts. We have dug a mile or so now, and have more to do. I took my Company out this morning, and halted them under a tree to wait for orders, and presently Col. Gibson, our acting Brigadier,[12] ordered us in; which command we were very glad to obey, as the need of Sunday work is hardly apparent enough to stop grumbling. We had preaching at 4 p.m. today and a prayer meeting in the evening. The Methodistical peculiarities were very prominent, and decidedly offensive to me - but of use, perhaps. I took no part save attending. I have been busy at one thing or another all day; meant to write a long letter, but have not time now, as I must turn out at 5 a.m.

I have acted as adjutant for the last three days on dress parade. It is the place where one has the most to do of any position, and not very desirable, unless a permanent arrangement. Our Adjutant will be present after this, I hope. Higley, I hear, is Adjutant of the Cavalry Rgt. They are somewhere in the vicinity of Alexandria, and the 10th is near by. We have heard heavy firing today from the Northwest. I sketched out a rough diagram of our position, which perhaps you will understand, and perhaps not. We have been singing a little tonight, and it seems natural enough. The nights are quite warm here; so much so that we lie without covering, and a cap on my head is quite suffocating. The days are very comfortable. My own health has never been better than since I have been in camp here. We have abundance to do. Yesterday afternoon I wrote letters and loafed, and mean to get along easier in future. The field officers are very kind to me, and I still call it a pleasant life, though I should be glad enough to get away, of course, if the occasion for staying were gone. The Col. has started an officers' school for instruction from the books of tactics. I am glad of this, as I have not learned much lately.

Our position around here is rapidly growing stronger. A masked battery has been laid out within ten rods of my tent. (Perhaps this is contraband, but I guess the rebels will never see it.) And others are being placed around us. Regiments are constantly passing us on the cars - from three to six a day. What disposition will be made of them, of course I don't know. We hear that our Vt. nine months' men are coming soon to this immediate vicinity. One of my company shot off the fingers of his left hand today. He deserted from us at Brattleboro, and reached Canada, but we got him back. We had trouble making him take the oath, and he said he would do us no service if he came on; so he has little sympathy, as every one thinks it was intentional. He cannot get away on account of this wound, however. Our mail last night did not reach us for some reason. I hope to hear again soon. Your last came through in two days, I believe.

I remain, Your aff. son,

Aldace F. Walker

Benning's Bridge, D.C.,
Sept. 27, 1862

Dear Father:

The last time I wrote you I was almost certain we should stay in the quarters we then occupied for some time; but we are comfusticated, as I then said might be possible. We had steady work for two weeks, and then Col. Gibson said we were to have an opportunity for drill, and we did - one day. We had a Company drill in the forenoon yesterday, and a battalion drill in the afternoon. At dress parade the Lt. Col. said we were to have a nice time drilling and made arrangements for the future. At nine o'clock orders came to divide the regiment into seven squads - two companies to Fort Lincoln, one to Fort Thayer,[13] some to Totten,[14] to Slocum[15] and another place, and one to Benning's Bridge.

We started for this place early this morning. The portions of the regiment detailed to the different forts are scattered through an extent of some five miles. We marched two miles directly toward Washington, and then a mile east, so that we are completely isolated from the rest of the regiment. The bridge is over the east branch of the Potomac. This river is subject to tides, and when the water is down there is one vast marsh half a mile wide. This is passed by a causeway, and the river proper by a draw bridge. At the time of Pope's skedaddle, a company was stationed here as well as at other outlets to the city, to stop deserters. It was relieved by a company of the 13th Pa., which regiment ours relieved. This regiment has been ordered to the field, I understand, and we may follow sometime.

Our duties here will not be very onerous, unless we are set to ditching. We have to examine passes in the daytime and stop everyone in the night, when the draw is up and a traveler would tip into the drink. It will take some six men and a corporal a day. We shall drill some, of course, and lay round considerable. The proximity to the sloughs cannot be very favorable to health - in fact, the last company say there was considerable fever and ague among them, but I am not afraid of that for myself. If blowing will avail we shall not stay here long, for the officers are after Gibson with sharp sticks. It don't suit. Well, this is a little taste of the fortunes of war. It is troublesome, but we can stand it. Our camp is pleasant enough - that is, there is nothing positively unpleasant, except the swamp. Our street runs parallel to the road, close by, and there is a good deal of travel. It is about a mile to the outskirts of the city.

I received the Atlantic today, and was glad to see it. The back numbers I shall have to return, as I can't transport them nor keep them clean. This last move we had two wagons for the company, and took everything we wished. We found some bunks, roughly knocked together by the last company, that will just hold my mattress and the Captain's tick. We have a table that we slip into the tent to eat on. I opened that bottle of cherries tonight, and found them first rate. We had beefsteak, potatoes, fine bread - and though you may not think it possible, we positively lived better than in Vermont. We may not be able to get supplied as well here as at Fort Lincoln, but I found a muskmelon patch across the river, where I tramped for a mile or two to report at Fort M[assachusetts,][16] and fruit goes by here in abundance on its way to market every morning. Meat we can't get so handy, but we have a ham on hand and shan't starve - beef enough for another meal, etc. I am not run ashore for money yet. Have perhaps $12 or $15. I think money will come perfectly safe, as I have not missed any of your letters yet. I don't know when we shall be paid off. Think you had better send me $25 as soon as may be. Of course direct to Washington, D.C. Our mail came in tonight with the victuals for four days. When we shall get another, we don't know. I am in good spirits, health, &c. Write as usual.

Aldace F. Walker

Fort Massachusetts,
Oct. 1, 1862

Dear Father:

We have moved again. We got to Benning's Bridge Saturday, as I wrote. Found nothing to do save to raise a draw bridge at 9 p.m., lower it at 5 a.m., and keep people from driving into the river. The location was terrible. Lt. Smith is now sick - fever and ague like. The scenery was dull and lonely - nothing visible in fact but marsh and niggers - and of those, plenty. Sunday there was a perfect stream of darkies on their holiday, flocking into the city with baskets of eggs, peaches, apples, chickens, ducks, doves - everything portable in the eating line, for their own private emolument. One Negro with a lot of ducks had come twenty-four miles. Said he was disposing of what little property he had, and then intended to make away with some of Mas'rs. There was a man, on whose farm we camped, who was a sort of market gardener, and we had abundance of vegetables, though we had just found out that tomatoes were twenty cents a peck before we left.

Sunday the Captain and I went to Fort Lincoln, (some three miles), and found that we were to be relieved by a company from somewhere else, and as soon as relieved we were to skedaddle. The other Co. came Monday forenoon, but our transportation did not come for us till late that night, and we started Tuesday morning at 6:30. We had no trouble in carrying everything we wished. Marched about four hours - some ten miles - till it got very hot and dusty, at any rate - and pulled up at Fort Mass. The situation here is very good. It is the extreme west of Gibson's line, Lincoln being the east. The Fort has just been enlarged, and is quite formidable. There is a house or so close by, and a post office called Brightwood. There are two batteries of a Pa. Artillery Regt. - Gibson's - here, and a Major Sadler of that Regt. is in command. The headquarters of both regiments are at Fort Lincoln - distant eight miles, up hill and down, a new military road and very dusty. The object of thus dividing us is to instruct us in the use of heavy artillery, with a probability that we shall be transferred to that arm of the service. Gen. Casey[17] is striving to bring this about, and we rather expect it. If it is done, it will require some changes in the organization of the regiment - two or three Majors (of which our Capt. will be one), three Lieutenants to a Co., &c. You need not mention this, as few in the regiment even know it as yet, and I do not care to have it reported from me. It will depend a great deal on the proficiency we attain, of course; but we are beginning to consider ourselves located for the winter. Nothing is certain, however. These two regiments expect this line, but Gibson's officers hear today that they are ordered to Florida.

There is great activity here; twenty-eight regiments have left Washington for Harper's Ferry via Baltimore within forty-eight hours. The first death in our company occurred today. An old man, with two sons in the Company, from Whiting - Sweet[18] by name - who was attacked with typhoid at Benning's Bridge. He died in the hospital at Fort Lincoln; will be sent home. Two others have died in the regiment since we came here. We shall have to do picket[19] duty here, though officers will not be sent out. I received your letter with the photograph, and was very glad to receive it. Shall acknowledge, of course, and send it home before long to put in my album, with Capt. H.'s and Dr. Porter's, which I enclose tonight.

Fort Massachusetts, D.C.,
Oct. 5, 1862

Dear Father:

I returned from a walk this evening after dark, and found three letters and the Herald; one letter from Uncle Joel, one from Charley Sheldon, and one from you with twenty dollars enclosed. I was not out of money, but should be before long. I find it rather expensive living here, but I make the rest do their share. We are very well situated here - a store near by, which furnishes us butter, eggs, sugar, potatoes, &c., and a patch of tomatoes, a quarter of an acre in extent, joining my tent; turnips, beets, apples, vegetables of all sorts handy by; meat, fresh, is the hardest thing to procure. The Rutland Herald is the greatest treat I have beside my letters. I have made arrangements by which I expect to have the Middlebury Register regularly, by writing a letter occasionally, and think this will do for Vermont papers. I was officer of the day a day or two since, and the next day I took the leave to which I was entitled, and improved it by a tour through the regiment.

I got the Lt. Col.'s horse, an easy riding, slow cantering beast, and set out for a ride. Had a capital time. I am not used to riding at all, you know, but I got along tip top. Feel a little stiff today, but of no account. I had business to do at headquarters - Fort

Lincoln, eight miles away. On my return after dark, I missed my way after leaving Fort Saratoga,[20] and kept galloping on, not noticing but what all was right, until to my great astonishment I brought up in a yard containing some three thousand army wagons, on the edge of the city. I figured along and around, and at last came on to familiar ground and got on a straight road to camp. It rained while I was in the city, but cleared away directly. I came all the way out, some four miles, without scarcely breaking gallop. I think I should make a good horseman, if I only could have as good a horse regularly as I had yesterday. Wish I was in the cavalry. Must have ridden twenty miles. The reason I have not visited the city, though only four miles out, is that passes are demanded of everyone by the provost guard, and it is quite difficult to obtain them. They have to be signed by the Company commander, by Col. Warner, Col. Gibson, and by Gen. Banks, Chief of Staff.

This forenoon the Capt. and I went off a mile or two to a brook for our Sunday wash, which I have never yet omitted. This afternoon we rode over to Fort Totten in an empty government wagon, and visited the Soldier's Home, some two miles from here. This is a splendid granite building, with beautiful grounds, for the residence of soldiers who have grown old in the service. They can claim it, I believe, after twenty years of service. There are many there - respectable looking, cleanly old men; but they pass away very fast, and the graveyard is one of the strangest parts of the place. Thousands even of bodies are there, constantly shifting as friends claim and remove them. President Lincoln has his residence in an elegant, but not at all extravagant, cottage, within the enclosure. He was not at home tonight. I went there expecting to attend church, but the countersign would be out (issued) before the service was over, and we thought we had better not stay, as we might have trouble getting home without it. It is rather cold tonight; the first time it has seemed so since we came out; but it has been very comfortable all day. Yesterday was as hot as our days in July. Lt. Smith has been quite feverish, but I think is improving now.

I am very well as yet. There seems to be great feeling in Vermont concerning the 7th. As near as I can ascertain the charges are substantially true after the death of Roberts.[21] Fullam[22] is a great fool, in whom the men had no confidence, and under his command the regiment went to pieces. Men who know him are glad that Maj. Holbrook[23] is promoted over him, and his retreating does not look much like a successful fight. Our boys are at work yet, though whether we shall go out tomorrow or not we do not certainly know. There is some ill feeling through the two regiments stationed through this line. There are many Germans in the Pa. Regiment, and they fight with the Americans. In fact, the regiment is greatly demoralized, and many of the officers are undergoing court martial now, Col. Warner being president of the Board. Our trouble is with the officers, who assume to give us orders in an overbearing way, and we assume to disobey as much as we choose when the orders do not come from Col. Gibson, under whom, of course, we are. They say the 11th Vt. has the "most stubborn set of officers they ever saw," and I reckon they won't succeed in running over us to any great extent. Our Col. wants to avoid trouble, but still to maintain our dignity, and the Lt. Col. swears he will arrest any officer who takes orders from a Dutchman. I don't anticipate anything serious, however. We are contented enough here, though lonely and glad to make and receive visits. I have no stamps, and fear this will not get away at once, but I will do the best I can.

Aldace F. Walker

Fort Massachusetts, D.C.,
Oct. 8, 1862

Dear Mary:

I suppose you are nearly through with your day's work now. It is most four o'clock. I don't have to work very much just now. We are not drilling, but chopping, and I don't have to take charge of the men very often. The most of the regiment moved in here last night, to dig rifle pits in execution of a new idea of Col. Gibson's. It is mean for them to keep us working so; we continually fancy we can see daylight, and then another job comes up. The artillery regiment is at work upon a new road close by - and we keep still chopping. We had much rather do this than work in the road, for it is cleaner, and we get out of sight and don't work so many hours. We are in hopes this week will finish - as usual. Our Col. is President of a Court martial for the trial of a number of these Dutchmen. The first case was a Captain, for embezzling public funds. He passed through some three days of the suit, and then skedaddled. No one knows what has become of him. Col. Warner bears himself very well, it is said. He is a very smart little fellow - rapidly growing popular. This General Court martial is quite an honor for a boy of twenty-six. I reckon he will come out high sometime. Our Lt. Col. is a lawyer and very bright. The Pennsylvanians think a good deal of him.

Yesterday noon a contraband came into camp full tilt, running as hard as ever he could, three men on horse back, with revolvers, after him. He had got away from his master's a month ago, and was at work for a man a mile from here. He was in the barn, and he saw these men coming in. His master asked him if he was ready to go home. He said he was not, but reckoned he should have to, and jumped down through a trap door into the stable below, and so out, the men after him. They found they could not catch him, and went for their horses. They got ahead and waited for him at a toll-gate. He saw them coming, and traveled over the lots; they over the fence and after him. He was afraid they would shoot him, but got into our camp - the men hollering, Stop him, Stop him. But our boys did not see it in that light, and the fellow is with us now. He is quite bright - about eighteen - can read some, and is very handy. He was not a slave, but illegally bound out, and his master wanted to sell his time; he did not just know what would become of him, and skedaddled.

I went toward Washington yesterday to visit the hospitals on the edge of the city. I went to three - Mount Pleasant, Carver, and Columbia College. They all seemed neat and well kept. The last in a good brick college building that looked natural enough. Carver was originally a set of barracks - has been painted white, furnished, and will hold two or three thousand. The most of these are wounded - paroled prisoners from the last Bull Run. The wounds are everywhere. Some are most shockingly mangled. I did not go about much, for I do not like such scenes. Boyden,[24] whom Father will remember, is there, sick. A young fellow whom I enlisted at Middlebury, and had transferred to the Vt. 2nd, I came across. The rooms are cleanly - all that I saw. The iron cots are comfortable, with springy slats, white cover lids, mattresses, etc. They are not so crowded as I supposed, and they say other hospitals in the city are in better condition than these. The men are cheerful, and seem as well contented as could well be expected. I saw also a regiment of cavalry drilling - that interested me much - moving by the bugle.

Fort Massachusetts, D.C.,
Sunday Eve., Oct. 12, 1862

Dear Father:

Things remain very much in status quo here; the greater part of the regiment came here last week to work on the road building here, and it is nearly done. We are still chopping, but hope to finish soon. We are in the first bad spell of weather I have seen in the district. Yesterday morning, I started for the city before breakfast. It had rained some the night before, and rained some during the day. Today it has been cloudy, and is windy and cold. I reckon we shall have a storm before we get through with it. We are very well prepared however; have paved both our tents with brick, and also under our fly in front, so that we have the size of three tents bricked. It sweeps easily and stays clean, and we are as proud as can be, as we are better off than any on the line. In the winter quarters we shall stockade - build up around the size of the tents with boards and put the tents on top, some four feet from the ground. This makes a very comfortable arrangement. I never saw such sights of flies as we have in our tents. This cold spell will trouble them. It is quite chilly tonight, but we have not got our stove up yet. I had a capital time visiting the city yesterday. Went down before breakfast, afoot of course; found the 12th in camp near where we went first, on Capitol Hill; got there about eight and stayed till three.

My friends there were all well. I found some whom I had no expectation of seeing; one, a classmate, Fitch.[25] Also the drum-major, Downer,[26] of the R. & B. R. R.[27] The regiment is not drilled much, but is of splendid material, and has much better guns than we. They had a hard time that stormy Friday night, for they had no tents but little "shelter tents" of cotton cloth, made to carry in the knapsack on active service, and not large enough to cover one entirely; so they got wet, but not one of my friends was injured. Their "A" tents came while I was there. I was lucky to see them when I did, for they probably will not stay long where they are now, though they hope to await the rest of the Brigade. They have a pleasant camp, close to the city - too close for comfort, I should say if I was an officer. The Rutland boys are proud of their company, but say they are going to throw away their knapsacks.

Button[28] and I went to the city at three - had dinner and looked about some. I was too late to get into any of the public buildings, and must take another day for that. Shall go very soon, if the boys of the 12th remain there. I can alter the date on my pass, and no one will be any wiser. I did not see any patrol, and think it is principally scare. It can't be that the crowds of army officers I saw have all passes regularly endorsed. It made a pretty long tramp for me. I got home late, and tired, but I stand such a jaunt first rate. This morning I slept till seven; got up and bathed, and went two miles to an Episcopal church. Had a very good sermon indeed - a little house and congregation, but very pleasant. The building was built in 1719 , and rebuilt 1789. It is quite near Fort Totten. I am officer of the day today - a sinecure in this little post. Have slept all the afternoon. My feet and I get along first rate. I am troubled a very little by corns - not worth speaking of. Wear my grain boots - have not unpacked the others since I left Brattleboro. I put on drawers today and find it a great relief. Smith and I keep warm as toast under our buffalo. He is quite well now; went to the city with me without a pass. Will send you mine for a curiosity when I get through with it.

I got me a hat and cord in the city. The cap was heavy on hot days, but it will be cold a while I reckon. We have not set up our stove in the tent yet, but can at any time. I am very well indeed. Have had only one bad spell of a few hours, when I followed a dish of honey by some cabbage and vinegar. They did not agree. If I am ever sick at all, you shall certainly know it. It don't seem as if you wrote as often as I do. I only heard once last week. A letter usually comes on Sunday, but I did not get any at all today. I will send the Atlantic's home when I come across some mucilage. I have enjoyed them very much. We officers have little enough to do now, but are waiting for the drill. I am very well contented here. It is not a life pleasant entirely, but I feel as though I ought to be here, and enjoy it as well as I can. I am much more pleasantly situated than many others; but have not struck the army as a profession, as Capt. Hunsdon has. It seemed good enough to see friends right from Vermont, I assure you.

Very truly yours,

Aldace F. Walker

Fort Massachusetts, D.C.,
Oct. 14, 1862

Dear Father:

I don't see why my letters are irregular, for I have written regularly every Sunday and Wednesday for some time. They may fail to leave here in our camp mails, or they may delay somewhere else. I shall keep writing, of course, and you may get what you can. I get yours all right, and pretty often; had one Monday, I believe. We have kept at work faithfully till night before last, when the Companies detailed to make road and encamped near here, had orders home and left. We had not quite finished our chopping, and I worked with them yesterday. About five yesterday, orders came to the effect that on account of the proximity of the enemy, the artillery must remain in the forts at the guns, and the 11th Vt. must have 30 men of each Company in constant readiness to turn out. We doubled our pickets at once, and told off our 30, which, with 14 pickets, 8 guard, and the sick, took nearly our whole strength. We issued 20 rounds of ammunition to each man, and got on the whole considerably frightened.

Capt. Hunsdon was officer of the day, and I took our Company out for the first time for action. About eight o'clock I marched them to the fort. The artillery Companies slept by their guns, and we had the floor of the implement room. We heard meanwhile that a new regiment was to reinforce us, but we have not seen it yet. We slept soundly till morning, and then marched back again. I suppose the process will be repeated hereafter for the present. I knew that it was pretty much all poppycock to think of an attack here; though it is true enough that, as lax as we had been, a thousand cavalry could ride into Washington any night, as well as not. It was well to increase our diligence, and there is a shadow of a possibility of a raid in this direction. It did the men ever so much good; the Major was somewhat scared, and on the whole nobody was hurt. If we keep 30 men in constant readiness, however, it will do away with fatigue, as we could send out but nine this morning, and I have started the balance out on squad drills; shall have a Company drill this afternoon. I suppose it is certain now that we shall be mustered before long - perhaps not till Jan. 1st - as artillery. I like the arrangement well. It strikes me favorably in every respect but this, that the heavy artillery will be the troops most desirable to retain for garrisons, should the war terminate before our term of service. I shan't complain, however, if I serve three years, as I agreed to.

The Col. dropped in upon us at dinner time a day or two since, and we had much other company the same day. We did not expect such distinguished company, but were able to give them baked pig, and vegetables of as great a variety as anyone could want. We have pickled beets now that are very nice. Tomatoes are played out. The nights have been colder lately, and we have had bleak days; but today is beautiful again, and will be hot. I have seen none of the 12th since I wrote before. Mean to go to the city again before long. I was hoping that that regiment would support us here, and it may yet, though I begin to think the authorities were humbugging us. Major Sadler got a bona fide dispatch to look out a camping ground for a new regiment, however. There must be a terrible screw loose somewhere, to allow a rebel force to run right around our army. Perhaps it could not be helped. Its very audacity was a great protection. I have not seen any paper this morning yet, and don't expect to be able to get one. I took supper at Blair's (Hon. for a title), the father of Frank and Montgomery, &c, Monday night. It is a splendid place, some two miles from here. I conjured up an errand, and got in just as they were sitting to the table. I was invited very kindly to come again, and shall, as there are young people in the family whom I have seen. No one was there on Monday but Mr. Blair and wife. The secessionists in this vicinity tried to hang him a while ago, but did not succeed, and probably won't now.[29]

It does seem as though Buell[30] had done something in the West at last. Whether his battles will remain fruitless is yet to be seen. Mr. Blair said that McClellan's army that marched by here and fought the battle of Antietam, looked perfectly unfit to do anything at all. He wondered that McClellan took them into action, and does not wonder at his present delay. He thinks that McClellan would surely have taken Richmond from the peninsula if he had not been interfered with, and stands by "Abe" and the proclamation. I am very well yet. Am troubled, as everyone in the regiment is, by blotches that itch terribly, caused by lying on the ground. In Light Artillery the companies are 150 strong, and each is an independent command. In Heavy Artillery, a regiment, full, consists of 12 companies, of 100 men each. Light A. has a Capt., two 1st, and two 2nd Lieuts. to a company. Heavy has a Capt., two 1st and one 2nd Lieut., to a company, and three Majors per regiment if there are 12 companies, two if 10. It is reported that two of the 1st Lieuts., present, will go to Vermont to raise two new companies to fill the complement; and if so, I can go if I choose. Hunsdon, however, will be Major if the arrangement is effected, and I had rather remain with Co. B than have a new one. Should like to visit home well enough, however, and shan't disobey my orders. The ambulance just drove up bringing two of our men from the hospital, who have been down sick. I am glad to see them, but one is so deaf that he is good for nothing. One man, a negro, we were just ordered to drop from our rolls.[31]

Very truly,

Aldace F. Walker

Evening - We see nothing of our new regiment, and have given it up. I hope to hear from you again tomorrow. I have got John Halifax,[32] and like it much. We find we have a little more work to do, but expect and end somewhere.

Fort Massachusetts,
Oct. 22, 1862

Dear Father:

It is a terrible windy day; the tent shakes and shivers, and the dust flies all ways. The nights have been cold lately, and reveille at half past five reveals a blue looking set, I assure you; but the days are comfortable, and we have very little rain. We fear a storm now. I have just got up from the dinner table - frugal enough, this time - and good enough, too - bread and milk. We can get all the milk we want for 7 or 8 cents. We have eaten a quarter of mutton this week. We continually make discoveries in the fodder line of new possibilities; slap-jacks was our last attempt, and if you will come to supper this evening I promise you as good a batch as you can get in Vermont. I have just suggested hasty pudding, and if we can raise some Indian meal, we will try that on - warm and fried. Smith is providing for the mess now, and I am glad to be relieved.

We have at last commenced our long anticipated artillery drill, and are doing famously. Monday and Tuesday morning the sergeants and corporals were instructed, and by Tuesday afternoon they were competent to teach the rest. The men take hold finely. We drill nearly five hours a day. It is a pleasant kind of a service; five or seven men work together on the same piece; each one has a number and a place and a special duty, and all the motions are on a double quick. The Pennsylvanians are astonished to see how readily we take it up. Col. Gibson has appointed the last day of the month to inspect the regiment, and we have got to buckle into it. If they will let us alone, however, I think we shall be ready for him. Nothing at all has occurred since I wrote before, that would interest you, as I remember. I hear often from friends. Aunt Minerva sent me a letter and papers last night. The last Herald has not reached me yet. The October elections seem to have gone completely by the board. The Democratic party in Pennsylvania is composed of men who will not support the administration or the war, and they have had their own way pretty much. So in the West. It is the most discouraging thing I have seen for a long time. An opposition to the war, organized and formidable, arising just as Emancipation is proposed officially, does not look as though the right move had been made. But the best will eventuate at last.

It is amusing to hear the provincialisms of the Pennsylvanians and of the people here. "Evening" begins at noon. "This 'ere" gun rests upon "this y'ere here" carriage. There's a "right smart chance" of a storm. "Where y'er going at?," &c. I presume our talk is as queer to them. The Pa. men with whom we are associated are gentlemen, and we get on with them swimmingly. Their men have rather a hard name for their "lifting propensities." We put a stove into the tent the other night. It is a very fine thing to have in a tent; but the first day it had to have the tent all to itself, for the smoke drove out everything else - even the flies. The next day the wind changed, and it went better. We had it so that I could lie in my bed and heat my feet most beautifully, and last night I went to sleep there; woke up in the middle of the night somewhat cold, if not more. This morning the wind blew exactly down the pipe, so we moved stove to the other side - made a fire - set the tent on fire

- and concluded to wait for colder weather. We have a cooking stove beside, that cost 75¢. Our brick came from an old meeting house torn down to make room for the fort, and the brick, seats, pulpit, etc., were "confiscated."

I may hear again from you tonight.

Aldace F. Walker

Fort Massachusetts, D.C.,
Oct. 26, '62

Dear Father:

I have waited till the mail came in this p.m., hoping to hear from you, but no letter came. One from Henry and Ellena,[33] at West Brattleboro. I presume I shall hear tomorrow. Our mail on Monday, however, is usually very small, as no mail leaves Vermont on Sunday, and there must be a hiatus somewhere. This is the first really rainy day we have had. It began about eight, and has rained steadily ever since. I have hardly left the tent. We are very dry here, however, and the boys are comfortable. Our stove drew the wrong way at first, but we put it on the other side of the tent and cut another hole, so that it is quite comfortable.

These lazy days are very long. I, of course, could not go to meeting. We had no inspection, and have nothing in fact on hand save to keep warm and dry. I have written a good deal, and the hours are wearing along. I hope it will hold up tomorrow, as we are to be examined in artillery next Friday, and we hate to lose any time. Another week will help us along some in the drill, but whether we are judged competent to hold the place alone I doubt; we hope so, however.

Yesterday a large number went to the city to see the new Vermont regiments. The 14th and 15th came in fifteen minutes apart. I was officer of the day, and could not leave camp. Heard from a large number of my friends, however. The regiments went directly over into Virginia into Camp Chase, under Gen. Casey, some six miles from the depot. I mean to go over next Saturday if I possibly can. I presume the 16th will go to the same place. It is rumored that the 12th is to be retained as a Patrol in Washington, but this is doubtful.

Yesterday I had every tent in the streets struck and thoroughly aired, and the ground policed. It needed renovating, and I am glad we got arranged before the storm. I have not been to any house in this vicinity except Mr. Blair's, and there a very little. I went first simply to look over the grounds, which are very fine, and met some of the ladies out walking - talked a few minutes with them. Awhile after I went out again; made an errand to inquire if our pickets were injuring their property, as I had heard they were. They said we did not trouble them in the least; the Pennsylvanians have some, however. No one was there then save F. P. Blair and his wife. They invited me to dinner, and vary cordially to call again. Said officers of this garrison often came there, and they were always very glad to see them. I left my card, and went out again last Friday p.m. Found no one but a daughter of Montgomery Blair, the P. M. General, who recognized me, and I had a very pleasant call. She has a beautiful Chickering, and plays splendidly; has studied in New York, and is really a master. I don't know who I had rather hear. Perhaps it was because I had not heard a piano for so long, but it was really a great treat. I don't take any great shine to the girl, however.

The people around here are very many - a majority perhaps, secesh, and rather decidedly dowdyish, moreover. I mean to find out that minister at Rock Creek, and know I can if I set out to, as my brass is in capital order. There is no doubt but that the artillery service will be much more pleasant and much less laborious than the infantry, and I think it is now "sure pop."

I am going to have some more stuff sent from Vermont presently. Lt. Smith has a box now on the way. We understand that if express is paid to New York, goods for soldiers come free the rest of the way, and our quartermaster brings them regularly from the city. I can tell more when his comes, and shan't want it for two or three weeks at any rate. He expects a tub of butter among other things. I want more particularly my overcoat. The one I have worn will do just as well as another, and better than these thinner ones. I think you had better have brass buttons put on, and a new collar. It may want rebinding; but, at any rate, Aunt Sylvia can easily fix it so that it will be just the thing for this winter. A pair of stockings or so, two or three towels, etc., and eatables as you choose. I am of a great mind to have you send on my trunk. If I do, it will be a convenience this winter, as my valise is crowded; and on any movement, I can easily store it or send it home. I shall have to have a new pair of pants presently for dress pants - I always was tough on breeches - but shall wait to see whether I shall wear the red stripes or not. My hat suits me very well. I shall have some photographs taken the next time I visit the city, if I have money enough. I hope to find some in the next letter, as my pond is almost dry.

So Buell is out in Kentucky. I am heartily glad of it. Our Col. has just returned from a visit to the Army. He says he had no comprehension of the enthusiasm of the soldiers for McClellan till he saw the spontaneous roar that arose as he passed along the line. I can't get over those elections. Why won't Northern men let the conduct of the war alone and look to their home affairs? I very much doubt the effect of the Proclamation. I foresee a reaction against the war, and fear that we shall break down, and that before long, from internal dissensions. But we hope for the best.

Very truly, &c.,

Aldace F. Walker

Fort Massachusetts, D.C.,
Oct. 29, 1862

Dear Father:

Your letter and paper started on Oct. 23rd reached me last night. It was a long time coming, and I was somewhat worried lest money should be lost. I found ten dollars enclosed, however, all right. I have nearly spent this already. Had to buy a pair of pants for my boy, and pay more money for food. We pay in $5 each, and use from it until it is all gone. We try not to be extravagant, but it has to come as often as once a week each. If we had not a boy apiece, it would be quite a saving in this line, I reckon. I suppose Uncle Sam is good for a handful of his greenbacks sometime, but I fear it will be a good while first. And, by the way, the Treasury notes are about all the circulation around here, and the postage stamp currency is all the change we see at all.

That storm of Sunday proved to be very severe. It rained full twenty-four hours, and with a high wind all Sunday night. The tents, some of them, came down, for the soil just where we are is very loose - no more than a mortar bed when wet - and the stakes would pull out in spite of driving. We lost some two or three during the night. The Pa. Co. lost all their big Sibleys. My own tent gave way about eight in the morning, but not till after the rain had ceased. We are all right, and beautiful weather now. The roads dried very quick, and are hard, not dusty. I hope McClellan will improve the present week.

Monday afternoon I went over to Fort Lincoln. Rode two thirds of the way on a hard - riding, high-stepping horse, and was glad enough to get off and go afoot the rest of the way. I went on, did my business, and slept there over night. Came back in the morning, riding two thirds again of the way in a provision wagon. When I reached home I found that we must have some tools from the city to fix up our guns for monthly inspection. So I started off without any pass, and walked to the city and back, getting home about eight I the evening. I went on to Capitol Hill and saw the boys. All are well. I visited the camp of the 16th. Found Eaton,[34] Capt. in Co. A, and Knapp,[35] also Pettengill[36] is a Company Clerk in the 16th. Another college fellow is Lieutenant. The 14th and 15th are, or were then, expected back from Arlington Heights to form a permanent brigade with the 12th, 13th and 16th, on Capitol Hill now. Col. Blunt is at present acting Brigadier. I presume they will stay in the city only long enough to complete their organization.

I have got a pass for next Saturday to go to Alexandria; I got it for the purpose of seeing the 19th, but shall go over and see the place, and try and find Higley. I will send home my old pass. It was originally for the 11th. I made it 17th, and then 27th - without using it however, but just to see how it would look. The one I have got now I can't change; and don't care, for I got along just as well without one yesterday. There is a patrol, however. I have often seen it, but it never stopped me. Four Burlington seniors got into the lockup the other day. I stood my long walk very well. In fact I have not felt so well for a long time as I do now. I have had but one attack of diarrhea since I have been here, and that lasted only a day or two. My feet are sound, and my boots are splendid. I hate to undertake to break the other pair.

Col. Randall[37] of the 13th got into a scrape the other day by abusing one of his men - knocking him down with a gun. If you send me a box presently, get a pair of buckskin gloves, or gauntlets, with wristlets say three inches long. I presume I shall think of more things presently. Charlie's box has not come yet. I have been making out charges against one of my men today. Mean to make a court martial of it, but may drop it.

I am full of business with our quarterly and monthly returns, and shall hardly get round by the 31st. I could not get blanks as I wanted, and have written all the time lately. I am going to have some hasty pudding and milk for supper, and expect to have a good one; for our cook, a boy, Doane, the Captain's waiter, is a good cook, and the other boys wait on the table. Lt. Smith is on detailed duty, building a battery in the woods near by. We have been practicing one of our big 24 pounders this morning. It shot pretty well, for green gunners. We have a target about a mile off, and plump at it. We get the line well enough, but have to get the elevation by degrees on a sight, and that we don't know so much about. The shot all went over. We could get the elevation exactly by our tables if we knew the distance, but we have to guess at that. I did not see the [Vermont] Chronicle last week. It has not come. I shall be glad to see it, however. Is Steel its editor? On pleasant Sundays, the Chaplain preaches at some one of the posts. He has got to be a sort of a cipher, and very little attention is paid to him. He is homesick, and talks of resigning. I think will do so before long. We of course have no regimental drills. The regiment was brought here a part of it, temporarily for fatigue service, but has returned long since. We have out two or three fatigue parties now, on batteries, etc. I suppose our monthly inspection is to come off Friday, the last of the month.

Our Col. is now in the city presiding over an adjourned session of the Court martial. A Dutch Captain skedaddled during the trial - was caught, and they are on him again. We are to be examined Friday also in artillery, and I hope a re-arrangement of the regimental position will be effected next week; I have some doubt, however. I have got to be quite proficient in artillery drill, not practice. The commands I can give, and execute, and I understand the names of the thousand and one parts of the piece and carriage. I have studied some concerning the fort and art of fortification, but have not got the books I wish. Meant to have got them in the city, but did not have funds enough, and besides, I forgot it. Shall make out sometime. Meanwhile, I borrow for what time I have. I can write no more this time. Shall expect a letter some tonight. Your letters I am always very glad to receive, and read them first when others come with them.

Love to Mary, Mother, Aunt Sylvia and all.

Truly,

Aldace F. Walker

----

1 See Appendix A.

2 Aunt Minerva; mentioned in several letters; lived in Hoboken, N.J.

3 CSA Gen. Robert E. Lee and his Army of Northern Virginia had invaded Maryland. Local Union leaders did not know where CSA Lieut. Gen. Thomas J. "Stonewall" Jackson and his 12,000 infantrymen were, and were justifiably concerned. Chester G. Hearn, Six Years of Hell: Harper's Ferry During the Civil War, (Louisiana State University Press, Baton Rouge, 1996), 146-7.

4 USA Maj. Gen. George Brinton McClellan's army had just won the initial battles of the Maryland Campaign, at South Mountain and Crampton's Gap, thus relieving the anxiety of an attack on eastern Maryland or Washington. Ibid.

5 USA Brig. Gen. Julius White, USV, had command of a brigade at Martinsburg, which had been forced in to Harper's Ferry on 11 September by Stonewall Jackson. Boatner, The Civil War Dictionary, (Vintage Books, New York, 1991), 914; Edward H. Ripley, "Memories of the Ninth Vermont at the Tragedy of Harper's Ferry, Sept. 15, 1862," Personal Recollections of the War of the Rebellion, (G. P. Putnam's Sons, New York, 1912), 133ff; Hearn, pp. 143-4, 173-9.

6 Probably Selah G. Perkins, Castleton, Capt., Co. H, 1st Vt. Cavalry. RR.

7 Lieut., later Capt., Edwin Hall Higley, Castleton, 1st Vt. Cavalry. MC 1868. RR.

8 Probably Nerva, Roman Emperor, 96-98 A. D.

9 USA Maj. Gen. John Pope, relieved of duty after the Union debacle at 2nd Bull Run, now commanded the Department of the Northwest. Boatner, 658.

10 Lieut. Henry S. Foot, Rutland, Co. C. RR.

11 William H. Seward, Lincoln's Secretary of State.

12 Walker uses the rank incorrectly here. Brigadier is only a rank in the British Army, not the U.S. The proper term is Brigadier General (herein Brig. Gen.)

13 See Appendix A.

14 Ibid.

15 Ibid.

16 Ibid.

17 USA Maj. Gen. Silas Casey, commanded the Provision Brigade and later the District of Washington, Twenty-Second Corps. Boatner, 131.

18 Private Allen Sweet, age 44. His sons, in the same company, were Eugene and Lafayette, 19 and 18, respectively. RR.

19 Picket = Picquet; Walker uses the English and French spellings for the word interchangeably throughout his letters.

20 See Appendix A.

21 Col. George T. Roberts, Rutland, MWIA 8/5/1862; he died two days later. RR.

22 Lieut. Col. Volney Sewell Fullham, Ludlow, resigned 8/26/1862. RR.

23 Maj., later Col., William Cune Holbrook, Brattleboro. He commanded the regiment until resigning 6/2/1865. RR.

24 Private Samuel B. Boyden, Guilford, 16th Vt. Infantry. He later joined the 11th Vt. Infantry in late August, 1864. RR.

25 Private, later Sergt., John Ashley Fitch (1839-1891), Fairfield. MC 1862. 12th Vt. Infantry. Robinson, 164. RR.

26 Private Perley R. Downer, Burlington, 12th Vt. Infantry. RR.

27 Rutland & Burlington Rail Road.

28 Private William Harvey Button, Rutland, 12th Vt. Infantry. RR.

29 Francis Preston Blair, Senior, one of the founders of the Republican Party and a confidant of the Lincoln administration, was involved in a number of events during the war, as Walker will comment on in future letters. His son Francis Jr., was a Missouri lawyer and politician, Maj. Gen., USV and eventually corps commander under Sherman. Son Montgomery was Lincoln's Postmaster General. Boatner, 67.

30 Walker may have been talking about USA Maj. Gen. Don Carlos Buell's invasion of Kentucky, in early October. Boatner, 96-7, 642.

31 Private, Calvin Billings, Whiting. Co. B. RR.

32 Probably "John Halifax, Gentleman," by Dinah Maria Mulock Craik. Accessed 1/7/2002; available from http://digital.library.upenn.edu/women/craik/john/john-I.html; Internet.

33 Henry and Ellena are frequent correspondents, somehow related to the Walkers.

34 Capt., later Maj., Henry Augustus Eaton (1838-1864), Granville, MC 1862. 16th Vt. Infantry, severely wounded at Gettysburg. Later, 17th Vt. Infantry; killed in action before Petersburg, VA, 9/30/1864. RR; Robinson, 164.

35 Capt., later Lieut. Col., Lyman Enos Knapp (1837-1904), Somerset. MC 1862. Later in the 17th Vermont. RR; Robinson, 165.

36 Private Edward Henry Pettengill (1837-1900), Grafton, MC 1862. 16th Vt. Infantry. RR; Robinson, 166.

37 Col. Francis Voltaire Randall, Montpelier. Previously Capt., 2nd Vt. Infantry; later Col. of the 17th Vt. Infantry. RR.

General
George B. McClellan
(Italo Collection)

3.
Defenses of Washington
November and December, 1862

Fort Massachusetts, D.C.,
Nov. 5, 1862

Dear Father:

I believe I have received everything you have sent me so far. I received a letter Monday containing a "V," and the Atlantic came a day or two since. It seems to be a very good number. I don't exactly know what to do about money, but I think your plan is on the whole good enough. The prospect of being paid off before long is better than it seemed a while ago, and I am in hopes of getting some money before the close of the month. We do not exactly know what is to become of us in regard to our denomination; one day we hear that we shall wait some time before being transferred, if at all, and the next (and most reliable story I have heard) is that Col. Haskins[1] is awaiting and expecting every day orders for its being done immediately from Gen. Thomas.[2] We know it is talked about in the official circles, for one of the department clerks, H. E. Miner of Manchester, was out looking for a chance for a commission here. So on the whole, I will wait and not worry, and when we have a new title we shall know it.

I don't know but it will be tedious to stay here through the winter. I am afraid it will seem like a perversion of our calling, but if someone must guard this line, why, we may as well enjoy its privileges. I had just finished writing you last Sunday, telling how tired I was, &c, with my tramp of the day before, when orders came for the Capt. and I to report at Fort Lincoln with our muster rolls; so we had to travel. Hunsdon was as tired as I, for he had walked to Lincoln and back the day before - but we walked over without resting - but very lame. I had a fine sleep there and came back the next day - walked, of course. I am well rested now, and feel very well - no doubt better for the exercise. I am nearly quite through with our Company business for the present, and just as I was finishing I found a clerk. I shall have an easier time the next trip, but I did not suppose there was a member of the Company penman enough to answer; I found a very good one, however.

Our election for sutler is now going on. There is considerable interest felt, and two candidates are very evenly balanced. I don't know how it will result. The election is in the hands of the officers. We need a sutler - can go on tick then till pay day, and there are certain articles that the soldiers should be able to get without ready money - letter paper and envelopes, tobacco, &c., - and it will be far better to have a regimental rather than to patronize the establishments the men are obliged to now. I have a strong preference between the two candidates - in favor of Haven, of Vergennes, a son of the Universalist minister in Shoreham. I was officer of the day yesterday - went the grand rounds at half past one, and found the sentinel in the gate of the Fort asleep. He is a member of my Company. I took his gun away, and sent a corporal with a man to relieve this one and put him under arrest. We shall punish him some here, and hush it up, I think. He felt very badly - is from one of the best families in Shoreham. That darkey of ours worked for Lt. Smith three weeks. He was petted so much, or something else was the matter, that he got good for nothing, and he has left now. Smith has a man from Vermont - a comical old fellow, but a capital cook. He made a first rate Johnny cake last night, and fried some of the batter for breakfast. We should get along tip-top if we could get rid of the Captain's boy. I don't like him at all. My Pete[3] and the old man (Winans) make a capital team.

I think people cannot complain of McClellan's sluggishness now. He seems to be pushing on very rapidly to me. I hope he will keep at it. His army must be in good order, and if the enemy will only fight I shall be sanguine of a victory - not decisive, but at least fruitful. If you can send Treasury notes instead of Rutland money, it will be much more convenient for me. I can pass those bills, but detectors have to be overhauled suspiciously first. I see by the morning paper that there is strong probability that New York has elected Seymour.[4] I would not have believed it possible, but our Administration must feel that the people are losing confidence and spirit in the war. Peace seems nearer by these home indications than by more Southern ones. Europe also is grumbling. The present Congress, however, lasts another year, and I hope we shall succeed ere the next fall. We have had a week of beautiful weather, but a storm is threatening now. I fear it will embarrass seriously our army movements. I am prepared for it myself.

Express per Adams & Co., if paid to New York, will be delivered to quartermasters in Washington free of further charge. I am not quite ready for it yet. A ham, if one can be obtained, and a lot of dried apples, will be especially acceptable. Gottschalk and Patti give a concert in the city tonight that I should enjoy very much, but I can't attend it as I see. Saturday is our only day of liberty, and I shan't apply for a pass this week. We are at work again by detachments on new batteries, &c. If Mac. is defeated, they will be wanted. My shirts are wearing very well, but shrink wonderfully. Perhaps another had better be made, longer than the others. I guess Mother's taste is the best about the overcoat buttons. Get some black ones that will wear, and it will be all right. I am pretty well rigged otherwise. Money will come surer in a letter than in a box. I have a good many letters to write nowadays. Enjoy writing them, and especially the answers.

With much love,

Aldace F. Walker

Fort Massachusetts, D.C.,
Nov. 9, 1862

Dear Father:

I received a letter from you yesterday, and another this afternoon. Ten dollars were enclosed and received in each, so that I am now unusually well beforehand. I shall have no trouble for a fortnight or three weeks; but if I should happen to be sick or in any trouble, I shall need some, more than a dollar or two. This occurs to me as I am not just in tune this afternoon. I said I would write if I was sick. I am not yet, but I did not eat any dinner, shall not any supper, and shall expect to come out all right in the morning. If I don't, I will write again.

There is a great deal of jaundice in the regiment. The major is quite ill with it - the only serious case - and as my water is yellow today and yesterday, I may have a touch of it. If, as I said, I am no better off in the morning, I will write. Now I am not ill enough to mention it, only for the want of matter to write. We have had a curious spell of weather of late - a freak for which I was totally unprepared. On Thursday it was cold, and Friday morning it began to snow. It kept at it all day and part of the night, and remained on the ground two or three inches deep. In the next forenoon it melted, and then grew cold. Today it is quite frosty. I did not expect such an operation at this season in this latitude, but I got along very well. I went with Thomas to church this morning - had a pleasant rapid walk - should have put on an overcoat if I had had one, but did not suffer at all. The sermon was by a stranger, and very much below par. I sat in the choir, or orchestra, and sang some.

Our men have mostly got stoves in their tents, and are taking this cold weather very coolly and comfortably too. It is rather hard on the sick, but they don't seem to suffer much. One of the tents partly burnt up last night; we don't meant to have that occur again. Lt. Smith's box contained a comforter, and now we undress to our woolens - it is a great improvement; and that reminds me - I think you had better dispatch my box at once, and I furthermore think you had better send the trunk, marked with something more than a card, precisely as you direct letters, per Adams Express. I think we shall spend the winter here, and if we do not, the trunk will be rather a convenience than otherwise. I have mentioned what I want mostly, I guess. Smith expects another box soon, with a tub of butter and a ham, and had a big piece of cheese in the one he had, so leave those out. There will be the overcoat, gloves, stockings, if any on hand, a ball of yarn, a pair of towels, four sheets, pretty well worn and of a large size, an old quilt or comforter if one is handy, (this is not at all essential, and perhaps had better be omitted unless you are very hard pressed to fill the trunk), a pair of slippers, No. 9, like my last, a sort of cotton velvet plush stuff, that I have worn since May, and they are not gone yet - shall keep the new ones in my trunk till the old ones are gone. My neck is pretty bare, and a few collars would be acceptable. I did not stir in this last storm, but if I had been obliged to even my tippet would have been a great help - and on the whole, send that.

If there is any dried beef around, we shall eat it, and I wish you would send a few pounds of good coffee, which we can't get. Anything in the line of condiments we shall be very glad of, as we have no sauce except apple sauce, and catsup, and this last is quite expensive. A few pounds of good sausage relishes exceedingly well. Apples of course, if they will bear the transportation. Our Indian flour here is white stuff that does not work very well - the Johnny cakes are a little heavy - still it does well enough. Supposing you put in a few quarts of cranberries; we can cook them (with directions.) Any sort of pickles - our beets are all gone. I think that, with what you will be likely to think of, will make quite an invoice. I had quite a deluge of mail matter tonight - your letter, the Herald, two Chronicles, the Register, and papers from New York. I wish the papers would be distributed a little more. I would return the Atlantic's if I had any mucilage. I hope you have got my last Sunday's letter, as it was a long one, and about my journey. I have had but one walk since the storm - to church today. Just before the storm began I traveled over to Fort De Russy,[5] our neighbor on the west, to look the property over.

We hear today that McClellan is superseded by Burnside;[6] whether to believe it, or what it means, we do not know. Also that the Vt. 13th, 14th and 15th are building tents for winter quarters - which they may do without using them. We are anxious to leave our location for the winter, but can't just yet. Our man was court martialled Friday; the sentence we don't know. We have some furniture in the tent that is rather unusual, and that I am enjoying now - a couple of dilapidated office chairs, that cost us nothing but the patching, but are great blessing in comparison with the camp stools. I hear from my friends occasionally; heard from Henry W[alker]. and Charley Sheldon Thursday or Friday. I have little to do now. Have finished my writing - found a good clerk just as I was getting through - shall know what to do next time. I write more carefully otherwheres than to you, but tonight I could not write well if I tried. I am not so sick at my stomach as I was at two o'clock, and shall be all right in the morning. We have had a good deal of company today, as we usually do Sundays. The Chaplain was here quite a while, but did not have any services, it was so cold. He says he got shot at a few days ago in Maryland - not hit of course, but terribly scared. I think he would do well to take it as an intimation to take off his shoulder straps, but he won't. Tell Lavonia that her cap has been in constant use and is very comfortable yet. It is the only one I can find that will stay on my head nights, and I have tried several in one place or another. With much love to Vonia, too,

Yours, &c,

Aldace F. Walker

Fort Massachusetts, D.C.,
Nov. 13, 1862

Dear Father:

Since I wrote last I have been rather pimping - not sick, around all the time - acted as officer of the day yesterday and was just relieved - but have just enough bilious difficulty or jaundice to make me feel uncomfortable, sickish, weakish, and to nearly destroy my appetite. I feel a little better this morning than I did yesterday, and when the doctor comes I mean to get a portion of physic, and think it will straighten me completely. We have had splendid weather since Sunday, but it is lowly this morning. I think it is sprinkling a little now. I am writing all alone in my tent - rather an unusual circumstance for me, but very pleasant.

Our doctors we like very well; remarkably well, I think for army surgeons. Dr. Kidder,[7] the principal one, is at Fort Saratoga, in charge of the hospital. He is a very nice, well informed man, but lacks energy somewhat; does not get all the comforts for his patients that an energetic man might, yet feels as bad about it as anyone. We have seven in the hospital now - rather an unusually large number, but no serious cases. On the whole, the health of the Company is improving. The assistant surgeons are located - Dr. Meigs[8] at Saratoga, and Porter at Totten, and visit the various Companies every forenoon. We like these very much. Both are young men. Meigs is liked by everyone, and always was. There was some opposition to Porter in Vt. He is from Cornwall, and I have known him a good while. He is wild, as doctors are apt to be, but indubitably smart, and rapidly growing into favor, for he is careful and successful. We are still on the anxious seat concerning our location for the winter.

Gen. Bernard was here a day or two ago, inspecting the Fort. He said he had applied for our transfer a month ago, but there was a drawback somewhere. Col. Haskins said he daily expected the order for that operation from Gen. Thomas. Col. Gibson said that we should be changed probably within a week, on Sunday, I believe, and stopped work of the Penns. here, who were preparing winter quarters. But why it is delayed, no one around here knows, and so about 15 men a day on fatigue, another 15 on guard and picket, another 15, the old guard or picket, excused from duty for a day, another 15 on drill, and the rest sick or on special duty.

Col. Gibson, in command, is a regular old tyrannical ninny - if it is our general. His own regiment hate him and fear him. He don't trouble us much individually, but we dislike exceedingly to see him around. He is forever finding fault, and is unreasonable in his fault finding - is exceedingly profane - a little withered man, about 50, I should think, lame from a wound in the heel, received in no noble way, the story goes - and a silly martinet, with no scope or width of purpose, save to plan petty batteries and swear at the officers who superintend their erection. On the whole we don't like him. He left his horse yesterday with a Paddy of the 170th to hold a few minutes, and the Irishman got on and galloped furiously a mile and a half. The Col. raved terribly, and the rest of the community were amazingly amused. Major Sadler, in command here, is an easy, shallow man, with no especial military tact, or any other kind. I shall be glad enough when we get under our own officers again.

Fort Massachusetts, D.C.,
Sunday Noon, Nov. 16, 1862

Dear Father:

I have had a rather miserable week; find on the whole that jaundice does not improve a man's temper in the least, besides not being especially conducive to present comfort; know what a bilious disposition means, and am on the whole in a decidedly disagreeable fix. As long as I can laugh at it, however, I shan't suffer much; and if the other matters would go as usual, I should keep my spirits in pretty good order, I reckon. The Capt. has had a very severe run of dysentery; was completely prostrated Friday, but is nearly well now, though having suffered some slight diminution of belly. Will fill up again soon, I reckon. This morning we woke up cold and uncomfortable, a mean north wind driving directly down our stove pipe; and the more fire the boys got, the more dense the smoke got - till I could stand it no longer, and vacated. We have moved our stove across the tent, and it behaves pretty well now. It was a very cold morning, but I found place where I could keep warm till nine o'clock, when I called around for some breakfast. I had a little appetite, having eaten nothing yesterday but a slice of dry toast with a cup of cider, but the meat was served with rancid butter, and the first mouthful turned my stomach. I cleared out instantly, and started for the tavern. Got a plate of raw oysters with plenty of vinegar, and a cup of coffee, and felt better. There are two very fair chances to hire board here, and if I knew what to do with my boy I should go in. I reckon I shall for the next week, experimentally, if this morning's experience is repeated. You see I am sour today. But Lt. Smith is in a much worse plight than I am.

We had a good deal of company yesterday, and among them the Sergeant Major, Wright, on the Chaplain's horse. He and Smith thought they would look the country over a little in this vicinity, and Wright got on to the Adjutant's horse, and Smith the Chaplain's, and started out into Maryland. They had got about three miles off when Smith's horse fell, throwing Charley head first into the road. He ploughed the dirt savagely I should think from the looks of his face; for it took the skin all off of one side, and puffed his upper lip out beyond his nose. He had a most interesting looking physiognomy, I assure you; no bones broken. We were considerably frightened at first, for he was crazy several hours, but he is all right this morning, though flat on his back in bed at a neighbors. His father would not know him; and if he does well, he will hardly show himself for a week or so. You see the officers of the Company are a set of poor sticks.

I have done nothing all the week but act as officer of the day once, and did not go the grand rounds then. Have laid around as weak as a kitten, and as yellow as saffron, trying not to take cold and waiting to get well. I felt worse yesterday than I have any time in the week, but am a good deal brighter today; presume I shall grow miserable again towards night. There is no danger, however, if I don't take cold, and it will wear away presently. It don't trouble me a bit, only as I hate to laze around, and there is always more or less nausea. I expected about a fortnight of it when it begun - the usual time; half the regiment has gone through the operation, and I presume the rest will. We know now definitely that the regiment is to move tomorrow, or at least very soon. There will be four Companies here under Lt. Col. Benton, four at Fort Slocum (head quarters) under Col. Warner, and two at Fort Totten under Major Chamberlain. This gives us three forts and the Dutchmen five - very much to the disgust of Col. Gibson, who did not have the arrangement of the matter. We shall have twenty teams at work for the Brigade, and are ordered to build huts. Lt. Col. Benton was here yesterday looking out a camp. So we shall work next week upon our winter quarters. When the "transfer" will take place, I can't tell. Unfortunately the three Companies that are to join us here are the three that I was most anxious to be away from, for different reasons. I am sorry they have been allotted so, and yet there may be some change - probably not, however. I shall be very glad to get away from these Pennsylvanians, and I presume they will reciprocate. We mean to have pretty comfortable quarters, and to be as much at home here as possible through the winter.

I meant to have written to Mary this time, but forgot it until just now. Received your letter with four others Friday, and $5 enclosed. I wonder whether you have got the lost letter or not. It was a description of my journey to Camp Seward and the camp of the Vt. Cavalry. If you don't get the letter, I will tell you all about it when I go home. I had a very pleasant time; found more friends than I expected, and came out all right. The Brigade was just moving when I got there, and yet it seems they were just moving to winter quarters. I hope not, now McClellan has been laid aside, yet I rather expect some blunder that will reinstate him in a month or two. Still, on the whole, I am pleased with the change; but I think the army generally lament it, and there is a good deal of feeling too.

I see the [New York] Times correspondent was much troubled at McClellan's leave taking, but I can't sympathize with such talk. I am satisfied, however, that the removal was the result of careful deliberation, as the pressure for the time being was the other way,

Mac's friends having carried the elections. Well, as you say, it must be for the best; and I hope for present action, as I don't believe the North will sustain the war another year. I hope to hear from you this afternoon, as I did last Sunday. Of course I did not go over to meeting this morning; nor did we have any inspection, as we officers were all sick. Our Chaplain is sick abed now. Our Maj. is hard up, at Reeve's; his father and mother are with him; but is improving, I hear. The quartermaster, Carleton, has had a hard turn of fever, but is improving. Smith don't remember a thing that happened yesterday, and is a little wandering today; was pretty severely jammed in fact, but will not be scarred, I think. His brain was scared some, I reckon. Your letters are always my best ones, though I am fortunate in a good many correspondents. Usually the mail goes to Vermont and returns in just a week, but delays are frequent. One day, a week or so ago, no mail at all got into Washington. It seems strange that the Capital of our country has no entrance save one single track railroad, but so it is. The mail has just come, and I have nothing at all. I hoped for some papers at least. I feel pretty well, however, and can write some more instead of reading, as I had hoped to. Truly,

Aldace F. Walker

Fort Massachusetts, D.C.,
Tuesday, Nov. 18, 1862

Dear Mary:

I am not too far from you to remember that your birthday has come around again, and you are now eleven years old, I believe. I remember I thought I was very old when I was eleven, and you seem to me to be getting along pretty fast. I don't know certainly as you are more than ten now, however, and I rather hope not, for I do not think so much of grown up girls as I do of little ones after all - they look ahead too much. I wonder how you are spending your birthday. I presume you will think of me sometime during the day; I have of you several times. It is a mean day here - chilly and cloudy, and often rainy. I got driven out of my tent by the smoke, which persists in going the wrong way every time the wind is in the east, and I am sitting and writing in Lt. Col. Benton's tent very much at my ease. He has a nice coal stove, and it is very comfortable. I feel pretty well today - better than I have before for a week, though I am pretty yellow yet. If I ever see anyone else with the jaundice, I shall recommend mercury, for I believe that it has been good for me, in the shape of blue mass pills. Everyone here, almost, is bilious.

Dr. Meigs, one of our assistant surgeons, who tents with Benton, is as yellow as I am. He is a capital fellow. He and I are boarding for this week in a private family close by - Mr. Butts[9] - to try it on. We like well enough so far, and I rather think I shall stay there all winter. It will cost $4 per week, and she is boarding my Peter this week for $2. That is about what it cost us in the mess, and it is a great deal healthier and less troublesome. I don't know but what I can make better arrangements about Pete. The Butts are, I suppose, secesh at heart, though of course they don't talk so. They owned a lot of negroes before the Emancipation Act, and are pretty well off I reckon. Smith is there with his sore head. Is rapidly getting well, and will be around in a day or two.

Our regiment moved yesterday, and the Penns. too, so now the garrison here consists of four Vt. Companies - our own, Capt. Templeton's[10] Co. I, Lt. Safford's Co. D,[11] and Co. C from Fairhaven, Capt. Hyde commanding - a son of the Sudbury Hyde - a fat, lazy, rough, inefficient fellow, with a capital 1st Lt., Goodrich from Castleton, and a miserable 2nd, Foot, from Rutland, a nephew of Solomon.[12] Safford is known as Brigadier General, and it shows him up pretty well. His 2nd Lt., Lewis,[13] is a college fellow, who came with Boyden, and is off from the same piece. The other Capt., Templeton, is a mean, sneaking sort of a fellow, no reliance to be placed upon him at all. He takes good care of his Company and has a good one, but is terribly jealous, and reckless withal. I could get him cashiered easily for what I could testify to, if I had the disposition. His Lieutenants are of no account any way. As I said before, I don't like the Companies stationed here, and could wish for any of the others; but I shan't complain; need have little to do with any of them, and don't care to, save with Goodrich and Meigs.

I like Benton well enough as an officer. He understands his business perfectly, but is very rough; rather eccentric, but undeniably smart as a lawyer at home, and capable here. He has appointed me Post Adjutant, which will give me almost nothing to do except a little writing. Has promised me a tent by myself, and I can be as independent as you please, thanking nobody for nothing. I do like to find myself alone here; it is a great relief. Benton has two horses, and without doubt I can use one occasionally. I mean to rig up my tent in comfortable shape, and live like somebody.

I have received all your letters to me, and all the remittances. They have not come regularly. This morning, I got Thursday's letter, the papers, and the Chronicle of two weeks ago, and a Register, with some of my lubrications this time. But they all get along, and I hope mine will most of them reach you. That Sunday's letter which you had not got last Thursday, asked you to send on the trunk at once. I presume you got the letter the next day, but as possibly you did not, I will try and recall the inventory. Overcoat and gloves, pair slippers, one shirt (long), stockings, blanket, quilt or comforter, two pairs sheets, any amount of preserves and pickles, nuts and apples. (Dr. Meigs has a barrel of apples from Vermont that are capital.) I can't think of anything else that I sent for, and hope you got the other letter, and that the articles will be here ere long. It often takes a fortnight for express matter to reach her, and I shall get another letter from you soon. I shall want more money to fix my tent, and should any way to arrange my winter quarters, say $25. I don't know how long credit old Butts will like to give. Believe I shall pay him at the end of this week, and then let him wait if I stay longer. I must go to dinner now.

I have just come down from dinner. We had roast beef and roast chicken, with all sorts of vegetables, and preserved peaches for dessert. I have not a very good appetite, but it improved wonderfully after I sat down to the table. People here do not live as we do, however; they don't know how. We had no napkins, and there was no butter knife on the table. We are ordered to build barracks for the men here. We wanted to make some six huts for a Company, but Col. Gibson would not let us; said we must make one for a Company, about 60 by 20. It looks small enough as we have got it staked out, and I don't like the arrangement at all. But we must obey orders, and all the reasoning of our officers could not persuade Gibson to give up his plan; and the more reasons for not adopting it, the more firmly he would stick to it.

I hope this letter will reach you in good season. It ought to on Saturday. I shall not write tomorrow, but will when I receive your next letter. I have not seen a paper of late. Hope Fremont[14] won't come to Washington, though perhaps he would do less harm here than anywhere else. I am glad Steph.[15] has got the position he has. He is well adapted for it, but will not be likely to be of much service to the government unless they give more cash to their paymasters than they have of late. Ours (Maj. Halsey) said he had $7.20 a few days ago, and did not know when more would come. It seems as though where money can be had for the making, it ought to come faster. Well, I have written quite a lot. I hope you find my letters interesting. I don't know how they are, for I never read them over. Let the trunk be directed just like the letters, per Adams Express. I can wear Father's gloves.

The Vermont troops are not at Fort Vermont, which is on this side the Potomac to the west of us, but at Camp Vermont, a camp of their own naming. Goodbye, and a happy year be yours to come. I hope I shall see you before another birthday, but I may not be able to. If I don't till then, I probably shall soon after the next Congress gets together. I mean to have a pleasant winter, and where next summer will find me I can't guess.

Aldace F. Walker

Fort Massachusetts,
Nov. 21, 1862

Dear Father:

I have time to write a little this evening - just to say that I received your letter of Wednesday tonight, with $5 and the key enclosed. This one came through very quick, and the one that Mary directed too. I will write again Sunday. It takes one day to get letters to Washington, and then they are delayed along, until more time than seems necessary is spent before they reach you. We have had three days of storm. It has rained a great deal, but we are encamped on a very favorable situation - sandy, where there is no mud at all, and probably will not be all winter. I am afraid that Virginia soil is not so favorable, and that Burnside will find trouble in the mud. But I hope it will be dry again when he gets his railroad ready. I shan't expect the trunk just yet, but shall keep a little watch on the city express offices. How much did you pay? As I am boarding now, the dried apples and coffee will not be so valuable, but they will keep, and the rest of the stuff I can dispose of soon enough I reckon. I am nearly well again - have very little jaundice, and feel pretty bright. I have worked a good deal of late, and that does me good; but I am in a way to have more leisure, and I shall hardly know what to do with it. And, again, I may be stuck in a place where I shall have more work; of that I won't speak, for in war as in other business we poor mortals "can't calkerlate." I have no more time now. Will write again Sunday. I have got to go and get Major Sadler to do some business yet this evening, connected with the transfer of the command, and it is bed time now.

Aldace F. Walker

Fort Massachusetts, D.C.,
Nov. 23, 1862

Dear Father:

I have just come down from dinner, and will write my letter now. It is very cold today; has clouded over since morning, and old Mr. Butts prophesies "falling weather," snow, if anything. I like boarding there tip-top. Have recovered from my jaundice in great measure, and have a capital appetite. The people here are great meat eaters. We have it every meal, and usually two kinds for breakfast and dinner, and cold for supper. Pudding and pies or something else for dessert; still it is not rich living, but good and wholesome, and I enjoy sitting at a table immensely. I went over to church this morning; sat in the choir, and chanted and sung at the top of my voice. Got back just before dinner. We are at work now in the woods chopping lumber and timber for our barracks. Shall have teams to draw them in, we expect, the forepart of the week, and then shall put them together as soon as we can. I shall be glad when we get this job done, and are ready for such weather as this; still, as we are situated, we do not suffer. I received the proceedings of the court martial today. Our man charged with disorderly conduct has been sentenced to a stoppage of $10 per month for five months, and hard labor with a ball and chain attached to his left leg for three months. It is rather hard, but I am glad of it. The proceedings above are rather voluminous, and I suppose I shall have to read them at dress parade tonight. I fear my fingers will be cold before I get through.

Capt. Hyde of the Fairhaven Co. C has resigned, and leaves for home tomorrow. Our Chaplain is quite sick, and I understand will resign in a day or two. If you know of any friend who would be a good man, and wants the place, he should apply at once to the Gov. and Col. Warner. I wish some decent Congregationalist could get the place - wish you were better. We ought to have an active man - not one like Steele - and hope we shall have a man before long. The pay of Chaplains has been reduced to $100 per month, and I think no allowance for forage. I can't think of anyone who might come well; perhaps you may. I mean to go to the city about Tuesday, and look for express - don't much expect it has come yet, however. I don't have much to do now except to get well. Shall have to rig up my winter quarters next week. Your cash has all come to hand regularly.

Four o'clock - I have just received another letter from you with $5 enclosed. It came very directly, but the Herald did not come. I have received a Chronicle for this week, or last rather. You must be about froze out today, for it is terribly cold here. I have worn my shawl every time I have gone out, and find it very comfortable indeed; don't care whether it is military or not. One of our Sergeants, and the color Sergeant of the regiment, is very sick with typhoid fever. We have got him into a bed at Mr. Butts, and are doing the best we can for him. I was very glad to see you drop an idea that you might visit me this winter. I had been intending to propose it myself, but was going to wait until I got fairly settled. I can make you as comfortable as can be, with a room and board at Butts; and a visit to Washington during the next session of Congress cannot fail to be pleasant. I shall rely pretty confidently upon your turning up in a month or two or three - regulated perhaps by the current of Congressional debate. My watch is a great convenience and runs well. I hope Mary has had a pleasant visit at West Rutland. Our Thanksgiving is this week. I don't expect to see much of it.

7:30 p.m. - I can finish this sheet before our mail is called for. There is a fellow who works for the sutler of the 10th in my tent now. They are stationed some 15 miles above Washington, 2 1/2 from the Potomac, doing outpost duty, which in their case means no duty at all. Learn some facts concerning them. John[16] is well. Lt. (2nd) Sabin[17] in his Company is sick, but improving. Young Noble,[18] of Tinmouth ditto. Post,[19] the orderly, has been reduced to the ranks for some turkey stealing scrape. Sheldon's 1st Lt. is to have a Captain's commission in a day or two in the Co. whose Capt. is made Major - and this is not Ed Frost,[20] as Vt. papers report. The Chaplain is very popular. Child[21] is respected, but thought rough sometimes in his treatment of patients, as might be expected. Hill[22] is all right, though in the trouble in which Post was disgraced; in fact, he and Post have rather fought each other, I reckon, and probably injured both. I don't see why some of these men are not sent to the "front." I hope Burnside has a big army, but I should hate to have him fail for lack of men, with such a force as there is within twenty miles of Washington.

I don't want anything said about it, but I have just transacted rather a curious piece of business. As soon as Hyde's resignation was accepted, my name was sent to Vermont with a recommendation for the vacancy. I did not want to get into that Company, for it is a set of hard tickets, and troublesome to manage. Still, of course the promotion was quite an honor, and I was pleased. I thought I had better tell the Lt. of that Co., (Goodrich) who of course expected the place, and who in fact might have been Capt. at the first if he had chose; and I found, as I expected, that he would be much troubled if I was put over him. So I got the Col. to defer the appointment for three or four weeks, and let Goodrich try; and if he suits and does well, as I think he will, he will have the position. The Col. said it was a piece of disinterestedness not very common in the army; but I guess I have lost nothing in his estimation by it, and it is quite a pleasure to know that he puts me first on the list for promotion. If we are transferred, I shall have a sure thing, and in my own Company, which was one thing I looked at. Meanwhile my present place is far pleasanter than Capt. in Co. C, and I am satisfied with the course of things, though probably some will laugh at me. Goodrich is, and has been, quite a friend of mine.

Very truly,

Aldace F. Walker

Fort Massachusetts,
Nov. 26, 1862

Dear Mother:

I went to the city yesterday, Tuesday, to get some lumber to use on my tent. I had a double team, and got boards enough for three tents, some 250 feet apiece - cost about $6 each. I have been at work today, with help of course, on my tent; and as Post Adjutant, I put it by the side of the Lt. Cols. The Capt. and 2nd Lt. have each one near the Company street. I have got mine up, or have got started in nice shape. Have laid a floor on some pine sleepers, and put up corner posts five feet and a half high, boarded up two feet and clear up in front, and in the morning shall draw the tent over it. I have put up a nice door in front, and some rafters and a ridge pole for the tent, and with the boards around the bottom it looks more like a pig-pen than anything else. It will be the nicest one in these diggings, however. These "wall tents" are nine feet square - room for a bunk, that I am going to make just big enough to hold my mattress, a stove, table and chair. The Col. is trying to get me an office desk by a requisition, and I think will succeed. I want to get a piece of grass (or this brown stuff, whatever it is) carpeting, and a coal stove, for we are furnished coal if we wish, a kerosene lamp, and then shall live by myself and be happy. I am going to put up a little tent behind mine for Pete.

When I was at the city, I went to the Adams office, and found nothing of my trunk. Went to the other office, and found that our Quartermaster had taken it the day before. So I came home rejoicing. I got it over from Slocum in the course of the evening. In fact it came just after tattoo - and I dug into it. I find my valise key will fit it as well as the one you sent me; wish I had known it before. I found everything all straight. The stopper had come out of one of the tomato bottles, and spilt a little - unfortunately the one done up in the sheets. Otherwise everything was safe. I am especially obliged for things you marked for Peter. The overcoat looks natural, and I have worn the gloves all day today, for it has been very cold, and is to be one of our coldest nights. They are a little heavy and stiff for this latitude, but are just about what I expected and just a fit. The cake is very fresh. I suppose the apples (dried) will keep, with the stuff in the bottles, and the coffee. How is it about the quince? The rest of the provender I shall immediately destroy. I am very much pleased with it all, the tippet especially. The slippers I shall save for my carpet, or matting. I find the duties of my office are not to be very arduous. If I had books enough I should be glad, but I can get hold of a good many in one way or another, and shall not suffer from ennui after we get at work again.

The men are progressing some with their barracks. It will take another week, however, I reckon, and then we have a battery to build; after that we hope to drill some, when I shall go at it. I am very well indeed now, no trouble at all, save a slight cold in my head. I rather like the jaundice for the excellent appetite it leaves after one gets well. I think I shall keep on boarding for the present. Messing is played out when it is not necessary.

I heard from Ab.[23] yesterday. He is well and happy enough. Part of that Brigade is under marching orders again, and I hope they will all move. I have seen nothing of Stephen. Well, I hope you will receive this in due season. I think of you and home very much, but am satisfied to be here. Col. Benton said I acted wisely about my promotion. He dislikes to see anxiety for office, &c. I think it was far the best move I could make.

Aldace F. Walker

Fort Massachusetts, D.C.,
Nov. 30, 1862

Dear Father:

Your letter of Thursday came to hand this afternoon. The one you refer to as being written a day or two before I have not seen, and as I expected it on Thursday and with money in it, I was considerably worried. I should really like to see the letter, however, even now that I know the money was not sent. I have not seen Post yet; hope I shall see him tomorrow, for I am dead broke. Will write when I do, and report receipts. I fear he will find trouble in finding his brother, for the 10th moved, I hear, last week, and no one here knows anything about where they are. I presume they are in Virginia somewhere. The

13th, 14th and 15th have moved from Camp Vermont to somewhere near Bull Run, and the other two expect to follow soon; are doing picket duty now near Mount Vernon. Capt. Knapp[24] and Lt. Clark[25] were here yesterday, from the 16th. They did not know but what they should find their regiment gone when they got back. They report friends as all well, in that brigade.

I hope Post will come around before long, for I owe some money now that I had to borrow to fix up my winter quarters. The prospect is that we spend the whole time of our service here, and at any rate I am in good order for winter. I expected money Thursday as usual, but borrowed without any trouble, and went to the city on Friday - borrowed $8. I should think that with what you sent by Post I could get along a month now, especially if old Butts does not come down for some cash on the board dicker. I have paid him for one week, and shall let him wait now. I like boarding there very well; there are there now, Capt. Hunsdon, Lt. Smith, Meigs and I. I am as comfortable as can be in my new quarters. I built a frame nine feet square and five and a half feet high - boarded up the sides part way and drew the tent over, so that it is raised some two feet from the ground. I have a board floor and have boarded up in front. The lumber cost me about $6. I got a grass carpet, 9 yards, for $3.60, a coal stove for $5.50 - the quartermaster furnishes coal if we choose in place of wood - have built a bed and stretched a bed cord - have a table and bookcase under way - a kerosene lamp, the cost of which I shall save in a month, instead of candles at six cents apiece, though kerosene is rising terribly - an arm chair - and on the whole have as good quarters as anyone. I am Postmaster for the Post, and have to attend to the returns and reports and details.

I was in the city, as I said, on Friday. I find no trouble going without passes, but still they are a good thing to have in the pocket. I have not had one lately; I don't know but I shall apply for one this week. Friday, I was getting out of the car on Pa. Avenue, and the first ones I saw after I struck the pavement were Steph and Charley Colburn. I walked with them to Steph's office. He boards near the Capitol. He says he is coming to see me soon, though I see his is a very busy now. I was glad to see him, and he seemed glad to see me, and was I presume. He said he was going to have his father visit Washington sometime this winter, and proposed that you and he come on together, and you must; I think you will enjoy it and grow fat together - though I should hope that Uncle C.[26] would not increase his corporosity in any great degree. George Boardman will come on at the same time. Steph says he can accommodate you as well as not at his boarding place, and I can find good quarters for you here. Amasa Walker and wife are boarding at Willard's.[27] He is member of Congress for the next short term.[28] Cyrus Thomas is having a run of jaundice now. I have him in my tent to sleep tonight. I never was better.

This promotion business is all in a muddle just now. The Col. got a letter from the Gov. granting the promotions he asked for - myself to Co. C, 2nd Lt., Austin[29] of F to my present place, and the Sergeant Major to his. The Col. has written meanwhile to have my appointment deferred, though I fear his letters will not reach Vermont until the commissions are on their way here; and meanwhile another 1st Lt. has resigned from ill health, of Co. I; and he has made the same nomination he designed to fill up my position, and this troubles the present officers of I. so that they threaten to resign - and all around it is in a muddle. We shall see it unravel in a few days, however, and I hope I shall be able to keep my present position at least till we are transferred - if that somewhat mythical operation ever comes to pass. I received the papers also today; have not had time to look at them yet. The Atlantic, also, has come for December. The November number was splendid - read the article on Russian Serfs. I have not read this one at all. Our Chaplain is very anxious to resign; has tried in fact, but couldn't without a surgeon's certificate - which I presume he got, though I don't know. I should like Olmstead, I think. He has a son who is a private in my Company. I will try and remember to send a plan of our camp the next time I write. Meanwhile, I must stop now, for the mail boy has come for the letters.

Love to all.

Aldace F. Walker

Fort Massachusetts,
Dec. 3rd, 1862

Dear Father:

We have not had any storm here lately; it is lowry and warm, and is pleasant on the whole for the time of year. Our Barracks are doing finely. We have the roofs all on, and are fitting up the insides. They will be more roomy than I supposed - accommodating 125 with ease. We have built a couple of chimney ventilators on top of ours, and I presume the others will follow the example. They are built of stockades, or logs on end, hewed on the inside, nine feet high, and a road roof. I reckon we shall have the best barracks in this region; at least they are the best I have seen. Our camp will beat that at headquarters; is better situated and arranged. I enclose a sort of plan of our camp, from which you may guess at our situation, and I enclose a piece of veritable red tape. I have got my tent arranged to suit me capitally. My stove works to a charm - saves bed clothes these nights; the only trouble is that it is too hot generally. I may, and am learning to run it a little better under control. Have cut a hole in the upper part of a gable for air. I sleep nicely, and feel capitally all the time.

It is getting quite common in our regiment for officers to bring their wives on to spend the winter. I don't know but it would have been a good plan for me to have attached myself before I came out, and so gone to housekeeping in the District. It is getting quite dark, so you must excuse illegibility. I waited till after the mail, but got no letter at all, and have not this week, save one from Charley. Post and somebody else from Wallingford got to Washington Monday morning, and came up here in the evening and spent the night. They had much trouble finding me - only knew the designation of the regiment. If they had only known that I was on 7th St., it would have been much easier. I was glad to see them, both on account of seeing a familiar face, and on account of getting the money which he brought. I am all right now on the money question, and shall be for some time I think.

That promotion business is not settled yet. I think, however, it will turn out as I wish, and the Col. thinks so too. The Governor's answer to his second letter is what we are waiting for now. The Chaplain's resignation has been accepted. I have not seen him, and don't know when he will go to Vermont. I have finished the Atlantic; shall probably lend it some. It is not so striking a number as the last, though there are some pieces interesting - The Fossil Man, in connection with my recent Geology, for instance - and others. I think I shall get Les Miserables for camp reading for the next few weeks. I have got a pass in for next Saturday, when Steph and I partly arranged to cross the Potomac. I fear however that all our friends are out of reach, and we may conclude not to go.

If McClellan had done what Burnside has done with his army, he would have been arraigned for treason; yet I presume it has been impossible for him to do differently. The fact is, an army is an easier thing to talk about than to handle. I like the tone of the Message rather better than its substance. Its author is evidently in earnest - thoroughly so - yet it all looks a little visionary, and as if the real result, practical, was a little more immediate. He don't refer scarcely to the "Proclamation," implicitly admitting that it was rather against his better judgment - which is the weakest point in his policy.

Fort Massachusetts, D.C.,
Dec. 7, 1862

Dear Father:

I have commenced on rather a large sheet, but perhaps I shall cover it. I have just completed my hebdomadal[30] wash, and am at leisure till dinner time. It is a very cold morning, and was a very cold night. I slept warm however, with my stove red hot till morning. Use my shawl and the quilt and the overcoat for covering. Pete sleeps on the floor with an overcoat and blanket and a straw tick - the latter under him. The men were comfortable, too, last night; all in their barracks, which they find far more pleasant than they expected. The bunks are arranged alcove fashion, and this gives room in abundance. They are nine feet high above ground, and ample ventilation - indeed too ample in the roof, for some snow blew in. They have small stoves and will be furnished large ones. Our favorite, Col. Gibson, refused a requisition for bed sacks and straw. Col. Warner took it to the city yesterday, up higher, and secured the articles. That is the way Gibson has uniformly treated us; and I am glad to find that there is some relief.

I had to turn out this battalion for inspection this morning. It was bitter cold - a sharp northwest wind - snow two or three inches on the ground - and we hurried matters as best we could. I am getting to like Lt. Col. Benton very much. He is a fine scholar (Burlington graduate) and is quite an ornament to the regiment in court martials, etc., being very well read in civil and martial law. He is a thorough officer, too; and I think we shall have a model camp here this winter. The worst fault of his is that he is quite profane; yet he has a care for others - is interested in the appointment of Chaplain. And by the way the Col. spoke to me yesterday of Johnny Labaree,[31] and I would like him very much; I reckon he would come, though of course I don't know. We had a hard snowstorm Friday, in the day and night; left some on the ground yet, and I said before. I presume and hope you have sleighing. The worst thing I have heard of in connection with the storm is the luck of the 13th, 14th and 15th Vt., who came back from Bull Run to Camp Vermont that day, and had no shelter for the night. The Brigade is together again. I saw General Stoughton[32] in the city yesterday. He said he had applied for the Vt. 2nd Brigade, because they were opposed to having him command them, and was going to join them tomorrow. He is evidently something of a swell; still, shows a good record as Colonel, and I think is a good officer. Should prefer Blunt myself, but we can't have our way always in these things, as our Brigade find to their sorrow. We hear, by the way, that Lt. Col. Haskins, who is at present acting as a Major General in charge of the whole line of defences north of the Potomac, is soon to be made Brigadier for this Brigade. He is a Regular, about fifty years old I should think. Lost an arm, (in Mexico, I believe), is apparently very pleasant and efficient. We are all hoping for the time when he will join us.

Col. Warner told me at Willard's yesterday that he had just been informed that Gen. Halleck[33] signed the order for our transfer the day before, that the proper officer had not been officially notified at that time, but in all probability would be speedily. He also said that my commission as Capt. had just come to his headquarters. I don't want to do any duty upon it till we are transferred, as that will give Goodrich a commission, and we can both take our own companies, the Col. says. So I don't want to start on Co. C and not expect to remain with them long. I think I can arrange it so, but I may be ordered to duty at once. C is one of the Companies at Massachusetts. Thanksgiving came and went. We had a turkey dinner. The men a holiday, and fortunately many boxes from Vermont reached us that day and the day before, so that almost everyone had a taste of a delicacy.

The evening dress-parade came off, and I read the Gov.'s Proclamation and the President's Sabbath Order, which was our only formal service. I thought of home that day, and doubtless many in Vermont remembered friends in the army, as Gov. Holbrook suggested. Of course we should have all liked to spend the day with our friends. It strikes me as the first thanksgiving when I have been absent from you, but I may not remember. I hope to get your Thursday's letter today. In the evening I rode to the city on Col. Benton's horse, and went to hear the opera of the "Enchantress." I had heard Sabin tell of this with the same performers, (Miss Richings for the principal part), and I was very anxious and very glad to see and hear it. She is a beautiful singer, and I enjoyed it very much. Dr. Meigs was with me, and we had a beautiful gallop that splendid evening from the city. Saw nothing of the Provost, and had no pass. I had to show my pass yesterday, however, and fortunately had one. I had arranged with Stephen to go over into Virginia visiting, but the traveling was so bad we thought it best not to attempt the journey.

Did you ever eat any steamed oysters? I reckon they are a new thing; at any rate, I was considerably taken down on going into a saloon with a friend and having him call for half a bushel. We found no trouble in disposing of them however, and another peck besides. They were good. Stephen had a private in one of his regiments come to him the other day and offer to buy the roll of the regiment. Steph was considerably astonished, and said that he had some doubt about the security of the operation. So the private went to Stanton, and arranged to lend the Govt. $31,000 to pay off that regiment. He has gone to New York for the money now, and the regiment will be paid next Wednesday. The private's name is Elias Howe, Jr.,[34] who has a yearly income of $200,000 on his sewing machine patent.

In the p.m. we went to call on Amasa Walker and wife, who are at the Washington House, near the Capitol - a pleasant room. They seemed glad to see me, and I shall call again. Frank Walker and his brother Robert were fortunately there. Frank is a Major (Asst. Adjt. Gen.) on Gen. Couch's[35] staff, who is in command of an Army Corps. Robert is a 2nd Lt. near Washington. Frank is a fine looking fellow - considerable swell and gas - just in for a day from Fredericksburg - says the army will cross in three or four days without fail. He, and other officers whom I have seen, join with Pope in denouncing Sigel[36] and Porter,[37] and rightly too I reckon. He says, however, that the best men are the worst spoken of at the North, because a good officer will exclude correspondents - something in this, too. He enjoyed Buell highly - did not mention McC., and spoke disparagingly of Burnside. He don't know anything more about it than anyone else however. Still I like to hear him talk, and he represents a large class in the army. Banks[38] is off - to Richmond, I hope, via Suffolk; still that would be a hazardous journey, and he probably has gone further south. I bought Victor Hugo's five new novels, serial, complete in one volume, Les Miserables, and probably the best new novel out, for reading this month, $1.25.

I hear rumors of approaching pay day, and they are getting distinct. At any rate, I can draw pay on my change of commission, and necessary muster out and in again. Thomas has had a run of jaundice in my tent, but is nearly well. Our Major is well again. Color Sergeant Parker has had quite a hard run of fever, but he is recovering gradually. Our hospital is simply large square tents - no board sides or roof - a board floor - iron bedsteads and straw ticks. They are not what they should be, nor managed just right. And there is a good deal of feeling against Surgeon Kidder - in fact endeavors are being made to take his place from him. He is a fine man, but somewhat inefficient. I don't like the Eclectic much of late. Think it will hardly pay to send it, though the Atlantic lasts me but a day or two. This is just the place where Frank's Brigade was stationed through last winter. There is little or no doubt but that we shall remain here through the season; in fact, we may through the war, which I think can't last over another winter - unless we should have foreign difficulty on our hands to excite us. Senator Foot I find is a very influential man here. Have not seen him. I took dinner at five last eve at Steph's boarding place - a capital dinner. You and Uncle Charles must come down in January. Goodbye for this time, unless I have to answer a letter from you this p.m.

4 p.m. - I have seen Col. Warner this afternoon, and don't see as there is any way for me to do but to go on with Co. C for the present. He virtually promised, however, that when there was an opportunity I should be transferred to my own Company. The commission reads "C." I shall let you know soon what I am doing. The Chronicle came last night, but no letter.

Aldace F. Walker

Fort Massachusetts, D.C.,
Dec. 10, 1862

Dear Father:

I had material for a long letter last Sunday; today I have nothing to say. I contrived to have that commission lie upon the table - or rather in the Col.'s trunk for the present - until we get further news from headquarters. I can use it when I choose, but don't choose just yet, for I could not better myself in the least. Cannon are firing from Fort De Russy. I don't know what it means, but we are not especially troubled. Your letter came along on Monday, and the Herald on Tuesday. I enjoy those Vermont papers very much. They contrast very favorably with the Clipper, which is our only food in the daily line. It is almost worse than nothing. I remember that today is Ellena's birthday, and that she will be at home before long. I heard from her yesterday, I think. We have had cold weather, very cold, since the snow storm of Friday. It is not melted much yet, though it has been very bright, pleasant weather ever since. Today however, it has gone some. I have not been able to keep warm hardly in my tent at night. I almost froze last night, and took some cold. Sent to town for a buffalo this morning.

We are continually suffering annoyances from our ridiculous Brigadier. He has reduced our transportation to one wagon, and the men have been almost without food for two days. It is a shame, and we hope for a change. The men enjoy their barracks very much. Still we lack some things to make them comfortable, which we mean to get if it is possible. Post got here Monday, and up to Thursday had not succeeded in finding the 10th. Whether he eventually made out or not I don't know - may see or hear from him again. Have got to go and run a dress parade, and will write more by and by.

I understand that C. B. Smith of Brandon, who was Chaplain in the 2nd, is willing to come out again, and I should like to have him very much. Also, C. C. Parker of Waterbury has been suggested. I should like either of them, or Labaree, better than Olmstead. There is an absolute dearth of anything to write just now, and I presume it will be so a great part of the time through the winter. This garrison duty must be rather monotonous.

I don't think I shall go to the city this week at all. There is really little there to make it worth the while to run the risk, unless I have business there. It is a miserable city - dirty throughout - only a few streets paved - scarcely any cleaning - public buildings very fine, but terribly scattered - and no good buildings save the governmental - no nice residences and no nice stores. The only enterprising thing in the place is the city railroads, just completed, and which are run with nice cars and good horses. It is a very easy city to navigate. I feel perfectly at home there now, though I have been in only a few of the principal streets. Frank Walker prophesied an advance about these days, and that we should force a general engagement. I hope it is so; still another defeat may be in store. Franklin[39] I find is a rising man, and one of whom everyone speaks well.

I shall hope to hear from you tomorrow.

Aldace F. Walker

Fort Massachusetts, D.C.,
Sabbath P.M., Dec. 14, 1862

Dear Father:

I have just finished washing me; did not have time this forenoon. First after breakfast we had guard mounting - at 8 - and I had to inspect the guard and arrange them for the day; then at 9 the usual Sunday morning inspection, that takes till 10:30; then I had to go into the Fort with some officers of the Engineer Department, and I did not get round till dinner time. The mail is just in, and has brought your letter of Friday. It seemed to have come very quick. I send also Lt. Smith's photograph, which I wish to have preserved. I have not found a suitable chance to get one taken yet, and shall wait now till I get my Captain's shoulder straps on. You may expect one before long. I shall sit standing, with my traps on. I went to the city yesterday, on a pass, to be mustered out and in as Captain. I succeeded, and am now strictly Capt. of Co. C. I made an arrangement, however, with the Col. that he should not assign me to duty at present, and shall go on as Post Adjt. for a week or so. Direct to Lt. Walker till further orders.

Folks here don't know that I have been remustered, and I don't care to have them. My principal object was to get my pay, of which I had exactly four months due, as lieutenant. I did not quite succeed. That is, the necessary routine for all that operation could not be gone through with in the time of one day. Expect to go down tomorrow and get the cash. Shall send you a draft at once if I am successful - have $440 due me. Col. Warner received a communication to this effect last Thursday: "Col. J. M. Warner, Commanding 11th Vt. - The Secretary of War hereby gives authority to change your regiment to one of Heavy Artillery" &c. so that we are in reality transferred. We shall receive a new numerical designation from the Gov. - Holbrook - who is expected to visit us this week. Col. Warner told me that he should recommend Capt. Hunsdon for Major at once, as we are entitled to another, and that I could be transferred to Co. B as soon as Capt. H. received his commission - which suits me. It will probably be a week or so first. I shall be able to keep my tent intact, with perhaps a change of position, nearer the Company.

Please get me up a pair of light blue pants at Chaffee's,[40] same measure as before, save to come up higher in the waist, with a red welt. I got a pair of Captain's shoulder straps yesterday, but of course have not put them on yet. I wanted to carry them in my pocket a while. I shall need another shirt or so by and by - when you come down perhaps - bigger and longer than the others, as they shrink wonderfully, and every time washed. The pants I need now. I don't think of anything else I need, save perhaps a pair of handkerchiefs, as I was pretty well rigged when I started. Shan't complain if you can think of more. The Vt. nine months brigade have left their winter quarters so much talked about, for Centerville, as we understand it to relieve Sigel, who has gone to the front. Gen. Stoughton is getting on finely, they say. Steph met them as he was returning from paying off Howe's Ct. Regt.

The city is in a fever over the battle at Fredericksburg. Military men agree that it was a bad move to cross there in the face of a fortified enemy, and that if he does cross, he can hardly subsist his army in its march of 60 miles along a single track railroad, and where teams can draw no more than their own forage. If Burnside could have amused Lee till Banks necessitated a division of his force, it would be easier. But perhaps he will make out to thrash him. We have the story of the Saturday battle in the Sunday morning Chronicle; but the fight is probably raging today.

Painful rumors reach us of the death of Bayard - of Sickles - of Franklin. I hope we have not lost the last named. He is a favorite of mine. Today will probably tell the story.[41]

I went into the Porter Court martial[42] yesterday. Saw Porter, McDowell,[43] Hunter,[44] Hitchcock,[45] and a snarl of Brigadiers - Reverdy Johnson,[46] too - Porter's counsel. Porter is an insignificant looking fellow. Hunter and McDowell look finely. McD. is here thought an able general, and true, but most woefully unfortunate. It is a splendid day. The men are not at work, and all seem happy. I wish we could have a chaplain and a meeting today, but don't see as it is possible. One of our Company, a nice fellow, nearly fitted for college, is very sick with diphtheria, hardly expected to live. One whom we left in Brattleboro reached us yesterday. I have been writing against time, before dress parade and the drum beats.

Aldace F. Walker

Fort Massachusetts,
Dec. 15, 1862

Dear Father:

I have spent the day in town running from one office to another in search of requisite documents. What troubled me especially was, that one paper and a very important one got lost, and I could get no track of it. The city around the White House is all rented to the Govt. for use of the Departments, whose usual accommodations are not sufficient. The Paymaster's is half a mile from the War Dept., and I had to oscillate. However I got my documents through to the officer who was ordered to pay from Aug. 13th - when I was politely informed that he had no money and would not have for a week. I supposed they always kept it there - but mine will come sometime. I found time to look into the Smithsonian, and to spend an hour and a half in the capitol. Heard Hale[47] speak in the Senate, and heard a hubbub in the house, of which I could translate nothing. The principal thing visible in both places were some dozen or so boys running around as pages. The city is full of talk of the battle. Wounded are beginning to come in. The general impression is that Burnside will do well if he can get his army back this side of the river. More is not hoped for.

There is a Corporal in Co. C whom there is some talk of making a Chaplain. His name is Macomber.[48] He is a Methodist, and a splendid fellow - young, but I should be very well suited with him. He is one of the best corporals in the regiment, and against whom there is no stain from any quarter. The idea was suggested by Lt. Col. Benton, and meets approval as far as it has gone.

Tell Mary that it is impossible to get furloughs out of this Brigade, and I don't think of it at all. Not that I should not like it, but I can't. I have no idea either of going home on recruiting service; should if I had not been promoted. The Capt.'s "commish" has not come yet. As I said before, I am in no hurry. He got a pair of Major's straps in the city today. I went into Porter's Court Marital again today. It was said that McClellan and Burnside were to testify, but I did not see anything of them. Heard Reverdy Johnson cross-question-witness, Ricketts,[49] I believe - and saw several other notabilities. Hunter is a splendid looking man. Porter looks like a calf, but I reckon will be sustained. I guess this will do, seeing that I wrote yesterday.

Truly,

Aldace F. Walker

Fort Massachusetts, D.C.,
Dec. 17, 1862

Dear Father:

I find it Wednesday morning again, and my customary dearth of news for this letter. I wrote a line in great haste on Monday, telling why I did not send the draft I promised the day before. I had quite a time running around among the offices, but I made out at last, and found no money in the Paymaster's hands. He, Maj. Rochester, said that his requisition for funds was the eighth in order at the Treasury; might be filled this week, and might not - probably not. Meanwhile, all discharged and promoted officers must wait - Bogart among the number, who is as nervous as a fish out of water - almost crazy to go to Vermont. I shall try again the first part of next week. I was asked for a pass the first time in the street near Willard's, Monday - never have been before. Had one - a bogus one - but it answered perfectly. As long as my own officers understood the occasion and the manner of my going, I did not care. We don't get our promotion business settled yet. Meanwhile I am acting as Adjutant. I think Capt. Hunsdon's nomination has gone to Vermont for promotion. It will unravel, any way, before very long. I did not see a paper yesterday, and have not today. Meanwhile, as near as I can discover, we have been pretty thoroughly whipped. It may turn out better than I hope, but no one here expected anything from the movement on Fredericksburg of profit, and now every one thinks we have met with severe loss.

McClellan is loudly called for, and very likely will have the army again. What a state of affairs - men and means, but no General. Regular officers all admit that the military talent all went with the South. Lee, it is said, plans all Jackson's and Stuart's[50] raids, and is a General. Who can we present to cope with him? Our most vaunted ones are failing. Porter is a simpleton, or a traitor. Sigel, a self arrogant weakling. Still we have good men – Sumner,[51] Franklin and Hooker,[52] have everyone's confidence now. When will they tumble? If we are really seriously defeated at F. propositions for peace will come, I think, from more than one source, and will be listened to. The war can't be a long one. The army will remove their support, if the North don't. They will give it up in disgust - 20,000 men thrown away for the clamors of politicians. It will ruin us. Still, as I said, I am writing somewhat on supposition, and we may not be as sorely situated as rumor says; I hope for little, however. The man in B. with diphtheria is alive yet, but very poorly; is hardly expected to survive. I am reading Hugo's Les Miserables, and enjoy it very much. He raves extravagantly about the infinite and the incomprehensible, but he tells a thing beautifully, and has a capital story and plot. Have just got a Clipper. Burnside this side the river. Better than I feared. The army is not completely disorganized, but has suffered another great defeat. Where are we drifting to?

Aldace F. Walker

Sunday Morning, Dec. 21,
Fort Massachusetts

Dear Father:

We are just through our usual inspection. We see a great improvement every week now. As the men are in barracks, they find it much easier to keep clean than when they were living on the ground; and we are beginning to get our guns, which were very rough when we received them, in quite presentable condition. The four companies are formed in line every Sunday morning, and the guns, cartridge boxes, knapsacks, clothing and equipment, examined. Then they form without arms in the barracks, and the quarters are examined; cleanliness being looked for, and generally found in good measure. We are in a special stew today, for Gov. Holbrook is in the city, and has sent word that he and his staff will visit our regiment today. Why he comes today, I can't imagine, unless he has a good deal of fatherly visiting to do in a limited time. Perhaps after the visit I will write more about it. It is a beautiful day. We have had cold nights lately - very cold. I find no trouble in keeping my coaler burning all night, and red hot in the morning, by simply filling it once or twice in the night. Though it was one of the coldest mornings we have had, I was comfortable to get up and bathe before breakfast. Once I a while, however, my fire goes out, and then the overcoat comes in play. I got a letter from Charley Sheldon yesterday, and expect to see him this week, and shall be very glad to. Mr. Worcester,[53] brother of the missionary, was here last night. He is Chaplain in Carver Hospital, three miles from here - just from Vermont. Has friends, relatives I think, in Co. B - desired to be remembered to you - seems a very pleasant man.

Charley Powers, the boy I mentioned as sick with diphtheria, has died. He was a very fine fellow - from Shoreham. Capt. Hunsdon telegraphed his father, and he arrived the day he died; took his body home at once. This is the second death in the Company. And what makes it seem worse to us - he had been detailed to nurse the Chaplain, and Bogart kept him with him and at work till Powers was far the worse off of the two. It was a shame, for Powers was worth a dozen insignificants like Bogart. I enjoy Mary's letters very much. Should have addressed this to her, but did not think of it in time. Am quite desirous of having the Atlantic next year. I have got the artillery red in my shoulder-straps (lieutenant's yet), and shall be glad to see my new pants. If you can send Peter any more stockings, I shall like it much - and perhaps a little bigger than before. I have not finished "Les Miserables" - am enjoying it very much. Perhaps you had better take it home. I did not go to the city last week. Shall go in a few days and try again for my money. The Chronicle came last night. I enclose a slip from last week's Register. I don't know at all what to make out of the present political and military muddle - have concluded to wait. We were very much bothered by not getting papers last week. The news was so exciting the boys sold all out before they got here, and in fact did not come at all. I have heard of Burnside's retreat and Seward's resignation, and see in both indications of a speedy termination of the war.

5 O'clock - Just through with dress parade. The Gov. has not made his appearance, and I am glad of it. We were officially notified to hold ourselves in readiness for his visit, and we did - with no very satisfactory results. I don't know, of course, why he failed. Rec'd your letter and one from Emily[54] tonight. Shall send Peter's wages up to time when I am paid to his guardian, Dea. Allen of Middlebury. It is gong to be another very cold night. Only to think that Christmas comes next week. This fall had literally flown away to me. The Cavalry regiment is divided over the appointment of Col. Sawyer to the Colonelcy again, but I think the majority cordially detest him. I see boys from the Cavalry quite often. The greater part of the regiment is mounted now, and on picket duty somewhere at the front. I don't know where the nine months men are. The 10th is still this side of the river, 15 miles from here. I mean to go there when Charley comes if it is possible. Very truly,

Aldace F. Walker

Fort Massachusetts,
Dec. 24, 1862

Dear Father:

It is a beautiful day - seems very spring like - and it has been fine weather all the week. Our men are all out at work, but I suppose will rest tomorrow, being Christmas. We have got a job on a battery near here that will take three or four weeks, I think. Capt. Hunsdon is to have charge of it, and I expect that when he leaves I shall have to carry on the job. We understand now that he will report at one of the other forts as Major in a few days. Nominations have gone to Vermont for lieutenants enough to make three to each company. The adjutant and quartermaster, however, cannot be extra lieutenants as heretofore, and consequently will have to be assigned to some of the companies. It is arranged that the Adjutant (Burrows) will be assigned to Co. B, and the Quartermaster (Carleton) to Co. E so that in fact, these will remain at headquarters as they have done, I shall have no more officers than before. My Orderly is to be promoted. I shall try and have a Roster published when we are reorganized. I am expecting to be assigned to duty every day, but am not anxious for it in the least.

The Governor has promised to grant all of Col. Warner's recommendations, and the commissions must be along before a great while. His Excellency did not visit us, or any of the regiments, but will be on again during the winter. I suppose his principal errand was to secure the transfer of his son's 7th to the North. Perhaps he will want to stay with Banks, however. We hope to have some recruiting done before long. I have not been to the city yet; am intending to go Friday, but may not get away. There is a Court martial in session here daily - full of cases, and they seem to be accumulating from what I can see, faster than they are disposed of. Nothing serious I believe however, and I don't interest myself much in its proceedings.

I am expecting Charley Sheldon, but have not seen anything of him as yet. There seems to be a thorough investigation in progress into the Fredericksburg affair, and it is a healthy sign. Burnside seems to be acting a manly part, and I hope will come out with honor in the end. Meanwhile, I don't expect any further army movements for months. You spoke of Smith's appearance. He is doing very fairly, but I think my Orderly (Howe[55]) will be put in as 1st Lieut. over Smith. I am rather sorry. Howe is the best fellow, but it will hurt Smith's feelings terribly. Many of the 2nd Lieuts. are served in this way, and in fact we came out with rather a sorry set; the orderlies generally were better. There will not be much new uniform required as Captain, save the shoulder-straps. I have got a nice new pair that cost $7.50; am going to have Capt. H.'s altered red for common ones. I think I had better have a pair of dark blue pants, like the coat, with a red welt of course, for dress pants - will wait a little.

Wednesday Eve. - our mail does not leave here till morning now, but I suppose it leaves the city as soon as before. Yours of Monday came this p.m. I see that the railroads are improving time tables and connections, and I suppose mail facilities will be bettered. At any rate, I am not so far from home as I was at Meriden when the mail came via Bellows Falls. I have been to see Col. Warner with Capt. H. about Smith's promotion. I find it is as I heard, - that Charley is "jumped," and we could not better the matter. Still I shall get along better with Howe for a right-hand man than Smith, and Smith's feelings will have to suffer. I presume we shall have quite a Christmas dinner tomorrow, as old Mrs. Butts is a zealous Episcopalian - not so zealous either, for we only just found it out. Old Butts has got a berth in the Navy Yard, and spends his time there. Many of the officers' wives are here and more are coming. We shall have a New England village presently. Love to all.

Aldace F. Walker

Fort Massachusetts, D.C.,
Sunday Eve., Dec. 28, 1862

Dear Father:

I did not receive the customary letter from you tonight. In fact, the one I had Wednesday was the last one I had - or two less than I expected by tonight. The Herald and Chronicle came in tonight, however, and I presume a letter will very soon. I got round with my morning duties in time to go to church this forenoon - had a very good sermon indeed. Col. Benton, Capt. Hunsdon, the Major, Surgeon, and many other of our officers were there, and the little church was filled with soldiers. Adjt Gen. L. Thomas has a pew there and was at church today. A strange minister officiated, and rather more of a man than Mr. Buck, the Rector. I have not had time or opportunity to see him yet, and he lives rather too far from here to make his acquaintance of much profit.

It has been a most lovely day today - just like May in Vermont - clear, warm and beautiful. It has been fine, in fact, for several days - dry roads and healthy weather. I fear your visit will just hit the rainy season. There is prospect of a fine day tomorrow - much to my pleasure, for I have a pass to visit the city, and want to enjoy it. I have not seen papers enough this week to know whether Congress has adjourned over the Holidays or not. Steph and "Aunt Hannah" called at my door just before I went to supper. Frank came out of the battle all right, though Couch's Corps suffered terribly, losing some 6,000. I like Burnside's manliness better than I do his general-ship. Got pretty despondent, but am beginning to recover. Don't expect much more this winter, however. I have not yet assumed command of my Company; expect to every day. Now that the Gov. has reached Vermont, he will doubtless forward the new commissions at once.

Am not very anxious to take the new honor and increased responsibility, however, as my present berth is a very easy one, and I am accumulating fat rapidly. Friends say I have gained twenty pounds since I left Vermont. I have not seen any scales, but think that is somewhat over estimated. Find a great deal of difficulty, however, in buttoning my coat clear down. We had some fun last night. Got proof against a man in the vicinity of selling whiskey to the soldiers. Went to his house with a guard - surrounded it - took the old man, and lugged him to the fort - searched the house - bayoneted a brace of dogs that were inclined to be unpleasantly familiar - and had things our own way generally. We are breaking up a large number of rum shops, so as to get ready for pay day. We send the criminals to the Washington Provost Marshall to take care of, and I reckon he thinks we are doing a big business here. Our pickets take deserters also occasionally, so that we have to send in a guard nearly every day, with some one in charge.

We had quite a time Christmas Day. A Holiday - and some twelve dollars in prizes were distributed for wrestling, running, jumping and climbing. We had a good deal of fun over a blindfold wheelbarrow race by the 1st Sergeants, and a greased pole. The officers ran a race - the one who touched a fence last, to treat - and the fast ones put in, and the slow ones did not touch the fence at all, so that the joke came on a 2nd Lt. who was not in the secret. I have not seen Charley Sheldon yet. Expect him every day, and he may come tomorrow and find me gone. I should have visited that (10th) regiment myself yesterday if I had not heard that it had moved. Thomas is well - is in my tent now. I am going to make him Quartermaster Serg't (of which rank we have one to a company in Artillery) in charge of the rations, clothing and Company property - an easy berth, with no fatigue or guard or picket duty. I think it will suit him, and he will do well. I am in somewhat of a quandary as to who I shall take for Orderly. My 2nd Serg't is not worth a fig, and I have nearly settled on the 5th. We shall be entitled to a large number of additional non-commissioned officers, and are anxious for recruiting to commence. Won't it drag rather hard? - or will our branch of the service be novelty enough to call in 600 men in Vermont readily? I hope so, but doubt.

With much love to all, I remain, as ever,

Aldace F. Walker

Monday Eve.,
Dec. 29, 1862

Dear Father:

Letters this way don't seem to work as favorably as they do the other. At least, both your last came in tonight, so that I had almost a surfeit after my waiting. I was very glad to hear, however, that you are all right. You speak of coming here, &c. It is my opinion, as I said before, that the sooner you come the better, and you must come. I can't think of anything I want save what I have mentioned before. I am very well fitted out now, and have good facilities here; so that need make no difference. The roads are splendid now, and may remain so for a fortnight - probably not much longer. It is beautiful weather here now. No one needs an overcoat - though you had better bring a couple.

I am writing this eve with my coat off and my door open, (though I have a fire in my stove - don't imagine too hot weather.) My pants have not come yet, though I am not troubled about it. Did not expect them till today, and they will doubtless come when our express team goes down in the middle of the week. I have been to the city today. My first errand was money, and I succeeded I getting $364.35 I was paid as 1st Lt. from date of muster, Sept. 1st, to re-muster, Dec. 12th. The pay from Aug. 13th to Sept. 1st must be arranged hereafter. Our regimental rolls were made out wrong, so that it will require a special order mustering us back, to reach that case. All the officers are in the same fix, and it will all come right some time. Of this 364.35, I have sent $40 to Dea. Allen as four months wages for Peter, and enclose an order for $100 to you - not as enough to pay my debt, but as enough to bring you down here at least. I have left $240 and some more of the former remittance, which ought to last me till another pay day. I wanted to send a chunk to you for this reason in part - that I could say that my money had gone in good measure to Vermont, and I have none to lend. I expect, however, that the regiment will be paid off soon. The 10th has been already.

I have not seen Charley. I did considerable shopping and visiting in town, and Charley Colburn gave me a ride out. I rode in with the sutler. I had a good pass, and had to show it. Steph is living in clover now. That "Elias Howe, Jr.." has three horses. He hires them kept in Washington, and Steph draws forage for them, to which he is entitled as Major, for the use of them. It will be a fine scheme for you when you come down, and I hope the roads will remain good till then. Please get this draft cashed soon, as I want to know if it is done readily. Halsey says it is good at any bank in Vermont. Try Rutland. I saw Capt. Hope[56] in the city. He has resigned. Broken down in health by the exposure. Has got a patent camp stove that he is going into, (not the stove exactly, but selling it) and is better since he left his shelter tent. Rollin Ward was his 1st Lt. at Fredericksburg, and I presume will be Capt. I wonder if I wrote that hospital chaplain's name Worcester? I meant Winchester. You know now who I mean.

Fort Massachusetts, D.C.,
Dec. 31, 1862

Dear Father:

This is one of our regular muster days, which occur on the last of each two months. A muster for pay. Every man must be seen by the mustering officer, and our post was mustered today by Lt. Col. Benton, Comdg. We expected Col. Warner, but he did not come. It has been very warm till today. It is more like winter - rained some last night, and turned cold towards morning. I am well prepared for cold weather, however, and should like to have it steadily cold rather than rainy, which I fear. I sent you a draft Monday, which I hope will be all right, and a letter. The pants came last night. They suit me very well save in one respect. I suppose they were made from the measure I had taken last summer, but I forgot my rapidly increasing corporosity, and can't button the top button save by great exertion. I conclude that my coat has not shrunk, for I have the same difficulty there. Two or three inches more waist would be desirable on all subsequent trousers while I remain on garrison duty. My cheeks are getting fat too. I must weigh a good deal more than I did in the summer. Still, the pants will answer very well. Shall have no trouble in wearing them out. Shan't want any more just now.

There are a great many reports due about these days - semi-monthly, monthly, quarterly and annual. I have to superintend the writing of the post. The ordnance reports are very voluminous, but are made out by Ordnance Sergeant, who is a Regular and a very good clerk, and a jewel - understands his biz thoroughly. He has been in the Army fifteen years; is a German by birth. His name is Gervas Loesch; can you pronounce it? I can't - but I don't know what we should do with our Fort without him. Tell Ellena that we had Vermont company yesterday - people from Shoreham and Bristol - and among them Mary Gale. Shep spoke of Ellena at once as a Brattleboro schoolmate, and wanted to be remembered, and is not going there this winter, but probably will in the spring. Her father was with her. Her uncle is surgeon in the Vermont Cavalry. It seems good to see friends from Vermont - next to going home. I learned some interesting news - to me - from Addison County, - that Washburn & Ticknor had broke down in the Addison house, which did not surprise me in the least. They got the ill will of the community by their high prices, and bad living, and bad care of teams.

My carpet has not worn very well. If I should ever move, which is getting somewhat apocryphal, I shall not put it down again. We have arranged an unusually large guard at this Fort, so as to allow some of them to drill in artillery. It is the only drill we can get, and is much better than nothing. All not on guard or picket have to work in the trenches, and so our buildings are not yet completed. The barracks are well enough, but the cook houses are not covered. We shall have to split shingles for them, and when they will come I don't know. I presume I shall get moved before you come down here, but rather hope not. Still, if we can get our new organization to running, it will be well. Please bring me a couple pair of drawers. These I have are nearly strapped. Get them pretty large perhaps, and they will last longer. Very truly,

Aldace F. Walker

Fort Massachusetts, D.C.,
Sunday, Jan 4, 1863

Dear Father:

I have just come down from dinner; was a little late today, because I did not get back from church till one. The congregation at the Rock Creek church is now principally military. From the regiments in the vicinity the church is nearly filled. Scarcely any others were there today. Hardly any singers at all. I played the little organ, and it seemed quite natural, though my fingers were somewhat clumsy. It was splendid weather last week, but a storm is now threatened. I think it will rain before tomorrow. Such beautiful evenings as we have had of late, I have rarely seen. Last Friday I went out for a walk, and made a visit. There is a family between here and the city of whom Frank spoke when I saw him, and I improved the chance to call - Blagden, a brother of Dr. Blagden of Boston - a fine place and fine people.[57] I had a very pleasant evening, and shall go again. As I wrote on Wednesday, I received two letters from you Monday, and another came yesterday. The journeys seem very irregular. You say that the party will probably start the 14th. I hope that is final, for I was expecting you the latter part of this week. I don't think of anything but drawers that I want, and be sure and get bigger ones than before. I shall be glad, of course, to see as many people from Vermont as can come with you; the more the better. I suppose you will want to visit the nine months men, and I will try and go with you. Don't know just where they are, but I reckon they can be found. I had a letter from Abner yesterday. They had quite a scare the other day, and turned out in what seemed to them gallant style. His letter rather amused me, as their conduct seemed like a dog barking at the moon. Still, their cannon actually fired four times, and that sounded martial. It was certainly more so than anything I have seen. I have not seen nor heard anything of Charley. Suppose he is making a full visit with John. I had heard that the 10th had moved, but not where to. I had a letter from Henry Walker a few days since. He is going to Portland in the spring to study medicine. A good enough selection for him, I reckon. It was the profession I have always imputed to him.

The Chronicle came yesterday. The Dr. Meigs noticed in an extract from a funeral sermon was the father of our asst. surgeon Meigs, of whom I see a good deal, and whom I like much. The Atlantic for January has also come, and is a capital number. I sent the December number home. Col. Benton has gone to visit his old company in the 5th at

Falmouth, and Capt. Hunsdon is Commandant of the Post. His Major's commission has not made its appearance, though daily expected. It has begun to rain already, with every prospect of a long storm. I have got some new buttons on it, with "A" in the center instead of "I." Mr. Winchester was here again yesterday, and took dinner with me. He has some relatives by marriage in Co. B. His brother, the missionary, married a sister of one of our Corporals - Jones.[58] His own wife also has a cousin one of our Corporals - Severance.[59] This last fellow has the dyspepsia, and wants to be discharged - probably will be. You may have seen something of a controversy in the Vermont papers concerning the Colonels of the 1st Vt. Cavalry, though of late it seems to be all on one side - that of Col. Sawyer. I know the truth, from Higley and others, and the fact is their "Regular" Colonels have been fine officers. Holiday[60] was with them but a short time, but Tompkins[61] was a careful, thorough soldier, and just the man to have charge of a regiment; while Sawyer, who was discharged, and then reinstated by political influence, is a worthless, unprincipled ignoramus, and many think him a coward.[62] He has some friends in the regiment whose favor he has bought by promotions, but very few; they generally clamor for a "Regular." Tompkins resigned because Gov. Holbrook would not commission the officers he recommended. There were three officers in one Co. the other day in the 14th Vt. discharged for cowardice.[63] This weeding is going on pretty thoroughly now, and with good effect. I saw no papers at all last week except a Philadelphia Inquirer yesterday. This told of Rosecrans[64] big battle.

I hear the President has issued a Proclamation of Freedom, but I have not seen it. I am convinced that negroes cannot take care of themselves so that they will be otherwise than a nuisance to the community. Want them freed, but should demand instant colonization if I was big enough to have a public voice. I was amused at a remark of Miss Blagden's - there were two of them - that she saw a well dressed young man in a New York City car give his seat to a negro woman and stand the rest of the journey. She "supposed he was a gentleman - he looked like one." But I am getting to feel a good deal that way myself - that the negroes are hardly human; any way they make us a good deal of trouble concerning the discipline of our troops, and they can't but be impudent. About recruiting - I find that many of our men have friends whom they are urging to come, but it will be slow work nevertheless. I am glad I have nothing to do with it, notwithstanding I should like to visit home so much. We did not pay much attention to New Years - the day before was "muster" and a holiday, so that on New Years we worked. These periodical "musters" are a great bother on account of the numerous lengthy and particular rolls they require, but practice will make these easier. Mr. Blagden read me a letter that he had had from Frank since the battle of Fredericksburg. He is a little gassy-blowy-sophomorical - but his letter was very interesting. He is intensely indignant at the battle and its results. Tells a pretty big story that I don't believe, of him and Gen. Couch riding in front of their corps, who were lying down forty yards from the rebel rifle pits, - and the balls coming at them - one hit Couch's saddle - which may be true. But he blowed to me about the excitement and pleasure of a battle, beautiful fights, &c., so much that I don't take much stock in that kind of talk. I do hope Banks is "coming north."

With much love,

Aldace F. Walker

----

1 Joseph A. Haskins, USMA 1839, lost his arm in Mexican War. He spent most of his Civil War career commanding the defenses of Washington. Stewart Sifakis, Who Was Who in the Union: A Biographical Encyclopedia of more than 1500 Union participants, (Facts on File, New York, 1988), 183.

2 USA Brig. Gen. Lorenzo Thomas, Adjt. Gen. U.S. Army.

3 Pete, Walker's servant, was a ward of Deacon Allen, of Middlebury. As a 1st Lieut., Walker received an allowance of $22.50 monthly from the army for a servant; he sent Deacon Allen $10 monthly for wages, and at least at one point $2 weekly for his board. Pete turned out to be more bother than he was worth, and became homesick, so Walker finally sent him home in March, 1863.

4 Horatio Seymour was elected Governor of New York.

5 See Appendix A.

6 USA Maj. Gen. Ambrose Burnside had refused command of the Army of the Potomac twice before accepting. Boatner, 107.

7 Surgeon Charles Kidder, Vergennes; replaced with Dr. Castanus B. Park. RR.

8 Dr. John J. Meigs, Hyde Park, Assistant Surgeon of the 11th until October 1, 1864, when he became Surgeon of the 3rd Vt. Infantry. RR.

9 Richard Butts and his wife hosted many of the officers in the regiment during their time in the defenses of Washington, and were one of "five or six families in the vicinity of Fort Stevens lost their homes to the battle." Benjamin Franklin Cooling, Jubal Early's Raid on Washington 1864, (Nautical & Aviation Publishing Company, Baltimore, 1989), 153. Walker's July 13, 1864 letter refers to the burning.

10 Capt. Robinson Templeton, Worcester. RR.

11 Lieut. Darius J. Safford, Morristown. RR.

12 Henry S. Foot, nephew of Vermont U.S. Senator Solomon Foot.

13 Lieut., later Capt., Charles Jay Lewis, Middlesex. MC 1864. RR; Robinson, 134-191.

14 USA Maj. Gen. John Charles Fremont. A failure in command of the Western Department; had just been relieved of command. Boatner, 314-5.

15 Paymaster Maj. Stephen Walker, son of Charles Walker, Aldace's 1st cousin.

16 Capt. John Andrus Sheldon (1839-1910), Rutland/Castleton, Co. C, 10th Vt. Infantry.

17 Lieut. William H. H. Sabin, Wallingford, Co. C, 10th Vt. Infantry. RR.

18 Sergt. Charles M. Noble, Tinmouth, Co. C, 10th Vt. Infantry. RR.

19 First (Orderly) Sergt. Henry G. Post, Wallingford, Co. C, 10th Vt. Infantry. RR.

20 Capt. Edwin Brant Frost (1832-1864), St. Johnsbury, Co. A, 10th Vt. Infantry. KIA 6/3/1864. RR. Brother of Laura E. "Nellie" Frost, who married 11th Vt. Infantry Chaplain Arthur Little. Relationship noted in later letter.

21 Surg. Willard A. Child, 10th Vt. Infantry. RR.

22 Comms'y Sergt., later Lieut., Daniel Hill, 10th Vt. Infantry. RR.

23 Private John Abner Mead (1841-1920), Rutland. 12th Vt. Infantry. MC 1864. RR.

24 Capt. Lyman Knapp (1837-1904), Townshend, 16th and 17th Vt. Infantry. RR.

25 Lieut. Francis Clark (1838-1921), Bridgewater, 16th Vt. Infantry, and Frontier Cavalry. RR.

26 Probably Charles Walker, elder brother of Aldace's father.

27 Willard's, the most famous hotel in Washington, D.C., 14th Street. "Its reputation had been made under the efficient management of the Willard brothers, who hailed from Vermont." Margaret Leech, Reveille in Washington, (Harper & Brothers, New York, 1941), 8. Today, the Willard Inter-Continental Hotel stands on the same site, 1401 Pennsylvania Avenue.

28 Amasa Walker (1799-1875) served a short term (December 1, 1862 – March 3, 1863) as a U.S. Representative from Massachusetts, to fill a vacancy. Lecturer at Oberlin and Amherst Colleges. Author. U.S. Congress, Biographical Directory of the United States Congress, 1774-Present. Accessed 1/20/2002, available from http://bioguide.congress.gov/scripts/biodisplay.pl?index=W000045; Internet. According to family records, Amasa and Aldace were 1st cousins, once removed.

29 Lieut., later Capt., Orlo Henry Austin, Brownington. RR.

30 Weekly!

31 Son of Rev. Benjamin Labaree. See Walker's letter, February 1, 1863.

32 USA Brig. Gen. Edwin Stoughton, late commander of the 4th Vt. Infantry, would get command of the 2nd Vermont Brigade, but fall victim to CSA Raider John Mosby, effectively ending his military career. RR; Boatner, 810.

33 USA Maj. Gen. Henry Halleck, "an able organizer and administrator, but an incompetent leader of field armies," had assumed duties effectively making him Lincoln's Chief of Staff in June. Boatner, 367.

34 Elias Howe Jr. was in the 17th Ct. Infantry. William H. Noble, The History of the 17th Ct. Infantry, excerpted from the History of Fairfield County. Accessed 1/20/2002, available from http://home.att.net/~DogSgt/history3.html; Internet. See also The Letters of Augustus E. Bronson, December 18, 1862. Accessed 1/20/2001, available from http://home.att.net/~DogSgt/bronson_Dec62.html; Internet.

35 USA Maj. Gen. Darius Nash Couch had assumed command of the Second Corps on October 7. Boatner, 204.

36 USA Maj. Gen. Franz Sigel commanded the Eleventh "German" Corps, Army of the Potomac. Boatner, 761.

37 USA Maj. Gen. Fitz-John Porter led the Fifth Corps through the Antietam Campaign, but was relieved and court-martialed "for disobedience, disloyalty, and misconduct in the face of the enemy." Boatner, 661. Walker followed Porter's trial with interest.

38 USA Maj. Gen. Nathaniel Banks was actually headed for the Department of the Gulf, to replace USA Maj. Gen. Benjamin Franklin Butler. Boatner, 42.

39 USA Maj. Gen. William Franklin (1823-1903) commanded the Sixth Corps during the Peninsula Campaign, and Burnsides's Left Grand Division at Fredericksburg. Walker obviously only had part of the story of Burnside's defeat at Fredericksburg, for which Franklin was blamed. Boatner, 303-4.

40 A hometown tailor.

41 USA Brig. Gen. George Bayard (1835-1862) was mwia at Fredericksburg and died the next day. USA Maj. Gen. Daniel Sickles (1825-1914) and Franklin survived. Boatner, 52, 303-4, 760.

42 For a complete transcript of the Porter Court martial, see U.S. War Department, The War of the Rebellion: A Compilation of the Official Records of the Union and Confederate Armies, (Government Printing Office, Washington, D.C., 1880-1901), Series I, Volume XII/2-Supplement, 821-1134. Hereinafter referred to as OR. Series I assumed unless otherwise stated.

43 USA Maj. Gen. Irvin McDowell (1818-1885) had commanded Third Corps, Army of Virginia at 2nd Bull Run, but had been relieved of command and was currently sitting on boards and commissions. Boatner, 531.

44 USA Maj. Gen. David Hunter (1824-1886), served on the Porter court-martial and investigated the loss of Harper's Ferry before returning to the Tenth Corps in January 1863. Boatner, 418-9.

45 USA Maj. Gen. Ethan Allen Hitchcock (1798-1870), grandson of Green Mountain Boy Ethan Allen, was commissioner for the Exchange of War Prisoners. John L. Barr, compiler, The Genealogy of Ethan Allen and his Brothers and Sisters, (Ethan Allen Homestead Trust, Burlington, 1991), pp. 8, 16. Boatner, 403.

46 Reverdy Johnson (1796-1876) was Porter's defense counsel. He had previously been involved as defense counsel in the Dred Scott case, and later defended Mary Surrat during the assassination trials immediately after the war. OR II/2-Supplement, p. 824; Boatner, p. 438; Leech, p. 412.

47 U.S. Senator John Hale, Republican, Maine. Biographical Dictionary of the United States Congress, 1774-Present. Accessed 1/20/2002, available from http://bioguide.congress.gov/scripts/biodisplay.pl?index=H000034; Internet.

48 Lieut., later Capt., John Macomber, Fairhaven. RR.

49 USA Brig. Gen. James Ricketts; wounded at Antietam; served on commissions and courts-martial from then until April 1864. Boatner, 699.

50 CSA James Ewell Brown "Jeb" Stuart, Chief of Cavalry for Robert E. Lee's Army of Northern Virginia. Boatner, 813.

51 USA Maj. Gen. Edwin Sumner was relieved, at his own request, of command of Burnsides's Right Grand Division after Fredericksburg, and died March 1863. Boatner, 818.

52 USA Maj. Gen. Joseph Hooker commanded the Center Grand Division at Fredericksburg, and would relieve Burnside as command of the Army of the Potomac. Boatner, 409.

53 Walker corrects himself later, the chaplains name was Winchester.

54 Apparently Emily Humphrey, daughter of a hometown Deacon.

55 Sergt., later Capt., George Howe, Shoreham. RR.

56 James Hope, 2nd Vt. Infantry, had just resigned 12/20/1862. RR.

57 T. Blagden lived at the intersection of Fourteenth Street and Piney Branch Road. Cooling, Jubal Early's Raid, 97.

58 Corp., later Lieut., Walter Jones, Shoreham. RR.

59 Corp., later Lieut., Philo Severance, Middlebury. RR.

60 Col. Jonas Holiday, Oswego, N.Y. Prior to the war he was a Capt. in the 2nd U.S. Cavalry. He committed suicide 4/5/1862. RR.

61 Col. Charles Tompkins, regular U.S. Army as well, also from the 2nd U.S. Cavalry. RR.

62 Details of Sawyer's shenanigan's can be found in Chapter Six of Elliot Hoffman's History of the First Vermont Cavalry Volunteers in the War of the Great Rebellion, (Butternut & Blue, Baltimore, 2000), 64-77.

63 Four officers from the 14th Infantry resigned, but not all in January. 1st Lieut. Theophilus Middlebrook, Co. I, resigned 7 January 1863; Capt. Alonzo Colvin, Co. K, resigned 10 February 1863; 2nd Lieut. Lewis Fuller, Co. K, resigned 9 March 1863; finally, 1st Lieut. John Woodruff, Co. D, resigned 13 April 1863.

64 USA Maj. Gen. William Rosecrans commanded the Army of the Cumberland from October 1862 to October 1863. Boatner, 708.

4.
Defenses of Washington
January and February, 1863

Wednesday, Jan. 7, 1863

Dear Father:

I am very tired, but you must not miss your customary letter. I have had a long ride this afternoon on a hard riding horse, and am pretty much jolted to pieces. We have orders to re-arrange our picquet so as to form a continuous line in front of us, instead of lying at a post or two on the road. I was sent to investigate the picquet line of the Brigade west of us, as it was desirable that ours should join theirs. I went over to Fort De Russy, and from there out through their line, coming on to 7th St. way out in Maryland, four miles from here by a by road across the country. The valley of the Rock Creek lies between the brigades. I had quite a time getting my horse over the stream, as bridges are scarce here, and the ford was at the deepest place I have yet seen in the rocky, shallow river - so deep that I dampened my feet by the horse's side. Should not if he had behaved himself. I came around down 7th St. to our picquets, who are in the neighborhood of Blair's, about four, completed my observations and visits to the stations, having succeeded doubtless in obtaining a great amount of valuable information - chiefly however, it seemed to me, of a negative character. Then I tied my horse and went into Mr. Blair's. Miss Blair is gone to Ohio, but I had a very pleasant visit with the old people and their daughter Mrs. Lee,[1] wife of the Commodore. It is very interesting to talk with old F. P. Blair, as he has had a vast deal of influence in the nation, and has still. I was there at dinner - in courses - soup, fish, fowl, beef, and the fixings - but the best part of it was to hear the old man tell about Fremont. He says that he got him his commission, but that he is intensely disappointed in him. That he is nothing but a mass of deceit, with no principle at all - no confidence to be placed in his word - nor in his brain - that Benton wrote all his books, &c., - and he gave instances that look hard for John C. I suggested that he might have been imposed upon in the purchase of guns and other things, but he scouted the idea; said it was willful misrepresentation to the government. His son Frank[2] turned against Fremont after he let Mulligan surrender, and he followed. He is hugely down on Halleck, and upholds McClellan, and vigorously. Likes Lincoln and the Proclamation, but lays all military blame on Halleck. His wife is a very lively old woman, and they are most social people. He says Silas Wright was an intimate friend of his, and inquired after his monument in Weybridge, of which I was very happy to be able to inform him. He gave me a yesterday's New York Times, which I have not read yet, but which will give me some days later news than I have yet seen. Our news boys have failed us, and we are dependent on Vermont papers - or at least I first saw the Proclamation in a Vt. paper, and other items also.

I saw Stephen in Washington on Monday. He has written very strongly to his father to come on with you, and I shall expect you both next week. He has very pleasant quarters in town, and an extra room that you can have; also the use of Howe's old "Whitey" for nothing, which will be a great advantage in the city of magnificent distances. I shall want to know the day to expect you. It is cold today; the first real winter day we have had for a long time. Still, it is clear. Rained a little yesterday, but it is all frozen up now. Col. Benton, as I said, has gone to visit the old Brigade. We now hear that he has got his pass extended to enable him to act as counsel for his friend and townsman, Col. Hyde[3] of the Vt. 3rd, charged and to be court martialed for misbehavior before the enemy at Fredericksburg; and I don't know how long the trial will take, but I know that Hyde has got a good lawyer. Meanwhile, Capt. Hunsdon is in command of the post. Col. Warner has applied for leave to visit Vermont to make arrangements for recruiting, and will probably succeed. The Gov. wants to recruit for the 7th, his son's regiment, and to let ours wait, and we don't like that just exactly; want to go to work now. The Col. said that when he went away he should send Capt. Hunsdon to command at Totten, but now Col. Benton's absence is prolonged he will stay here. I expect every day to put on my new shoulder-straps, but am not anxious at all for it. I reckon the reason the Capt.'s commish as Major does not come, is that another person is trying to get struck into the regiment. Should think mean of Washburn if he should do this; he never has used our regiment just right. Please remember me to friends.

With much love.

Aldace F. Walker

Fort Massachusetts, D.C.,
Jan. 10, 1863

Dear Father:

I received a letter from you last night and one this afternoon, and am assured that I shall see you next week. I shall not try to meet you at the city, but shall expect you Wednesday and afterwards. When you come into the city, if it is between nine and three you had better go to Stephen's office. Get into a horse car at the depot and ride up the Avenue to 14th St. On the further corner, right hand side, is Willard's Hotel. Opposite, third story, over the Mercantile Bank, is Steph's office. His boarding place I am not so sure of. I have been there, but only to the door in a wagon, and did not get the number. It is on F. St., which runs parallel to Penn. Ave. I think between 12th and 14th, on the south side of the street - may be between 11th and 12th - a very high house comparatively, standing by itself as it were - the west door of the house. I hope you will be able to hunt it up after this not very lucid direction, but I neither know the number nor the name of the family. Washington is a very easy, plain city; the lettered streets run east and west, and the numbered ones north and south. The Avenues are rather "promiscuous like" - none of any consequence, however, save Pennsylvania - and there is hardly another street of mark in the city; cars go every four minutes, and it is really quite a busy street.

We have actually been paid off today. Maj. Halsey, our paymaster, is a very pleasant man - very much disposed to oblige - and a good business man withal. He paid off Co. B in twenty minutes. I got $65.30 as my pay for the month of August - worth saving. This makes $429 that I have received in all; seems like a big pile - more than I ever had of my own before. Maj. Halsey thinks that we shall be paid more regularly hereafter, though I believe the Paymaster General means to keep continually two months behind, to save clothing from deserters and persons dead and discharged, &c. When I was in the city last I weighed myself - 182 pounds - twenty more than ever before, and thirty more than when I left the state. Col. Benton has just come in from his visit to the army. I am very glad to have him back - just now especially, for some of our men will make trouble after payday fills their pockets.

Our regiment will not be as bad as many, I hope, and I think will not give us much trouble. Col. Warner goes to Vermont soon to arrange recruiting matters. For the last two nights it has snowed a little. Today it has rained nearly all day. Will not keep it up long I hope. I have really got to having a good deal of confidence in this southern weather. You can come from New York in ten or twelve hours. I shall write Stephen what you said, and suggest that he expect you about dark on Wednesday. I don't know the hour that the train will arrive, but presume he will meet you at the depot. Love to friends in Hoboken.

Yours,

Aldace F. Walker

Fort Massachusetts, D.C.,
Sunday Afternoon, Jan. 11, 1863

Dear Mother:

I received a letter from Father yesterday saying that he proposed starting hitherward tomorrow, but I suppose you will want to hear from me just the same, and I don't feel at all inclined to give up writing. I wrote to Father last night, directing to Hoboken. Whether he will get it or no I some doubt, but I think a mail leaves Washington on Sunday as on other days. We had a rainy day yesterday - the first one for some time - but our camp is dry today. We had also yesterday our first visit from the paymaster. We were very glad to see him, and hope he will call again soon. He thinks the Govt. will be more punctual in future, but I reckon they always intend to keep two months pay behind us. Maj. Halsey paid us off - is a very accommodating, pleasant man, and he dispatches business with a rush. He paid Co. B in twenty minutes. I received $65 for my August pay, making $429 in all that I have got from the government. Col. Benton got back from Falmouth last night. I believe he succeeded in clearing his friend, Col. Hyde. At any rate, he is in capital spirits. I enclose his photograph. Isn't he fine looking? I hope to get more of our regimental officers presently. Col. Warner is hoping to go to Vermont soon. I think I shall remain in my present position till he returns, and am glad of it, for it will give me leisure to visit with Father, and, I hope, to navigate some. The War Department as decided that we can't muster in our new officers till the Companies are full. I suppose, however, that does not affect Hunsdon's promotion, though the State Authorities seem to have so regarded it. I don't wear my shoulder-straps now. The last time I was in town I weighed myself - find that I weigh 182 pounds, 20 more than I ever did before, and 30 more than when I left Vermont. Don't worry, however, for I am not a fat man yet, and shan't be till I touch 250. I mean to apply for a pass to go to town on Friday, and hope to visit Congress with Father. At any rate, you may think of me as there in the afternoon. I don't know as I shall be able to go around much, but I have not been from camp much yet, and mean to try to visit the 10th if they are not too far off. Our men are kept at work all the time on our battery. We have commenced a new bombproof in our fort, that will take several weeks to finish. It is in charge of Lt. Whittemore of a Maine battery - a capital fellow, who boards with us at Mrs. Butts. Meanwhile we have so much fatigue to do that we are hardly ready for winter ourselves. Our cook-houses are not roofed yet, and tents have to answer. I shall want to hear from you and the girls as often as from Father. Have no idea as to how long he means to stay here, for he has said nothing about that. Still, I know no reason why he should cut his visit short, and shall expect a fortnight at least. Uncle Charles will like to look over our peaceable fort, and I hope neither of them will get any nearer war than our situation is - and I can't realize that I am in the army. I hope to get a paper or so this afternoon. Did not get around with Inspection, &c, in time to go to church this morning - the first Sabbath I have missed for some time. If it was not so muddy walking I would go down to Mr. Blagden's this evening, but 14th St. is made of clay. I think I did not tell you that old F. P. Blair told me that Halleck said to the President at the time of Pope's defeat that he could not save Washington. He told McClellan the same, and McClellan said he would try, and fought South Mountain and Antietam. This Blair had from Lincoln and McClellan personally. But McClellan was removed in the face of the enemy, and Halleck is chief in command of the army. A strong movement is being made to reinstate McClellan, and I think it will succeed. The army has no confidence in Burnside, Burnside has no confidence in himself, and our eastern campaign will be of no avail under such circumstances, I strongly fear. Well, perhaps now Lincoln has said that the niggers shall be recognized as free, we shall be favored. Hope so, but hope I shall see as little as possible of those same niggers.

With much love, in good health and capital spirits, truly your son,

Aldace F. Walker

Lt. Battery B., 11th (Art'y) Vt. Vols.

Fort Massachusetts, D.C.,
Jan. 14, 1863

Dear Mary:

I have just come down from dinner. This forenoon I went to headquarters at Fort Slocum, and drew my supply of stationery for the current quarter. It is not so good, you see, as what I have been using, and I suppose paper is not as good anywhere. I got a picture that will give you a sort of an idea of the camp at Fort Slocum, though it is nearer wrong than right generally speaking. It was printed from a very rough sketch, and is by no means exact. Fort Massachusetts does not lie in the position represented at all, but way to the right of Fort Slocum. The barracks, which are in the center, to the right of the two trees together, should be represented much larger. The triangle this side [of] the barracks is a frame where the boys air their blankets and overcoats. The large house to the left in the distance is where Col. Warner boards - a Mrs. Walker's. The officers' quarters are in two groups of tents over the wagon. The Adjutants and Quartermaster's quarters are on the left towards Fort Totten. It is very rough and inaccurate, but you may like to see it for all that. I wish I had a picture of Fort Massachusetts and our camp. And by the way, the officers' tents in this picture, and the tents on the left, are all being moved this week into one row, just beyond the men's quarters.

Charley Sheldon came here yesterday morning, and stayed till this morning. I had a very peasant visit indeed with him. He has been with John a long time. They are at Poolesville, 35 miles from here; all well, of our friends. He is going to visit Harley tomorrow, and will return to Vermont next week. I hope you will see him and find out something about my condition, though probably Father will get home before you get a chance. I suppose Father will get to Washington tonight. I wish I could go down and meet him, but I can't very well. Shall see him in the forenoon tomorrow without doubt. I presume that he and Uncle will take one of Howe's horses that Steph keeps, and will drive out. I shall keep him here tomorrow night at any rate, and expect to have a pass to go into town with him on Friday. I doubt much whether I shall be able to go about much with him, as I am more busy than I have been. Col. Warner went to Vermont Monday. Found before he went that we should have to wait for our regiment to be filled before we have any new officers, so that Capt. Hunsdon cannot be Major at present; and I fear it will be a long while before we can recruit 800 men. Meanwhile, I have been assigned to duty as Captain of Co. C. Goodrich is made Post Adjutant, the 2nd Lt. has resigned, and I am left alone with the roughest company in the regiment just after pay day.. Some of them are off on a bender now. I think I shall get along with them, for they seem to like me pretty well, but still I am full of business. I hoped that I should not have to go into that Company, and did what I could to avoid it, but could not help it. Still I mean to take hold and have a good time if I can; at any rate, to do the best I can. I went to Mr. Blagden's last Monday night. Had a good visit, and a chance to play the piano and sing with the girls, and enjoyed it very much. I presume you will get a letter from Father soon, describing my quarters here, &c. My tent is twice as large as it was before, for I have two together; but it is lower and darker. Still, it is better on some accounts, and I am glad to have more room. Please write as usual.

Love to all.

Direct to Aldace F. Walker

Battery C., 11th Rgt. (Art'y) Vt. Vols.

Fort Massachusetts, D.C.,
Jan. 18, 1863

Dear Mother:

I am having a capital visit with Father, and he is writing to you now in my tent. I think he is pretty well pleased with my situation, but he will tell you about that better than I can. I rode one of Steph's horses up from the city yesterday morning, and took it back after inspection this forenoon. It is a splendid little animal, and I wish I could have it all the time. Charley Colburn brought us out this afternoon with old Whitey. I think I like my boarding place better than I do Steph's on the whole. He has a good room, but the table is shammy - little to eat and poorly waited on; while at mine there is a large abundance, though it will not always bear the closest scrutiny.

The clothing Father brought is just what I wanted. The drawers are capital, though

I imagine they will shrink - not more than six or eight inches, I hope. The new stockings do not wrinkle on the heel; said wrinkling being decidedly prejudicial to easy navigation. When I wrote before I did not think of Mary's being in New York. I am very glad she has gone. Was sorry to disappoint her last summer, but could not see how to avoid it. You can hardly imagine what lovely weather we are having now here. It is a little cold. Steph and Colburn find it very cold, but I don't mind it at all. Have not worn the overcoat a very great deal, because I have not felt the need of it, but it feels very natural when I do get it on.

We met Mr. Button and Mr. Martindale at church today. They are going to Fairfax tomorrow. I tried to get Father to go over with them, but he had no pass and could not get one in time. The boys are thirty miles off, and he would have to stay over night, and I am somewhat apprehensive as to what quarters he would find, though I did not tell him so, and think it is as well perhaps that he could not go, though the boys would have been very glad to see him. I am getting along well enough in my new company. Don't trouble myself much about them while Father is here, but shall go to work harder when he leaves. Still while the regiment is on fatigue duty I shan't have any very great work to do. There are a good many sick here with colds and so on now. I have no serious cases in my Company, though there are thirty excused from duty by the surgeon, - more than ever before. As I said, it is pretty cold weather here, but you need not be troubled about my ability to keep warm. I have two tents now, making a room 18 x 9, but Father is complaining of being too hot. There are lots of Vermont people in Washington. We saw Silas Hodges and Mr. Tilden[4] Friday, and John Osgood today, and called on Mr. Hope, and come across Vermonters most anywhere. Well, Father I presume will want to write a good deal by this time. I expected he would send a letter yesterday, or I should have done so; am afraid you will get lonely, but this long one must make up for it.

Your son,

Aldace F. Walker

Fort Massachusetts, D.C.,
Jan. 21, 1863

Dear Mother:

I suppose Father is traveling today towards home. Think he enjoyed his visit, though he said he got tired of camp life so quick. I don't wonder at that, for everything one can see here can be seen in half a day, and after that it must grow monotonous to one who has no part nor lot in this matter. For me however, I find enough to busy myself about, and have little time to think of nothing and bother about things away. After Father left me yesterday morning, I went to work inventorying the Company property. There is a good deal of clothing on hand ready for distribution when called for, and that was turned over to me yesterday forenoon. I have not receipted for it yet, but shall have to do so. In the mean time, it is in my charge now; and the Company property is one of the greatest bothers of a captain. If a man wants a new shirt or pair of stockings, we have to issue it and keep an account; and many captains have been broken because their accounts could not agree with the quartermasters. I have no fear but that I shall be all right, but there is no wonder that ignorant men in organizing a Company get under the weather in some of the twenty or thirty distinct issues of clothing and ordnance to be made to a hundred men. It is much easier to take hold of it after all are supplied for the first time.

Yesterday evening I went down to Mr. Blagden's. Mr. B. has gone North, but the young people are at home, and I bowled in their private bowling alley till after ten. I am not very huge at that game, but got along after a fashion. Mr. Blagden is a lawyer, I should think. He is one of the directors of the National Monument humbug - with the best intentions, of course, and the strongest hopes; but I don't think that monument will ever be completed, or will be worth looking at after it is done. I left there, as I said, between ten and eleven, and it had begun to rain then. It grew worse and worse through the night; blew and stormed, and shook my tent so that it was hard work to sleep; and has been a terribly stormy day today. To add to my trouble I am officer of the day, and had to tramp afoot out the muddy road two miles, and then a mile and a half at right angles across 7th St., to visit the eight posts on our picquet line. I had my rubber coat, and my rubber cap with the cape which protects the neck, so that nothing got wet but my hands and feet. My gloves and boots I find are not waterproof, but I have on dry stockings and my other boots, and am not afraid of taking cold at all. These rubber clothes are a great institution - much ahead of an umbrella. It is no fool of a job to have the care of.

Fort Massachusetts, D.C.,
Jan. 25, 1863

Dear Mother:

Here it is, a month after Christmas. One of our captains who went home last week (it seems) on a twenty days leave, returned last night. It is wonderful how time flies, and more especially so as I expected it would drag heavily in the Artillery line. Our steadfast position and little to do, I expected would be productive of ennui. But I find no such disposition; time slips along in some fashion, and is gone before I know it. I have been over to the Rock Creek church this forenoon. Sang as usual. I enjoy the visit there very much, though the church is small, the service odd, the choir ignorant. The organist (Miss Walker) is a very fine player. But the singers all run their words together and talk flat - "sam" for psalm, like the Methodists at home. Col. Dana of the 13 Pa. is now in the choir regularly. His regt. was paid off yesterday, and is now in a very diffuse state - and seeking to diffuse itself through other states as much as possible. I believe our picquet fired on some of the deserters last night - without effect. My prisoner has returned from the guard house, and his ball and chain.

Went to the city the next day, and got into the guard house. Came back just now. I think I shall let him go this time, and try him once more - but he has got to walk the scratch.[5] My Company generally are doing very well for them. They passed a very good inspection this morning, as they always do, and I am getting to think quite well of them. I find that the Regimental Quartermaster (Carleton) has been assigned to the 2nd Lieutenancy in Co. C, as the only vacancy in the regiment. I told the Col. that I was left all alone in rather a hard place; so he transferred Lt. Lewis temporarily to my company, and he is helping me now. Col. Warner returned last week from Vermont. He does not feel very much encouraged about recruiting. Washburn thinks something can be done, but the Gov. thinks it will go hard. The Gov. has heard of the bill to consolidate regiments which

Father and I heard discussed, and was fearful that the 7th and 8th would have to be united; and as they are terribly jealous, he wants his son (Col. of 7th) to avoid it. So he proposed consolidating the 7th and 11th. The Col. looked upon this as probably the only way that could be done, and we are now waiting to hear from Pensacola. It does not strike this regiment very favorably, however, as the 7th has earned rather a bad reputation, and besides trouble would of necessity arise among the officers, and non. com. officers, as to place, rank, &c. Perhaps these things could all be adjusted, but it is one of the evils of the consolidating system that internal difficulties in regiments must arise. I don't know, of course, what will be the final determination, but I presume we shall unite. My boys are on their muscle tonight, I find. The officer of the day has got seven in the guard house, and two more are away yet. I hate to have them sent there, and don't think it does much good; but then, I have nothing to say.

After supper - I have just sent two more to the guard house, who had leave of absence till four and did not come till six, drunk at that. It is rough, but I have got to come down on them hard to make up for Capt. Hyde's silly laxity or laziness. That is the most unpleasant part of my present situation. I shall get most of them out in the morning, but shall prefer charges against four. We can have regimental court-martials now, with a smaller penalty, and I think it a good plan. I send another little slip out of the Register. I don't see but what you got my address as well as though you had been used to it. I hear that Dr. Phelps is complaining about the soldiers sent home from the nine months brigade; says that there is nothing the matter with three-fourths of them. The fact is that a good many soldiers do play off; it is hard to accuse them of it, but I believe it. I hear Steph has gone to Falmouth with money. That rain last week seems a most unfortunate thing for army movements. It was a terrible storm. Did Father send me a Testament? I have not received it yet. I am glad now that you can hear of my situation from Father. Perhaps it will make you more at ease - perhaps not. I received a letter today.

With much love,

Aldace F. Walker

Fort Massachusetts, D.C.,
Jan. 28, 1863

Dear Father:

I received a letter from you with Ellena's picture last night, and in fact your letters have been quite frequent of late. Still, the postal arrangements must be out of gear in some degree, for I have not received a Herald for the last three weeks. I have seen them in camp, however. The Atlantic came last. I am going to write for them to change the address, and to enclose a receipt next time. I was in the city Monday, getting boards, &c., for my company. I had some castings made for the cooks, and shall get a good kitchen to going after awhile. Teams have gone down for our stores of this nature today. It was a good day on Monday, and I had quite a pleasant time. Found Clement[6] and Johnson[7] of Woodstock, Meriden classmates, who are, Clement in the Treasury Dept.,[8] and Johnson, clerk to the Comm. on Postal affairs in the Senate, of which his grandfather, Collamer, is chairman. Saw John Osgood and other old acquaintances - one fellow, Butterfield, from Sabin's class, who was expelled from the service - a Lt. in the 6th - was reinstated a month ago, and has been in the city ever since. He was dismissed unjustly, but deserves it now. I learned there of Burnside's resignation and Hooker's installation. Of course that throws Sumner and Franklin out, as they are senior to Hooker. I have heard no news since. It is astonishing how much feeling there is in favor of McClellan; the current all sets that way in the city, notwithstanding the resume of Holt in the Porter case.

The Tribune seems to be trying to scare the army into exertions, and I think it may almost be regarded what that Pennsylvania fellow imputed to Cameron - that Southern independence is certain - to be true. I don't know but it's treason to say so, and I don't know but it is darkest before dawn, but I can't see as we can subjugate the South, and what is worse, the Army of the Potomac can't see it either. I have talked with men in the streets, and men in the hospitals, and though all are willing to fight for their country, still the idea of the "best attainable peace" will be a taking one, and I fear will prevail - who knows? It rained yesterday, and it snows today. Yesterday I was officer of the day, and had another wet tramp. I have got a new pair of boots from the general clothing store-house; red boots like the wrong side of leather, made in England at $15 a pair (so said) from Russia leather for the Southern market, caught by the blockading fleet and sold to officers for what they bring at auction, $3.38. They are sewed, and are very thick and high - must be water proof - but are awful looking things.

My company is getting along well enough now. Sundays and periodical holidays it breaks loose, and some of them get bit. I have got charges in against four now, and shall pinch them as fast as they try to run over me, for that is the only way to get along at all. The rest like me well enough I guess, but they must walk the chalk whether they like or no. These fellows won't be sentenced very hard, but enough to hinder the rest from any such fooling. That man with the load of whiskey had to pay $20 or lose the rum. We broke up another hole here yesterday. They sent six from Slocum yesterday at $20 apiece. If we keep hammering we shall get free from the nuisances in time. The Dutchmen that were here before did not care, and had a mean set of men as a consequence. We are trying to get our regiment in good order, and to do that we have to purify this part of the District. I understand that the name of our regiment has changed again. I am now in Battery C., 1st Art'y, 11th Reg't Vt. Vols. That picture is rather a mean one, and besides that it is incorrect; but you have a better photograph, and Mother must do the best she can.

There is a man in my company by the name of Wells, who lives about a mile and a half south of Wallingford village; says his wife is sick; had a letter last night which said she was very dangerously sick. I wish you would look her up, and write concerning her. He is a good man, and I would like to have him have a furlough if it is possible and necessary. I think his name is Oscar E. Wells, and think that you can easily find him or her. The disease of his wife in the letter was spelt "Inflammation:of the lungs." Is there a Sabin from Wallingford in the Cavalry? If so, he is quartermaster at present. I am sorry you misunderstood my answer to Lt. Whittemore. The fact was, I was a little vexed at his inquisition, and the more because he knows, as well as everyone else here, that "I never use it," and was just pumping me before you because he thought it would bother me, and it did - without any particular reason, I suppose, but we can't account for our mental states always. No one here ever asks me to drink now, so that I have no particular temptation in that regard.

With much love,

Aldace F. Walker

I have just received yours of Thursday eve., but none of the papers which you mention sending. Holt's presentation of the Porter case seems, as you say, insurmountable; but his own defence seemed also very plausible, and one side should not be looked at alone. Mother, Col. Benton was reading Les Miserables when Father was here. I will send it by mail presently. I like it, though it is extravagant and Frenchy. I did answer Henry's letter from Brattleboro. Presume the letter miscarried; was misdirected, perhaps. Please send his true address, and I will try it again.

Fort Massachusetts, D.C.,
Sunday, Feb. 1, 1863

Dear Mary:

We had a hard and long snow storm last week, and it is so muddy now that I can't go over to meeting. As I sit and write I can hear the city church bells ring, and it makes me think of home. I should enjoy going to church with you - you can think how much - and I hope I shall have such an opportunity at some time or other. I can't but think that this war will end before my three years expires, and much sooner I hope. The snow I spoke of does not melt very fast, and though there was not enough for sleighing, still it looked natural enough. My big red boots are a fine institution for such weather. I got a great lot of clothing for my company the other day, and have issued a good deal of it, and the rest is piled up in my tent - a stack from my table to the door as high as the roof. I got 50 blouses, 100 shirts, 100 pr. socks, 90 drawers, 25 pr. shoes, 25 pr. pants, 50 caps, and canteens and such things by the quantity. I got a letter from Prex. Labaree[9] last night. He says that his son John is engaged, so that he can't leave. He (the Prex.) is coming to New York this week, and may visit Washington. I would like to see him very much. Col. Warner was formerly a member of his family.

We were to have our monthly inspection yesterday. Lt. Col. Oberteuffer of the 112 Pa. was to inspect us. So we got as ready as we could in so short notice as we had and waited. He came about 5 p.m., and we could not show off to any great extent of course; but we made him think we did tip-top. He said he never saw so good a set of officers as we have, which I thought was laying it on rather thick. He is a good old fellow, and not like Col. Gibson at all. Col. Warner inspected the 112th; don't know what success he had. Those Heralds came along both together last Thursday. I moved into my new cook-house the day (Wednesday) that Father went to New York. It rained so here that a brook ran right through the fire place in the old ground, and we had to move in the rain in order to get dinner at all. I have got it all covered now, and have got boards for the ends. In a few days more I shall have it in as good shape as need be.

I had a photograph, or "potograph" as Mrs. Butts calls it, taken the other day. Have not got any printed yet; but shall be able to send you some the next time I write, I think. I had it taken in a little shanty near my tent, and think the man made out very well for a camp picture. I send back Ellena's today. Am very glad to have seen it, but have no place to put it or keep it. I think it is very like indeed. There is an immense drove of government cattle going by now - 1000 I presume. They come in from Maryland on this road in enormous quantities, and I presume our men will eat them presently. That returned deserter came with no story at all. I arrested him, but he was guarded very loosely and got away Friday night. I presume we shall not see him again. I have had no trouble the last week at all, but presume some of my men will get drunk today; shall be most happily disappointed if they don't. Capt. Hyde used to let the men go and be gone two or three days and take no notice of it; but I shan't. He would not report his absentees at all. Goodbye for now.

With much love, your brother,

Aldace F. Walker

Sunday evening - My men have behaved very well today. I gave leave of absence to several of them, and they all came back on time and none of them drunk. I presume there will be occasional difficulties, but the money of last pay day is almost gone - few have any left, and it is hard to spend it to any great extent without any dosh. It is raining tonight, and our snow is almost gone - will be quite before morning; meanwhile, the roads are a soft, pasty mud, sort of semi-fluid, six in. deep, and getting deeper. I think Father chose a very good time for his journey South, but I shall be contented to stay pretty closely on my present dry spot, and wait for the roads to dry. Marching orders now would be rather unpleasant, but these we do not fear. We hear that the Army of the Potomac is to be divided. I should think it was about time to give up taking Richmond. I get a morning paper regularly now, and early too - usually before I get up. I have the daily morning Chronicle, which comes Sundays and all, and is the best paper in the city by far.

Aldace F. Walker

My Company is doing very well now. I expect to make it a model one, but don't just see my way clear how to do it. I heard from Major Austine last night, that a deserter who left the Co. at Brattleboro and who has been at home since (Hampton, N.Y.), whom I wrote about to Austin a while since, has been retaken and will be sent on here soon. He will count us one more at any rate. Steph says he means to get Henry on here for a little while after he leaves Jonesville. I shall be glad to see him of course. Wonder if Henry and Steph will agree as usual. I do enjoy hearing them jaw each other; neither are stubborn only when talking with the other. Your last came as usual. W. Rutland seems to be getting into a queer way. One bad man has more influence than ten good ones. I pity them all; well, the good preponderates there yet, and I presume all will be well sometime or other. I hope to get papers or something from home tonight. My Chronicle comes regularly now, Sundays and all - nothing new this morning save Napoleon's nigger soldiers.

Fort Massachusetts, D.C.,
Feb. 4, 1863

Dear Father:

It is late tonight - 10 o'clock. I have been busy all day, and this evening have been to Fort Slocum. I had a man, one of those in the hospital, who received his discharge today. He is quite feeble, and I wanted an order from Col. Warner to go to the city and start him off. I found another captain, however, who was going on the same errand, and I let him do my business too; am glad of it, for I had no other business in the city. I don't mean to go again till the latter part of next week unless something breaks. I have got my cook-house covered and boarded, and it is quite a comfortable affair. Have not got any new chimney done and my range at work, but shall before long. My company is doing very well comparatively now, and the number of sick is comparatively small, only 13 today off duty, and none in the hospital. I had men enough today so that I took three detachments to the Fort and drilled this p.m. It was the first time I had had a chance, and I felt like a king on a small scale. They are poorly drilled, and I mean to take every chance. But the weather has been very cold of late. It was terribly frigid last night; not so bad tonight, and I guess will snow tomorrow. I have been very comfortable, however, and the men are so too; but I pity the poor boys in Virginia. We have a new order now, which provides for an officer with the picquet, so that the officer of the day will not have that tramp to take.

I have received the Times you sent last week, but none of the other papers, and no letter since Sunday. I have got a dozen photographs taken at the shanty near the camp. How do you like them? And had I better have him print more from this negative, or go to the city and try there? We don't find out about our 7th yet; but time, a fortnight perhaps, will unravel the knot. Meanwhile we can wait, and are doing it with very great success. Capt. Hunt[10] and Adj't Burrows are at home. They are from Brattleboro, or Vernon, and got the Gov. to order them home for 30 days. If you want to see bad enough to do that, I will go; for I always mean to obey orders. We have got that old guard house torn down, and the tent on the parade moved, so that we are looking quite slick. The dust blows terribly here in the summer, but the absence of mud in the winter compensates for that. I enjoy my morning Daily very much, though there has not been much news of late. I hope they will keep the army still for the present, for a movement must leave them in the mud sooner or later. I have just signed a requisition for my coal for February; only 4750 pounds - enough to last until summer. Well, I must go to bed. I am well; eat hearty and sleep late - that is till half past seven, which is late enough. Hope to hear from you tomorrow. Have got no letters of late. We have no snow, and the ground is frozen hard; rough in the roads, as you can well imagine. I commanded at Dress Parade for the first time tonight. With love to all,

Aldace F. Walker

Fort Massachusetts, D.C.,
Feb. 8, 1863

Dear Father:

I have just finished my company inspection and it was well done too. My boys are getting into pretty good shape. I had rather they would work by love than by fear, though I presume they will not do as well quite; still it will be much more pleasant for me and for them. I have only two in arrest now; one who was tried before a regimental court-martial, consisting of Lt. Col. Benton, yesterday, and is now awaiting sentence; and the other, Jerry Callahan, who wore the ball and chain so long, and who is so far gone by the use of liquor that he can't control himself at all, and is rather to be pitied than blamed. Still he is a nuisance, and we can do little with him save keep him from strong drink. It is a terrible case. He had an attack of delirium tremens last night, or night before, and stayed out under a pile of cornstalks, so that we thought and hoped he had deserted. Well, there is a black sheep in Co. B too, and on the whole I think that is the very best company. I think, however, that I had better go back there if I can, as it will be much the easiest berth. There is one nuisance in that company - that is, there is more familiarity of the men with the officers. In this company of strangers the men let me alone unless they have business with me, and I enjoy that; still, B would improve in that respect. Capt. Hunsdon has gone over to Stoughton's Brigade for a couple of days, and I mean to go in a few weeks.

I had a line from Ab last night, saying that he and H. were coming to Washington Monday, and asking me to meet them. I applied for a pass at once, and hope it will get round, as I am very anxious to see them. It is a most beautiful morning, and was a fine day yesterday, but in the last week we had two snow storms, two rains, and two freezes. These changes of weather don't affect me much, however. I never was so well for so long a time as I remember, and my company is well too. The measles are at the Post in Company D., and I expect my boys will have them before long. The small-pox is in the neighborhood; is very thick in Washington. Our regiment has all been vaccinated. I understand there is a case in every block in the city; it is a mild form of the disease, however - varioloid. I think Mary's picture a very good one. I have not got the papers of week before last yet, though Feb. 3rd Chronicle came last night. I suppose that list of promotions has been printed, but I have not seen them. My Register comes regularly.

Lt. Lewis does very well indeed; he is faithful, and it does not trouble him to get up to the morning roll-call. He is out on picquet now, in charge of the line of the 11th Vt. He has given up his tent to the sick ones of his company, and is in the tent with me now. There are some dozen cases of measles in his company. I think Capt. Hunsdon and I shall stop boarding at Butts' tomorrow, and go to messing with Goodrich. His wife is here, you know, at the house just across the road, and is to have a white woman to help her - the wife of one Pelkey[11] of my company. She, Mrs. Goodrich, is a very pretty woman, and I think we shall live cheaper there than with Mrs. Butts, and in a fashion more like New England. And especially I am heartily sick of nigger cooking; I get disgusted every meal, and if I don't like I shall go back - still I think the change will be a good one. Wells was very glad to hear of his wife from you, and can't understand the first report. I presume they wanted to get him home, and took that way to do it; not very kind in them, for he felt very badly. Please write again concerning her. We do not learn anything conclusive concerning the consolidation. I presume the 7th has not been heard from yet. Meanwhile, everything remains in status quo, and we can do nothing but wait as patiently as we can. I have no idea of going home myself, for Col. Jim says he won't send captain's, so I have no particular interest anyway. I have not much idea of a furlough either before summer, for Col. Warner had very hard work to get his ten days granted.

We are where it is much harder to get away than it is in other brigades, for Gibson won't approve any furloughs except with special intercession. So let it go for the present, and the war will end sometime. I think at least I am not where there is any danger of getting shot, and there is no visible possibility but that we shall stay here till the conclusion of the war. Well, I must stop and go to dinner. Shall write more perhaps.

Goodbye,

Aldace F. Walker

4 P.M. - The mail is just in with your letter. I have given up trying to see ahead in politics - and don't have much of a chance, for my newspaperial happiness was short lived - the price went up, and the enterprise went down, so I am all afloat again. Col. Warner spoke very favorably of Mr. Olmstead as Chaplain to me the other day. Our inspections are all at the several Posts. hittemore is here yet, though fretting terribly because he cannot get his battery sent to the field. His job does not progress very fast in the late bad weather. We have stopped chopping for the present, but are to go at it again soon. Some fifteen tons of coal were delivered here yesterday for us officers. I shall keep Mary's photograph for the present, with that of the "two girls." Our cook house is very convenient and comfortable now.

With much love, Your son,

Aldace F. Walker

Fort Massachusetts, D.C.,
Feb. 11, 1863

Dear Father:

It is very late tonight - half past ten or so - but I must write tonight in order to get my letter off in the morning. I have been officer of the day today and very busy all day. I had to turn out all the men here and see to their drilling in the fort both forenoon and afternoon, and have had many other botherations, so that it is late now as I said. I have had four letters today, but none from you. My correspondence comes in a freshet when it gets started. One was from Sue at Brattleboro, where she seems to be enjoying herself very much, and I hope will be profited. My papers have got to coming again, for which I am rejoiced, as there seems to be a prospect of work in South Carolina. I am boarding now, as I suggested, with Goodrich, and enjoy it much. We only eat twice a day, but have enough at those times, and can have what we want. Capt. Hunsdon is a little sick, threatened with fever, but I hope will get well without it.

I went to the city Monday as I suggested. My pass was mislaid, and I got leave of absence and altered my old one; got along all right. I met Ab and H. at the National,[12] and had a pleasant time. H. is corporal now, and will have the first shake at a higher position. They are very well, as also the other boys - all my friends in that brigade. They came out with me and spent the night and the next forenoon. William Shaw was also in the city, and Major Kingsley. I also saw young Post, who I believe has been in a hospital - at least he says so. He says he is transferred from the 10th to the Regular Army, with the promise of a 2nd Lieutenancy - which is excessively dubious. I also stumbled on to old Prex Labaree, and I was very glad to see him too. He came out on Tuesday accompanied by John B. Page and Joseph Warner, the Col.'s father - all old acquaintances, and Warner just from Middlebury. They did not stay long, but I was glad to see them all, I assure you. Today while I was drilling, three ladies came down from Blair's, and I had the honor to introduce them to the fort, &c. Miss Blair has returned from Ohio, and I am going out there soon.

We have had ugly weather this afternoon, but capital for several days previous. There is a rumor that we are to be paid again soon. Steph has got back from the army with $100,000 left - half what he started with. He was a good deal amused at the result of his first estimates. There is a young lady, niece or something of Rev. Harvey Leavitt, a Miss Miner, twenty-three years old, who has just married an old widower of seventy-two. Perhaps you have heard of it; it was a curious operation any way. One of my letters was from Charley Sheldon. He speaks of a surprise at Ralph Hascall's, just before he left for Maine, which was all right I suppose; but I wonder if Emily went. Rollin was there of course. But I must go to bed - am tired and it is late. The last newspapers have come.

Truly your son,

Aldace F. Walker

Fort Massachusetts, D.C.,
Feb. 15, 1863

Dear Father:

It has been a rainy day today so far, though it has been most beautiful for the last few days; the roads were nearly dry. I don't think there will be much of a storm now. It has been a long time since we have seen any snow, and inhabitants think there will not be much more cold weather. Still March is often stormy. We can find out nothing about our recruiting, and have pretty much made up our minds to - wait for developments. I don't know but this has been our practice for some time, but its necessity in army dicker becomes more and more manifest. I am getting along famously at Goodrich's. It seems kind of human - like to have Vermont eatables in lieu of Mrs. Butts' beef and cabbage. We can get anything we choose of the market teams that pass here every other day to the city; have a great lot of Carter potatoes, &c. Capt. Hunsdon has returned to camp all right, having escaped the fever. I have now three cases of diphtheria; all seem to be mending however. My Corporal, Macomber, is seriously sick with fever. Still my company is very much more healthy than when you were here, and more so than most other companies. I did not go to church today on account of the rain, nor could we have any inspection. I have bathed, &c., and feel capitally. I eat only twice a day now, at 9 and 3, and lay abed a little later in the morning, as Lt. Lewis attends all roll calls. We have now to inspect the barracks formally every day, and visit them after taps. Our fatigue is very much diminished, so that there are quite ample opportunities to drill, and we have to do it, much to our satisfaction. You may remember that battery unfinished over on the hill. I am at work there with twenty men from Slocum. I don't like the job at all, but as they send a Lt. with them, I give general instructions and vamoose. An order has been issued allowing two officers to a regiment and one man to a company ten days leave of absence, so now the great question is, Who will go? I have a Corporal with a sick wife, and an Orderly Serg't with a sick father, and am in doubt which to send. Think it will be the Orderly, however, as other circumstances have a bearing on the thing. Perhaps I shall get a chance next August. I don't want to try just yet. I went down to Mr. Blagden's last night, and had a very peasant call. You may have seen an article afloat praising Mrs. Hooker, Joe's wife, to the skies for her devotion to the soldiers and exemplary character. Of course the fact is that he is a bachelor. Equal to the story of McDowell's intemperance. Seward seems to have put his foot down at last. Glad of it. Hope it will stop some mouths that have questioned his devotion. We are waiting on the Carolinas now it seems; at least - I was interrupted there, and forgot what I was to dogmatize about - no matter. I have sent in a furlough for my 1st Serg't, Meeker.[13] My 2nd will do very well in his place.

We have had our inspection which should have come off in the morning this p.m. at 4, and a dress parade afterwards. I received your letter this eve, and the last Chronicle, and the Herald and Chronicle that were mailed together Jan. 30th. It is queer what becomes of this sort of mail matter, but it seems to turn up eventually. My men are all on hand tonight, and as orderly as I could wish. Their money is pretty much gone; after another pay day I shall have another siege I expect, and we hear that this may be soon, - not this week nor the next, I reckon. I settled with old Butts for my board, and our accounts did not exactly agree. He charged $15 where I was expecting to pay $24. As he had it down in black and white, I did not know but he might be right, and was glad to settle it so. You speak of Aggie's playing. The fact is, that is a miserable piano. It is utterly impossible to give any execution upon it, save the most "brilliant" or boisterous. Still practicing upon such a rackety machine must of course destroy any taste or cultivation that ever existed, and as to that I have very serious doubts. There is not much fun for me in hearing her play at any rate. My fingers do not grow as stiff as I should suppose they would. I have lost a good deal of their elasticity, but still I can hammer away a good deal after all. I have got up quite a reputation at Blagden's as a song singer - on a very slender basis of anything save brass.

You are correct about Sherman, and he is a capital fellow. I keep trying to get over the river to the 14th and thereabouts, but can't get a pass through, and shan't be able to for some time yet. We have been formally announced as in the 22nd (Heintzelman's) Army Corps.[14] I have kept scribbling. Have got several letters in the past week, and must write more this week than the last. If it is pleasant weather, I shall be occupied the most of the time out of doors; but we cannot expect as good weather for another week as the last has been. Pete has had a very hard cold, and I was somewhat alarmed concerning him last night; but Meigs fixed him up some syrup and gave him some Dover's powders,[15] so that he is better today. Miss Bettie Blair has returned from Ohio; I am going there some evening soon. I hope you will be able to pick this out from among the numerous pieces, and remain, with much love, Your son,

Aldace F. Walker

Fort Mass., D.C.,
Feb. 18, 1863

Dear Father:

We had a beautiful day Monday, but four inches of snow Tuesday morning, and it kept coming all day; did not get very deep however, and it is not storming today, nor melting much. Of course we can't drill nor work, and so I am in Capt. Hunsdon's tent writing. Monday I worked very hard; had to see to that battery, to police the ground around my camp, and to drill my company four hours - so that I got pretty well tired. I enjoyed having something to do, however. We have orders that the Department commander will inspect us some time before long, and that we must get ready for it. We don't know just what that means, and have not much time to do it in; but are not especially troubled. The 143rd Pa., encamped over towards Slocum, left in the storm yesterday to report to Hooker. I am glad I am situated where there is not much danger of a start like that, for they must be having a terribly rough time. There are fine men in the regiment - the Col. is a capital man, - and I hate to see them in a hard fix. "Such are the fortunes of war." "Such is life." I suppose they will go by boat to Aquia Creek (pronounced, by the way, with the accent on the second syllable) and then hoof it to Falmouth. Our Surgeon, Kidder, has just passed through his trial or examination before a "board." He was pumped for two days, and eight hours each day. Came through all right - better than anyone else this winter, they said. I am glad of it, for I think him a good physician and I don't just like the clique that has been trying to oust him. The men at the hospital think very much of him as a surgeon and a man. There is no trouble about his knowledge. The only difficulty is in his lack of energy and determination. He will go without what is needed, because he believes all that lazy department clerks tell him. He is learning the ropes in this regard however, and will come out all right I think. Two died at the hospital yesterday, making 14 in all, I believe. The 10th has lost over 60. I have three there now; two recovering from slight attacks of diphtheria, and one (Macomber) has a fever - not very dangerously sick as yet. There is a case of small-pox in Co. K at Totten. There have been several accidents with guns of late. While we were at Lincoln we had two hands injured. A corporal in Co. H was accidentally killed awhile ago; a man in F was shot through the arm; in through the hand, ramrod and ball; and in C shot his thumb off; these last all on picquet. My man was not badly hurt at all; will be all right soon. These accidents always occur. It seems sad, and queer - but a man with his gun in his hand all night gets careless. The man in Co. I had just fired at a deserter, and was loading again. I presume there was fire left in the gun. I hope to hear from you this afternoon. My Orderly's furlough came back disapproved, because it was not written on a full half sheet of paper; so I tried it again, being a little more liberal in my use of stationery. We hear nothing more about recruiting. My boarding arrangements continue to please. I have my cook house in pretty good shape - a bunk in it for the cooks, a tent behind for the Orderly, and I am going to move my company clothing in there in a day or two. Our comforts continue to increase and presently I shall not be able to enjoy myself in a house.

Aldace F. Walker

It may interest you to know how we got our requisition through for hospital buildings. We have been using tents, you know, heretofore. Our Quartermaster got the necessary papers signed here, and took them to the city - 8000 feet boards, scantling, tar, lime, etc. He took them to Col. Rucker, head of some bureau in Washington. He peremptorily refused to have anything to do about it. So Carlton took his papers to the Medical Director's, and after a long parley he signed them. Then he went to Halleck and got his name on, and returned to Col. Rucker and told him that he reckoned he had got him that time - and he had.

Fort Massachusetts, D.C.,
Feb. 22, 1863

Dear Father:

We have a veritably stormy Sunday today. It was pleasant and clear yesterday and the day before, and had got passably and clear yesterday and the day before, and had got passably dry, but last evening it commenced to snow and blow, and it is really Vermontish today. I have hardly left my tent except for breakfast. My tent is warm and dry and comfortable. Lewis and Pete were out on picquet last night, and came in this morning in the storm looking decidedly blue. This snow is different from any we have had here before; it is dry and fine, and would promise good sleighing in New England, but it will all be cut to pieces and melt in the morning.

I received the Chronicle and Register last night, and have had four papers from Uncle George[16] the last week. They came very pat, as I have not seen a single city or Baltimore paper. Still, there is not much news save the backing down of Western secessionism in obedience to the voice of the army, and perhaps to the fear that they were getting too far to secure subsequent "Democratic" triumphs. I am expecting to hear from Uncle Joel on the New Hampshire elections soon, but have not of late. We have had a rumor here that Mercier had been ordered home, but have not seen it in print. I got it yesterday second-hand from so high an authority as the President's coachman - who ought to know of course.

Our sick and deaths here have been increasing somewhat of late, as we might have anticipated. I now have four in the hospital, though none of the cases are regarded as very serious. The disease that is troubling our surgeons now most is that which took away so many in the Vermont regiments last winter - the measles, falling away into a lung fever. It is almost invariably fatal. There is no regimental news, save that two of our lieutenants have been before a board of examiners, and probably dismissed the service. My Orderly, Meeker, has received his furlough, for eight days, and will start this afternoon, I suppose. I fear he will not find his father alive, the document has been so long in getting around. I think Col. Benton expects his wife before long. He is going to build a house and live like home.

We have commenced to whitewash our barracks, and by and by (that is, in a year or two) shall be perfectly settled. What do you Vermonters think of the general enrollment? The money clause is quiet a saving idea, and if the thing was managed right might furnish funds to prosecute the war. But these negro regiments I don't take much stock in. I would rather not come into very close contact with them, especially if there was any fighting going on. Those Bucker articles you sent me from the Independent are keen enough, but still I think Weed is nearer right than Bucker; don't you? But one can't trust any body nowadays. When is the war going to cease? Who can tell? It certainly don't look so near its end as it did at the first Bull Run, and I am beginning to think that the North are waking up again. Action and reaction will ebb and flow, of course, but they always seem to come at the wrong time as regards army movements. The "wayward Lister" idea is mostly dropped, and even by Prince John, its author, who has described a curious somersault. I shall expect Seymour[17] next.

That Miss Miner is a daughter of Mrs. Leavitt. Has always been very highly spoken of, though quite an invalid. Saw her husband first at Saratoga. I have not received the Greek Testament you sent so long ago; perhaps it will turn up at last. Papers have come round after a fortnight and more, and I do not call it lost yet by any means.

I have got money enough left yet. When I get short I shall apply for more, but I felt that my safest way was to put the $200 in your hands. I am spending a good deal, but have to in order to be comfortable, and it is best. I am on pretty big wages, however, and hope to save something if I stay long enough in the service. I don't know as my mail will get along regularly this stormy day, but it has never failed of coming yet save when the ice freshet blocked up the Susquehanna.

I may add more in the evening.

Your very truly and with much love,

Aldace F. Walker

Fort Mass., D.C.,
Feb. 25, 1863

Dear Father:

We have had a beautiful day, but the snow is not yet gone. It is very sloppy traveling. The fort - which is clay, and not sand - is so muddy that it is almost impossible to navigate there, and drilling is impossible. You remember a bomb-proof which they were building in the fort. They have got the sides all up and sawed off, and the roof partly on. I suppose when it is done that one of the companies at the post will have to move in there, and be relieved by another at the expiration of a month. I don't know what will be the effect on the health in living six feet underground, but time will tell. I presume it will be as healthy as the plan adopted at Fredericksburg. I had a call the other night from Charley Colburn and Sam Burnham of Manchester, who came out as 2nd Lt. in the 5th - was promoted to Capt. - resigned last week. The men on the Rappahannock, he says, have nothing but shelter tents. "Wedge" or "A" tents were issued to the line officers some time ago - a month perhaps - and one to a Company - for three. When they found they were like to remain in one place some little time they "fixed up," and this "stockading" was done by digging a hole in the ground and setting the tent over it, so that the floor was perhaps three feet below the level. He says he took the trouble to measure the water in the hole the last night he stayed there, and found it eight inches deep. I can't vouch for this last story, but the digging I have heard of from other sources. It is not such like our style of living, at any rate. Sam says the army is in pretty good order as a general thing, but he got fearfully demoralized.

We are getting towards another muster day - the last of each two months, or next Saturday. This time we have three muster rolls to make out, each half a day's steady work, and two muster and pay rolls, a little longer. These last are to be made out for four months, with the expectation of getting pay on them sometime in March. I have money enough on hand yet. I think that Peter will not stay with me much longer. He thinks he must visit his friends in Vermont again, and I think if he goes home he had better stay. It will cost him

$15 to come back, and besides I can get a nigger for nothing that will be of as much use to me as Pete. I had a visit last night from one of my college classmates, Converse,[18] who is a private in the 14th. Pitt W. Hyde, of Hydeville, has also been here, taking some interest I suppose in his nephew's company. Monday, Higley and Smith of the Cavalry were over here. I was very glad to see them of course, and had a little sing with him and Thomas. Hig. is fat as a pig, and looks very tough and hearty. Has quite a crop of whiskers and is quite a soldier.

Dwight Smith[19] was alluded to in a recent Washington letter to the Herald, as having "come to grief." He was a classmate of Higley and Mead.[20] Had risen to the position of Sergeant Major. When Col. Sawyer was expunged, he took off a horse with him that belonged to the government. Major Collins ordered Smith to get the horse. Sawyer was at the National in Washington and refused to give it up, so Smith arrested Sawyer. He got the horse, as he would be sure to do anything he undertook, but Sawyer's first order reduced him to the ranks. He takes it coolly - says he is in the direct line of promotion, as he is the junior private in the company.[21] It is rather hard, but Sawyer is managing by promotion, &c., to get the majority of the officers in his favor, though I think him a mean man.

It is late tonight, and I have got a business letter to write, and besides there is nothing more, as I think of, to say; so Goodnight.

Aldace F. Walker

----

1 Elizabeth Blair Lee, wife of Commodore Samuel Phillips Lee; Virginia Jeans Laas, ed., Wartime Washington: The Civil War Letters of Elizabeth Blair Lee, (University of Illinois Press, Urbana, 1991), 1-3.

2 USA Maj. Gen. Francis Preston Blair, Jr., Missouri politician and division commander in the Fifteenth Corps. Boatner, 67.

3 Col. Breed Noyes Hyde (1831-1918), resigned 1/15/1863. RR.

4 Probably Capt. George G. Tilden's father.

5 Mark the scratch, and later 'toe the scratch,' meaning walk a straight line, to keep out of trouble.

6 Charles Russell Clement (1840-1881), KUA 1858. KUACat, 56.

7 William Edward Johnson (1841-1917), KUA 1858. KUACat, 56.

8 Treasury Department, 15th Street, Washington, D.C. Leech, 6.

9 Benjamin Labaree (1801-1883). KUA 1824. President of Middlebury College 1840-1866. KUACat, 4.

10 Capt. John Hunt, Vergennes, resigned 8/10/1863. RR.

11 There were three Pelkey's in the company, David and Lewis of Fair Haven, and Samuel of Benson. RR.

12 National Hotel, Washington, D.C., on 6th Street. Leech, 8.

13 William V. Meeker, Poultney. RR.

14 USA Maj. Gen. Samuel Peter Heintzelman commanded the Twenty-Second Corps and the District of Washington during this period. Boatner, 392.

15 A pharmaceutical preparation of opium and ipecacuanha, a purgative. C. T. Onions, The Shorter Oxford English Dictionary, (Book Club Associates, London, 1983), 1:599, 1111.

16 An older brother of Aldace's father.

17 USA Maj. Gen. Truman B. Seymour, a Vermonter, commanding the Tenth Corps. Boatner, 733.

18 John Rollin Converse (1842-1864), Panton, 14th Vt. Infantry and 17th Vt. Infantry. MC 1862. Killed in action before Petersburg, Va., 7/30/1864. RR; Robinson pp. 163-4.

19 Henry Dwight Smith (1841-1923), Middlebury, 1st Vt. Cavalry. MC 1864. Enlisted as Quartermaster Sergt., Co. K, 9/18/1861; promoted to Sergt. Maj. 5/5/1862, reduced and returned to his company 12/24/1862, subsequently promoted to Sergt. 5/2/1864. Taken prisoner during Wilson's Raid on Richmond, 6/29/1864 and held at Andersonville, Ga. Paroled 12/10/1864; mustered out 2/6/1865. RR; Robinson, 134-191.

20 John Abner Mead (1841-1920), Rutland, 12th Vt. Infantry. MC 1864. Post-war physician, state legislator, Lieut. Governor and Governor. The Political Graveyard. Accessed 1/21/2002, available from http://politicalgraveyard.com/bio/mead.html; Internet. Mead roomed with Walker in Starr Hall, room #23, during Walker's senior year at Middlebury. Eulogy of ex-Governor Mead by Dr. Ezra Brainerd, Fine Tributes Paid Late Ex-Gov. Mead, unidentified news clipping dtd January 16, 1920. Mead was later a Trustee of Middlebury College, and the chapel, built c1914, is named for him. History of Mead Chapel, accessed 1/22/2002, available from http://www.middlebury.edu/~chaplain/meadhistory_new.html; Internet.

21 Hoffman, 68-70, relates the same story, but indicates Smith failed to return the horse to the regiment. He was, nonetheless, busted by Sawyer for his efforts.

5.
Defenses of Washington
March and April, 1863

Fort Massachusetts, D.C.,
March 1, 1863.

Dear Father:

It rained this morning, so that we could neither have our usual inspection nor leave camp. Cleared off about noon, and we were inspected at one; have just come in. Yesterday, as I wrote you before, was our muster day. We were mustered for four month's pay. When the money will come, I don't know of course, but I understand Halsey has money enough when he gets time to cipher out the rolls. We have not sent in our rolls yet. They are quite serious affairs, and our clerks are at work today copying them. The musters are preceded by inspections; all of which are necessary enough, we find, to keep up the appearance of the men, as well as the discipline. We have got now so that we look pretty well, and we are all feeling well too. I am a little off the hooks today for some reason. Can't say what is the matter with me, and don't exactly know as there is anything, though for some reason I don't feel as though I should like to walk forty miles this afternoon. Presume I have taken a little cold.

One of the best boys in Co. B died this morning, of measles followed by lung fever. I am thankful I have nothing to fear in that line, for I had the measles pretty thoroughly in Meriden. I have applied for a pass for Tuesday, and mean to see Congress towards its close. Wednesday is the 4th, I believe. It is rushing through the big bills now with commendable vigor, and I am beginning to realize the ability of some of the members. I have been able to get the Chronicles again this week - enjoy them very much. Their Congressional reports are very full. That Scott letter is rather a damper on McClellan. These damaging things keep coming up; yet the army still worships him, and the Washington people too. Any allusion to him in the city is always cheered enthusiastically, and how history can be written I don't know. Meanwhile, events interest us, and the why and wherefore we are partially content to have hidden.

You know I told you that I might lose half my house at any time. Well, the time came last week. Austin took the tent that Goodrich has been using, and I had to give Goodrich one of mine. I gave him the back one - dark and black - tore up my stockades, and moved my old frame right on here - built an addition behind, and raised an "A" tent as high as the other, and have as much room as I had before, and much higher, lighter and pleasanter. I am rather glad on the whole that it happened so. My old furniture fits in first rate, and I never knew that there was so much room in one of the small tents. The fact is, I have stretched it immensely. I still continue to like very well at my new feeding place. The fact is, I have things to eat that look clean and are, and the variety I care less for. I think it will cost us much less. We bought half a 150 lb. hog the other day, and find fresh pork agreeable for a change. I have a good deal of business to do with J. B. Page of late.

The allotment rolls of our Company were made out by Hyde and Foot at Brattleboro, when they were both pretty drunk most of the time, and contain a great many mistakes. When Page was here he agreed to correct these for me. I am righting the machine up, and I have to see to drawing the State pay for the boys too. I have received a receipt for the Atlantic from Tichnor & Fields, which I will enclose. The Chronicle came last night. I would like to have you see my new tent, and see how much pleasanter it is than the other. It is smaller, I think, but it is so light and pleasant. I have not received the Greek Testament yet. It may turn up yet, however, as I received a letter last week from Uncle George that was written in January. I started to go down to Mr. Blagden's last night, but it began to rain and scared me back. Capt. Hunsdon has just come in, and I will wait till after dinner. I hope to receive a letter from you this afternoon too.

Evening - Your letter came this afternoon. I get your Monday's letter Thursday and your Wednesday's letter Sunday quite regularly now. Come to look at the Chronicle it was an old one - Feb. 17th. My rolls are getting along well - nearly finished. My company clerk is a fine young man who has just fitted for college at Poultney and was going to Ann Arbor. The wind has risen and it is blowing very hard - trying my new tent pretty effectually. I left one place unbraced, I found, and it came near blowing over. I feel better now I have finished a good dinner; have a little cold, and shall probably feel it more in the morning, but my head has stopped aching, and on the whole I am well enough. I have not been off duty since I came out, though jaundice gave me a pretty hard pull.

I have just been out to see the officer of the day about one of my men who a Sergeant arrested for insolence - I shall have him released late in the evening. Pete's picquet business has been done for the fun of the thing. Our picquets are so comfortably arranged and provided for that it is rather a pleasure than otherwise on pleasant days. Wells, I have just made my company cook for the next two months. I expect Pete will go home this week. He has set his mind on going to Vermont to visit, and though I should not dismiss him, still think it best for him not to come back. He works well enough for me, but is a good deal in the way, and a nigger who would cost me a great deal less would be just as useful. Lt. Lewis was a classmate of Mead's, who came from Morrisville with Boyden. He labored under the depressing influence of that association at college, but I find him to be more of a man than I thought, though his intellect is by no means of the first order. He is faithful and ready, and gives me valuable assistance. He is out on picquet again today. My company clothing took up a good deal of room. When we are full we shall have a Quartermaster Sergt. to look after such matters, and he will tent with the Orderly. So for the present I have left it there; there is a lock on the door, and it is all right in every respect. I expect my Orderly back Tuesday. The report of the Board on the two lieutenants examined has not been made yet, though without doubt they will be dismissed the service. It will be no particular loss either. They are at the other Forts, and I know but very little about them, but they are both inefficient and dull.

Smith's father has not come yet. Meeker's father lives in Houghton, N.Y. He was and is now a Methodist minister, though he studied medicine and practiced in Middlebury when I was there. Meeker I knew before; he was Orderly in Hayward's company in the 1st, and is a capital fellow. Sherman does very well indeed, though he is on the sick list today. My third Sergt., a brother of Col. Nichols,[1] is also sick, and I have had my fourth as Orderly. He is a pretty bright Irish boy, Peter Donnelly.[2] That General Enrollment measure is very popular in the army, and we all hope to see it put through, and see no other way of supplying the places of the nine months volunteers. The company do not as yet eat in the cookhouse. I mean they shall by and by. That ration selling dicker I think I am all right in. My own officers know that it is the only way to secure a company fund, which they are very anxious we should have, - besides I can find nothing which prohibits it. I have never sold any myself, nor directly authorized it, though I have spent a good deal of money procured in that way.

Aldace F. Walker

Fort Massachusetts, D.C.,
March 4, 1863

Dear Father:

It is pleasant out today, though quite cold and windy. I am very well, and enjoying it. I am officer of the day today, but my duties are not very laborious, as perhaps you know by this time. Still I am confined to camp, of course. I did not get my pass around to go to the city yesterday, because the paper got torn; but I started another at once, and got it last night, for tomorrow. So I shall have to go then and lose Congress. I have a good many errands to do, and shall make some calls. I meant to have called on Mr. and Mrs. Amasa, but I find they are to leave tomorrow. I have had considerable company of late. Yesterday two of my classmates and another college friend from over the river came in. Eaton and Smith were the classmates. They are looking well, and bring favorable reports from the other boys. They spent the night with me, and went off about noon. I slept with Capt. Hunsdon to make room for them, and there was a disturbance in camp about a load of govt. property we had taken. The owner came about one or two, and wanted his stuff, &c. Hunsdon was in command, and so we had to do the biz and not sleep - nothing serious. Today Steph. and Charley Walker were up to dinner with me. Charley has been all the winter near Chain bridge, not half a dozen miles from here or the city, but had never looked up Steph or I. He looks well, and is just about starting for Falmouth. I never saw him but once or twice. He is quite a fine looking and appearing young man. Steph has had his regiments all changed. He came out $7 behind on his paying scrape - pretty well, I think. He drew $65,000 more than he used.

Evening - I have been having more trouble of late - tonight - with disorder in my company. Have got my foot down again, and mean the men shall see I am in earnest. We have had a pretty easy time for the last few weeks, and things had got to running pretty loosely, but I have brought up one or two of them with a yank. Lt. Smith's father came in this evening. Looks just as he used, and is happy as you please to see his son. Charley is a perfect image of him. One of the Fletchers from Bridgeport [sic] came with him. I had a letter from Susan this afternoon. She seems to enjoy herself pretty well at Brattleboro. There has been a movement started in regard to a chaplain. Our Major has circulated a paper, and has obtained the names of most of the officers of the regiment in favor of Arthur Little,[3] who you may remember at Thetford. He is at Princeton now. He was an old college crony of the Major's, and from what I saw of him will do well enough. Tenney will know more of him. The Major does not know as he will come certainly, even if appointed, but thinks he will.

With much love,

Aldace F. Walker

Fort Massachusetts, D.C.,
March 8, 1863

Dear Father:

We have an inspection ordered for today again at one, owing to rain in the morning, so that I cannot leave camp to go to church. I went to the city Thursday, as I expected when I wrote last. We had the most pleasant day of the season and a capital time. I did a good many errands, and then went to see Steph. Found Charley Walker, and visited him the rest of the day; though I found time to call on Hodges and wife, who wished to be remembered. I also found Jim Slade, or rather Lt. Gov. Slade, of Middlebury, in the Treasury Dept. That building is much more imposing than I thought, and is well worth a visit for the sight of the building. The attorney General has rooms there, and there are other fine apartments.

Charley has got his men out of prison. Did I tell you about it? He had loaded his stuff on to a sloop, with a lot of sutler's stores, for transportation to Falmouth. The sutler had a little milk punch that had passed the custom house inspection, and someone sent word to the gun - boat at Alexandria, who stopped her and brought the whole concern back. Took the crew and all to the old Capital Prison, and would give them no place to see friends or say a word to anyone. I wish secesh got treated half as rigorously. While I was there Steph's little horse got away from a post where a man that he had lent him to had hitched him, and went home to the stable. A Paddy caught him, and a couple of boys came along and claimed him and took him off. The last I heard the police were after him - specially the boys.

There is a court-martial, or examination rather, of one our Penn. friends at the city that is attracting a good deal of attention. Hunsdon and others are before it as witnesses, Benton as counsel. Don't know, of course, the result or tendency, but it will be apt to unearth things that will make considerable of a smell - and rank too.

Peter leaves for home at once with a man from Monkton who has secured a furlough. I am glad on the whole to get rid of him. He made more bother than he was worth by far, and cost a good deal. I shall strike for a nigger, and expect to be suited some way. It has taken all my money to send Pete home. I shall have to apply for more according to your promise. I don't know, of course, when we shall be paid off, but it may be some time - and may not. The Paymasters have nearly all changed regiments of late, and become brigade officers. Steph has lost all his old ones, and I think it very doubtful if Halsey pays us. Still I don't see much chance for any great expense in the month to come.

As soon as the weather gets good I am going to have some new clothes throughout. I have seen nothing of the Greek Testament yet, but am going to run the risk of sending for one more book, and should like it as soon as possible - Loomis' Trigonometry.

On second thoughts, however, I believe I have sold my copy that I used at Middlebury, and think I will send to the city tomorrow, as I wish to use it at once. We are going into a system of triangulation, to estimate the various distances to prominent objects in this vicinity. I won't trouble you to get the book then.

Evening - Your letter just received, and one from H.E.C. The Chronicle came yesterday. The Herald has not reached us, nor last week's one either. Please send Dea. Allen $6 (six) for Pete, as you suggest. He has been in the way a good deal more than he has been of use lately. Charley Smith's Bill, the one who ran away into our camp, has returned to him again, and I think I shall have him do my little chores too. He is as lively a nigger as I have seen, except one who works for Col. Benton.

There is some prospect that I shall be summoned to the city on that court-martial business tomorrow. Don't know though. As to Sunday work, I always try and get along with as little of it as I can. The writing on the muster rolls I regarded as necessary. We had the sheet we were to copy from given us Saturday at dusk. We made out one copy that eve, and the other three the next day, as they were required on Monday. In fact I did not finish till about Monday noon. Then all had to be revised and corrected at headquarters, and they left for the Adjt. Gen.'s Tuesday morning.

Today we have all had to have the Articles of War read to our men per Brigade orders. I have five men - six - in the hospital. Two Corps., one Sergt., three privates. Corp. Macomber is going finely; in fact none are dangerously sick except Corp. Gardner, a very fine young fellow, who has had the measles, and took a cold resulting in pneumonia. I am very afraid we shall lose him. We have had a case of small-pox at this post. The patient was removed to the city hospital today. I have been vaccinated anew, and all the men beside. Our new hospital is going up over toward Fort Slocum. Meeker found his father alive, and left him in about the condition he found him - very low. I am glad to have him back, as he runs the wheels very smoothly, and with little trouble to me. I have applied for a pass for one of my privates to Sudbury. Think I shall get it, as Hunsdon got one for one of his men.

My tent is my front wall tent on the old adjt.'s frame - the back knocked out and ripped up, and an "A," canvas, common, soldier's tent, put up on a pig pen four feet high behind, so that the ridge poles join. Lewis and I sleep in the bed room, and live in the front tent. The tent that was up by the side of the Col.'s was one that belonged to the officers of Co. I, and was not in use when I took it. Lt. Austin has put it up next to Charley Smith's, and gone into it himself. Goodrich has fixed up my other for an office, while he lives in his house. I hear that our barracks have all got to be moved up to the side of the fort in the spring. I am sorry about that, for we shall have to live in the mud then like other folks. We are too far from the fort, though, to be of any use. Well, I must close. I am well now - feeling well. Am glad to get your letters so regularly and so long.

With much love,

Aldace F. Walker

Washington, D.C.,
March 12, 1863
Stephen's Office

Dear Father:

I am in rather a curious scrape this week. Was summoned to appear as a witness on that case I told you of. Came down on Tuesday morning, gave in my testimony, was only asked one question, and expected to go back at once. The prosecution had closed its evidence, and I was on the defence. After the defence had closed, the prosecution brought in more witnesses, and Col. Benton kept his; so I am not dismissed, and shall stay I don't know how long. I get $1.50 a day extra, and am having a capital time. Spend my nights with Steph, and navigate in the day time. Find lots of friends - on every corner. I hear from my company often enough to know that it is all right, and have nothing to do but to enjoy it.

Charley came up from Falmouth last night. Has not got to running yet. Some of his boxes were thrown off by mistake and detained, and he came on to look them up. Found them all right this morning, and will return tomorrow I suppose. I had a fine chance to see Gen. Burnside yesterday. He is some like his pictures, though with heavy hair, when he is represented bald. Gen. Rousseau, the fighting man from the West, is in town and looks finely. That was a big thing on Stoughton. He is universally condemned, and will probably lose his place in consequence. I see this morning that Stannard has been confirmed as Brigadier - in Stoughton's place, I suppose. He is worth a dozen of him. I never saw such a place to find people as this is. You are sure to run across someone on the avenue you did not expect to see, and anyone you know turns up twenty times a day. The fact is, there's only one street that anyone goes on, and there you find every body.

I heard yesterday that my Corp. Gardner was dead. I am very sorry to lose him, for he was a capital little fellow. The measles is a very dangerous disease in camp. I knew he would not live when I left. Don't know whom I shall put in his place. Smith's father went home this morning. Said he had had a capital time, and I never saw a man appear to enjoy himself so well. When I get back to camp I can write more fully.

Till then, yours with much love,

Aldace F. Walker

Sunday Noon,
March 15, 1863

Dear Father:

By some unaccountable chance, although letters north have been delayed of late, yours of Thursday with $15 enclosed reached me Saturday. It is a beautiful day. Lt. Lewis is a little off the hooks, and I had to get up to roll call this morning; so had plenty of time to wash and change my clothes before breakfast. I was intending to go to church, and should but that on account of the illness of Capt. Templeton I had to take his turn as officer of the day. We have had our usual inspection - all right - have just issued cross-cannon letters and figures for the men to put on their caps, so that they look quite brassy. I have my barracks whitewashed, a brick walk laid from the quarters to the cook-house, a range in the cook-house, and a brick oven just put in operation, so that the men had baked beans for the first time today, and were as happy over them as a lot of magpies.

On the whole we are very comfortable now, and our only trouble is that we have got to move up to the fort door, or perhaps I should say sally-port. The new bomb proof gets along bravely - is covered, though not with dirt yet; perhaps a month's more labor will be required with the force now at work on it. The hospital is nearly done - over towards Slocum. Of course there are men to look after our magazines - an Ordnance Sergt., a Corp., and three men, are there all the time to take care of the guns and ammunition, and it is very well done too. Our Quartermaster has been promoted to Brigade Quartermaster, rank of Capt., regular army, - and I suppose I shall have a promotion in my Company soon in consequence. I made my company Clerk, Lewis,[4] a Corporal to fill the vacancy caused by the death of poor Gardner. I came up from the city Thursday afternoon. Was not called into the court again; and in fact, it was all knocked in the head by the resignation of the President of the Board, Col. Murphy, so that the case will all have to be gone through with again. It is rather a mean affair. I hope I shall not be summoned again, though I had quite a pleasant time, as I told you.

I saw Hemmenway[5] and others from Stoughton's brigade, and George Cheney and Hall from Rutland - other acquaintances without measure. Everyone condemns Gen. Stoughton - "Stouton," as the newsboys call him - for his carelessness, and probable disobedience of Casey's orders - though Johnston was to blame for the negligence and inefficiency of the picquets. And apropos of Generals, rumor says we are to have a new Brigadier - Gen. Davis Tillson[6] of Maine, an accomplished artillery officer of Gen. Heintzelman's staff (Chief of Artillery), formerly Capt. of a Light Battery. Did not know that he had any chance of a Gen.'s position till he saw his confirmation in the papers. I am glad of his promotion and hope he will come here, though Col. Warner has arranged things so that he runs his wheel pretty much his own way and has a virtually independent command.

Did I tell you what Lincoln said of Stoughton - "that he was sorry to lose the horses, but could make another general easy enough"? - too true. The Chronicle came last night. My daily Chronicle keeps coming now, and chronicles accounts of forward movements being ordered at Vicksburg and Port Royal - perhaps they are. Col. Warner's court-martial is in session at "Jakes," or our hotel, and will be for several weeks. I have four victims, and perhaps five. I heard from Emily the other day, giving a story which probably she has given you, and the same or the reverse from Cousin Charley. They agree well enough - interesting though. About our magazines again. There are a dozen ventilators in each, and the one where the powder is kept is perfectly dry. I should have very much enjoyed the opportunity of getting acquainted with Wallingford people at your Donation if I had been able to attend. It must have been a pleasant gathering to you, and I hope you had enough acquaintances to feel at home. I don't think you need send me anymore money at present. I had a letter from Charley Sheldon awhile ago, at Poughkeepsie Commercial Institute. John is favored with a "leave." I suppose I could get one if I was to make an urgent application, but I don't think it best just yet. I presume the same chance will be open next August, and I should like to attend commencement. However, I will not lot on that too much.

I have heard just now that the 13th, which is with the 12th at Wolf Run Shoals, had a little brush yesterday - a reconnoitering party of the enemy - nothing said of it in the paper, but there are rebs in that neighborhood and enough of them, and the stores at Fairfax Station would be a great prize. I see the Chronicle reports the number of men in the 11th as 709. I presume it means the number for duty, not counting those "off" with colds, &c.; but it ought to have said so, for other regiments are evidently not reported in the same manner. Our number is considerably over 900. I see persons quite frequently from the Army of the Potomac. Capt. Johnson,[7] of Hope's[8] old company in the 2nd, has been here today. He tells a very favorable story. That Hooker, by increasing and changing the ration, and giving furloughs, and other such little things, is fast becoming popular; though they know that when he starts some one will be hurt. The ground is frozen there now; but it is not safe to trust to it, of course, for any extensive movement, as it must thaw soon. You did not send me the catalogue you promised, but I got one from Tuthill the other day. In that Roll of Honor I counted twenty-one mistakes - not much value in such a list.

With much love &c.,

Aldace F. Walker

Fort Massachusetts, D.C.,
March 18, 1863

Dear Father:

I did not know but I should get your Monday's letter tonight, as I did your last; but it did not come, so I shall have to write without it. I got a letter from Thomas tonight. He thinks he is getting along well in his studies, but is doing a vast deal in the musical line as usual. Sabin[9] is leading a choir in Chicago on $500 a year, &c. It is a beautiful night. We have had a snow storm this week, but is all gone and in its place reigns mud. The 20th is coming soon, and after that I hope for settled weather. I never saw thunder, or heard it rather, in such perfection as in the two of our snow storms, and it sounded queer enough. Our papers have stopped again, and I have been without news for the past two days. We have a good deal manufactured in camp, but it is not very satisfactory. Lt. Lewis has been out of camp sick for the past two days, but is back again tonight. I am glad to see him of course. The health of my company is improving much of late; men are returning from the hospital, and are getting better in camp. I think we shall turn out all right in the spring, though it has been rather sickly of late. Our hospital steward has the diphtheria very dangerously now.

I have been reading military books of late - scientific - and am much interested. A Shakespeare has also turned up in camp, and I enjoy it much. I am ready now to have a new suit of clothes; my old ones are getting rather shabby. Perhaps I will give you a few directions, and leave the rest to you and Chaffee. The dress coat on the old measure, but two inches bigger at the lower button; the lower button - holes, or place where they are rather, faced with morocco, to keep them from tearing out; buttons on coat and vest to be artillery - letter A in center. I want a good coat; no shoulder straps; two inside breast pockets. Blouse of fine beaver cloth; no lining; like one made for Capt. Hunsdon; same buttons. Pants and vest also of dark blue cloth (light blue soils easier, and does not look so well); red welt on pants; three inches bigger waist; vest with an inside pocket. A pair of boots on same measure like the finest ones I had before; calf double and sewed; slugs in the heels. Boots do not wear out as fast here as in Middlebury. Those nice ones are perfectly good yet; not worn much, and very easy. Some way or other my stockings are reduced to two pairs, and my handkerchiefs are a little short. Let Mother pick me out a pretty necktie, narrow; they are very high here, and I wear paper collars all the time now.

If you have any books you want to send me, I should be glad to see them. Classics I am not familiar enough with to enjoy without a dictionary or a pony. I have found a book with the necessary tables for the computation of distances - remembering that the sides of a triangle are proportional to the sines of the opposite angles - but have not gone into it yet on account of the weather. We have had a regimental court-martial in camp today. I have had three victims before it for absence without leave. No sentence rendered yet. I have a couple more who will have to go to the city before a general court-martial. I hope to get them to realize that there is a law for sinners before pay day. That court, or board, which I told you was knocked in the head, is alive again with a new president. They are hammering away at the same old case, but do not allow the victim any counsel as they did before. I presume, however, I shall be summoned again in his behalf, and am ready to go for another day or two at any time now. Goodbye, with much love.

Your affectionate son,

Aldace F. Walker

Fort Massachusetts, D.C.,
March 22, 1863

Dear Father:

It is now Sunday evening. Your letter has come in, and I am all ready to answer. It is a splendid day. Our Equinoctial has passed with a two day's storm of rain and mist, and now I hope we shall have a "spell" of settled weather. It is wonderful how the ground in this vicinity dries up. We had a very pleasant parade this evening. Have our companies assigned to guns in the fort, and the member to particular guns. Formed in detachments after parade, and shall do so till all know their places. We have a compass, and are going to work at once in Trigonometrical measurements. I do hope we shall have pleasant weather for awhile, for March so far has been most dismal. I have been over to church this morning, and busy all the rest of the day.

As I told you, that "case" of ours - Lt. Lewry of the 112th - Gibson's - Pa. Regt., has been tried, or is being tried over again. Capt. Hunsdon and I were summoned down Friday; gave our testimony by having the old testimony read, and agreeing to it; then stayed over night, and came up the next (Saturday) afternoon. I thought as I was splashing along through the mud and mist last evening about six - mud six inches deep, and mist thick enough to carve - what you imagined I was doing - if you were thinking of me at that time. I thought at any rate that you would not be apt to get it very near right. The mud here is good on one account - it is very thin - of no more constituency than so much water - and though I was covered from head to foot, it was not very hard for the horse.

I found that I could draw my pay on the "summons" as on detached service, and that was the reason I waited till Saturday. I got an order from the Paymaster Gen'l, hunted up Maj. Morrell, our new paymaster, found him out of funds, and patched up an arrangement with him and Stephen, so that Steph furnished the cash for Capt. Hunsdon and I, or an order on New York, which we were fortunate enough to get to the bank just as the doors were closing. I got $320, pay to Feb 28th. Received $10 more from you, making $25. Hope you were not inconvenienced by sending it, as it has proved to be unnecessary. I will send you some when I can get a draft; was too late Saturday, but shall be in the city again soon I presume. I have learned the ropes some of late, and shall be able hereafter to draw my pay pretty promptly after the rolls are made out. I think we shall like Maj. Morrell, our new paymaster. He is in hopes to pay off our regiment before long; is not a green hand at the business; has the rolls all ready, and expects funds in a week or so.

Steph had orders to make out his rolls at once, as money would be furnished him this week to pay his brigade. He heard at the same time that the whole of Smith's corps, 9th, was about to move from Fort Monroe, west, and was expecting that the payment would be the last thing previous to their departure. But while I was there officers from his troops came with the news that they were already in motion. Broke camp Wednesday, and were en route via Baltimore for Tennessee. It will be a valuable reinforcement to Rosecrans. I don't know whether Steph will go west to pay them, or whether they will be assigned to Western paymasters.

I saw Col. Nichols of the 14th. He says he has promoted Harley Sheldon to a lieutenancy, and speaks very well of him. Those two lieutenants of ours that were tried before that examining board have been dismissed the service. I went Friday evening to hear Shakespeare's tragedy of MacBeth. Enjoyed it very much. Davenport, one of the best in America, acted, and was very fine. I had just been reading it, and enjoyed it all the more, as it was acted verbatim. I had a fine view of Seward, who was present, the papers said, for the first time. I rode up on Steph's old Whitey, and shall keep him in camp a few days. He is a powerful, tough old fellow, though not as easy a riding horse as the other. I rode him to church this morning. Keep him at "Jake's" as we call our little tavern. I had the pleasure of ordering him to shut down on selling beer to the boys the other day, while I was officer of the day. It was the pleasantest task I have had for a good while. One of my men had got drunk on it and into trouble the night before, and I was especially vexed at him. If the roads dry off I shall enjoy the horse.

I have got the Chronicle as usual, and the Atlantic. The Herald for some reason never reaches me till the last of the second week, though the Chronicle comes Saturday. I think it is rather a curious freak, but it is very regular in its irregularity. There still is a good deal of sickness in the regiment. The sick are moving to our new hospital now; and if the weather changes we shall do better. My men are continuing to improve; no dangerous cases at present. I was sorry to be away when Gardner died. His father was sent for and came on. Of course it is a Captain's business to look after such things, and to forward the corpse when requested. I did not see Gardner's father, as I believe I told you. It was a great deal easier for me to have him here of course, as the care of the dying and dead is among the hardest duties of a Captain. My company has been lucky - or perhaps something better, favored - only two have died in all. B. has lost five, one last night. I presume this spring will see our armies in motion in earnest again.

I understand Hooker makes great threats, and I hope he will do great deeds; but I reckon he is a good deal of a swell, though not of so bombastic a nature as Pope. This court-martial business is a great nuisance. I presume I shall get stuck on to one sometime, but I hope not. We had some men tried in the regiment a few days ago - three of mine - and I presume I shall have to go to the city before long with some before the court-martial of which Col. Warner is president. I shall hope for letters as usual.

With much love, as ever,

Aldace F. Walker

Fort Massachusetts, D.C.,
March 25, 1863

Dear Father:

I have nothing especial to write this afternoon. It is a beautiful, though we had a rain last night. I still keep old Whitey. Was down to Mr. Blagden's last night, and came home in the mud and rain. Had a pleasant visit, however, and did not take cold. I just received a line from Stephen, who says he is ordered to Cincinnati, and wants to see me before he goes. I presume he will make his office there. I hate to have him leave, as it has been very pleasant for me to have him in the city. Shall try and go down on Friday. He is to leave Friday evening. The 9th Army Corps is composed of Burnside's old men, and will compose Burnside's army I suppose in Ohio and Kentucky, where he is to supersede Gen. Wright.[10] I presume this is done on account of the rebel talk of another invasion of Kentucky, and certainly it is well to be on our guard against such a contingency. There is a very great probability that the Vicksburg and Fort Hudson armies will be withdrawn and turn up in that direction, and that Rosecrans with all his éclat will have to reenact Buell's glorious movements. If we can get the Mississippi open, however, it will be a great compensation for another foray on Cincinnati. We shall never believe how much danger that city was really in last fall.

The three days this week I have spent in surveying. My compass has been a very poor one belonging to Mr. Butts, with only one level and no vernier, and I could only approximate; still could do much better than guess work. I have made a little map, and it is much thought of by the officers at the post. We have got several Irishmen at work by the day in our fort, and I understand more are coming; of course we like that. We have been able to drill some of late, though our detachments are small. The health of my company continues good. I have got a man standing on a barrel on the parade today, for getting drunk repeatedly, and he don't like the fun. Shall make him play it till his legs ache and again.

Fort Mass. Evening - Since dress parade Lt. Lewis and I have been having a gallop in the dark; rode some six or eight miles I presume. I am getting quite in love with horseback riding, and wonder why folks in Vermont ever got so out of the way of it, so that the horses don't know anything about it and there is no one who can teach them. I suppose cold weather has a good deal to do with it, as there is more exposure, and our roads are so good with a good horse and an easy saddle there is an excitement about it that is very pleasurable. This old Whitey is not as easy a rider as the other, but he does very well and is very different from horses at home, where the only way to make them gallop is to drive them out of a trot.

It is getting towards the time when I shall have to be at work on my quarterly returns. I am quite anxious to see how I come out; don't anticipate any trouble, however. I had a letter from Emily tonight. I reckon that the affair is hurt beyond patching. She speaks her mind very freely, and is decided as usual. It is rather too bad, but matters look to me pretty well defined. I am, to speak the honest truth, rather more sorry for his sake than for hers. Am sorry I got so unfavorable impressions on my last visit to Bath, but I certainly did not feel that it would be a very pleasant home. I suppose Stephen's move will deprive us of a visit with Henry.

With much love,

Aldace F. Walker

Evening - The mail has come, and has brought a letter from you and one from Uncle George, with the March "Atlantic." It seems to take just a week for a letter to get around from here home and back. I am glad my letters go through sooner than they did. The Herald did not come. The storm has abated somewhat this evening, though it is not clear yet; still we shan't enjoy the sleigh-ride that we should tomorrow if we were in Vermont, for the inevitable result of snow here is slush. I should rather enjoy a severe spell of cold weather now, though I fear it would tell on the health of the company. Our barracks are in rather a bad condition today, for the snow has drifted through the roof a good deal. I must contrive some way to floor them. We do drill in the infantry movements, marching, &c., when we get time, and can't be at the big guns. We have so much other duty on hand that we can never get out over about twenty-five to drill at all, and the fort is often very muddy indeed; but our parade is always sandy. When there is no snow on it, and when there is no getting about elsewhere, we can drill there with ease. Capt. Hunsdon is very well now. Mrs. Goodrich is a very companionable sort of woman, though not very intellectual. I have written a long letter to Emily this evening and my hand is tired, so Good - night again. Lewis wants to write at the table, and I am using his pen.

Aldace F. Walker

Fort Massachusetts, D.C.,
March 29, 1863

Dear Father:

It is another Sabbath afternoon. We have a clear sky today, but rather a chilly wind, so that it is a little unpleasant. Yesterday it rained again. I was officer of the day and had to visit the picquet, which, by the way, have been reduced in strength of late, and the Lieutenant who used to be out with it has been taken off, so that it makes an addition to the duties of the officer of the day. It does not come very often of late, however, as we have nine officers to divide it among. I was up and visited the fort at two this morning to see that the guard was in shape - "Grand Rounds" we call it. Our inspection this morning was quite satisfactory, as we had more men out than at any other time this winter. I have only 13 sick now, besides the three that have been sent to the Campbell Hospital. I have had only one in hospital the last week, and he returns to the company today. I was in our new hospital on my way from church. Am much pleased with it. It must be better than the tents used before, and the ventilation seems ample. It is in a windy place, but that will be an advantage rather than otherwise in the coming hot weather. There is room for forty odd patients without crowding; the same iron bedsteads are used as before, of course. I went there on my return from church. I am not able now to get there quite in season, as we have our inspections at 10 a.m., but the services are very long, especially now, or in Lent. I always sing. The lady who plays is a Miss Walker; plays very well. The minister is decidedly shallow; talks very generally of sin and contrition, and very vaguely too.

I did not get my pass, as I expected, to visit the city on Friday, so I rode down and back Thursday evening; and not finishing my business with Steph in relation to the vouchers for Hunsdon's and my pay, I got a line which got me a pass from Haskins' headquarters Friday afternoon. Steph and Charley left for Cincinnati via New York and Binghamton. Steph had sent Charley to Newport News to pay off a couple of regiments yet remaining there; he paid one, and the other started taking the rolls with them. I suppose he will take an office in Cincinnati when he gets there, and attend to his brigade. Gen. Tillson, whom I think I have mentioned to you, has also been ordered to the Department of the Ohio. We hoped he would be assigned to our brigade. I went to the Treasury with Steph, and counted over his money, $250,000, which he sent at once West by the Quartermaster Dept. It was more money than I ever saw together - so much paper that it lost its money look entirely. I was riding down the Avenue on old Whitey, and I met Uncle Abe. I knew his carriage, and recognized him from the pictures. He was all curled down in one corner, and looked tired, as I presume he is. I made a few purchases - a $150 draft, which I enclose - a copy of Benet's Military Law and Court martial Practice - a copy of the "National Almanac," which I shall send to you when I get through with it, and there is a vast deal of matter in it too. I presume you have seen it reviewed. I have the April Atlantic - a capital number - much better than February or March.

Your letter came last night, and Chronicle. Herald came Monday last week; soon enough, if mailed on Friday. Register came yesterday with nothing in it. I don't feel much like writing for it when I am not in an Addison Co. company, and besides there is not much to write. I will enclose Steph's photograph, and also my Lt. Lewis'. I had a letter from Benny a few days ago, which I shall answer of course. I can't think of any books I want sent to me. I am well provided for just now, and don't see but what I shall be. Don't have so much leisure any way as I did when Post Adjutant, and my labor is increasing every day, as we are getting to drilling more and more. You were right about the boots; plates will do very well on the heel and toe. I wanted the good ones, as I said, for summer wear, and they will last me much longer here than in Middlebury. I don't think I lose any of my handkerchiefs, though I find them wearing out, - but where my stockings go to is a mystery. I wore a pair of army stockings - the "thin" kind - last week, and finished them with a big hole in the heel.

I presume our railroad makes less certain connections and less rapid time since the adjournment of Congress. The agitation of a line to New York stirred up the animals, and a train was run some two hours quicker since Jan. 1st. I don't know that it has been taken off, but it is certain that it is less sure. We get daily papers now by our mail boy, who comes this way from the city to Fort Slocum. Take the Chronicle, F.'s paper, and the Administration "organ," which puffs everything gov't does. The mail has brought the Herald and a letter from Henry announcing the fact that our Chaplain Little would be with us soon. I shall be very glad to see him, and have strong hopes that he will do well in his place.

It is a shame about that Capt. Huntoon scrape. He was a brave, good officer - I knew him well - though a wild fellow. He may have been careless in the place where he was taken. If so, it was because he was not afraid, and it was impossible to scare him. I know Capt. Woodward too, and there is a man here, bugler, who was taken in the same place, and who says Woodward ran like a deer at first, and till his horse was shot. He was paroled because he had no horse and could not be taken off, not on account of his bravery, as he would have Vermonters believe. I don't know but he was wounded himself - perhaps he was - but he is a regular gassy swell head - like Drew - and a good deal of a puppy. He is a son of the Chaplain, and a '62 man in Burlington College. The fact is, that a man that gets out of such a scrape has much the advantage in having the story to tell. They say Stoughton has been dropped from the army rolls. I am glad of it. It is said that his secesh sentiments led him to arrange his own capture. Don't believe that; but he is, I think, a humbug - K. K. Child to the contrary notwithstanding. Pray tell what Edward Walker's "book" is about; and if convenient at any time, present my congratulations, or whatever is the right thing, to Katie.[11] I wish Mother could see a letter I had from Emily the other day. I laughed till I cried, and then began again; but the cake is all dough.

With much love,

Aldace F. Walker

One of my men, Erskin S. Grover, started for Sudbury today on a ten day's furlough; one of Hunsdon's too. It is said that Higley will be dismissed on account of his conduct in the scrape where Maj. Wells was captured. It is said he told his men that he would "go as far as they would," giving no orders to go or stay. I hope the rumor is false, and hardly believe it of Higley. It is certain however, that our officers have to toe the scratch now-a-days, and are held to a strict account.

Fort Massachusetts, D.C.,
April 1, 1863

Dear Father:

We have a queer streak of weather now, and in fact have had for some time. March went out in a snow storm - six inches deep yesterday morning, more through the day, but melting all the evening, rain at night after I went to bed, and a cold morning - colder than any we had in December, and so cold all day that we have not been able to work or to leave camp at all. I hoped for sunny weather, and we have got it - but frigid enough for polar bears. I wanted to go down to the big union meeting in the Capitol last night, but it was so stormy that it was impossible. I have been revising my Trigonometrical performances of late. I set my compass up on a corner of the parapet, and find now that a certain 24 Par. barbette cannon affected my needle so much that it will all require revision. It is a good joke - like the rat trap. The mail has come, and I will stop to read the paper and the news.

Well, I did not find much news in my Chronicle. I am interested in our great Union meeting - but the rebs are getting the ranges from their various batteries on the Mississippi most dreadful accurately. I don't know but they will annihilate our Western gunboat fleet. At any rate, I am dubious about our western operations, though the preparation has been made on so grand a scale. One of my deserters took advantage of the President's proclamation, and came back Sunday and reported. Of course we cannot punish him, and I hope he will behave himself at least till pay day, when I expect he will run away again. Another of my men, who has charges preferred against him that would subject him to severe punishment by a general court-martial, left last night. Our guard house in the fort is damp and unhealthy, and Col. Benton has been in the habit of letting the prisoners stay in quarters with a guard. He took the chance to skeddadle, and turned up missing. We found he had written to his wife the night before. Hunted the letter out of the mail. Found that his intention was to deliver himself up to the Provost to be sent to the 22d N.Y., from which he deserted some time before, and where his time would be up the 6th of June, being a two year's regiment.

I have stopped since writing the above, and have more news about him. Lt. Goodrich went to the city after the letter, and to telegraph to his home. Got on track of him, and brought him back to camp. His name is Charles A. Moulton; is a tough, hard fellow from Whitehall. He never gave me much trouble, though always a troublesome fellow to have around. He was charged with breaking into a house and assaulting the inmates one night when he was drunk. This attempt at desertion will probably send him to the Rip-raps for a while.[12]

What makes this scrape worse is that the officer of the day is blamed for his escape. It was Lt. Smith. I presume he will have to leave, though probably he will get an honorable discharge. He was certainly careless, however. I have commenced on my rolls. Have finished my Ordnance returns all right. Shall have more trouble with the clothing rolls, and presume it will bother me a week or so. These reports are all well enough and right, but it puzzles me some to know whether they are ever to be audited or not. One of our lieutenants, Fleming of Co. D, has been detailed to act as Quartermaster.[13] Meanwhile I hear that our Commissary Sergeant has been nominated for promotion to that place. Since five o'clock I have been on a horseback ride to Fort Bunker Hill,[14] some four miles. I went on a little errand and on the Col.'s horse. Had a good ride, though somewhat muddy.

My company is very well indeed now; only eight off duty today; none of them so but what they are around all the time. There was a new case of small-pox in Co. A today. The new hospital is capital and works to a charm. I am very much interested in my book on military law. Don't know as I shall ever have occasion to practice, but I may get a taste as a victim. Meanwhile the knowledge won't hurt me. The sentence has not yet been passed on that lieutenant whom I testified for in the city. I have written this by spells and by jerks, and now will finish.

Benny Thrall told me in the letter he wrote me that Uncle Joel had sold in Lebanon, and bought Charles Boardman's place. How is it? He would have hard work to find a political mate in W.R., wouldn't he?

With much love to all,

Aldace F. Walker

Fort Massachusetts, (Stevens) D.C.,
April 5, 1863

Dear Mother:

We hear that the name of our Fort has been changed as above, but have had no "order" to that effect; so I will use the old style with an appendix. The weather here outstrips the memory of the oldest inhabitants. People say that their oats ought to have been in a month ago, but the ground has seen nary oat yet, and there is no prospect of a spring at present. Thursday and Friday were fine, and the roads had got into pretty good order, save here and there an unfathomable hole; but on yesterday the sky grew black, and it kept growing blacker and blacker; the wind rose and blew terribly, first clouds of dust which made outdoor life almost impossible, then snow - and the storm through the night was terrible, the worst by far we have had. It is ten o'clock in the morning, and it is snowing yet. It is a melting snow, however, and acts as if it was almost played out. I presume a foot of snow has fallen in all, but it is drifted in a manner that looks real Vermontish. Such is April weather in the sunny south.

My tent is tight generally, though some snow got in through the cracks. I have no trouble in keeping a good fire all night. Hunsdon stayed with me because he thought my tent was the warmest. His got afire the other day, and burnt a big hole in the top. I am rather glad of this storm on one account - Col. Gibson is absent on furlough and Col. Warner commands the Brigade, so Benton commands the regiment. We have no time through the week for anything but fatigue, and Benton ordered a regimental parade and inspection at Slocum this morning instead of the usual company inspection. I did not care to go, though I think my company can beat anything in the regiment. I presume it will come off next Sunday.

"Little Jim" is still in the city most of the while, where he presides over a Department Court martial. He is as dignified as an owl, and looks as wise; though they say he does not speak much - another good trait. We like him more and more all the time. He has got the regiment in some way so that he has an almost independent command. Gibson lets him do as he pleases, and never comes near us. We could not be better situated in any respect, as I see, and be in the service. There are several vacancies among the officers, but Jim keeps his own counsel and asks no advice, and no one knows who is to be promoted, though we probably shall this week. When Holbrook and staff were here, Gen. Phelps[15] remarked to Jim that he might perhaps in view of the large number of officers to be appointed call a sort of a council of officers, and take their sentiments on promotions. Jim said that he supposed he was commissioned to command the regiment - when he was thought incompetent he wanted to give up his commission, and let some one else run it. The Gov. told him he would fill all his recommendations, and we are satisfied to leave it all to our little Colonel. Washburn, Adjt. Gen. of Vt., was in the city last Thursday, and we were ready to parade in his honor for a day or two, but did not see him. I understand he came to Totten, and that he was going to try and urge on some recruiting for us when he went back. I hope so, though I have not much confidence in his showing us many favors or in him anyway. Fleury,[16] 2d Lt. Co. K, is very sick, not expected to live. He is the first of our officers that has been seriously ill.

I have not seen our chaplain, though I guess he is near by. That is, I saw "Chas. Little, Vt." in the list of guests at the Avenue house; don't know as it is he however; don't know his Christian name. We have an order allowing 25 rounds a month to each company for cannon practice, on Tuesdays and Fridays, so we shall get up some tall firing I suppose; that makes 100 rounds for this post, and it is just what we want to go into. We have been using that coffee for some time in our mess, and it is much better than any we can get here. I wish I had thought to send for more, but I didn't. The tomatoes and cherries we ate at Butts. We have gone back to three meals a day; the days are longer and we get hungry; eight, one and seven are our hours now. We have a very pleasant table indeed. Goodrich is a very good fellow, as I found at Brattleboro. Capt. Templeton, Co. I, has gone to Vermont on a 30 days sick leave.

Our Vermont Cavalry have cut up another bright operation. I believe they are all a parcel of fools. Detachments of six companies, 125 men in all, under Capt. Flint,[17] called the best Captain in the regiment, went out one morning to take Moseby, who was heard of in the vicinity. They were marching carelessly in columns, with no flankers or advanced guard, and came upon him before they expected, behind a high barnyard fence. They got a raking fire, which killed Capt. Flint and two lieutenants at once. Charged and had to fall back - lost some 60. This is the story of parties that were there. Higley is out of his other scrape, I understand, and commended his company in this. Came out all right. One of the lieutenants killed was Woodbury,[18] a brother of our Capt. Woodbury,[19] Co. D. He has gone home with the body on a ten days leave. A few more such scrapes as these last three have been will use that regiment up. Col. Sawyer is not in the regiment, being on a court-martial in the city. Its headquarters are now at Fairfax, Maj. Hall commanding. Of the 2d Brigade, the 12th, 13th and 14th are at Wolf Run Shoals on the Occoquan, the 15th and 16th are at Union Mills, a little beyond Fairfax, and the 10th remains as it was.

Capt. Woodward of the Cavalry had his horse shot under him, and pretended his leg was broken, and so was paroled at the time Huntoon was taken. The officers of that regiment are all quite young now. Cushman,[20] a Meriden classmate of mine, is a captain. They hope to get into the city on Provost duty, as they are so poorly mounted, and I rather hope they will. They have seen service enough at any rate - most of it honorable, till of late. I was officer of the day Friday, and had to visit the picquet line.

Saw old F. P. Blair. I like to talk with him on national affairs, as he is right up among the circles. He told me of a letter he had just had from his son Frank, in command of a division at Vicksburg, which he showed to the President, which says that Grant[21] is weakening himself by dividing his forces and that the whole is endangered - don't send strong enough force anywhere to accomplish anything. Porter nearly got caught in his expedition to Haines Bluff, and was lucky in getting out at all. Things don't look so pretty as they did a month ago. We are scattered and have no head. Some one of our columns will be cut up before we know it, or the South are not as smart as I give them credit for being. But when this winter is done - if it ever is - we shall see.

I stick by McClellan yet. His last report reads well - considering what Blair told me - that at the time of Pope's defeat McClellan urged Halleck to go into Virginia and reorganize the army - that he (Mc) could not on account of his personal relations with Pope - but Halleck was afraid, positively afraid to. Blair says he is an arrant coward, who never smelt gun-powder at all, and that he fought more as a savant than as a patriot. I expect the report of the "Committee" will throw cold water on him at a great rate, and perhaps overthrow his pretensions. I don't think he is to blame for being adopted by the copperheads as their type. Of course adopted by them, he was dropped by the Radicals, and at the North a man can't fraternize with his enemies - still in some aspects this does look hard.

Your letters come very regularly now on Thursdays and Saturdays, so that my long letter must be written Sunday, and Wednesday letter writing is usually dull. In response to yours of 29th - I hear Chaplain is Arthur Little, so I guess he has not come on yet. Stephen was always very kind to me. I shall miss him much, and probably shall not visit the city now except when business calls me. My quarterly returns differ from my muster rolls in that we have twenty days to make them in. I have sent on my Ordnance report, but may not get the clothing return ready this week. I have to obtain signatures of every man to my vouchers or receipt rolls, and it is a great bother. Shall come out a very little behind, which of course I shall have to pay for some time, if it is ever called for.

Father tells about your going to a "goose party." Our goose parties are all gander parties. I wish there were a few more geese. I doubt if it would be hardly fair to let anyone see Emily's letters, though perhaps I might if you were here. They are keen, I tell you, and well worth reading; but I doubt if I ought to show them, and I presume she will tell you herself the whole and more too, as she might me if I should see her. I have no faith in any sort of a patch-work. It can't be did. She has got so she makes fun of John, and I reckon it is all over. I wish Mary would take all the lessons she can. If she can do more with twice a week, why go in; but she ought to practice twice as much of course. How does she like it? I wish she had a piano, but I stick to my idea of getting a good one when you get any. I am about tired of the melodeon, though it is well enough in its way.

I have finished reading my book on military law, and am going to borrow some more if I can.

I think I have written a good deal in the snow storm, so with much love, Goodbye,

Aldace F. Walker

I have just been reading the fine article in the Chronicle, "How a Free People Conduct a Long War." Have enjoyed it much. You will find many good things in the Atlantic. I send the Almanac also today, and it is well worth preserving. Steph left his vouchers for Hunsdon's and my pay to collect of the paymaster here and forward. I don't know when our pay day will come - expected it before this; rather dread it, for though I have got some of my worst ones out of the way, I have others who will bother. There is, I understand, a letter in the Herald from my company. They sent a box of old clothing to someone in Fairhaven against whom they had a grudge, with the express to pay; and by their story it was quite a good joke. Co. C is rather queerly constituted. It has more roughs than any other, and more church members too I think - some very fine men. Only eight off duty today.

Fort Massachusetts, D.C.,
April 8, 1863

Dear Father:

As I expected, I have not much to say tonight. I have had a busy day with my accounts and my drill, and am somewhat tired. I have footed up all the amounts due the men in my company, and as the price list has been recently changed this has been quite a bother, and have drawn it off into my ledger. The "Clothing Account Book" has to be signed and witnessed like other rolls, and I shall get around within the twenty days I guess. I found a missing pair of breeches today, and shall have a pretty good account I think - a few pair of socks and a shirt or so minus perhaps.

We have had an affair brewing in camp some time that has troubled me a good deal; but as the cat is all out of the bag now, I shan't have any compunctions in telling the story, though I don't want it to get out in Vermont from me. It has relation to Lt. Smith, who has gone overboard completely. When I was in the company with him, Hunsdon and I had to keep blowing him, and urging him to be careful or he would get into trouble. Benton has thought a good deal of him, and Charley has relied on this too much. Some three weeks ago he got into a scrape - left for the city, &c. - so that some notice had to be taken of it. Benton advised with Hunsdon and I, (we have saved him from being ordered before the Board by Warner) and we let him try it again under penalty of the old charges and others - such as gambling with the men, &c. But a day or two ago he was officer of the day and let one of the prisoners escape, and great carelessness was apparent. Benton said he could get along with the boy no longer and must have a man, so Charley sent in a resignation founded on youth and inexperience. But Heintzelman saw that something was concealed, disapproved the resignation, and asked for charges. So they have gone in, and a court-martial will follow, and Smith will probably be cashiered. Smith is a good hearted fellow, but weak and inefficient. Hunsdon and I have helped him all we could, but now are called as witnesses against him. I presume the trial will not come off for a fortnight or so, but of course can't say. There are a great many cases before the court - Warner's. I was cheated out of the pith of that Report of the War Committee. My papers were changed. Monday I got the Inquirer with the report to the Battle of Williamsburg, and Tuesday the Chronicle, where it was in Monday whole, so I lost the last half. I may see it around here, but if I don't please send me the Times or something else with the whole. We have had no storm since Sunday. Drying some, though cold.

I am very well, and send much love to all.

Aldace F. Walker

My man absent on furlough has got back all right. I have applied for one for

Corporal Macomber.

Fort Stevens, D.C.,
April 12, Sunday Morning

Dear Father:

I reckon I shall have enough to say tonight to fill the big sheet I have taken. I reckon I get more on to a page than you do, but your letters don't trouble me in the least by their brevity, and are a very great source of pleasure to me. The last one came on Friday, the other one Thursday, bringing the two for this week pretty near together; Thursday and Saturday are the usual days now. I have received both papers this week. The box has not come of course. Imprimis, you see I date from a new place - and not from a new place either, but from an old place with a new name. The fort is named Stevens in honor of Gen. Stevens, killed at Chantilly, formerly Gov. of Washington Territory. It will take less ink than "Massachusetts" at any rate.[22] You may have seen orders published in the papers for a muster of the army on the 10th, for the sake of ascertaining the number of conscripts required to fill the various regiments. Our muster took place at Slocum, when the regiment was brought together for the first time in many months. It was at one o'clock - a splendid day - the weather is all fine now-a-days - and the review was preceded by the inevitable inspection. We hear that we are to go to Slocum for a regimental inspection every Sunday morning now in fine weather. But we enjoyed that show very much, and the men are getting to know how to take care of themselves. Col. Benton says he never saw so good an inspection.

Warner was at the city on his court-martial. Old Blair was there. I had the satisfaction of hearing my company pronounced head and shoulders ahead; whether we shall be able to keep so I don't know, but my guns are beauties now. I presume the others will come up to us, but they can't get much ahead. Our detachment from this fort made quite a show, and went through evolution's that the others would have difficulty in doing. But if we can get together ever, with any chance to drill, there is material for a splendid regiment in our Eleventh. We had our colors out and it looked natural and good to have a whole line of ten companies. I am the junior captain now - am in the center of the left wing. We got home about five o'clock - some tired, but feeling pretty well. Saturday the event here was the announcement of promotions recently made. My 1st Sergt., Wm. V. Meeker , is 2d Lt. in my company - much to my satisfaction. I shall give Sherman his place. Lewis goes back to his old company. I have liked him very well here, and L. has been more pleasantly situated than he will be, as his Captain is an unpleasant man to be with; but I think Meeker will be a better officer. He has been a Captain, and is very well drilled - a fine penman, and I shall make him do a good deal of my writing, he is very popular with the company. Our Commissary Sergeant (Clark[23]) is made Quartermaster, and assigned to Co. G in place of one of those dismissed by the Board. The other similar vacancy was filled (a 1st Lt.) by the promotion of its 2d (in K.), and Todd,[24] a Meriden classmate of mine, and a Captain in the Vt. 2d, wounded at Bull Run, and played out, was put in 2d Lt. I don't think very well of him, though he is undeniably smart.

But the circumstances of Lt. Fleury, 2d Lt. in K., promoted to 1st, were very sad. He died the day the commission came and before he had seen it, of inflammation of the bowels. He was a very fine young man and deserving of promotion; young, but very energetic, and had seen service before in the sharp-shooters. This is the first death among our officers, and was felt very severely in the regiment. The services connected with the funeral were held at Fort Totten this morning at 10 a.m. It was our first introduction to our new Chaplain, who came on yesterday he seemed very plain, and ready - a little formal, as young men are; but we were pleased on the whole, though not surprised by any special excellence. I hope he will wear well, however, and trust he will. He will stay at Totten with the Major. Major Chamberlain is a very fine man. I did not know before that he was a church member, though I have often thought he might be. I wish you had seen him. Both these men are Dartmouth, and of the same society. You see this sticks, and in several instances since I have been in the army I have found it an advantage to me. Shall never repent it. Fleury's father and mother were both on. He thought he could not die till his new commission came, but it was ordered otherwise. He was terribly emaciated. I would not have recognized him. After the funeral I went to Rock Creek church, and came home by the hospital. I have two men there now; one an old man who might have been a good soldier fifty years ago, but who is worth nothing now but to chop wood - not dangerously sick however; and the other a fine young man, Kilborn from Castleton, who has the diphtheria severely, and will probably not recover. I telegraph to his father tomorrow, but the boy don't know himself that he is dangerously ill.

Am glad we have a chaplain to see to the good of the sick in hospital. The accommodations are very good however. Contagious diseases have to be kept in tents by themselves - diphtheria among the number. We have a case or two of chicken-pox. The death you saw from Co. C was a misprint. None have died from my company since Corp. Gardner. We have eight off duty today. Kilborn is the only one severely sick. One of my men was discharged from the Campbell General Hospital last week - Cassavant,[25] a Methodist minister and a humbug - has been playing sick, the surgeon thinks, to get out of the service.

We have had a big scare today. Orders reached us to leave our present home tomorrow, and go into camp in the city to do Provost duty, as the regiments now there were ordered to the front. So we got together our duds, packed boxes and barrels, and tore up generally in a wonderful manner for Sunday. The men were elated with the idea of going away - anything to stir - but we officers did not fancy the new duty. However, we got ready through the afternoon to turn over loose property, take up our pegs and start. I got my company in good trim according to orders, but smelt a very large mice, and did not do anything towards arranging my personal traps. The Col. went to the city, and came back with the facts, and orders to be ready to march at any time, with one day's cooked rations, to replace the Washington patrols if they are ordered away - which is about as likely to happen as a trip for our whole regiment to Africa. It may though, and we are positively under "marching orders."

Have assurances from Heintzelman that if we do go to the city it will only be for a few days. The amount of the matter is that Hooker will fight soon, and if he is licked he must be reinforced by troops from this vicinity, and that will move us. Charlestown news is exciting, isn't it? I enclose Col. Warner's photograph. We have got a $200 sword and trimmings for "Little Jim," and mean to present them at a social supper tomorrow night, at Safford's house on the hill. They are a splendid set, and I would as lief he would have them as anyone this side of the Hudson. I will tell you about the supper next time. I think I will follow your suggestion and write another letter for publication. I don't think it is too late to print yours now, and if I were you I would shove it on. Who is Mr. Hull? That Times article interested me much. Have not seen the whole report yet, but McClellan has gone down of late. Opinions will always be divided, I presume; have no doubt but he wanted a big war, but I can't but think he meant it to be earnest and successful. I get my washing done now by one of our laundresses, who does it very well. Double woolens have been uncomfortable the last few days.

I am very glad to have Mary write. I think of her as often as of anyone, and take a good deal of comfort in her photograph. I wish I could have some card pictures of you and Mother. I wish she had a piano, but as I have always said I want a good one. I don't doubt but there is much money made on the high priced pianos, and that cheap ones may sound as well at first, but they don't wear .. get to tinkling with age. Grovestein's are well spoken of however, and if I could get a good judge in New York to approve (Ernest or someone else), I might be satisfied with one of those. The patent "attachments" don't amount to much. The best parlor piano I ever saw is one of Chickerings at Blair's. Miss Bettie has been to visit the army with Mrs. Lincoln, &c. Don't know whether she has returned yet or not. I remain very well, and comfortable as usual.

With much love,

Aldace F. Walker

Fort Stevens, D.C.
April 15, 1863

Dear Father:

Your letter came today, a day earlier than usual. The Tribunes did not come. I have not seen the Report yet, and shall be very glad to get it tomorrow. The box has not come yet, and I have not expected it. Our team will go for express stuff on Friday I suppose, and I presume it will come then, if it has reached the city. As there is nothing perishable I don't care, though my old coat is looking rather seedy. We have another rainy day today, and little to do. I have written some and done some business this p.m., and since dinner have read the paper which reaches here at about half past one. Meeker tents with me now, though I presume he will have his wife here before long, now he is in a situation to take care of her.

I have a negro for a waiter, Billy, - the boy who ran into our camp in the fall. He came awhile ago to work for Charley Smith, and does my chores too. He is about seventeen, and a good fellow. We found awhile ago that he was supplying the soldiers with liquor a little, and had him in the guard house a little; but he has learned better, and is above the average of darkies. Charley boards him, so that I have no trouble about that. Smith's trial has not come off yet, and the court that has been in session has been dissolved. Another goes into operation at once I understand. You see that we have not moved yet, and the probabilities are that we shall not. One of the patrol regiments was ordered off, but its place was supplied yesterday by a regiment of the Penn. Reserves, so that we don't now expect to leave here. The "marching orders" have not been retracted however, and I presume they will continue in force all summer. I am very glad we are not going, for it is a disagreeable duty any way, and it is hard enough to take care of our men here, let alone the city. The men are all anxious for a change, and would be glad enough to go anywhere, but on the whole I am content for the present.

One of my men, Frank Kilborn of Poultney, died Monday night. He was sick but four days. Monday morning we telegraphed for his father, and he reached here today. Meanwhile we had sent the body home. I am glad to have someone here to turn over the clothing to, as it saves some bother. Mr. Kilborn says he knows you, and seems a good sort of a plain man. Frank was baptized by Chaplain Little before he died. In such cases the attendance of a chaplain seems very essential, and it is a great pity we have been without one so long. His father's name is Hiram Kilborn. He was a good boy - young, but faithful, and I was very loath to lose him.

The sword presentation I spoke of came off as we expected on Monday night at the house (Safford's) on the hill south. All the officers were not present, as we expected them certainly to move in the morning; but there were enough so that we had a very pleasant time. Several ladies, &c. The presentation was made without much formality in a little speech by Col. Benton, complimenting Jim on the rare combination of qualities he possessed for a regular, uniting discipline with an appreciation of the peculiarities of volunteers. Warner said but a sentence or two in reply - what I don't know, but I do know that it was just the neatest thing I ever heard on such an occasion, and just what he ought to have said. I think a good deal more of him than I ever did before - it was remarkably happy. And then we had an oyster supper. The present was an elegant sword with two scabbards - one gilt and carved for ornament, and the other of burnished steel, gilt mounted, for service - a sword - knot – belt - cartridge - box and strap to hang under the right arm - and a sash that cost $30. The whole cost $200, and was very cheap as such things go.

Mrs. Lee, Blair's daughter, Miss Blair (Bettie) and Miss Martin were there. The last two have just returned from a visit to Hooker's army with Mr. And Mrs. Abraham. Bettie says the army is in splendid order and going to move. Of course she knows. She said that something happened on Sunday night that she would not tell, but the papers would before long. Mystical, of course, and probably humbug. I am going out to see her before long if we stay here. Mrs. Lee is the wife of the Admiral in command of Fortress Munroe. He says that he is not at all discouraged by Charlestown failures - that they would try it again before long - that the Keokuk was in his fleet for while, and he condemned her as unable to stand heavy fire, and advised Rhind[26] not to take command of her. What puzzles me is those big chains and piles and things that our vessels could not get by, and the way so many vessels are said to run the blockade there. How do they get in? Grant is a humbug I reckon. Wish Lew Wallace[27] or some live man could run that Vicksburg wheel.

Yesterday I spent at Fort Totten seeing their target practice. Col. Haskins was there to direct. They fired with a 100 Pdr. Rifled Parrott five times - the shell nearly two feet long, and distance two miles and more. It was fun to see them fly, and there was no particular delay about the way they went. The screech was awful. Folks in houses fired over hung out white flags sudden. Col. Haskins is coming here Saturday if pleasant, to shoot, and then we shall have some fun. Col. Benton's wife in not here. Safford and Goodrich are the only officers at our post who now have ladies in camp. There are several at Slocum. Capt. Hunt and Adjt. Burrows have gone to Cincinnati in charge of a lot of convalescents for the 9th corps, with twenty men from this regiment as a guard. The rain still continues this evening. Capt. Hunsdon says it always storms when he is officer of the day - or rather that he is always on when it storms. I can stand it if he can. I am quiet anxious to get the papers tomorrow. I made Sherman 1st Sergt., Macomber, Sergeant, and Patch[28] Corporal.

With much love as ever,

Aldace F. Walker

Fort Stevens
April 19, 1863

Dear Father:

I have not time to write as much as usual tonight. This forenoon right after breakfast we all fell in and had a regimental review and inspection, conducted by Col. Warner. It was quite long and tedious, though quite interesting and successful as such things are. It must be a terrible task to go through with a Division review, for the soldiers, but they did not have their knapsacks on today, and their absence was a great relief. It has been a beautiful day - one of the finest we have seen - but it is going to be terribly hot in July.

After the inspection we formed a hollow square - had a meeting - not too long and quite interesting, though the Chaplain has a way of dealing in generalities quite natural and easy in extempore speakers, but which I do not very much like. I notice that the older good men grow, the more practical they become, and I wish all our ministers were forty years old and over. I don't know a minister I really like younger than that.

This afternoon I have spent one way or another reading and resting - we got back about two - and this evening I have been up to Safford's on the hill till quite late singing. Some of the ladies can sing just enough to make it hard work to sing with them, and I get entrapped occasionally. Yesterday we had the first of our target practice at the Fort - blazing away a good many times, and with pretty good success. It was quite satisfactory on the whole, and I presume we shall repeat it before long. The day was cloudy, but good enough, and I find that it is no hard matter to see any kind of shot after one learns how. It is rather noisy fun, but we don't think there is any danger in it, at least for those in the fort. We could make it pretty hot for an enemy in front though, and I would rather see balls go than come. You don't seem to realize the permanence of our location here. The other regiment of our brigade has been here ever since it was raised - over a year and a half.

I saw Dr. Allen today, formerly of Vermont. He told me of a fellow by the name of Underwood, an old student of his whom I used to know, who came out in the 10th as hospital steward, and who is now in the old Capitol prison under sentence of a court-martial for stealing rings and money from dead soldiers, he says unjustly of course.[29]

Gen. Stannard is assigned to the new brigade.

I got the Chronicle with your letters last night. The Tribunes came in good time. The box has not reached me yet. I expect to go to the city tomorrow, and if I do I shall try and look it up. I am very much obliged for Mother's picture. Have got quite a lot here now, and have sent home several I believe. I mean to sit again in the city. Things are moving very nicely here now. With our Irish Laborers at work, we are able to drill more than usual, and that the men and officers of course like much better than the fatigue. The idea of our leaving has all blown over.

Lt. Smith's trial does not seem to be inclined to come on yet. I don't know when the court will get around to it, as I suppose they have considerable business. Warner and Benton are both on a court-martial, Warner presiding. I suppose that is a place where they do well, but I think they don't enjoy it much. I don't think much of the new lately. See against bravery, but these old officers have an awful prejudice against innovation and distrust any new invention. "Carlton's" story of the Charlestown affair is different from some of the others whether just or not, I don't know of course. He seems to think they ought to have tried it again the next day.

I don't see anything in your letter that require an answer, and it is bed-time, so Good-night.

Aldace F. Walker

Fort Stevens, D.C.

Dear Father,

It is late this evening and I am very tired; can write but little. I wrote confidentially about a performance Sunday. Monday morning at three we got marching orders and left. Went to Cliffburn Barracks near the city, in the rain, and had a desolate time I assure you. Will tell you about it Sunday. Meanwhile, we came back tonight, more firmly convinced than ever of the permanence of our location. Find things all right, and am at home again, though I have not had time to make my bed. I am well, though we had more exposure than usual. The march was quite a good thing on the whole.

With much love,

Aldace F. Walker

Fort Massachusetts, D.C.,
Stevens, I should have said,
April 23, 1863

Dear Father:

It has been a rainy, dull day today, and as I wrote you so little last night I may not be able to do better than continue my story this evening. I have worked all day today counting and arranging my company ordinance stores, which I had boxed, collected in mass from the barracks where they had been kicking around, when we left so suddenly. I had dreaded this job, but I went at it in earnest with Sergt. Sherman and Corp. Bigelow,[30] and was very happily disappointed as to the result. I selected 84 full sets guns and accouterments - enough to equip my company as it now is - and counted the rest to turn over to the

Washington Arsenal. Find that I have an over-plus of every article, except that I am deficient to bayonet scabbards. It was very gratifying, as I expected to be $20 or $30 dollars out. I can't imagine where the surplus comes from, and shan't trouble myself much to find out. I only receipted for what Lt. Goodrich found on a very imperfect inventory - he was not so careful as he might have been, because Hyde left no accounts, and he was responsible for what he chose to take up only - but I find more of some things than the company was ever entitled to, and understand that more than the legitimate number were armed at Brattleboro in some manner.

But to return to, or to begin on our journey. Our orders came, as I said, early Monday morning. I did not pay much attention to them - turned over and went to sleep - got up as usual about seven o'clock, and found that Col. Benton had his things packed and ready to start, so I had to hustle around. Had time enough, however, for the company of the, 2d Pa., which was to relieve us did not come till about 10 a.m. We did not know where in the city we were going, and went over to Rock Creek church to unite the regiment, supposing it most likely that we should camp on Capitol Hill. It was muddy, very, and rainy to, and marching was hard work. I was at once made officer of the day, and turned over my company to Goodrich.

I had packed all my necessary articles in my valise, but as the waggoner seemed somewhat surprised when I carried it to him, I added my trunk, mattress, and a big bundle of blankets that I intended to have my nigger carry - in fact, all my property except my chairs and stove - even my water pail and wash basin. Our sticks we left here. The company that relieved us took up quarters in the new bombproof, and the camp was mostly deserted.

Our regiment marches well. There was very little straggling, although we marched six miles to get there - a highly military proceeding; for while we were forming the battalion near the Soldier's Home, Col. Benton, who had gone with Warner to the city to look for quarters, came back with orders for us to go Cliffburn Barracks. These lie west of 14th St., on 21st I believe, a mile this side the city limits, so we had to wade across 7th and 14th, and still on even West of Fort Stevens. These barracks were originally built for hospital purposes, but have been occupied through the winter by the 2d. D.C., whose Col. Alexander is in command, and some detached companies. We did not think them very attractive in the mud and rain, moreover they were decidedly dirty. We were not put together, but decidedly scattered. The bunks were not floored, but built with slats for bed-sacks, so that the men woke up in the morning striped - and on the whole it was comparatively rough. I had to see to the prisoners, and took them to the Post guard-house, which was of such a nature that I was unwilling to put them in it; so I sent for the Major, and he let me give them a corner in one of the company barracks - except two, Moulton of C. and Edwards of B., who were awaiting sentence by G.C.M. Their sentences, by the way, came while we were there - Edwards one year, and Moulton three, at the Rip-raps. Edwards' was mitigated by Gen. Heintzelman to three months in camp, and Moulton shrewdly escaped from the 2d District guards, and we shall never see him again.[31] There were no quarters at all for the officers, so I slept the first night in the company barracks - not very well, for the mattress did not fit the bunk, and the blankets kept slipping off through the slats.

The next day I enjoyed bed and board at a house near by, and a nice place too; was rather sorry to leave so soon, as I had quite a good wheel running. The Major commanded the camp; Warner and Benton are both on court-martial. Major is a good man - somewhat of a martinet, and somewhat of a coward too, as I could give instances if I chose. We had no orders to do any provost duty - in fact a brigade came into the city for that purpose the same day we did, and I more than half opine it was a mistake taking us there.

We had battalion drills all the time, which we enjoyed much, as we have not drilled together at all before. Major Chamberlain is a very good drill master, and the regiment is quick to learn. I hear, by the way, that in point of discipline we are far ahead of any regiment this side the Potomac. I went to the city Tuesday. Got a new hat and some other things. Looked for my box, but it has not come. I am getting anxious about it. How was it marked? But it may turn up nevertheless yet. Our recruiting officers started on Tuesday - two lieutenants to raise the new companies, and a non-com. Officer from each of the old ones, with two Sergts. extra to help the Lieuts. I have a good deal of curiosity as to their success. My Sergt. Nichols went with Lt. Safford, and Corp. Lewis also from C. Company. We came back yesterday afternoon, with nobody hurt, and all as glad to return as they were to leave.

On the whole it has been a good thing for us, though I don't care to repeat the experiment. We came home by the shortest road - found everything all right. I had a big invoice in the mail tonight - four letters, two papers, and a catalogue. May Atlantic has come. Sherman makes a very good Orderly. Lt. Meeker is the one you remember who went home first. (Macomber has gone now.) Meeker's father was a Methodist minister who practiced medicine in Middlebury. He, Wm. V., was Orderly Sergt. in the 1st Vt., then Capt. In a N.Y. company, and now out again. Is a printer by profession, from Tuttle's office. Is not a professor, but a steady fellow. Has sent for his wife, and I presume she will be here soon.

I have written a good deal for an extra letter, so good-night.

Aldace F. Walker

The women were left here, and were glad enough to see us back.

Fort Stevens, D.C.
April 26, 1863

Dear Father:

I am again crowded this evening into a few minutes after taps, but as I wrote you a long irregular letter this week you must pardon a note this time. We have had splendid weather of late, and are quite dry. Had artillery practice yesterday, and Col. Haskins present. The first shot I sighted, and hit the target. Today we had a long inspection this forenoon - a call from the chaplain the p.m., but no service - a walk - and at five a march to Slocum at the head of my company to attend the pay-table. We started unexpectedly and in a great hurry. Have only just got back. This pay was to the 1st of March. Of course I got nothing, but had to see that the Company were fairly treated. I expect to have trouble now somewhat, though I am not afraid of anything serious. I have only two in arrest now, whose sentences both expire on Tuesday, but shall fill up this week I presume. Sergt. Nichols is in Vt. on recruiting service. Sergt. Macomber, home on furlough, has been telegraphed to stop with the same intent.

Aldace F. Walker

Fort Stevens, D.C.
April 29, 1863

Dear Father:

I mean to find time to write you a full letter before long, but I can't tonight, for it is past bed-time. I have been absent from camp all the day, in charge of my company on a fatigue detail at Fort Slocum. We did not work very hard, but the standing round was decidedly leg-wearisome. Our fatigue has been increased of late. It had gradually got quite light, and we were drilling a good deal, but now we have to turn out every man - don't know of course how long it will last. Since I came back I have had to make out a big duplicate monthly return and other company papers, which took a good deal of writing; besides tomorrow is our muster-day and the rolls must be forthcoming, and accurate too. My company are very well now, and are behaving quite well. I have instilled a wholesome dread of any unusual dissipation, and am having for a wonder an easier time than some of the other captains. I presume it will break out however sometime, but my worst men have behaved themselves quite decently thus far since pay day.

Your letters all came in good time. Got yours of Monday today, which is decidedly quick I think. I am glad you saw our recruiting officers. The Sergt. of B. Co. was Sergt. Gage[32] of Monkton, and a good fellow too. In fact I think the selections on the whole were very good; men were sent who will make a business of recruiting, and not of spending time in enjoying it. Still my expectations certainly are not very sanguine as to their success. We have not heard from them yet.

I saw a Sergt. today from Higley's Co., in the Cavalry. He says Higley is in the city trying to get restored, and that there are strong likelihood's of his success - that he was accused by a Pa. Major, in command of the picquet post, who must blame someone to shield himself, and that the feeling in the regiment is in his favor. I am glad to hear that it was exterior influence, as I had attributed it to Col. Sawyer, and have no doubt but that he would be glad to be rid of him. Just before I sat down to write I took a candle and went through my barracks; found the men all in their places and asleep. This precaution that I very often take now - more particularly as I know the location of all and it is thus so easy. We are making arrangements to close certain dens around here; if we could only kill certain irresponsible darkies, we could get on easier.

Had a line from Ab Mead yesterday. He is well, and the others - under marching orders, but not very apprehensive of a move. Hooker started on Monday, and Tuesday was a rainy day. Such a spring - wet, late and cold - has not been known here for a long time; but the peach trees are beginning to blossom, and the grass is beginning to look green, and I hope weather for military operations is at hand. I have not had time to read my paper yet today. Suppose Charlestown is threatened again.

The box has not come. I think you had better institute inquiries of the Express Co., though it may be in the city now, as our teams go very rarely; but I was at the office two weeks after it left Wallingford. I shall try and go to town the first part of next week, and look it up if I can, or get some clothing. Charley Smith has got into additional trouble, when there was a strong probability that he would get off easy, by bringing in frivolous charges against Capt. Hunsdon - his best friend here. Of course no notice was taken of them, as a person in arrest can do no official act; but it turned in a very bad way for him, as I will explain sometime.

----

1 Sergt., later Capt., Henry J. Nichols, Sudbury, brother of Col. William T. Nichols, Rutland, commanding the 14th Vt. Infantry. RR.

2 Sergt. Peter Donnelly, Castleton. KIA 6/23/1864. RR.

3 Arthur Little (1837-1915), eventually became the regiment's Chaplain. KUA 1856, DC 1860. ATS 1861-1862 and PTS 1863-1863. Died in Newton, Mass. RR; KUACat, 48.

4 Corp., later Lieut., Judson A. Lewis, Poultney. RR.

5 Probably Private Lewis Hunt Hemenway, Rutland, 12th Vt. Infantry. RR.

6 USA Brig. Gen. Davis Tillson was Inspector of Artillery until April 1863. Boatner, 840.

7 Capt., later Lieut. Col., Enoch E. Johnson, Castleton. RR.

8 Capt. James Hope, Castleton. Resigned 12/20/1862. RR.

9. Albert R. Sabin, Rockingham, ex-Captain, 9th Vt. Infantry, Co. C. Information courtesy of Donald H. Wickman.

10. USA Maj. Gen. Horatio Gouverneur Wright, here as commander of the Department of the Ohio, and later as commander of the Sixth Corps. Boatner, 949-50.

11. Katie Child and her husband, Edward Ashley Walker.

12. Private Charles A. Moulton, Poultney, deserted later in the month, 4/24/1863, returned 11/15/1863 under Presidential pardon and mustered out with the regiment 6/24/1865. RR. Rip-raps is a pile of rocks placed beneath the foundation of a fort or other large building, most often in shallow water. Its not clear whether Walker is talking about a specific place, i.e. the Rip-Raps (Fort Wool) at Hampton Roads, Virginia, or just using the term loosely for prison.

13. 1st Lieut., later Maj., Charles K. Fleming, Rockingham. Listed in Co. G in both the 1864 and 1892 Adjt. General's reports. Regardless, he had gone back to Vermont, recruited Company M, and returned as its Capt. RR; Benedict, 2:348-9.

14. See Appendix A.

15. USA Brig. Gen. John W. Phelps, a Vermonter, resigned in August 1862, and was apparently an informal advisor to Vermont Governor Holbrook. Boatner, 650.

16. William D. Fleury, Isle La Motte, 2d Lieut. Co, K. RR.

17. Henry C. Flint, Irasburg, Co. I, 1st Vt. Cavalry. RR.

18. Charles A. Woodbury, Co. B, 1st Vt. Cavalry. RR.

19. Urban A. Woodbury, Elmore. RR.

20. Capt. Oliver Tucker Cushman (1841-1864), KUA 1859. KIA 6/3/1864, Cold Harbor. RR; KUACat, 60.

21. USA Maj. Gen., later Lieut. Gen. Ulysses Simpson Grant.

22. Walker obviously did not think much of the name change, but USA Maj. Gen. Isaac Ingalls Stevens had been a contender for command of the Army of the Potomac before he was killed at Chantilly. Boatner, 796.

23. Sergt., later 1st Lieut., Charles W. Clark, Montpelier. RR.

24. Capt. Edward Augustus Todd (1840-1913), Brattleboro, Co. C, 2nd Vt. Infantry. KUA 1858. Post-war physician. RR; KUACat, 57.

25. Henry B. Cassavant, Poultney, PVT, Co. C; discharged for disability 4/9/1863. RR.

26. Commander Alexander Colden Rhind commanded USS Keokuk from October 1862 to April 1863. Mark F. Jenkins, "The Iron Captains," Ironclads and Blockade Runners of the American Civil War, accessed 2/18/2002, available from http://www.ameritech.net/users/maxdemon/ironcapt.htm; Internet.

27. USA Maj. Gen. Lew Wallace, future author of "Ben Hur," was investigating Don Carlos Buell's military operations, and would later unsuccessfully try to stop CSA Maj. Gen. Jubal Early at Monocacy, in which the 10th Vt. Infantry played a significant role in July 1864. Boatner, 887.

28. Ransom M. Patch, Weston, eventually 1st Sergt, Co. C, mortally wounded 9/19/1864, died 11/11/1864. RR.

29. Thomas G. Underwood, Castleton. RR.

30. John L. Bigelow, Benson. RR.

31. Charles A. Moulton deserted 4/23/1863, but returned under Presidential pardon 11/15/1863, and served until the regiment mustered out, 6/24/1865. RR.

32. Sergt., later 1st Lieut. Co. F, William W. Gage, Monkton. RR.

6.
Defenses of Washington
May and June, 1863

Fort Stevens, D.C.
May 3, 1863

Dear Mary:

I wonder if you are as much interested as I am in events now transpiring in the army before or behind Fredericksburg. Probably before this reaches you the results will be known, but now we are in great suspense. Our papers are allowed to say little, officers and men coming from the army are put on their oath to say nothing, and the most they do say is that there is no bad news. The President is very cheerful, and beyond this Washington knows nothing. I have been able to keep up with what is known in the city, but tonight's boat will be looked for anxiously. We are having fine weather for a wonder, and I cannot but think that though the movement commenced Monday last today may be the day for the grand battle of the spring. Hooker has certainly maneuvered well; and if he is in sufficient force and keeps up his own communications he may be able to cut off the lines of the enemy and take them at a disadvantage. The evening papers Friday had it that Hooker was defeated with 1000 loss, but e have heard nothing of it since and I presume it is false. All we got this morning in the "War-organ" is Hooker's "Order" of April 30th - nothing authentic since. Yesterday's New York papers are as unsatisfactory, and this absence of information is the beauty of the movement.

We have resumed fatigue again with our whole force, and I have had to go to Fort Slocum the last few days with my whole company. Meeker is on duty in Co. B, as Hunsdon is in command of the post, Benton being on a court-martial, so that I am alone again. It is very tedious business, and I presume will last a month or more. It is hot too, very, and my thick clothing is vastly uncomfortable. And that reminds me that my box has not yet come, though I don" wonder at it, as no team has been for express since I was in the city to look myself, though it is true enough it ought to have been there then. I expect to go again this week, and if I do not find it I shall try and make a fuss. I think stuff from the west side of the mountain is reshipped by Hamden's Express ... know it is usually. Meanwhile I am getting ragged, and if I don't find the box I shall buy some clothing; almost everything is giving out.

We had our usual muster April 30th, together at Slocum. Were inspected and mustered by Maj. Anderson of the 2d Pa. Art'y. Our rolls are not all done yet, but will be completed tomorrow. We had a visit from Gen. Stannard and staff, who took dinner with our mess on that day. Also yesterday we had a call from Dr. Woodward[1] and others of the 14th, and from Col. Jewett,[2] Capt. Frost, and others of the 10th, besides other company. I imagine this will be quite a fashionable place of resort when the roads are good. I see Father is a little in the mist about our ordnance, or "ordinance" as he spells it. There is to be no ordnance sergeant to take any responsibility - only a commissary sergeant to do the work for the captain in the matter of rations, clothing, ordnance, &c. We are obliged to take up additional property found, and can get no credit for it; though of course we can keep it on hand to make up subsequent losses, if we say nothing. I have found an error in my count that don't leave me in quite so good a fix, though I am in no serious trouble; have just drawn a new lot of clothing.

I have been having a little trouble with a corporal, who was enlisted by Hyde while a paroled prisoner, and discharged besides. He claims that he has never been exchanged, and that we can make him do no duty. How it will turn out I don't know. Corp. Lewis was expecting to go home, but had an attack of diphtheria and could not get off with the rest, and the result was did not go at all. Macomber was telegraphed to stop on that service. Lewis is a very fine fellow from Poultney, fitted for college; but was not known in the Co., and came out private. I made him corporal the first chance, and shall promote him as soon as I can. He is now detailed as Adjutant's clerk. Has heretofore made all the papers out for the company, which I am having Meeker do now. Meeker is a fine penman. I must go to Slocum this p.m. and see Warner on certain matters of business, and so will stop here. Col. Benton's wife has come - a very pretty woman with four children - and his mother. With much love, and good luck to the Latin,

Evening - I expected to get along without much Sunday work on these rolls, but they were sent for unexpectedly this afternoon, and Meeker and I have been at work from four till ten - just finished - and sent them off by a night Orderly. It is quite a task, and quite a knack to fold them even, after they are made out - very few captains can do it. Nothing new. The whip-poor-wills are singing very loudly this beautiful evening, and I must try and go to sleep. I have to get up to morning roll call at sunrise, but I usually take another nap.

Aldace F. Walker

National Hotel, D.C., Washington
May 6, 1863

I am spending the day in the city, but will write a line to let you have your usual letter. I have been very busy, but am about through. Shall be in again in a day or two on Smith's trial. We are all crazy over the news - have heard two or three times of Hooker's total defeat - but the news on the whole continues good, and I understand the President is satisfied - but the rebs will fight till the last this time, and I don't know what may happen yet. The 2d Brigade has gone to Falmouth. My pen won't go, and I shall have to wait till another time. Am well and all is right. I got the box at the express office today. Have not opened it of course.

Aldace F. Walker

Fort Stevens, D.C.
May 7, 1863

Dear Father:

I wrote you from the city yesterday, but as it was only a line I will try it again today. We have had a steady rain of two days, and it is not clear this morning; is muddy and nasty generally everywhere but on our camp, and I had a pretty hard time getting home last night, although I was on horseback. Perhaps I will give you an account of my day's work, so that you can have a little more insight into my business. I went by Slocum to get some blanks for Company Savings that were waiting for the Col.'s signature. He had not been up from his court on account of the rain, and I failed there. Then I went to Totten, and got $40 borrowed money paid to me. Then went into the city by North Capitol street. Went first to the Paymaster's to draw the money on Steph's vouchers for Hunsdon and I - and by the way had to cancel my allotment before I could get the draft. Paymaster was not at home.

Then I went way off beyond the War Dept. to see about some Company Savings vouchers, given while Goodrich had command of the Company; left them for examination with the promise of the money tomorrow. Went back to near the Capitol and put up my horse. Went to the express office - found my box - had to quarrel fifteen minutes before I could get it, as I had no documents to substantiate myself, and they are more particular than at a bank - but I hung to them and got it at last - carried it to Barr's on 9th St. for our sutler to bring to camp. Bought eight dozen white gloves for $15 for the Company - carried them to Barr's. Went to Brady's and got my photographs (enclose one). Got my watch from a jeweler, who has cleaned it and set it running (only $2).

Then I went up to the War Dept. again, and hunted up a clerk from whom I had a line the other day - Hall from Portland; was at W. R.[3] last summer, and is engaged to Lizzie Shaler or Mary Hascall, I forget which. He promised to get me their photographs any way. He is in a good place - the money requisition office - all applications by the War Dept. on the Treasury for funds have to be made out by him. Then I went and hunted up Col. Somebody, Commissary of Exchanges, and found out that my Corporal who claimed to be a paroled prisoner not exchanged, had been and was liable to do duty.

Then I went to the Court-martial rooms to find when Smith's case was coming on - tomorrow - and got into the car and started for Georgetown. Found by inquiring that Georgetown Forest Hall was a prison, and went there to find one of my men who had been sent here from a general hospital, (the one sent on by Maj. Austine), found that he had been remanded to the hospital, or to another one. Went back to Washington - got my money of the Paymaster and mailed it to Steph, and as it was about four o'clock I got some dinner. Got the evening papers and read them, with bully news. Went to the steamboat landing and saw Duryee's Zouaves[4] come in on their way home. Lots of prisoners are coming, and going to our old camp - Cliffburn Barracks.

About dark I began to hear whispers of bad news, and then went to the Opera - the best Italian singers in the country - here for two nights only - and I enjoyed it immensely. After that I went to the National, and found that the news was all over the city that Hooker has retired, or been driven, this side the Rappahannock. So I rode home in the mud and dark and rain feeling blue enough. Our morning papers have not come yet, and I am still in suspense. We sent a nigger to the city for papers, but he has not returned (noon), and for all that we know the army is annihilated - not very pleasant waiting any way.

I got my box and opened it this morning. Found everything all right, except the apples half rotten. The sugar is good, and tastes natural enough. The boots are the best thing in the lot - have worn them all the forenoon, and they don't pinch a bit, and still are close fitting and good looking. The pants are good enough in fit, but not very fine, and I don't believe they will last long. My others that were sent to me are very much worn. I have got a tailor at work on them now - the first chance I have had, for I have had no change. The vest is too high in the throat, and I shall have to have it cut down. The coat is a very good fit indeed; I was astonished to find it so good, and it looks well - is much wrinkled of course, but I am satisfied with it. I have got a new pair of straps for it, and shall "swing out" soon. The blouse is not beaver cloth by any means, but is better for summer wear than that would have been. But it is so short that I can't wear it; I look like a bob-tailed Indian with it. Shall sell it and get another. The other things were all very good, and very acceptable; especially the stockings, for I was almost barefoot. I feel like a man again now, and shall resume some of my acquaintances among the neighbors, if we don't go to reinforce Joe.

Higley has been restored. I may have told you before. Senator Foot took it up, and made the Col. help, and so they got the order through. Smith's trial is fixed for tomorrow - Friday. He is sorry about his stir against Hunsdon - did it under the influence of bad advice; will plead guilty to the charges, and call on H. and I to say what we can for him. The fact is that he has felt just as he was brought up to feel at school and at home - that if he could get along and have a "good time" and not be found out, it was all right - and did not feel that he was in a position of any responsibility. I pity him - still his loss will be a gain to the regiment.

Hunsdon is doing finely. If we had officers all as good as he we should be vastly better off, still he is not a perfect man by any means. Hunsdon has gone to work to beat me on guns, but he will have to dig for it. The Chronicle says that Hooker has "withdrawn in safety," but that means he was forced to do so. The fact is he had no business to divide his army and take so small a number with him. He was virtually whipped Saturday and Sunday, losing ground each time. Col. Warner told me months ago that Sedgwick[5] was big enough to run that army, and I hear well of him elsewhere. Warner was under him at the West. Bully for Banks. We'll make a president out of him yet.

Well, I have written an extra letter again. Hope you will get it and read it. I understand Maj. Austine has ordered all of the recruiting officers to recruit for the two new companies. We don't like it much, and they won't do well I fear. Nichols says he has talked with three men. They are starting a negro regiment here - Col. and Lt. Col. - two chaplains. Billy wants to enlist.

Aldace F. Walker

Fort Stevens, D.C.
May 10, 1863

Dear Father:

It is now about eight o'clock. I have just come in from a meeting held out of doors by our chaplain and attended by almost everyone at the post. It was very pleasant. A prayer meeting was appointed for Thursday evening. Mr. Little evidently wants to do something, but we have been without a chaplain so long that we hardly know how to accommodate ourselves to the services of a new officer. However I doubt not that he will work into it before long, and we too, and that he will be a good man and do well. It has been a most beautiful day, and has been all the more pleasant for the stormy time we had last week - three days steady rain, and more too - mud in abundance, &c. - but I presume it will dry soon. I was in the city, as I expected, on Friday. Lt. Smith plead guilty to all the charges, and the witnesses were not called on. So the only work I had to do was to collect some Company Fund money that has been due sometime. We are pretty well off now.

I have not much to write now but war news, and I presume you will have the start of this letter in regard to that. Friday the news of Hooker's recross, that I heard of on Wednesday night, was generally known. But I was surprised to see how little despondency was felt. Reasons enough were cited for his "change of base" - exhaustion of food and ammunition - the rapidly rising Rappahannock - the necessity of uniting with Sedgwick, if not at Chancellorsville, at Falmouth - absence of tidings from Stoneman,[6] &c. - and all felt that it was with reason and not a serious defeat, though an acknowledged failure. But Friday night I learned that Hooker had again recrossed, though the papers were silent, and are. Last night I saw a person who had seen the movement, and who said that on Friday all correspondents, sutlers and newsboys, were sent to Washington; and when we shall hear again I can't tell. In the meantime we hear that Richmond has fallen into the hands of Dix[7] and Keyes.[8] This is only a rumor. If the war had ever been prosecuted with decent vigor I should think it probable - as it is, it is a bare possibility, and we can only hope for good from Hooker's last forward movement. Now is the time if ever, and we hope for success. We had quite a time on inspection here today. Have fixed up wonderfully, and had Col. Warner over to look at us. The men pleased him very much - one of the best inspections he ever saw, &c. Col. Benton had agreed to give the best man at the post a visit to the city. So we sent five from a company for examination. He could not decide, so threw them all out, and gave a pass to each company. I have concluded that the blouse is about right after all, and am pretty well satisfied with the whole kit.

With much love,

Aldace

Wednesday Evening
May 13, 1863

Dear Father:

It has been very hot hitherto this week until this afternoon, when we have had a thunder storm, or "gust," as it is called hereabouts. The weather seems like July, and our woolens are quite oppressive. Monday was my birthday. I was on fatigue all day, and got nearly tired out. Did not think as it was the 11th till evening, and then did not have any sort of a celebration. Don't know as I experience any different feelings now that I am a "man" - in fact I feel pretty much the same, though it seems a little more appropriate for me to be in command of a company. I have felt that it was rather a responsible place to put a boy, but still the peg is not a very big one and the stair not very high. Tuesday I was officer of the day, and today I am resting. Have been at work tinkering and fixing all day.

Have arranged the sides of my tent to lift up and let the air come through, and the boys have set out some big pine trees before my door for a shade. It is quite an improvement this hot weather, and looks real picturesque from the road. This afternoon I have been down to Blagden's. Had a pleasant call.

I like my new clothes very well; but unfortunately for myself and others, we now find that the black pants are not "regulation" and will not do for inspection. I shall get another pair in the city before long. I received your letter tonight and one from Alice. I hope you will see Macomber, as he is a very fine fellow. If you do after this, ask him for his address, and I will send him a Sergeant's "warrant." I think this weather must have been pleasant for your visit, and that you must have enjoyed it. Should like to have seen Uncle and Aunt myself, but it seems hardly possible at present. Charley Smith stayed in the city for two or three days after his court-martial, and got on considerable of a bender I reckon. He has returned now, and is put under guard in his tent. No admittance, and no exit. Why will he be a fool? Meeker is restored to my company tonight, and Austin of I. given to B. So I shall not be so busy, though I expect to have to go on fatigue tomorrow.

Our reveille is at 4:45 a.m. now, and after attending roll call I get back to bed; but now I shall not have to get up till I choose. We continue to get on very well in our mess. It costs about $4 a week, but is much pleasanter than it was at Butts. We have started a little garden, and shall have some green stuff of our own if we stay.

We are now in a great doubt to know which side of the Rappahannock Hooker really is - this side probably, though I saw a man who says he saw them cross back again. John Monahan has gone to Vermont wounded. The Mead boys and others in the same company are all right. Frank Walker had his left hand shattered, &c. What is to be, or is being done, I can't guess, and don't bother about it. This is a great country for dogs. I can now hear them howling by the score. I don't get many letters of late - fear my friends have deserted me. I have two classmates in Heckman's Brigade,[9] that is vibrating between Port Royal and Newbern, and am anxious to hear from them - Hobbs[10] and Beaman;[11] and they have "seen service" - were under Casey at "Seven Pines."[12] I think I shall have to be excused from writing much more tonight.

With love to all,

Aldace F. Walker.

Fort Stevens, D.C.
May 17, 1863, Noon

Dear Father:

It is beautiful weather - finer than I am accustomed to. The first few days of our present "spell" were excessively hot; but the air got toned down by thunder storms, or "gusts," so that the last three days have not been uncomfortable, but simply enjoyable - a cool breeze - cloudless sky, &c. We are doubling up on the inspection. Yesterday our newly appointed Brigade Inspector, Maj. Anderson, inspected us at Slocum at 3 p.m., then a dress - parade, &c. And this morning our usual Post inspection, which was quite fatiguing, as the breeze had not made itself manifest. We got through about 11 - have not seen the chaplain today, but presume he will be along after supper. Our meeting in the middle of the week failed from some unaccountable (to me) reason. But "Dinner is ready" is announced by our seven by nine thick headed little pickaninny, and I must cross the road. Of course we live in our shirt sleeves when not on duty.

Just back from dinner. Had a sort of Sunday meal - cod fish and potato and cold boiled ham, apple pie - simple, but healthy. Our mess is very pleasant now - Hunsdon, Goodrich, Austin, Lewis and Meeker. I presume Meeker's wife will come this week; at least he expects her. I have arranged my tent for hot weather, and have the most comfortable place in camp. Loop up the sides on to the eaves, leaving a hole 18 inches wide each side, allowing circulation enough certainly. Then in front, over my brick pavement, an old "fly" has made a very good awning, with nothing to fear from heat, as it opens to the north and laps down on the east and west sides; and pine trees set out around this, so that it looks real romantic, and is amazingly comfortable.

Not much to do just now either but to sit I the shade and enjoy the breeze. Our Fort here is looking much better than it did when you were here. We are laying turf over the magazines, &c., and it will be a very pleasant place a month from now.

Hooker has at last and veritably re-ensconced himself in his old camp. I see officers from the "forwards" occasionally. The last is a brother of Col. Benton,[13] Adjt. of the 5th Vt. He says that troops are leaving on account of the expiration of their time, at the rate of a regiment a day. Three came up with him Friday. Well, all Hooker can do then is to stand fast through the summer I fear. Everyone says they were not defeated, and that if it were not for the defection or failure of the 11th Corps they would have been eminently successful. Meanwhile, nothing can be done until more and permanent troops can be had. I hardly think we shall be taken from Washington - Halleck is too much of a granny for that - but as the conscription is of no value till July, and the troops raised thereby until September, - why things look rather blue, I confess. So we turn to other quarters.

I wonder if nine months men were raised in the West as in the East, and so generally - though New Hampshire has only two regiments; if so, Grant must be paralyzed soon. You speak of work on our guns. Guns have been taken on our inspections - and you know how bad they looked when we got them - not fit for a garret - and a white handkerchief passed over them, inside the barrel and hammer and screw heads, and in fact everywhere, without being soiled in the least. If we could only get Springfield rifles[14] we should be happy.

That blouse is not beaver cloth like Hunsdon's at all - not half so heavy; still for this time of year, I like it better. John Monahan,[15] I may have told you, was wounded at Fredericksburg. The other West Rutland boys are all right, though the S.S. did "feats" &c. The Chronicle came yesterday, and the Herald today. The article from the 11th is from Corp. Lewis of C., now Adjt.'s clerk at Slocum.[16] My number of men is gradually falling away. I have 89 men now here, besides officers absent .. can see a smaller look to the company. Well, I will write again soon. I have learned to expect your letters regularly, and they are a great pleasure to me.

With much love,

Aldace F. Walker

Fort Stevens, D.C.
May 24, 1863, Sunday Noon

Dear Father:

Last night's "Extra Republican" brought a dispatch from Gen. Hurlburt,[17] who had seen a "reliable gentleman," who said that a "good man" told him so and so, - facts encouraging on the whole, but not very satisfactory. So we were in suspense as to what has become of Grant since he left Jackson [Tenn.], and as to what he would do when he came to the Big Black with Pemberton[18] entrenched the other side. Today our Morning Chronicle has just come in, and for once I bless a Sunday paper. It gives official dispatches, the most interesting one from Grant's Adjt. Gen., giving an account of the five battles and the investment of Vicksburg. If the city does not fall, the campaign is the grandest one of the war, and it looks as though the opening of the Mississippi was to be the crown of the enterprise. I have always distrusted Grant, but I have got through. Even if he is finally defeated, which looks very improbable now, he has shown a determination to move on the enemy's works unequaled.

It is hot, very. No rain at all last week - dust in abundance, and sultry weather and shirt sleeves generally. I have got off my underclothing, and am pretty comfortable; but the tents are much hotter than the barracks. There is a trotting course half a mile from here, with frequent races and a large attendance of the "fancy." One of my corporals got into a mess there yesterday, and will have to be reduced. We have a regimental court-martial tomorrow, for which I have four or five cases. Our inspection for today is at 5 p.m. at Slocum, without knapsacks. Presume we shall have a parade and a meeting. We are beginning to reap the advantages of a warm climate in the early vegetable line. Have had green peas from Norfolk, asparagus all we want, lettuce, radishes, &c., and have a strawberry shortcake cooking for dinner - three quarts for 40c. But I am too hot to write now, and must go out of doors and cool off. Your letters come all right, and papers too. The last (June) Atlantic is a good number, and I shall be ready to send it on before long. Charley Smith is still under guard, and most roasted in his tent.

Evening - Since I wrote the above Lt. Smith has been released from guard, and again has the liberty of the camp. His sentence has not been published. This p.m. Montgomery Blair rode into camp on his way to his Sunday dinner at his father's, and said that Vicksburg had fallen and that Grant's victory was complete. Of course it seems authentic coming from a Cabinet Minister, and doubtless is. We turned out on the parade ground, and gave three cheers for Grant and his army with a will. This morning as our guards were discharging their pieces, a horse came between the guns and the target and was shot through the heart. Nobody to blame but the man who hit him. We have been over to Slocum - hot and dusty, very - and had a decidedly mean time. I don't want another such scrape, but we shall probably keep having them all summer.

This evening the wind has risen, from the south - dust is flying terribly, and I hope we shall rain. Mrs. Harper and husband, who have been annoying us by tempting our boys, have been arrested and are now is the guard house awaiting transportation to the city tomorrow, to experience the tender mercies of Capt. Todd, Provost Marshall. Well, things are very much as usual here - work and drill, principally work. I get blue sometimes, but seldom - for I never was in the habit of letting my mind wander far from the thing on hand, and don't mean to. Our men have got a notion that Vermont's quota was full before we were counted, and that we are to be reckoned as nine months men and go home in June. All folly, of course, but still many really believe it. The 10th, by the way, have the same story. Capt. Sheldon and Capt. Salisbury[19] were here the other day. With much love to parents and sister, I remain as ever,

Your affectionate son,

Aldace F. Walker

(Not "company" now) Battery C.

1st Arty. 11 Vt. Vols.

Fort Stevens, D.C.
Wednesday P.M., May 27, 1863

Dear Father:

I did not receive your letter today as usual, and in fact did not last Wednesday till Thursday (there are a good many Irishmen around here), so am not much disappointed. It has been cooler of late (since Sunday) and very much more comfortable; though we have had no rain, and the grass which we have "set out" in the fort is nearly dead for want of it. We are going to hauling water tomorrow. I have been at work all day today in the fort, and we can see daylight ahead at last. I think this week will finish the work inside, though it may not. Slocum is getting along some too, and on the whole we are not so much in the mire as we might be. After today we are to work forenoon's only - from 6 to 12 - and have a drill in the afternoon at 4:30; a very pleasant programme if we must have the fatigue.

Lt. Meeker's wife came today - a day earlier than she was expected. I have not seen her yet, however. She is to live for the present at Mr. McChesney's, out 7th St. half a mile or so. I mean to call after supper, and see how tired she is. We had a regimental court-martial Monday and Tuesday, before which I took several cases. Sentence not announced yet. Maj. Chamberlain was the Court. I don't get any news, or anything to write at all. It is as quiet here as in Greenland. Vicksburg looks dubious. Col. Benton is building a house near the road just beyond my barracks. He will go into it in a few days, I suppose. I understand they are getting more recruits in the north part of the state than they are your way, but not enough to amount to much. I don't see how time flies so fast when there is so little of interest here, though I usually find something of some sort to do.

A few days more and I shall have been in the service nine months full, or a quarter of the time of enlistment - not much encouragement of returning then, but something nevertheless. I don't know about a furlough. One for ten days is not of much account, except about commencement time, and then I should be at home so much the less, and it is very doubtful if more are granted this summer. Well, you have been here and know how we are situated, and that is almost as good as my going home.

Love to all. As ever,

Aldace F. Walker

Night - We have orders to be especially vigilant and look out for a surprise. What it means I don't know. Probably Moseby is "raiding" somewhere in Virginia. At any rate we are not much scared. Have sent 50 men into the fort beside the guard of 25.

Fort Stevens, D.C.
May 31, 1863
Dear Father:

I am living in our new bomb-proof now, with my company; and they are very pleasant barracks - cool always, though fronting the south - plane thus a little longer, so that my room is square, 12 x 12. I have the Orderly, Sherman, with me. The company is just handsomely accommodated. We use our old cook-house in camp. Have built a table through the old barracks, and eat there - and on the whole think we shall like it much. Moved in yesterday, and are to stay a month. I have forgotten how far along our bomb - proof was when you were here. The rooms are high and well ventilated, and six feet of earth on top and on the north side. I am more comfortably situated than ever now, save being so near my company, so that I shall have to keep them still nights. I am officer of the day today, while the men have gone to inspection at Slocum.

We are living under high pressure just now. I don't know whether it is really on account of danger, or for purposes of drill - but our guards are doubled at night - have a regimental officer of the day - passes are forbidden - the roads, except the main roads, are obstructed with fallen timber - everyone leaving the city is searched - after parade every night the men are marched at double quick to the guns (quite a run from our parade ground) - ammunition is inspected. Men are roused at 12 midnight and drilled at the guns ten minutes by moonlight, &c. Last night was the first night this was done, and two of the companies, D and I, let the men know it before hand, and turned them out in readiness for the surprise, greatly to the displeasure of Hunsdon and I, who managed the thing squarely, so that the men did not know of it, and of Benton too, who nearly put them in arrest - the officers, I mean. This is to last till the 3d proximo. I suppose Lee is feared a little just now, and we are losing so many men by the expiration of the term of enlistment that he may reach Washington. Vicksburg is not taken so much as it looked to be last Sunday, but I hope it will turn out all right sometime. I have not seen today's paper yet. We have got guards over two of the beer saloons near us - much to the disgust of the proprietors, and the increase of my travel as officer of the day this hot weather.

Our barracks here have good floors to them - a great improvement on the others. We have officers of the guards too, lieutenants, so that we Captains have to take our tour of duty quite often - in four days. I am well, and so are my boys. Meeker's wife is a pretty sort of a plain thing, with a bright baby. Very much to our astonishment we were paid off yesterday for two months. My share was $53.75, some of which I will send home when I can go to the city and get a draft. I want to get my debts paid and get some money laid up if I can, and the only way I can do it is to send it to you as fast as I get it, what I can spare. The mail has just come I hear, and have sent to camp for it, expecting a letter from you.

Afternoon - Your letter came as I expected, but I got no papers. Must remain in ignorance as to Vicksburg and elsewhere for the present. Our men are getting well over the nine months idea, and the recent visit of the paymaster will help to content them. It is hot here yet - no rain for weeks, and I am afraid the turf we are laying will all wither if we don't get some wet weather.

Our fort is very much changed, and I think we shall call it done in the inside this week sometime. Next month we have artillery practice again. Have to make up what we didn't shoot in April, and that gives us over 170 shots from this post - on Tuesdays and Fridays. This month don't take much writing to wind up; only the muster, or even months, bother us, and the ends of quarters, which come together June 30th - then I shall have a streak of business, I assure you, with my moving back to camp and all. We in the army don't have much squeamishness about such miscreants as Vallandigham.[20] It was better to send him South than to Fort Warren, but it would have been better yet to have hung him.

I feel vastly more bitter to Northern "sympathizers" than to Southern secessionists. If the army could go home for ten days en masse, it would come back leaving a different state of feeling I reckon. A Southern traitor may be, and doubtless is, honestly so; but a Northern traitor, or one who even fears Lincoln and hinders the necessary war measures, is a villain.

The men came back from Slocum about noon. I understand there was a little service after the inspection. But the worst of it is that they are ordered to go again at five, though I hope that this will not be thought necessary. Billy is still here. There is some hitch about the D.C. nigger regiments, but I think several will be organized about here. How is Mary going to work with her Latin? According to one of the new "methods," or the old fashion of cramming the senseless grammar? I hope she has not got to the second conjugation in Andrews & Stoddard, in course for that is a disagreeable and miserable way of learning a language. I will write to her sometime before long.

With much love to all,

Aldace F. Walker

There is a little event going to happen next month, rather queer in some of its relations to me - of which more anon.

Midnight - The men went to Slocum this p.m. Are making preparations for reviews &c. for our inspection by Gen. Barry[21] next Wednesday. We understand that six companies of cavalry are coming here to do picket duty out on the roads; this looks like work. I am about to start the alarm and bring the post to the fort on a double quick. Don't know how many anticipate this "alarm," but shall have a lively time for a few minutes.

Hoping I shall have success, I remain,

Aldace

Fort Stevens, D.C.
June 3, 1863, Evening

Dear Father:

Not much time to write tonight. We still continue under arms, as it were, but not much scared. Six companies of cavalry went into camp on Monday in the woods opposite our little hotel, and are doing picquet duty out the road - 2d Mass. (or California Battalion.) All soldier's wives are ordered to leave the camp at once. Officers cannot leave their posts without leave from Department Headquarters, (Heintzelman), &c. Culpeper Court House is supposed to be the rendezvous of rebels who will make a grand attack on Washington; but is can't come as I see without our knowing it a week before hand. We had our grand review by Gen. Barry today - a very nice man. The whole regiment came here for a wonder, and much to our satisfaction, for we get sick of going to Slocum; but it rained this morning, so that they did not have the dust to travel in that we have usually had. We had a review, inspection, and artillery drill - all very good but the artillery, which don't speak very well for us as an artillery regiment, but the fact is we have had so much fatigue to do that we have had no opportunity to drill. Our night alarms continue, though tonight is the last time. It is fun to see the cavalry turn out. They think they are in a very exposed situation - alarms every night, &c. I was officer of the day again yesterday, and am to come on once in three days now. Hunsdon and Woodbury are on courts-martial. I cannot write more. Will try and give you a letter Sunday.

With much love,

Aldace F. Walker

Fort Stevens, D.C.
June 7, 1863

Dear Father:

I have been over to church this morning, and am now in my room in the bomb - proof waiting for five o'clock, the hour when our inspection is appointed. After that I believe our chaplain means to have a service here. I am getting along very well in my new home; like it well enough, and am as contented as usual. Nothing more has turned up to alarm us. The extra guards have been taken off - officers can get passes now, two a day - and on the whole we are subsiding into comfortable quiet. We have comparatively little fatigue to do, and what we have is light - five hours a day - and are drilling a good deal. We have target practice this month too. Fired some thirty shot at our old target Saturday, and hit it sometimes. Pretty good practice I thought, and everyone else - much better than we have done before. We have got the range of the top of that hill pretty well earned, and could make it pretty hot if it was occupied. It is a little bigger business than rifle shooting - more scientific, and full as interesting. Shall shoot again Tuesday.

We had quite an exciting time yesterday over Lt. Smith. He has been waiting sentence sometime you know; in close confinement awhile, and then the liberty of the camp was given him. The court adjourned a week ago, but the proceedings have not been confirmed yet, or at least have not reached us as confirmed. Charley is of course terribly uneasy. Has had a private staying with him, a smart young fellow, an old friend of Smith's, and foolish enough to be led by him. Well, night before last Hunsdon went to bed leaving his wallet with $550 in his pants on the trunk near an old stovepipe hole, and in the morning the wallet was gone. Several things led suspicion on to these boys; and though the case looked pretty hard at fist, Benton got at it, and got a confession from Curtis.[22] When Smith found he was discovered he thought it would ease the matter off a little, and so he returned the money, which he had hid under the foundation of Mr. Butts' barn; and now he is begging and pleading that they will not prosecute him. He measures the punishment he will get by the amount Capt. Hunsdon and Col. Benton are "mad" at him, not by the amount of his guilt at all - that he never seems to appreciate at all. I shan't have anything more to say to him. I pitied him awhile as a boy, but have got over it, and now am ready to leave him to his fate and hope it will be a severe one. He was handcuffed for a few hours yesterday - a treatment to which we have been obliged to subject only two privates in our post. But I do pity the fellow who has been engaged with him. He is the clerk for Co. B - a bright boy, and one who deserves better companions and advisers. He took the money, and Smith made way with it. Still Smith was the one to blame, and I hope Curtis will get off comparatively easy; and I think he will, as Benton is the only one who can criminate him, and he won't. Altogether it is a sad affair, and Smith is ruined. He is really the most vicious boy of his age I ever saw - only twenty, and hardened enough to steal all the money of his best friend in the face of almost certain detection. He is mean enough for anything, but not smart enough to be a successful villain.

I don't know as I want his photograph in my album any longer, though I don't want it destroyed. I should hate to have to exhibit it, and you may lay it away. I send one tonight that you may put in its place, my 1st Sergt. Sherman. A capital fellow, doing better every day, and good enough for anyone. He is faithful and thorough - takes a good deal of responsibility - blows up the boys, so that they are as much afraid of him as of me - and yet all like him, and he is not rough at all. He is much more of a fellow than Meeker.

I have got a very easy and unceremonious way of dealing with my refractory cases now - just keep them in the guard house all of the time. I have quite a grist there now. Had six court-martialed, regimentally, the other day, though their sentences have not come yet - one of them a corporal - and have others in arrest, one of them waiting for a general court-martial, and some that I shall release when I come on officer of the day, as I shall tomorrow.

Col. Warner leaves tonight for Vermont on his wedding tour. He is to marry in Middlebury - Tillie Allen of whom you have heard me speak, and my old "flame." I shall be very glad to see her in camp. Presume he has a ten days leave, and that I shall have the pleasure of renewing the acquaintance before long. Mrs. Goodrich is here yet, and a very pleasant lady too. Mrs. Meeker and family are at Mr. Butts now. She is rather a motherly little thing and on the whole quite an improvement on the women we had here last winter. Mrs. Benton is a very fine woman indeed, and has a pretty family, four small children, and very well behaved. Capt. Templeton was a tavern keeper, and his wife is a coarse woman, like himself.

Fort Stevens, D.C.
June 11, 1863

Dear Father:

I received your West Rutland letter this afternoon. You do seem to be pretty much on the go just now. If you are not pretty much tired out when you return from Middlebury, I shall be much mistaken. I shall want to know where you stop, and any items from there that you can give - college, village, choir, &c. And that reminds me that the Congo.

Choir will suffer quite a loss today, or has this morning, from Col. Warner's marriage to my friend Tillie. I expect to see her in camp next week sometime. Chaplain Little is trying to get a furlough to enable him to be married, to Nellie Frost[23] of course.

If I only could make a selection I don't know but I would try and do the same; perhaps I could go home and make my pick after I got there - but I reckon it is best not to be in a hurry. Everything connected with me and my company remains in status quo, though there is some prospect of a change. Capt. Woodbury of Co. D, who lost his right arm at the first Bull Run, is well aware that there is a strong feeling against him in his company and in the regiment, (owing to a mean streak in his disposition) and so he is trying to get a position in the Invalid Corps, now being organized, and without doubt will succeed. This is rather an honorary organization, and I presume he will accept a lieutenancy. If he gets the appointment, Goodrich will be made Captain probably, and will want and expect his old company. In that case, I shall have to take D until Hunsdon is promoted. Nothing will be done, I presume, however, till Col. Warner returns; and before that something may turn up. That will be an easier company to manage than this; and as I have succeeded so much better than I expected here, I may do pretty well if I take that place.

We hear that there are almost men enough in Brattleboro to organize one of the new companies. I presume they will organize with 83 and fill up. It is slow work recruiting, but they are gradually gaining. I presume we shall get some of the first of the drafted men, and if so we shall be all right in the course of a month or two. We are to change our guns soon for better ones. When we do I will let you know. This will be by Gen. Barry's request, who said that he could whittle better guns out of a shingle than the ones we have.

I was out drilling part of my company this morning, and Col. Benton told me to drill them in the Skirmish drill and Bayonet exercise. I did not know anything about either; so I got a book and tackled the "School of the Skirmisher." Made it go pretty well for a green hand, and shall try it again. Lt. Smith's sentence has not come yet; and when it does, he will not know what it is. After his theft and confession, a guard was placed over him again - and one morning he was gone. Had crawled out of the back side of his tent, and gone no one knows where. Rather an inglorious termination of a military career, but we are well rid of him. We fired again yesterday, but it was so windy that it did not amount to much, and we stopped soon. I see that one of the magazines over the river blew up yesterday. It must have been from carelessness; probably a percussion shell was dropped and exploded. The officers' wives are not going home as I know of. There was a rumor that such an order was to be published, but we haven't seen it, and shan't at present. We have a white woman for cook now, wife of a man in Co. B, and I think she will do well. Goodbye, it is almost time to drill again. Love to Mary and all.

I have taken a great fancy to the laurel blossoms which grow very profusely around here. We have lots of flowers, and they boys keep me supplied. I was down to Mr. Blagden's Sunday evening. Had a pleasant time - music, &c.

Aldace F. Walker

Fort Stevens, D.C.
June 17, 1863

Dear Father:

This is a very sultry day, and I am on duty as officer of the day. I was only relieved yesterday at noon, and today at seven went on again. Well, I may as well be wearing my dress coat, sash, belt and sword as well as anyone else for ought I know, but still it is vastly uncomfortable. I have stayed since dinner close in my room in the bomb-proof, and find it very much more comfortable than camp would be. I had quite a visit from Higley. He went back Monday morning. I think he will be reinstated, but it will take some time, and he feels his position a good deal. He is not as fleshy as he was last fall, and though by no means gloomy is sort of blue. I don't wonder at it. He has a long beard (yellow, of course,) and looks very like an officer. Col. Warner and lady reached Fort Slocum last night. I have not seen them, or anyone who has seen her. I believe that Nellie Frost is coming on here to marry the chaplain, and before long. He and Warner board, or are to board, at a Mr. Carpenter's near Slocum.

The complement of officers at this post is three now. In B, Hunsdon is alone, and he is detached on court-martial. The regiment Adjt. is his 1st Lt., and Smith's vacancy is not filled. I is full. In D the captain is on court-martial, and expects to join the Invalid Corps soon. The 1st Lt. is Post Adjt. We have officers of the day and of the guard, so that our turn comes regularly once in three days. I understand that a Lt. has just come from Slocum to take temporary command of Co. B, which will help us a little. We had quite a time firing yesterday. Began at five, and finished our number, over a hundred in all, yesterday. Got through about noon. We have improved very much in our practice. Have got the range of the guns and various places about, and are pretty lucky on our hits.

Do you begin to believe in a rebel journey North now? I have all along, and glad of it. It is waking up the North in good earnest, and I am glad of it. It is frightening the weaklings, who are too lazy and too fond of their own comfort to do anything to put down the enemy, and I am glad of it. It is showing up the designs, infamous designs and deeds of the Northern copperheads and consigning them to their merited doom, and I am glad of it. It is pointing out the spies and traitors and K. G. C.'s,[24] whom Northern philanthropy has feared to touch save with double gloves, and is turning public opinion toward and in favor of the glorious vigor our Executive has shown regarding habeas corpus, &c. - the only thing in which it has gone before public opinion - and worth all the rest - and I am glad of it. It is weakening Lee's army, and I hope and trust that Hooker will fight him while Ewell[25] is gone, and if we could only be successful at last with our Army of the Potomac, and at the time when it is reduced so small, - but I fear we can only act on the defensive at the East.

That nine months measure was bad, though some of the regiments have done good service; and our Congress in framing a bill for a draft in July did a deed very much like treason. I don't know what this will amount to - probably a repetition of Stoneman and Grierson,[26] on the other leg. There is a strong supporting force evidently near Harper's Ferry, but I don't think much infantry will cross the river. Can't tell of course. We don't have any fears here, nor is their any in the city; as they won't think of attempting to force so strongly a fortified line as this, unless with their army in force. But their presence will make the powers that be only more anxious to protect Washington, and we are only more likely to stay here. Vicksburg is played out.

Our order of exercises here now is for one third of the men to work at Slocum from six to eleven, the rest to drill from 6 to 7:30 and from 8:30 to 10, and all from 3:30 to 5, with parade, &c. - the drills all artillery. I believe we have some sort of an inspection tomorrow. The cavalry are here now, but expecting every minute will be the last. They won't do much fighting, for their horses are active, and the men can't stay on - rather a bad fault in cavalry. Well, I have written more than I expected to. I sweat so that it is rather hard work. I am lucky in not having some job on hand that would take me out of doors to work today, for it is very hot. It has been six weeks since we have had any rain, and no signs. Love, &c.,

Aldace F. Walker

Fort Stevens, D.C.
June 21, 1863

Dear Mary:

Another fighting Sabbath - and not exactly that, for the day doesn't fight, but we have heard cannon and musketry since early this morning, gradually becoming more and more indistinct; the rumors that come from the city are that Hooker is driving the rebels. I hope so. He certainly can now if ever; for the rebels are divided, while he has the assistance of Abercrombie's,[27] and Casey's and Stahl's[28] Divisions of Heintzelman's army. Still, the noise is louder and plainer today than it was last fall at Sharpsburg, though in Virginia still. It is barely possible that we shall go over and help them, though not at all probable. The Pennsylvania raid I think was nothing but a feint, with the hope of distracting attention and troops from the real point of attack - Washington - but it has not succeeded. We are ready for the big army, and the bigger the better. Now is one of the trying times. Our force is so much depleted that it is a hard case for us, if the rebels had not advanced so far as to throw Hooker on his reinforcements. It was cool and cloudy this morning. Has rained some through the day, though not hard at any time. We have plenty of wet weather now, and it seems refreshing. It is cool and comfortable. It may seem strange, but our greatest annoyance here is the swarms of flies; they bite as Northern flies don't know how to, and spoil one's morning nap.

I have been transmogrified again, sooner than I expected. Am now in command of Battery D, where I want my letters directed. I have moved into my old tent for the present, but shall re-occupy the bomb-proof next month with my new company. Goodrich is in command of C, and has been recommended for promotion. In my new company the 1st Lt., Safford, is in Vermont recruiting.[29] The 2d is my old college acquaintance Lewis, and a good officer. He has been recommended for promotion into Battery C in Goodrich's place; and in his, Dodge,[30] the 1st Sergt. of Battery D. This will be a much easier company to get along with. In C. there are twenty more or less of the worst men I ever saw, and the rest can't be beat anywhere for intelligence or ambition. In D they are nearly all steady, but not of so much ability or vigor as the good ones in C. They can't pass so good an inspection, for instance, though Capt. Woodbury has left them in very good shape and discipline. He is now 1st Lt. in the Invalid Corps. It is a great bother to shift companies so, as receipts and invoices have to be made out for all the property. There are so many bothering little articles that it is a great nuisance. Still, I shall get things into shape, and shall be a little more particular than I have been heretofore. I presume I shall be $10 or $15 short on the final settlement of C accounts.

I don't know but I shall take cold tonight sleeping under canvas again, but I have got hardened to almost anything, and I have not had a cold hardly since I left Vermont - never since winter. Our chaplain has had three meetings here within a week, but none today. I have been over on invitation to Slocum to see Mrs. Warner. I found her just as she used to be, and had a very pleasant call. I think she sings better than she did last year, and she is just as lively and pleasant - a fine woman. She has not been out at all since she came on. I had quite a scrape day before yesterday.

I was ordered by Col. Benton to take a guard and go and clean out Mrs. Harpers establishment - a grocery near by which has given us considerable trouble. Her husband is with her, but she runs the concern and is a vile old woman. So I took a corporal, two men from the guard, and six men from the company, and loaded all her merchandise on to a wagon and hauled it up to camp and put it in the bomb-proof. Col. Benton sent me back to finish the job and clean out the whole concern. So we put out the tables, chairs, counter, stoves, beds, and last of all the old woman herself, who had to experience some very plain arguments before she would budge. It was a thorough job.

I got your letter last night, and one from Father at Middlebury. I hope you will like "Her Bright Smiles, &c.," for it is a pretty air. Well, I must stop and go to bed. I am glad you are not within sound of the enemy's cannon, but it does not trouble us much after all, save in the anxiety which you of course feel as well as we.

With much love,

Aldace F. Walker

Capt. 1st Vt. Arty., Comdg. Battery D.

Fort Stevens, D.C.
June 24, 1863

Dear Father:

I am getting on very well with my new company. In fact there is not much to do to get on with it, for it is the easiest company to manage in the regiment. All that is necessary is to see that they keep clean in quarters, grounds and equipment, and the rest they do of themselves. It is a great relief from my hitherto constant vexation. The men are from the back towns of Lamoille county; never have lived in or near any large villages or cities, and are accustomed to behave themselves. They are rough - childish - not at all bright as a whole, but rather feeble - still a good set of men, and one which I think I shall like, and if I do I mean to keep, for I need not have left C. unless I had been willing. Col. Warner is very good to me; has always used me well, and I am satisfied with his treatment of the regiment. The firing of last Sabbath turns out to be principally from a Cavalry fight.

I think that few rebels are east of the Blue Ridge, but I think they are just where they want to be. I rather hope they will get north of the Potomac in force. The Cavalry regiment that has been near us so long has left.

Went today out the road to Poolesville to report to Col. Jewett. I presume they will have work to do there before long, though Lee may cross between them and Washington. I believe that Baltimore is what he is at, for he can't meditate a siege at this distance from his supplies. Still, he may carry Washington by assault. If so, well and good, and bully for him; but I don't think he can do it. This northward movement at a time when the North felt so safe shows the value and importance of our line of fortifications, and increases the probability that we shall stay here through our term of service. If we do I shall get sick of it I reckon, and I know the men will; but we have to stay where we are put, and go when we are moved. It is so dark that I can't see the lines at all, and had better give up trying to write for the present. The weather has been splendid the past week - cool and enjoyable.

I want to go home and shoot six or eight of those Irishmen.[31] I don't know where they will get a proper military force in Vermont to squelch them; they may call on our Brattleboro recruits. We are expecting a company of new men down here before long; hope so at least. Capt. Hunsdon still remains on the court-martial detail. Woodbury is gone, and Templeton is also on the court, so that I am next in rank to Col. Benton and have to command all reviews, parades, &c. We have quite an evening ceremony now - a review every night, dress parade, and double quick to the forts and guns. It takes about an hour I all, but comes at a pleasant time of day. We are working our whole force now half a day on Fort Slocum, and with some prospect of completing that monstrous work. They have begun to mount the new guns already. Our mess has broken up, owing to the impossibility of getting competent help, and I am boarding at Butts again. It will be a nice place through the summer, as they have a big garden under way. I have learned to be content almost everywhere.

With much love to all,

Aldace F. Walker

Fort Stevens, D.C.
June 28, 1863

Dear Father:

It is now 10 a.m. I have been pretty busy so far this morning. Got up, washed, and to breakfast at seven - a very comfortable and respectable hour indeed. After breakfast, cleaned out my room, &c., tent rather - and by the way, I have the most comfortable tent in the lot - arranged to loop up the sides and have a free circulation, which these days means a strong breeze, with a tendency to disarrange my numerous papers. Well, we had a company inspection, and since then I have been writing - business, I am sorry to say, but necessary nevertheless. I have got my C property all transferred, and my D property all receipted for, but the final accounts of C are not sent into the Depts. yet. I shall get off the clothing returns in another day I guess, and the ordnance as soon as I get the necessary blanks. I think I must work on them some today, as the muster rolls are to be made tomorrow and next day, and then another quarterly return must be made for the few days

I have had command of D - almost as much work as for a whole quarter, though not quite.

So that for the next fortnight I shall be busy enough, and if we should move or be attacked I want to get the C. business off my hands; so I propose to put it through. I sent to the Ordnance Dept. for a set of blanks, and they sent me a set for a battery of field artillery. I am not half as big a man as they took me for. But it has delayed me about the settlement. When I get through I will tell you how much I am short - some $20 I presume. In addition to all this, we have double and treble work to do - fatigue to finish the forts - extra picquet and guard - officers of the day, and of the guard besides, sot that my turn is once in three days - when we are forbidden to sleep the whole twenty-four hours - and the next two days it will take to get rested in - on the whole, we don't mean to be surprised, though we may. Col. Gibson is here this morning to look over the roads in front with Benton. Col. Benton came up from the city last night feeling better than he has for a long time.

We had positive information in the morning yesterday from Poolesville that Hooker's whole army crossed at Edwards Ferry and went up into Maryland towards Antietam. He took the Vt. Nine months Brigade in the 1st Corps, Reynolds, Penn. Reserves, Stahl's Cavalry, and all in fact of Heintzelman's loose troops. There are only artillery regiments in this dept. now, with one or two Provost regiments in the city. The lines are drawn in to the forts south and north, Fairfax being abandoned; and Lee will soon find a flea in his ear, or rear.

You remember John Osgood? Well, everyone who goes to Washington sees John Osgood. He is always nosing round after news - gets it all - takes a great pleasure in telling it, and is generally pretty reliable - is a sort of dictionary of facts in fact, and I never asked "What's the news?" without learning something. Benton saw him last night, and he had just seen a gentleman from Fortress Munroe, who said that Dix with 50,000 men was beyond the white house on the way to Richmond. That's the way to save Philadelphia, even if Richmond is not taken; and if Lee falls back to protect Davis, Hooker will give him the most awful flanking he ever saw anywhere - that's what we hope now. About pianos - I go in for letting cousin Alfred get one at once. There is no doubt but that Steinway's are the best in the country, but very high. You would want a seven octave of course, not fancy, but substantial, and I think it a good scheme to let him get it now, if you have the cash to spare. Lt. Austin is Post Adjt. I was over to Slocum yesterday. Saw Mrs. Warner. Had a letter from my classmate and crony, Scott,[32] last night. He is in Nevada City, Colorado Territory, for his health and money. Means to study law in Chicago next fall.

With much love,

Aldace F. Walker

Evening - We have had a big scare here today. A Capt. Quartermaster in charge of a wagon train that left W. for Hooker's army via Tennallytown, three miles west of us, came into our camp saying that he had been attacked, &c. I was ordered to get out an extra picquet and get the men into the fort. Benton went on to the piquet line. I got the fort ready for action - powder, shot and shell on hand, and could have commenced firing in one half minute - but saw no rebs. We hear that they took the train entire. Whether they will stay at Rockville over night, or go back at once to Virginia, of course we can only guess. If they stay we shall see them tomorrow perhaps. Our picquet is very strong. All stay in the fort tonight.

In haste.

Aldace F. Walker

Rebs. were within five miles of us.

Sunday Evening 10 P.M.

I have sealed and mailed one letter to you this evening, but as I am in my tent ready for bed and not sleepy, perhaps I will tell a longer story. We have been considerably excited today, and no wonder, as it is our first scare and quite an event. I told of the Quartermaster who brought us the news. It seems now that Benton had a message from Col. Haskins about the same time, saying that the rebs were at Rockville and on the rampage, 2000 strong. As I said, we started off 20 new picquets and the rest of us went into the fort. There are two roads from the city to Rockville, thus - If you can understand it - dubious. They crossed I suppose last night at Coon Ford or thereabouts. Camped at Rockville. Sent a body towards the city on the road west of us. Caught the wagon train, a big one, three miles from Reno. Have since burnt it, as we hear, and saw the smoke - saving of course some 500 miles. There is a big drove, some thousands, of government cattle out to pasture that way somewhere. Col. Becquith sent for them this noon. The drovers have just come back - met the rebs nine miles out this road and had to return. They have force enough to hold that place awhile, and send over and cut the railroad, and then strike for Penn. And Lee. I hardly think they will return as they came. If they do, it will be tonight and we shall hear nothing more of them.

I don't think we shall see them here either, for they won't come within range of artillery except by accident; but they will ravage the country in front, and property of all sorts is being run within the lines. Another force was sent out at night under Lt. Austin to guard Blair's place. Benton went out there this p.m., leaving me orders to, if I heard any firing from his party, drop a couple of shells over there, which I was ready to do. Tonight C is in the fort of course, and enough from the other companies to man the guns. Benton is there too. If there is an alarm, I am to get the rest of the battalion there sudden. But I don't at all anticipate it. What I most fear is that the railroad will be cut, and you not get my letters. I enjoy this, I tell you.

Fort Stevens, D.C.
June 29, 1863

Dear Father:

When I finished writing last night I lay down and went to sleep, but did not make much at that game. Had just got to napping when a cavalry regiment came along and woke me up. We sent one company out on picquet, and the rest into camp. That took some time, for cavalry, strange as it may see, is the slowest moving of all arms of the service - especially this (13th N. Y.) which had only got their horses that day. Then for a diversion, Col. Baker, head of Baker's detectives, who we knew had gone up the road in the p.m. with

20 men in disguise, came into camp. Had struck the rebels, and had a muss - lost one man - and been pursed to within four miles of our fort - and probably we should be attacked at once. The guns were loaded, and I was aroused to rectify the sighting. Then I got the rest of our battalion into the fort, then posted them, and lay down in the implement room Was soon roused for something else, and the first thing I knew a full regiment of infantry came into camp - 14th N. H., of which Sam Duncan[33] is Major and the working field officer - very popular. I had to go as a guide to deploy the regiment through the rifle pits along the hills each side of the fort, and as it was dark and rainy it wasn't a very lovely job. Then I was put in charge of the fort, and kept stirring and watching till morning. About five another cavalry battalion, 15th N. Y., came in, but no rebs. And we soon learned that they left Rockville about two a.m. for the northward. The 14th N. H. went back (Provost Guard), and the cavalry stayed.

We have heavy picquets out, and patrols - shall push a reconnaissance to Rockville this p.m. This was quite a flare last night. Benton had a brigade under him - four regiments - or parts of four - some 2000 men - and we felt perfectly safe. We got all the news ahead of everyone - kept sending dispatches to Warner and Haskins. Have stopped all travel out of the city for the present, though there is no more immediate danger. Haskins has been out this p.m. Is well satisfied with our vigilance. The road is full of stragglers and civilians, who were paroled by the rebs at Rockville last night. All corroborate our news as we got it and transmitted it from time to time. The rebel force was a big one, 6 to 12,000, under Stuart, Lee, Hampton, &c. Came more to pillage than to fight, and they made a pretty good haul of niggers and mules. They left Rockville in a mighty hurry.

Goodbye for now.

Aldace F. Walker

The 2d Mass. Cavalry captured a Lt. and three men, their rear guard, at Rockville, and sent them through here to Washington.

----

1 Adrian Theodore Woodward, Brandon, Surgeon, 14th Vt. Infantry. RR.

2 Col. Albert B. Jewett, Swanton, 10th Vt. Infantry. RR.

3 West Rutland.

4 5th N.Y. Infantry.

5 USA Maj. Gen. John Sedgwick, "Uncle John," was commanding the Sixth Corps at this time. Boatner, 730.

6 USA Maj. Gen. George Stoneman commanded the Cavalry Corps of the Army of the Potomac at this time. Boatner, 801.

7 USA Maj. Gen. John Adams Dix commanded the Department of Virginia and the Seventh Corps from June 1862 to July 1863. Boatner, 242.

8 USA Maj. Gen. Erasmus Darwin Keyes commanded the Fourth Corps at this time. Boatner, 458.

9 USA Brig. Gen. Charles Adam Heckman, whose brigade was in the Eighteenth Corps. Boatner, 391.

10 Edward Harmon Hobbs (1835-1907), Ellenburgh, N.Y., 98th N.Y. Infantry. MC1862. Died Brooklyn, N.Y. Robinson, 165.

11 Fernando Cortes Beaman (1836-1911), Burke, N.Y., Capt., 98th N.Y. Infantry. MC 1862. Died Knoxville, Tenn. Robinson, 163.

12 Also called battle of Fair Oaks and Seven Pines, Va., 31 May–1 June 1862. Boatner, 272.

13 Caleb Henry Benton, Johnson, was actually 1st Lieut., Co. D, 5th Vt. Infantry at this time. RR.

14 The regiment was initially armed with inferior Austrian muskets. Benedict, 2:344.

15 Private John J. Monahan, Rutland, 1st U.S. Sharpshooters, Co. F. He was wounded 5/5/1863. RR.

16 Judson A. Lewis's letters to the Rutland Herald have been compiled and edited by Donald H. Wickman, Letters to Vermont From Her Civil War Soldier Correspondents to the Home Press, (Images From the Past, Brattleboro, 1998), 2:122-147.

17 Actually, USA Maj. Gen. Stephen A. Hurlbut. Boatner, 420.

18 CSA Lieut. Gen. John Clifford Pemberton would be Grant's victim at Vicksburg. Boatner, 631.

19 John Andrus Salsbury (1827-1887), Tinmouth. Haynes, 391-3 contains a short biographical sketch.

20 Clement Laird Vallandigham, Ohio politician, active in the Knights of the Golden Circle and Sons of Liberty. Boatner, 864.

21 USA Brig. Gen. William Farquhar Barry, Chief of Artillery of the Defenses of Washington from September 1862 to March 1864. Boatner, 47.

22 Identified later as being in Co. B, the only Curtis in that company is Charles S., of Ferrisburgh. RR.

23 KUACat, 48, says Arthur Little married Laura E. Frost, 15 Aug., 1863.

24 Knights of the Golden Circle. Boatner, 864.

25 CSA Lieut. Gen. Richard Stoddert Ewell had returned to duty May 23, 1863, after recuperating from losing his leg in battle, in command of Robert E. Lee's Second Corps. Boatner, 268-9.

26 USA Brig. Gen. Benjamin Henry Grierson, a cavalry commander in the Army of Tennessee. Boatner, 359.

27 USA Brig. Gen. John Joseph Abercrombie commanded a division in the Defenses of Washington until the end of June, 1863. Boatner, 1.

28 USA Brig. Gen. Julius Stahel, a native of Hungary, commanded the cavalry division of the Defenses of Washington until the end of June, 1863. Boatner, 791.

29 Capt. Darius J. Safford recruited Company L, which mustered in July 11, and joined the regiment five or six weeks later. RR; Benedict, 2:348.

30 Sergt., later Capt., Chester W. Dodge, Morristown. RR.

31 Walker is refering to the draft riots in Rutland.

32 Lauren Anson Scott (1840-1896), Bristol, MC 1862. Died in National City, Cal. Robinson, 166.

33 Maj., later Bvt. Maj. Gen., Samuel Augustus Duncan (1836-1895), Meriden, N.H. KUA 1851; DC 1858. KUACat, 28.

7.
Defenses of Washington
July and August, 1863

Fort Stevens, D.C.
July 1, 1863

Dear Father:

We are all as quiet as usual again. When we hear from the Front, which is now our Front, we can guess better what will become of us. Meanwhile we are lying on our oars and in our accustomed tranquility. I have been on fatigue to Fort Slocum this morning - in fact have been on duty pretty steadily lately. Sunday night I was up, Monday I was officer of the day, and no sleep; so that Tuesday morning I was pretty well fagged out - in fact, "played." The worst trouble I had was with my feet, which got so sore that I could not wear my boots; but I am all right again now.

The court-martial is adjourned for five days. Hunsdon went on as officer of the day yesterday; so that we have a little relief. Fort Slocum is nearly done, though I presume we shall have small details there for a month yet. We have had no hot weather lately till today. It is not nearly so hot now as it was in June. My company is in the fort. Lt. Lewis is with them, and I am still in my old quarters.

I saw Wm. Whiting, solicitor for the War Dept., yesterday or day before. He expressed himself very strongly in favor of Meade.[1] We shall hear from him in one way or another soon, and then can guess what will become of us. It seems Stuart made Baltimore almost as near a call as he did us. Whiting said that he had 80,000 men and Meade 130,000, and has no fears for the result if we manage things decently. Hooker got afraid of the enemy - "Was relieved at his own request," of course. We have all sorts of stories of further changes - that McClellan and Butler[2] were to run the machine awhile - but we can't just see it, though may wish it. Halleck and Stanton are by no means popular. I received your last today. I am anxious to see what is to be done in Vermont in the line of raising new troops. The time for drafting has come. Everyone around here, negroes and all, were enrolled yesterday.

I hope all will have a chance to enlist, will or nil.

Aldace F. Walker

Fort Stevens, D.C.
July 5, 1863

Dear Father:

I don't know exactly how to write today - not but that I have time enough and disposition enough, but I don't just know how to feel. The news we have got of late has all been good, but we have been so much in the habit of late of seeing good news from the

Army of the Potomac turned into defeat, that I have no heart to trust a victory from that source. When Hooker was at Chancellorsville, I was in the city. At 3 p.m. we got extras and bulletins announcing the most astounding success, and before evening I learned that the army had been withdrawn to Falmouth. But at Gettysburg nothing wonderful has been claimed. Meade's dispatches are modest, and read like those of one not wishing to claim too much for fear of a reversion. He forced Lee to attack him, and stood his ground, and that is all we know now. Whether Lee is in enough of a strait to fly, or whether in such a case we are able to pursue, we have no manner of inkling.

Today we were able to get no papers. The whole edition had been sold in the city when our mail boy got in, and none could be had for twenty-five cents a copy. He said the news was all good, and that is all we know of it today. Last night's paper brought intelligence up to the end of Friday's fight. He said something about Lee's retreat being cut off, but that is something I have learned to take no stock in. The slaughter must have been awful, as it seems that the position Friday was such that artillery could be used freely. I suppose that all the Vermont regiments, except the 7th, 8th, 9th and 11th, are engaged, including the cavalry. Our forces have been admirably massed, and I hope for a decisive victory. We are busy of course in making our arrangements in case of a defeat. Gen. Barnard[3] ordered work on yesterday and today, though we do not work our whole force, and that only five hours a day - part forenoon and part afternoon. We shall send a fatigue party to Slocum but a few days more - none, I hope and think. We are now busy felling trees and brush in front of our rifle pits, while we have a big gang of niggers and Irishmen building new batteries and rifle pits, which when completed will make us completely secure. But I hope we shan't have to use them, though This week will tell the story.

Yesterday, the 4th, I principally spent in sleep, having been up all the night before as officer of the day, and visited the picquets among other things. Our picquets have a muss once in awhile with a stray bushwhacker, and occasionally bring one in, but there are no rebels in force on our front that we can find. Mr. Blair's place is almost deserted, as they all have gone in town. The rebs would be glad to get hold of some of that family. We have got a telegraph office and operator her, but as it is a direct line to the War Dept., and not connected with any other line, we get no news at all - the only office on the line in fact, and it has not been used since it was opened. The operator thinks it is rather dry picking. We have a cavalry picquet of 80 men now from Col. Wyndham's force, in camp near Alexandria. Quite a comfort to us. George Howe, 1st Sergt. in Co. B, has been promoted to 2d Lt., in place of Lt. Smith. The other commissions have not got round.

We have not heard from Smith since he ran away, and have no idea what has become of him - nor care. I am still in my tent, and Lewis with the company, though I slept in the fort all that I slept last week. While the other companies have to sleep by the side of the guns, mine is allowed to remain in their bunks in the bomb - proof - much to their satisfaction. We are almost eaten up with flies. They are excessively annoying. We have to get net to sleep under, to take any manner of comfort. I did not know that Button had been at Howard, or Harewood (I suppose), Hospital. If so, he is probably there yet. I would go and see him if my feet would hold out better, and may as it is. I can't do much more now than tend to my knitting here. Well, I am well and contented yet. We are a very harmonious family here. My D. is all right and pleasant, and Mrs. Butts is liberal as usual with her table, and as stingy with everything else. Goodbye. Love to all.

Aldace F. Walker

10 P.M. - I have seen a Daily - the news is good. I have also seen old Mr. Blair and his son, the PM. Gen. Got information concerning those intercepted dispatches which the papers may not reach. They were from Cooper,[4] Davis' Adjt. Gen., to Lee, announcing that Davis was unable to carry out his part of the program contemplated in the invasion, and saying that he must protect his communications endangered by Dix. This plan was for him to attract the Federal army into Pennsylvania - for another army to be concentrated at Culpeper under Beauregard[5] from South Carolina and from Bragg,[6] which should march on Washington, and either draw Hooker back, leaving Philadelphia and Baltimore uncovered, or capture Washington itself. This was a splendid scheme, but out aggressive movements in other directions forbade its consummation. Lee is in full retreat, but Meade is unable to pursue owing to lack of rations and the exhaustion of the army. Smith failed to come in time from Carlisle.[7]

Fort Stevens, D.C.
July 8, 1863

Dear Father:

I am sleepy tonight. Was up last night, and though I have slept a good deal today I have not yet made up the loss. I have to get up at six tomorrow, and go into the woods with a fatigue party. We work but thirty men at a time now, and 30 more in the afternoon; quite a let up from our old detail. Last night there was something of a fear that prowlers would make a descent on Blair's; so we sent out an extra guard, and I went on the picquet line myself. I got a horse and rode all alone up among the cavalry picquets in Maryland - rather a lonely ride for midnight. Only two nights before a guard had been shot in the ankle on that road, and the night before that one had been fired on several times. I was well armed and mounted, and had no fear. Yesterday a corporal bringing dispatches was fired at on 14th St., between here and the city; the ball passed between his leg and sword and into the horse, which will die. Rather rough, isn't it? But the leaves and underbrush are heavy, and it is impossible to see or find him. We are all quiet here now generally speaking. The loose troops in the vicinity have gone to Frederick to hunt Lee. I don't anticipate that he will have any trouble in re-crossing the river with the majority of his command. But I don't see well how the army could have done better. Gen. Stannard is in the city, wounded in the thigh, not seriously. The 2d Brigade are complimented in general orders for their behavior at Gettysburg - "like a dress parade." The 12th and 15th were not engaged. The other three regiments lost about 350 in all. Those two were guarding a train. But I believe the 12th has gone home, and I presume you will have particulars from them which I shall be glad to hear.

I see Lt. Rounds is reported wounded slightly. Gen. Davis was here tonight, but he could give no names of the injured. The 1st Brigade was little engaged. It is a marvel how that brigade has seen as much service as it has, and won so good a reputation, with so little comparative loss in killed and wounded. Savage Station and Lee's Mills were its two severest blows. We heard of the fall of Vicksburg about one yesterday afternoon, by a line from Montgomery Blair to Benton. It rejoiced us of course. I did not receive a letter from you today as usual.

Must go to sleep.

Aldace F. Walker

Fort Stevens, D.C.
July 12, 1863

Dear Father:

It is just after morning inspection. The chaplain is here, and will have a meeting soon. I was officer of the day again yesterday - up all night, and as a consequence feel probably better just now than I shall at any subsequent time; so I will write a few things I have heard and seen concerning recent events, hoping that when you see our friends returning from the war you will send on to me their tidings. I see my classmate Eaton is wounded. I am anxious to know how severely, and where he is. Gen. Stannard has been in the city. He was wounded early in the fight. Gen. Doubleday[8] sent for him twice to leave the field, but he could not see it. He is a splendid man, a little rough and uncouth, but perfect in tactics, thorough in discipline, and brave in the extreme. He wore an old straw hat, a blouse with a single star on one shoulder, no straps, pants as they were torn by the shrapnel, and carried an old crooked stick for a cane while in the city - an attire which made some of the incipient, foppish staff officers who fly around the hotels like so many butterflies, stick out their eyes, though they did not dare to turn up their noses, for Stannard was quite a lion. Was serenaded one night at ten, when he had left for Vermont in the six o'clock train. Stoughton is as brave, I presume, but is very different in other respects - is a dandy with airs, while Stannard is courteous to everyone. Stannard is immensely proud of his "boys." He had but three regiments in the fight - had detailed the two weakest elsewhere - but with these he had brigade enough. The fire was hot and severe. There is a maneuver which regiments very seldom undertake under fire, which Stannard performed three times that day with his whole brigade - a change of front. (I just hear that or meeting is postponed till evening on account of the intense heat.) We had a meeting last Friday evening. The old brigade was lying back as a reserve; only one man was hit. It is said that they were called on for a final charge at the end of the day. The rebs ran as soon as they saw them. The "would not fight those fellows." They are highly complimented this morning for their conduct in the skirmish Friday. What these movements amount to I can't fathom. Lee has the lead I fear, but Meade has the men. Lee has been reinforced - Meade has still more. Lee I think can cross the river when he chooses, though I hope he means another fight. If there was one yesterday, or is one today, we have heard nothing of it. But if our men are decently managed, we can beat them in a battle. The "bag" game is another thing. Immense reinforcements have gone to Meade - all the available troops around Washington, Baltimore and Harrisburg, except the artillery. Even, as near as I can learn, Dix has been recalled, and his forces sent to Harper's Ferry - for I know that ten transports at least have passed up the river with troops from Fortress Monroe or beyond, and Gen. Naglee[9] is in command at Harper's Ferry. I imagine we have a cavalry force "raiding" in the Shenandoah Valley, though I can't hear for certain. The Cav. Regiment is with Kilpatrick, and going good service, though I hear that Kilpatrick is like to lose his command for his rashness, having been three or four times in places where escape seemed impossible. I reckon the boys will rue the day they ever came across Kilpatrick - unless they like him. Lt. Higley has his shoulder straps on again, and was trying yesterday to get to his regiment. I drew my quarter's stock of clothing yesterday - shall be busy for a few days now issuing - mean to keep the business in my own hands. We have direct information that Gen. Stuart intended to run this line that Sunday under the spur, and sack Washington - but found the defense stronger than he expected, and had no support as he expected. I had seen that letter of Wilkesons. He is a fine writer and correspondent, but was ousted from the Tribune some time since for his radical views. His son (killed) was a promising young Regular. The beauty of Meade at Gettysburg is in the fact that his victory was so much better than he represented. I have hope in that man. But what our troops have endured in the past fortnight is hard to imagine. An invading campaign would be almost impossible. So I hope for something decisive at Williams port.

Fort Stevens, D.C.
July 15, 1863

Dear Father:

I will write tonight, though it can be but a line, and there is little probability of your getting it in any season. Mails this way have been detained by the freshet, destroying bridges on the Baltimore R. R., and now I suppose the New York mob is stopping communication. What a shame it is to trifle with that mob as it seems to have been done - blank cartridges - and Gov. Seymour said they should have their rights. I am in hopes to hear soon who were drafted in Vermont of my friends. The cavalry regiment has lost very heavily - over 100 killed and wounded. Among the killed was Capt. Woodward, son of the chaplain. I have been in the city today. Came back before dark. Got my savings. The Invalid Corps goes tonight to Philadelphia, as trouble is anticipated there. Col. Benton is on a court-martial, so I am in command of the post till Hunsdon gets off from his. I did not see anyone in particular in the city today.

With love,

Aldace F. Walker

Fort Stevens, D.C.
July 19, 1863

Dear Father:

This is a beautiful Sabbath morning. I am officer of the day, and of course tied to camp, though today will be exceptional in one instance. An infant child of Lt. Meeker's died yesterday morning, and I am going to Rock Creek churchyard this afternoon as one of the bearers at the funeral, leaving a temporary substitute with the sash. It was a very pretty, bright baby, some ten months old - died very suddenly, and we all feel the loss and sympathize with the youthful parents. They show a great deal of sense in their affliction, especially Mrs. Meeker - a very bright little woman. Lt. Sears, who has been on duty at this post, has been relieved and sent to Vermont to organize our share of the drafted men, with two other lieutenants and six non-coms. So we are three again, who take our turn as officers of the day - I wouldn't as commander of post, unless to help the other two. We hope to have a brace of new lieutenants here soon, as Safford is Capt. of Bat. L in Brattleboro, leaving a vacancy in my D, while he stood in the way of Goodrich, who will now soon leave a vacancy in his C. When we have some new appointments I will let you know.

I send a little pamphlet, which I would like to have you preserve. I am well, and we have no news. The war is going on finely. I am satisfied with Meade, though the North won't be I fear. They will blame him for not capturing Lee, and laud Lee for his escape - but why did not Lee capture Burnside and Hooker? I suppose it was understood Lee had no boats and could not cross till Tuesday - but I more think that the driving him back into Virginia was all that was hoped for. It certainly was all that I hoped for, and thoroughly done. I don't think the army will move at present. What is going on elsewhere we don't exactly know. Charleston isn't taken yet, though we heard it was, but I think our generals there are going to work the right way, and will fetch it this time, if operations elsewhere do not prevent Beauregard to be rapidly reinforced. There's the rub.

Our mails have been very much delayed of late. We have only got two Philadelphia papers in a week. What a shame that New York riot was; and the greater shame was the manner in which it was handled. If I had been in Gen. Wool's[10] shoes I should have hung Seymour on the spot. He had a fine opportunity to make himself President, but lost it palpably enough. I want to see the draft go on there, and I believe it will. Senator Foot is in town. Was to apply to Lincoln yesterday for Springfield rifles for our regiment. We have not heard with what success. Col. Warner has the Enfields on hand yet, but does not want to issue them. We are to have an inspection by the brigade inspector at 3 p.m. today, at Fort Stevens. I have got one man in arrest in my new company, for drunkenness on guard. I am sorry, for he has a wife who is laundress, and I fear it will go hard with him. Still, the bother is nothing as compared with my old Co. "C."

The mail has come, and I hope to have a letter from you.

Aldace F. Walker

11 P.M. - I have been very busy ever since I stopped writing this morning. The funeral, the inspection, the parade, a meeting this evening, and the Herald you sent me with news from the Addison County draft, have kept me on the tilt pretty much all the time. I don't understand why the draft was not proceeded with, but perhaps I shall know sometime. In Middlebury it struck on the whole the very ones I wished, but 50 per cent. Will not begin to cover the number who will fail to come. I have acquaintances who are hit in almost every town in Addison County, and I see Willie Stimson is on the list from Waterbury. The first name from Middlebury is Brainerd Kellogg,[11] Prof., I would like him in my company - he would make a bully corporal. But such men will ante the $300 of course. There is one number of the class of '63 and two of the class of '64 whom I have seen so far; also Rev. L. A. Austin of Orwell, my former tutor; some of the business men of Middlebury too; some manifestly unable to come, and more manifestly able to pay. But it is fun for us to sit here and read the names. It is worth a fortune to the soldiers now here to see others harnessed. I hope there will be no trouble in Rutland, and I want to see the list.

About pianos - I do not feel like speaking dogmatically at all. I like the letter you sent me. Chickering I know best (most favorably) from an instrument at Blair's - a splendid, superb, best, piano; but what he says in no doubt true, and I incline to give them up. Steinway also is just as he says, and the knowledge that his pianos were uniformly so high has kept me from urging that maker. It is paying pretty dear for a name. Nims I know nothing about, though I believe that is the make of Ernest's, is it not? The name is as new to me as that of Worcester, in fact more so. Worcester is Sabin's favorite manufacturer, and he has a fine ear if nothing more. With you, however, I have no fondness for the "double volume," and should regard it under the circumstances as rather a nuisance than otherwise. Still I suppose mellow tones can be evolved also. If they can't, I don't want it, for "brilliancy" is a humbug, in a small house. If Nims is what I think it is, I incline to that, for the Worcester recommendation rather scares me than otherwise, and I see you feel so too.

The plan I propose then is this - to write to Alfred for the expense of a plain piano, seven octave, (the extra one third is of no account) of Nim's make. It should be less than $290 - to you. And yet get an instrument that he is perfectly satisfied with. Still that name would be as new to Wallingford as Worcester - and that consideration is of no consequence any way. But I want the mellow instead of the brilliant. I want to play the Portuguese Hymn and such music, not "O, Hail Us," and this, I know, is your feeling. And if he can't do as well as I suggest in regard to Nims, why take the Worcester. I am going to have a shake in paying for it. I am of age now, and making considerable money.

We officers off the day don't sit up all night now. After midnight I shall go to bed and sleep till seven. He says Nims are "unrivaled for parlor use." We don't want a piano for anything else, and that is recommendation enough. If he will be decent on price I shall be satisfied there I think.

With much love to you and Mary and all.

Aldace F. Walker

Fort Stevens, D.C.
July 22, 1863

Dear Father:

Your last about pianos was received yesterday, but as it did not change my views in any respect I have nothing further to add. We were paid off today again. Your letter did not come as I expected. There is nothing new at my post, save that the fort is pretty much finished and grassed, and I should like to have you see it a fortnight from now. Tomorrow we turn out the whole force at work on some new rifle pits. I am not very well tonight, though not sick - have been at work all day and yesterday - and am tired out, with little disposition to eat. I am going to rest a day or two, as I can if I choose. We have nothing at all new, strange, or remarkable here, and I have nothing further to say but to send love to all. My classmate Robinson[12] is drafted.

Aldace F. Walker

Fort Stevens, D.C.
July 26, 1863

Dear Father:

This is a hot Sabbath morning, though there is a little breeze, and in my well ventilated tent I get the full benefit of it. We had a delightful shower last night, and our fort looks nicely this morning. I was officer of the day yesterday - pretty warm work. We do not have to keep vigil now, and there are seven of us to take the tour. I go on, though in command of the post, to help the rest. We have had some trouble, as usual, since pay day; but my company makes none at all. I have had only one man leave camp, and he came back sooner than I expected. Goodrich's commission as Capt. Came yesterday, and we are all glad of it. I am formally transferred to Bat. D by special order No. 2, P. T. Washburn. Lt. Lewis is my 1st Lt., and I have no 2d, and am afraid I shan't for the present, as a new order has been issued allowing no 2d Lt. to be appointed when the aggregate of the company falls below 86. Mine is 88 including officers, but I fear the order will be construed to mean enlisted men and shut Dodge out. I shall be very sorry if it proves so, for he has been expecting promotion a long time.

I have about given up trying to get a furlough at present. It is impossible now to get anything but a sick leave except in very urgent cases, and I certainly am not sick, and don't know what excuse I could put on an application except the "sickness of my father" - and I doubt if the facts would hardly warrant that - so I believe I must wait. I am not much of a hand to crowd in with officials and get favors for myself - in fact I can't do much at it. All I can do is to take what comes to me and be thankful. I presume Col. Warner would endorse a furlough for me, and if he was in command of the brigade it might go through; but as it is I see no possibility of going home at present. I had forgotten till I received your letter that your semi-centennial had passed. I presume you don't feel any older than you did a week ago, and probably it is as little of a step to you as my 21st birthday - I scarcely thought of that.

I got the list of drafted men yesterday in a Daily Herald. It seemed to strike a smaller number of influential men than anywhere else. Still I presume few of them will come. Government assures us very plainly that "the place of those who pay the $300 and exempt themselves will not be filled by drafted men," meaning, I suppose, to buy veteran volunteers with the money; but I can't quite see it so. I think that unless other states show more patriotism and less money than Vermont, another draft will be made at once - supplemental perhaps, though this would be contrary to the promise in terms. I understand there will be very little drafting in New Hampshire through arrangements with the Gov., but I reckon the reason is they are afraid to try it - the copperheads are pretty thick there. There are a good many names I see in Rutland who will have to come however - Irishmen, railroad hands, &c. - Patrick Egan, the accommodating switch-tender at Sutherland Falls among the number. For our regiment, one new company, 152 men, has been organized, Safford Capt., Macomber Senior 1st Lt., &c. - are now in Vermont watching copperheads - may be one of the regiments of "regulars" at Rutland, as they supposed that to be their destination. The other company the Gov. expects to fill with "veterans," and it is partly full now. We now number 993 mustered in.

Gov. Holbrook wrote to Lincoln, and Foot took the letter in, requesting Springfield rifles for our regiment. An order came to that effect from Stanton, and Col. Warner took it to the Arsenal. They had none but second - hand ones and he would not take those, so they promised to send up the first lot of new ones they had. It is a sure thing now, and

Gibson feels rather crestfallen at our success, for he has been trying to do the same thing and can't make it work. I admire Mr. Seaver's pluck - would like him for a corporal.

I had a letter from Ab yesterday - no news. Also from Emily. I got a carriage and took Mrs. Goodrich to call on Tillie day before yesterday - came back by Blair's. told Mrs. Warner about Davis, who was one of her old friends. Meade seems to be watching Lee, but I don't expect a collision.

Willard Child is in Washington, a little sick. I ought to go and see him I suppose, but I have not much disposition to, and presume he would not care to see me especially.[13]

With much love to all,

Aldace F. Walker

I have nothing further to add about pianos.

Fort Stevens, D.C.
July 28, 1863

Dear Father:

I received your last today. It is strange my letters are delayed, as yours come through so promptly. I am very well now, and things are moving smoothly for all that I know. We have very little trouble, and small bother generally at our post - are as happy and comfortable as one could well be in the army. We are to go to work grading for our new barracks tomorrow. I don't suppose they will be anything very nice, but I reckon our boys in the "front" would be glad to get into them. I will describe them when I know more about them. I enclose a check for $150, good at any bank. These allotment checks are the ones used in arranging allotments in other states; the soldier who allots is paid in money and a check which he sends home. Given to me as a draft, they cost nothing. I want $100 of the money to go towards the piano, and so divide the $300 between you and Mother and I, if you like to call it so. Our batteries are full at 150 men. That was Safford's number when he organized. We are discharging a good many now, hoping to get our number filled with whole men. I have applied for a discharge for one of my Sergeants who is broken down with heart difficulty. Hunsdon's court-martial is on its last case we understand, and he is not on that as he was absent when it commenced. It will be a long one - and then a new detail I suppose, in view of which I tremble. Benton's court is in my empty barracks yet. I see very little of it save the members and victims as they come and go. Warner is on another detail - commission or something in regard to "Stoneman's raid." Maj. Chamberlain will have a regimental court-martial soon I suppose, as the cases are being prepared.

With love, Aldace F. Walker

Fort Stevens, D.C.,
Sunday P.M.,
August 2, 1863, 2 O'clock

Dear Father:

This is a most intensely hot day. Thermometers are a scarce article in camp, so that

I am unable to give you the exact Fahrenheit - and the worst of it is, I am officer of the day. I wear my blouse, however - which by the way I like very much, though it is somewhat heavy this warm weather - and am sitting before my tent under the awning, where I get a little breeze occasionally. One of the unpleasant things of our business has just occurred, since I have been writing. One of Hunsdon's men, a rough, ugly surly Frenchman, got drunk and got into a fuss the other day with a neighboring Dutchman - and into the guard - house. He is the same one who shot his hand last fall. His wife is in camp, and is a very pretty, neat woman - the best appearing Frenchwoman I ever saw. She has just been to me interceding on her husband's behalf. I was about to give her very little encouragement, and in fact have nothing to do in the premises - and she feels badly, poor thing. The chaplain had a service in Bat. I barracks this forenoon. It was very hot and few were there. He does not succeed in getting a furlough, and has about given it up. I moved my battery into camp yesterday. I goes into the fort next. Am glad to have them nearer by, and they are glad to get back. I have found a mill dam in Rock Creek a mile and a half from here, where there is a fine chance to bathe, and it is quite a luxury this weather - I wish I was there now. Hunsdon was relieved, or rather is not wanted any longer in his court. They are on their last case, and he was lucky enough to be sick the day it commenced, and so unable to sit on the case at all. He has returned to duty here, and is in command of the post of course. By the way, where did you get that remark of his about being "promoted or disgraced" &c. It don't look very pretty written or repeated, but I can imagine him saying it in a jocular way (as it must have been) that would make it appear very different. Furthermore the last clause is a quotation from Maj. Chandler of the 10th, and not original with or natural to "Tub," as we call him.

It seems you are considerably indignant over the Congressional nomination. I feel nearly as much, or more, pride in Addison County than in Rutland. Still Kellogg[14] was the best man up, and came near securing the nomination as the ballots tells. Woodbridge[15] is a smart, energetic man - is a member of the Congo. Church in Vergennes, though not a very reputable one, I fear. Is much more of a man than Stewart,[16] who has become the man in Middlebury owing to the dying off of the smarter ones. He is well read and pleasant, but so insufferably lazy as to make his friends hate him at times. Still I should have been glad to see him put forward, as he is a good friend of mine. Kellogg is the best man west of the mountain, except perhaps Edmunds[17] of Burlington. Still I think Woodbridge will get more of a name - be a better "member" as the reputation goes, than either of the others - and his principles will be found a good deal above the average. In fact, he is a man to whom I have taken considerable of a shine of late years. I have not so much fear of railroad influence as you have. I guess the candidate for Governor [J. Gregory Smith] is a good one, though I should have preferred Dillingham.[18] It is expected that regiments will have an inspection on the last day of the month; so Friday we were assembled at Slocum at 4:30 p.m. Hot I tell you - knapsacks, &c. The Major took command, and he is a curious man. He likes to command - is ambitious - likes to work and show off, and go the whole figure - do things up in style. So he preceded his inspection by a review, which was quite unnecessary, and followed it by a parade, which was as much so - nearly tiring us all out. There is considerable sickness her now - mostly dysentery. Mrs. Templeton has been quite sick, and is now; Col. Benton's children also. One of the best boys in Bat. C lies at the point of death. I have none seriously sick, and am very well myself.

With much love to all, as ever,

Aldace F. Walker

Fort Stevens, D.C.,
Tuesday, August 5, 1863

Dear Father:

I received your piano letter last night. I sent on a week ago a draft for $150, which I hope you have received before this. What Alfred writes don't seem to alter your feelings much, and I pretty well agree with you. It seems he got the price of the Worcester $5 less than he had it before. But we all have a feeling that the other is a little the bet, (as he seems to intimate also,) and I think we shall be better satisfied hereafter to have got it. The cover and stool you will have to have of course, but the stool need not be very expensive. Aunt Sylvia can knit a cover for it. I am very glad you are going to have a good piano, and wish I was to be at home when it arrives. It will have to be tuned, of course, before it is used; and it is well to be careful who tunes an instrument of that nature. Merriam can do it well if he tries, but I have known him to be a little tricky - vexed because a person did not buy of him, he has "tuned" an instrument out of tune so as to disappoint the purchaser. Lavonia can tell more about this than I can, but the is an old chap from Burlington that I think is good. Last night Goodrich and I went on to Capitol Hill at 5 p.m. to see a grand review of light artillery by Gen. Heintzelman and Gen. Barry. There were thirteen batteries - some new ones just in process of instruction, and some played out in the service and recruiting in Camp Barry. It was a splendid sight. I have never seen anything of the kind, and it was grand. Six guns and six caissons make a battery - six horses to each gun and caisson, besides those of the officers, sergeants, forges and wagons. The Generals drove up horseback, with some fifteen staff officers and as many orderlies, a salute was fired, and the whole line cheered as they rode before them. They passed up and down the line, took their place in front while the batteries wheeled into column - battery front - and passed in review, first at a walk, then at a gallop. Then part of them left, and Gen. Barry drilled the rest awhile, covering "front into line," "action front," and firing right at the crowd. I have been under fire for once, and got some idea how it looked. Reckon my sensations would have been a little different if I had known the pieces were to be loaded with grape and canister. I certainly should have felt a disposition to skedaddle. As it was, I drove my buggy right towards the firing, as near as I could get my horse to go. I would not have missed the occasion for a good deal. Seventy-eight guns are enough to equip an army. Gen. Barry is a splendid man - fine form and figure and face - active - perfectly at home - a captain in the regular army, but chief of artillery now in the U. S. A. - and he is well worthy the position. He inspected us a while ago, you may remember. I have a very high opinion of him indeed. Heintzelman I saw for the first time. He is a shortish, thickset man, some sixty I should think - grey considerably - but looks like a soldier. I should be willing to go into battle under him. He has quite a command in the Dept. of Washington. Can't take the field, for he ranks everyone there - though he may have the army sometime. The review was commanded by a young Lt. Col. from Rhode Island - and a Lt. Col. of light artillery is a pretty big man. I have written so much that I think I shan't write tomorrow, unless something happens. It has been very hot of late, VERY yesterday. Today is more comfortable. Capt. Rich of Bat. H has resigned; so now I am eighth in rank, which is a point on which I borrow very little trouble.

With much love to all, Aldace F. Walker

Fort Stevens, D.C.
August 9, 1863

Dear Father:

Your letters and papers of the last week have all come to hand, and were much enjoyed as usual. We have been having an exceedingly hot spell - 95 today and for the last week. Some smaller annoyances also - secondary - bugs, flies and mosquitoes innumerable, eruptions on the skin that come in big blotches and itch - O, how they itch - dust and sweat and grime everywhere; still the weather agrees with me - in fact I am thankful that almost every style of weather seems to agree with me - and I remain well and comfortably happy. Some news to write this time. I have at last for a wonder two lieutenants under me. Dodge's commission as 2d came today. Tucker[19] of I. has been promoted to the Goodrich vacancy in C., and Orderly Foster of I. to that vacancy. We now have eleven officers at this post on duty, besides Col. Benton and Lt. Burrows of B, Regimental Adjt. We never have been so favored, and our labors are much lightened this hot weather. At Slocum they are cramped. Another captain has resigned - Hunt of E - leaving me seventh; so I keep getting promoted you see. I fear we shall have to temporarily detach some of our officers to help them. We are doing some fatigue now - give the men stints, which they finish about 9 a.m. - and have no drills. Not very hard duty, is it? But it is a scheme that gets a good deal of work done, and our rifle pits are almost finished. I give you a section, to show you the kind and amount of work. The figures are feet; so the ditch is three feet deep. When it comes in the woods among the roots it is rather hard for a man to dig his foot a day, and the drainage has to be looked to also. We have not gone to work very seriously on our new barracks yet. They will be better than the present we hope, and put close to the entrance of the fort, on the hill. I will show you how when we get them laid out. The draft for this subdistrict was on Friday. Took some acquaintances, and lots of niggers. I have gone into business at last. Am joint owner of what I never owned before, but often wanted to - a horse. Goodrich and I are together in the purchase. He is not a very valuable beast - is of the somewhat apocryphal age of nine - grey - or white, with little red spots on him - neck straight out in front, and tail straight out behind - no beauty, but no faults that we can find. He is a very easy rider at a gallop or trot, and it is said he goes well to harness. Walks very fast, and can run like smoke. Is very kind, and not very lazy. Still he can't be a very great loss to us in any event; and his sale was no great gain to the Lt. we bought him of, for the cost of horse, saddle, bridle, spurs, new shoes, &c., was $70. We hope to let him enough to pay his keeping, and he don't seem to be an enormous eater. We got him in the idea that one of us might be on the next court-martial, but we ain't. However, we shall find enough for him to do, as I have contrived to keep him on the go pretty much all the time so far. Thursday Goodrich went to the city on old Pompey, Benton's, for a Dr. (Allen), for Benton's child. I went with him; could not go into the city, but went around Boundary St. to Georgetown, and from there up the Potomac to Chain Bridge, four miles, and around home through the forts. It was a very pleasant ride, and the old horse showed considerable endurance. This morning I went over to Rock Creek church with him. Our inspection was at 6 p.m. Meeting here is over it is thus nullified. I could say a good deal on these and kindred subjects if I had time - but I haven't.

With love,

Aldace F. Walker

Evening - Col. Benton's little boy died this p.m. The funeral of the babe was postponed, and both will take place tomorrow at 8 a.m. I have been up to Mr. Blair's to inform them of the deaths, and some of them will attend the funeral. Our new guns have come and are issued - new Springfield rifles - the best arm in the service. Gov. Holbrook applied by letter to Lincoln for them for us, and Senator Foot carried in the letter. We got the order, and would take none but the best, and new ones. They were issued today. It is a good deal of work to change, as all the accouterments have to be exchanged and papers made out, but we shall get through it and be much better off.

Aldace

Sunday, 4 P.M.
August 16, 1863

Dear Father:

I am waiting for the bugle which will summon us to march to Fort Slocum for inspection, as a sort of preparation for the Brigade Inspector, who is to visit us on Tuesday. It was hot this morning, but is now cloudy with a breeze, and we shall have quite a comfortable and I presume pleasant time, as it will be our first appearance with our new Springfields and the men like to shine. We have one new acquisition that I think will prove a nuisance - brass shoulder scales. I can't well describe them - they are intended to guard the shoulder against cavalry saber cuts, but are never worn but on dress occasions to set off the uniform. They look well enough, but scratch the guns, chafe the shoulders, and wear out the patience and elbow grease of the men. We have been very busy the latter part of the week putting our new guns into shape. They are beauties, I assure you. Col. Benton has moved his family "into the country" for the hot weather. If he had done so sooner, he might have had more of it to move. He is in a house of Mr. Blair's. Hunsdon and I are living in his house. I have the upper room and find it very pleasant - much cooler than a tent, and a good circulation generally. I reckon Gov. Seymour means trouble, or at least that the authorities here think so. All the Regulars in Meade's army have been sent to New York, and the old Vermont Brigade is now at Alexandria waiting transportation to the same place - as I presume you will learn before this reaches you, though the first story that we heard was that they were en route for Charlestown. It is quite a compliment to the Vermonters, though I suppose they are as good a brigade as any in the army. Their feat at Funkstown was unparalleled. A whole brigade on the skirmish line, two miles and a half long, men twelve feet apart, were charged on three times by a rebel brigade closed in mass, and the line was not broken. If New York troops had done that we never should have heard the last of it. Lt. Lewis and Foster have been temporarily assigned to Slocum, so I have but one Lt. again. We have eleven officers here, they but five; hence the change. But they expect more every day. Two lieutenants in Vermont for conscripts have been recommended for captains. I suppose they will be on before long, and new lieutenants made for their places. Chaplain Little was married yesterday p.m. at five in the city, by Miss Frost's brother, Rev. Of Middlebury, who came on with her - Episcopal service of course. Henry F. and Dr. Allen were here a few minutes ago looking after the couple. I was in the city Friday (was invited to the wedding, but could no go of course) for stuff to work up our guns with. While I was gone Frank Walker, Lt. Col., called here. I was very sorry not to be able to see him. Col. Benton has another child quite ill. He is very much afflicted. I went over to church this morning on the old horse, who holds his own well. Patronize Rock Creek extensively for purposes of cleanliness. This paper is furnished by government. We can't buy as nice anywhere around here. I don't know what Steph means by talking about owing letters, &c. We never exchanged letters except on business, and he has never acknowledged the receipt of a check I sent him long ago. He is blowing, as usual. But I must quit.

Evening - Inspection is over - well enough - did not get back till after dark. Nobody knows for certain where the troops now at Alexandria are going - perhaps to Charlestown yet.

Love to Mother and Mary and all.

Aldace F. Walker

Fort Stevens, D.C.
August, 1863
Wednesday Eve.

Dear Father:

We are having beautiful weather of late. Just comfortable night and day. We are at work grading our future barracks ground in the early morning, and have a drill at artillery in the afternoon. I have a pass for the city tomorrow to visit a dentist. I found out from Miss Blagden who this dentist was - Dr. Noble - and have engaged his services for tomorrow. I have several teeth that are badly in want of filling. I am still feeling very well, though I think I am not exactly. I was quite costive a while ago, and had a touch of one of my old troubles, which I feared would annoy me in the army. Took some physic and more fruit and cucumbers, and now have a slight diarrhea, though no more than is good for my general health. The hot weather brought on a humor peculiar to the army called ground itch, which is very annoying.

We are little troubled with vermin, by the way. I never saw a louse, though I have heard of them once or twice. We have a good deal of diarrhea, as a consequent on the summer weather and the hot spell - some quite severe cases - and some fever. I have six in hospital - none dangerously sick however. I called on Mrs. Little with Mrs. Goodrich the other night - Monday. I recognized her at once, and she seemed glad to see me. Looks very well, and I hope will be happy here. I am quite anxious to hear more from Uncle Tenney's folks. She came down into camp with her husband last night, when I was officer of the day, and went with me into the fort - which, by the way, is looking very nicely now. We are still at Mrs. Butts' table, which is fully loaded as ever and as slovenly managed. We have all sorts of fresh vegetables however, and they must be good. Our season is earlier than yours of course. We have had all the tomatoes we could eat for a month, and other things in proportionate season. Peaches are delicious now. Apples have been good some time. We have at the table Capt. Hunsdon and I, Lts. Austin, Howe, Tucker and Meeker, with Mrs. Meeker, which couple however are going to keeping house tomorrow in a shanty in camp. Mrs. Goodrich has gone up to Blair's to live with Mrs. Benton a few weeks. We had an inspection by brigade inspector at Slocum Tuesday morning at 5 a.m., which brought us out of bed at half past three. Rather an early start for one of my habits, but a good idea after all. Had breakfast before we went, and got back in the cool of the day.

Lt. Smith's sentence reached us tonight with the endorsement and approval of the President. He is sentenced to lose all pay and allowances, and to be dishonorably dismissed the service to date from July 16 - quite a while after he ran away. I received your long letter today. I suppose ere this the Vermonters have reached New York, though I have seen nothing of it in the papers. I hope and believe the draft will be put through, and I rather half wish a little muss just for the fun of seeing it squelched. The news boys came out tonight hollering "Fall of Sumter," but the dispatches hardly carried out their assertions - fighting however.

As to resignations, it makes considerable difference who resigns. If the Col. endorses a resignation, "Better out than in," it will be pretty apt to go through, as in the case of Lt. Morse who resigned for incompetence. That and a surgeon's certificate are the only things that will get a man out of the service now. John's probably was not laid on thick enough. My "matin service" that you wonder about as a "big thing" was a mistake of yours in deciphering my hieroglyphics - "swim" was the word. I congratulate you upon the trust reposed in you by my Alma Mater, but don't think it need prove much of a burden. Pierce was valedictorian of '61, though not the smartest fellow in the class. He is a good scholar, but not a big man, nor a very valuable tutor.

With love to Mary, Ellena and all,

Aldace F. Walker

Fort Stevens, D.C.
August 23, 1863

Dear Father:

We have a brigade order for a regimental dress-parade every Sunday afternoon; and this hot p.m. we are waiting and sweating for the time to come for us to start - about half past four. It is a little rough, but all right I suppose. Your letter came this noon, with the Atlantic. I will send you the August number in a few days. There are several who like to read them. I am getting considerable reading on hand now. Have the "Bivouac and the Battlefield" by Capt. Noyes, our Brigade Commissary, and Fanny Kemble's experience on a Georgia plantation, which I may send you sometime. We hear that some new commissions were in today's mail. I presume so, for there are several vacancies, mostly at Slocum. We have several barrels of whiskey on hand, furnished by the Medical Dept., or Sanitary Commission, I don't know which, liberally adulterated with quinine, which we are giving to the men twice a day, half a gill to a ration, after being one half diluted. It is purely for medical purposes - not enough for anything else - and I think will prove a good scheme.

Hope it will have some effect in counteracting the summer complaint that is so frequent now. We have a good many sick; but the health of my company is on the whole improving, and our regiment is not nearly so badly off as some others in our immediate vicinity. And I see a good deal of talk, as there always has been and I presume will be, about these volunteer commissions that are accessory to the army. I presume no one is fully satisfied about the practical workings of any, but here at Washington I can see something of all. The State Agencies cannot be compared one with another, as they contemplate different objects. Some obtain pensions for soldiers; other have nothing to do with that branch of assistance. Some run hospitals of their own here; others send the wounded and sick to their respective states. Some visit battle fields (rather injudiciously many think, as the regular field help is ample); others have other instructions. In any of these fields they may do good. Still I think Vermont is not well represented; in fact that Holbrook is utterly unfit for the post, though I have never seen him or heard of him save through Vermont papers.

I hope John G. Smith, who is represented as an honest, energetic, Christian gentleman, will put a man in this post who will be a credit to the state. We've got them. The Sanitary Commission is on the whole a good thing, though it has provoked the ill will of army men by its unnecessary flings at the bad organization and maladministration of the Medical Dept. In the army it is very seldom well spoken of. Many of its agents are imbeciles, silly, &c. still I regard it as a good thing; though in some of its branches it expends money needlessly, and in others it doesn't see holes where it might put in chinking. It is in the hands of - primarily - good and practical men; and if it has not good agents, it is because the right men cannot be found who are willing to take the post.

But the Christian Commission, so called, I am sorry to say I regard as an unmitigated humbug. Its agents are mostly Methodist ministers who can't be trusted with congregations North, and are a pretty slim set necessarily. I am really at a loss to know whether the distribution of tracts in a camp is for better or worse. So many treat them in such a way - by ridicule, &c. - that there is more sin than if they are kept away. The Testament is always received gladly where it is not frequent, and never with scorn or scoff, but tracts are treated differently. Money paid to this last body in my opinion only helps to support a worthless set of imbeciles, who can't get their living anywhere else.

I remain very comfortable in my new quarters, though it is no wonder to me that these hot days that the Col.'s children died. The others are better now they are in a grove - out of doors most of the time and in a cool shade. I was in the city Thursday. Had those teeth filled - one of my front ones where the filling was lost - and two big holes in back, with amalgam. Found a very good dentist - Dr. Nobel - charge $5. These young women in camp seem to trouble you a good deal. But the chaplain's wife is as comfortably situated - in as good a house - as he ever was at home - with Northern board too; and as her brother was the member of the family selected to accompany her on, I can see nothing out of the way in his performing the ceremony, even though an Episcopalian - and on the whole, I think well of the whole affair. You had said nothing till your last of Mr. Chellis' coming on, though Ellena had. I hope she will find things "out West" to her taste, and that she will not be disappointed this time, for "hope long deferred maketh the disappointed the heart sick" you know. My clothes are in good shape for the present, though I shall want some new drawers by and by. I think my overcoat will do.

With much love,

Aldace F. Walker

A big watermelon for dinner.

Fort Stevens, D.C.
August 26, 1863

Dear Father:

I have a little time which I will spend in writing, though it is after bedtime, and there is not much to say. Yesterday was a comfortable sort of a warm day till towards evening, when for a wonder it rained, and we got a good deal before we got through. I was officer of the day and considerably exposed. Caught a little cold; otherwise I am all right. Today has been cold - no dust - and the pleasantest day of the month - though so cold that I have worn my heavy coat all day - no vest. I have been over to call upon Mrs. Warner. Have called on Mrs. Little this evening with an old acquaintance of hers - Henry Miner of Manchester - now in the Pension Office. The regiment is in a stew about our surgeon. Last winter while he was before the board he took hold and tried to do what he could, and I rather pitied him; but he has been growing slacker and slacker and more and more disagreeable, till at last the feeling culminated in a set of charges and specifications - neglect of duty, &c., - preferred by Col. Benton. He got wind of it, and has anticipated them by resigning this evening. I sincerely hope his resignation will go through, as we shall thus get rid of him the quicker. We are so sure that he will go that we have already begun to canvass for his successor. I have not time to give the details of the accusation, but they are pretty rough. What an amount of knowledge newspaper correspondents show in artillery. "8 inch rifled Parrotts playing on Charlestown." He has one 200 Pdr., several 100 Pdrs., and mostly 30 Pdrs.; but an 8 inch rifled gun has never been made. The rifled projectiles are all elongated.

With much love, &c.,

Aldace F. Walker

Fort Stevens, D.C.
August 30, 1863

Dear Father:

Busy again. I have passed the day some way - part of it at Col. Benton's "in the country" - and his children are well again. Inspection at Slocum at 5 p.m., followed by dress-parade. Back after dark, and then to work on our monthly returns, and putting the finishing touch on my muster roll - which I completed as far as possible yesterday - for the muster at Slocum at 8:30 a.m. tomorrow. This roll is especially difficult, as the clothing account for the last year has to be settled on this roll. Then I have had to prepare a long list of absentees with reasons - and on the whole I have not much time to write. Tomorrow we have four copies of this roll to make, and a sheet of paper two feet square and more mostly written over on both sides is no fool of a job for one man. Fortunately I have a very good clerk in my new company - a Corporal Pike[20] - steady as a clock - a good penman - and a faithful worker. I have relieved him from all other duty with the company, and given him charge of my ordnance and clothing and policing and cooking and writing, and he is a good hand - Acting Commissary Sergeant. It has been the finest day of the season. Not too warm - clear and beautiful. A year ago this week I spent a few days at home - hope to spend more there some time. Battery L, Capt. Safford commanding, reached Fort Slocum last evening. They are rather boyish looking - "light" - but good men I guess. I will try and say more next time. Till then I remain, with love to all,

Aldace F. Walker

Wednesday

Dear Father:

I can write but a line. Have a hard cold in my head, and my eyes are so much inflamed that I cannot use them. All right otherwise.

Aldace F. Walker

----

1. USA Maj. Gen. George Gordon Meade, replaced Hooker as commander of the Army of the Potomac just in time for the bloody conclusion of the Gettysburg Campaign. Boatner, 539.

2. USA Maj. Gen. Benjamin Franklin Butler, the "Beast of New Orleans," a totally incompetent political general. The editor.

3. USA Brig. Gen. John Gross Barnard, Chief Engineer of Washington until June 1864. Boatner, 44-5.

4. CSA Gen. Samuel Cooper, the highest ranking general in the Confederacy, one of the few West Point graduates from the North who sided with the Confederacy. Boatner, 175.

5. CSA Brig. Gen. Pierre Gustave Toutant Beauregard had command of the defenses of the Carolina and Georgia coasts. Boatner, 54.

6. CSA Gen. Braxton Bragg commanded the Confederate Army of Tennessee. Boatner, 78.

7. USA Brig. Gen. William Farrar Smith, "Baldy," had command of a division at Carlisle, 30 miles from Gettysburg, in the Department of the Susquehanna. Boatner, 775. Walker is too lenient on Meade, who could have pursued Lee more aggressively, and too harsh on Smith; a division of Federal troops would not have made much impact.

8. USA Maj. Gen. Abner Doubleday commanded First Corps, to which the 2nd Vt. Brigade was attached, at Gettysburg after Reynolds was killed on July 1. Boatner, 244.

9. USA Brig. Gen. Henry Morris Naglee. Boatner, 578.

10. USA Maj. Gen. John Ellis Wool commanded the Department of the East.

11. Brainerd Kellogg, Middlebury College Professor of Rhetoric and English Literature, 1861-1868. Robinson, xlii.

12. William Albert Robinson (1840-1910), Morristown. MC 1862. Robinson, 166.

13. It does not sound like they were kissing cousins!

14. Daniel Kellogg, a Vermont Democrat, unsuccessful candidate for the U.S. Senate, and Presidential Elector for the 1864 election. Crockett, iii:430, 616.

15. Frederick E. Woodbridge, U.S. Representative from Vermont 1863-1869, succeeding E. P. Walton.

Crockett, iii:551.

16. John W. Stewart, Vermont delegate to the 1860 Republican National Convention. Crockett, iii:485.

17. George F. Edmunds, State Senator, 1861-1862. Would be involved in the St. Albans Raid aftermath; post-war U.S. Senator. Crockett, iv:15-17.

18. J. Gregory Smith was elected, but Paul Dillingham would be elected the Republican Governor in 1865. Vermont Governors since 1778 and Their Party Affiliation. Accessed 1/21/2002, available from http://users.aol.com/frotz/governor.htm; Internet.

19. Silas B. Tucker, Northfield, eventually Capt., Co. C.

20. Corp., later Lieut., Paphro D. Pike, Stowe.

General
George G. MEADE
(Italo Collection)

8.
Defenses of Washington
September and October, 1863

Fort Stevens, D.C.
Sept. 6, 1863

Dear Father:

I am now living in a dark room at Mr. Butts', suffering from acute inflammation of the eyes. The doctor forbids both reading and writing - an unpleasant arrangement. Otherwise I am quite well and altogether in good spirits. The inflammation of my eyelids has somewhat subsided, though the inside of my eyes remains quite sore. I hope, however, to get round within a week. I keep my eyes continually bandaged, with various applications, as sugar of lead, sulphate of zinc and opium, boiled flaxseed and rose water, milk, &c. Salts and pills internally. I hope Uncle Joel is better by this time. Dr. Meigs is taking care of me. Dr. Porter is sick, and Surgeon Kidder is "played out."

Will the failure of Mr. Parker to get dismissed make any difference in your plans? I think it very kind in Mr. Nims to make a piano expressly for you. I hope you will be satisfied with it when it comes, and that it won't keep you waiting much longer. I take my meals regularly, and have a good appetite. Owing to the present distracted state of the country I don't think it best to write any more this morning.

Your son,

A. F. Walker, Per Scribe.

Fort Stevens, D.C.
Sept. 9, 1863

Dear Father

I am still unable to use the pen, although I think my eyes are slowly improving. I presume it will be a week or so before they will be good for much. The inflammation of the lids has pretty much subsided, but the balls are very red and inflamed, and I have to keep some sort of a cooling application on them all the time. It is pretty hard living with nothing to do but to count one's fingers. I hope to get out of it before long. My eyes do not pain me much now, except when they are exposed to the light, or the doctor puts acetate of lead in them.

I reckon Uncle Abe gets along about as fast I putting down the rebellion as though I was around; at any rate our regiment seems to do very well without me. I have not heard from you since Saturday, and don't know when you were to return, but presume this letter will find you at home. I am quite anxious to hear from those whom you visited - presume I shall today. The Herald and Chronicle came Monday. I see that "Parson" and Batchelder (another college boy) have paid the commutation money. One in ten was the ratio I thought would come before the draft, and I guess it was not much out of the way; but I still believe men can be bought for the army, and expect we shall have them at last. What is Ab Mead going to do this fall? And what is Button about? I shall want to keep posted on the movements of Mr. Challis if he comes on - a consummation which I fear is somewhat dubious. Can you find how many freshmen the Prex. has got? I have been thinking about getting a furlough, but as I have to depend upon other folks to do my business for me, I could not make it work. It is just as well I guess, for I don't believe I could travel very extensively if I had one.

Yours truly,

Aldace F. Walker

Sept. 13, 1863

I am getting better. Hope to write more next time.

Aldace F. Walker

Sept. 16, 1863

Dear Father:

I am living in camp now - in the Col.'s house again. Have been glad to receive several letters of late, from you and from Wallingford. Am getting better, though not on duty yet. My right eye still remains so tender that I have to keep it covered with a handkerchief. The other is comparatively well. I have had a sweet time of it on the whole, and can't do much now but sit around. Can't bear any lamplight. Can see well enough to read the papers; that is some comfort. We have all sorts of rumors - Meade everywhere - Lee retreating on Foster[1] and Burnside both at once - Franklin in Mexico - Metamora - Heintzelman going there Sickles coming here - &c.

Aldace F. Walker

Sunday P.M., 3:30
Sept. 20, 1863

Dear Father:

I have received your last letter, in which you mention before you conclude of having received mine of last Sunday, containing news of improvement on my part. I am now some better still, though sometimes I think my eyes are no better than they were last Sunday - on the whole I know they are. I have no doubt but that I use them too much, but how can I help it? I never was famed for prudence in taking care of myself. I have lived in camp the last week as usual, for I could not live alone any longer - traveling around with a handkerchief over my eyes till today. I got a pair of green goggles last night from the city, which I find a great relief. I have been "on duty" a couple of days, but could do nothing save go into the barracks, and had to excuse myself from dress-parades. Am not trying to do anything now, though with my glasses I have no trouble in navigation and could do most anything. In fact, while I have them on I feel as well as usual.

It is cold weather - the stoves and coal are great comforts - but the north wind accompanying the Equinoctial is rather hard on "Conjunctivia." I tried a week ago to get a furlough. Got a certificate from our surgeon, and it would have gone on well enough, but the brigade surgeon would not sign - "An acute disease of so short standing would hardly warrant such an application." He had not seen me - is six miles off - so that I could not see him; so I gave it up for the nonce. I mean to try again this week however - that is, I may if I see any chance of success. Still it takes a week or more to get such an application "through" headquarters, and you need not think much about my coming until you hear from me again. Of course, I shall do all I can in the premises, and all that can be done. I had given it all up however, and may not renew the attempt. We are to be paid again this week.

With much love to all, and luck to the piano, I remain, as ever,

Aldace F. Walker

Wednesday, Sept. 23, 1863

Dear Father:

I don't get along much - am about the camp loafing most of the time, unless I can get someone to visit with me. My eyes are very tender - ache some. Though the goggles ease them much. I have a sty coming on one, which the doctor says will be a good thing - no fun any way.

We were paid off today. I drew $258.43. Pretty good pay for such a two months work as I have done. I have an application for a furlough signed by Col. Warner and the surgeons - our own and the brigade - for twenty days. Col. Gibson has it today, and if it is not returned disapproved tonight, I shall have some hope of its going through. If it is, I will add a line and tell you; if it is not, there is a possibility that I shall get home the last of next week - not before. You will hear from me again first I presume, if I make out to go; and if I don't I shan't be very much disappointed, and shall try again when I get well.

With much love to all, and anxiety about Rosecrans,

Aldace

Fort Stevens, D.C.
Sunday Eve. [October 18th]

Dear Father:

I got along faster than I expected, and write from my tent. I found that there was a train that left Jersey City about 11:30 p.m., so I took that and came along. Got to Washington at nine this morning. I wanted to be back on time seeing I could so conveniently, and am all right now. I went over to Hoboken - saw the folks and got a lunch. Got a plate of oysters and cup of coffee too at Poughkeepsie. The cake got squashed. We got to New York at nine, so I stayed at Hoboken till half past ten. Uncle says his schemes are working well.

I find things just as usual here - the new quarters not quite finished - delays in getting the stuff. I am not very tired tonight, for I made out to sleep more than I did the other time. I found a deaf and dumb brother of Ed. Phelps (clerk in Pension Bureau) coming to New York on the train; also his deaf and dumb wife; also his sister Hattie, who is neither deaf nor dumb, but a very pretty girl of about eighteen - one of my Middlebury acquaintances, and I was very glad of the company. I cannot write more - am well - have taken no cold - though I don't know how I shall sleep in my tent tonight.

Aldace F. Walker

I attended church at Dr. Gurley's. Came up when the horse came for me, about five.

Dear Father:

I received your of Sunday and Monday this p.m. It is very late tonight - midnight or after. We have had a big party at Slocum in honor of our new barracks. I was one of the committee of invitation and have been at work all day, and the evening of course. Am sorry I can't write more, as I meant to have said a good deal this time, but I shall have to defer it till Sunday. I am very well. Find things in good shape, and am ready to take hold again.

With much love,

Aldace F. Walker

Fort Stevens, D.C.
Oct. 25, 1863

Dear Father:

Sunday has come round again, and finds me very well. I don't see but my eyes are all right. Still I don't use them much at night, and don't write at all in the evening - trying to be careful. I am sorry I had to write such short letters last week, but expect to have some time today - the more sorry as I have received two long letters from you.

I have had a very busy week. Monday I spent in making our my ordnance quarterly returns, reporting at headquarters, doing some business with the quartermaster, drawing my stationery, and calling on Mrs. Warner. Tuesday I was in charge of the work on the barracks - in fact I have been in command of the post all the week, as Benton and Hunsdon have been a little sick. Benton is also president of a court-martial, and Templeton home on a sick furlough, leaving his wife here - a queer arrangement, for he is very feeble.

Wednesday, as I said I was at work getting up our big party - which was a most decided success, though too much of a ball to suit my clumsy extremities. We had splendidly trimmed rooms in two of the new barracks at Slocum, and a good many invited guests, fine supper, and got a good name. By the way, our band is a big thing. They had not got their instruments when I went home, and it surprised me more than anything else on my return to find that they could and can play twice as well as ever the West Rutland band eve did. It is wonderful to me - is called now the best band on the line - but the men are all old players, and they have a beautiful set of instruments.

Well, to resume my story. Thursday I was officer of the day, and was some tired beside. It was the first time I had worn my sword since the first day of September. We have no dress-parades now, the men are all so busy on the new quarters and on the ditches. Friday I took charge of target practice in the morning, and in the p.m. worked getting out and getting up the frame for the officers' quarters, when I and eight men worked hard and accomplished a lot. Saturday it rained hard. I had a pass and went to the city. Took down Tilden's shoes. Went for some company savings, of which I have three months due me; but did not get them, as Capt. Wright who pays them was sick and not in his office. Came back about dark after waiting all the p.m. for the rain to stop - wet and cold - but did not experience any evil results at all.

Our new quarters are all well along except the officers' rooms, which are gong along now. We could have been in them long ago but for delay in furnishing material, lumber, &c. We have not the windows, nor the timber out of which to make the bunks. They are all done besides this. Are made very well, and in fact are the best set on the line.

You see I brag a little, but I have reason to do so I think. Today I have got ready for inspection, at 4 p.m. and now am waiting and writing. I find my boys generally in good condition, and they have been well taken care of I think. Lewis is still sick, though so far recovered as to be around camp once or twice a day. He tried to get a furlough, but did not succeed. Mrs. Goodrich is also sick, with a slow fever. "Dinner's ready, Cap'n," says the little negro who answers for a bell to our mess - so hold on.

I am boarding with Austin and Foster at Sweetland's, an assistant sutler. We get along well enough - find it much pleasanter than at Butts'. Mrs. S. is Foster's sister, and a nice woman and good cook - though our stock of tools is rather slender. I am living in my old tent yet. Am comfortable at least for the present. The weather was much warmer last week than while I was in Vermont, but is cold today after the storm. There is no sign of a chance to move this fall as I see. I am glad Rosey is out. Have heard more than I can write, and know whereof I affirm. In a tight place he isn't there - don't know what to do, &c.

We have had our inspection. I was the senior officer present, and of course did the work, - then a dress-parade. I have several things that I might say, but no time, as I am writing by candle - light now. In fact, I have not had time to visit my boys in the hospital. But I will tell you a story of one of my boys, who would be pitied by one who knew the circumstances as they appear, without knowing him or the truth.

His name is Handy. Before I went home, he had applied for a situation for his wife as laundress, which I refused, as there was no vacancy. Orders are strict and understood against wives of enlisted men coming to camp, but she came on with two small children; he said without his knowledge, but I don't believe it. He had no place provided for her, and Butt took them for a while - then they went somewhere else - and to a dozen places - paying nowhere, and no means to pay, as he owes a year's wages now. At last she was ordered from camp. He got a place for them down 7th street a couple of miles - never expecting to pay - and last Sunday he was missing. I kept watch of his family, and Thursday he was apprehended there. The company raised money to send the family home, and I have preferred charges against him for desertion.

But Goodnight.

Aldace F. Walker

Fort Stevens, D.C.
Oct. 28, 1863

Dear Father:

I received yours of last Monday with Ellena's enclosed. I am glad to hear from her, though the letter contains no very positive information. It is the best written letter however that I have ever seen from her, and I am glad to know that she can at least write sense, if she don't talk it very extensively. I am glad also that Mr. Powers has fixed our piano. His judgment is worth something. The felt instead of buckskin is true probably. That is what ails Chalon's piano I suppose, i.e. the felt has become worn off. Still it can very easily be replaced, as it is only gummed on.

I knew very little about Wells, save that he was a good man, never made any trouble, and was usually on duty. We first knew of his death through the published list - knew that he was at Kalorama small - pox hospital, but supposed that he was on the gain. I am office of the day today, and have found a good deal to do. We are putting the finishing strokes on to some of our big jobs; are where the work tells, but where it has to be very carefully done. Our barracks are done ready to occupy, all but the windows and the bunks, and for these we are waiting for lumber. The boards for the officers' quarters came today, and the sides are now going up. When our camp is done, we shall have the best one in the line. Col. Haskins is petting it already. We have moved so much dirt that the great objection I had to the new place - clay sand - is obviated by the super - imposed sand.

We finished our target practice Tuesday - Bat. D firing 25 rounds. We do all the mortar firing at the post, and though the least showy on the tabular result, it is the best fun of the whole. Mortar shells are rather fickle things however, and I would not depend upon them much in actual service. Our party was a regimental affair, given by the officers of the regiment to friends from without, and at Slocum as headquarters. The barracks are uniform through the division. The privates had one a few days before - the non - commissioned officers last night - both at Slocum ... and one is to be given here tomorrow night by the enlisted men of this command - and at Totten too, I presume. They enjoy it.

You say you fear you shall not hear much about my journey. Well, there's not much to say. T'was a very quick, pleasant, tiresome ride, and that's all. I got a lunch at Poughkeepsie and Hoboken, and a late breakfast at Washington, for which I was amply prepared. I fell in with my friends, of whom I told you, at once - two deaf and dumb, and a pretty girl; managed to get a seat behind them on the Hudson river, and was ready to find their hotel for them, which they would have had trouble in doing I fear. Rode into New York with a "dummy," which went slower than horses do, and not half as steady. Had a miserable time of course in the horse cars, and slept almost to Havre de Grace. The train seemed to be express to Baltimore; this side of there it stopped everywhere, but got in at last - and wasn't I hungry? I reckon the National waiters thought so. I got my 75 cents worth any way.

The only drawback about the service at Dr. Gurley's was my sleepiness - and his, perhaps. He is a very pleasant, quiet man - a great contrast to Dr. Sunderland, who is sometimes extravagant. The organ playing and music were splendid. I expect to go to the city tomorrow to get a young man mustered who wants to enlist - a brother of one of my sergeants, who looks like a very nice fellow. I hope I shall be able to get my company funds at that time. Well, I have written a sheet without telling a story that I meant to about Rosecrans, so I will defer, and perhaps forget it. The movements of Meade and Lee are just what I anticipated, as you will perhaps remember. But I have official duties and must close.

As ever,

Aldace F. Walker

----

1. USA Maj. Gen. John Gray Foster (1823-1874), commanded 18th Corps and Dept. of North Carolina. Boatner, 301-2.

General
John SEDGWICK
(Italo Collection)

9.
Defenses of Washington
November and December, 1863

Fort Stevens, D.C.
Nov. 1, 1863

Dear Father:

Yesterday was our muster day. It rained hard in the forenoon, and we were mustered in our new barracks. I finished my rolls last night - took them over to be examined and accepted this morning. Acted as officer of the day while Foster took over the rolls of the Bat. I went to inspection and dress-parade at four, and have just returned. We are to have a meeting at seven. The new batteries turn out four times as big as the old ones - little regiments. Our aggregate now is 1164, and we hear of men joining in Vermont occasionally.

I saw that Wallingford Allen the other day.[1] He is in the band - which, by the way, is a perfect marvel to me. I wish you could hear them play. Capt. Adams seems to have hard luck. I presume he is brave, and I understand he is "tough." My rolls were all right, and I got some credit for their being free from mistakes. My Corporal, Pike, is a capital fellow for such business - steady as a clock, and very correct and careful. I have given him full swing in charge of my company property. Have a room in the new barracks twelve feet square for him, with a big cupboard with lock for the clothing, and another such room for the Orderly. I have a young fellow as 1st Sergt. who is doing first rate. He came out as Corporal. Has a fair education, and tends to his biz straight. Lt. Lewis will be ready for duty in a day or two. Mrs. Goodrich is so as to sit up some.

I am well suited with my board now; but think when we get moved I shall board with Dodge, and so have all the officers of the company together. I enlisted a brother of Sergt. Bedell Thursday,[2] and took him to the city in the afternoon to be mustered. He received $60 bounty down. Quite a dose. I don't see but that my eyes are perfectly well; used them for the first time to write evenings last night and did not hurt them any, and am now writing by lamp-light. Batteries B and I have moved into the new barracks without bunks. We are waiting for windows for the other two. We are having beautiful weather now, but cold nights. I shall be glad when we have our tents. The three papers came today. I see the day of issue of the Chronicle is to be changed, and am afraid it will not get here by Sunday - But I must go to meeting.

After taps - I am sorry to say that our meeting proved a failure. The congregation - a smallish one - waited for the chaplain three quarters of an hours, when we disbanded, as he failed to come to time. I had just returned to my tent when he came in to inquire which building we were to use. His time was half an hour slower than ours, and he had been waiting some too for the Major, who had promised to come over. I think he will learn a good lesson any how. I have just received a detail ordering me to act as a member of Gen. Court martial convened at Fort Stevens, vice Capt. Goodrich relieved. Col. Benton had the change made, as Goodrich and Tucker, both of C, were on the detail, and he wished to equalize the thing; but more especially as Goodrich fell back on his dignity, and would not do anything else. The order is a perpetual pass to the city anyway, but I don't care to use it in that way however. I can draw my pay on it, however, tomorrow if I choose. The court is adjourned over this week to Monday the 9th, as the Judge Advocate and several of the members have gone home to New York to vote. The duties are nothing but to sit and hear what is done, and vote occasionally.

I believe in my last I said something about Rosecrans. I saw a man in the city the other day, Col. 10th Missouri, and commanded a brigade under Rosecrans at Corinth and Iuka, and under Grant at Vicksburg. He says that at Corinth Rosey was fairly surprised; and during the engagement, as some regiments gave way, he sat on his horse near him apparently paralyzed, not knowing what to do; and that he is no master of battlefield tactics. That his fault at Chickamauga was in having his men in such shape in front of an enemy that a line of battle could not be formed with any facility or promptitude, and in fact was hardly formed at all. Grant he thinks not so big a man intellectually, but a general throughout. He was candid, and I believed him. He is in for the "Committee" in Missouri. Likes Schofield personally, but he went there committed to a mistaken change of policy. Well, Goodnight.

With love to all,

Aldace F. Walker

Fort Stevens, D.C.
Nov. 4, 1863

Dear Father:

I have been rather afflicted of late, having had a big boil on my lower lip, which gave it twice its usual size, and made it look worse than any nigger's. It has ached incessantly, and I slept little last night and begged off from a tour of duty today on account of it. It has just burst however, and I have spent the evening - part of it - squeezing it - feels better. I have to hear the recitation of the officers of the post every other evening - this evening was one. Col. B[enton] used to hear them, but says he is sick. I don't know why he did not give the job to Hunsdon, who attends, and out-ranks me - but he didn't. Hunsdon will put on his new straps in a few days I suppose, as authority has been obtained to commission another Major for the regiment, and the recommendation went to Vermont Saturday. 1st Lt. Lee[3] of A is to have B. I don't want to swap with him. There were quite a lot of recruits gathered at Brattleboro Saturday for our regiment. Gilman[4] took 17 for my Battery, and I think we shall now get some more men - am quite sanguine, in fact, if we can only keep it before the people. What a fine position we are in. I have enlisted (here) two men in my battery of late. About papers - I think you had better send the Herald Friday and the old religious papers, as I get them Sunday and like them that day. The age of the others will make no difference. I moved my battery into the new barracks on Monday - on to the floor; the bunk lumber is promised us every day. The windows have come. Boards for bunks and floors for the officers' quarters are now all that are lacking.

With much love to all. I am writing without a fire, and must go to bed.

Aldace F. Walker

Fort Stevens, D.C.
Nov. 8, 1863, 8 P.M.

Dear Father:

This has been another of our busy Sundays. Our inspection was at Slocum at 10, and there was previous to the inspection a dress-parade, at the conclusion of which a presentation was made to Col. Benton of a sword, sash and belt, the counterpart of the ones given Col. Warner last spring. The reason for having this ceremony on Sunday was, that the money was raised in the first place by the non-commissioned officers, sergeants and corporals, assisted at the last by the officers to raise the desired amount, and Sunday was the only time when they could possibly assemble. The Major was expected to make the presentation, but was detailed as brigade officer of the day, and just before we went over I was informed that I must take the job. I sat down and scratched off a page of note paper, committed it pretty much, and got it off with variations; so did not break down, nor quite make a fool of myself - "creditable," they say. Benton responded well. After the parade, which Benton commanded, the officers formed in the center - some thirty - the non-coms behind them - some hundred and thirty - and marched to the front. I went out - with a corporal, Moses Lee of C., a very small, short fellow, nicknamed "Mote" - to carry the box; all presented arms, and then we slobbered.

This evening we have had a good meeting in my barracks, which have no bunks in as yet, and by bringing in boards make very comfortable chapels. There were more there than have been out before, and the chaplain preached a written sermon - on leaves - quite good - and he began promptly on time too. I have been all through the two brigades from Fort Lincoln to Chain Bridge, some fifteen miles, lately; find some bigger forts than ours, and better situated, but none where so much taste has been shown, or care and pains taken; our camp is ahead of all, and when all are done we shall be not ashamed of ourselves at any rate. It has been windy of late - too windy to ride with comfort - but my overcoat is a big thing. I went out to Bladensburg and the Maryland Agricultural College - a semi-classical, semi-literary, semi-scientific, semi-barbarous institution; not that it has four halves, but it is a compound - seven years course - fine building - 63 scholars. Don't know whether Vt. Ag. College will be patterned after this or no - might do worse.

Of course I want a catalogue, of Middlebury. And speaking of Middlebury reminds me of something which I would like to have you tell Button. I had a letter from Tuthill last night. He is at Vicksburg; went to see his brother and to enlist. Gen. Logan, his father's friend, got him a place in the Quartermaster's department - what place he did not say - so he is "grated" &c. He found one of my classmates, Simonds,[5] whom I supposed was teaching in northern New York, editing a paper in Memphis, and corresponding with northern newspapers. I have found a thoroughly honest man in the army, and am happy to say he is in my own company. Corp. Pike had a cousin sick in a city hospital - a member of Col. Benton's old company in the 5th. I got him a pass to go and see him. He was very sick, and crazy to go home - unable to go himself. The surgeon wrote a letter asking me to let him (Corp. Pike) go with him, urging it very strongly. I applied, attaching the letter, and the furlough came. Pike had been a long time anxious to go home - to save his business from ruin and to see his family - and I should have given him the first chance when furloughs began to be granted in muddy weather. But the day his leave (for ten days) came, he got word that his cousin was dead; and he did not deem it honorable to use a pass obtained on such special reason for his own private business. Diogenes may hang up his lantern. I am free to confess that I told him to go, but he could not see it, though very anxious to. I have applied for another without his knowledge, and I hope it will be granted. He is the one that takes care of my clothing - safe, isn't it? Gen. Martindale's provost regiments[6] are to be replaced by Invalids - are in fact now. "Condemned soldiers," we call them. They are not considered fit to do "field service" - and ours comes under that head. In field fortifications. They say Sumter is taken; we heard so last night, and it is apparently reliable; but the 144th Pa. will have a hot place, unless Dahlgren moves at once and successfully on the enemy's works. The first case on our court tomorrow is my Handy, and I am a witness.

With much love, as ever, to you and Mary and Mother and all, I remain,

Aldace F. Walker

Fort Stevens, D.C.
Nov. 12, 1863

Dear Father:

It is coldish weather - windy - but yet fine in the day time - evening brings chill - and morning, frost. We were paid off today ... marvelously quick. I think Chase[7] was right in going to Ohio to vote. I will try and forward a chunk to you the next time I write. Our regiment has grown so big that the paymaster can't get round in a day; and more are coming this week - quite a "respectable squad," Maj. Austine writes Col. Warner. I will tell you how many I get next time, for I presume they will be distributed then. I hope they will come uniformed, for I have not a very great supply of blankets and overcoats on hand just now, and those are rather necessary for bed clothes this weather. Cpl. Pike's furlough came tonight. I am going to the city tomorrow to get transportation for him and start him off. Col. Benton took rather a queer way to tell him of it - gave him a hundred dollars, and told him to give it to a man in Hyde Park. His eyes peeled, for he was not expecting it - "Why, where shall I find him?" We are all interested in the case, and very glad to have him go. Our court did not sit today - "no cases ready." Some on the docket for tomorrow however.

I don't like your college plan so well as Adams' - Agricultural and Academical separate - and so use both sites. Still, I hope some arrangement may be effected. I have not much to write tonight. I am very well now, and have not completely resigned my company as Goodrich did, on account of the court-martial. Still, I am not confined at all unless I choose, save during the hours of its session; and I suppose I shan't have to bother myself with Sunday trainings. Mean to go into the city to a decent meeting. I heard from Uncle Tenney last night. He speaks of Hardy - wants some sort of place for him around our hospital; but I can't promise much. Our new surgeon is doing very well. We are putting up a new hospital building like the first, and so doubling our accommodations. Still delay about our lumber, though the bunk stuff has more of it come, and we have got a few stacks up. They are arranged thus: Bunks three tiers high - two men - four feet - to a tier - and all to be movable. We are putting drawers under them as sort of cupboards.

With love to all,

Aldace F. Walker

Fort Stevens, D.C.
Nov. 15, 1863

Dear Father:

We have been enjoying our Indian summer for the past week, but I fear it is over. It began to rain last evening, and today it rains terribly. There is not much wind however, and my tent makes a very fine protection; though it is getting weather worn in some places, so that I had to move my bed last night to keep the rain off from my face. I was expecting to go to the city to church this morning, but don't see how I can.

Our men are comfortable in the storm, and I am very glad, for our old barracks leaked sadly. The new ones are tight - felt roof. The pitch has not arrove. The officers' quarters are covered and plastered, but no floor; the timber is coming soon I trust, however. The man who has contracted to furnish and build the new quarters for the line, Mr. Allard, is hardly competent to carry on so big a wheel; though he tries to accommodate everyone, he can't quite do anything. He gave me an order yesterday for 30 lbs. "roght nales." I got the nails, but no thanks to the orthography. We have got up in D barracks 11 bunks, for 66 men, and used up all the lumber on hand. The storm increases as the morning passes on. My fire is good, and I don't particularly care unless the wind rises enough to lift my house over.

Our morning papers come regularly, rain or shine. I think I will send you this morning's Chronicle, though the Sunday morning issue is the poorest of the week. There is a thing or two in it that I should like to have you see. Our court is a big thing. We tried two cases Monday, one Tuesday, and none since - the witnesses in others being home on furlough. I presume we shall have more to do next week. I was in the city yesterday again, but I am sick of it now and leave when I get my business done. I hope our court will last till into December, so that I can attend a session or so of Congress.

Col. Benton has been quite sick for a day or two - feverish &c. - sick abed. I have not called or heard from him this morning. Mrs. Goodrich has had a run of fever; is convalescent and going home this week. Our new surgeon is doing well, and the hospital is well managed. I got a copy of Cicero De Senectute and Amicitia the other day - can read it "right smart." I received your letter last night. It seems Vonia and Waldo are married. I shall want to hear where they live, and how. Hope he won't die. I never had any vast liking for him, but he is a clever man I presume. Our old barracks have been completely dismantled to furnish the new, and will be cleared away - all but part of one, which the Col. is, with the sutler, roofing and using for a barn. We shall have enough lumber left to fit up some quarters for laundresses I think.

My overcoat is much nicer than Goodrich's, and I think will wear better. I am very well fitted out for this winter. Enclose a draft of Riggs and Co. for $140. I think I will enclose the letter Charley Sheldon wrote me, as I know it will interest you; it certainly did me, and did me good.

Middlebury college is running pretty thin on Faculty now. The Prex. and Seeley[8] are the only ones that amount to anything. Burlington has lost all of any consequence too; the whole concern needs remodeling, and I hope will receive it, though I fear not. I have received several letters of late; one from Emily, Friday. I don't say much about war matters lately, for I don't know anything. Meade is at Culpeper again. Charlestown is merely a side show, of no account anyway. Our prisoners at Richmond occupy the principal part of my war thoughts, and yet their suffering tells of trouble for the Confederacy.

Aldace F. Walker

Fort Stevens, D.C.
Nov. 17, 1863

Dear Father:

I have not much time to write this p.m. and am engaged for the evening. We have a new lot of material, and are pushing on the remainder of our work today. Shall be done sometime if nothing happens. I doubt if the engineer work is ever finished however. I am still living in my tent, but Mrs. Goodrich expects to go home tomorrow, and I talk of going in with the Capt. for a season. Lt. Dodge and wife move into Bat. D officers' quarters today. I expect a room in Col. Benton's when it is finished. We have had cooking ranges furnished each company mess of a very good description, and the men are beginning to think they are living in clover.

A squad of 43 recruits came on Monday; 32 of them joined my battery. They look like good quiet, steady fellows most of them; though some of them are quite boyish - too much so - only a few of these however. Col. Warner promises me all he can get for me out of the next squad - that is, all that can be ordered here without going too much against the grain - such as have relations &c. elsewhere; and another such squad will fill me up - my aggregate now is 118. I think it is "real mean" of Gen. Washburn to issue such an order as he has in regard to recruits for old regiments. The design is to save some of them from consolidation which are near the mark; but hardly any will volunteer for the 7th, 8th and 9th, and after ours is filled there will be enough for the rest. We need but 6 or 700. Still I don't think it will have much effect.

Our court-martial met today. Tried one case and adjourned till Friday. Col. Benton is still sick abed. We have delays in getting our cases ready, as the New York men have not all returned from their furloughs, so that I have sat on but three cases. I expect that we shall be dissolved before Friday - hope so. You would know none of the members, as they are all but Benton, Lt. Tucker and I, from other regiments - New York and Pennsylvania. Our new surgeon is Dr. Park of Grafton, or Weston, or somewhere.[9] Was surgeon of the 16th - is a very nice man. The rest of our medical staff remains unchanged. I hope you are all well and happy. I have never been more contented since I have been in the army than I am now, and think I can see the "broke of day." I send my draft of presentation speech, written in

2:40 Sunday morning. Please put it with my papers.

With love to all,

Aldace F. Walker

Fort Stevens, D.C.
Nov. 22, 1863

Dear Mary:

My Sunday has not been spent in any military duties, thanks to my court-martial; but it is now nine o'clock, the first time I have found to write. After breakfast I went to Slocum to arrange a little business with Col. Warner, and thence to the city. Went to Dr. Sunderland's church, and into Mr. Blagden's pew. Found a stranger in the pulpit however, as Dr. S. had gone to Shoreham to attend the funeral of his father. After service I came across John Osgood and went with him to dinner. He boards with a Vermont family, Buck of Chelsea - son and daughter of the M. C. - Father will know about them. Then I went on the G. Street and called on Dr. Allen. Found some acquaintances there. Went to the Avenue House to find Chaplain Hale[10] of the 5th - an old classmate - but he was out. Got home about dark, and have spent the evening in making necessary arrangements for to-morrow, and reading the budget of papers from home.

By the way, tell Father that I think three papers for one cent is rather an improvement on the old rate of postage. I don't know as my Sunday afternoon made out as well as the morning promised, but I reckon it is about as well to visit among such friends as those in the city as to loaf among the officers in camp, as I should have to have done here. Our chaplain did not preach here today - the first omission for some time - and he has preached written sermons of late. Henry Frost[11] is to leave Middlebury - Dr. Allen says on account of his health - his sister says to get a bigger salary. But he is a slim stick. I saw a man from the army, who said it had all broken camp and gone on - a diversion, I presume, in Burnside's favor. Col. Benton is getting better.

Mrs. Goodrich has gone home, and I have moved my bed over there. Find it much warmer o' night - but keep my table in my old tent. Hunsdon's commish. and the rest, do not come. We can't see why the delay occurs. I did not expect to get into print about Pike; though as I did, I almost wish the number of the regiment had been inserted.

Col. Warner expressed himself sorry that he had not made the time of the furlough granted him 15 days instead of 10, as he had acted so honorable about it. He has not yet returned - time is out today. We have got hanging kerosene lamps to running in our new barracks, and they light them up splendidly; shall save money at it.

The Atlantic came today. We are going to drilling next week on alternate days, in view of Gen. Barry's next visit. We have just learned that Gen. Pitcher,[12] Provost Mar[shall] Gen[eral] of W[ashington], has issued an order forbidding recruiting for our regiment. I can't learn why, and Col. Warner goes into town in the morning to see about it. I am afraid Pitcher will get snubbed, for Jim is popular in all the city offices, and influential. We have 70 more recruits at Brattleboro.

Fort Stevens, D.C.
Nov. 25, 1863

Dear Father:

Tomorrow is Thanksgiving Day. I have been wishing all day that I could be with you, and thinking that I would have a most pleasant time if I was to be there - but I ain't, so what's the use of "greeting." I am undecided as yet how I shall spend the morrow. I believe our mess is to have a turkey. There is a parade at Slocum at 8:30 a.m. And I am in doubt whether to stay in camp and enjoy the parade at Slocum at 8:30 a.m. And I am in doubt whether to stay in camp and enjoy the parade and the turkey; or to go to town, hear Dr. Sunderland on the Nation, and Graws Opera Troupe, who give a concert in the afternoon. I may do the whole. At any rate, I can't get a Vermont Thanksgiving out of it, the best I can do - so I'll not try. Lt. Dodge had a pass in for town tomorrow with me, but it was disapproved. Our court has had no cases yet this week, and is adjourned till Friday. I am having a very quiet, easy time, with very little to ruffle me. Our new boys are doing well, though they (some of them) ought to be in their mothers' laps yet, and find it hard work to run a siege 24 Par. "from battery." I drilled a squad of them today. They take hold well enough. We have got to the full enjoyment of our new kitchens and mess rooms - a $50 range with suitable cooking utensils. Tables all around - kerosene lamps - capital stoves - and all clean and new. It will not look so well in the spring, I fear. It has rained a good deal of late, but has turned cold tonight, and we shall have weather for Thanksgiving that will seem natural at any rate.

I presume there is fighting this week, though I doubt if the results will come round in time to inspire ministerial eloquence tomorrow. My Co. is the first to be filled, as having the biggest squad of recruits, not for "training" purposes, but to fill one Co. and get the new officers, and then take another. I suppose that there are recruits enough at Brattleboro to fill my battery. Gen. Barry has taken the matter in hand about our filling up, and Pitcher may get squelched. It is a shame the 17th regiment was saddled on to the state, especially in the hands of Randall.

I am cold in my tent, and must go to my room. Goodnight, and a happy Thanksgiving when we meet again.

Aldace F. Walker

Fort Stevens, D.C.
Nov. 29, 1863

Dear Father:

This Sunday morning seems a little like winter. It rained yesterday - in fact it has rained for the last three Saturdays - and in fact we would rather have it rain on Saturday than on any other day, because it hinders our work less and makes the roads so muddy that the regiment cannot be got together on Sunday. These inspections however trouble me not at all, and I am excused by virtue of my court from going to Slocum occasionally to recite in the "School of the Battalion." Said court, by the way, being a humbug unmitigated; has done nothing the last week, principally I suppose because the Judge Advocate has got lazy and wants to be relieved - I presume we all shall be at the end of the month. I was hoping it would last till the session of Congress, but have about given that up. Thanksgiving Day I was rather lonely. It seemed as if I might be at home as well as not - and I might, if I had not been here.

I went to the city in the morning - let the regiment go. Went to Dr. Sunderland's, but found another man there; a good sort of an old covey - don't know who it was. But ministers, and everyone else here, will persist in calling "psalm" "sam" and "calm" "cam," and very flat at that. A pretty good little choir sang old "Denmark" - "Before Jehovah's throne" - very finely, and I wanted to join - did some.

After meeting I found a brace of Middlebury friends, got half a dozen fried oysters, and went to hear the Italians sing; and I verily believe that the hearing of "The last Rose of Summer," "Home, Sweet Home," and "Kathleen Mavourneen" by these artists did me far more good than the meeting. I was much more impressed by it any way. There was a good deal of Italian singing too, which I relished probably more than you would. Then I got my Thanksgiving dinner at "Willard's," with the turkey and plum pudding of course, and hurried home. I have been setting up my company cooks in housekeeping; have got table room, and plates, cups, spoons, knives and forks for 125 - as many as I shall be likely to want to feed at once.

Hunsdon's commission came Wednesday night - or Thursday night I guess - so he is wearing his coat and shoulder straps that have lain in his trunk for the last twelve months. He has not got a horse yet, and is moderately happy. Lt. Lee of Bat. A takes his place. This finished up all our original 1st Lts., and in fact Lee was at first a Sergt. is an Amherst college boy (Delta Kappa Epsilon) from St. Johnsbury. Our 2d Lts. are all promoted too, and our original 1st Sergeants either promoted or reduced. You may tell Mr. Nicholson that his friend - or nephew, I think - Lewis, whom I found a private in Co. C, has been made Sergt. Major, and I presume will have a commission sometime. Still, there are five of our original Captains holding that place still. I am sixth in rank. The other changes have been made by resignations, the two new batteries, &c. I don't suppose we are getting any recruits now. It is a shame, and will hinder the state in regard to filling their quota. Rutland is extravagant on bounty. Soldiers now in the field ought to be exempt from taxation on such wheels. A member of the 3d told me the other day what his tax was on the nine months men. It is too bad - no bounty for them, and a tax for the cowards who waited.

Our news is all good of late. Meigs gives Grant great praise for a "well delivered battle," and Chickamauga is virtually regained. How far it will do to press on Ulysses knows better than I do, but the whole country will have to be overrun sometime. I wish J. D. would skedaddle, and think he will by and by. The papers are trying hard to make out that Meade is on his fight, but we can't quite see it. Don't know but he is however. The army is getting to think very much of Meade. He moves so quick - has uniformly got the better of Lee - in short, understands his biz. I send a paper to Mary for the big picture inside.

With love to all,

Aldace F. Walker

Fort Stevens, D.C.
Dec. 2, 1863

Dear Father:

I have been very busy today. One of my men, Potter, died last night, and I have had to make out divers papers, &c., besides making arrangements for the funeral, which is to be tomorrow. And then I have made my property returns for the last month - went to the court-martial - nothing to do - drilled some - heard a recitation, &c. Your letter came on in spite of the new mail arrangements, and I was glad to hear from you and Ellena. It is strange how Mr. Chellis manages. The lumber for Col. Benton's quarters came yesterday. Austin and I are to occupy them for the present, but it will be a fortnight first. Meanwhile I am very comfortably situated. I am very well yet; expect, or hope, to remain so. My new recruits are mostly doing very well; some of them are very fine fellows. We have news from Gen. Meade that puts us full of hope. He has cut loose from all his communications, and is off for Richmond on his own hook. I was in the city yesterday, and heard that he was at Orange Court House, and had intercepted Lee's communications. The railroad is in good order from Aquia to Falmouth, and if he is worsted he will fall back on Fredericksburg. If not, it is supposed that either the White House or City Point will be his base of supplies. It evidently is such a movement as the army has never before attempted, and we Augur success from this and from Meade's known caution.

With much love, for I must go to the barracks and look over a new invoice of blankets, &c.,

Aldace F. Walker

Fort Stevens, D.C.
Dec. 6, 1863

Dear Father:

It is rather late this evening, and we have had a busy day. Our officers are trying to edge in a little battalion drill among our other exercises. Yesterday we had one at Slocum, of course, and today our Sunday inspection was ordered at 2 1-2, and we had a drill substituted, which we had a great deal rather have than an inspection. I have drawn guns for my recruits and take them out on the drills. They do better than I would think. Port Baxter[13] brought on a son who has been at Norwich awhile, and who is going to enlist in my company in a day or two. I don't know but he will be rather a trouble than otherwise, but he won't if he is anything of a fellow. Our chaplain has a meeting here in the morning and evening of each Sunday, when he preaches a written sermon. The evening meetings are very fairly attended, but in the morning the attendance is slim, for the men are busy. Our court adjourned last Thursday. Another is ordered to meet tomorrow at brigade headquarters - Fort Bunker Hill. Lt. Austin and Capt. Lee are the detail from this post. Col. Benton has had a relapse and is quite thin; is getting run down considerably, but I hope he will get up again soon. My house (Col. B.'s), which is to be occupied by Austin and myself, is getting under headway, and I hope it will be finished by the last of the week. I wrote you that one of my men was dead. He had a sort of a malignant typhus fever, with inflammation of the brain. One of my men has a son - comparatively a small lad - who has been driving team in the city of late. Came out here to see his father. Was taken sick in the same way, and now lies at the point of death. I fear he introduced the disease from some of the teamsters' camps. Another of my men is at the hospital sick in the same way, and will hardly live through the night; and still another is taken today, and what it will result in I am afraid to think. All is done that can be. I don't know but it is to run through the company. All the cases were in one corner of the barracks till this last, which is in another part. It can't be contagious, but it seems to be malarious. Surgeon Park is quite startled I see; but he is skillful, and I hope the worst is over. You had not mentioned that Miss Waldo was with you till the letter I got last night. I should think she would board with Vonia. It is pleasant weather, though a little cold. We don't mind that though, and I think it is healthier. I have got something to send Mary; but as I am writing in Austin's tent, and it is up to my old domicile, I can't put it in tonight. Will wait till next time; meanwhile she may guess, and ten to one she won't guess right. Meade is played out, I fear.

With much love,

Aldace F. Walker

Fort Stevens, D.C.
Dec. 9, 1863

Dear Father:

It is queer that there is delay and difference in the time required to take my letters home. Yours are as regular as the sun. In fact, I have had to much to do this week that I had lost a day, and the reception of your letter this evening was the only thing that put me right. I have been shoving along my quarters as best I could. Met with one drawback, for after the frame and sides were all up we had to raise it two feet and alter the grade - "dress" it - so as to be military I suppose. It is now enclosed, partly lathed and partly floored. Hope to get into it by Sunday, but don't know as I shall. We are to drill the rest of the week, as we have worked the first half - Battalion drill Thursday and Friday at Slocum, and Brigade drill Saturday at Fort Bunker Hill.

I believe you are not posted on the present condition of the horse. A Vermonter came here a while ago with quite a good horse, and offered Goodrich the use of it if he would keep it through the winter. So he took it. The next day we saw that the man was arrested for stealing horses, and is probably under sentence by this time. So Goodrich has the horse, and is so sure that he never will be called for (he has told the police of the circumstances) that he has sold his share of the old White to Lt. Lewis. We have been building a barn for our equines, of stockades, &c., and have quite a palace - comparative. I imagine recruiting is resumed for our regiment. Gen. Washburn telegraphed to Warner yesterday inquiring how many men he needed to "fill," and was answered of course. A squad of 100 left Brattleboro Monday for us, and they are expected tonight or tomorrow. I hope to get some more - enough I presume.

I find some very fine fellows among my new men; some that will make first rate corporals, &c. Gov. Holbrook promised two regiments (veteran) to Stanton about Gettysburg time, and the 17th is one of them. It is the one Conway[14] is in, and I think is now about half full. My sick men (some of them) are better. None have died, and I have no new cases;

hope the worst is past. There is one of them whose case in now extremely critical. I think our surgeon is very skillful.

I read your sermon with a great deal of interest. Of course you could have multiplied examples if you had chosen. Mrs. Little told me her husband expected to see his Thanksgiving sermon in the Chronicle, but I have not seen it. The recruits are at Slocum now, I understand.

Goodnight.

Aldace F. Walker

Fort Stevens, D.C.
Dec. 13, 1863

Dear Father:

It rained this morning early, but has cleared away and left us one of the loveliest days I ever saw. It is some muddy under foot, but on our sand we don't mind it, and it is so warm that dress coats are uncomfortable. I suppose I have been one of the busiest mortals entirely for the past few days. Another squad of recruits has come on, and my company has been filled. I suppose wee shall have the new officers and non-coms. Before long, as application for authority was immediately made by the Col. to the Adjt. Gen. I have now 147 enlisted men and three officers, and I have had and shall have sights or work in getting them in order, fed, clothed, armed and equipped, and then drilled. It is a job, I tell you. But I have got my first squad so that they go on guard, &c., with the old men, and I shall have the new ones so in a short time - a fortnight or so. They are a better set of men than the first ones were, larger and older. Recruiting is going on very fast for us now in Vermont. There are nearly enough there to fill the regiment, if not quite. Two of the Wallingford men are in Bat. C. I have not found them out yet. We shall be fully organized, I think, in a month from now. Baxter[15] is with us. Is a young, slim fellow. Looks like Lt. Smith, but I hope he will not prove like him. Of course his father expects him to be commissioned; but I shall oppose it for the present, as it will be hardly fair for the rest. We are to have a man from Vermont commissioned as 2d Lt. and detailed to lead the band - a common practice; but I fear he will be commissioned in my battery. Maj. Hunsdon is still here. Col. Benton is still ailing; I fear he will not be well for some time.

One of my men died Thursday. I took his body to the city, and sent it home. He was a good fellow - married. I have a good deal of sickness now, but nothing serious. Several of my new men are in the hospital, and I suppose they will be sick a good deal all the winter, until they get acclimated. To add to my labors, we are having regimental drills every day - which I enjoy very much, but am getting a little foot sore. We had a brigade review yesterday at Fort Bunker Hill, and are soon to be reviewed as a brigade by Gen. Barry, and all our drilling is in preparation for that. The battalion drill is fun however. Col. Warner drills us, and is very particular - a good drill master.

We had our usual inspection here this morning. I am officer of the day today. The "Russ-hims" and Gen Augur came up to Fort Totten the other day.[16] That is the showiest fort, and in the best position of any on the line - near the Soldiers' Home too. I send the last Atlantic. Will try and send Mary's present today. It is Capt. Goodrich's "Jack." We had a pull back or two on our house. Had to raise it two feet. Took one day. When we got ready to plaster we found - or could not find rather, the hair for the mortar. Took us two days to find it. So we plaster tomorrow, and get in the latter part of the week.

I saw the 2d Brigade reviewed and drilled the other day. The Division will have to get together sometime, I suppose.

Fort Stevens, D.C.
Dec. 16, 1863

Dear Father:

Your letter and Mary's came tonight. Finds us pretty much in status quo - busy as bees for a wonder. I shall move into my new house tomorrow. We are considerably agitated just now about certain of our officers, but it will end in smoke I think. Authority has to be granted by the Adjt. Gen. To appoint the extra officers and non coms. in my battery.

Application has been made, but no answer has been received as yet; no doubt it will be granted. We have a great deal of drilling to do nowadays. Regimental drills every forenoon at Slocum - a mile and a half off, Mary, and we go there because there are others as far the other side, and it is central-headquarters too. But we enjoy them very much, if it is something of a jaunt, and we are getting to be somewhat proficient I think. Can form squares and all such thing, that are considered rather difficult in artillery regiments.

My new recruits are getting on well as a general thing, though there is one of them very sick, and I am afraid he will not live - diphtheria and scarlet fever combined. The last squad drill, or learn to drill, more quickly than the first, and are not so boyish and inattentive. In fact, they are much older and better men. I have not received guns and equipment for them yet. Expect them by the last of the week. But they go on dress parade with the rest.

Last Monday night I had quite a treat - Shakespeare's Henry IV, with Hackett[17] as Falstaff - the best actor of that part in the world. The one whom old Abe wrote the letter to, which was copied so extensively, and commented on by English papers. Lincoln was there with his wife and sons, and Major Gen. Sickles was in the box with them. Austin and Lee and I were there together, and had a seat exactly opposite the presidential squad. Abraham was vastly tickled, and is quite a family man.

Col. Benton is getting better; and if he is well when his furlough comes round he will not go, as his family are all here, and it would be very expensive to make a family journey to Vermont, and he would not do as Templeton did - leave them here.

About the 5-20's - I will write when I think more about it.

Charley Thomas of Brandon was one of my best friends, but I see no place here for him.

With much love to all, I remain as ever,

Aldace F. Walker

Fort Stevens, D.C.
Dec. 20, 1863

Dear Father:

We are having very cold weather these days. You must be completely frozen up. But have had no snow as yet. Last year we had a severe snow storm on the 7th of November; this year we have not seen a flake. I am fairly moved into my new quarters, and am as comfortable as can be. We kept a hot coal fire till we got the plastering fairly dry, so we took no cold. You know, I suppose, something of my chum - Lt. Austin of Bat. I; I believe I have told you that he is a Burlington collegian of three years standing, and a consistent church member. I have learned to think very much of him. He is quiet, but of a good deal of determination - one of those fellows that would understand danger, and dare to face it. Is a scholarly fellow withal - much more so than my Lt. Lewis, who, though he has had a good many advantages (most of them of his own making, by the way), is never meant for a scholar - nothing literary about him. I am very much pleased that circumstances have placed me with a fellow like Austin, and I know you will be. It seems less like army, and more like home. He is on a court-martial now at Bunker Hill, four miles off, but lives here still; has transportation in an ambulance with Capt. Lee. He has had considerable trouble. Was promoted into a battery against the wishes of everyone in it, but has worn well, and is very much liked by all its members now except Capt. Templeton - a worthless fellow, a disgrace to the service - and on or two of his "set." Templeton has tried every way to rid of him - by transfer, &c. - but Austin won't go, and I admire his spunk.

We are kept busy in spite of the cold weather. Yesterday Maj. Chamberlain inspected in artillery, preparatory to the coming inspection of Gen. Barry, and he is so faithful that we nearly froze to death. My company did very well I thought. Today we were ordered to Slocum at 9 a.m. for inspection, which we understood to mean drill. The major was in command, and had "charged front forward on first company" - the men rubbing their ears, and taking no interest in the drill - when Col. Warner came out, and ordered us home - "too cold to drill." A battalion means from two companies to twelve, and a battalion drill is a drill of two or more companies in regimental maneuvers; usually the same as a regimental drill, but we can have a battalion drill at our own fort. You have probably seen in the papers of Buford's[18] death and the obsequies. The officers of the Division were requested to attend, and so we went down the p.m. I rode old Grey, and was very comfortable in my big overcoat and cape. We were ordered to assemble at Division (Haskins') Headquarters, and go from there to the church, and the consequence was (intended perhaps) that we could not get in, as there were three times as many present as could be accommodated in the church. I succeeded in getting on to the threshold of the door towards the close of the service. Saw lots of big generals. Sickles is the finest looking one in the crowd, and is quite a lion here - quite a change in his social status in the last two years. There was an escort of Infantry, Artillery and Cavalry under Gen. Stoneman, who has a voice like a lion; and a big procession of military men, Cavalry officers, &c. But I cut for home when I had seen it pass down the Avenue. It was quite a show, and Buford deserved it. One of my new recruits turns out non compos. I have made out papers for his discharge, and shall write a letter to the selectmen who enlisted him freeing my mind. It is a shame, and he should not be enlisted on their quota. I think I shall apply to Washburn to that effect. That nigger I sent Mary is a genius. The picture is good, but don't express his character. I sent the same to Miss Bugbee,[19] much to her amusement. I have received no letter from Henry or Ellena. I think Mr. Chellis is keeping them from correspondence with us - don't you? In our drills, the field officers are mounted.

I have considered that matter of the bond, and am in favor of getting it at once. Of course the coupons should be cashed as fast as due, as gold must fall to its normal condition sometime.

With much love, as ever,

Aldace F. Walker

Fort Stevens, D.C.
Dec. 23, 1863

Dear Father:

Your letter with the watch guard was received tonight, though as we had a new mail boy on he did not get around till dark. I think the chain quite pretty, though it dispenses with the hook, which I have been in the habit of regarding as quite an ornament. I have lent that to Austin, but will turn it over to you if you wish it. I got "Tales of a Wayside Inn" today, and will send it to Mary for a New Years present when I get through with it - Longfellow's new poem, you know. We are having bitter cold weather - just a sprinkling of snow last night - the first of the season. It is cold weather to drill, and cold to dig, and we are not doing much except drilling our new recruits. Squads of these keep coming - two a week, of a hundred or more. Our aggregate yesterday was 1618. Batteries D., I. and B. at this post are full, C. lacks 20. A mistake was made in the application for additional officers for me, and it had to be renewed to satisfy the red tapists of the War Dept., so we have not received the authority yet. I don't care much about the officers, though we need the corporals and sergeants very much. Still, I don't want them appointed until after Gen. Barry inspects in artillery, which we expect every day, as it is the N.C.O.'s that he is principally "after." He reviewed our brigade Monday at Fort Bunker Hill. It was not as cold as days before and since, and we got along very well. After review, the Pa. regt. drilled. Did not do much - nothing but a simple maneuver or two, and those not very well. And we went at it - got along first rate, all but one big blunder made by one of the captains, which mortified us somewhat. We can drill quite decently as a general thing. I was in town today. Got an order for the balance of our bunk timber, and shall send team for it tomorrow. Drew my company savings for last month - got some gloves and a thing or two besides, and came home to diner, at 3. It was bitter cold riding horseback, but warmer than riding any other way. I throw my big cape over my head, and let the old horse kite. He stumbled and threw Lt. Lewis the other day, bruising his cheek badly. I am boarding now at Sweetland's for $3.50 per week, and we live well enough - have buckwheat cakes very often in the morning, and they seem good and natural I assure you. I have got a clerk writing for me tonight, and I must tend to him.

So goodnight, with love to all,

Aldace F. Walker

Fort Stevens, D.C
Dec. 27

Dear Father:

It has come off warm after our cold spell and rains today. We went to Fort Slocum for an inspection; but as it began to rain quite hard, we came home again without forming the regimental line, very much to our satisfaction. I took over to Slocum 77 enlisted men, and had some dozen others that I had excused because I had enough, and they had some slight reason for staying at home. My battery is all armed and equipped. My nominations for non-commissioned officers went in yesterday, and the appointments are made today. I have now a 1st Sergt., Quartermaster Sergt. and six duty Sergts., 12 corporals, and 2 artificers - these last at $15 per month - sort of company carpenters. I had 7 new corporals to make; 5 of these are men who did not come out with the battery, though two have served some months with us; two of the others are "veterans," and the other is Baxter. I don't know who are to be my lieutenants, though I expect to know soon. Do you remember Norton Dudley, who used to run the depot at Center Rutland? I saw John Osgood the other day, as I often do, and he told me about Dudley. He enlisted in a Regular regt. at Chicago under a fictitious name - deserted - was apprehended, and is now under sentence at the Tortugas ... having a pretty hard time, of course - been there six months. Osgood was trying to get Foot to procure his pardon. I am surprised, for I always thought rather well of the fellow. I have been in town several times of late, after our bunk lumber; but though I have had the promise of it, and have had teams in for it, the contractors ailed to come to time. I have an order for the 7850 feet due us, and am going to follow it up - keep watch of the mill till I get it. The health of my company is much improved. We have a case of small-pox in the regiment. A squad of 160 came on today. Our aggregate is 1730 or thereabouts. My battery has been full, 147 enlisted men, once, then one deserted - three more sent to Invalid corps, and another will be as soon as he returns from a furlough. I sent one to the insane asylum yesterday, from whence he will be soon discharged, and so we dwindle. I don't want to get any more till after the next muster. I am dreading this next week a good deal, as our monthly, quarterly and annual returns must go in, with our big muster rolls that will make a great deal of work. They are so much larger, &c., that we probably shall not be paid as soon the next time. I am about broke, but shall get a big Company fund about the 10th of next month, and can get along till then. I was in the city yesterday on my lumber wheel, and as Othello was to be played by Davenport, Wallack, &c. (the best troupe in the country) I staid in. Enjoyed it very much indeed. There were several of my Regt. there, Austin, Hunsdon, &c. Hunsdon has got him a nice $200 horse. I met N. B. Smith (Parson). He promised to come out today, but I presume the rain prevented him. I am getting on nicely in my new house. Have not had any cold at all. My old horse is a great institution; holds his own and is quite a comfort. Mrs. Goodrich has returned to camp. Have not heard from Col. Benton.

Love to all.

Aldace F. Walker

We have had a meeting in my barracks tonight - quite well attended, some 200 - and attentive.

Fort Stevens, D.C.
Dec. 30, Midnight

I have not found time to look into my morning paper yet; but am well, and getting on well with my papers. Returns are all in but the rolls, and those more than half done.

Aldace F. Walker

----

1 George Charles Allen, Wallingford. RR.

2 Moody Bedell, Barton, brother of Sergt. Henry E. Bedell, Westfield. RR.

3 Lieut., later Capt., Edward P. Lee, Waterford. RR.

4 Sergt. David H. Gilman, Westfield. RR.

5 David Kendall Simonds (1839-1917), Peru, 3rd Regt. Tenn. Vols. MC 1862. Editor, Newport Express, 1864-1868. Died Manchester, Vt. Robinson, 166-7.

6 USA Brig. Gen. John Henry Martindale, Military Commander of the District of Columbia, Twenty-Second Corps. Boatner, 515.

7 Salmon P. Chase, Secretary of the Treasury in the Lincoln Administration until July 1864; replaced by William P. Fessenden. Boatner, 140, 279.

8 Henry Martyn Seeley, Middlebury College Professor of Chemistry and Natural History, 1861-1895. Robinson, xlii.

9 Walker was correct the first time; Surgeon Castanus B. Park Jr. was from Grafton.

10 Chaplain Charles S. Hale, Brandon, is not listed as an alumnus of MC.

11 Henry Frost is not listed among the Faculty or Staff of MC. Robinson, xxxiv-lviii.

12 USA Brig. Gen. Thomas G. Pitcher, Commissary and Provost Marshal in Washington. Boatner, 654.

13 Portus Baxter (1806-1868), Derby Line. U.S. Representative from Vermont 1861-1867. U.S. Congress, Biographical Directory of the United States Congress, 1774-Present. Accessed 1/11/2001, available from http://bioguide.congress.gov/scripts/biodisplay.pl?index=B000246; Internet.

14 Capt. Daniel Conway, Sherburne. Previously 2nd Lieut., Co. H, 14th Vt. Infantry. RR.

15 Sergt., later Capt. and Bvt. Maj., Henry C. Baxter, son of U.S. Representative Portus Baxter. NU 1866. RR; Poirier, 291.

16 USA Maj. Gen. Christopher C. Augur assumed command of the Twenty-Second Corps October 13, 1863, replacing Heintzelman. Boatner, 34. The "Russ-hims" were from a Russian ship docked at Alexandria. Fort Totten had been selected, according to Lieut. Col. George Chamberlain, "'from among all north of the river as the one for them to see.' Bands played, thirteen-gun salutes fired, and there was 'quite a crowd to see the strangers,' he recounted." Cooling, Mr. Lincoln's Forts, 172.

17 James H. Hackett played Falstaff in Washington the previous year, prompting Lincoln's letter. Lincoln entertained the actor at the White House Sunday evening the night before the play opened at Ford's Theater, which is when Walker attended. Lincoln was reportedly so enamored of the actor and his rendition of the part that he attended the presentation four nights running. Leech, 278.

18 USA Brig. Gen. John Buford, a cavalry officer, one of the unsung heroes of Gettysburg. He died of typhoid fever December 16, 1863. Boatner, 97.

19 Louise King Bugbee (1838-1910), Plymouth. KUA 1858. KUACat, 56.

10.
Defenses of Washington
January and February, 1864

Fort Stevens, D.C.
Jan. 3, 1864

Dear Father and Mother:

I am waiting for dinner (3 p.m.) and will commence my letter. Have just received yours, which usually comes on Saturday. Have been to Slocum with my battery for review and inspection. As arms have not yet been issued to the rest of the new recruits, my battery is the largest in the regiment on drill. I have, as I think I told you, all my non-commissioned officers. Corp. Pike is my Quartermaster Sergt., and is the best man I could have. He keeps my clothing under lock and key - none is issued by anyone else, nor by him without a receipt at once. He also takes care of my ordnance, &c., the cook house, and the policing of the barracks and grounds. He is a very valuable man, and faithful; is a good penman, and makes out most of my rolls, &c. Nominations have gone on for my new lieutenants - Dodge to be 1st Lt., and my 1st Sergt. Dunham,[1] and Sergt. Bedell to be 2d. We still lack about a hundred men, and Maj. Austine has stopped sending them on. I presume, however, that they will come sometime. Meanwhile, all our batteries are full enough for the new organization except two – A and F. It is queer how men drop away; my aggregate now is 144 - has been 150. I had a man discharged today for mental imbecility. It is a shame that selectmen will enlist such men in their anxiety to fill their quota. I am going to free my mind in a letter to them, which I expect will be a literary curiosity.

We have a good deal of sickness in the regiment, and disease is unusually fatal. I lost a man Dec. 31st. We lost 14 last month. One of my men went to City Hospital yesterday with small-pox; the first case I have had in my company, though it has been in the regiment several times. Measles have made their appearance among the new recruits, and the surgeons fear this more than small-pox. The most fatal diseases of late have been pneumonia and a malignant camp or typhus fever. I got my rolls in yesterday morning, with no mistakes to be found. Pike and I made them out. This week I have made and sent in five big muster rolls, each good eight hours work, monthly return, return of men joined, quarterly return of deaths, monthly return of deserters, return of deserters from muster in Sept. 1, 1862, annual return of changes and casualties, besides morning reports, and various descriptive lists and final statements of men transferred, discharged, died, &c. The coming week I am going to make my returns to the Quartermaster Gen. And the Ordnance Dept., and then I shall be free again for a while. I presume we shall have our pay about the 20th or 25th of Jan., and I can get along till that time; could easily if I could collect what is due me. I got a telegram today, which frightened me till I got it open and found a dispatch from Gen. Washburn asking for information in regard to certain men whom I had enlisted here, and whom I had requested credited to certain towns in Vermont on quota for town bounties. It was very cold yesterday, but is quite pleasant today; no snow.

I am very much pleased with Mother's $70 furs; but that would not buy a decent overcoat in Washington. About our house. Col. Benton has a good two story building, which he erected at Mr. Butt's expense last summer; so he has no use for his quarters. Lt. Dodge has a wife here - Lewis lives with them; and to accommodate Dodge and the officers of Co. I, who also have families, Benton let Austin, Post Adjt., and I have his shanty - a very good arrangement for all concerned. We enjoy living together very much - read aloud a good deal evenings, and lie abed mornings, and have a good time generally. I have not received the Atlantic. You had better write to Tichnor & Fields; perhaps the direction was misunderstood. I am accountable now for about $6000 of property; ought to give bonds, oughtn't I?

With much love to all,

Aldace F. Walker

Baxter was up a day or two ago with his wife, Miss Collamer,[2] and two Strafford ladies - one of them Mrs. Morrill's sister,[3] and the other one who talked of you - heard you preach last summer - but I have forgot her name. I think I shall call on our delegation at 470 7th St., as I have been invited to do several times. I persuaded the Col. from commissioning young Baxter, as unfair to the old men. Presume he will get the next lift. I also persuaded him not to appoint my Sergt. Gilman, who is home recruiting, and got my "slate" accepted, much to my satisfaction. I am very much pleased also with my new non-commissioned officers. Austin has gone to town to church today. His court adjourns tomorrow.

Aldace F. Walker

Fort Stevens, D.C.
Jan. 6, 1864

Dear Father:

I came very near forgetting my letter to you tonight, because your letter for the first time for months failed to come. The trouble, I suppose, is with the ferry at Havre de Grace, ice, &c.; besides a freight train ran off the boat into the river yesterday. It is so late now that I feel very little like writing. Austin has gone up into Maryland to a party. I have been reading till I am very sleepy, and was just preparing for bed. I began to take a little "note of time" on the 1st, and my diary to my surprise said Wednesday. We have some three or four inches of snow now, and very cold weather - no sleighing of course. The cold weather is rather a benefit in a sanitary point of view I think. I am getting the rest of my bunks up. Have put the two windows that were lacking to my private domicile in this week, and hung up some curtains-green, with big geese on them that are meant for swans I suppose. Our men are allowed furloughs now - two to a company, and it is hard to choose which two to send - no lack of candidates. We don't get much news nowadays. I think we shall do well if we sit still this winter and organize. I have great faith in the efficacy of such weather as this to promote the welfare of our cause. I still trust the spring campaign, and think our regiment will not have a shake in it. But I have a business letter or two to write, and must close so as to retire in some sort of season. It is long after eleven now.

With much love,

Aldace F. Walker

Fort Stevens, D.C.
Jan. 10, 1864
Sunday twilight

Dear Father:

I received your letters last week on Thursday and Saturday, so I think the mails must be getting regular again. There has been a great deal of detention of the trains of late around here. Lt. Austin left here for Essex, Vermont, on a 15 days furlough on Friday p.m., and I have some doubts as to whether he got any further than Rutland last night. So I am alone in my new house. This has been a long day - very pleasant weather though. We had a company inspection at 11. This evening we are to have a temperance lecture by somebody. I have got my returns all in, and all right I think. Have only my common business on hand, but that is enough for week days, as we have got to drilling a good deal. We have had quite severe weather of late; more snow than all last winter - enough for decent sleighing. Persons were here from Vermont last week-say there is more ice on the Susquehanna than on the Otter Creek, and that we have the coldest weather. New Years Day I mentioned, which was cold here and followed by a very cold night. In fact, it has been so cold the past week that drilling has been almost impossible, and that ice is being cut in large quantities from the Potomac.

I took occasion to speak to my company about gambling the other night. Did not like to forbid it, as some of the officers indulge in it, and as the men are apt to go away and gamble elsewhere if it is not allowed at home; but I said that I did not like to see it - though less of those who played for money - and that it was wrong - have not seen any since, and don't think I shall.

I have sent away my Bill, and Austin's darkey does the work for us both. My boys take care of the old horse, and he draws water for them. It is a very good arrangement all round, especially as Billy was getting to be a very poor stick of late. The horse will get better care, and I shall get better attention, and especially the men will be saved some work, as the carrying water from some distance for 150 men to drink and to wash in is no slight job. Each of the companies now here has a horse, and we use a cart on two wheels with no body and the axle bent down so as to hold a barrel. I don't know but I told you about the horse before.

Later in the evening - I reckon our temperance lecture did not amount to much; at any rate, I did not care to hear much of it. I enclose some photographs - Lt. Lewis I think you have, but this is a better one. Dodge is the one with the chin whiskers, and the Capt. is Safford, formerly 1st Lt. of this Co. and now of L. I hope to have some more lieutenants to send on shortly. I think Mary must have enjoyed her Christmas eve. From her description, with the presents. Emily writes me that she is getting so that she plays "right smart" as they say around here. But about the dollar - I shouldn't know what to do with it if I had it myself. Col. Benton, who is now in Vermont on sick leave, has, I understand, arranged it so that we shall receive the rest of our men. Maj. Austine has managed rather queerly towards us. There have been so many from other regiments wanting a shake at the recruits that he is overrun with applications, while we have not had anyone there to tease for us. I expect to go to town Tuesday after my Company Fund, and if I do I mean to call on the Congressmen, or their wives. I have no doubt but that Morrill is the smartest of the representatives, but I don't think he begins to be as much of a man as Judge Collamer. I can't see much in Baxter any way, but a well-dressed, nice sort of a man. Morrill is certainly a working man, and as such is of value to the country. There is a little political log-rolling going on, I find, about our next Major. Don't know whether the candidate of the politicians is the one the Col. will select or not. He is our senior Capt., Rice of F. The chaplain and wife have moved into their new quarters at Totten.

With much love to all, as ever, your son,

Aldace F. Walker

Fort Stevens, D.C.
Jan. 13, 1864

Dear Father:

My last quarter's supply of stationery is on its last legs. I suppose I can have some more when I get round to go to Slocum for it; meanwhile, I must use scraps. We have warmer weather today, and our snow is melting. A little rain spoiled our dress-parade. I never was in better health than at present, nor ever had my affairs and responsibilities in better shape. I went to town yesterday, as I expected. Drew my Co. Fund of $93.93 for December. Expended some of it, but have money enough on hand now. Don't expect to be paid off before February. It has been over two months since we were last paid, but they want to pay the Army of the Potomac before they do the troops inn the Defenses, and funds are now a little short.

Went into the Capitol a few minutes. Called on Hon. and Mrs. Baxter after dusk, Mr. Morrill came into the room, and I conversed with him a few minutes. I knew about the Strafford arrangement, and they seem glad to find a little hook for acquaintance with their son's captain. I called on N. B. Smith; found him at work, though not very hard at work I reckon. My old horse was smooth, and the roads were very slippery. I had Lee with me in the Col.'s buggy, and the horse fell down once on the way, flat, and got up again without breaking the thills. I don't see how he did it. Had to get him sharpened to come back with. I am rather lonely now Austin is gone, but can endure it I reckon.

I understand that the rest of our recruits left Brattleboro on Monday. I don't think the soldiers will care much about specie payment; it is recognized as a measure to embarrass the government. What they want is a regular pay day, and an increase of pay to all but the big bounty men. Edgerton of Wallingford called today. Has a commission in a negro regiment, as I presume you know already.[4] The new commissions for our regiment have not yet reached us. I don't know whether any body will notice my article in the Herald, but

I wanted to free my mind. I would like very much to be informed whether men transferred to our regiment, for instance to the Invalid Corps, get this $7 or not, for I am in the dark as to the ruling. Did I tell you that young Barrett of Strafford, who was at W. Rutland at school a few days ago, has a place as Quartermaster Captain, and is stationed at Alexandria? I have met him once or twice. His father has been up to our camp, and spoke of you as a friend, &c. Jed Baxter, who has been in charge of Campbell Hospital, is relieved and assigned to duty as Medical Inspector Provost Marshall Gen.'s Dept., and is organizing a bureau in the War Dept. All the surgeons examining recruits, &c., and the Invalid Corps surgeons, report to him; rather a big thing. His hospital was the best in the city.[5]

With much love,

Aldace F. Walker

Fort Stevens, D.C.
Jan. 17th, 1 P.M.

Dear Father:

Our inspection today was by company at home, very much to our satisfaction. We have been having warmer weather of late, and the snow is almost gone generally a thin layer of mud nowadays that is rather disagreeable. We are getting things to running first rate now; are provided with bunks all around, and the new men are learning to "come to Limerick." In fact I have the advantage of the other captains in the longest time to drill, &c., and my new men many of them are now as good as the old. I suppose the last squad to fill our regiment left Brattleboro on Friday. I now lack seven, but it will be comparatively a slight job to put them in shape. The new commissions for our regiment came last night. I have now my four lieutenants that I have been wishing for: Lewis and Dodge, 1st Lts.; and Dunham and Bedell, 2d Lts. These last were both corporals a few months ago, but on the principle of the best man for the best place I have shoved them ahead. Bedell had not the faintest idea that he was going to be promoted, and when Col. Warner sent for him he was pretty much beat. We had lots of fun at the expense of his "phelinks." He did not fee very bad, of course; but is modest and faithful. Just the man I like to promote.

I have the two new ones in Austin's part of my house for a day or two till they can make other arrangements. Of course this leaves me some more to promote among the non-coms. Hudson[6] will be my 1st Sergt. at Brattleboro, but was left sick and did not come on till April. Meanwhile as the company needed a sergeant, he was reduced to the ranks and another appointment made in his place. I have appointed him successively corporal, sergeant, and 1st sergeant, and think he will do well - he always has. The only trouble is that his health has a way of breaking down quite often. I shall make Baxter a sergeant; had to promise that to keep him from having a commission. Think he will do pretty well, however. He is young, hates to have the boys think he feels his "posish," &c., and is not thoroughly reliable I fear. On the whole, however, I am as well satisfied with my company and its arrangements as I could well be, as I have had it all my own way entirely and throughout. The greatest bother is with the boys who came in my first squad, and who are always losing and stealing and playing schoolboy tricks generally. I had a letter from C. N. Thomas the other day, with a photograph which I may as well enclose. Randall[7] is the third of my Middlebury classmates who has taken "orders." Two of them, he and Harris,[8] were Congregationalists when I first knew them - or rather Harris was a Baptist and then a Congo. - he is a fickle chap and not worth much. I had a letter from Ellena last night - the best one I ever read from her. She told some news which I won't repeat, as she spoke of writing to Mother at the same time. I am very glad, however, that Henry has entered the army. Think it will be a good school for him, for I have seen more young men improve under army discipline than the reverse.

In my own battery, some of my non-coms. that I most trust and confide in were worthless almost a year ago. One in particular, who I am just making a sergeant, and entrusting with the whole care of the discipline, &c. of the barracks, was a gambling, drinking fellow - reduced from corporal once; but show a really open hearted fellow of such a temperament some confidence, and he will repay it sure. This man's name is Atkins. I am suffering from a queer botheration today. Was officer of the day yesterday, and went to bed at midnight with cold feet, and this morning my calves are so sore and lame that I can hardly stand. My feet have an impressible tendency to be cold always - much to my disgust. I have no very sick men now except with the measles, and all doing well as yet; two in small-pox hospital who are recovering. The Atlantic came the other day. Seems to me the Chronicle is rather flatting out. Its imitation of the Observer's "Secular" &c. is bad; destroys the character of the paper, and in fact it is pretty much all secular now, and not so good as the Herald either. I am expecting Mother and perhaps Mary to come down and see me about next May, when things get settled &c. I have no idea that we shall leave here in the spring. We hear that Col. Benton is not so well since he went to Brattleboro to get the rest of our recruits. Will stay North another thirty days.

With much love to all,

Aldace F. Walker

Fort Stevens, D.C.
Jan. 20, 1864

Dear Father:

I received your long letter today. Can't get up as much of a reply as I would like, as I am rather down in the mouth today and want to go to bed. I went to town yesterday to see about correcting muster-in rolls of those of my men who have enlisted here, some six. Found a good many friends in town, ate a big dinner that did not agree with me, and today I feel pretty much bunged up. Think I shall be all right, however, when my stomach gets settled. I have now got my full complement of officers and non-commissioned officers, all armed and equipped and ready for duty - quite a corps of us. Still my battery now lacks seven of being full. We are expecting another squad every day. The measles are running like wild fire among our recruits; none have died yet however. I have one whom I fear will not live - quite an old man, and the measles go hard with him.

About the new Majority - there are three or four possible candidates, with not much show for any of them to "do anything" about their chances. Col. Warner keeps his own counsel, and in fact I rather doubt whether he has made up his mind as to whom he wants. I knew of course that I had been talked of in connection with the matter. Benton is very anxious that I should have it, but does not have much to say. I had not heard of the Col.'s remark to Hyde, and have never supposed my chances were worth figuring on, or paid any attention to the matter at all. If it falls to me, it won't be the result of any scheming; and that don't do much good in our regiment any way. Still, I think I am like to retain my present position, for the circumstances are as follows. The senior captain, Rice, has been pitched upon by men from Orleans Co. and pressed upon the Gov. as a candidate for promotion, claiming it as a county thing - rather for another regiment, but of course including this if a vacancy should occur - and I think Gov. Smith will be likely to lay some stress on the matter. Still, there are some drawbacks against the man, and if Col. Warner chooses he can bring good and strong reasons for not appointing him. Still, I had rather have him than either of the others. The 2d captain, Buxton, is thought of some, but is not much of a "military" character. The other captains above me are nowhere. I am 6th.

A great many think our Adjutant stands a good chance to obtain the position, and I don't know but he does. Still, I should be rather sorry to have him have it - should prefer Rice by far. By a rather singular coincidence, I had a line from Jed Baxter today speaking about a sergeant's "posish" for his brother, which I had given him before, and suggesting that I apply to his father for assistance in getting the Majority. I don't think I shall, for I don't like the style; think it will do more harm than good, and besides Baxter's name is on Rice's paper. So I think I shall just sit still - expect nothing - and won't be a bit disappointed. I think Mary had better keep on with her "lessons," and hope before long she will strike a teacher who can "finish," with taste and style. I can't see for some reason or other, and don't know what sort of marks my pen makes, so will stop scrawling.

With love to all,

Aldace F. Walker

Fort Stevens, D.C.
Jan. 24, 1864

Dear Father:

I have had rather a busy day. We had our inspection of the Post at 10, and that took till noon. And, by the way, 10 was just as soon as I had got up, had breakfast, bathed me and changed my clothes, for I have got into the habit of reading or writing late nights and rising at eight or half past as I used to I college, and I should like abed just as late if I went to bed at nine, so the evening arrangement is clear gain. Mr. And Mrs. Baxter came up during the inspection, and from them I learned that Col. Warner's father had reached here. As I knew Emma Allen was coming with him, I got on my old horse, rode over to Slocum, and made a call. Found her just as she used to be, and glad to see me. She is to stay a couple of months to "learn housekeeping," and I presume I shall see her again. I got back to dinner - found Austin back again, he having come in on the same train that I did - and had a capital time of course. My lieutenants moved out at once into a little place fortunately vacant.

Dress-parade as usual; and after parade a four hose load of clothing came to be counted over and receipted for, and not all my requisition filled either. I drew, by the way, 144 pairs of mittens. Then I had my next month's supply of fuel for self and company to look after, and make requisition for, which took some writing. Then Major Hunsdon dropped in, and soon very unexpectedly Wm. T. Nichols, late Col. of the 14th, who has been visiting with us through the evening. Add to it all that I am not just well, having a cold with a little feverish tendency - not sick of course, but I have been just a little off the hooks for a week. I am to be officer of the day tomorrow; but as our new 2d Lts. Act as officer of the guard now, shan't have much to do. Sherman is on tomorrow. And by the way again, please tell Nicholson that his friend Lewis is a 2d Lt. in C., and Patch is a Sergt. and doing finely. Circumstances were such that I don't think anyone felt very much hurt at the promotion of Bedell, except perhaps Gilman, who is recruiting and who is not fit to be even a sergeant. Baxter may have expected it some, and my 1st Sergt. Hudson some, but I don't think either of them had set their hearts upon it much.

We are drilling all the time now that the weather will allow - and the weather is splendid, like a Vermont April. We have rather slighted artillery of late, drilling at infantry for the benefit of the new men, and on account of the mud in the fort. I have drilled my company a good deal at the skirmish drill, and yesterday a battalion drill was ordered at the post, and the Major set me at it. I divided into eight companies, and had a very respectable regiment, and a good drill. We have over 600 at the post. Regiment has 1836 - just full. I presume the new Major has been recommended, but I have no idea who it is - the Adjutant, I presume. My February Atlantic has come before I got the other fairly read. One of my men died Thursday of measles - quite an old man, and I saw from the first that they would go hard with him.[9] Most all of my recruits are having the disease, and it is rather a bad season. Several have already completely recovered however.

With much love to all, as ever,

Aldace F. Walker

Fort Stevens, D.C.
Jan. 27, 1864

Dear Mary:

I am rather tired tonight - have had a hard day's work - but feel very well in other respects. I don't see where Father got his idea about my sore eyes, for I certainly have not complained of weak vision since last fall. I received your long letter and his long letter this afternoon - our mail comes about three now - and of course was very glad to receive them and read them. I am glad on the whole that I find so much to busy myself about, for army loafing is neither very pleasant nor profitable. I wonder if you are enough of a grammarian to decide whether that "nor" should be "or" or not, and whether you are enough of a Latin scholar to decipher the old "puzzle," "Equus est in stabulum, sed non est." I rather enjoy what writing I have to do now, for I am using a bottle of "Arnold." Well, this forenoon the Brigade Inspector was around on a tour of condemnation, examining all of our accumulated stores that had been broken or damaged by us, &c.

It was quite a job to get the stuff together and look it over, and there were quite a lot of papers to get out. My right bower, Pike, is a little off the hooks - sick a bit - and I have found a boy among my new recruits that takes his place and does my clerking very well. His name is Williams, from Dorset, I believe. I know he was in Sergt., now Lieut.,

Gage's office in Rutland when I was at home. This afternoon we had another Battalion drill here, and I was again delegated to do the drilling.

It is rather hard work any way, but all the harder today on account of a rather peculiar circumstance, namely the heat, which was really oppressive. We sweat as we would in June. But I presume we shall have to pay for our fine weather next month. Perhaps this is a "weather breeder." The ground is now perfectly dry, and the weather and all is the finest I ever saw - too good to last. Of course there is some mud in some localities, but we have none. I went to Slocum last night, and had a visit with the "Allen girls" that seemed like old times. Mr. Warner is here yet. I am very glad you are getting on so well with your music, and take such an interest in it. I want you to try and find out the meaning of every piece you play, with particular reference to the expression. Your piano is susceptible of a great deal of variety, and that is the beauty of good playing - the soul of it. I want you to love good music for the sake of it, and when you can play the minor symphonies of the Masters well I shall call you a good player. In order to do that, it is necessary to be master of the instrument and music, and not let them be master of you. Feel that you can and will take what liberty you please with them. A great many players play as some soldiers drill - as if the gun was too heavy for them. You want to be perfectly assured that if you feel that you want to retard or accelerate or swell or diminish you have a perfect right to, and will, and the notes and the piano have nothing to say about it any way. About the photographs, you will have to put some of them aside. It will be hard, I hope, to find albums for the countenances of all your friends, for the more friends one has the better off they are generally. Some of them must lie on the table or in the basket - and just about as well off too. The Tales of a Wayside Inn I will send on by and by. The Atlantics too, as fast as we get through with them. I have taken quite a shine to playing chess lately. Always like it, but enjoy it more than ever just now. Mr. Sherman from Clarendon Springs is in camp. He now has three sons in Battery C.

With much love to all, I remain, &c.,

Aldace F. Walker

Fort Stevens, D.C.
Jan. 31, Noon, 1864

Dear Father:

Another month has nearly gone, and our "three years" are nearly half expired. I don't exactly see how I am going to get away, however, at the end of the three years if the war should continue, for my company the new part of it, will be then big enough to require a captain for another eighteen months. We have had splendid weather the past month. A few days the latter part of the week were so hot that we had to seek the shade, and a dress-parade at Slocum Friday p.m. made us suffer more with the heat than many summer days that seem hot. I have had to have battalion drills all the week except Saturday, when it was drizzly. Am getting to be quite au fait in the trade. We have not had our inspection today - are waiting for Col. Warner at 1 p.m. I am pretty well nowadays; don't feel exactly natural, but am well enough for comfort. One of my corporals went home on furlough a while ago, and now has the small-pox in Stowe. I have had one man die of small-pox in the city hospital - another there who is convalescent. The measles have nearly run their race, and the health of my company is improving. I send two Atlantics today. I enclose a new photograph taken in camp. How do you like it? Also one of Major Hunsdon. Our regiment now numbers 1836. The new commissions have not come. Chaplain Little lives at Totten now, and we don't see him as often as we did. He had a prayer meeting Friday evening.

Evening - We had our inspection at one. Col. Warner ordered two of the batteries to report to him at Slocum tomorrow for another inspection, as they were deficient. Mine got along somehow. Mrs. Baxter was up to see her boy today. Also Morrill and wife. That Miss Somebody and young Barrett, who is stationed at the Washington Arsenal - in charge of the transportation, I suppose, which is quite a wheel, as they deliver all their issues. For instance, I make requisition for a dozen guns - they send them out here, and I receipt to the Quartermaster for them - and so of all issues. I went into the Fort with Morrill, and they were present at our inspection. We had a meeting here this afternoon. I wish we could have a building to hold meetings in, as our barracks are not at all comfortable now convenient, filled as they are with bunks. If we had $200 it would build us just what we want, and if you were in West Rutland I should ask you to raise it. I have procured an additional furlough for a man to go home with my crazy man now in asylum. Shall get him discharged tomorrow. The business connected with that institution is done at the Adjt. Gen.'s office, and is very prompt.

Fort Stevens, D.C.
Feb. 3, 1864, Evening

Dear Father:

We have had a windy, cold day today - quite uncomfortable. I am officer of the day, but my duties have been principally confined to staying in the house and keeping myself warm. It has been rainy since Sunday, but has all froze up again now. Nothing especially new here now. It is getting to seem like home again, or at last - this camp life; and well it might, for we have (Bat. B) been here for sixteen months and more - are acquainted in the vicinity - know the surroundings and the by-paths - and on the whole feel located and localized. I have been interrupted by some fifteen or twenty non-commissioned officers coming in to recite in tactics - hear a lesson every other evening - rather enjoy it, for I have a bright, studious set of boys and men, and I learn something myself withal, as I always do teaching. But I like to "set the boys up," and I hope we are all improving in the knowledge of our duties.

Col. Gibson, we are very much gratified to hear, has got into trouble. I send a slip from the Chronicle giving the statement. I understand that Gov. Curtin is at the bottom of the matter, and if he don't succeed, that two of his captains have a string of "charges" ready to "shove." Curtin has wanted to get rid of him for some time, as he has found him decidedly obstinate, and by no means a ready political "tool." Don't blame Gibson so much for some of those things as for some others, but hope he will go back to his regiment in the Regulars and we shall see him no more. I went to the city yesterday. Had been trying by proxy to get a man discharged from the Govt. Insane Asylum, and succeeded in getting the whole matter into a snarl, which I had to unravel myself at last. Saw Col. Townsend, and blew the thing through with some bother, and started the man for Vermont with an attendant - getting home by one p.m. Rather a lucky forenoon's job on the whole. Govt. pays a discharged soldier's fare home in rather a queer way - allows them to foot it at twenty miles a day, and give $13 a month for the time, with 30c. a day ration - good mileage on a journey to Vermont. I think I know someone who may teach your school - my friend Miss Bugbee. I don't know what you can give, and don't know as she wants to teach - perhaps she don't; though she is teaching, to give her sister a few weeks rest, in Hartford, Ct. now. She was in my class at Meriden, and a good Latin scholar - has studied French some. I will write to her tonight, and find out something more soon. She is undeniable "smart" any way. But such schoolmaams as Emily don't grow on every bush; she is rather a marvel in that line.

With much love to all,

Aldace F. Walker

Fort Stevens, D.C.
Feb. 7, 1864, Evening

Dear Father:

I am feeling very well this evening, and much like writing. Am experiencing but one inconvenience - I am too hot; due not so much to the outdoor temperature, which is quiet mild, as to the coal stove at my back. My bedroom door, however, will soon remove the trouble, as the window there has not been closed for a fortnight. We had a Post inspection by Maj. Hunsdon, Com'dg. At 11 this morning. He is living just now in Col. Benton's house, though he has a house ready for him at Slocum. I opine, however, that he will stay here, and the new major go to Slocum when we get one - in which case he will have an additional building, probably at the left of mine. His rule here is very easy, and everything moves smoothly as possible. He is now holding a Regimental Court-martial, in which he finds more work than is his wont, for he has to be President, Recorder and Court. I enclose photographs tonight of my two lieutenants, Bedell and Dunham and Capt. Lee of B. He, by the way, was a delta kappa at Amherst. Bedell is the one with whiskers on his chin. Dunham has on rather a ridiculous smile, which is not exactly natural.

I went to Slocum yesterday about noon and visited at the Col.'s till five or so, staying there to dinner. And there was one thing connected with the dinner that reminded me of old times - Tillie's coffee. It always ran in that family to make splendid coffee, and she got something out of what our Commissary furnishes that was infinitely superior to anything I ever saw evoked there from anywhere else. I have got to go to the city tomorrow on rather a strange errand. We received notice a day or two since that one of my men was discharged, for which I had applied. The discharge, however, has not come round, and as it generally reaches us before the "notice" in such cases, Col. Warner thinks it must be mislaid in some of the city offices, and wants me to go and look it up or get a duplicate. The mortality among my new recruits rather frightens me. I have lost six since January 1st - two yesterday, of pneumonia; one of them died of small-pox. I have one or two more quite sick, though my sick list is not nearly as large as it has been. The proportion through the regiment has not been as large - of deaths, I mean - though many companies have had more men sick. I hope, however, we have got nearly through with it, as the measles have been round, and the small-pox seems to be played out. We keep sending men home on furloughs, and I am very glad of it of course. Hope it will last for some time to come. There is no telling what form the military operations of the spring will take, but it would be really wonderful if we did not get moved away in May or so.

Meanwhile we must enjoy our comforts as best we can. Unless the rebels-"Lee's Miserables" or Longstreet's[10] - succeed in piercing Grant's line, it seems as though the military occupation of Virginia must cease. If so, goodbye Washington for us. I hope and trust we shall be able to hold 'em where they are, for if we do they must certainly fall back further. So late a winter will bring a late spring, however, I fear in this vicinity. It is perfectly dry now. Col. Benton is improving, and is expected back on the 18th. There is another Gen. Court-martial now at Totten, with Maj. Chamberlain for president. I am not affected by it in any way, as none of my lieutenants from this Post are engaged on it. Well, I must doze again. Think of me as contented and comfortable and moderately busy, and accept much love for all.

Aldace F. Walker

Fort Stevens, D.C.
Feb. 11, 1864

Dear Father:

I did not write my usual letter home yesterday. It was a busy day for me, and I really found no time when I could wedge it in. I am afraid that its failure to come on time will cause you some anxiety, but will try and not let it pass again. In the forenoon yesterday I drilled the battalion here. I am now president of a board of investigation into certain claims made by a farmer in Montgomery County, Maryland, for damages done by our picquets last spring in the burning of rails, &c. He sets his damages at $313. We visited his farm and measured the fence destroyed on Tuesday. Yesterday at noon we met at Slocum and took testimony from soldiers there. Today we rode out to the farm again at ten, came here and made further investigations, assessed damages ($131), and meet at Slocum in the morning to agree on our report, and sign. We shall try and come to terms with him however, and I sent my recorder there again this p.m. to tell him of our appraisal. I presume that Mr. Brashear, the victim, will be at our session tomorrow, and that further action will be deemed necessary. I attended parade last night, heard a recitation of my class in the "School of the Skirmisher," and then we were unexpectedly summoned on a mock court-martial, which lasted so late and tired me out so thoroughly that I did not feel like writing and concluded to postpone.

We had lots of fun last night. Capt. Templeton was the criminal, and the charge was chewing tobacco in violation of an agreement between him and Lt. Lewis. The one who was detected in the first violation was to forfeit his watch, which was the sentence we rendered against the captain. I enclose Maj. Hunsdon's order convening the court, that you may see a specimen of our camp fun. It is a wonderful "spell of weather" this. A little cold, but pleasant as can be. I am beginning to hope that our winter will be comparatively mudless. It seems Butler's Richmond expedition failed. I can't see why it need not have been successful. I received today Morrill's speech on the reciprocity treaty under his frank, so he has got me located it seems, and perhaps will remember me if I should ever want anything of him which I hope won't happen. We have heard nothing as yet of our Junior Major. I see Emma Allen quite often, and it seems quite natural too. I supposed I had done with the society of those girls when I left Middlebury. We hear nothing of any imminent pay day. I have spent over $170 since Jan. 1st, and none of it my own money - not much of it spent for myself, of course. I rather thought you would take to wearing spectacles before long, but I think it will look funny to see you. Do you write any sermons now? I have written this between dinner and parade. Must close now.

With much love,

Aldace F. Walker

Fort Stevens, D.C.
Sunday, 5 p.m.
Feb. 14, 1864

Dear Father:

We have been decidedly on the go of late, for troops doing garrison duty. This fine weather has stirred up the exhibiting proclivities or our superiors, and they seize upon every opportunity to show of us and themselves. Friday and Saturday forenoon we had to march four miles or so to Fort Bunker Hill for Brigade review, drill, &c., which is a kind of exercise that may be very valuable and profitable in a military point of view, but is very apt to produce a feeling of weariness in the lower limbs of those of the subjects who are neither "Field nor Staff" and have to pedestrianize on all such occasions. It may be augured from this that we are to take the field in the spring, but I can't see the connection. It is very likely, however, that the theater of war will change its base the coming season, and that we shall be located somewhere nearer the rebellion. If it does not turn out so, it will be strange - as I thought last spring when it didn't. Col. Gibson is in command of the Brigade still, though the odds are against him very decidedly.

Today we heard nothing about any regimental maneuver, and had fallen in for a quiet inspection at home, when an order came for us to appear at Slocum at two o'clock "without knapsacks." So we went at the proper time. Meanwhile, the wind had risen, wonderfully, extraordinarily, and the dust blew almost miraculously. It was with the greatest difficulty that we formed our line under the storm of sand - (I think now, by the way, that our men will stand bullets) - we got off - got the regiment together - and could hardly stand in our places. The inspection was very brief, and we got home to dinner at three. We are having lots of company nowadays. The fathers and relatives of officers and men are visiting us and other friends too numerous to mention. Today, Clement and Johnson, two of my Meriden classmates from Woodstock, came out, with a brother of Clement. They are all city clerks. Johnson is secretary for Collamer's Post Office Committee, being Collamer's grandson. My Board have adjourned and reported - compromised with the old man by cutting down his claim from $313 to $148.70, and assessed the damage on five companies, mine not included. I have no doubt but that the claim is just, and hope the money will be promptly handed over. I began my talk by requiring him to take the oath, which he did without much reluctance. Otherwise than our drills, &c., all is progressing very well as usual.

I call on the Allen girls occasionally, and they returned one of my calls last evening. We expect Col. Benton again on Wednesday. New commissions have arrived, filling our complement of line officers, but the new Major is not appointed. I mistrust that the Col. recommended Burrows, and that Rice has applications, &c., on file there of considerable influence, and a discussion is in progress; but I don't know anything at all about it. I suppose Hunsdon will go to Slocum when Benton returns. I should hate terribly to have anything occur which would throw Maj. Chamberlain into the command of this Post, for we find a good deal of fault with his excessive martinet ideas of discipline, &c., and he is an unpleasant man to be with, though a good officer in many respects.

The 3d Vt. Battery is at Camp Barry, near Fort Lincoln. They are already well spoken of. I have seen a good many of them - find that I am acquainted with some of the officers. They are to get their guns this week - I understand sooner than usual, on account of their proficiency in the preparatory drill. The old regiments are returning. I see them occasionally in pieces. I am going to town tomorrow for company savings. I presume we shall have some cold weather when this mammoth wind subsides-rather hope so for varieties sake. It is getting dark and I must close.

With very much love to all of you and Aunt Minerva, I remain as ever,

Ald'ace F. Walker

I have not come across Charley. Should think he would call around if anywhere in the vicinity.

Fort Stevens, D.C.
Feb. 17, 1864

Dear Father:

Our weather has changed, most emphatically changed. Today has been the coldest day of the season, and the coldest I have seen in the District. It is possible that the thermometer may have been lower at some other time, though I doubt it; but we are having a piercing, driving north wind, before which clothes are of no account whatever, and which chills one to the marrow in a moment. It really seems quite natural for winter weather. There is no snow, though some fell Monday and some yesterday; but it has all blown away, not melted, and the dust is blinding. I have been hearing my class recite tonight. We have finished the company drill, and I am going on with a part in battalion drill, and am to turn over the rest of Dodge in artillery - those that have not hitherto recited so much. My coal stove is a jewel tonight. It is red all over, and I am as comfortable as you please. I was in the city with Austin on Monday, (He is reading Addison out loud, and bothers me). Drew savings for January, $86.75, and visited Congress in the p.m. The House was voting and bothering, but the Senate was at work; and there was the neatest little spar between Fessenden and Wilkinson I ever saw, in which the Minnesota man came down on the Army of the Potomac and cracked up the West, and got handled pretty roughly - in fact, effectually used up. It seems that a campaign has commenced in the south-west. I am glad to see our army take the initiative in anything. Hope it will do.

With much love to all,

Aldace F. Walker

Fort Stevens, D.C.
Feb. 21, 1864

Dear Father:

I am in rather a resting than a writing mood tonight, which is not very pleasant of a Sabbath evening. This forenoon we were expecting orders, and I improved the time by having the men fall in and inspecting property, getting a roll of articles lost to be charged on the next muster roll. It was quite a job, amounting in fact to a complete inventory of all my ordnance stores; but I could not get the men together on any other day, and it occupied the time while we were waiting. We reported at Slocum at two. Had a drill in the manual and firings, an inspection, and a dress-parade. Got home about five, and in good order for my dinner. Lots of company today, for it has been a most beautiful day, and the Washington holiday - Baxter and wife, though the son is just now in Campbell Hospital, a little, not much, sick. I presume Portus is intriguing a little about our new Major. It seems to be settled that the Governor has refused to commission the man the Colonel recommended. What will happen next I don't know, nor care much. N. B. Smith was out, and North, and others, Vermonters, but strangers to you, as perhaps these are. This weather is really wonderful. It was terribly cold last week, but has smoothed off again, and no mud yet; last year a month before this we were wallowing in a continual slough.

We have got up a drum corps at our Post within the past few months that is already a rival to the regimental band. The Drum Major of the 16th is a recruit in B, and he has got together four fifes, four drums, a bass drum and a pair of cymbals, and they rattle it off in style. I believe he intends to add some cornets. We have had quite a good meeting here this evening. The chaplain preached on, "If a man die, shall he live again?" Not as a matter of proof, but of inferences and lessons - very good too. I want another pair of boots - meant to have written you about it a week or more ago, but forgot it. Those I got last April are played out, and the top boots won't do for dress occasions for an officer of the line. I want a nice pair made at Valiquette's[11] on my last measure, like those he made last March, double calf, sewed, &c. You and he will conjure it up - what would cost me here from eleven to fifteen dollars, probably nine or ten there. I will find a chance to send for them by some of our furloughed men - Sergt. Thomas perhaps, as I understand he is going next from his company.

Col. Benton came home on Thursday morning with his wife and children. He was feeling pretty well; but took cold, and yesterday and today has been sick abed again. His doctors hardly think that it is his old disease, and hope that he will get out of it, but I fear that he will have to leave us. It is too bad, if so, for he runs this thing very smoothly, and Maj. Chamberlain is a bitter dose to take. I see men from the 3d Vt. Battery very often, and inquire for Hardy, whom I have not seen. He is a private, and is at present detailed in the hospital connected with Camp Barry, where the Battery is stationed. I had a letter from Sophronia Conway[12] the other day, making inquiries for a man in our regiment - brother to her hired girl. I looked him up, and answered last night. Tell Aunt Sylvia that my new shirts and drawers are the best I ever saw; don't shrink a bit, nor rip, nor wear out yet.

With much love to all,

Aldace F. Walker

I hardly think Miss Bugbee will wish to teach your school, though perhaps her sister would like it. I think Mother wrote me, however, that Mr. Congdon was to have it again.

Fort Steven, D.C.
Feb. 24, 1864

Dear Father:

I have not received your customary letter today - the first time it has missed for a long time. It still continues very pleasant and dry here today, though it has been very windy. We got over to Slocum in the forenoon, but it blew so that it was impossible to hear commands, and the drill was postponed. We are rather getting ready for a Division review or drill or something which is to occur sometime. There is nothing new here. Col. Benton is better. There is some considerable interest in a Fair at the patent office[13] for the benefit of Christian Commission and families of District soldiers. Mrs. Baxter is quite prominent, and Emma Allen is at work behind one of the tables. Well, I have nothing especial to say. We are anxiously expecting news from Mobile, and think it will be good when it comes. Goodnight. Love to all.

Aldace F. Walker

Fort Stevens, D.C.
Feb. 28, 1864, Noon

Dear Father:

This would be the last day of winter in an ordinary year, and the air seems most spring-like. I have been sitting in my house this forenoon with windows and doors open, as officer of the day, while the rest of the camp have been to Slocum for inspection; and they have just returned, so I have sent my Pike, who has been at work with me on the muster rolls, to dinner, and commenced to write to you. We have got our rolls well under way, but the muster is tomorrow, and we shall have more to do today. I began on mine Friday - as early as we dare, on account of the constant liability to changes. We were not paid on the last. Shall get four months pay on these as soon as they can be made up; but as we have to reinsert all the voluminous remarks of the last muster, with new ones besides, it is a vast job.

I am very well and continually busy. We went to Bunker Hill Thursday and Saturday - all for preparation for our Division review, which I suppose is to come next week - or this week rather. Yesterday we got away at eight, marched our four miles or more, passed in review, and drilled till we all were tired, and marched home again. I was immensely hungry for our three o'clock dinner, but not at all tired out. In fact, I think I am getting pretty tough. I know I am much more rugged than I used to be. Last night I rode over to Slocum; and as I wanted to consult Maj. Morrill about our new rolls, I got into an ambulance and rode to town with the Col. and the "Allen girls." After I did my business I went to the big D.C. and Christian Commission Fair, where Mrs. Baxter has charge of a booth, and Emma Allen, Julia Hodges, and others of my acquaintance, are table waiters. I had a capital time. The thing is got up in very good shape and taste - in a gallery of the Patent Office. I saw Foot and wife, who seemed glad to see me; also Winslow, B. F., and others. Julia H. is as lively as ever, and I shall call. Miss Swan, Mrs. Morrill's sister, was there, of course. Gov. Smith has been here, and has gone to the front, where the 6th corps is on the move. Adjt. Burrows will be the Major in all probability. My Sergt. Baxter is still at Campbell Hospital, but well enough to come back, and will after muster.

Evening - There has an order reached us to send home any New Hampshire voters on a twenty - five, I believe, are to go from our regiment, including Chaplain Little. I have got on with my rolls very well - Better than anyone else-and am feeling quite content tonight. We have an order to go to Bunker Hill for Brigade muster - hope and think it will rain. We did not have any meeting here today. When we do, I start the tunes, and the boys sing "right smart." Maj. Hunsdon still sleeps in our quarters. Don't know what is to be the final arrangement of our "Field."

With much love to all, as ever,

Aldace F. Walker

----

1 Sergt., later Lieut., William G. Dunham, Morristown. RR.

2 Probably daughter or granddaughter of Vermont's U.S. Senator Jacob Collamer (1791-1865). Available from Discovery.com. Accessed 9 January 2002, from http://school.discovery.com/homeworkhelp/worldbook/atozhistory/c/723277.html; Internet.

3 Probably sister of Ruth Swann Morrill, wife of Vermont's U.S. Rep. Justin S. Morrill. Available from FamilySearch International Genealogical Index v4.02, accessed 9 Jan. 2002 from http://familysearch.com/Eng/Search/frameset_search.asp; Internet.

4 Sergt. Charles M. Edgerton. Co. C, 10th Vt. Infantry. Later commissioned 2nd Lieut. and assigned to the 25th U.S. Colored Infantry 1/8/1864.

5 Dr. Jedediah H. Baxter, NU 1856. Served as a Surgeon in The Army of the Potomac, and 12th Mass. Infantry. Also served at Judiciary Square and Campbell Hospitals in Washington, and as Chief Medical Officer, Provost Marshal General's Bureau. Son of U.S. Representative Portus Baxter. Poirier, 290.

6 Sergt., later Lieut., William Hudson, Stowe. Co. B and D. Wounded 10/19/1864.

7 Edward Herbert Randall (1837-1918), Northfield, MC 1862, ordained 1864, rector of Grace Church, Randolph, 1863-1866. Died Poultney, Vt. Robinson, 166.

8 Charles Clarke Harris (1837-1886), West Brattleboro, MC 1862. Ordained deacon 1862, priest 1866. Died Parsons, KS. Robinson, 164.

9 Private Gardner W. Chase, Jay, who had enlisted 11/7/1863, age 38.

10 CSA Gen. James Longstreet.

11 Chaffee, a hometown tailor?

12 Probably wife of Capt. Daniel Conway, 17th Vt. Infantry, mentioned in Walker's letters several times.

13 Patent Office, 7th and F Streets, Washington, D.C., across the street from the Post Office. Leech, 8.

11.
Quite Ready to be Sent Somewhere
March to mid-May, 1864

Fort Stevens, D.C.
March 2, 1864

Dear Father:

I am late this evening - time to say that I am well - got my rolls all in straight - am getting up my monthly returns. We have snow on the ground. It will be sloppy for a while, I expect. As ever,

Aldace F. Walker

Fort Stevens, D.C.
March 6, 1864

Dear Father:

Before I commence to write anything else, I want to say that my sheets are played out, and when my boots come I want about three more; and also a dark blue vest from Chaffee's; so there will be something of a bundle. Perhaps I shall think of something else next time. We are to be paid as soon as Maj. Morrell can get his rolls figured up - first of his regiments. So I shall get a little lump of $500 and odd - your yearly wages. I have had money enough all along, though none of my own since December. Still in January and February I have had and spent over $200. I have kept a close account, and shall come out square, though it will cost something to pay my debts. I have my company fund audited to date, and my monthly returns in and on the whole am as square with the world and the government as one in my poverty stricken circumstances could well be. It has snowed and rained some of late, and though it is dry around here it is muddy elsewhere, and our regiment has lain on its oars of late. Inspection this p.m. at two, at home. I am writing about noon.

Board with Foster and Sweetland now. Have two meals a day still. The days are long enough for more, but I can't persuade myself to get up any earlier in the morning, and the rest are very much of the same mind. We keep pretty late hours here - both night and morning. There is a Board of Field Officers in session in the regiment now, trying to get rid of some of the recruits that the Vermont scare foisted on to the service. We have some fifty or so whose enlistment was a perfect sham. I am having a book case and writing desk made, nicer than anything of the sort you ever had, and mean to send it home sometime - black walnut front, &c. Our recitations are doubled now - every night, and of officers every other night. I have kept pretty close in camp the last week; have not even been to Slocum; but find something to busy myself about most all the time. Yesterday was a dull, rainy day. I read "Lear" out loud, and completed the March Atlantic, which is a very good number. We have more or less small-pox around here now - two deaths in the regiment of it lately - two carried away with it to general hospital from here yesterday - negroes around here having it all the time, and no way to keep the men from becoming exposed. In the house where my little nigger lives there is a case; of course he is kept out of camp. I have not had a death in my company for a month, and not much sickness now, save one or two cases which have been sent to Harewood Hospital. I hope we shall get rid of some of the chronic cases, and would like to prosecute the examining surgeons.

Evening - I have been to Slocum since parade, and made a few minutes call on the "Allens." Emma is to go home this week. Maj. Hunsdon has a fifteen day leave, and will start tomorrow. We are giving furloughs now at the rate of five per cent. of the enlisted men, which I hope will give them all (that is, all the old members) a chance to see Vermont. They are all anxious to go, of course. I have a pass to Washington tomorrow. Think I shall see Col. Streight, who is to speak before the Union League. I send a late "Harper," principally for the article on the President, which I suppose to be by George W. Curtis, its editor, and is very well written. There is an immense and very general feeling in the army for Lincoln. The soldiers all love him and esteem him, and want him kept in office. Though, by the way, this last abortion of Kilpatrick's was authorized by Lincoln, in opposition to the judgment of Meade, Halleck, Pleasanton, Stanton, &c. It was an experiment worth trying perhaps, though it proved a costly one. It is well, I think, that Dr. Child[1] has left Castleton, for the people there were becoming painfully conscious that he was failing. The grand-daughter is a big thing, and stands a very fair chance to be spoilt in the raising. I have also had a letter from Aunt Minerva, saying that Cousin Charles was at Fort Sumner. That is at Chain Bridge about five miles west of here, and where he was last winter, with the 1st Maine Art. I shall try and ride over when the going and weather get settled. I think I shall try and find Henry. I know where to look for Baker's Cavalry.

Aldace F. Walker

Fort Stevens, D.C.
Wednesday Evening [March 9, 1864]

Dear Parents and Sister:

I have been spending the evening with the "Allens." Emma leaves for home tomorrow. It has been a beautiful day. We expected to do a good deal of drilling, &c., but at ten we got orders to stop drill, put our flag at half mast, and go to the city if we chose, to attend the funeral of Lieut. Caldwell, artillery officer on Haskins' staff. Almost all our officers went, but I did not care to and staid in charge of the camp - no very arduous job. We have a sort of a reading club - buy books in a lump and exchange - have just commenced - I got the first lot of books Monday. We have Blackstone, Charles the Bold, &c. I have read but one, the new novel, "Peculiar," which is very fair.

I went down to the city Monday, as you may infer from the above. Turned over some stuff to the Arsenal. Did not get my savings, but made a good many purchases. Found J. B. Page, Col. Nichols and Mr. Bliss of Brandon, and a heap more Vermonters. Went to hear Col. Streight with Smith, and to the Fair. Streight is no great shakes - a good looking man-without much education, though perhaps smart in a way. Called on Julia Hodges in the afternoon. Found Mrs. Robinson, a sister I believe of Mrs. H., who said she knew you. Her husband is a Paymaster - also Mr. H. - and gave him your message.

The fair is a capital place to go and is crowded, but the receipts are principally at the door. Rumors are rife of changes of all sorts, resulting from Grant's promotion, &c. - in the army in general, and in our condition. Gen. Fry[2] suggests that battalions of the artillery regiments be sent to the field, as they have been the favorites in the recruiting, and as they are now so full. Gen. Canby[3] told Col. Warner of 10,000 men who are going on board gunboats soon - Col. Haskins, of two companies from our regiment on Provost duty, &c. We shall see.

Bully for New Hampshire if first reports are true. Hunsdon has gone home. I have got the best desk and book case in the regiment - worth, I guess, twenty dollars, though it cost me but two for the trimmings. No new Major's commission yet. Thank you for your kind offer about the "bond," but be sure and not let the mice get at it. I expected the North would be disappointed about Sherman,[4] when they came to find out what I learned from an authoritative source ten days ago, that his demonstration was only a big railroad raid, and not a military maneuver save as a distraction. Still, I suppose the cavalry made a failure. Well, I have been up till after midnight the past two nights, and it is eleven now, so I must bid you goodnight.

With much love,

Aldace F. Walker

Sunday P.M.,
March 13, 1864

Dear Father:

We have had a most beautiful morning, and an order for inspection at Slocum at 2 p.m. Had a shower about noon, which gave rise to an order countermanding the other. This reached us when it was clear again, and we had fallen in ready to start, so we formed line for a post inspection. Another shower drove us in at a double quick, and now it is pleasant once more. So this has been rather an easy day in that line, but our pay rolls came up last night, and today they have been signed, preparatory to pay day tomorrow. I shall get $506.03, quite a little sum after my debts are paid. Nothing new in camp nowadays. The story of two batteries going to the city for provost duty is probably true, but the order has not come yet, and when it does I shall not go according to present arrangements - at the request of Col. Benton. He is comparatively well now, and much as he used to be of old. I never had any trouble with him - in fact, am rather his "right bower," drilling his battalion, &c. About those things-get them together, and then when I make up my mind I will give directions about the transportation here. I want full, or nearly full, width sheets, partly worn as good as any. I think one of my men will take them at your depot on his way hither in a fortnight or so - though I am in somewhat of a hurry for the boots. We are to be full of money tomorrow - over $100,000 coming to the regiment. I would like very much to comply with Mother's suggestion and spend a few days at home now, but on the whole think it best to wait till August or September. I know the ropes pretty well now, and can get what I want if anyone can. Charley Walker called here the other day when I was in the city. I shall go and see him when the traveling gets better that way - the roads are mud.

Fort Stevens, D.C.
March 16, 1864

Dear Father:

We have had rather a cold raw day of it. Not so much so, however, but that I had one of my battalion drills this afternoon; and towards evening was sent unexpectedly to the city with some over $7000, going home from this post. I saw M. B. Smith, who is all right; has a good comfortable boarding place, and a nice time I presume. We were paid off on Monday as we expected. It took about $120,000 to pay the regiment. No news as I know of. I think I told you that Chaplain Little was at home. He has had his leave extended for fifteen days to raise money for a chapel, &c.

With much love, as ever,

Aldace F. Walker

Fort Stevens, D.C.
March 20, 1864

Dear Father:

We are having pleasant weather thus far in our Equinoctial - a beautiful day, and on the whole a quiet one. Our inspection was by company at 4 p.m. Yesterday we went to Fort Bunker Hill. Got some tired, though not much. I have not been doing any especial of late but my usual routine. We have commenced target practice again on Tuesdays and Fridays, which will probably last a month or so. I am detailed on another General court martial, to convene at Fort Stevens tomorrow. Col. Benton is president, and Lieut. J. A. Lewis, Judge Advocate. This last for Nicholson's benefit, if you choose.

I have been intending to send for Mother to make me a visit sometime this spring; meant to wait till the season was a little further advanced, but as my court detail will give me some advantages which I shall not have by and by. I think that, as she says she wants to see me, she had better come on. I can get a comfortable place for her to stay close by, and can visit more with her than I could at another time, and go about more too. I shall expect her to start about next Monday. Is it sudden? So much the better. A little visit at Hoboken won't be out of place, though probably better going than coming. I would like very much to see Mary too, if you think it is best.

I will send home what I can spare of my money when I can get to the city for a check. I have got my debts nearly paid. Now I want Mother to be sure and start for these regions the first part of next week. It will furnish a fine chance to bring on my boots, you know. Capt. Fleming of Battery M. has received his commission as Major. Adjt. Burrows has his place. No other news as I know of.

With much love to all,

Aldace F. Walker

Fort Stevens, D.C.
Monday Evening [March 21st]

Dear Father:

I send herewith Riggs & Co.'s check for $200. I want Mother to take it and use what she needs in making me a visit, and be sure and come on the first of next week. I think probably that Mary had better come too. I want to see her ever so much, and it will be pleasanter for Mother to have company. If anyone happens to be coming this way so much the better; if not, some of the Hoboken folks will put her on to a train at Jersey City, and there is not trouble - I think no change of cars now - in getting to Washington. I may be able to meet her at the depot. If not, just get into a hack and ride out 7th St.

Aldace F. Walker

Fort Stevens, D.C.
March 23, 1864

Dear Father:

I received your last today. Shall be impatient to hear from your next regular letter, to find what you say of my proposed journey hitherward. I have quite got my heart set upon it now, and Mother must be sure and come, and Mary too I hope. Our court convened on Tuesday and tried five cases - none on hand today. We had a big snow storm last night, eight or ten inches, but it is drying off rapidly and will leave no mud. Maj. Hunsdon came home tonight. He will be located here; and I am quite pleased with it, for he is a very clever man to have around. Nothing new. I am very well. Have been looking for Henry C. some, but got misdirected. Know where it is now, however.

With love, goodnight.

Aldace F. Walker

Fort Saratoga, D.C.
March 27, 1864

Dear Father:

I have succeeded for the past two days in getting pretty effectually tired out by this time of night - the why, I will proceed to detail. My legs ache, but that need not hinder my writing; my hand is tired, as I have been writing since candle light and it is after taps, but that shan't stop me from writing a letter from my new headquarters. Two artillery regiments from across the river have been sent to the "forwards." Two from Haskins' division relieved them, as the north side is generally considered I believe to be less exposed. One of these relieving regiments was Col. Gibson's 2d Art., and ours was spread through the line of eight forts, so that now Col. Warner is a brigade commander, with one regiment in his brigade. Beginning on the east, Major Chamberlain with Batteries B. and L., garrison Fort Lincoln; Capt. Rice, F., Thayer; Capt. Walker, D., Saratoga; Maj. Fleming, M. and H., Bunker Hill; Maj. Hunsdon, A. and K., Slemmer[5] (one half of Co. A here) and Totten; Col. Benton, G. and E. at Slocum and C. and I. at Stevens. Col. Warner expects to locate his headquarters at Bunker Hill, in the center of the line. We are evidently located for the summer. I have an independent command, so does Rice - two little forts, eight guns each.

We receipt for all property, &c., and report to no one but Warner, and he won't trouble us. I am vastly pleased with this part of the arrangement. As there were quarters all along the line, we have double room now, which is also pleasant; besides being much more healthy, as the men were crowded before. At Saratoga, there were two line officers' quarters, an extra concern smaller, and one field officer's quarters, where Maj. Saddler had his office. Lieut. Lewis and myself have taken this last - three good big rooms, government furniture, &c. - and the lieutenants have divided the rest of the accommodations. Dodge has his wife here, and my 1st Sergt. Hudson has his wife also in the quarters next to the fort, (a 2d Art. P. V. Capt.'s quarters) and will board us. She is a very nice woman and cook. Lt. Lewis left today for Vermont for fifteen days. Our court-martial is dissolved, as some of the members have gone with the Pa. Vols.

I got notice Friday night at midnight to start my battery at 7:30 a.m., entirely unexpectedly, and to precede my battery and come over early to receipt for property. Went to bed and slept till reveille - told the boys to pack knapsacks, and was over on time. But there was a vast mess of plunder to move - most of which we should leave of course if we were to march further. In fact, I have had seven wagon loads come over, and have three more to bring. I have been vibrating over the five miles between here and Stevens on my old white horse, which is a great institution nowadays, though I imagine I look rather ridiculous.

I find the camp here in a very bad shape - very dirty - barracks poorly built-and more especially, the ground not at all graded. I have quite a serious job before me to get a good looking camp out of this. I have been cleaning and washing hitherto; shall go at the shoveling in the morning. I can accommodate Mother just as well here as at Stevens; in fact, she may like it better, for I have a room for her in my house while Lewis is gone, though she may think the bed rather hard. I can lodge her here, and feed her a few steps off at my boarding place, and visit generally. If she does not come, send on the things by Allen-and send them by him any way. I'll warrant him. By the way, he is a member of the brass band, which is now at Stevens. I have a little drum corps on my own hook. I have an adjutant (Dunham) orderly, &c. My candle is just going out, and my lamp chimney is missing.

Goodnight.

Aldace F. Walker

Fort Saratoga, D.C.
March 30, 1864

Dear Parents:

I was expecting to write you a long letter this evening, but at dusk an orderly came in with a heap of blanks and papers to make out, and I have been busily at work with Pike to help me from that time till now - nearly ten - and we are not through yet. It is the end of the quarter, which is always a busy time, and I have the fort returns on my hands this time, together with my usual company affairs. It has been the worst day of the season - snow and rain and sleet and wind and altogether. We have staid in the house mostly. I have improved the time by finishing the first volume of Charles the Bold. I enjoyed it very much. We are hard at work here every pleasant day in reducing our camp and surroundings to some sort of system. There were a dozen or so shanties and tenements for such of the men as had wives; scattered promiscuously anywhere and everywhere. I have moved such as I need for my laundresses on to a line with the quarters of the Ordnance Sergt. (a regular army sergeant, attached to the fort), and shall tear down the rest. I am grading outside, fixing and turfing the inside of the fort, tearing out the bunks in quarters and rebuilding them, and tearing up things generally. The men take hold with a will, for it is for our own comfort, and we are as happy as a mess of swallows building their nests under the south eaves of a New England barn.

I have received your letters announcing Mother's decision to stay at home. As Father suggests, there is one good thing about it - I got more letters from her than I ever did before in my life; but I can't quite see any reason for her not coming out, even yet. In fact, she has not tried to give any, only that she thought it wasn't best. Well, I suppose she knows; but I wish if it really wasn't best, that she didn't think so. I don't want to apply for another furlough, for there are still a good many officers that have not been home at all. I mean to by and by, however, when I get around to it - in the summer or early fall. I rode down to see Henry last night. He is only some four miles from our new camp. I would have brought him home with me, but he had no horse. He has a hard cold, but is looking well; and doing well, the officers say. I have got a new horse, left with me to keep and ride by Jed Baxter - a nice big bay, with saddle &c. complete. He agrees also to draw forage for him so I am in luck generally. We have been so busy here that I have not had time to be lonely, and don't mean to be. It will be a nice place to stay; and if we are to remain around Washington, I don't want to leave it. It is a great deal more retired than where we were before. Don't see anyone but what passes over the military road. Have communication with headquarters twice daily by mounted orderlies - in forenoon, and at dusk when the mail comes. Have our daily papers about noon.

Goodnight.

Aldace F. Walker

Fort Saratoga, D.C.
April 3, 1864

Dear Father:

We have had a stormy time of it for the last week. Have not been able to do as much toward fixing up our new camp as we wanted to. I don't know but it is sugar weather in Vermont, but this continual rain and snow and wind can be accounted for in these parts only by the supposition that the Army of the Potomac proposes to go somewhere. Still, we keep busy - in doors, if we can do nothing out. I have completely rebuilt the bunks in one of my barracks, and shall attack the other this week. I am gong to paint them, and on the whole do the best I can with my camp and its surroundings. Maj. Sadler, the old Post Commander, comes around here occasionally, and it astonishes him to see how we go to work. He is the one who commanded at Massachusetts when we first went there.

I keep very well, and am much better contented here than I was at Stevens. I am my own boss, you see, which is a pleasant arrangement. The men like it better too, for I am disposed to grant all the favors I can, and they understand it so, and are much less disposed to take advantage of a free giver than of a stingy one. They behave first rate, and come to time right along. As you and I expected, my young Baxter has proved more of a bother than an advantage to me. He is smart, and tries to learn moderately well; and so gets on pretty fast, though not nearly as fast as he might. Still, he is making now a good duty sergeant. But of course it causes dissatisfaction among the other boys - and then he has his company - and they intercede and take him off - and he was sick once, and went to the Campbell Hospital and staid a good while after he got well. And did not take to his work very well after he got back - and he is considerably "tough" in the metaphorical sense of the word, besides.

Well, Col. Warner told me the other day that he was recommended for a vacant 2d Lieutenantcy in Bat. I, told him I was "glad of it," and he said he "thought I would be." He hasn't a very high opinion of the youth. Still, he was under some obligation to his parents, and he cared less about Capt. Templeton than anyone else in the regiment. Won't the I folks grumble when it gets out. He will make a very passable officer I think, but I had rather have him elsewhere. It has given me an acquaintance with all our Congressional delegation except Collamer; but it is not my style to run after big men, and I have not been near Chipman's, where our delegation board, except when I have had business there.

I was in town on Thursday. Fortunately, the clouds did not shed water, or rather they did shed water - any way, it was cloudy and didn't rain. I had a nice time. Saw more acquaintances than I ever have met in the city at one time before; among them, Wm. Y. W. Ripley, with whom I had a long conversation. By the way, I have heard that efforts were being made to brigade us with the 9th and 10th, and form a command for Stannard. I should like that well enough, for I think a great deal of Gen. S.; but don't know anything about it of course, and no more does Col. Warner. There are other stories around here - of the Veteran Reserve Corps being about to relieve us - of Col. Warner having his choice to go or stay, &c., &c. I give them for what they are worth, and meanwhile go on making myself comfortable. Col. Warner is about to build himself new quarters at Bunker Hill.

I have not been to Stevens for a week, and find enough to do and keep contented meanwhile at home. I have wandered a little from my city story, I see. I was going to say that in the evening I had the greatest treat I have had lately, in hearing Edwin Forrest play Othello. I don't care a fig for theatrical performances generally, but when I heard him, the most perfect elocutionist living, I enjoyed it thoroughly. The other parts were well carried out, and it was thoroughly enjoyable throughout. It is worth while to hear Shakespeare's sentences spoken by one that understands them knows how. I went with Capt. Lee, the present commander of Bat. B. Did I tell you of him? An Amherst Delta Kappa Epsilon, as big and tall as I am, and a thorough good fellow.

I am a little lonely now without Lt. Lewis. He is a capital fellow, and will help me a good deal. His furlough is now about half out. Send on those things by express, if you can't by Allen. I had a letter from Ab Mead last week. He says there is a good deal of religious interest in college, something of a revival. He writes well, and is a whole-souled fellow too. He says that Frank (B. F.) Blanchard is very sick.

About that Majority - I wasn't expecting it, principally on account of your "3d" - that Hunsdon and I were from the same company and county, and that the Col.'s own. I know he thought of me. Fleming is a fine fellow, and a good officer - from Bellows Falls way - has been in New York as a clerk-and was out three months in the 71st as a 1st Sergt. He wasn't made captain till after I was, though there was quite a debate at the time between his merits and mine. I reckon locality and the favor of Col.'s father and friends had something to do about that. I presume these "posts" were given to Rice and I as a sort of recompense for what we might have expected, as our command is now as independent as Fleming's - though to tell the truth, I don't know who else he could have trusted as well as us, with our steady companies.

I don't care much about the buttons on the vest; such bother is played out. I send the photographs Mother asked for, and the book. I have a good boarding place now, with Sergt. Hudson and his nice wife - three meals a day. I have got a new big sponge, and use it. We are now only three and a half miles from the city - a little nearer than at Stevens. These forts lie in a sort of a circle around the city. I have been answering up your old questions.

Love to Mary and all.

Aldace F. Walker

Fort Saratoga, D.C.
April 6, 1864

Dear Father:

I did not get your letter as I expected today. I presume the late immense storms have impeded mail navigation. It has rained or snowed almost incessantly here for ten days. Today has been comparatively pleasant, however, and I have improved it this afternoon by riding over to Stevens, &c. I like my new horse very much - he is stylish. I think I shall buy; he can be got for $75; would be worth $150 easy if it were not for a little trouble with his wind. He has been sick the past winter, and is not yet recovered quite, I think. We are getting on much as usual lately. Don't do much but read and loaf. But when it don't rain, we are busy enough. I have got in my property returns, all of them, this week, which has been quite a job. My responsibilities in this line are very much increased of late by the charge of post property, but these sort of things are generally in very good shape. I am very well, save a little of Job's affliction; which is a good thing, I suppose, though rather disagreeable. I wish some of my Vermont friends could see my new quarters. Many of them did see the old ones. Is Grant going by the Peninsula? It is evident on all hands that the spring campaign is going to be novel and vigorous. Burnside is getting up a big expedition, for Mobile perhaps, the 3d Vt. Battery included; and it is rumored that Hancock[6] will move on the Peninsula. We shall see. Perhaps I shall be a part. The officers left at Stevens are so many of them assigned to courts martial duty now that but three are left to do the work. I have more than that myself.

With much love,

Aldace F. Walker

Fort Saratoga, D.C.
April 10, 1864

Dear Father:

We have had more rainy weather, and when it rains it pours nowadays. Still, Friday was a fine day, and I improved it by riding my big horse to Fort Sumner, Bedell accompanying me on old Grey. It was some muddy, but we had a nice time, coming home by way of Chain Bridge and Georgetown, making a ride of some 30 odd miles. I liked the horse first rate, but sold him for Baxter the next day to Dr. Porter, as he wished. And by the way, he sent me out another tonight. Don't think I shall like him as well however. Well, I found Charley very well, and very busy, and he complained of being very ragged. I sat for some photographs by way of experiment, thought I don't much expect he will better the last, and he took an ambrotype, which I send you. He expects to hear that John is married, but has not heard so yet. We are all excitement nowadays concerning the "forwards" - more than usual, for reasons which I will proceed to develop.

Gen. Grant when he made his Vicksburg campaign felt the need of men to man his big guns, had to extemporize them, take them from gun boats, send north for them, &c. Well, he don't mean to be caught so again in a like contingency, and has ordered that an artillery (heavy) regiment be attached to the reserve artillery brigade of each army corps (now three). The two regiments that left this department a fortnight ago went in this capacity to the 2d and 5th Corps, but Sedgwick, in the 6th, has not got his heavy artillery regt. yet. Col. Warner served under him out west. Our regiment has a good reputation too, and last Thursday he made application for us at the War Department, telling Warner of it at the time. He got the promise that if any other regiment left the defenses this would be the one. Meanwhile Augur and our immediate commanders are complaining of the depletion of their forces, and Haskins and Gen. Barnard are going their best to keep us here. Warner wants to go very much. It is certain that if we go we shall have as good a "posish" as there is in the Army of the Potomac. Meanwhile, we are on tender-hooks. I think, however, Warner expects to take the field. Benton is certain we shall, and Sedgwick told Portus Baxter last night that the 11th was going with him; and Baxter is going to try and get the 9th assigned to the same corps.

I am so far from headquarters that I have to feed on rumors, but mean to ride over and see Col. Warner in the morning, and try and find out what he knows of the matter. I am getting things in shape; and if we do go, we shall have time enough, we are assured. Of course I shall let you know when the "marching orders" come. Meanwhile, I am as comfortable as can be here, and don't care particularly whether we go or stay. The worst thing is the foolishness and ridiculousness of our serving three years in an active army in time of war and never seeing an enemy - I can't quite swallow that, so shan't be annoyed if we move. Still, I like to let well enough alone. To answer a few questions. The north and south road by here is called the "back road to Bladensburg" - is an old road, and a very good one to get into the city on, though rather a hard one to find in the night. I was over to Fort Thayer today. Found a little four octave melodeon in camp, and was as happy as you please for fifteen minutes. I can run it nearly as well as I used to could. There is a good deal of interest now about the Harris affair in Congress; also about Emancipation in Maryland.

Maryland planters near here, and south-east, are letting their farms grow wild this spring, expecting the slaves all to be proclaimed free in May, by the "Convention." I send with this a couple of photographs of officers - names written on backs. I presume I may write a line tomorrow evening; if there is any new development in regard to the move question, I will. Don't worry. I will take care of myself the best I can, and I have the reputation here of being pretty good at that. The women in camp are in quite a fidget. I like to plague 'em, but am a little uneasy about it all myself.

Well, goodnight.

Aldace F. Walker

Fort Saratoga, D.C.
April 11, 1864

Dear Father:

I scratch off a few lines this evening, which I fear you won't be able to read, because I said I would, not because I have anything to say. I have been to town today to settle some of my old government account; succeeded in doing so; waited till four p.m. to find some news about our future, but failed to learn much. Col. W. saw Gen. Sedgwick just before I came away. He is to return to the front tomorrow, with no positive knowledge whether we are coming or not; though with the assurance from Augur that we shall go if any other regiment is detached from the defenses. He is to ask Grant about it, I believe. Well, this don't amount to much. We are all in the fog yet, but it don't seem so much like a start as it did - don't know why, however.

Goodnight. I saw Mr. Fisher today.

Aldace F. Walker

Fort Saratoga, D.C.
April 13, 1864

Dear Father:

We are having pleasant weather this week. Are enabled to finish our target practice and do some little drilling. I am not feeling so much like working on my camp as I was; don't like to lay out any especial labor for other folks to enjoy; so we drill and play ball. I was in the city on Monday fixing up my old accounts, as I believe I told you. We don't get any more news about our going to the "front," though Col. Warner still thinks we shall go. None of us expect to spend the summer here any way. Lt. Lewis has returned, and my military family is all about me. It will be quite an improvement as to work and pleasure. Well, I have a do deal to do, and mostly pen work.

Goodbye.

Aldace F. Walker

[Walker went home on a short furlough between April 13 and May 1.]

Fort Saratoga, D.C.
May 1, 1864, Sabbath Evening

Dear Father:

I am once more in my old quarters and writing to you as I used. I am very busy as I expected, and will give you a little account of my travels and labors, reserving a more detailed account for another time - which may never come. I got left at Troy as I expected, and had the pleasure of passing the night at the Troy House - only five minutes too late, and might have been in season just as well as not I think. Presume the hotels subsidize the conductors in such cases, as they hurried up right smart as the last end of the route when there was no chance of getting in. I got into New York at noon on Friday; ran around some with Charley Sheldon, whom I found after some trouble; took tea in Hoboken, and came on at 7:30 in a splendid train with no change of cars. (I did not see Aunt Minerva.) I got a good berth in a very nice new sleeping car, and did not wake up till I got to Washington depot. I started for camp on foot, and got out here at 7 a.m., before breakfast. I found the boys all right and everything straight; the muster rolls further along than usual - in fact, so that they were finished yesterday before dark. I was some footsore and did not go to the muster, which was at Bunker Hill, acting as officer of the day, while the Co. went. Had a lot of things to see to, however, and more today. We had our morning inspection, and then I had to compare the rolls here and take them to Slocum for final acceptance, which took nearly all day, so I went to Stevens to supper.

I am retained as counsel for one of our lieutenants, who is to be court-martialed soon, and shall have to work a good deal on his case. I have a lot of property returns to make out; my company savings returns also, and four sets of quartermaster's returns; also a requisition to get up of stuff necessary to complete the armament of the Fort - with other work too numerous to mention. We have lots of drill now. The regiment is organized into three battalions in order to have brigade drills. Now we are crowded in artillery for our inspection by Col. Haskins. We have no orders to go to the front, but the Invalid Corps is organizing for the forts, and Col. Haskins and others expect us to leave "after the first battle," and I think so too by what I see. I positively can't write any more tonight, as I have three other letters to write and it is after nine - and mean to get a bath before I get to bed.

Love to Mother, Mary and Belle, &c.

Aldace F. Walker

Fort Saratoga, D.C.
May 5, 1864

Dear Father:

I did not succeed in getting a letter off yesterday as usual. Was in town and did not get out till late in the evening; and when I did come, I did not come home but went to Fort Stevens to spend the night. I drew some Company Fund and did a good deal of other business; visited the Senate; had a long visit with N. B. Smith; found J. A. Lewis, who is judge advocate of the court-martial now in session at Fort Stevens, and who informed me that Lt. Gage's case was to come off today. So I rode up there instead of coming home. Today I have been busy with the case. We finished the prosecution, and the evidence on the defense, working all day for it. Tonight I have got to prepare the argument for presentation tomorrow. It adds a good deal to the labor of such as occasion, as everything has to be reduced to writing. It is lovely weather here now. As I was riding to the city yesterday, I passed several fields of grain over two feel high. All sorts of fruit trees are in blossom, and the trees are green. Around the President's and La Fayette Square it is cool and shady - and on the whole, the weather is thoroughly enjoyable. We have greens and such things in abundance.

We understand that the army moved yesterday, though the embargo is complete, no news at all getting in from the front. It is surmised that Burnside will lie around Manassas and Centerville to cover Washington while Grant outflanks the enemy. It is also rumored that Hooker and his Corps are at Harper's Ferry. This last is doubtful. Well, I am glad we know so little, and hope and trust we shall be signally successful. I saw Henry Post yesterday. He has finished his examination, but says he don't know whether he was successful or not. I opine he was not, because he told what an examination they gave him in Ancient History, &c., and made excuses - still he may be all right. Well, it is late in the evening. I have been hard at work writing my speech, and have got it into a sort of shape. I am really interested in the case, for I don't think him at all to blame, and I really hope he will be acquitted. Am sure the sentence will not be very severe; though if he was found guilty of what he is charged with, he would be cashiered. My big horse is lame - I believe I told you. I am riding old Grey now. I have got a nigger, in partnership with Lt. Lewis, and am ready to take the field on that head. But I am amazing sleepy.

Goodnight.

Aldace F. Walker

Fort Saratoga, D.C.
May 8, 1864

Dear Father:

It seems as if July was upon us before its time. The weather is most sultry - from 90 to 100 degrees in the shade. Well, the hotter it is the more out door work we have to do. Yesterday, the hottest day of the season so far, we had to brigade drill at Bunker Hill at ten a.m., which kept us from home till two, and then we returned nearly melted. For this drill, our big regiment is divided into three battalions, commanded by Buxton, Chamberlain and Hunsdon, and each battalion is subdivided into eight companies, a tactical regiment, though they are usually larger in our service. So we maneuver like a brigade, and the drill is good, though very tiresome for a company that happens to be, like mine, the 8th Co. of the 3d Battalion - or on the extreme left. I act as Major of Maj. C.'s battalion, and being field officer on foot isn't pretty play.

This morning it was hot again. I had my inspection at 9 a.m. to get it over with, and was just finishing it when an order came to go over to Fort Lincoln for a battalion inspection with knapsacks on. It was hard, but we went, and probably are the better for it. Don't know what we shall do when we are ordered to march into the "Wilderness" some of these fine days. I send you a slip from the Chronicle to show you the way in which our news reaches us - not "By Telegraph," and rather scanty information; we have to steal New

York trains for the details, but authentic as far as it goes, and so satisfactory. We are anxiously, most anxiously, awaiting further developments. It seems Smith is on the James instead of the York - glad of that - it looks like more pre-certainty of success. And Burnside is with Grant, and Sigel in the valley. Everybody here says that Hooker is there with his corps, but we don't get it in the papers, and don't know whether to call it so or not. Sherman is playing Patterson's game at the first Bull Run, and I hope he will be more successful. Well, a few of these days are of immense importance. The country is hanging in the balance. We feel more and more our liability to leave these diggings. In fact the new Mass. Heavy Art. Regiment, now at Alexandria, is rumored to be the one about to relieve us. When we get the result of the battle, in three days perhaps, we shall know whether we are to go or stay; and very likely this will be our last Sabbath in the "Defenses North."

Of course when we get any news of that sort I will let you know, for they aren't sending many letters from the "forwards" these days. I have had an incessant stream of business on hand the past week, as I expected; but am nearly out of the woods. I finished up my legal job on Friday; when the verdict is published, I will let you know. We have a breeze this afternoon that feels quite refreshing, and the scenery around is as lovely as green forests and fields can make it. Blossoms are everywhere too, and every color. I am sorry about that college pickle. It seems like not only folly but extravagance to run two, and because Middlebury has the most students now they are on their high heeled boots. My post sutler is in town today, and I expect news on his return. I can think of nothing else today but the army and the shooting. Love to Mother and Mary and Belle.

Aldace F. Walker

Evening - I have a little more news tonight. We have the extras, which report favorable news from the army. Still, they haven't been at it long enough to have any very serious bad news. I trust it won't come. We hear a rumor that Sedgwick is dead. Hope not, very much. Our city papers print a good deal of stuff that is mere rumor. The Star and Republican we get in the afternoon. The last is most absurdly unreliable. Still there is no use "greetin" till there is bad news. Col. Warner was along this p.m. Showed me an order from Col. Haskins to prepare quarters for one Co. of the new Mass. Heavy Art. At Stevens, Slocum, Bunker Hill and Lincoln, and the order said: "This is preparatory to removing your regiment from this command," Which is equivalent to "marching orders."

Two regiments of the Invalid Corps are also coming in here. Of course I shall go to work at once, and make all necessary preparations for a start. We can't tell when we shall go, or where; but without doubt we shall move soon, and somewhere - "across the river," Col. Haskins says. I am feeling very well, and am quite ready to be sent somewhere. With love,

Aldace F. Walker

Fort Saratoga, D.C.
May 11th, 1864

I have just time to say that we move by boat to Belle Plain, near Falmouth, as soon as transportation can be provided, which will perhaps be at reveille. I am getting things together. Sent a big box to you. Have worked a long while on returns, &c., and am going to try and get a little sleep, though orders may waken me at any time. I am well and send love.

Aldace

----

1 This is not Surgeon Willard Child, but probably another cousin of Walker's.

2 USA Brig. Gen. James Barnett Fry, A.A.G., Washington, D.C.

3 USA Brig. Gen. Edward R. S. Canby, A.A.G., Washington, D.C.

4 USA Maj. Gen. William Tecumseh Sherman, commanding Federal forces in the western theater, soon to begin his famous Atlanta Campaign. Boatner, 751

5 See Appendix A.

6 USA Maj. Gen. Winfield Scott Hancock, commanding the Second Corps. Boatner, 372.

Colonel
Asa P. BLUNT
6th Vermont Infantry
(Italo Collection)

General
William Thomas H. BROOKS
(Italo Collection)

General
Ambrose E. BURNSIDE
(Italo Collection)

Lieutenant
Charles W. Clark
11th Vermont Infantry
(Italo Collection)

Major
Richard B. Crandall
6th Vermont Infantry
(Italo Collection)

Captain
Chester W. Dodge
11th Vermont Infantry
(Italo Collection)

Colonel
George P. FOSTER
4th Vermont Infantry
(Italo Collection)

General
William B. Franklin
(Italo Collection)

General
George W. Getty
(Italo Collection)

Captain
Charles G. Gould
5th Vermont Infantry
(Italo Collection)

General
Lewis A. GRANT
(Italo Collection)

General
Ulysses S. GRANT
(Italo Collection)

General
Joseph HOOKER
(Italo Collection)

Colonel
Charles HUNSDON
11th Vermont Infantry
(Italo Collection)

12.
The First Vermont Brigade
By Aldace Freeman Walker

[Transcript of a speech by Aldace Walker before the Illinois Commandery, Military Order of the Loyal Legion of the United States, later published in Military Essays and Recollections, Chicago: McClurg, 1894.]

One of the greatest embarrassments of the Northern army throughout the war was the lack of permanence in its organization.

Immense armies were demanded, and were produced. Their efficient organization clearly required stability. The Division should have been the smallest permanent unit, to be solidified and preserved. Upon the usual basis, this would have furnished a body of ten thousand men constantly present for duty — a military unit easily handled in the camp, on the march, or in action and always ready to fuse and throb with mutual sympathy and self-reliant pride. As the years went on, more was heard of this or that Division; the reputation of many of our most successful generals was made while holding such a command. It is difficult to conceive what would have been the result if a given number of Divisions had been organized in 1861, and their ranks kept full to the end. But nothing of the kind was attempted.

There were, however, a few brigades in different portions of the army, the integrity of which was to some extent preserved. One of these was the organization known as the "Old Vermont Brigade." The adjective "old" was at first used to distinguish this particular brigade from a second Vermont Brigade of nine months troops, whose only battle was Gettysburg. At the last, the word involved the secondary idea of respect and affection, as when employed by the soldiers in speaking of "Old Grant," "Old Sherman," or "Old Sedgwick."

The first, or "Old Vermont Brigade," was organized in October, 1861, upon the soil of Virginia, a few miles south of Washington. After nearly four years of constantly active service, it was disbanded in June, 1865, at almost precisely the same spot. Its formation was suggested to General McClellan by Colonel William F. Smith of the 3rd Vermont, a distinguished engineer of the regular army, who was its first brigade commander. The command of General Smith soon took on the proportions of a Division; he afterwards became commander of an army corps, and was known familiarly as "Baldy Smith."

The original components of the Old Vermont Brigade were the second, third, fourth, fifth and sixth Vermont infantry regiments; all of which were enlisted in the summer of 1861 for three years' service. These organizations were represented in its ranks to the close of the war, by re-enlistments, though their ranks were not kept full, and at the last their numbers were greatly reduced. The 11th Vermont, after eighteen months service as heavy artillery in the fortifications on the North of Washington, joined the Brigade May

12, 1864. It had but two regularly assigned Brigadier Generals; there were many occasions, of course, when a senior Colonel was in command. Its first Brigadier was General W. H. F. Brooks [sic],[1] who afterwards commanded the Tenth Army Corps. His rule was firm and efficient, and his regular army education and experience were of great value. After his promotion, the command presently fell to Colonel Lewis A. Grant,[2] of the 5th Vermont, then the senior officer of the Brigade. He was subsequently made a Brigadier General, and led the Brigade to the end. Gen. Grant was afterwards Assistant Secretary of War when the Secretary of War was Redfield Proctor, who was at one time Major of the same regiment and is now a United States Senator. Gen. Stannard entered the army in the Old Vermont Brigade, and subsequently commanded the Second Vermont Brigade at Gettysburg.

A body of men like this, when subject to the stringent demands of active campaign service, soon becomes self-reliant and coherent. The touch of elbow which gives united action is felt throughout the organization. A sense of solidarity is developed, bringing the assurance that the fractions are not merely individual regiments, but are parts of a greater whole; and a continuing consciousness exists that support and assistance will not be wanting, if required. The Old Vermont Brigade received no factitious support from war correspondents. Metropolitan newspapers seldom found space to advertise its deeds; illustrated weeklies published no alleged pictures of its charges; but in the Army of the Potomac there was abundant appreciation of its merits. Its chief characteristic was not dash or display, but steadiness. There was no elaboration in its drill. The skirmish-line was its delight. The secret of its acknowledged preeminence on the battlefield was its extraordinary tenacity. Although its active service embraced more important engagements than almost any other similar command in the Northern Army, it was seldom if ever driven from its position by assault. It was famed for a certain quality of steady, quiet, intelligent courage, comparison with which was high honor.

At Sheridan's[3] famous battle of Cedar Creek, October 19, 1864, Getty's[4] Division, known as the Second Division of the Sixth Army Corps, was the furthest from the point of Early's[5] fierce attack at daybreak. Getty's second brigade was the Old Vermont Brigade, which held the center of the Division through the day. Getty's was the last division to come into the fight. It was moved by the left flank a mile across the field, and fronted to the right, thus forming its line in the face of the entire rebel army, which by that time had passed over the camps of the Eighth and Nineteenth Corps in Early's successful charge. Three of the Vermont regiments were at once ordered out as skirmishers into the dismal fog which enveloped the entire attacking line, and amid the tumult and dismay which covered the field with disaster. They deployed through a broad cornfield, diverging and gradually taking proper distances, then across a little watercourse, through a pasture, aligning instinctively and almost without a word of command, forward into the scattering grove even then occupied by the advance of the enemy, and on its furthest margin, where the rolling ground sloped away. There, with an open view to the front, five or six hundred skirmishers arranged themselves for battle, prepared to cover for a time the defensive position which Getty with the remainder of the Division was endeavoring to find and assume. It is believed to have been the first moment on that disastrous morning when the rush of the surprise was confronted by a skirmish-line well out in front of a line of battle; and by eight A.M. there was no other organization which could be seen or heard holding ground against the enemy.

Although the position was practically chosen by the men themselves, in the center of confusion and dismay, it was maintained in perfect steadiness, and with an entire understanding of a skirmisher's duty. The grove was held, with some loss, for an hour or more, until artillery was brought up by the enemy, and two lines of rebel infantry were distinctly seen advancing to drive back the Vermonters' skirmish-line. Then, receiving the order to retire, and assembling as they went, the three regiments took position with the rest of the Brigade, in the center of Getty's Division, — the only Union troops then in line of battle with their front to the foe. A determined stand was here made; a terrible artillery fire was silently submitted to; three successive line-of-battle charges were repulsed; and, after a desperate conflict, the Division eventually received and obeyed an order to retire, when two rebel divisions had executed a flank movement around its right. Moving back once more, this time in line of battle and with well-dressed ranks, Getty's Division presently faced about again, a mile north of the village of Middletown, and took up a new defensive position, with every regiment in perfect order. A new skirmish-line went to the front, and once more the true battle formation was presented. This was perhaps ten or eleven o'clock A.M. The fog had lifted and the day was bright. Cavalry formed on either flank. Two or three batteries of artillery rallied in the rear. Then the unexpected happened. General Sheridan, whose absence was known and deployed, was seen dashing down the pike, in hot eagerness to find the front line of his scattered army. The first infantry troops before which he halted were those whose movements have been hastily described. "What troops are these?" were his first words; and "The Vermont Brigade" was the first answer, amid cheers and hells that filled the air. Colonel Tracy of the 2nd Vermont, then commanding the Brigade, rode up to salute, and said, "We're glad to see you, General Sheridan." "Well, by God, I'm glad to get here! We'll have our camps by night!"

How vividly a scene like that burns itself into one's memory! Words cannot describe it. The artist's brush cannot paint it. But it stands distinct in the chambers of the mind; and, when its vision is awakened, the eyes fill, and the throat swells, and the soul thrills in quick response.

I have no hesitancy in saying that Sheridan's greatest victory was very largely, if not chiefly, due to the cool and dogged steadiness of the Vermont Brigade during those house before he arrived upon the field. It is generally conceded that Getty's Division remained in the fight of that morning at least two hours after every other organization had been successively defeated. When at last it retired, a position was deliberately selected where the fight could be resumed. It thus became the nucleus on which the army formed. The Vermont Brigade was the center of Getty's Division during all that day. The first Brigade, on the right of the Division, was commanded by one of the Vermont Colonels, permanently assigned, General James M. Warner, a member of this Commandery. It was composed of the 62d New York and four Pennsylvania regiments. General Bidwell, of Buffalo, commanding the third Brigade, upon the left, was killed about nine A.M., while repulsing one of the rebel charges made upon the semi-circular crest which the Division occupied; soon after this his men began to waver under the fierce attack, when the appeal was heard, "Don't run till the Vermonter do," and they stood steady to their work. This brigade embraced the 43rd, 49th, 77th and 122d New York, together with the 7th Maine and the 61st Pennsylvania.

Sheridan, in his official report of the battle, makes the situation clear. He says: "On arriving at the front, I found Merritt's and Custer's divisions of cavalry[6] and General Getty's division of the Sixth Corps opposing the enemy. I suggested to General Wright that we would fight on Getty's line, and that the remaining two divisions of the Sixth Corps, which were to the right and rear of Getty, about two miles, should be ordered up, and also that the Nineteenth Corps, which was on the right and rear of those divisions, should be hastened up before the enemy attacked Getty." And again, in the same report, he says: "Getty's division of the Sixth Corps confronted the enemy from the first attack of the morning until the battle was decided." In his Memoirs he writes as follows: "Getty's division, when I found it, was about a mile north of Middletown, posted on the reverse slope of some slightly raising ground, holding a barricade made of fence rails, and skirmishing slightly with the enemy's pickets. Jumping my horse over the line of rails, I rode to the crest of the elevation, and then, taking off my hat, the men rose up from behind the barricade with cheers of recognition. An officer of the Vermont Brigade, Colonel A. S. Tracy, rode up to the font, and, joining me, informed me that General Lewis A. Grant was in command there, the regular Division commander, General Getty, having taken charge of the Sixth Corps, in place of Ricketts, wounded early in the action." Sheridan proceeds with the story as follows: "I crossed the depression in the rear of Getty's line, and, dismounting on the opposite crest, established that point as my headquarters. Crook[7] met me at this time, and strongly favored the idea of fighting, but said that most of his troops were gone. General Wright (of the Sixth Corps, who had been in command of the army) came up a little later, when I saw that he was wounded, a ball having grazed the point of his chin so as to draw blood plentifully. Wright gave me a hurried account of the day's events, and when told that we would fight the enemy upon the line which Getty and the cavalry were holding, and that he must go himself and send all his staff to bring up the troops, he zealously fell in with the scheme; and it was then that the Nineteenth Corps and two divisions of the Sixth were ordered to the front." The subsequent advance of the army and the total rout of the enemy as the sun went down, are known to all.

This was by no means the first occasion on which the Vermont Brigade had exhibited the cool and persevering steadiness and composure under extreme difficulties which distinguished it so highly in the Army of the Potomac. Its conduct at Cedar Creek was not accidental, but was habitual. There was never a time after the Peninsular campaign in 1862 when the knowledge that the Vermont Brigade was holding a point of danger did not give confidence to all the army, or when its absence from the fight was not a cause for regret. Its troops were commonly known as "the Vermonters." When brave John Sedgwick, the beloved organized and command of the Sixth Army Corps, marched his men thirty-two miles in a day to the sound of the guns at Gettysburg, he issued an order, as reported by his Adjutant General, which has since been often repeated: "Put the Vermonters ahead, and keep the column closed. up."

I remember a group of troops from other States, whom I found conversing around a picket-fire in front of Petersburg, while making the grand-rounds as "Officer of the

Day," one night in the early spring of 1865. The story was evidently of some desperate occasion, when the danger was extreme; for the narrator concluded, with the hearty approval of all the group, as I approached: "Then is when we wanted the Vermonters."

In the summer of 1864 Early was knocking at the back door of Washington, and the Sixth Corps was ordered to move by water from Petersburg to its relief. When the first boat arrived, President Lincoln, silent and careworn, was standing on the wharf. As soon as its landing was made, he inquired what troops were on board, and was told the name of the General who had occupied the steamer as headquarters during the trip. The anxious President turned away with evident disappointment, saying, "I do not care to see any Major Generals; I came here to see the Vermont Brigade." And he was at the landing when the Vermont Brigade arrived.

To give the story of the Old Vermont Brigade in detail would be substantially to write the history of the Army of the Potomac. Its proper presentation would require a volume. Upon an occasion like this there remains only time to hastily sketch its services, pausing to speak more particularly of two or three matters perhaps not generally known.

The 2nd Vermont regiment was in the first battle of Bull Run, and witnessed Lee's surrender at Appomattox Court House. The first important campaign of the Brigade as an organization was with McClellan on the Peninsula. The first assault upon an entrenched line made by the Army of the Potomac was the celebrated charge of a detachment of the Vermont Brigade across the mill-dam and into the enemy's works at Lee's Mills, near Yorktown. The battle of Williamsburg followed, and the army trailed its slow and tortuous way until it finally halted astride the Chickahominy. The battles in which the Vermont Brigade honorably participated in this ineffectual demonstration against Richmond were Golding's Farm, Savage's Station, and White Oak Swamp. At Savage's Station in particular the men fought desperately and the loss was enormous. The 5th Vt. Regiment had not exceeding four hundred muskets in the battle, and its killed and wounded numbered 206. General D. H. Hill,[8] in his "Century" article describing this action, says that a Vermont regiment made a desperate charge upon the division of McLaws,[9] and was almost annihilated. "Baldy" Smith's Division did its part well through the whole campaign of disaster, and was among the last to leave Harrison's Landing when the army was recalled to Washington. It did not arrive at Alexandria in season to participate in the Second Bull Run, although it marched out towards the south through Fairfax Court House. It was active in the Antietam campaign, taking a brilliant part at the battle of South Mountain, known in its annals as the storming of Crampton's Gap. Its next serious engagement was General Burnside's unfortunate battle at Fredericksburg, where its experiences were painful and its losses large. When General Hooker, shortly after, repeated the experiment, in what is known as the Chancellorsville campaign, the duty assigned to the Vermont Brigade, with a few other troops, was the storming of Marye's Heights. The hill was carried by a brilliant and successful charge, and Sedgwick's part of the battle was a complete success. At Gettysburg the Sixth Corps was the last to reach the field, and most of it was held in reserve. The position occupied by the Old Vermont Brigade is marked by the marble statue of a crouching lion. Speculations have often been made concerning the possible result in case Pickett's charge on the third day had proved successful; but such conjectures are of little value unless the fact is kept in view that Sedgwick's command was under arms in readiness at any moment to participate in the battle. In the course of Meade's pursuit of Lee, a so-called skirmish took place at Funkstown, Maryland, in respect to which General Sedgwick's official report says: "The Vermont Brigade were deployed as skirmishers, covering a front of over two miles; and during the afternoon repulsed three successive attacks made in line of battle. The remarkable conduct of the Brigade on this occasion deserves high praise." Soon after this, General Sedgwick was asked to detail his "best brigade" for duty at New York City in connection with the draft riots then in progress. He designated the Vermont Brigade, which spent August and September, 1863, in and about this city. Returning to the army, it was received with music and military salutes, and took part in Meade's Mine Run campaign, including a severe engagement at Rappahannock Station.

The next spring the army was reorganized for active service under General Grant, and on May 4 it crossed the Rapidan. On May 5 and 6, 1864, the Battle of the Wilderness was fought. Getty's Division was detached from the Sixth Corps and sent to occupy and hold the Brock Road, at the crossing of the Orange Plank Road, until the Second Corps, under Hancock, should arrive. It was a desperate duty, and the circumstances were such that the service performed was little known outside the army. The assault, under Lee in person, was sustained for hours by Getty's Division without support, and the entire loss of the Second Corps on May 5 was not equal to that of the Vermont Brigade alone. On the second day the Second Corps took the front and delivered a successful advance, but reinforcements of the enemy presently enabled Longstreet to sweep down its flank in apparent victory. "We thought," he afterwards said to Mr. Swinton, "that we had another Bull Run on you." But two brigades from Getty's Division were waiting, and the steadiness and nerve of the Vermonters were never more signally displayed. The Brock Road was held, and on the evening of the 7th the Army of the Potomac took up its march to the South. The Battle of the Wilderness was an enigma; it has even been doubted whether, in fact, it was a Northern victory. But the troops engaged had no such doubt. It was the last occasion when General Lee made an attack in force upon the Army of the Potomac. The losses on both sides were nearly equal. Getty's Division sustained at this time the heaviest loss experienced during the war by any Division in any battle, a total of 2994. The Vermont Brigade suffered one-tenth of the entire loss of Grant's army. It crossed the Rapidan with 2800 men, and its casualties in the Wilderness aggregated 1234 or 44 percent. Of the officers present for duty, three-fourths were killed and wounded. Twenty-one officers were killed, or died of their wounds.

The army moved on towards Spotsylvania, and the Vermont Brigade, by a forced march, was brought to the right of the Sixth Corps once more. It was directed to take position on the left; and as the Brigade, reduced to half its former size, began to move down the line, the men nearest broke into spontaneous hurrahs, and its march was made under a continuous roll of cheers.

The fighting for a time was now almost constant. General Sedgwick was killed, and General Wright succeeded to the command of the corps. General Getty had been severely wounded in the Wilderness, and was in a Northern hospital. Three of the Vermont regiments were engaged in Upton's famous charge, which captured what was known as the "bloody angle." Ordered to withdraw, they refused at first to do so. But the position gained was abandoned, and was the scene of a terrible conflict two days later on. Then the Vermont Brigade for nearly eight hours was engaged in a hand-to-hand fight across the breastworks. A tree was here cut off by bullets, described by the Confederate General McGowan[10] as an oak tree, twenty-two inches in diameter, which injured several men of the Seventh South Carolina regiment when it fell. Mr. Swinton says: "Of all the struggles of the war, this was perhaps the fiercest and most deadly. The musketry fire had the effect to kill a whole forest within its range." In these engagements about Spotsylvania Court House the Brigade lost nearly four hundred men more; and when it was reinforced, on May 15, by the 11th Vermont, fresh from the defences of Washington, the new portion of the command out-numbered the old. One hundred and fifty recruits at the same time joined the older regiments, and the men were still stout at heart, feeling that they were moving to the South and had at last left Fredericksburg behind them.

Several other collisions with the enemy occurred, of which time does not permit mention; the region about Spotsylvania Court House was soon abandoned in a movement by the left flank still southward across the North Anna. Thence a like manoeuver repeated brought the Sixth Corps, on June 1, in face of a prepared line of earthworks near Cold Harbor. The Brigade participated actively in the desperate but unsuccessful attempt to carry the rebel position, fortified the ground gained, and was under fire for twelve days without a moment's cessation. Then, moving by the left flank once more, the army crossed the Chickahominy and the James, and pushed forward to the attack then in progress upon Petersburg. After constant fighting here for twenty days, including a battle on the Weldon Road that cost the Brigade a loss of over four hundred and fifty officers and men, and a raid to Reams's Station on the south, the Sixth Corps was suddenly ordered back to Washington, then threatened by Early, who was approaching through Maryland with considerable force. The Vermont Brigade was near the head of the corps as it marched up Seventh Street from the landing and pushed straight out to the presence of the enemy. The entire population of Washington thronged along the line of march. The day before had been one of almost absolute panic. The morning saw the streets filled with old campaigner, whose rapid steps and easy swing told the story of veteran experience. Before sunset there was a "right smart" fight within five miles of the National Capitol, and the next morning Early's army was gone.

Then followed a weary month of marching and counter-marching, by night and by day; across the Potomac, through Leesburg and Snicker's gap into the Shenandoah Valley; back again to Washington; out once more by way of Frederick to Harper's Ferry; back to Frederick, and on to Harper's Ferry again. The men were weary and worn by continual hurrying to and fro, with no apparent object or result; until one day a new command was announced, and a new order of things presently began.

General Sheridan's campaign was cautiously conducted until he received authority to "go in." One of its early incidents was a falling back some forty miles from Strasburg to Charlestown, at which place an unexpected attack was received by Getty's Division, which was covering the movement. This was once more the Vermonters' day upon the skirmish-line; and though no other troops were engaged, and the affair finds no mention in the histories, it was for them as bitter a little fight as could well be imagined. The brigade held its ground all day against several attacks of infantry and a severe artillery fire, without asking for support. Two divisions of the enemy were in its front. General Early, in his "Memoir of the Last Year of the War for Independence," says of this affair: "I encountered Sheridan's main force near Cameron's depot, about three miles from Charlestown, in a position which he commenced fortifying at once. Rodes'[11] and Ramseur's[12] Divisions were advanced to the front, and very heavy skirmishing ensued and was continued until night; but I waited for General Anderson[13] to arrive before making a general attack." Although the rest of Sheridan's army was in position some distance in the rear, the only troops engaged on our side upon this occasion were the regiments of the Old Vermont Brigade. A comparison of the accounts given by both the opposing commanders clearly shows that Early was endeavoring to bring on an engagement, and Sheridan was quite willing that he should; but the unusual tenacity with which the Vermont Brigade held the skirmish-line prevented the battle, though both Generals desired it.

Sheridan's first serious engagement in the Valley was the battle of the Opequon, named from the Opequon Creek. This encounter is often spoken of as the battle of Winchester; but as that City was taken and retaken some eighty times during the war, its name is useless for any special identification. After the battle of Opequon, however, the rebel army saw it no more. On the morning of September 19, 1864, the army broke camp at 2 A.M., and the Vermont Brigade led the column of infantry, marching straight to the west.

If there were time, it might be interesting to describe this action sufficiently to call attention to a series of accidents which upset General Sheridan's calculations and caused him to wholly change his plan of battle during its progress. In his Memoirs he says:

"The battle was not fought out on the plan in accordance with which marching orders were issued to my troops, for I then hoped to take Early in detail, and with Crook's force cut off his retreat. It was during the reorganization of my lines that I changed my plan as to Crook, and moved him from my left to my right. This I did with great reluctance, for I hoped to destroy Early's army entirely if Crook continued on his original line of march towards the Valley Pike south of Winchester; and although the ultimate results did in a measure vindicate the change, yet I have always thought that by adhering to the original plan we might have captured the bulk of Early's army."

In conversation during the later years of his life, General Sheridan expressed himself still more strongly, saying in substance that he had always regretted the change from his original plan, which sacrificed the opportunity for a much more important victory than the one which he in fact obtained.

General Early criticizes Sheridan for his failure to take advantage of the opportunity open to "have destroyed my whole force and captured everything I had."

During this engagement the writer had an excellent opportunity to observe the condition of affairs on the extreme left of our army. The opportunity to envelope the entire rebel force from the south was perfectly apparent and was freely discussed in the ranks; the appearance of troops in that direction was anxiously expected. They failed to come, and the battle was ended by an attack from the other flank of the army which the whole line took up in turn; but I have never seen the least reason to doubt that if Crook's command, after the reorganization of the line, had pursued the direction originally contemplated, and come in on the south of the rebel army, there would either have been an entire surrender by the enemy or a quick retreat into the North Mountains.

A brief allusion only can be made to the battle of Fisher's Hill, three days later, in which the enemy was driven from the strongest position in the Shenandoah Valley, by a secret movement executed by Crook, who marched his two small divisions all day through the woods and along the mountain side, and delivered a complete surprise upon the enemy's left flank about 5 P.M. The Sixth Corps at the same time charged in front, directly against the works occupied by the rebels at the crowning points of the line of defence on the high hills that here cross the Valley. General Early says that he intended to withdraw that night, but when his left was turned his men abandoned their position and "my whole force retired in considerable confusion." He omits to notice the fact that their haste was so extreme that eleven hundred men and sixteen pieces of artillery were left behind. The heavy artillerists in the Vermont Brigade enjoyed the exhilarating sensation of turning the guns of a captured battery upon the retreating foe.

After the pursuit to Staunton, the army returned leisurely and camped on the north side of Cedar Creek. Early presently again occupied Fisher's Hill, from which his movement across Cedar Creek was made against our army in Sheridan's absence, which has already been described, and which ended the war in the Shenandoah Valley.

In December, 1864, the Sixth Corps returned to the Army of the Potomac and was assigned a position at the extreme left of the line on the south-west front of Petersburg. The Vermont Brigade occupied works previously constructed by troops which it had relieved, facing northerly, near the furthest point at that time held by our army in that direction. Picket duty had an occasional skirmish occupied the days and nights until the latter part of March, 1865, when active work was resumed.

At daybreak on April 2, an event occurred which is well worth a careful description. The battle of Five Forks had just been fought and won. The time had arrived when it was considered necessary to break through the entrenched line of the enemy. General Wright was sure he could do it, and told General Meade that whenever he got the word he would "make the fur fly." The enemy's line was closely studied. General L. A. Grant discovered an opening in the rebel entrenchments, where there was a little ravine which their works did not cross. This was opposite the furthest point to the west then held by our army. He describes what took place as follows: "Knowing that a vulnerable point of attack was sought for, I called General Getty's attention to this place, and he in turn called the attention of Generals Wright and Meade. All came down, and we went out together to examine it as well as could be done at a distance. It was decided to make this the point of attack, and the Old Vermont Brigade was selected to form the entering wedge. Orders were given the night previous for my brigade to move out at twelve o'clock, and to take the position that I might select as most favorable for the purpose, and for the other troops to follow."

The plan thus outlined was closely followed. While the troops were being massed for the assault, a general bombardment was in progress all along the line, which continued throughout the night. The Vermont Brigade moved out, under strict orders to hug the ground and observe the utmost silence, and laid down three hundred yards from the enemy's picket line. The other brigades of the division took position on its right. The other Divisions of the corps were in echelon on either side of Getty. Each brigade was massed in columns by battalion. Axmen were in front, to cut away the abatis. General Getty's official report says that Grant's Vermont Brigade "was made the directing column." It was ordered that upon the firing of a certain gun from the whole Sixth Army Corps should rise and charge together, silently and without firing a musket. For three hours after the preparations were complete the Sixth Corps waited for the signal gun. The night was very dark and cold. The ground was damp, and the men were almost benumbed as they lay upon it without fire or light. Cannon shot were frequently exchanged, and the projectiles whizzed over the heads of the troops in both directions. By some unlucky chance, a picket fire was opened, to which the rebels replied sharply, and many casualties occurred in the prostrate ranks of the corps. General L. A. Grant was wounded in the head, and Colonel Tracy again took command of the Brigade. Colonel James M. Warner, of the 11th Vermont, had for some months commanded the third Brigade of Getty's Division. The cannonading was so heavy that the signal gun, when fired, was not recognized. The order to advance was finally given. The troops rose to their feet, and the massed columns moved out silently into the night. The entire corps took up the movement as directed. The blunders of the Mine were not repeated. Twelve thousand men were formed into a living wedge, to penetrate the strongest line of works ever constructed in America. Suddenly the enemy's pickets heard the tramp of the approaching army, opened a scattering fire, and fled to the works behind them. Silence was no longer required, and a mighty cheer arose, while the Sixth Corps rapidly pressed forward on its charge. The rebel works were almost instantly manned; the enemy had evidently also been under arms through the night; musketry and artillery swept the field, but the column moved on. There was disorganization and confusion as the lines of abatis were pulled aside, and the men were on their mettle; dashing into the ditch, they climbed the parapet, and poured a resistless torrent, across the enemy's defenses, as the day began to dawn. There is no dispute that the first man to mount the parapet was Captain C. J. Gould of the 5th Vermont, who was bayoneted in the face and back as he jumped within the fort. The first mounted officer to cross the works was undoubtedly Colonel Warner of the 11th Vermont, who led the charge of the third Brigade. The scene, as it appeared to a non-combatant, was described by Surgeon S. J. Allen, of the 4th Vermont, Medical director of the Division, who was standing on the parapet of Ft. Welch, in rear of the attacking column, anxiously peering into the night. He could hear the muffled tramp and rustle of the moving host, but could discern nothing. He saw the flashes of the first volley, heard the answering shout from ten thousand throats, and then he saw, stretching across the front for half a mile, a line of flashing fire, crackling, blazing and sparkling in the darkness, more vividly lighted up by the heavier flashes of artillery; shells with their fiery trails sped through the gloom in every direction. While he was intently watching that line of deadly fire, suddenly in the middle of it there appeared a tiny black spot, a narrow gap, which spread and widened, moment by moment, to the right and left; and then he knew that the line was pierced and our men had carried the defences of the enemy.

It is claimed by historians on the other side that this feat was rendered easy by reason of the depletion of the troops upon the rebel line. This hardly accords with known facts. It is certain that the entire line of breastworks against which the charge was directed were fully manned, and that a seemingly solid wall of fire was maintained until the charging party reached the works and broke through, that all the artillery commanding the line of march was in full play, including many enfilading guns; that three thousand prisoners were taken by the Sixth Corps; and that it lost eleven hundred men killed and wounded in the charge. It was no boys' play. If the line of attack had not been well chosen and quickly traversed, the corps could not have succeeded. No mistakes were made by officers, and the spirit of the men was superb.

The results are well known. The Sixth Corps pressed forward without a moment's delay, and before nightfall had cleared the entire country between Hatcher's Run and the Appomattox River. General Lee in person attempted to stem the tide, and narrowly escaped capture. The news was telegraphed to Richmond, and Jefferson Davis with his cabinet took a special train for Danville at 2 P.M. in the evening Petersburg and Richmond were evacuated, and the end of the war was near.

A few days later, I heard General Meade say that the gallant and successful charge of the Sixth Corps on the morning of the 2nd of April was in his opinion "the decisive movement of the campaign." Candor compels me to add that he called it "decisive," but the peculiarity of pronunciation did not weaken the value of the praise. It was undoubtedly the decisive movement of the final campaign of the war, which soon resulted in the surrender of the army of Northern Virginia. The importance of the part taken by the Vermont Brigade on this occasion may safely rest upon the facts which I have stated.

The next day the whole of Grant's command started for the west with a new objective, — Lee's flying army. Sheridan and his cavalry pressed the pursuit with such vigor that three days found them in advance of Lee's left wing. He planted General Crook and General Merritt, with their cavalry, directly across the road which the rebels were taking, and then hurried round to their rear, where he met the Sixth Corps, which he had been trying for several days to get under his orders. When the men found that Sheridan was putting them into the fight, their enthusiasm was indescribable. They charged across Sailor's Creek, attacked the enemy furiously, and forced the surrender of General Ewell and eight thousand men, caught between the cavalry and infantry lines.

A few days later, almost identical tactics were repeated at Appomattox Court House, the remainder of Lee's army surrendered, and the war was over.

No doubt many remember an article by Colonel Fox in the "Century Magazine" of May, 1888, entitled "The Chances of Being Hit in Battle;" an article which, while purely statistical in form, was intensely interesting, and was subsequently expanded into a volume.[14] One of the tables given was a list of infantry regiments whose loss during the war in killed was two hundred or more, embracing every regiment in the Northern Army in which two hundred or over were killed in action or died of wounds received in action. This list contains only forty-five regiments, it includes the 2nd, 3rd, 5th and 6th Vermont. His roster of "three hundred fighting regiments" of course embraces the entire brigade — 2nd,

3rd, 4th, 5th, 6th and 11th Vermont. A list of 103 regiments losing 63 men or over, killed or mortally wounded in a single battle, includes five regiments of the Old Vermont Brigade at the Battle of the Wilderness, and another at Savage's Station. The total number of deaths in the Brigade during the war, including killed in action, deaths from wounds, from diseases, and in rebel prisons, was twenty-four hundred and seventeen, being about 25% of the total membership of the Brigade, original enlistments and recruits. Its losses in killed and mortally wounded in action are eleven hundred and seventy-two, a greater number than any other brigade in the Army.

The Brigade was engaged in thirty different battles, the names of which are embroidered on the colors of its regiments. It was fortunate in its officers. No unnecessary sacrifice of life is chargeable to reckless handling. It was fortunate in its officers. Its casualties were evenly distributed; their severity was simply owing to the remarkable personal character of the rank and file. They were called on for the hardest work; they never knew when they were whipped; they stood together like men, and they fought every battle to the end; not one of their colors was ever in a rebel hand, their appearance was quiet, and their speech was often homely; but their hearts were stout and their aim steady. They were never surprised or stampeded; no panic ever reached them; their service was intelligent, faithful and honest; they had the full confidence of their commanders; and their countrymen will forever honor their memory. In the words of General Martin T. McMahon,[15] the well known Adjutant General of the Sixth Army Corps, "No body of troops in or out of the Sixth Corps had a better record. No body of troops in or out of the Army of the Potomac made their record more gallantly, sustained it more heroically, or wore their honors more modestly" than the Old Vermont Brigade.

----

1 USA Brig. Gen., later Maj. Gen. William Thomas Harbaugh Brooks.

2 Colonel, later Brig. Gen. and Bvt. Maj. Gen. Lewis Addison Grant, would lead the First Vermont Brigade until being wounded at Petersburg in April 1865. He was Assistant Secretary of War from 1890-1893. Boatner, 352.

3 USA Maj. Gen. Philip Henry Sheridan, "Little Phil."

4 USA Brig. Gen. George Washington Getty. Boatner, 329-330.

5 CSA Maj. Gen. Jubal Anderson Early, commanding Robert E. Lee's Second Corps in the Shenandoah Valley Campaign. Boatner, 255-6.

6 USA Brig. Gen. Wesley Merritt and USA Brig. Gen. George Armstrong Custer, commanded a division of the Cavalry Corps, during the Shenandoah Valley Campaign. Boatner, 216, 544.

7 USA Brig. Gen. George Crook, commanded Army of West Virginia in the Shenandoah Valley Campaign. Boatner, 209.

8 CSA Maj. Gen. Daniel Harvey Hill. Boatner, 401.

9 CSA Maj. Gen. Lafayette McLaws. Boatner, 536.

10 CSA Brig. Gen. Samuel McGowan, commanded a brigade at the Wilderness. Boatner, 533.

11 CSA Brig. Gen. Robert E. Rodes. Boatner, 706.

12 CSA Brig. Gen. Samuel Dodson Ramseur. Boatner, 677.

13 CSA Lieut. Gen. Richard Heron Anderson, temporarily commanding the First Corps while Longstreet recuperated from wounds. Boatner, 14.

14 Lieut. Col. William F. Fox, Regimental Losses in the American Civil War 1861-1865: A Treatise ..., Albany Publishing Company, Albany, N.Y., 1889)

15 USA Brig. Gen. Martin Thomas McMahon, born in Canada. Boatner, 537.

Colonel
James M. WARNER
11th Vermont Infantry
(Italo Collection)

Captain
Judson A. LEWIS
11th Vermont Infantry
(Italo Collection)

Captain
John H. MACOMBER
11th Vermont Infantry
(Italo Collection)

Surgeon
John J. MEIGS
3rd and 11th Vermont Infantry
(Italo Collection)

General
Philip H. SHERIDAN
(Italo Collection)

General
William F. SMITH
(Italo Collection)

General
George J. STANNARD
(Italo Collection)

Colonel
Edwin H. STOUGHTON
4th Vermont Infantry
(Italo Collection)

Captain
George G. TILDEN
11th Vermont Infantry
(Italo Collection)

Major
Wheelock G. VEAZEY
3rd Vermont Infantry
(later Colonel, 16th Infantry)
(Italo Collection)

Captain
Elizah WALES
2nd Vermont Infantry
(Italo Collection)

13.
The Overland Campaign Spotsylvania to Petersburg
Mid-May through June, 1864

On the Field, Sunday Morning
May 15th, 1864

We have been at work pretty hard of late. I have had not time to write since I sent my hurried note of Wednesday night, and don't know as I can get this off. I am now, 9:30 a.m., sitting in front of my Battery on the ground with my back against a knapsack. Guns are stacked. We are the extreme left regiment of the army, and are drawn up thus waiting for developments.

Well, you will want to know what has been done and is doing. I was up all night Wednesday night. Thursday morning at 5:30 we assembled at Bunker Hill, filed off for the "front," embarked and were off by 10, down the Potomac to Belle Plain. Nice ride, only it rained as it did Wednesday night. We got down and ashore about 5, and landed in a big mud hole entirely - lots of troops coming down with us. In fact, Grant is getting heavy reinforcements now-a-days, and he needs them. The newspapers have got him along altogether ahead of the time.

Well, we got our shelter tents, put them up in the rain, and slept pretty comfortably Thursday night, though it was wet. We could get but one team to come on with our regiment to carry medicines, so all baggage was left at Belle Plain. I travel with a haversack of hardtack, and a little coffee and pork when I can get it, (I love it now, but haven't got any - we started with six day's rations,) also a canteen, rubber coat and half a tent in my blanket straps, pair of socks and a towel in my pocket, and a flask with a little whiskey the surgeon furnishes, and which I feed to the boys when they get fatigued and faint. Have found it of use once or twice myself. Have on my new boots, which do nicely. Feet are all right, though I slept with them so near the fire last night that I burnt them badly; could hardly walk when I got up; am all right now. I change my socks every night, and so have a new pair on all the time. Well, Friday morning it rained and was muddy.

We marched to Fredericksburg, stopping the north side of the Rappahannock. Met 9,000 rebel prisoners on the way, who looked well enough, well clothed and hearty - taken on Thursday at Laurel Hill, the hardest fight of the campaign so far, and the most successful. Yesterday we had a hard walk, from that place a mile across the river to Headquarters of 6th A. C., Army of the Potomac. It rained more or less all day and the roads were frightful - through the Wilderness, you know - and awfully cut up and muddy. I can't begin to describe them, but I never saw or thought of the like before. We came in about 9 p.m. very tired, having marched about 20 miles to the neighborhood of Spotsylvania Court House, which is not occupied as yet. Encamped as usual, only we did not pitch our tents, but used them for blankets, - and this morning moved out to our present position on the left of the front line, as I said, and are waiting orders to advance or to meet the enemy. I brought into camp here every man I started from Belle Plain without a straggler. There are 118 in my Battery - about 1500 in the Regt. We are attached to the old 1st Brigade, which has been complimented by Grant as the best in the Army, and which has suffered fearfully, now numbering only 800 men all told, much more than half having been killed or wounded - two thirds, I guess.

It is very woody hereabouts, though a little cleared just here. The fighting has been terrible, but I never saw men in better spirits; all say they will use up Lee before they get through, and all full of faith in Grant; say that any other general would have fallen back first part of the fight, but he won't be beaten and wouldn't know it if he was. Yesterday the line advanced a good deal - Headquarters two miles. We are now where the rebs occupied last night, and the report is that they have run for good, but doubtful. Our loss so far cannot fall short of 50,000, and the rebels fully as much. We have taken many times the most prisoners, 42 guns, - and have gradually forced them back from position to position. They seem to be short of artillery, as we shelled them out of here last night and they made no reply; may be moving back, though some apprehend a flank movement upon Fredericksburg. Men all feel well and are ready to see the greybacks. I saw Haynes this morning - all right and going to his regiment, which is in the extreme front and has suffered but little. The 17th was said to be badly cut up, but it is recruiting fast as skedaddlers come in, for they broke and ran and haven't all got back yet. Eaton and Knapp[1] are both slightly wounded. Lots of other friends are wounded or killed, but the rest are full of courage, and I think we shall get through to Richmond some time. I don't know when this can go, but will get it off as soon as possible. We may stay where we are all day - may move in half an hour.

Meanwhile, with love to all, I remain as ever,

Aldace F. Walker

Capt. 1st Vt. Art., 11th Vols., Washington, D.C.

We are now in the 2d Div., 6th Corps, but may not remain so. The above address is enough.

At the Front, Thursday Noon
May 19, 1864

Dear Father:

I shall write whenever I can get a chance, which I fear will be only semi-occasionally for the present. We have received no letters since we left Washington, though the old regiments do. Presume ours will come sometime. I am very well and all right. We have been under fire once only so far. The old men said it was the hardest artillery fire of the campaign, and some say the hardest they ever experienced. I believe I wrote you Sunday that as our 2d Battalion, the one I am in under Maj. Hunsdon, was ordered off half a mile to support a battery in position to cover our picquets, (this was Monday instead of Sunday,) had a good place for our camp, nothing to do and no picquet details.

Tuesday Grant, Meade, Neil and the Corps commanders, had a convention at a house close by us and I saw them all. We were on the 1700 acre plantation of a rich secesh, who calls himself ruined. His farm won't bear anything this summer - that's certain, and I hope will be confiscated in the end. We are just south of the Wilderness, though by no means out of the woods. But about our fight. The plan was to drive Lee out of his works at Spotsylvania, which are better than those at Yorktown. An apparent movement of our forces was made from the right to the left, the 2d Corps feigning to withdraw to withdraw, but sent back in the night, and our 6th besides. Lee wasn't fooled and the plan failed, partly because our march was impeded by wagons and we did not get up till 5 a.m.

We left camp at 8, marched all night with no sleep at all, way back and around, muddy and dark and cold and tired, deployed in the rifle pits we took from the rebs last week Thursday and others we had thrown up since; but, as I said, we were late, and before we got into line the rebs opened with shell. We went in in good shape however. Went forward half a mile out of the woods under a hill to support a brigade in rifle pits on its crest. The elevation was very slight, and the shell and canister played around us terribly - also minies from sharpshooters in the trees. The men behaved admirably all the time till the attack was given up. We came together at noon, marched back to the left again, and got in to camp about 8. I was put on officer of the day and did not get much sleep. This morning at three we marched again, straight forward about two miles, and are entrenching now. Burnside's Corps is now on our left, and I presume the intention is to throw forward our left and so flank the Johnnies out of Spotsylvania. I have been asleep this morning some, and as I said feel nicely. It is rumored that we are to go on picquet tonight, guess not however.

Our loss was light in our fight, as shelling is of use principally for its demoralizing effect. But one was sent to the rear in Co. - a French boy, Ladeau, who had a little wound in the top of his head, but is with us again today. I presume fifteen were hit in their clothing, knapsacks, &c., or received flesh wounds. Dodge was hit in the boot - Dunham's sword, &c. But other companies were worse served. Col. Warner was shot through the neck, not dangerously wounded. He is the coolest man I ever saw. Was standing on the top of the pit ordering the 3d Battalion to advance, when he dropped his sword and put his hand to his neck. He was shot on the right side - was facing the men. Should think the wound was about four inches through. Went back and had it dressed, and came on to the pit again, marched the regiment off and back to camp. Has gone to Washington today leaving Buxton in command. Will be all right in a few days if he is not foolish. Lt. Glazier of "A" lost his left arm - a very fine officer, too. Five men hit in "C," &c., &c. Maj. Hunsdon was fired at several times, but all missed. I wasn't scratched, but there were lots of narrow escapes, and I don't see how we got off so well. We did not fire a gun. We got a great deal of credit for our behavior in our first engagement; everyone expected to see us run, but we couldn't see it. The hardest thing to do in a battle is to retire under fire. Twice I happened to get the left wing of our Battalion ahead of the right, and marched them back as coolly as you please. Other Art. regiments (all are on from Washington now) broke and ran, but we were as steady as anybody. Two of our colors were hit. A big detail was at work carrying rails for breastworks under the heaviest fire, but were as easy as could be about it. We did not leave till the enemy's fire was silenced. It is rumored that we took the works in the p.m., but I don't believe it. Have seen lots of friends, Frank Walker, &c. Weather is delightful. I lost a rubber coat, wool blanket and tent; have since got hold of a tent and overcoat and am all right again.

As ever,

Aldace

Send me some postage stamps.

South of the North Anna
May 24, 1864

Dear Father:

Since I last wrote you (and I fear you have not heard at all) I have endured more than I could have thought possible, and feel well yet - only a little footsore. I think I last wrote of our shelling scrape, when Col. Warner was wounded. We advanced a mile or so and threw up earthworks for a line of skirmishers to hold while the main army went off on a flanking scrape. It was my fortune to be on the picquet or skirmish line the time that this movement was made. I was in charge of a detachment of 200 men and four Lieutenants from four Companies of the Mass. 37th, on account of my inexperience, and he proved a very fine fellow indeed. We went out on Friday night, the 20th I think, about 900 in all, relieved our predecessors about 11 p.m. I took charge of the reserve. Posted the men about a rod apart through the woods and opposite the skirmishers of the Johnnies. Had rather a quiet night, though no rest of course. I did not happen to have any meat on hand when we started, and so was all the more exhausted when I got through with what I am going to tell about.

I changed the videttes about six in the morning, and just as Capt. Loomis and I had reached the end of the line, we were fired on seven times in succession by sharpshooters, while we stood still expecting that they would stop to load presently. We were not hit, though some shots passed between us - poor marksmen, I think. They did not accelerate our departure in the least. About two p.m. we got orders to withdraw our line to the trenches, as the Corps had fallen back. This was done. Meanwhile the rebs pressed us closely with considerable skirmishing and shooting, but no casualties on our side, except one man in the 3d Brigade killed. About 5 p.m. however, they charged on our line with two Brigades, 10 regiments, and we had a hot season till dark, I tell you. Maj. Hunsdon was on the line, but I did not see anything of him, as he kept with the Corps Officer of the day. I was alone with my detachment, had sent 50 men to the extreme right, 30 men and Lt. Bedell[2] I sent to support the Mass. 37th on my right, and the 10th Mass. lay between us. My line, what I had left, was extended about 50 rods, I think - perhaps not more than 40. I broke three charges in my front, but on the right they were not so fortunate. They got over and came down the pit flanking us right out clear to the line of the 10th Mass., and they all ran with no reason at all. My men stayed fast and did not leave our position. Bedell's party were driven out, but got great credit for staying by as long as they did. In my Co. two men were killed and one wounded. The slaughter of the enemy was immense - not less than 500 killed and wounded - and we took some 20 prisoners. They took none - 10 would cover our total loss. Our breastworks were capital. We were completely covered and fired (my detachment) 3000 rounds. Those driven out fell back to a second line and the rebs did not hold their posish five minutes. We threw out videttes and kept on the alert till 4 or 5 a.m., though I let the line sleep all they could.

I buried my two boys together after midnight, and felt very badly. One, Corp. Stevens, was shot through the heart; the other, Priv. Larock, through the breast.[3] These are the only two men we have had killed in the regiment so far. We were all withdrawn at 5 a.m. and made a forced march toward the southeast to catch our Corps, which we reached about noon at Guinea Station. I was so exhausted when I got there that I could not stand. They had heard that I and my command were captured, and were very much surprised to see us come in. I got rested some, however, and we marched five miles further that night, - our 6th Corps being the tail of the army. I got a lift of a mile on the Chaplain's horse and contrived to get into camp. Had a good night's rest, but still no meant, and started the next morning with the regiment for the South. Stood it about four miles and broke down. Waited for the ambulances. Found that Maj. Hunsdon had played out and was riding in an ambulance, and got on his horse. Rode five miles or so and felt a good deal rested. Came across Capt. Sheldon, who expects his resignation to be accepted in a day or two. Found Capt. Goodrich - thought he was worse off than I, and gave up my horse to him. And then we had the hardest march I ever saw. There was firing ahead, - Warren[4] crossing the North Anna - and we were pushed on to support him if necessary. We had a terrible time, but I stuck to the head of my Co. - how I don't know - but we reached the north bank of the river about 9 - slept till 4 a.m. and crossed. Are lying now as reserve, waiting for other's to move.

We lost about 300 men on the march; most of them have come up, as we are having a splendid rest today. I am in command of the 2d Battalion now and ride Hunsdon's horse. Presume it will last but a day or two. It is amazing how the prisoners come in. Whole lines of battle lay down their arms and come over, and squads have passed through our lines here all day. I should think 5,000 have given themselves up yesterday and today.

I had a swim this p.m. and feel like a new man. There is heavy firing on our left, where Hancock is today, but we are not needed or we should go. 900 gave up to him at once this morning. A whole regiment came in here today. I am messing with the "field" now and they have got some ham, which is very acceptable. I could not find my little red testament when I left Saratoga in such a hurry, and was without one, but have picked up one since.

With much love to all,

Aldace F. Walker

Camp South of the Pamunkey
Sunday, May 29th, 1864

Dear Father:

I have had no opportunity to send the letter I wrote the other day and so will add another sheet, hoping that you will get it sometime. Have nothing especial to write, however, save the details of another big flank movement we have come over Lee. When I finished writing before, we were south of the North Anna. And, by the way, Maj. Hunsdon came up contrary to the expectations of everyone, so that my riding did not amount to much.

On Wednesday we moved south a couple of miles, crossing the Va. Central (Gordonsville) R. R. at "Noel's Turn," and entrenched half a mile below it, while our pioneers most effectually chawed up five miles or so of it. These railroads we find in better shape than those in Vermont. And by the way, the Johnnies are well enough off as to food and clothing; but it is true that they are terribly disheartened. We have taken about 12,000 prisoners in this campaign, some 5,000 of whom voluntarily surrendered. Well, we lay there some time while Hancock and Warren were making demonstrations on the Junction, where Lee had fortifications Grant had no intention of bucking against, and didn't try.

On Thursday night at 8 p.m. we broke camp for a long race. I don't know much about the army in general, only the operations of our Corps. Sheridan came in from and went back to Hanover Town with Russell's 1st Division[5] of the 6th Corps in time to arrange and secure the crossing on Friday, with no opposition, though a small force if it had been here would have stopped us most emphatically. The rest of us, as I said, moved off quietly on Thursday night for the hardest march we have had yet. It rained that p.m. We went back across the North Anna, and up to Chesterfield on the Potomac R. R. to breakfast, making about eight miles in the whole night. It was the worst time I ever saw. Very dark, and half of the way the mud was up to the top of my boots. We could scarcely drag ourselves along, but got through some way.

When we halted we dropped to sleep in half a minute. Some of the time it was very slow, and sometimes very fast, and at all times very exhausting. We left Chesterfield about six, and marched all day - struck sandy, dry roads, but very hot and dusty. Went nearly 20 miles I should think. I got a little footsore but am all right now.

We did not go clear down to Hanover Town for our crossing, but about four miles above, where we crossed yesterday morning, marching about four miles and then a couple more this side. We came up on to the heights and entrenched, some six miles from Hanover Court House, and fifteen or twenty from Richmond. I suppose that the other Corps are below us, though I think the 5th crossed where we did, after us. We are in a beautiful spot this beautiful day. I am rested and happy, and thankful that I have endured so much so well. I have 102 men in camp of the 112 I started from Belle Plain with - two dead, three or four gone back to Washington sick, and the rest with the ambulances and I presume will be up today.

I think we have done remarkably well. The men are green at this business and have been improvident with their rations, and are short now when they have drawn for three more days. "No hardtack." I have a few crumbs still on hand. We get fresh beef every day. I got hold of a liver last night, and had a breakfast as was a breakfast. The Commissary has been ordered up, and we shall get another issue today I hope; though he is a good way back. We have not suffered for water much, though we have drank almost anything, (mud is of no account at all,) but here it is capital and clear. Only one trouble here, the sun rises in the west. With much love to all. Oh how I do want to get some letters - I have not had a letter and scarcely seen a paper since I left Washington.

Aldace

May 31st, 1864

I will add another line. Received mail for first time last night - four letters from you, to May 23rd - amazing glad to get them. A mail leaves in ten minutes. I have had a chance to send off two letters before this; hope you have got them by this time. I am all right - feet sound. Rations issued last night. Communications opened with White House. We are on the extreme right of the army. Were on the old Hanover C. H. battle ground yesterday; are nearer Richmond now, just where I don't know. Something of an action on our right last eve. - don't know what it was, and we don't pay much attention to firing elsewhere now.

It is a shame to see the papers and the accounts they give. The campaign has been a most magnificent success so far - first nine day's fighting driving Lee through the Wilderness and ending with the glorious 12th, when he retired behind his forts, &c., at Spotsylvania. Then a week of waiting, some mud, some skirmishing, some fighting, much reinforcing, resting and reorganizing. Started again with army as good as ever - outflanked Lee, who fell to junction between the Annas - an attack not attempted, but railroads destroyed, and Lee befooled till we were ready to outflank him again and move beyond the Pamunkey on the Peninsula - changing our base from Belle Plain to Port Royal - and White House. Time up.

Aldace F. Walker

Under Fire, 6 P.M.
June 3d, 1864

Dear Father:

I don't know exactly where we are - somewhere about a mile this side of the Chickahominy near Cold Harbor and about ten miles from Richmond, in front of strong rebel works, the first lines of which we have carried, and judged so strong that further storming will not be attempted. The firing now is skirmishers with an occasional shell, and the bullets whistle over the rifle pit where we lie, thick and fast. We are in a pit that was taken from the Johnnies night before last and has been turned over, or faced about, for our use. Our position is a good one, I should think; but it will probably be months before we get to Richmond. Since I wrote last we have moved up around Hanover C. H., and destroyed R. R., &c., then by a long march day before yesterday moved to the left of the army. That was the hardest time we have had; it was hot very, and dusty extremely, and I thought awhile that I should peg out, but I got through the feel all right now. That same p.m. we went into a fight and lost a hundred men or so, mostly wounded - some half a dozen officers, mostly in our 1st Battalion. I am in the 2d. This morning we opened the fight at four - took one line in our front. We were in four lines, and our regiment in the fourth, so got nothing of damage as we were under cover, but the army lost heavily. We were moved to the front and ordered to charge, but this was countermanded on account of a swamp in our front and the strength of the army's position. We have been on the move ever since we left Washington - have slept tow nights in the same place but once - that was just after we crossed the Pamunkey, while the other Corps were crossing. I suppose the army is in position now for its advance. We have been joined by the 18th and half of the 10th Corps under Smith. Butler is played out for field service most effectually. His boys all blow on him.

The country where we are is quite rolling; we are on the top of quite a hill, and there are hardly any marshes around, though I suppose that there are some nearer the river. It is very woody; we are in the woods now, and most of the time. All the ground not woods is ploughed and sowed to corn or wheat. When we march over it, it makes a terrible dust. This fighting in the woods is pretty rough business. It is almost impossible to preserve any line. Regiments get mixed up, and Generals have hard work to know where their brigades are. I can't see why we are not well managed - as well as possible. Hancock is now on our left. If the field was clear and the ground open, we could finish the thing in short meter; but, as I said, it will take a long time. There is no need of anxiety, however, as the rebs are not in a situation to come any such game as they did over McClellan two years ago. They attack very little, and with time enough we shall fix them. Don't trouble yourself about newspaper stories, for any skirmish is magnified to a battle, and they get us along altogether too fast. I have seen some glowing descriptions of our little affairs at Spotsylvania that were quite ridiculous. Send me all the papers you can. If you can forward the Journal daily, that is in bundles for awhile, it will be a great pleasure. We expect another mail tomorrow. I have the Atlantic and enjoy it much.

Our regiment has lost about 140 so far in killed and wounded. We are terribly dirty. Have short rations sometimes, though we shall be all right now - such as they are. I don't know much about the rest of this army except our own Division, and nothing of the rest of the country at all; never felt so isolated. We had rain last night and it is cool and comfortable today. I presume after dark we shall move out a little and dig again. We can cover ourselves with a good rifle pit in an hour. I never want to hear anyone speak against smoking again. It is the greatest comfort I have - keeps one occupied, saves anxiety, is a great rest after a march, and when we are under fire it helps immensely to keep one cool and composed. I have had my pipe alight a good deal today. We confiscated tobacco in the leaf from the dry houses. I don't think I could have endured our marches either without an occasional taste of whiskey. Such habits at such a time are not habits. I'll look out for them.

12 M., June 4th, 1864

We worked all night last night in entrenching as near as possible to the enemy, and now we are lying in a perfectly safe position under fire from the rebel first line. A man who exposed himself carelessly was wounded five minutes ago two rods from me, though the shots are mostly random. The Artillery has been pegging away. It is the understanding that we are to dig 'em out. We have struck rebels further from Richmond that McClellan did, and if nothing happens we shall worry them out in the course of next fall. I wonder if I wrote in my scribbling yesterday of the great tendency one has to go to sleep under fire.

During that first shelling we were under, I had a nap. Yesterday I slept a good deal. Today I have slept all the morning - and needed it, for we worked all night. We are in the second line now, the 6th Vermont directly in our front. There are half a dozen lines back of us, and the men are plenty. We expected to charge yesterday, but didn't - believe I wrote that before. We have apparently more leisure today than we have had for some time before, and I believe I will transcribe so much of my dairy as relates to our marching, &c., hoping you will get it sometime. And by the way, I am very glad you have got that big box I sent. I think it will pay the expressage. I left my trunk with some other clothing, &c., in charge of Michael Donovan, Ordnance Sergeant at Fort Saratoga. I am surprised that I feel so well and happy; best of spirits all the time.

Well.

Thursday, May 12. Started at 5 a.m. Marched to city 1500 strong. Embarked and got away by 10 a.m., and rode to Belle Plain. Rainy and awful muddy, great confusion, wounded coming in, &c. Camped in the brush, in shelter tents and the rain.

13. Took a good while to get away. Started at 10:30 with one team, all baggage left with prisoners and a guard. Marched to Fredericksburg, 17 miles. Met 9000 rebel prisoners. Camped north of the river. Find pork fried on a stick is good.

14. Left camp at 7 and marched 15 miles or so to the 6th A. C. by Headquarters. Got in about 9 p.m. Roads almost impassable - through the Wilderness; got every man through, however, and all feeling well; hardly a straggler left from the regiment. Slept out of doors on the ground.

15. Moved up a mile on the left of the old brigade, and are now part of the 2d Brigade, 2d Div., 6th A. C., under Gens. Grant, Wright, Meade and Grant, on the extreme left of the army and I suppose nearest to Richmond. Nothing done. Wrote home. Reported that Lee has left our front.

16. Laid in camp till 2 p.m., when we (2d Battalion) moved over to the right of the Div. To support a batter, and encamped with nothing to do. Are on the plantation of a rich secesh, Anderson, 1700 acres, a nice house close by here. Troops to the right of us advanced during the day, our corps lying still.

17. Sergt. Baxter made 2d Lt. in Co. I (Now on Grant's staff as aide.) Nothing done till evening, when the 6th Corps was moved around to the right by a long road, all night on the march. The 2d was feigned to move away from front of Spotsylvania, and it was expected that we should break Lee's line. (Some said a reconnaissance in force was intended.)

18. Did not get around in season by reason of wagons and mud. Deployed at 5 a.m., but before we were fairly in the line rebs opened a very heavy cannonading. Troops stood the fire, but did not advance far or attempt to charge, and were drawn off about noon and marched home very tired. Behaved very well under the heaviest Art. fire of the season. Col. Warner, Lt. Glazier and others, wounded. Slept some under fire.

19. Broke camp and marched at 3 p.m. I was officer of the Day and had no sleep of any consequence, thus being up for two nights. Marched south as far as possible without engaging and entrenched. At 6 p.m. an action began on the right, 5th A. C. Our bands were playing, and with roar of artillery, made as exhilarating a time as I ever saw.

20. Lay in camp all day resting, &c. At 8 p.m. detailed on picquet with 195 men.

50 of them, Bat. M separated from us. Maj. Hunsdon in charge of Brigade line. Deployed on a skirmish line, rather than picquet. Slept a very little. Lying in charge of the reserve.

21. Relieved line at 6; fired at seven times in one place, but not hit. Rebs grew ramptious in p.m. Our army withdrew for a change of base, and the skirmish line drawn back _ of a mile into a rifle pit. Pressed hard, and at 5 attacked by two Brigades, five regts. Each. Lt. Bedell with 30 men sent to help the 37th Mass. 3d Vt. broke on the right, and they flanked us out of the pit nearly to where I was; we held our ground, doing well. Corp. Stevens and Priv. Larock killed - Priv. Marsh[6] wounded.

22. Up all night - buried the boys. Picquets all drawn in at 4 _; two hours after the last of the army moved, and we started for Richmond. It was very hot and we marched very fast to overtake our Div. When I reached there abut noon I could not stand. We marched five miles more. I got a ride of a mile on Chaplain's horse.

23. Breakfast at 4 1-2. Slept again till 8. Started. Marched four miles and could go no further - footsore and exhausted. Found Maj. H.'s horse and rode about four miles with boots off. Gave horse up to Goodrich, who was worse off than I, and footed it on a terribly rapid march to the North Anna, with heavy cannonading in front. Don't know how I got along, but dropped down at last with part of my Co.

24. Had a fine rest all day. Fell in to move at 4 p.m., but did not go. Had a swim in North Anna, which we crossed before breakfast. Firing on the left in front of Hancock. Prisoners coming in all day by squads - must have been quite a number in all. Wrote home, but no way to send it.

25. Hot, with a hard thunder shower at dusk. Moved south about two miles, crossing the Va. Central R. R., which is being destroyed. Lay in line of battle all the p.m. in hot sun. At dark advanced along the crest of the hill and entrenched. Rebs in sight all day, and sharp firing on the skirmish line.

26. Marched till 5 a.m. over the muddiest road imaginable. Made about eight or ten miles during the night to Chesterfield Station - bore off east after breakfast and down the Anna, to and down the Pamunkey. Had a tiresome time, very. Pulled up about 6 p.m., and went to sleep with a good appetite for it. Found two or three strawberries.

27. Marched at 4 1-2, four miles south to the Pamunkey and across and another mile beyond, where we entrenched in the p.m. - not very tired. Men short of rations through their own fault. I have enough and have got a liver for tomorrow. We lie, as I understand it, midway between Hanover C. H. and Town.

28. Lay in camp all day and night, being the first time we have spent two nights in the same place. A beautiful place, good water, &c., but no rations. Got a liver last night, and lived on it today. What will be done tomorrow for grub don't know. 1st Div. Advanced in p.m. and we stood to arms. Nothing done. Added to my letter home.

29. Hungry all day. Marched five miles to and around Hanover C. H., and lay there while R. R. was being destroyed; then marched back a piece and south. Quite an action going on on the left. We are on the extreme right of the army and facing west and

north to avoid flanking. Got rations at 7, then moved out half a mile. Big Mail came in - 9 letters and lots of papers.

30. Very hot and dusty. Laid in camp all day. Moved towards night a few rods to support a Battery. Had a good place for the night. 3d Battalion on skirmish line with heavy skirmishing. One man killed in Bat. I and several wounded. One suspicious wound - detailed a court to examine. Finished my letter home and started it off at 7 a.m.

June 1. Marched at 5 a.m., clear around the army to its left - took till 3 p.m. Was terribly hot, very dusty, woods afire, &c. The hardest march we have had. At 4:30 we deployed for battle. Went up a piece in second line and lay under an artillery fire, which was silenced by our artillery. Then a big charge on our right by 3d Div., driving rebs, and we advanced half a mile and dug.

2. A good night's rest. Skirmishing in morning, but no fight. Our 1st Battalion lost heavily yesterday. (120) Moved to the right and entrenched in rear of others and lay for the night. Reinforcements arriving. Rations issued at night for two days. John Sargent got a horse for us. This written under fire on the 3d lying on my back in the woods.

3. Quite a severe action all through the lines. Can't hear of what was done anywhere but in front of our Division, which carried one line. We were in the fourth line of battle and lost very little. Were moved up to the front and lay through the day, entrenching on the second line during the night. Cool on account of rain night before. Under fire all day and night, but well covered.

There you have our history to date, and I hope you will get it soon. Have seen two men slightly wounded while I have been writing.

Love to all.

Aldace F. Walker

We hear there is a mail for us at Brigade Headquarters

June 7th, 1864

Dear Father:

We have been under fire every day since and including the 1st. This morning we were relieved and withdrawn about a mile into a pine wood. Nice place for a rest - and very much to our satisfaction, for this lying in rifle pits, crawling around, kneeling and sitting, but no standing up, is real hard work. It is a great rest to be able to stand up and walk around, with no fear of a minie. We have probably lost in killed and wounded 175 since the 1st.

Half of our Brigade, including two Battalions of our regt., were sent to the assistance of the 2d Corps two or three days ago. We hear nothing from them save that they are in the front line, as we have been and probably lost more. I don't know, of course, now soon we shall be sent out again. I sent you my diary up to Friday, the 3d. Saturday we lay in the pit all day, rainy and sloppy. We were in 2d line, and continual firing, of which we got the most of the benefit. Good cover, but boys careless, and some hit. Big reinforcements coming to the army. Rebs charging on lines around, but repulsed. Heavy cannonading. Sunday we lay in camp and wrote letters. Men hit all around me all day. At night we went out to the front line 300 yards, or 250, from enemy and entrenched. I was in charge of the job, and it was rather a scaly one. We undermined the old front line, run out a zigzag to where we wanted to go, and put up a big breastwork with the traverses, &c., strong enough to resist cannon.

At daybreak Monday we moved in, and occupied through the day. Sharpshooters were distributed through the line, who opened and maintained fire all day. At noon we raised a flag of truce, under orders that a formal amnesty of three hours was arranged for the burial of the dead. The Johnnies knew nothing abut it, nor other divisions, but we had a little visit and exchange of papers before it played out and wee were whacking away at each other. I fired once, and made a good shot too; but mostly laid low for ducks. A battery was built just there, in which guns are to be placed tonight. After dark we were relieved and drawn back a few rods, and this morning brought back here.

We get a daily mail now, and can send; so I will write twice a week as usual, and perhaps oftener. My articles of comfort and convenience now consist of my clothes I have on, a private's overcoat, half a tent, a rubber blanket, my haversack, knife, fork (my silver one is lost, but I have smoused another,) spoon, cup and plate, handkerchief, towel, extra pair of socks - and that's all by my comb and toothbrush. I took off my shirt to wash it for the first time this morning; wear my undershirt, a blue one, meanwhile. Washed myself all over for the first time since the bath in North Anna.

The 2d Pa. Art. has come in, and is as green as we felt at first, in 18th Corps, Smith's. Sheridan's Cav. And a pontoon train has left to join Hunter. We are having a capital rest today. Rather expect our Art. To open tomorrow. And so goes the siege of Gaines Hill. We hear rumors of a siege train for us, but it is too good news to believe.

Love to all.

Aldace F. Walker

Yours 30th received last night. Don't want the handkerchiefs. Plenty of pork and hardtack now. Please send me five bags of strong white drilling, or something else, about eight inches long and five wide, to hold sugar, coffee, tea, salt, &c., with stings at top to tie them tight. My new boots ... one of them is all right; the other I burnt one night, so that there is a big crack across the bottom and jammed a hole through the toe night before last, so it is nearly played out without any chance to cobble. I have a pair of shoes in my valise; and there is an effort being made to bring them up for one look at them, to dig our clean shirts, socks, &c., which I very much hope will be successful. It was only the 1st Div. Of our Corps which secured the crossing of the Pamunkey.

Well, you letters do me a great deal of good. Please keep sending them; and write everything, for little things interest me full as much as the war. I see enough of that here.

Love to Mary, Belle and all.

Aldace F. Walker

Peninsula, Va.
June 8th, 1864

Dear Father:

I have not much to say this beautiful morning, but I will write a little, and send it sometime, as I know you like to hear often. We are still resting. Had a good night's rest last night for the first time, almost, since I can remember. On the front lines our engineers are still at work and will open soon, tomorrow perhaps, with batteries so unpleasantly near the Johnnies that I think we shall hold the Chickahominy by the close of the week. I presume we shall take another turn at the front tonight. Meanwhile we are making the most of our pleasant, comfortable posish, and shall be in good shape for another two or three or seven day's work in the front line.

We are out of the range of the minies, but not of the shells which are sent over our way occasionally. I had a man scratched by a fragment here yesterday. We have been figuring up our losses so far: killed, 23; wounded, 154 - nine of them being officers. Some of the wounded will die, some of them have already returned to duty. One of the officers, Lt. Wilson,[7] is not expected to live. Capt. Goodrich has gone back to Washington, played out. Orlando Liscomb, Qm. Sergt. in Bat. M, went to Washington with a flesh wound in the thigh, as happy as a man well could be in getting out of the campaign with nothing serious to bother him. One of our Battalions is still at the front. The Major of the 6th was killed yesterday,[8] Capt. Ed. Frost of the 10th the day before. Our loss since the 1st of June has been very heavy, 10 or 15,000. We hear rumors of heavy fighting yesterday by Warren, who swung around towards Bottom's bridge.

I believe I sent off a letter to you last night, but have not decided whether to forward this tonight or wait a little. About midnight last night we were wakened by the welcome news that our valises were up and accessible for a few minutes. So we got them open, and dug out what stocking and towels and handkerchiefs we wanted. I got my paper and envelopes, but did not find as much as I expected to, so want yours sent as I requested.

I have entrenched a little hole to set my tent over to keep off the shell fragments, and have it arranged so high that it seems like living; in fact, I am taking more solid comfort now than for a long time before. We sent out Lt. Dodge with a working party to the front last night, who finished the little fort in the front of our Brigade. The guns are not in position yet.

Our mail failed to come up last night; but four day's rations came and were issued. I got a few beans, which I expect to have boiled for dinner. I had my shirt washed yesterday, and my undershirt and drawers are in the wash today. I have not quite made up my mind to put them on again, however. There is one difference in our climate here from yours - the nights are always cool, and no matter how hot the days, one wants an overcoat at night. There is not any vast amount of fun in all this, however. How glad we shall all be when it is over. The Johnnies have just opened on us with shell, and I have incontinently sought cover. These shells are not very dangerous, but are excessively demoralizing. The 2d Pa. Regt. seemed to take it as a matter of course that a line of battle should move when a shell came. I am very glad and thankful I am so well and safe, and can but hope the time will come when we shall get out of this scrape satisfactorily - successfully.

Aldace F. Walker

I shall want some more stamps, as I am writing to various friends in the hope of getting letters, which I crave.

4 P.M.
June 9th, 1864

Dear Father:

We are still in the same place from whence I wrote you yesterday, back in the woods resting. We sent out a big detail to work last night. I expect part of us, if not all, will have to go to the outer line tonight. I take this opportunity of writing again, because I suspect it is the last chance I shall have for sometime.

There is another big move evidently in contemplation. Our works here have been constructed with the simple intention of holding our ground and amusing the enemy. Our Generals have given no attention to them. All has been done by subalterns; and, though apparently crowding the enemy, it has been done in self-defense. Orders have been issued to clear everything from the White House, and within a few days we shall be across the James.

The capture of Fort Darling by Butler would have been a great help to such a movement. I don't know whether we shall wait for its reduction, or move around it on to the Petersburg R. R. It is a big thing, any way, and attended with immense risk; just such a movement as Grant has so many times successfully carried through. I don't profess to be officially informed of the program, but I guess that City Point is our destination, or perhaps Bermuda Hundred which is close by. It will be a hard, weary march. The weather, however, bids fair to be cooler than it has been on our previous migrations; and I have got on so well hitherto that I am quite confident in regard to what is to come.

There is a new development in my case of late - a most ravenous appetite; I can hardly eat enough. We are learning to fix up our hardtack so that it is very palatable; make beef stews of our fresh beef that are first rate, and fries of our port grease that are quite good; and then we pound them up and cook them over again in the form of slap-jacks to eat with sugar. Our officer's supply train has just come up with a wonderful lot of stuff - potatoes, pickles, ham, beans, &c., dried apples; I don't know how we shall survive the infliction of such luxury.

Well, I have not time to write more, as our mail goes soon. We are anxious to hear from the Baltimore convention.

With love to all - and I think of home, home friends and home comforts, ever so much - and with great hope that our labors and trials will result in great and lasting triumph to our cause,

I remain, affectionately,

Aldace F. Walker

Peninsula, Va.
June 12th, 1864
Sunday, 7 A. M.

Dear Mary,

I received your nice letter of last Sunday day before yesterday, and was very glad to see it in so good season. We are still in the pits in front of Gaines Hill. Did not move as soon as we expected, though we understand that the White House has been abandoned, that the trains are moving around by Tunstalls, that the 2d A. C. has gone and the 5th probably, and we don't know how much more. The fact is, we are in a position that we can't get out of as easily as we entered upon our other flank movements, and very movement has to be made circumspectly. Our Brigade has relieved the 3d Div. Had relieved the 2d Corps; though I don't know anything about the arrangements, save that it seems as though we were being left to cover some sort of a movement; and we all suppose that the whole army is to be thrown south of the James, though this line may be still held - and in fact we don't know much about it any way, probably not as much as you do today.

I am very dubious about letters getting away, though they are still collected by the mail carriers. We got a mail this morning, but I got nothing but a Middlebury Register. We are now in the front line of works, with a picquet in front of us, which keeps blazing away, and the enemy's answers pass over our heads with the peculiar sing of a minie, that we are so well used to now. My headquarters are in an angle of a rifle pit - dug out and well protected, nearly high enough to stand up behind, with tents spread over the top to guard from sun and rain. Comfortable enough, though rather unpleasant to sit or lie down for days, with no chance to stand up and stretch without risk of having your head bored by a bullet. A ball just hit my tent over my head, at which we all laugh, as it is three feet too high, and in front of us we have ten feet of earth.

We get enough to eat now. I have on hand nearly ten day's rations of hard bread, pork, ham, beans, tea, coffee, sugar, salt, dried apples, flour, a few potatoes; have eaten up all our pickles; have some vinegar left for the beans, which are the greatest luxury we have now. My dinner is to be a soup of fresh meat, potatoes, bread and flour. We have plenty of salt and pepper, and feel as though we were living on the fat of the land. My appetite is huge, and my health of the best. My boys have cabbaged a horse and a mule to carry our stuff, and if our outfit of dishes was a little more complete we should be in first rate shape; we are rapidly "finding" these. How the woods around here are riddled by shot and bullets and shell. Every tree is marked, some of them fifty times. Col. Benton's health broke down, as everyone expected it would; he is unable to stand the climate, and chronic diarrhea has a strong hold of him. He is now at the hospital, and will doubtless resign at once. He has not done well in command of the regiment. He has been unwell and surly; has a very rough side naturally, and that has been the one he has exhibited. So his enemies have much increased, and all are wishing for Little Jim.

If Father wishes to see my name in print, he may send the following to the Herald. I don't care anything about it, but the arrangement of our regiment has been misstated in all the Vermont papers, and it may be well to have it right in one.

The 11th (1st Art.) is at present commanded by Maj. G. E. Chamberlain, Col. Warner having been wounded on May 18th, and Lt. Col. Benton being unfit for field service on account of chronic diarrhea. It is organized into three Battalions of four Batteries each, and either of these Battalions is larger than the old regiments of the Brigade. The first Battalion, Batteries F, L, K, and H, is commanded by Maj. Fleming; the second, Batteries E, C, D and M, by Capt. Walker of Bat. D; the third, Batteries A, B, I and G, by Maj. Hunsdon.

The regiment has lost (June 12th) about 180 officers and men, about 25 of the number being killed. It has participated in four engagements, besides being continually under fire in the front line of rifle pits from June 1st to date. Its conduct is highly complimented.

Well, this arrangement is highly satisfactory to me, as Col. Benton has turned over his horses to me, and if we have any more toddling to do I shall ride; that is, till Col. Warner comes back, when we shall have three Majors. I presume Col. Benton will at once resign. We hear that Gen. Getty has nearly recovered and will soon take command of his Division; which is good news to us, as Gen. Neill[9] has few friends, and few who respect him very extensively.

There is one very annoying circumstance connected with our lying in our pits - we have to get up and be ready for an attack at 3 a.m., which very much abbreviates my usual sleep. We make it up in the daytime, however. We are on hills now; Chickahominy swamps are a myth so far as we are concerned.

Well, I have scribbled off a pretty long letter. Good bye. Love to all,

Aldace F. Walker

P. S. Evening - Col. Seaver of the 3d has just been assigned by Gen. Grant to the temporary command of the 11th, so I am in my Co. still. We have rumors of a march tonight. I have Col. B.'s horses in my charge yet.

Charles City C. H.
June 14th, 3 P. M.

We left our line at dark Sunday eve., moved back a piece and lay till 12, covering movement of 9th and 18th Corps. Marched till next night at 8, getting around the big swamp and across the Chickahominy at Jones' Bridge, 25 miles. Not a very hard march - good roads, no tems, and cool day; many rests till the last six miles, which rather tuckered us. We started at 3 this morning and came on here. We are bout three miles from the James, lying deployed to cover the march of the rest of the army across the river. Having a good rest.

I am all right; some tired. Walked all the way, though I could have rode, but while I command a Co. I shall stay by them as long as I can. Our mule and horse played out. They were rather thin specimens. But I got my grub, &c., on to the Col.'s horse.

Aldace

Turkey Bend
June 15th, 1864

Dear Father:

We are having a nice time after our march that I hastily described to you in the letter I sent off last night. We laid still till 9 this morning, when we fell in and moved a couple of miles nearer the river, and deployed again. We are now lying facing northerly, like this across the peninsula, at the end of which the army and the wagons are crossing on lots of transports and one bridge. We understand that the 2d Corps, which started a day before us, has occupied Petersburg. We are to be the last of the army to move again, and are talking of entrenching our present lines. The 5th Corps is now passing through close by me, and teams innumerable. How long do you think it takes for an army Corps with its artillery and wagons to pass a given point? Perhaps six or ten hours. So we have to use all the roads available, and it takes some time to move an army of five Corps at that. It is marvelous to me how systematically these great masses of troops are handled. There is no clashing, no running of one body of men into another, or racing to see who should reach a point first and have the road, as there has been on other campaigns - see Casey and Fair Oaks. But every General knows where he is going to stop, and when he is going to start, and what he is going to do when he gets there, and everyone is kept toddling almost all of the time.

Our Corps seems generally to be detailed as rear guard; perhaps there is intention in it, as it has suffered most, and is the smallest in the army, and it is a good safe place usually. But the bother is, they make us hurry on and get in ahead to cover the next river crossing or something of the sort. Well, if I get on as well as I have hitherto, I shall be all right and shall be thankful. We were a little short for grub - the men; I know better than to get out again - but have had an issue today. Got some splendid pickles and potatoes and flour. Shall have some slap-jacks tonight, though the saleratus is lacking. Col. Benton has resigned. He says I shall be Major soon, and wants to sell me his horses, but I can't quite see that. I doubt if we can have three Majors now, though I don't know the law on the subject. I don't know as Col. Warner would present me for the position, and if he should it will take a month any way. I have had good luck through the campaign, and have made a hit or two, and stuck to my work generally in a manner that I have got some credit for; besides Col. Benton has rather a shine for me, though I don't reciprocate very extensively. I am proposing to keep quiet at any rate and wait for "something to turn up."

We all like Col. Seaver very well. He has much more field experience than Col. Warner can show when he comes back, and the loss of such service he will fell, and we too I fear. The country around here is very different from what I expected to find. It is capital just here - rolling, no marshes, and splendid clover fields. Almost all the open country, however, has been planted or sown this spring, and immense crops will be raised in the South. In the interior of the Peninsula it was more woody, and our marches lay in the shade principally. The Chickahominy is very insignificant where we crossed it, though I presume that above in the White Oak Swamp it is wider. When we get across the James we are thinking of occupying Petersburg, sending a Corps to cut the Danville R. R., and waiting for developments. What Grant and Lee intend I don't know, but I think on my individual responsibility that Lee will have to strike first in the next battle.

Love to all, and keep writing.

Aldace F. Walker

If you haven't sent any P. O. stamps, send some along, as I am all out.

Petersburg, Va., not exactly at,
but a mile and a half east of it,
and trying to take it this 18th
day of June, 1864, 7 A. M.

Dear Father:

We formed the line I told you about across the Peninsula east and south of Charles City C. H. on Tuesday last. We held it, contracting it occasionally half a mile or so, till Thursday eve., when we marched down to the river and crossed on a bridge of 101 pontoons, just at dusk. We left Burnside's niggers to see the rest of the stuff over, the main portion having crossed before. The 1st and 3d Divisions of our Corps went by transports up to Bermuda Hundred. We (2d Div.) marched all night and till 5 the next day, when we relieved the 18th army Corps in the front line before Petersburg, making 25 miles. A hard march, as it was very dusty and hot, and we were guarding trains, which interfered with the marching of the troops sadly. We passed some Ohio 100 day men on the road. Well, we find that a big thing has been done here.

One Div. of the 18th left Cold Harbor Sunday morning, went to West Point, took boats, came around here, were joined by a colored Division, and charged these works long before the rebs expected them, driving them from a strong position that might have been held against anything; and we are now a mile or so within the outer line feeling our way to the city. The darkies did splendidly.

It is rumored that Sam Duncan, who commanded a Brigade of them, will get a star for it. Since then the 2d, 5th, 9th and part of the 6th have come up, and the 18th has gone away. They had been fixing up a place they could hold, and planting batteries which perfectly commanded the city. The other troops were ordered on a grand attack at four this morning, and of course we were up and ready to participate. The 2d advanced over a plain in front of us in three lines of battle, expecting to have a terrible fire opened on them every minute, but found nothing but a light skirmish line. They are now pressing close to the city. We shall advance soon.

The prevailing impression is just now that the rebs have mostly left. What the result will be of course I can't say now. Our skirmishers are certainly very near the city. The spires are in plain sight and look beautifully. Col. Seaver has been returned to his regiment, on account of a disobedience of orders in posting us last night. We had got to liking him much, and don't think him to blame under the circumstances. Maj. Chamberlain now commands the regiment, Benton having sent in his resignation, and being at the hospital. Hunsdon also went to the hospital last night. I command the 2d and Capt. Buxton of G.

the 3d Battalion, but these are changing every day. We expect Hunsdon back soon.

We are in the yard and garden of a splendid residence, but the country between here and the James is pretty rough.

With much love,

Aldace F. Walker

Sunday Morning
June 19th, 10 A. M.

Dear Father:

We are, very much to our surprise, still in the same place we camped in when I wrote you yesterday morning. We are not in the front line so much as we were, however, for our advance is a mile in front of us, and our skirmishers are at the edge of the city. On the left, the rest of the army has not been so successful. Yesterday they found heavy interior line, and they are hammering away today, while we are comparatively quiet. Our Division was not much engaged yesterday, and can't be today as I see, for it is reported from our front that we can occupy the city at any time; though of course it won't do to get into positions that are still commanded by the artillery of the enemy. So we are waiting for developments on other places where our forces are nearly south of the city. I think no shell have been fired into the city, and I hope none will be. This siege is quite a thing, and will tell immensely on the campaign. I have just got New York papers of the 17th, and am immensely vexed at the stories they tell of a small force before us, &c., - probably in our hands at that date. Smith's Corps did a splendid thing, coming up so unexpectedly and going over their outer works so handsomely. Still, it was something of a surprise. The works were manned by home-guards, and the three lines of battle debouching from the woods were more than they could stand, though one line of us could have held it against anything. Now there are plenty of Johnnies before us, and days may elapse before we take the place.

I thought yesterday when I saw our skirmishers at a run, followed by our battle lines moving solidly over the plain between the hill on which we are supporting artillery and the city, that we should all move in by night. But, though they met nothing but skirmishers and sharpshooters in houses, still they were getting into range of certain batteries not yet taken, and we secured a good night's rest in these splendid grounds. This has been an aristocratic place - this plantation - for long years. We find in an outbuilding piles of letters and ledgers, from which we gather the details of a heavy business done by the family back to 1755, one transaction involving the purchase of tobacco to the amount of 125,000 pounds sterling for a London partner, &c. It is very interesting to look over these old documents.

Maj. Hunsdon returned from the hospital this morning. He was assigned to the command of the 3d Battalion, and I was left in command of the 2d. I don't know but what these changes are all essential. The organization of our regiment is now the same as what I wrote suggesting its publication. I don't know either why I am put in command of a Battalion rather than the four other captains senior to me in rank, and one of whom was removed from our Battalion to make room for me to command. Co. I exchanged for Co. C. This was done when we were at Noel's Turn. Since when I have not commanded Battalion at all, save for a few hours at a time, until yesterday; and now I presume Col. Benton will be up today, though his resignation has gone in and will doubtless be accepted soon. Maj. Chamberlain is liked better here than he was in the defenses. Still, he is old maidish and particular - very for a young man. Col. Warner will be around before long probably.

We got two mails yesterday. One, a little mail, in the morning; another, a big mail, in the evening. A letter from you in each, and in the last the bundles of stationary and papers. I got five letters and half a dozen papers; and also New York papers came, so that we are in clover in the literary line at 10c. each for the Herald, Times and Tribune. The 2d Vt. is just relieved from service at the front, as its time expires today. Great rejoicing among its members, and great envy among the rest of the Brigade. Men would re-enlist in last winter's camp, but such a campaign as this makes a man think that three years are enough. That account of Carleton's of the battle of the 1st is very good, though he thinks Neill stayed still, whereas he advanced full half a mile. There has been a call sounded for church just now, and I will stop for the service.

Of course I have written to the parents of those of my men who have been killed - only two thus far. As to lists, if I sent any home it would be to the News Dealer at Hyde Park, which you would not see. And in fact, I see by the N. Y. papers the names of two of my Co. reported as wounded, whom I had not seen since the 1st. Supposed were simply stragglers. They certainly were not in the fight with us. The fight of the 3d was harder than of the 1st. We did not get it so hot, however; but those ten subsequent days in the pits were very tiresome and hazardous. Knowing, as we did, that it was not the plan to go to Richmond by that route.

With much love to all,

Aldace F. Walker

Near Petersburg, Va.
June 21st, 1864

Dear Father:

I am decidedly puzzled. What we are about I am at a loss to know. We see by the Rutland Herald of last week that Petersburg is taken, but the point we fail to see. It is true we command it, but the rebs command it too, and rather a more immediate command than ours. I presume we have 300 guns that might play on the city - some of them in our line of battle - only half a mile from the suburbs, and one of these is playing close by this morning; not on the city, however, for I have never seen a battery open on a house but once, and of course it is of no use to us to burn the place - it is the position we are after. That once, by the way, was a day or two ago, when Gen. Neill was fired on from a big white house by sharpshooters, and came raving back at a gallop. "By G-d, I'll burn that house - I'll burn it," and a few shells burnt it to the ground.

This same Neill is a pretty small specimen, and I shall be glad when he is relieved by Getty, whom we know nothing at all about. We were first sent off her, you know, our

Division by itself, under "Bucky Neill," and we were in fear and trembling. He kept quiet, however, and on Sunday Wright came up with the rest of the Corps, which had been on a big railroad expedition with Butler.

The 1st Div. relieved Martindale of Smith's Corps, who by the way is one of the most energetic working men I ever saw - always on the go, and apparently to some purpose. We went on the front line Sunday night, relieving in our own division. Where the 3d Div. is I don't know, but last night we relieved the 2d Corps on our left, getting into a place where the bullets are a little thicker, though no danger in our pits. We think the 18th Corps has gone off in the direction of the Hundred, but where the 2d is gone is a mystery; perhaps on to the south side of the city; perhaps somewhere else, for we hear of fighting at Drury's Bluff. Where Lee is we don't know, and in fact we don't know much about what is going on.

We don't know whether we are besieging Petersburg in feint or in earnest. Our works now look just as they have before on our flanking scrapes. Still Gen. Barnard was over the front line yesterday and siege guns are being placed - 30 Pdr. Parrotts. But again, our lines are not advanced by night, as one might expect. And on the whole, we are in complete state of mystification. The only plausible solution is that we are working on to the south side, and are trying to come a big brag game, by an attack there while annoying them here.

It is queer how we accommodate ourselves to circumstances. Here we are with a like rebel line 100 yards or so across an oat field; sharpshooters in little holes in front picking away at each other; the rest of us lying quietly in the shade, waiting for an attack or "orders." We dig ditches back from the main pit so to make places for cooking, and live like pigs in the good, clean dirt. I have got the most comfortable place for my Battalion Hd. Qrs., with Lt. Lewis as my Adjt., that I have found in our rifle pit experience. A big hole, three feet deep, dirt thrown up to the front, with an old cart body for a support on two sides, or "revetement," boughs over the top, the sides cut down for seats or sofas - and on the whole quite a comfortable house, and high enough to stand up in, the front side being the front of our pit at this place, and the other protected side being towards a battery that enfilades us.

We start with a day's rations, and keep close till night. Capt. Frost was buried by Cap. Little, his brother-in-law; and he said he was excited he thought nothing of sending him home. Did not think it possible until the next day, when he found it might have been done; opened the grave, but it was too far gone. He was feeling bad about it. Still it is a thing that I care little for personally, and feel differently about from most. I have no care for the disposition of my body, and I feel that sending home the corpse of a friend only aggravates the pain and is useless expense. It is a custom the value of which I fail to appreciate. Of course I should follow your wishes in giving directions in my own case.

With love to all,

Aldace F. Walker

We are close to where the Petersburg & City Point R. R. enters the city, on the right of the army. Keep sending postage stamps; I am out again. Yours of 16th I received this morning when we were under arms at 3 a.m.

Petersburg, Va.
June 23d, 11 A. M.

Dear Father:

My letter of the 21st has had no opportunity to go out, and I will add a little. Grant has found a hard nut to crack here; and I presume it grows harder every minute, by reinforcements from Lee, and by new shovelfuls of dirt - for spades are big things I tell you. I am more mystified than ever at the position of things around here. We have moved to a new position, but I don't know where we are or what we are here for; bt I will try and tell you as well as I can. The night of the 21st we were relieved about midnight by Martindale of the 18th, marched back a piece, drew rations, and the whole 6th Corps marched way around to the left, on to the south side of the city. It will be an interesting task sometime to find from my diary how many of these night marches we have made. They are very fatiguing, slow at times, then very rapid, blundering along through the woods and byways, across fields, open sometimes, sometimes full of stumps and underbrush; but on the whole, though sleepy and weary, we endure them better than the heat and dust of noonday. By way of an episode, a New Jersey regt. that relieved us, sent out to relieve the videttes, and the party was fired on, as is very often the case. No one was hurt, but the whole regiment broke and ran in the most disgraceful manner. As I said, we came around to the south side of the city, I suppose striking for the Weldon R. R., but we have not reached it yet, though crowding on as fast as the Johnnies will let us. My Battalion was detailed as picquet reserve yesterday, and though the rest of the regt. were congratulating themselves, we have got the best end of the bargain. The line that we support covers the extreme left flank of the army. In fact it is so far refused and doubled around that it faces south. We are in a clean pine wood, near a farm where we get cherries and apples, for sauce, and beets, &c., and mulberries and blackberries are plenty around. We are in no danger at all, but the line is to be advanced today, and we follow. I sent 140 men on to the skirmish line this morning. One of them has just come in wounded by his own gun. There is no firing in our front. The rest of the Corps and regt. is charging down through the slash on to the railroad gradually. They went in with a big yell on to a rifle pit last night - found it empty. We heard the hollering, but nary gun. I think they took two prisoners. I am afoot yet, because I can't get a horse. Col. Benton has gone home, a citizen. My watch is played out - something broke - but I carry another. My boots are nearly gone up - have seen hard times, I tell you. I wonder if there are any cobblers in Petersburg - and if we shall ever get there to see. We must be four or five miles south of the city. I got papers this morning, but no letters. Have had quite a good time reading, however. Keep writing as usual.

Much love,

Aldace F. Walker

June 24th
Morning, 11 A. M.

I am still on the picquet line, and no letter sent. Will try and get this off, for fear you may hear bad stories from the regt. and be alarmed. The performances hereabouts yesterday were very bungling. The R. R. was taken and some of it destroyed, but being held by a skirmish line with no supports, it was easily taken back by Ewell's Corps, which charged clear through down to where we were. The 1st Battalion of our regt. lost heavily. We don't know how much, though there are rumors of a good many prisoners taken. I have seen no one who knows. One Co. of the 3d lost somewhat. In my 2d, I never have been so vexed as at the part it was forced to play. I sent 140 men under Lt. Chase, a very fine officer of "E," and Lts. Sherman, Bedell and Lee, in the early morning, the rest of us staying back at our reserve.

And by the way I have not been under fire myself. In the p.m. this line of my men was advanced one-half mile, and the troops on the left failed to make connections, and this is what vexes me; for the Division Officer of the Day sat by and did nothing. The line then ran thus with the break as represented. It was attacked in force. Stood two charges, under cover of piles of rails, then was outflanked on the left and had to skedaddle. Lt. Sherman was killed trying to reestablish the line, which was done on the old ground. Lt. Chase has not been heard from.[10] About 25 of the men are killed, wounded or missing. This morning the line was advanced again and in good order, and I am now with my reserve in the spot where the charge was made last evening. We expect to be relieved every minute. Nothing to be seen of the Johnnies.

In haste,

A. F. W.

Sunday P. M.
June 26th, 1864

Dear Father:

We are still where I sent my last letter from and hope for a few days rest here. We have entrenched a line facing west and south, and are covering the left of the army. Our picquets hold the railroad. Our regimental headquarters are in a nice place under a group of trees, and we are resting as much as possible this terribly hot weather. And if ever men needed rest, we do. It seems as though we could do nothing else, though the men are perfectly willing to try and do all they can. The great event of yesterday was a call from Henry, who is attached to the 1st Div. 2d Corps Hospital, which Corps lies on our right, and so he hunted me up. You may imagine how glad I was to see him. We rode over to the 10th regt., which is camped near us. I saw Salisbury, John S[heldon], and others. John is better, doing duty now. Had not heard directly that Kate was married. I hope to see Henry again soon. He says that I am changed, but I reckon that I am only bronzed and dirty. Our regt. looks pretty small now, but its colors are all right, and its reputation good. Is said to be the only "Heavy" regt. that has done credit to itself, and is called as good as anybody's regt. I opine that troops are weighed principally by the number of men they lose.

I was mistaken about the body of Lt. Sherman. It was disinterred to be sent home, but was not sent; owing to, we think, the conduct of the Division Medical Director, who did not keep his word in the matter. What we are doing around here I don't know - planting batteries, I suppose. Lee's army is in our front, and I suppose the two armies are in about the same relative position as to spirits and strength as when they started. Though we have been reinforced heavily, Lee has too - though probably less. We have got in a position where we can hear absolutely nothing of what is going on, and so we hold our lines in tranquility. Perhaps we shall cut Lee off from Richmond some of these days. That affair the other day was a mean thing. It was all bad management; though who, is not determined. Probably the fault lies among certain Staff Officers and certain Officers of the Day. The Corps Officer of the Day, Lt. Col. Pingree of the 3d Vt., I think did badly. Well, we number now 860 men, the 4th Vt. only 60, as the result of that scrape. I think I told you of my present command and arrangements generally. I still mess with the officers of my Co., and we have one of the best messes in the regt. We had soft bread issued to the army yesterday.

As ever,

Aldace F. Walker

----

1 Capt., later Lieut. Col., Lyman Enos Knapp, Townshend. MC 1862. Wdd 5/12/1864 and 4/2/1865. RR.

2 Sergt., later Lieut., Henry Edson Bedell, Westfield. RR.

3 Privates George O. Stevens, Stowe and Joseph Larock, Westfield, both of Co. D, were killed in action 5/21/1864. RR.

4 USA Maj. Gen. Gouverneur Kemble Warren, Commanding 5th Corps. Boatner, 891.

5 USA Brig. Gen. David Allen Russell. Boatner, 713.

6 Private Zelora Marsh, Westfield, Co. D. He was wounded in the eye. Henry E. Bedell Diary, May 21, 1862. Italo First Brigade Collection. Accessed 1/21/2002, available from http://vermontcivilwar.org/1bgd/11/bedell-diary.shtml; Internet.

7 Lieut. Stephen R. Wilson, Morristown. Mortally wounded 6/1/1864 and died 7/6/1864.

8 Maj. Richard B. Crandall, Berlin. 6th Vt. Infantry, killed in action 6/7/1864.

9 USA Maj. Gen. Thomas Hewson Neill, commanded the division while Getty was recuperating. Boatner, 586.

10 Lieut. Henry R. Chase, Guilford; taken prisoner, 6/23/1864. RR.

14.
Early's Raid on Washington
July and August, 1864

Camp in the Field
Sunday Morning, July 3d, 1864

Dear Father:

Our Corps has been off on a raid to Reams's Station, as I wrote you before, and has returned, having lost but one man, who was gobbled while "foraging." We are back with the army now. Went off Thursday night, and formed our lines, advancing over the railroad and fortifying. Friday we had a nice time in an oak grove, where was situated a church and a schoolhouse. And, by the way, about once in five miles around this region you find a very pleasant grove with a church and a schoolhouse, both brown, but both very decent indeed. We saw more of the real Southern country on this trip than we ever did before. It is very woody, but where there are clearings almost all is under cultivation; no grass land; corn and wheat, with a few potatoes. The cultivation this spring was very hurried. Corn was planted by running a furrow through and turning it back, leaving the space between the rows unplowed. When we came across a grain field it had to suffer. That Friday we took desks from schoolhouse, made rolls, and were mustered for pay. The movement was a complete surprise to the inhabitants.

One of the most intelligent men at Ream's, a Scotchman, drafted, but employed on the railroad at $7 per day, saw fit to return with our train. The rebs held our skirmish line pretty well, but when our Brigade, which led the Corps, deployed and advanced in line of battle, they incontinently skedaddled. Well, at dusk we started and came back on a terribly slow, weary march, about five miles, where wee fielded the whole Corps in a big corn field. The next morning we moved out into the woods, getting headquarters in another church and schoolhouse, and lay there waiting orders, which told us to return here yesterday, as I said. On passing this time in review, I find I have reckoned one day too little, and that we started the day before the date I fixed. We were run off at last into the woods behind the hospitals, and I suppose our Corps is now held in reserve - which, although we are liable at any time to be moved off on a march like the one we have had, still is preferable to being in the front line, where there is still occasional firing, if not more. A sort of Corps of Observation, as the French call it. Our sutlers are here - our baggage wagons, with our clothes and dishes. Our tents are pitched in style, with tables and beds. And, on the whole, our present situation is gay.

I am only a quarter of a mile from Henry; saw him last night, and he promised to comer over today. I was on horseback on that expedition, and I find that, although I got along well enough I thought on foot, it is preferable by far to ride. But it is so hot, and the dust, fine and deep, is stirred from its profoundest depths by the march of troops, cannot be described at all. Supper last night - potatoes, mackerel, soft bread and butter, canned strawberries, tomatoes, tea, earthen ware; as long as we are here we are well enough off. I presume we shall have service today sometime. We have been busy so far today fixing up our camp. It is about noon now. Our mail is just being sorted, but I don't expect anything from you today; I got your last Sunday's and Monday's letter on Friday, somewhere south of here. I hope you were not in suspense long about my being a prisoner, cause I didn't go.

Aldace F. Walker

Monday Evening
July 4th, 1864

Dear Father:

I am actually writing by candle light; the luxuries are beginning to come in. We are still in the place from whence I last wrote you and no signs of moving, and I hope there won't be for sometime to come. We have a beautiful place for this sort of weather - a fine grove, if such a thing there be; but if it gets wet there is a swamp in our rear that will trouble us on the fever and ague line, but for the present we can call it a capital location. We have made pretty good arrangements as to our personal comfort, and are ready to rest if the powers that be are only ready to let us. Our Brigade band, a very good one, is just playing, "Rock Me to Sleep Mother," and playing a beautiful air well. If I had the least tendency towards homesickness I should take a shake at it now, but I fail to see it; for I am well and happy and ready for what comes, only I very much prefer that there don't be any more campaigning just at present. This is the glorious 4th of July. Grant is not in Richmond - not by no means; and won't be at present, though I hope he will by next year. But he has good news from Sherman, even if it means powerful reinforcements to Lee. It has seemed like Sunday today around here - so still and quiet lying in camp, with a dress parade at evening. We are where we see no other troops. Still, today I have seen a good deal of company, or been a good deal.

After breakfast I saddled my horse and rode by Henry's establishment to the headquarters of the 2d Corps, and called on Frank A., who was very glad to see me apparently. At any rate, I ate another breakfast and had quite a visit with him. He told me of the news from Sherman, and a good deal of other gossip, which I may retell sometime, but can't stop tonight. Then I rode to the 10th and called on John, who has been appointed Commissary Sub., but has not yet received his commission, and will have to serve with his regt. for the present. Had a visit and a ride with Chaplain Haynes. And then Henry was here to dinner; spent the afternoon and was here to supper. I was able to give him a very good one, as in addition to our present facilities for good eating, (which I love so much to talk about, for it is a novelty and a capital one,) we have good cooks, enlisted men; their coffee is capital. Eugene Mead called on me last night. He told me of Charlie's death, and the circumstances, which I meant to have told you; but I see by your last, of Thursday, which came today, that you have heard already as much as I know. He was a good boy. Genie feels badly, but keeps up good heart; has improved much, and is quite manly. It seems as if this campaign was coming nearer home than others have. Several college friends have been killed. And yet some have suffered all the time. I do hope we are in a position to rest. Much has been gained - not as much as was hoped. Banks failed to back out of the Red River and demonstrate on Mobile. Butler and Sigel failed. Grant failed, in fact. But we are much better off than we were two months ago – immensely - and I am sorry the croakers made so much fuss over the little Weldon R. R. affair.

Love to Aunty, Mary, Belle and all.

Aldace F. Walker

July 7th, 1864

Dear Father:

Our nice camp was broken up very soon after we commenced to enjoy it. At 3 a.m. yesterday morning we were routed and marched a mile or so before breakfast, going into position behind rifle pits which we dug some two weeks ago when we first came into these regions. We relieved the 3d Division, which it is understood has gone to Harper's Ferry. The great question now is, Shall we follow them? We rather expected to go this morning. Still I did not think we should get away so soon (if we went at all) as the transportation could hardly be furnished so rapidly, if it is true, as we understand, that our transports, a good many of them, have gone to New Orleans after the 19th Army Corps. We think more about it, as we are quite anxious to get out of these regions. Such an expedition would be hard before we got round, but still we have been just as far South and just as much of it as we want. It is so dusty and so hot. We have had no rain yet, but it is a little cooler this morning. A nice breeze is blowing, and we are feeling quite comfortable.

I have got my muster rolls made out and accepted, but some of the Companies which lost their rolls when the Captains went South will delay us till we can get a copy of the last roll from Washington, and our pay will be some time coming I fear. I have got a pretty good house here, compounded of tents and boughs. The only trouble is the dirty sand which composes the floor. I shall be pretty well satisfied if we do as well every time however. We get news pretty reasonably early now. I am sorry for the scrape which has resulted in Chase's resigning - principally on account of the effect which it will have on this country and others - as though he felt that he could not carry it through. And yet I rather think he did not expect his resignation to be accepted. I hope Fessenden will take the job, for he certainly understands the situation. There is a great dearth of news from these parts now. There is more or less cannonading all the time, but none near us. We are a good way from Petersburg, and on the left flank, refused to prevent its being turned. This position of ours is rapidly becoming impregnable. I think that one of these days when it is strong enough to be held by a simple picket line, and it is nearly so now, that one Corps will be left to keep the posish, and the rest of us will "move." We must rest first, however, and wait for cooler weather I hope. We have daily dress parades, and the bands are in their glory.

The Brigade purveyors, or sutlers, are here and doing as lively a business as the limited amount of cash afloat will permit. I never want to hear sutlers universally condemned again. It is nearly time to hear from you again. Our mail is daily now, and quite regular. The 3d Vt. is to leave for home in a few days, and the leaving of these old regiments makes the rest of us homesick. Still, it can't last always. I expect sometime to be out of the wilderness and to drop the sword.

Love to all.

Aldace F. Walker

Evening - No news and no letters. Am trying to arrange my papers and returns, but find it quite a job with my slim conveniences. Wish I had my desk and old arrangement of papers. Love to all.

On Board Steamship S. R. Spaulding
July 11th, 1864

Dear Father:

The 6th Corps has fairly on its travels gone. I wrote sometime ago that the 3d Division had gone, comprising about half the corps. Because it was very large to begin with, and because it has never been able to lose its proportional numbers in battle, mush to the disgust of the rest of the Corps, who call it cowardly, and with some justice, I fear - but that's neither here nor there. The point is, we follow them. Where they have gone, we don't know, though we understand we are to land at Washington. We are intensely glad to get out of the heat and away from the dust and flies that made our position so insupportable near Petersburg; but I fear a hard campaign is before us. Saturday morning I rode over and called on Henry, finding him well, and by the way leaving him my July Atlantic; the June number I think was lost. In the p.m. we fixed up our quarters in gay shape, building an arbor and a bed. The nights in this region are always cool, however hot the day may be, and we made arrangements with our shawls for a good night's rest. I bunk with Lewis, my Adjutant. We had been resting just about a quarter of an hour when the order came to "pack up," and before we were fairly awake we were off. Went a piece and waited to get the Brigade fairly arranged, and got off at half past eleven, pulling up from the extreme left of the army, at City Point, in just six hours, 5 1-2 in the morning. It was a very rapid march with no rest at all, but much better than marching in the daytime such weather as this. We were the last regiment of the Division to embark, and did not get away till 6 p.m., lying sweltering around all day, and expecting to move every minute.

It was a hard Sunday, I assure you. I got a chance to wash and a breakfast with a former sutler's clerk of our regiment, who keeps an eating house at City Point. While there I saw two college acquaintances, Williams[1] and Partridge,[2] and Jack Hurley of Long Sue fame, who works for government on the railroad. I got my men aboard, Maj. C., the horses and baggage, and two of Hunsdon's Companies going here, and Hunsdon and three Companies going on a smaller boat. This is one of the finest transports in the service - good staterooms, meals, and accommodations generally, and we are not at all crowded. A boat we just passed with a Brigade on looks miserable enough. The 1st Division came after us, niggers relieving us. I came on board with less than a dollar in money, but we happened to catch a mail just as we were starting and I found your twenty dollar bill. The other things did not get along. We came down the James, passing our old crossing place before dark, and the Atlanta moored near by. Then we turned in and had a good night's rest, and in the morning were up in time to see Newport News, Fort Monroe and the riffraffs, having anchored during the night on account of fogs. We are now, 3 p.m., just turning into the Potomac, passing Point Lookout, where they keep the Johnnies. It is a longer journey than I thought, taking the mail boats twenty-six hours, and these transports longer of course. We expect to anchor in the Potomac tonight and get up to Washington in the morning. Still we are sailing right along and may get around tonight.

Col. Warner is at Washington, being assigned to his old command in the defenses for a week, to get the militia into shape. There are two Ohio regiments there. I presume he will join us when we get there, however. Your letter hopes Grant will not weaken his army, &c. Well, I don't think he has. We were the fifth wheel at Petersburg - of no account save as a reserve, and what is wanted of a reserve but to go where it is needed? I don't anticipate it is so much of a defensive movement however - for I don't take much stock in any vast number of men being detached by Lee - as a movement in force on a point we have twice failed to get this spring - Lynchburg. I don't know about this of course; hope not, for it would be an awful march; but it may be the case. Even if we go to Frederick or Harper's Ferry or Hagerstown, we shall sweat some little, I reckon. But it will be better all round than lying in those rifle pits, (how we hate 'em,) and not on this account so much as on that of the weather. I don't think much of the Vermont Cav. was with Wilson;[3] we have not heard of it. We did not start till they were driven back from Ream's, still Kautz[4] came in while we were there. Henry Chellis, by the way, is under Kautz. There was a strong skirmish line at Reams's that held our skirmishers, but when our Brigade deployed and advanced on the railroad they marched. I inquired for "Luty" in the 2d Ct. last night, but did not find him. Love to all.

Aldace F. Walker

Fort Stevens, D.C.
July 13th, 1864

Dear Father:

I have a familiar dating place, but am amid unfamiliar scenes to some extent. We got into Washington about eight Tuesday morning, and were ordered to Fort Stevens at once, as there had been heavy skirmishing the day before, and the rebel line was only 500 yards in front of the Fort. We found the rest of our Division here, and massed our Brigade on 14th St., half a mile down the road, near Rohrstown. Our Brigade was the last in, and at four the other two Brigades advanced, deployed into a strong skirmish line and charged. We drove them, of course, the Forts firing heavily, (they had fired at intervals all day.) The Generals and President and Secretaries, &c., were in the Fort looking on, Lincoln with a hole in his coat sleeve. After dusk our Brigade went out and relieved the picquet line, and soon after we formed we could hear them leaving. There were, I should judge, 50 killed on each side, besides the numerous wounded. Our Brigade was not engaged at all, except a few detailed as sharpshooters, three of whom were wounded from our regiment.[5] But the fighting was heavy, and the rebs meant to take the Fort too. The magic word "6th Corps" was what started them. The prisoners (we have a number, 50 or so) all say they thought they were fighting militia, but when they saw those Brigades advance and deploy they recognized the style of men that had been there, and soon they could see the cross of the 6th Corps, and then they knew it was all up. They said the last they heard of the 6th Corps it was at Reams's Station. And it was considerable smart moving.

Sunday night at City Point, Tuesday fighting in the District of Columbia. These houses around here, Butts and the rest in front of the Fort, are burnt, by our folks as a military necessity.[6] The inhabitants take it well and fall in and fight too. The rebs have all gone now, to Baltimore perhaps. What will be done with us we don't know. They are trying to keep us in the defenses. Col. Warner is in command of the Brigade west of here across Rock Creek, Col. Haskins of this Brigade, and Gen. McCook[7] of the whole line north. We rather dislike to be serving as infantry around here, and these Ohio hundred day boys in the Fort; but can't help it much. There are some dismounted Light Ord. Companies serving part of the guns, however.

I was sick yesterday, an attack of colic and diarrhea night before last and through the day that nearly played me out; so I laid around and did not do more than I could help; did not come out here last evening, but slept back at the tavern. I did not eat anything and am weak today but feel much better and am around. I have been out to Blair's. Find the old man's house all right. The P. M. Gen's burnt to the ground, still smoldering.

Poolesville, Maryland
Friday Morning, July 15th, 1864

Dear Father:

We are on the rampage, for a wonder of course. The 6th Corps is bound to travel for a living, and that seems to be about all the good it does. When I wrote last we were on picquet in front of Fort Stevens. The men ate their dinner as usual about eleven. We were relieved by a mess of men from the convalescent camp just after, marched back of the Fort, and put under marching orders. The Corps 1st Division had started - we were to follow, our Brigade in rear of the whole and of all the trains. We tried to get away at 3 p.m., but could move only by inches. Got to Fort Reno, Tennallytown, where we saw Col. Warner, who is in command of the Brigade there, about 9, only three miles. Then we began to move the trains, new mules and green drivers began to break down, and we went by them. Our regiment in rear of all when we started, and on we went and went, and at 7 a.m. we were 21 miles from Washington, and had nary mouthful to eat. If we weren't pretty well played out - but few of us left; most have got up now. We rested two or three hours, and pushed on through the heat of the day, by Seneca Hills to Poolesville. We were there ahead of our Brigade and ahead of the 1st Division and ahead of everything except the cavalry. How it all happened I don't know, but I do know that we deployed here before the rebs had all crossed the river, but the rest of them did cross mighty sudden. We were too late after all.

We got to Fort Stevens in good time, and in time. There was quite a smart fight there Tuesday night. It was much more of a thing than I supposed. I think the loss on both sides must have been 500, and I saw lots of dead Johnnies and many of our own, and this in the District of Columbia. In Mr. Blair's house I found a photograph of a young lady with this writing on its back. I replaced the carte and took a copy. "Taken from a pilferer for old acquaintance sake with Miss Emma Mason, and left at 11 p.m. here by a Rebel Officer, who once knew her and remained behind to prevent this house from being burned by stragglers, as was the neighboring one. 11 p.m., and no light. July 12, 1864." Rather romantic.[8]

This country is beautiful. Has not been greatly injured by the raid save in the loss of cattle and horses and grain. The rebs made a pretty good haul. Still the raid was not so great an exploit as was Sherman's or Wilson's when they circumnavigated the rebel army.

Wilson's cavalry came up last night and has gone after the rebs, some of the Vt. Cav. among them. The 19th Corps is here, part of it. As I said, the 6th could easily be spared from Grant, and both Corps can be returned in six days if needed. We left Sunday and were engaged here Tuesday. What we shall do now I don't know and can't guess. More of the valley perhaps. I am all right.

Aldace F. Walker

Leesburg, Va., or rather on the top of a high
hill about three miles west of Leesburg, Va.,
Sunday, July 17th, 6 A. M.

Dear Father:

I have had no chance to get my other letter off, and add another sheet if we don't get routed before I get it done. We lay at Poolesville one day, Friday, as I suppose for other troops to come up - the 19th Corps and more cavalry - and also to get orders. A staff officer went to Washington and brought back an order from Gen. Grant for us to make up an expeditionary force of our own Corps, the 19th, Hunter's and Sigel's forces, men from Baltimore and all about, all under Wright, to follow the rebs and live on the country. This is as we understand it, at any rate. There is nothing with us as yet but the 19th, and only two small Divisions of our Corps, with some cavalry and artillery; but we seem to be headed toward Winchester, or somewhere where we shall join the forces in the valley. You probably know now more about the dispositions of the troops for the campaign than I do. We marched about 20 miles or over yesterday, passing above Edward's and Conrad's Ferries, as the water was too deep, and wading the river at White's Ford.

When we got to the river we saw the Johnnies across, shelled 'em out and put after them, a battery of artillery crossing among the first, which kept them all the way here in continual trouble. Still it was only their rear guard of cavalry, the main force having passed through here a day or so before, and a big force too, as their tracks showed. Our two poor little divisions, though called the two best in the Army of the Potomac, would not stand much show against their big army - but we shan't catch 'em I reckon. Fleming's horse was sent to Washington by the 3d going home, but I got another of the surgeon which I think I shall buy - a beautiful riding mare, and for sale cheap on account of a little doubt as to the possibility of a U.S. brand, which I am willing to risk. I took off my coat, vest and suspenders, and had the most comfortable day I have had on the march as yet. The men stood it well too. The country here is very like Vermont; hilly, and yet the soil is not exhausted. The grass is heavy and crops good. I rode through corn fields where the corn was up over my head on my horse. The water is good and abundant, and the air is most invigorating. I had far rather be campaigning here than lying still at Petersburg. With very much love all round,

Aldace F. Walker

Shenandoah Valley
Tuesday, July 19th, 1864

I don't know as we shall have anything more to do with Uncle Sam's mail, either giving or taking. It is just a week now since we had a chance to do either. It don't trouble us so much as it does the good people at home I fear. We are still chasing Johnnies. We understand now that Wright's orders are to follow them carefully until he sees them well off up the river, and then return with his 6th Corps to Washington. Still, this is dubious. We have quite a little army here now - 6th and 19th Corps, Hunter's and Sigel's and Crook's Cavalry - and can hold them if we can't drive them. I don't know which is intended.

We had a nice rest last Sunday. Lay in a beautiful grove all day waiting for others to get up, and among them our 3d Division came up from Baltimore via Washington. I went with Dodge out in front of our picquet line in the p.m. and got some butter and chickens and blackberries, &c. We are living pretty well nowadays; have just learned how. No forage is furnished for horses, but we have a few days rations along in the trains. Yesterday morning we set out and had a very nice easy march of about twelve miles, taking all day for it, and passing through Snickersville and Snicker's Gap into the Valley of the Shenandoah. We were coming down the mountain in rear of the army, and heard cannonading, which we found resulted from one of Hunter's Brigades having crossed the river without supports and getting into trouble, losing a good deal. I presume the rebs have all left before this time; but don't know of course, as we halted half way down the mountain in a clearing, with another hill between us and the river.

I see the 8th Vt. occasionally. Capt. Pollard[9] is all right, as well he may be, that regt. having lain at New Orleans all the spring. He is about the only one in that regt. I ever saw before. Chaplain Haynes has just come into camp, and I am going to try and find out something about the 10th and the fight of the Monocacy, where the 3d Division didn't distinguish itself.

I saw the Chaplain awhile, and now we are about to move somewhere - perhaps only into the woods to rest, perhaps on picquet, perhaps to form a defensive line, perhaps to fight; but this last is highly improbable, for I don't think they propose to make any stand in their retreat up the Valley. My horse has cast a couple of shoes, and I have been riding around to find a chance to have him reshod, but didn't succeed. It is rather hard to see a horse barefoot on these rough roads, but is can't be helped it seems. Well, time is passing. Yesterday the boys were telling of thirteen months and thirteen days. If nothing breaks our term of service will end sometime, whether the war does or not, and I hope for a more speedy termination of both. I hope, however, that in any event we shan't go to Petersburg again, for I have a great horror of that region. Hoping I shall hear from you before long, and with much love to all, I remain,

Aldace F. Walker

Thursday
July 21st, 1864

Last Tuesday week, the 12th, was the date of the last mail we have seen or sent; but we are on our way back to a base and reliable communications again. What has been done meanwhile we know nothing of, and of what we have done we know little. We followed the rebs into the Valley of the Shenandoah, cautiously avoiding a general engagement, though with considerable skirmishing. I suppose it was a sort of grand reconnaissance, and I should think a very successful one. Tuesday night the rebs left the ford they had held during the day, and Wednesday morning we crossed, our Division going the least distance of any, a couple of miles perhaps towards Berryville, and at dusk we all started back towards Washington. We waded the river again, re-passed Snicker's Gap, had a mean time getting to the top of the mountain, started down about one, and got to Leesburg to breakfast at nine, having made 19 miles. Then we came on six miles more, and are to spend the night, I suppose, and try to get to Washington in the morning, or rather tomorrow night. It has been a hard march so far, and rapid. I got a couple of shoes tacked on to my mare at Leesburg. She is a much more valuable beast than I thought. I enjoy riding, I assure you.

Love, &c.

Aldace F. W.

Fort Stevens,
or Brightwood, D. C.
July 26th, 1864

Dear Father:

I have not had a chance to write a line since I sent my last on the march back to Washington, for reasons which I will tell in a great hurry. Friday night when we had halted my Battalion was sent on picquet, and I was up and around a good deal. Found capital quarters in a Virginia mansion, and made myself at home. Saturday we came on, and the Corps went into camp near Fort Gaines in rear of Georgetown. Sunday I spent the morning in getting my horse shod at Tennallytown. We had an inspection, then I went to Saratoga and obtained possession of old Grey, which took me till 11 p.m. in a rainy night - some 12 miles and back. During Sunday we received an order detaching us from the 6th Corps, and ordering us to report to Gen. Augur. Col. Warner joined the regt. and reported Monday morning, and we were ordered to our old line. We moved over. I was assigned to the command of Forts Lincoln, Thayer and Saratoga - Hd. Qrs. at Lincoln, in a beautiful big house, the best place on the line. It took till after dark to get things arranged, and then I could not get a candle, and so had to go to sleep. The commission you saw announced in the papers reached us Sunday, and I now wear a Major's cap.

Today as soon as I could get away, Capt. Lewis and I went to town to be mustered. We did not succeed, and I was just hunting for the paymaster to try and get some money, when I was met by an order to join my command, as the regt. was ordered to rejoin the 6th Corps. Wasn't I in a happy frame of mind? I made a few purchases, and went to the Metropolitan and ate as big a dinner as I could get into me, spent all my money, and started for Fort Lincoln. Found them gone an hour and a half. Followed to here, six miles, found them still half a mile ahead, got mad and concluded to stop at Sweetland's for supper, feed my horse and write this letter, and as supper is about ready I must stop soon. It seems that after we left Snicker's Breckenridge and Early turned back, gave Hunter's forces at Winchester a good thrashing and again menace Harper's Ferry. The Corps has moved toward Frederick via Rockville, and we are to follow them and join them "for temporary duty with the Corps," the order says. So we hope to get back sometime, and I think before long. We were happy as clams in our good luck in re-entering the Defense, and now we are equally vexed at our removal. But we can stand it all I reckon. I pity the poor exhausted men, though.

Aldace F. Walker

Monocacy, Md.
July 28th, 1864, Noon

Dear Father:

I wrote you a hurried line on Tuesday as I was rushing after my regiment from the city. I followed on with Col. Chamberlain and the Chaplain for company, and caught up about eleven, finding them camped by the side of the road half way from Tennallytown to Rockville. The next morning we got off bright and earl and marched twenty three miles to Hyattstown, where we caught the old Brigade. This morning we came on here and are resting on the old line of battle of the 3d Division some weeks ago. Frederick is in sight, and the railroad and river are just in front of the ridge under which we are covered. I suppose we are to lie in this vicinity and await further developments. It was a stunner to us to be ordered out of our old barracks again so soon and so unexpectedly. We had just got home and were so confidently expecting to stay awhile, and had congratulated ourselves so much on our pleasant prospects, and now we had to go back and join the troops commencing a campaign, and especially to get laughed at for the blighting of our hopes - "How are you, Heavies?" Well, we can stand all that.

But, meanwhile, while we were changing to the Forts and back again, the rest of the Corps were clothing themselves and shoeing themselves and getting paid, while our men are ragged and penniless, and many of them barefoot, which makes it pretty rough. I borrowed $25 as I came by Fort Stevens, so I am well enough off. As to shoes or boots, all I had played out at Petersburg, so I bought a light $4 pair of shoes of a sutler, which do me very good service for horseback wear in dry weather. My boots are good yet if I can get them mended. As to my new position, it is one of much more ease than my former on, very much - no accountability and nothing to do, like the fifth wheel of a coach; especially now, when Col. Warner commands the regt., Chamberlain the 1st and Hunsdon the 2d Battalion, leaving me all alone in my glory. I shall have a job in settling my Company accounts, but it must wait awhile.

I have learned one thing by two very successful experiments - that it won't do to rise at one jump from hardtack and coffee to good living. I tried it once on the boat coming to Washington, and again at the Metropolitan Tuesday afternoon, and it made me sick each time. I am all right now and won't do it again. A story for Mary. I went into a house in Clarksburg yesterday to get a pie or so; wanted to wash; saw a wash basin, soap and pitcher of water; asked permission, but folks didn't hear, so took it; had got my hands washed when young woman asked if I got the water out of the pitcher; told her I did; said the baby had the erysipelas and that was a solution of sugar of lead; as I didn't have the erysipelas, I threw the rest of the water out of the window.

Harper's Ferry, Va.
July 29th, 1864

Dear Father:

I wrote you yesterday from Monocacy, at noon. Today noon found us at Harper's

Ferry. We are now some three miles or so out on the Winchester road forming the Corps. Our Division was ahead and got here hours ago. I have heard about marching, but I never saw of heard of an army moving as rapidly as our 6th and 19th Corps have done this week. From Washington to Harper's Ferry through Frederick, full 70 or 75 miles, in four hours less than three days - and I don't want to see it again.

We expected to stay at Monocacy yesterday, but instead we forded the river and marched to Jefferson, twelve miles. Got in about 11, away at 5 in the morning, and fifteen miles before we halted brought us here, with the loss of half our Division left by the wayside, and expected to come up as they get able. It is pretty rough, this hard marching, especially for a regiment nearly shoeless, but I see we stay by as well as the rest after all. Wonder if we are to move out toward Winchester. We came here in a great hurry any way, that is about the only thing I am positively sure of now.

I am very glad to have seen Harper's Ferry and its surroundings, but don't like the circumstances of the visit - to cross the pontoon and march through the town at the head of a lot of dusty, grimy, sweaty, tired, straggling men, who can scarcely get over the ground, much less keep up any semblance of marching - I don't want to do so any more. Personally I get along well enough, but I do hate to see the men suffer so. If the Johnnies were to try and come such a game as this, I think they would make out: for instance, cut across through White's Ford, or thereabouts, and Poolesville, between us and Washington. They would take the city without any trouble, for there is nothing left of a garrison, and how we would have to hump it towards Washington again.

With love, but somewhat demoralized,

Aldace F. Walker

Saturday Morning
6 A. M.

Mail going out. We drew shoes and pants and socks last night and feel much better generally, but from 70 to 75 miles in 68 hours is no joking matter. Hope we shall rest; there are no signs of a move this morning. My horse stands it pretty well, though more grain and more regularity about its feeding would better her condition very much. How strange it is that we don't get some rain; from the 15th of May we have seen none, except the Sunday night we were near Washington, and no mud at all. We shall get weather bound in some of our expeditions scyugling round one of these days. Well, the mail is off. Goodbye.

With much love, as ever,

Aldace F. Walker

Frederick, Md.
Sunday, July 31st, 6 P. M.

Dear Father:

Our army has gone up the hill, and down again; and why it came up, and why it came down are alike mysterious. We were at Harper's Ferry when I sent off a letter Saturday morning. That morning I went off to the Ferry, (we were in camp at Halltown, four miles toward Charlestown,) and bought some chickens and eggs. It was a very hot day, and an additional investment in butter resulted in grease. We moved out on the back track at 3 p.m., but there was such a crowd of troops and wagons (6th, 8th and 19th Corps) that ours, the rear most Division, did not get across the pontoons till 11 p.m., and the heat was so great that many fainted, and it has been worse to - day. We marched on till 3 a.m. and then rested till 9, then marched back over the mountain, all in the heat of the hottest day of the summer, men falling out at almost every rod, reaching our present posish, a mile and a half southwest of Frederick, at 4, and camping in the most beautiful grove, and the most beautiful section of country we ever laid in. But the march has been awful. We have had a good many cases of veritable sunstroke, and seen many others. I hope it has been necessary. I know nothing of the general situation of troops and rebels, but from what we can see the management of things seems most absurd, and the troops seem to be handled without mercy. It is getting to be dark and I must stop soon - wanted to write a line, as a mail goes out in the morning. I am all right, and comfortable as could be expected under the circumstances.

With much love,

Aldace F. Walker

Camp Near Frederick
Aug. 2d, 1864

Dear Father:

I am writing in the open air by candle light with a little breeze, and fear my tracings may be somewhat hieroglyphical; but I feel like writing, for we have just got our week's mail; and must trust to your wit to decipher the scribbling. Much to our surprise we are this Tuesday evening in the camp we formed Sunday afternoon. It is the best camping ground we ever had, and we are wishing to stay as long as we remain in the field. We were rushed back Sunday, it seems, to cover Baltimore and Washington against the column which went to Chambersburg, but which proved a very small one, and now we seem to be waiting for further developments of the enemy. If they should throw a good column over at Poolesville they might take Washington with no trouble, still I suppose our forty miles is considered as supporting distance.

We were ordered out this morning, and our 1st Division had got under way headed for Washington, when the order was countermanded and we camped down again. I took the opportunity to go into Frederick, where I got a good dinner, and spent the best part of the remaining fragment of the $25 I borrowed at Washington in a clean shirt, pair of socks, &c., &c. You need not send any more money at present, however, if ever we get to Washington for an hour or so I can get my pay. Your letter came in tonight with the muster roll - a very quick response, but in the field they don't stand so much on ceremony as in Washington, and I had been already mustered without it, to date from July 1st, twenty-three days earlier than would have been possible in Washington - a saving in a financial and military point of view - rank, you know. On July 1st, we were returning from Reams's. I was acting as Major then, and mounted for the first time on that trip.

My commission dates from June 28th, so I only lost three days, and that as the mustering officer could not go beyond the last muster of the regiment. It has been intensely warm here of late. We go around in shirts and drawers and sleep in same with a blanket at hand to keep off the chill of the morning. We are living well, and in hopes of reseeing Washington sometime. Our men are all up now and well rested. More clothing for them tonight, blouses, &c. I think the secesh must think the 11th Vt. a slippery set. I have forgotten, or omitted, to tell of how Capt. Eldridge[10] jumped from the cars with Capt. Morrill,[11] for I presumed you had seen it in the Vermont papers. Morrill was shot and died the next night, we hear in this mail. Eldridge saw Morrill to a house, and in good hands from whom he received a decent burial, and then struck off around Richmond, getting off on a raft at Aquia Creek, and is with the regiment now. It is a hard story and a deeply interesting one in its details. Tonight we have a letter from Capt. Safford, another of the 23d of June prisoners, stating that he and Lt. Fleury have arrived in Washington, having left the Johnnies at Lynchburg and struck for the Ohio, coming in via Wheeling. Lt. Griswold[12] started at the same time. "Bully for them all" say we, and everyone that hears the story. That description of our Shenandoah campaign is good, and correct as far as it goes. Love to Mary, and tell her to tell Belle that "Codfish Aristocracy" is played out. The papers are at hand and very acceptable, also the August Atlantic. I hope we shan't go into the valley again, but shall return to Washington; but how do we know what's up? I got measured for a Major's coat in Frederick today - $35, ten or fifteen cheaper than is possible in Washington. I am messing in my old crowd and not with the "Field" on this campaign, and we live better and cheaper.

Love all around,

Aldace F. Walker

Halltown, Va.,
Saturday, Aug. 6th, 1864, 5 P. M.

Dear Father:

Yours of August 1st was received last night in the camp from whence I last wrote you, across the Monocacy. At nine or ten the order came to "pack up and be ready to move at a moment's notice" - which means work - and off we went three miles to Frederick Junction. The B. & O. R. R. leaves that city four miles to the west. There we took the cars, and were at Harper's Ferry before we fairly knew it - a much more comfortable way of accomplishing that distance than either of the other trips we have made over it. We moved out after breakfast at once to a little beyond our old camp in this vicinity, where I have spent the most of the afternoon in making up lost sleep. We have been marched and countermarched and fugled and bamboozled round since we left Petersburg till everyone is disgusted; but the general impression is that this move means something. Hunter commands the army in lieu of Wright, which everyone regards as a blessing. U. S. Grant was at Frederick last night. Hooker is talked of as to command this army, which is now quite a respectable little force; and in any event, it seems as though we were likely to have a sight at the Johnnies this time, as their picquets are only four miles from here, and said to be in strong force. I am afraid when you get my former letter, you will be sorry you sent the $10, but it was a very lucky hit.

I have been so sure that we should not enter Virginia again till I had a chance to be paid off that I thought I should not need any more from you; but yesterday as I was returning from a good swim in the Monocacy I came across a sutler who had some very fine mackerel, and I invested my last fifty cent note in three big ones. Had a cent left, just. Got home and found a letter with ten dollars in it, and it seemed as good a hit as the dose I got on the boat. I don't know what our postal facilities are to be for the next week, or month - rather slender, I reckon - but I think you had better send me another bill, and am confident it will reach me sometime, and probably before we are paid off. Our saddle horse came in on other trains, and our pack horses and mules "overland," so we all were dismounted in the last four mile march. I have "Old Grey" along. Sick and wounded officers report to Surgeon Antisell, Washington, and are uniformly put in print as "wounded." Capt. Pollard is sick, but I understand not at all seriously. Nearly all the 19th Corps is here now. Have not seen the 8th for sometime. This sheet is all the paper I could get hold of. We had a little rain this morning, the first for some time; everything is terribly parched. Fruit is coming into season hereabouts. With much love, as ever,

Aldace F. Walker

Sheridan has been put in command of this army. We expect a hard campaign, but "better doings."

Halltown, Va.
Tuesday, Aug. 9th, 1864

Dear Father:

I think I sent you a letter from this place the other morning. Since our terrible march of a week ago last Sunday we have been comparatively quiet. We moved at one time five miles across the Monocacy, and when we came out here three miles to reach the cars and four miles this side of the Ferry. The rest for the remainder of the week has been very grateful to man and beast. That hot Sunday played out my horse, stiffened his shoulders, and I am afraid he is spoiled; still she, for it's a she, gets better some as we rest, and may be good for something yet. I was to have her for $100 if she showed lameness in the shoulder. I bought another - a little bay mare - yesterday, that has been through the wars in the 6th Vt., for $90, to rest the one I have been riding and because I want two. It don't seem wise to me to have any great amount of money invested in horseflesh while engaged in an active campaign, but when we get back to the Defenses you know, I'll sell out and buy bigger. Col. Chamberlain and self have had a wall tent sewed, made of shelter tents pieced together, and it seems really palatial; will be perfectly tight if we ever get any rain.

We have had a change in our commanders that we think well of, though the boys are a little afraid Sheridan will think they are Cavalry and rush 'em. Yesterday we had an order from Sheridan, assuming command of Hunter's, Augur's, Wallace's and Couch's Departments, with Hd. Qrs. for the present at Harper's Ferry, which means where the army is. Whether these other generals will continue to serve under their junior, as there may be a special act of Congress, or not, remains to be seen. It looks as though Sheridan intended firstly to rid his Dept. of rebels. A Div. of Cavalry is here from the Army of the Potomac. And it may make some difference with the fortification arrangements too. What is to turn up nobody knows. The 6th Corps goes by the name of "Harpers Weekly" now. I have written this while the mail boy is collecting his mail and must close.

With love to all,

Aldace F. Walker

Sunday Morning
Aug. 14th, 1864

Dear Father:

This is the first chance I have had to write a line since I sent before, and when this can be sent I don't know, though I shall try and get it off by the supply train which is to return to Harper's Ferry this morning. It came up last night just as we were all out of grub. We expected it would bring out a mail, but we have not seen anything of it yet. We have got up the Shenandoah about forty-five miles. We came out through Charlestown, when struck across the country, passing through neither Winchester nor Berryville, but between them, and moving mostly through the woods and fields, - which, as the woods in that region are free from underbrush, and the fields are quite level, made very comfortable traveling indeed. We struck the main "pike" from Winchester to Staunton at Newtown, and came on through Middletown to our present position. We are on Cedar Creek, about half way from Middletown to Strasburg. We got up here after a hard march, night before last, found the enemy in line on the hills beyond the creek. Sent over our 1st Brigade as skirmishers, and they had quite a lively little time till dark. We were on a hill overlooking the whole ground. In the morning they had vanished, and the 6th corps pushed on a couple of miles toward Strasburg, and found the enemy's skirmish line just beyond the town. We made no attempt to drive them, but stood there looking the matter over till dark, when we moved back to our old hill this side of the creek.

What we are about I don't know. We were short of rations, and may have had to come back to meet the train. The enemy may have been in force and entrenched, so that it would not have been wise to attack them - one hypothesis. Or it may have been discovered that only a rear guard of cavalry was holding the position and that the main body had gone. So little do we know of what our own army is doing. It is raining a little this morning, and I find the tent a great comfort. I am traveling with more conveniences than ever before - have two horses, and take a carpet bag right along, with all the worldly possessions I have accumulated. My valise was left at Washington by a lucky mistake, as now it would be back in Harper's Ferry with the baggage train. We have very few wagons with us indeed. I wear a linen coat with no vest, a long duster, and am as comfortable as one well can be on such a campaign.

We all suffer from the plague of soldiers, the grey backs, - body lice, in plain English. Have to keep busy to keep rid of them. None of us are entirely exempt. We wash and change our clothing as often as possible, and generally keep as clean as we can, and so keep them in subjection. What this army is to do I don't know. The papers said that Sheridan was to clear the rebels out of his command. Whether or no this has been done I can't say, certainly they are above the gaps. The Shenandoah is divided her into two valleys by the Massanutten Ridge. The enemy and principal road are in the "north fork," or western valley, the entrance to which our present position commands. I am inclined to think we shall go no further, but return to Petersburg as many of our troops as can be spared from this Dept. Some think, however, we shall push on and make a big campaign up the valley still further. We got three days rations last night, and were notified that they must last us four days. Whether this results from the necessities of the case or from part of our train being captured by Moseby last night, as is rumored, we don't know - and we don't know much any way.

I enclose, that you may have some idea as to how things are conducted in the army, the "order of march" under which we moved from Harper's Ferry. The different regiments take turns in leading the brigade on the march, and the Brigades in the Divisions, and Divisions in the Corps, also take turns in the lead each day. It is, of course, much easier to march at the head of a column. I hope you will receive this some time.

With much love to all,

Aldace F. Walker

Tuesday Morning
Aug. 16th, 1864

Dear Father:

I wrote a letter to you in a hurry last Sunday morning and gave it to an officer of the escort going to Harper's Ferry with the supply train returning. A little while after I found that a mail had come up on the train and that another was to return. I received your letter and some others, but had no time to write any more.

This morning I have been answering my letters, and will write a little to you - which can't go out before Thursday, and perhaps not even then. We are still where we were when I wrote on Sunday, near Strasburg, on the hither side of Cedar Creek. We drove the rebel skirmish line off a piece Sunday p.m., and they returned the compliment in the afternoon of Monday; so matters may be said to be in status quo. There was quite a little skirmish Sunday afternoon.

I have been lucky enough to be honestly out of all such affairs since June 23d, and even then I didn't get shot at. Our skirmishers advanced, and the Johnnies held their position till our men were within three rods of them, and then "got up and dusted," in army slang, leaving their tents and their supper. Last night they ran up a battery, and drove our line back with grape and canister. They have a strong position over there, and I don't think we intend to attack.

It is said that part of the army has moved, and I presume the 6th Corps will soon follow. We are quiet longer than usual now. A hundred of the wagons of the last supply train coming out were burned by about fifty of Mosby's men. The train was about six miles long, and the Brigade of Marylanders escorting it ran to the head of the train, leaving the rebs to burn the tail. It was a most disgraceful affair. Gen. Custer hung a spy yesterday in a most summary manner on his own confession. Col. Warner has just come in from somewhere and reports that we are to go back to Winchester, which is satisfactory, as it is towards our base.

Near Charlestown, Va.
Aug. 19th, Friday

Dear Father:

No chance yet to send out my letter, and some doubts as to whether the other sent on the supply train has gone along, though I think it has. The train came up to our camp on Cedar Creek, issued three days' rations to last four, and it was five before we got any more, which was a sad arrangement for the pigs and sheep in the Valley of the Shenandoah. The train had eight days' supply on board, came back toward the Ferry, and has been wandering around the country since, though empty wagons were sent in, and the mail wagon perhaps. It was discovered that the enemy were 30,000 in our front and in a very strong position indeed. As we had but 28,000 guns we thought it prudent to let them alone.

We have had no news of any sort for nine days. It is reported that Longstreet is this way, that Lee is transferring the seat of war, &c. all of which you know far more than I. At any rate, one night we just pulled up and left - "got up and dusted," you know - without much noise of drums or bugles, and we made splendid time to Winchester I tell you. The roads were fine - a big "pike" - and much labor has been expended on these Virginia pikes. This one has a telegraph line - of poles - milestones - is thoroughly macadamized - hard as a floor. Our Division brought up the rear, one Brigade in the road, and one each side, and waited for the picquet before we started. We got breakfast at Winchester, a place of more size than I supposed, and came on five or six miles further on the Berryville pike, where we expected to get rations, but didn't. Left the Jersey Brigade to cover the rear and Col. Penrose, com'g, contrived to lose about half his men. Glad 'twant the Vermont Brigade.

Yesterday morning we started in the rain and marched all day, with the understanding that the supply train was three miles ahead, and I guess it was, and traveled as fast as we did. We cooked what we had left, and could steal, at noon, and called it breakfast, and then pushed on. Lost our way, made a critical survey of all this portion of Virginia, and got rations at about ten o'clock at night. It was a good day to march after the rain stopped. This morning we are waiting orders. I had chicken, potatoes, beets, green corn, cabbage and vinegar, and slap-jacks for breakfast. And it cost nothing at all save the sugar on the griddle cakes. I have two horses, you know - "Lady," the one I got first, which lamed herself that hot Sunday, so I got "Nellie." Both are capital riders. "Lady" is all right now. I rode her yesterday for the first day. She is about 150 lbs. The biggest. I think we shall see Maryland again today.

Aldace F. Walker

Camp of 11th Vermont
Near Charlestown, Va.
Aug. 20th, 1864

Dear Father:

I sent you a letter yesterday morning in something of a hurry, while we were waiting orders to move; which, much to our astonishment, did not come - and we are still here, in a most beautiful spot at the edge of a grove, and likely to stay for all we know - so

I will write a little to send out tomorrow morning. We got a mail yesterday - three letters from you, and some others, with the papers, which were unusually acceptable, as we had been without new so long. I got hold of a paper this morning of the 19th, which is nearly up to date, and am beginning to feel posted again. I got hold of the last letter of yours before the others were distributed, and as it alluded to a ten dollar enclosure, and as I knew nothing of any more mail, I did not know but it had gone up, but I found it all right in a couple of hours. We are about two miles southwest of Charlestown. The rest of the army is scattered around at different places within a dozen miles or so, and is busy hunting guerrillas as near as I can find out. We have a big barn full near by here.

Every able-bodied man around here belongs to the C. S. A., and they are picking them up where they can find them. Gen. Duffie[13] shot one yesterday, who undertook to show a party of our men in Johnny uniform where they could capture him, and put the inscription, "A Traitor to his Country" over the grave. There are various indications of our operating in this vicinity for some time yet. The railroad track is being relaid from Harper's Ferry, is finished to our old camp at Halltown now, and even there the working parties are annoyed by guerrillas, who are very bold indeed. I see by the papers that Sheridan told Stanton that there were no rebels this side the Blue Ridge; which, as it comes in Stanton's dispatch, I take to mean the east side the Ridge, and that they are all in the Valley. There are enough of them above us at any rate. Some of Longstreet's men were found to be outflanking us through Front Royal, which the papers assign as the reason of our retiring, and which I take to be the true one. Meanwhile I don't think a fight is imminent. The rebs are satisfied if they can keep the 6th and 19th Corps from Grant, and we have just men enough to watch them, not to attack them in any of their chosen positions. If we had attacked at Strasburg we should have got most woefully shipped, I am thinking. Perhaps this move of Grant north of the James will relieve us, as Lee will have to extend his line very extensively. If they will let us stay where we are now, I would as lief be here as any where. We don't hear of any pay day yet, but I think we shall be paid off before Aug. 31st, as if we are not there will be six months pay required. I rather hope we shan't, however, now.

I got a letter from Aunt Minerva last night, giving me "Luty's" assumed name, Morris, and I rode over to the 1st Division and looked him up this morning. He is a slender little fellow, and says the marches are wearing him out. I think he is pretty well discouraged. Did what I could to cheer him up. He said he did not know that I was in the army. He has not fallen out at all, he says, which shows a good deal of pluck; but he is too small a boy for campaigning - don't look as I expected to find him. I heard from Ellena a few days or weeks ago, which is perhaps later than you have heard. She wrote in pretty good heart; only wished she "had been here last years," and thinks her father is not appreciated around there, and that the place is running down. Henry is at home with paralysis of a hand. You wrote me a while ago that President Labaree had resigned. I don't understand your last letters in connection with that. Noble is without doubt the best writer in the class that has just graduated, though perhaps Brainerd is as good a scholar. I always gave Button more credit for ability than you were inclined to do. I think he is very much of a thinker - a good writer, and quite effective as a speaker, and should suppose he would do well with much a theme as his at the Commencement. Tillie mentioned in a letter to the Col. that you called on her while she was out. I wish you had seen her. I saw Chaplain

Haynes today and Hill. Both are well. Salisbury is at home it seems. John Sheldon is in the 5th Corps at Petersburg "temporarily," which he does not like. I also saw Charley Hilliard[14] while we were at Cedar Creek. He was looking very well. Our Chaplain is along, but is developing, I am sorry to say, very decided inefficiency. A Captain's coat is single-breasted, a Major's is double-breasted - quite an essential difference in a military point of view. The blouse is alike for both, and as we wear no dress coats in the field I am well enough off for the present. With much love,

Aldace F. Walker

Haynes told me we had marched 600 miles since we got back from Petersburg.

Halltown
Monday Morning [8/22/1864]

Dear Father:

Yesterday was a Sabbath which I shall always remember, and painfully too. I wrote you Saturday intending to send it out Sunday, but did not get a chance for reasons to be detailed. I was somewhat unwell Saturday night with a slight dysentery, and ate no breakfast, laid about and slept till half past nine, when I was awakened by an order to pack up, and to my surprise there was heavy firing on the picquet line. This was a little beyond Charlestown, you remember. Our picquet was driven back almost to camp. It seems to be a complete surprise all round. But our Brigade soon had its orders, and was well handled all day. It was ordered to retake the ridge from which the picquet had been driven - the 3d, 4th, and part of the 6th, were deployed as skirmishers, and the rest of us followed as supports. Lt. Col. Chamberlain was hit in the bowels while going on to the field, and is probably dead ere this. I took command of the Battalion, and we pushed on - drove the enemy a mile, and then had to fall back ourselves in turn. While falling back the line was contracted, so that it left me on the front line near a house known as the Packett house - a splendid place. I filled the windows with sharpshooters and occupied every available spot around the grounds, built a covering of rails, &c., and held the position all day, under a terrible fire. The house was the key to our position, and they ran up a section of artillery and shelled two hours. It was hit nine times while our men were in it, and set fire to twice. The last shell that struck it exploded in the room I occupied with my men. I was in the room in the rear. Killed one, perhaps two, and shattered everything. I concluded to evacuate, but everybody admired the pluck of the men who staid by so long. We held the ground till dark - our old picquet line - and then the army fell back to Halltown. Some firing by the cavalry in our front now. I feel well and am all right. We lost about ten killed and nearly forty wounded. I feel very bad about Col. Chamberlain.

With love,

Aldace F. Walker

Halltown, Va.
Tuesday Morning, Aug. 23

Dear Father:

I am afraid the letter I sent you yesterday morning speaking of "skirmishing in front" may cause you anxiety, and so will try and show you how little danger we are in just at present. We have not seen any rebs since the affair of Sunday. Our position at Charlestown was a poor one, selected rather on account of its proximity to water and other conveniences, than because it was adapted to repel an attack. The camp was commanded by ridges on which the skirmishes took place, and if we had been driven in I fear the Corps would have indulged in a general skedaddle, though it entrenched heavily during the day. The rest of the army meanwhile was moving back, the 19th Corps ignorant of the proximity of an enemy, &c., though some of the Cavalry was engaged - Wilson, I think. As I said, in the night we fell back to Halltown, where the whole army is in a very strong position on heights running across from the Shenandoah to the Potomac four miles from Harper's Ferry. We have thrown up a rifle pit on the front ridge, and are to entrench on the second ridge today.

Our Brigade, in consideration of its Sunday fight, is placed in the fourth line, on the second crest, and will be the reserve in case of an engagement. We don't know what to make of these operations. There is no doubt but that our army is a little larger than the one Early first brought North, say 35,0000 to 30,000, but he has been reinforced by two Divisions of Longstreet, and unless Grant's movements compel their return we shall have to keep shy; and that is what's the matter now, though we are ready for them in this position. We were out ready for a move at three this morning. "The enemy," it was announced in the order, "have been divided into two columns, part in our front," and part somewhere else, I suppose, and so we are not much wiser for that. Still, if the rebs had intended an attack they lost a very good chance when they failed to pitch into the 6th corps unsupported, and I think they would if our Brigade had not given them such a slap in the face. We accomplished all we were ordered to, and got a good deal of credit as usual. Our regiment lost 32 - five killed. Of the wounded, some have died and others will, few however. I think there are none missing. Lt. Col. Chamberlain is dead - lived about 30 hours - was in little pain, except while being moved around, and was conscious to the last, and firm. He died at Sandy Hook across the Potomac. Chaplain Little, his friend and classmate, was with him all the time, and is making strong efforts to take the body home. There are no facilities for embalming here, and the railroad will not take a corpse without that process, so that I fear he will not succeed. He expects the Col.'s wife this noon. I was not able to see him after he fell. The wound was directly through the body. No other of our officers were wounded. The 6th lost 39, four officers wounded, including all the field officers.

We did not lose proportionally, but had only half our men under fire at any one time, and far the hottest place on the field was the house I held; the cover was good, and I took pains to protect the men all I could by rails, &c., so that we saved many, but all our loss except Col. Chamberlain was just there, and those upper rooms where the sharpshooters were - were bad places to be in, I assure you. Other regiments, who did not know who the sharpshooters in the windows were, cheered their pluck; and as I said, we stayed there through a continual rain of bullets fired at the windows, and while nine shells struck the house. I don't want to try it again any way, and am surprised that we escaped so well. We did fearful execution too. The Brigade fired 40,000 rounds of ammunition that day. I fired 7000 from the house and grounds. All is quiet in our front now, although we have heard some firing. We are so far back under this second hill that we can see nothing. I hardly anticipate an attack here, and think that the enemy will soon develop some plan that will compel us to cross the Potomac. Your letters and papers continue to come and are a source of great pleasure to me.

Halltown, Va.
Aug. 25th, 1864

Dear Father:

I received yours and Mary's letters of last Sunday this afternoon, with the Herald and Congregationalist, all of which were very acceptable. We have been here quite a little while now, and our former intimacy with the locality makes us feel quite well acquainted. We have been hoping that the rebs would fight us here, as it is a position that would give us an immense advantage, but there was no such good luck in store for us. Today Wilson's Cavalry have been up toward Shepardstown, and judging from the cannonading have been gradually pressed back. The Generals have been together today, and I presume have a plan. And just now we were notified that four days' rations would be issued, and as we have three now on hand, this means something; and it is rather an unwelcome order too, as the haversack is the soldier's heaviest burden. We indulge in no speculation now concerning future movements - for we have learned better - but don't expect in the least another trip up the valley at present. Our trains are said to be crossing the river, and perhaps we shall evacuate tonight - How many of these night marches we have to make. - We shall, of course, if the enemy has succeeded in crossing above.

We have had an easy time since Sunday. Our sutler has been out, and will bring in a load of goods soon. I sent for a rubber coat and some other essentials. Says the paymaster is coming this week, which I consider decidedly doubtful, though I think we shall be paid before the 30th if we are accessible. I got $10 on an old debt the other day, and $10 from you today, so that I shall not need anymore just now if we are not paid even. Will send word as I write from time to time. It will take nearly all my money to square up my accounts, which are of long standing you know, and some of them of a good amount. We have had a good deal of rain lately, and so can't complain of drought. Our officers who get to Washington on account of wounds or sickness are retained there; we have six or eight there now in one capacity or another. Gen. Augur won't give them transportation here, as the regiment is to return there soon. I presume there is some contention among commanders as to the disposition to be made of us. Still we are regarded at Corps Hd. Qrs. here as simply temporarily attached and belonging to the Washington garrison. This campaign bids fair however, for all I can see, to be of an indefinite extent.

I shall be immensely glad if we ever do get back to Washington - on account of the comfort and the safety of the service in part, and in part because I am anxious to get rid of, or "get shut," of this Brigade. We are not well treated - are regarded as interlopes, and slighted and sneered at, though the latter has stopped of late months. But Gen. [L. A.] Grant and the rest of the Brigade, though second to none in the fighting line, are very far from being gentlemen; Grant don't know how to treat anyone well. There is no one in the brigade who is suited with or suits him - and in our regiment especially. When Col. Warner told him of Col. Chamberlain's wound, on the battlefield at the time, he went to recounting his faults and errors, as much as to say the loss of that fine officer was a gain to the service. He is at loggerheads with every field officer in the brigade. Unquestionably he handles troops well in action, but he don't know how to use officers. We have earned a position among the other regiments, and now experience very little of the difficulty I alluded to in relation to them, but we heartily join in the opinion that "Aunt Lydy" is a very appropriate name for our Brigade commander.[15] Col. Warner is doing well - is going to work to rid the regiment of some inefficient worthless sticks, and continues to be well liked all round.

With much love to all,

Aldace F. Walker

Charlestown, Va.,
Monday Morning, Aug. 29th, 1864

Dear Father:

I have been hindered from writing for a day or two by various considerations. Meant to have done so yesterday, but it was Sunday, and of course we had to march. While we were at Halltown we had a nice time - a good camp, and quiet from Monday morning till Sunday morning; we even got to drilling some. We have learned the science of living well, at least enjoyably, in camp. The reconnoisance that Sheridan threw out so vigorously and so persistently were made by other troops - I suppose in consideration of our exertions of the previous Sunday; and with the "Old Curiosity Shop," "Harpër," "Atlantic" and "Rory O'More," I passed a very comfortable week of it. In the Atlantic I find a piece by Katie C. Walker, judging from the internal evidence. You will doubtless discover it if you choose. I want you to get the Sept. Harper and read a piece about somebody's experience on his first battlefield in Louisiana. It is to the life. I never saw my feelings so well depicted before, and the idea that the more fights one gets into the less he likes it is quite correct. Well - so much for literature. We had no mails or papers yesterday, and I presume shall not today.

The Johnnies found that they were playing a decidedly losing game watching Sheridan, for beside some half dozen picquet lines of theirs which he gobbled, he had a larger force detached from Petersburg than we, and we could well afford to have it equal. So Early pulled up stakes and left - the inhabitants say for Fisher's Hill beyond Strasburg, where we found them before - though Custer was fighting yesterday, and is this morning, at Smithfield, four miles from here. We came out here yesterday and went into our old position. My Battalion was detailed as picquet, and I am now holding the line of last Sunday.

I have been looking the ground over, and understand the position better than I did before. I find in front a good many graves of the enemy; their loss was at least double ours, and they had a much heavier force than we put into the fight. We worked the whole brigade, and they supposed we had supports as usual, whereas we had nary one, except back to the camp. On the whole we are very well satisfied with the little fight. Col. Chamberlain's remains were taken to Baltimore by the Chaplain, put in a metallic coffin, and sent on. His wife and her sister and father got here in time to accompany the body home. I have up my tent and am comfortable. My cooks are frying doughnuts close by. My breakfast was fresh pork, salt pork, liver and chicken, corn meal hoe-cakes, cabbage and vinegar, onions, &c., &c., and we have splendid coffee, and a pail of butter, and a peck of beets. I hope the rebs have been recalled to Richmond, and think it very likely. Goodbye.

Aldace F. Walker

Tuesday Morning [8/30/1864]

We are still on picquet, and shall be I suppose till tomorrow night unless the army moves. There was a mail went out from camp this morning, but we knew nothing of it till it was gone. Our Cavalry, Merritt's Div., was at Smithfield, four miles in front, yesterday. Our line faces westerly, toward Bunker Hill, as near as I can remember. Well, Merritt was driven nearly back to our lines yesterday. I don't think he tried to make much of a stand; did not lose much, but would turn and let him artillery play at intervals, and so about three p.m. he had got pretty near up. We were thinking it likely that we were in for a brush on the old line, but Sheridan and Wright and Ricketts, rode out with the 3d Div., 6th Corps, and Johnny fell back; so I understand the matter we occupy Smithfield again, and the prospect of an immediate fight is about played out. We are having the nicest time on picquet imaginable, men enough to make the duty light, pleasant weather, and on the whole had rather be here than in camp. The general news of the campaign I am oblivious to.

Wednesday Morning, 31st

We expect to be relieved this p.m. Are to be mustered early this morning. The last muster was at Reams's Station, the scene of Hancock's fight. It seems that Frank W. is missing. We are not to be paid just yet. The paymaster tried to get funds to pay us on the last rolls, but could not, and we are to have the first show as soon as the new ones are made out. We have not got blank muster rolls yet however. Expect them today. I think you had better send on another X,[16] and that will last me out of this scrape. Nothing new from the front. I got sentimental last night. Lay under the lee of a haystack with my blanket, and the stars over me, and listened to Ricketts' splendid band performing "Rock Me to Sleep," a mile and a half away. The north star was shining into my face square, if that adverb is proper in the connection, or is an adverb at all, - and I fell to computing the angle between the due north, and the Vermont, direction. I got cold before morning though. The dew was heavy - must have another blanket.

----

1 Possibly John Kilborn Williams. MC 1860. ATS and ordained 1866. Robinson, 134-191.

2 Sylvester Baron Partridge (1837-1912), MC 1861; 92nd N.Y. Infantry, later Chief Signal Officer 25th Corps. NTS and ordained 1868. Robinson, 134-191.

3 USA Brig. Gen. James Harrison Wilson, commanding 3rd Division, Cavalry Corps, Army of the Shenandoah. Boatner, 930-1.

4 USA Brig. Gen. August Valentine Kautz, Chief of Cavalry, Twenty-Third Corps. Boatner, 448-9.

5 The wounded were Privates Joseph Burke and Lafayette Sweet, Co. B, and George Everts, Co. D. RR.

6 Cooling, Jubal Early's Raid, 153.

7 USA Maj. Gen. Alexander McDowell McCook. Boatner, 526.

8 Elizabeth Blair Lee, daughter of Francis Prescott Blair Sr., and wife of Admiral Samuel Phillips Lee, was living in the family house with her parents and young son, Blair Lee. Just before the battle, she had taken her mother and son, and went to another family house, at Cape May. In a letter to her husband on 16 July, she said her father told her of a note left behind, "A confederate officer has remained here until after eleven - to prevent pillage & burning of the house - because of his love of (Emma Mason Mrs. Wheaton) - who found in this home good & true friends." Virginia Jeans Laas, editor, The Civil War Letters of Elizabeth Blair Lee, (University of Illinois Press, Urbana, 1991), 405.

9 Capt., later Maj., Henry M. Pollard, Ludlow, 8th Vt. Infantry.

10 Capt. James Edward Eldredge, Warren. Co. H. Wounded 6/1/1864. Taken prisoner 6/23/1864; escaped 6/29/1864.

11 Capt. Edwin J. Morrill, St. Johnsbury. Co. A; taken prisoner 6/23/1864, wounded while escaping 6/29/1864, died 6/30/1864

12 Lieut., later Capt., Edward F. Griswold, St. Johnsbury. Co. L; must have been recaptured, since records indicate he was paroled 9/26/1864. RR.

13 USA Brig. Gen. Alfred Nattie Duffié, born in France. Boatner, 250.

14 Private Charles L. Hilliard, Wallingford, Co. C, 10th Vt. Infantry. RR.

15 Aunt Lydy or Lydia, the brigade's nickname for Vermont Brig. Gen. Lewis Addison Grant, provenance currently unknown.

16 Probably shorthand for $10; the previous Thursday, August 25, Walker thought he had enough pocket money for the present, but appears to have second thoughts here.

15.
The Shenandoah Valley Campaign
Winchester and Cedar Creek
September and October, 1864

Charlestown, Va.
Sept 3d, 1864

Dear Father:

I was relieved from picquet after a three days' tour, and found the regiment in the camp of Sunday night, and we are there yet. We don't know what's the matter, or why we are quiet, but we do know that since Sheridan took command of this army we have had a very easy time for an army in the field, and also that as far as we can see he has been exceedingly successful in foiling the plans of Early. Of course our campaign has been defensive, and we have covered Maryland successfully with an inferior force to that of Early - have refused battle when we were weak, and offered it in strong positions. Sheridan expected to fight here on Wednesday, but on the advance of the 3d Div. Mr. Reb incontinently retired to Bunker Hill. Where they are now we have no sort of an idea, though Cavalry officers who have been navigating in front say they find nothing of Johnny. If they have really left for Richmond, matters are arranged here to transfer the 19th Corps at once to City Point. The 6th will remain here for the present I think. I rather wish the 6th was going, for in that case I am sure we shall stop in Washington, and I want the 6th where we can't be "temporarily attached."

Still, in any event, I am inclined to think our fighting is over for the present, though till we are assured that Early has left the Valley we can't say what a day will bring forth. We know this, however, - that Lee's plan to raise the siege, which succeeded in '62, couldn't be played on Grant. It is strange that a battle has been fought in those old rifle pits at Reams's; we built them upon honor.

I am decidedly encouraged by the later movements around Petersburg. Men is what is wanted - 75,000 would take Richmond. Our Corps is being reinforced now about 400 a day by recruits and convalescents, and I presume the rest of the army is like ratio, will be a faster rate for the next two weeks, then a lull, and then the drafted men will come on. It won't take long to make soldiers of them in the old regiments. I find my old Meriden room mate Wilson, in the 14th N. H., 19th Corps, a Sergeant.[1] I received a letter from you yesterday with $10 enclosed. If we are allowed to remain quiet through tomorrow we shall nearly get our six months rolls in condition to go to the Paymaster. If we move, we can form no idea as to when we shall be paid.

Our sutler has arrove, much to the general satisfaction, as owing to the "order" system, men can get their tobacco without money, and he gives credit to the officers. He brought me out a camp chair that I find a great luxury, and shall carry on my led horse;

and I shall have a rubber coat and new blanket in a day or two. These nights are getting really cold. We are to have an inspection in a few minutes, and I must close.

With much love to all,

Aldace F. Walker

Capt. Burrows of "M," formerly Adjutant, has just been discharged for Physical Disability, as an easy way of putting the thing. He left the last battle field with "cramp in the leg." Sherman on Enlistments in the South is the ablest state paper of the year, and the Chicago Platform the poorest. Still McClellan will run strong unless Grant is successful.

Clifton, Va.
Monday, Sept. 5th, 1864

Dear Father:

The last letter I sent out was from Charlestown, with a scratch on the outside saying that we were to move at 4 a.m. on the 3d. We did. Came on here, six miles perhaps, and the army formed line of battle through Berryville, the 6th Corps bending round to the right and rear, and the 2d Div. in reserve. There was quite a fight that Sunday by the 8th Corps, judging from the sound of the guns; and the enemy appears to have got so much that they didn't need any more, and have left us alone since. We are here I suppose trying to find out how much of the enemy are here - have a fortified front, but as I said, our Div. in reserve. It rains a good deal and is not very pleasant, of course. There is a story that only Breckenridge's force is left here; if that is so, of course they annoy us all they can. I am inclined to think that we shall get out of this by and by. Our papers and mails don't come up. We only have the news that Slocum[2] is in Atlanta. Last night at midnight in the rain we were all routed up and moved on to the right to build breastworks. Had an immensely pleasant time till morning fortifying, and then came back. It was so dark and rainy, and wet and disagreeable. I don't take cold at all, however; feel tough and hearty all the time.

6th - All right. Rainy weather. Election today, which I bossed. Voted for F. E. Woodbridge. No rebs near us. Have the Atlanta and Mobile news. Hope Mac won't stand the platform.

With love,

Aldace F. Walker

Clifton, Va.
Sunday Morning, Sept. 11, 1864

Dear Father:

We have been here now a week. Our camps are located and seem permanent - like home a little - but on the whole I don't like the posish. Principally because our communication with the outside world is merely what might be called semi-periodical. We are fed, clothed and informed by the "supply train," which is our great and peculiar institution - the caravan of the Shenandoah Valley - a train of wagons four miles long that plies between here and Harper's Ferry, bringing us rations and mails once in three or four days. It is due tomorrow, and on its return I propose to forward this letter. It came up Friday, bringing a letter from you, among others. My pen works so poorly what I will change to pencil. The 2d and 11th Vt. had to go back some four miles to Rippon to escort the train in, and it is supposed that their so doing saved Moseby a good gobble, for he was in sight of our men. I didn't go, for I was on picquet; and that same circumstance prevented my writing, as I did not know of the opportunity till it was too late. I am trying to forestall punctuality this time.

I was detailed as Division Officer of the Day on a three days' tour - had a detail from various regiments, all on a long line toward Bunker Hill. No excitement, except when the 8th Corps changed position, causing me to throw forward my line; and in so doing I ran it into the best orchard I have found in Virginia. I was relieved yesterday, and I hope shall do no more picqueting at present. We have had some wet weather of late - a good deal. Last night we sat in front of our tents till quite late with our coats off, so beautiful was the evening. It reminded me of Saturday nights when I used to take the long way home from choir rehearsal at Middlebury. But we had hardly got to sleep when a thunder storm came up, and was continued at intervals all night most furiously. My tent did very well. Col. Warner's came down in the heaviest of the storm, and Hunsdon and I amused ourselves by laughing at his frantic cries of "Orderly," and thought how he would feel crawling out of the wet linen into the storm. Lt. Hicks,[3] of the 10th Vt., called this morning. He is now on the Staff of Col. Emerson, comd'g their Brigade. Says the Wallingford people, Hill[4] and H. &c., are all right. We get our daily papers, however, with a good degree of regularity. The newsboys don't seem to be suitable game for the guerrillas, or else they purchase their passage by a free distribution of intelligence. At any rate, our Baltimore American reaches us about 6 p.m. each day. So we are posted about McClellan's crafty letter, (and yet honest, I hope) and are waiting eagerly to see how Pendleton will Dovetail his peace and his olive branch into McClellan's war policy and powder barrel. I have dropped speculation and prophecy, and wait for events. If they are as favorable as the Mobile, Atlanta and Vermont news of last week, we have good reason to keep hoping. My election resulted - 237 votes, 2 opposition. Our muster rolls have been forwarded and we shall be paid on them sometime, but it will be a big job to prepare them for payment.

With love to all,

Aldace F. Walker

Clifton, Va.
Wednesday Eve., Sept. 14th

Dear Father:

Our supply train is to make us another visit tomorrow, and as I have a little story to tell I will get it ready. Yesterday was the only pleasant day we have had for some time. It has rained again today. Well, we, the 2d Division, being in reserve had a special job on hand for yesterday. We broke camp at 5, moved out on a reconnoisance, went six miles, "developed the enemy," and came back after dark. Meanwhile, Custer's Cavalry took a few prisoners on our right, and Wilson took a South Carolina regiment on the left, penetrating to Winchester. The enemy lies in force still between Winchester and Bunker Hill, and scattered thereabouts. That's what we did. Our Division lost eight-one killed and seven wounded. That don't sound like much of a time, but there was a good deal of interest about it nevertheless. I wasn't hurt at all, but I never was so thoroughly scared I my life as I was for about ten minutes - didn't run, or see anyone else, but was terribly demoralized. I'll tell you about it. We went out towards the west and the enemy and the Opequon, our Brigade leading the Division, Getty in command, and Wright and Sheridan taking observations. This Getty is a fighting man all over, very quiet, but always on the skirmish line, and seems to think bullets are of no account. He was wounded in the Wilderness, the first battle in which he commanded the Division, joined us at Reams's, and since then we have learned to almost venerate him. The first question always is, "Is Getty along?" and the answer as invariably, "Yes, on ahead."

Well, as I said, our Brigade was in advance, got out beyond our picquet line and deployed, the 3d and 4th making a mile front, and the 5th and 6th a half mile flank, thus and the 11th and 2d in the center as support, by Battalion following the immediate advance, and the other Brigades and artillery coming after, - Getty on ahead leading the whole. So we advanced for four miles pushing the enemy across the Opequon. There is very commanding ground on each side of the creek. We did not attempt to cross, save a few sharpshooters, and couldn't if we had tried, but our skirmishers and the Johnnies fired at one another across the stream, and the rest of us lay back in the woods where we couldn't see or be seen. Johnny had a Brigade there, and pretty soon two more came along. We got a battery at work, and filled fourteen ambulances for them right away, besides the wounded that could walk to the rear. This was all very nice, but after dinner I got on to my "Lady" and rode to the front where I could see the opposing skirmish lines, the reserves of each side being concealed - and the Johnnies didn't know where ours were. While watching Cowan's artillery practice,[5] I saw in a little interval in the woods on the other side, men and horses in abundance, and a little observation convinced me that the rebs were planting a battery. They had tried it before, but Cowan had shelled them out. This time he did not see them. I tried to go and tell him, but couldn't get my horse near his battery on account of the noise and the gunpowder; so I rode back into the woods again, and told the folks that they would awake from their slumbers presently, though I didn't think we should take it in just the shape we did.

Presently they opened fire, at our battery, not us, and as they fired over, as they always do in commencing an action, the shell came screaming plump into the woods where we were. How so few of us were struck is a mystery. It only lasted a few minutes, and big trees where at a premium I tell you. I was sitting on the ground on my blankets - rolled them up and strapped them on to my horse. Went around to the front of the Battalion and saw that two men had been fearfully wounded by the second shell; one had lost an arm and a leg and was carried to the rear; the other was Lt. Bedell of D., who lay on the ground some ways from his company with no one to help him, and a most ghastly wound - his left leg torn through above the knee, and bleeding frightfully.[6] I let go my horse, who was off at a run, and hastened to Bedell. Succeeded in getting on a tourniquet, but the rope broke, got another, and at last saw him on a stretcher and off. I looked around for my horse and found that it had been recovered, and then took care of myself; but the sight and handling of that wound gave me such a shock as I never received before. Meanwhile, I had orders first to move my command away, then to stack arms again, and had to give the necessary orders; so among the whole I was in a good deal of confusion. I was glad I saw Bedell and knew what to do, for he would have had to wait some time I fear if I hadn't. It was comparatively a very small affair. When the rebs got range on the Battery their shots gave us no trouble, and the Battery got out of the way; but I was more excited than eve before. The fact is, as a general principle, shells are demoralizing. We are back on the old grounds, and all is quiet. I have given you this $36.16 on my books. Think you have sent me $60, isn't it? I hope we shall be paid sometime before long. At any rate, need no more money just now.

Lt. Bedell is alive, with his leg amputated, and will have to lose part of his right hand. The chances are against his living. He is in a house near by, and will have good care as long as we stay in this vicinity. The 5th Vt. Is to be mustered out today what have not re-enlisted - and I think I shall send this off by then. We expect some wall tents up tonight - can come then - two, in the Brigade team, which will be up every night.

With much love,

Aldace F. Walker

Clifton, Va.
Saturday, Sept. 17th, 1864

Dear Father:

We are still in the region we reached two weeks ago today. Have had a splendid rest, with the slight exception of the reconnoisance I told you of in my last. Have laid out a fine camp - room enough, clean and regular - and are willing to stay here for sometime to come. We thought yesterday that we should - that the rebel plan was to keep this threatening force in the Valley till after the election for political effect, and that we should simply stay here and watch them. But, alas, how human expectations fail. A little circumstance occurred last night which sets us afloat again. Gen. U. S. Grant reached Sheridan's Hd. Qrs. On a visit. Now this means something. Either this army is to be reduced for the sake of the Petersburg campaign, or we shall fight here, or something else will happen. In either event, we shall probably toddle, and possibly we shall reach Washington sometime. The summer's campaign has been on the whole a grand one, and the rebellion is crumbling away. We get deserters daily, and prisoners quite often.

The other day while on the skirmish line, some of the officers took occasion to go into a house near by. Two men were found sick abed. Several guns, rifles, carbines, and a large amount of ammunition for small arms and cannon. So the men had to get up. One of them, quite old and infirm, was left and the other was marched into camp by our Brigade pioneers with very little appearance of sickness. I have not moralized much on the political campaign, because I don't know what to think, but I trust Lincoln will be re-elected with little difficulty. New York is copperhead, but the Wood split may save her vote. The great trouble is, we don't know where to find the Democracy, and it will operate against them. The army is all right. Some say McClellan, but they are either the ignorant or the obstinate; sensible men know better. I saw Haynes yesterday, who says he contemplates resigning soon. Capt. Pollard[7] called on me this morning. Seems very well. He has been mounted all through this campaign, serving as a Staff Officer; is now Provost Marshall for the Division to which he belongs. We are getting some recruits nowadays - 37 last night, and more are on the way. We want 200 yet.

Lt. Bedell is still alive - the left leg amputated at the upper third, and the middle finger of the right hand taken out way down in the hand. His chances are slim, however, and if we have to move I don't know what will become of him. He is cheerful, however, and will take every chance there is.

It is splendid weather now all the time, and I think will remain so, for the autumns here are beautiful. Our supply train is due again tomorrow, and then I shall have another mail. This is worse than the back woods of Vermont, for they have a tri-weekly mail there everywhere.

With much love to all,

Aldace F. Walker

Sunday Morning - All right. Five days' rations. Think we shall move. Have got big tent, rubber coat and blankets, new hat, &c. Let 'em move. Great is credit. Paymaster coming - so is Christmas.

Strasburg, Va.
Sept. 21st, 1864

Dear Father:

I fear you will be very anxious at not hearing from me at once after the battle of the 19th. When we started from Clifton that morning we had five days rations, and it will be Friday night or Saturday morning before we get a chance to send letters I fear. When you do get this you will be happy to hear that I passed through the terrible ordeal in perfect safety - did not receive a scratch, and was not very essentially frightened. I am interested to see the stories of the papers, for it was a hard fought battle and a brilliant victory. It was on open ground for the most part, and I could see more of the fight and the enemy than I have ever been able to before. I will give you my story, and you may compare it with the versions of the correspondents. We started at 2 a.m. Monday morning, our Division leading the army, marching on the Winchester pike, reaching the Opequon at daybreak. Beyond the creek the road runs for two miles through a long ravine, woody, and a terribly mean place, but Wilson had driven a rebel Division across the creek and beyond the ravine, back on to their main body, so that we were enabled to form our lines of battle under cover of a skirt of woods half a mile from the enemy and three miles from Winchester. Our Division was on the left, guiding on the pike, the 1st Division on the right of the pike, the 19th Corps beyond them, and the 8th still farther to the right, with Cavalry on either flank.

We were on higher ground than the Johnnies, so that our batteries, coming into position in front of the skirt of woods as we advanced, did splendid execution, and were of great help to us. It seems that the rebs did not expect a front attack, but supposed a feint was being made, as they could not see the force we were bringing into position. It was eleven or twelve before we got our men all up and in position. When we did, not time was lost - the whole line advanced in one grand charge. We had half a mile to go over open country before reaching the rebel position - under an awful fire of musketry and artillery -

and our cannon rushed up and fired over our heads. About half way to their skirmishers we passed transversely through a ravine, which was completely enfiladed by a rebel brigade drawn up at its foot and firing directly on us; but they were driven away in the rush of the 3d Division. But we scrambled out of that gully in a hurry, losing severely of course. I forgot to say that Col. Warner commanded the Brigade. Hunsdon pegged out, was sick, and turned over the command of the regiment to me, (in a manner that did not strike me as being peculiarly honorable at the commencement of the charge.) Capt. Safford commanded the 1st Battalion, and Capt. Buxton the 2d. Well, our advance was over the highest ground of all right in the face of the rebel battery. We rushed on and the Johnnies ran. Every place where there was any cover they would hide till we came up, and surrender. We got crazy with the excitement. On, how they ran.

In that first charge my regiment took a Colonel, a Major, several officers, and full 200 prisoners. We pushed on a mile full, till we were completely exhausted. We didn't pretend to keep any line - it was pell mell, and I was ahead of everybody. The lines on our right and left kept well up, till at last we halted. The rebel battery had moved three times and I was trying to catch it. When we pulled up I found myself in a trench, pretty good cover, way to the front - Capt. Brown of the 4th (comdg. the 5th), Capt. Templeton, Lt. J. A. Lewis, acting Regt. Adjt., and one or two others, with perhaps 40 men. They were all tired out, but we fired away all we could. I saw the Johnnies rally. Some of the men were too tired to shoot, and I fired their guns for them. There was a hill, so that we could not see the line on the right, but we knew that we were ahead of it, and on our left the line ran obliquely back so - and we in the apex. The fact was, we had gone too far and our ranks were too much disorganized. Still we could have held the position all right if we had been supported and the rest of the line maintained. My colors had not been able to keep up, and my regiment was everywhere - a good many at the rear, but none but those who went back with wounded and with prisoners, - quite a good many of course - five color corporals wounded. At this time the 19th corps on the right gave way and fell back with a rush - most shamefully, we think.

Of course the movement backward was carried through or all would have been captured, but the 6th Corps only retired enough to save themselves. As I said, I could not see the right, and did not know of the falling back till it was carried on by the men of the 1st Brigade of our Division on my left, then I told the men in our party to get up and get out, and supposing the movement to have commenced on the left and that a rebel charge was coming from that direction, I ran towards our right; and to my surprise when I got so I could see over the ridge the Johnnies were right where I was headed for. I obliqued the other way, looked around again, and saw two horsemen about eight rods off pegging away at me with revolvers. I was tired out - could not run another step - thought of surrendering - partly decided to - but concluded to keep pegging. Those on our right who were behind us did not see us, and some way we got away, all but those who were wounded. It was a most marvelous escape.

I held on and rallied in front of the second line of battle - 1st Div. you know - in a ravine where they were shooting over us. Got them to advance to the ridge in front of us, and then as we were out of ammunition and badly scattered to the right and left, we waited to reorganize. I got quite a respectable regiment together before long, and we reformed the Brigade, unfurled our colors, made our connections, threw out skirmishers, and waited for orders. The 6th was strayed away into the 3d Div., but in the least disorder of any regiment in the Corps I guess.

About half past three Gen. Sheridan rode through the skirmish line on a dead run, sometimes inside and sometimes out, coming back between our Brigade and the 1st, (which was on our left,) shouting, "Crook and Averill[8] are on their left and rear. We've got 'em, by G-d." He isn't a profane man, but was excited immensely, and it gave us all new courage. We weren't a bit demoralized before. Very soon we got orders to advance, and on we went - full Corps line, with the extreme left retired and the rebs pressing it, which made our position rather a precarious one. A battery there, too, enfilading us; but we went on so fast that their shot would plow through just behind us. We didn't run this time though. Would go on till we got a little cover, reform and go on again - quiet and cool, skirmishers ahead - till we got into a garden near a big brick house. There we got a fire from a full rebel line of battle in our front that looked strong, I tell you. We rushed up to the further edge of the garden, where was a paling fence of hard wood boards, and opened the hottest fire I ever heard from the same number of men. Our Brigade was there and there it stayed, and the men worked like heroes. The left was in great danger, as I said, being retired and partly flanked. The regiment on our right went tumbling back, but soon rallied - not up with us, however.

I got orders to retire to a ridge just behind the garden, but I could see the reel line waver, and Crook's flags way on their flank across the plain, and couldn't see the falling back; so the Brigade held on. Soon T%. Perhaps we had fired 30 rounds in fifteen minutes - the rebels ran. Our Cavalry rushed down upon them - it was Averill on their left - and over went the fence, and though I did the best I could to halt and form a line it was forty rods before I could stop the regiment; then we dressed, and the whole army with flags flying, heads up, and cheers passing from one side to the other, proudly advanced over the plain. It was the most glorious sight I ever saw - and the rebs pushed to the south in the greatest disorder. It was then just dusk.

Sheridan rode up to where we were halted just at the edge of the city, and we gave him nine cheers. He remarked, "I guess we'll go to Winchester." We were by a big vine-yard, and the Brigade ate their fill of luscious grapes - the first we had eaten since morning; then we moved south of the city, went into position, and to sleep. As we understand it, we took 5000 prisoners, five guns and fifteen flags. We know we gave them a most conclusive thrashing.

But now we are counting our loss. Capt. Buxton, to have been Major in a few days, was instantly killed in the garden. Lt. Duhigg, to have been Capt. of "M," was also killed. Capt. Eldridge, an extremely gallant officer, was wounded - it was supposed, mor-tally; but they say he has a chance and means to take it. Several other (four) officers were wounded slightly, six men killed, 82 wounded, nine missing, total loss 103, out of 400 that we took into the fight. We had nearly half the loss of the Brigade, and the brigade over half that of the Division. Gen. Russell was killed - the best general in the Corps; but balanced by Rodes. At daybreak Tuesday we pushed on, (I was on foot through the fight of course, and got very lame, but my horse came up in the night,) made a very rapid march to this position, south of Cedar Creek, north of Strasburg village - the extreme south place we reached before - and find the rebels in their stronghold on Fisher's Hill, in our front. Don't know whether we are to fight again or not, but rather think not; if we were, it would have come off today, it seems to me - be we can't tell what's in the future for us.

I have been over to the 10th. Major Dillingham is dead, Gilbert Hill badly wounded, Hilliard and Wellman all right. I haven't heard of any other acquaintances of yours who were hit. Gen. Wheaton[9] of our 1st Brigade has been assigned to command the 1st Division, (Russell's old command,) and Col. Warner detached to command Wheaton's Brigade. Col. Foster[10] of the 4th is in command of our Brigade, Gen. Grant being at home on a twelve day leave. On the whole, I have been safely through a big battle, and shall always be proud of it; and the country has reason to rejoice at the victory we have gained. I am perfectly satisfied with the conduct of the regiment, and believe they were willing to follow me - but I shouted myself hoarse, completely.

I want two shirts and two pair drawers made right away, some socks and handkerchiefs. Let Chaffee make another blouse, and Valiquette a pair of top boots, double sewed, with stiffer ankles than the others, not so apt to sag, and I shall want my black pants sent to me when I send for these things. We have received Stanton's and Grant's congratulations. I hear cannonading at the front, light and distant. I very much doubt another battle in the valley; at any rate, a victory here is no longer a thing to wish for.

With love to all,

Aldace F. Walker

Thursday Morning - I wrote this yesterday forenoon. At noon the army went into line of battle - the 6th Corps moving toward the right - lay near the skirmish line through the afternoon - just at dusk moved still further to the right to support Warner's brigade, which charged and took a crest in his front. Then we went into position on his right and entrenched. We can see a strong place for the Johnnies this morning, very strong; I hardly think it is the intention to attack them, but to work on their communications. Crook is moving to our right this morning, and just opening. Will advance, I presume, and possibly we may also. The valley is about six or five miles wide, and we extend clear across - no chance for flanking.

Woodstock

Friday, 5 A. M.

We utterly defeated the enemy last night, with hardly any loss. Their position was the strongest I ever saw, and the whole affair seems simply providential. After heavy cannonading and skirmishing through the day, Ricketts got his three Brigades into a good place, close to the enemy. We got down into the woods not very far off. Crook got on the enemy's left close to the mountain, and swept down their lines to the east, each Brigade and Division of us in the front falling in as the tide reached us, and joining in the chase, screaming and yelling like a grand fox hunt ... ran them off five miles without stopping. Prisoners, flags, guns, were taken in abundance, and we followed them all night. My regiment (Hunsdon's obesity troubled him on the double quick) formed and got into shape to advance up the pike the first of any in the army, and was soon joined by the rest of the Brigade and led off in the pursuit.

After a mile we stopped for supper, and the 19th Corps passed us. We are now 12 miles from Strasburg. Early is thoroughly whipped and will give us no more trouble. Our Brigade took several guns, a General, flags, and lots of prisoners. Bat. F of the 11th reversed the guns in one Battery, and let the Johnnies have the benefit of their own ammunition; but they soon got out of range. We were under heavy fire for a few minutes, but lost nothing. A skirmish line could have held their position against an army.

Aldace F. Walker

Harrisonburg, Va.
Sunday, 5 P. M.,
Sept. 25

Dear Father:

We are getting well up the Shenandoah, as you will see by consulting your map, about 62 miles from Winchester. Quite a way to pursue a retreating army in these days, especially with the detention we experienced at Fisher's Hill. I hope you will receive speedily the letter I forwarded Friday morning from Woodstock. It gave as full an account of the battle of Winchester as I can afford to give till I can do it verbally, and a little about the battle of Thursday at Strasburg or Fisher's Hill. That was the greatest marvel I ever saw. The position of the enemy seemed impregnable, reaching from mountain to mountain.

We got up Tuesday evening. Wednesday the 19th Corps took a threatening position directly in front. We went to the right, and Warner's brigade took a crest, which we fortified at night, and which proved a fine position for artillery. Then Thursday, Crook left his knapsacks, filled canteens, allowed no one to leave the ranks, and crept around into the woods on the enemy's left. We swung forward our 3d Division, so that it appeared to be the extreme right of our lines, and no doubt the rebs thought it was; but it was in just the position to join Crook when he made the rush from the crest. When Early heard that his left was turned, he said it was impossible, for it couldn't be turned - that he could hold his position against a hundred thousand men. But his men were panic stricken. They ran like sheep, and we should have taken lots of prisoners if we only could have caught them. As it was, we got a good many and almost all the artillery there was.

Sheridan is a driver. He ordered pursuit that night. Emory remonstrated - don't understand Northern fighting, but had to take the advance, and we went on to Woodstock, 12 miles, and very dark ... pretty risky, but it just suited Sheridan. He told our Chief of Artillery Monday morning that he "wanted to see some dead horses before night," - and he did.

Friday P. M. we came on the Edinburg. Averill was ahead and came back reporting "two Divisions of Infantry in front." Sheridan relieved him, but it stopped us over night. The next morning (yesterday) we pushed on through Mount Jackson, where we found rebel hospitals and wounded, and the rebels making a stand this side. We formed, and they left; but it took some four hours. Then we came on and struck them again near New Market. Got out a skirmish line and drove them five miles, our artillery being constantly at the extreme front and shelling them x x x x x x. They apparently don't like that usage, for they didn't try to make a stand in our march today, and what is to become of us next we don't know; but we are in good hands, and are ready to go either way. We hear of other columns, but know nothing definite.

With love,

Aldace F. Walker

I am tenting with Dodge in a wall tent tonight.

Harrisonburg, Va.
Tuesday Morning
Sept. 27th

Dear Father:

We lay quiet all day yesterday, and are likely to do so today for all that we can see. It is understood that we are waiting for the supply train; at any rate, our rations are about played out. We don't know what the intention is, of course, in this region. It is certain that we have cleared the valley of rebel troops, have beaten them hard, and pursued them vigorously for seventy miles, till we compelled them to take to the woods with orders to assemble at Richmond. All able bodied men in this vicinity were ordered to assemble at Harrisonburg yesterday to go to Richmond, but of course they didn't, as we occupy it. The citizens here unite in saying that the C. S. A. is "played out." Still they can make a desperate struggle for Richmond yet, unless it caves before the surrender of that city. They have a hundred thousand men they say, though probably the accessible number is very much less, styled exempts, men who were engaged, "detailed," at various occupations considered essential to the welfare of the Confederacy - overseers, railroad employees, artisans, &c.; these they are trying to collect now, though they are decidedly loath to go. While coming here our soldiers committed some disgusting acts of vandalism - burnt two or three barns, and at Mt. Jackson, where were some barracks built by Gen. Shields',[11] and used by the rebels as hospitals, well fitted up too, one of these was burned - no inmates, but a good deal of valuable hospital furniture being contained. The Reb cavalry told the citizens that we were burning everything, and they generally understood that this place was to be destroyed in retaliation for Chambersburg. But there has been no damage done here. There are several hundred wounded rebels in the churches and other buildings of the place. I visited the 14th N. H. yesterday, doing provost duty in the village.

My old chum Wilson was a Serg't in Co. A. I inquired for him and found that he, with another of his Co., had been left wounded on the field at Winchester on the first advance, and when we advanced again they were found dead with bayonet wounds. I never believed these stories before. I inquired for Col. Gardner, Col. Chamberlain's wife's brother. He was mortally wounded at the same fight. It is quite cold today and has been. I have some cold in my had, but am pretty well on the whole. Did I tell you that we had a cow? We have a very good one, and it is a great help in our mess. Five of us find hard work in disposing of ten quarts a day. Biscuit[s] that we make are capital, and apple butter isn't bad to take. I hope I shall have a chance to forward this today.

Aldace F. Walker

Harrisonburg, Va.
Oct. 1st, 1864

Dear Father:

We hear that another supply train is near by, and so I will write a little with little to say, and perhaps be able to add something after I get the eight days mail that we expect, and old at that. I am in a state of great disgustity this afternoon - partly because I am Division Officer of the Day in charge of the picquet in a terrible rain, though loafing in camp just now; and especially because the paymaster is coming on the train, who is to pay the rest of the Brigade and had our rolls, but who was ordered to turn them over to somebody else just before he left Washington and so we are not to get any money. It is a shame to be bandied around this way, and we are proportionally indignant. But we may as well "take things by their smooth handle, sin' there's no use gripping at thorns." It's a terrible provocation to profanity on the part of swearing men - seven month's pay due, and nary red. Since I wrote you last from this place the 6th and 19th Corps have been off on a seven mile journey to Mount Crawford, principally as a grand foraging expedition I suppose, for we went to work with grist mills and then burnt them up, and stole cattle and sheep and honey and everything we could find, and then moved back here the next day.

The enemy have been fairly driven out of the valley and I suppose we shall retire in good order as fast as we can satisfactorily destroy all property than can in any way aid or comfort the enemy. Meanwhile, the last paper that that we have seen was Sept. 23d, and that was the Richmond Enquirer, so that we are in a state of very dubious uncertainty as to the general welfare of our great and glorious Union. We could get Richmond papers here of quite early date, only the daily stage from Stanton has not made its trips with regularity since our advent, and the railroad tunnel and iron bridge near Staunton are in bad order since our cavalry visited them. We get rumors enough, however - Petersburg taken sure - 8000 prisoners, 100 guns - also Grant repulsed with a loss of 50,000 men - Lynchburg evacuated, &c., ad nauseam. How much we shall learn when the supply train comes. I inquired for "Luty" of a Serg't of his Co. I found straggling in the march of yesterday, and learned that he was well - a great favorite in his Col., and fights like a lion, - runs in the family, I reckon. Only Steph. and Henry seem to prefer the peaceful part of war. I saw Luty afterwards, and he is looking very much better than before - is fat as a pig. I shall write this to Aunt M.

We have got a lot of recruits and convalescents since the battles, and so our regiment is larger than then. We miss those officers lost, however; and also Col. Warner, who is permanently detached with a very good prospect of promotion. In fact, he has been recommended - though that is a secret here yet. "Twinkle, twinkle." We are making a very clean sweep of things in this section of country. I pity the citizens here very much; don't know what they will do; but is all under orders from Gen. Grant, who doubtless regards it as a military necessity.

We have burned fifty mills in the twenty miles above here, and have no trouble at all in making three days' rations last four. Our Gen. Grant will feel rather ridiculous at being in Vermont through the most brilliant campaign our Brigade has ever seen. And, by the way, it is all Sheridan's. Averill failed here. Torbert[12] did at Winchester. But Sheridan has shown an immense deal of vigor, and the campaign is a bigger thing than the papers I saw represented; for Early, we know, confidently expected to beat us both at Winchester and Fisher's Hill. He was fairly outgeneralled. The 6th Corps has been on time every round, and has earned great credit - is in fine spirits and in very good repute. Crook's command has done very well, too.

Sunday Morning - A detachment of 500 picked men from our Brigade has gone out hunting guerrillas. I was very much provoked at my ill luck being on picquet. Just as well, I guess; but I don't like to have the Brigade in and I out. 100 were from our regiment. It don't rain this morning, but is lowery, and I fear we are to have a wet season.

Yours of 19th and 22d received, ten days old. Those cattle were not near Reams, but way round toward the James, and the greater part of our Cavalry are operating in the Shenandoah. We got a dispatch from Grant, dated the 29th, telling of his advance and success; hope he will keep it up.

Bedell has a father and mother, a wife and three children, just in moderate circumstances. I have not heard from him since we left Clifton. Capt. Eldridge is expected now to recover. The ball passed through his body above the vitals.

We are very glad of this trip up the valley, as we see the country. Have good foraging ground. A fine country for campaigning, and it keeps us away from Petersburg, our great bug bear. Lincoln must be reelected, and though the Southerners will hate to submit to him, people here think they will have to soon. A letter also from Ellena.

Love to all.

Aldace F. Walker

Thursday, Oct. 6th, 1864
5 P. M.

Dear Father:

We have marched twenty five miles today, from Harrisonburg back through New Market nearly to Mt. Jackson. The supply train we hear is at the latter place and presume it will be out here soon, so I write a line to say where we are, and all right; though if we keep on down the valley as we have today we shall get to Harper's Ferry before the train does. But who knows whether we are going to Harper's Ferry, or where we are going, or whether we are going anywhere. We supposed when we started this morning that we were going to Culpeper, but we have got by the gap we should naturally pass through to get there, so we are afloat again. We are certain of but one thing - that we have made a clean sweep of the Valley, even to the hay as well as the Johnnies. I hate to see buildings burn, but I suppose it is a military necessity. The papers will tell you of the murder of Capt. Meigs and of the retaliation. Gen. Grant returned to the Brigade on this train, or with it. Nothing further. I am too tired to write, but hope I shall have some letters and papers to read soon.

With love to all.

Aldace F. Walker

I hope you got my letter requesting shirts, drawers, socks, boots, blouse, and those black pants. I want to add a pair of undershirts. Send on as soon as possible to "F. Evans, Sutler 11th Vt. Vols., Washington, D.C."

Strasburg

Saturday 8th

We have made big time in our movement down the Valley so far. Stopped last night at Woodstock, and came here this forenoon, where we are to meet a genuine supply train. Last night and the night before an apology met us with a very small allowance of rations, but we are now about two days "shy." The train is two miles from here, with a big mail aboard, the third in three weeks. We met papers of Oct. 3d five days old, but were very glad to see these. It is an intensely cold day - sharp wind; our big tents are very comfortable, but would be more so if a stove was added. I have been over to part of the battlefield; always enjoy the second visit to such a place better than the first. We hear just now some "bumming" of big guns up the valley, and infer that we were pursued by guerrillas or something, and don't know but a Division or two of Johnnies may be together above us. We don't care much, for we left the 19th Corps in position across the road four miles back. We should have starved if we had stayed at Harrisonburg, and have utterly destroyed everything save dwelling houses on our return, and the green corn fodder. Wish we knew what is in store for us. Some say a trip through Manassas Gap.

Front Royal, Va.
Oct. 12th, 1864

Dear Father:

We have been having very cold weather of late - three hard frosts, and a cold drizzle today, which dampens my paper as I try to write by an out door fire. I haven't anything particular to say except that we marched round to this place two or three days ago. Pretty rough country where we are, but two miles on, around the village, it is very pleasant. I am very glad you sent me the papers, for we can get them very rarely. I was interested much in the World account of the battle of Berryville. Why Berryville? - as it ended in Winchester? With a few corrections it is a very good account. Torbert gave Gen. Rosser[13] a good blow last Sunday. The country around here is full of guerrillas, who are very murderous in their proclivities, and necessary retaliation begins a terrible system of warfare. We have been suffering a good many deprivations of late. Have not seen our valises since we left Clifton, so that clean clothes would be a luxury indeed. I had my shirt boiled once as a sanitary measure, and am ready to do it again if it wasn't so cold lying around waiting for it to dry. We are all out of saleratus too, and have to live on hardtack. Hardtack is good in milk, like cracker and milk you know, but you have to crumb it up with a hatchet or a stone. We got hold of some yeast today however, and shall get along better. We hear that the railroad is being put in order from here to Washington; if so, we shall be likely to remain hereabouts for some time; but we don't know what to believe. We would be as well satisfied with that arrangement as any. As the season passes, campaigning grows less pleasant and we long for winter quarters.

P. M. - The train is in and your long letter is received, with several papers. I have seen no dailies yet later than the 5th. I am glad you got my account of the battle, and am of course willing you should publish parts of it if you deem it worthwhile. The 19th Corps could not have advanced as far as we at first, for the general line was very much refused where they were; but they met a much greater resistance, as the enemy were more prepared for an attack in that part of the field, where it was more woody - did not expect troops would dare make the charge we did so successfully, but with so much loss. In all the fighting we have had our regiment has never fired a round standing up in two ranks, regimental front, as one would suppose all battles were fought. I saw the rebels do it twice at Winchester. We always lay down; so generally that "lay down" is a great by word with the boys, a command they are very willing to obey too. We laid down behind a fence at the hardest point of our second advance, and we made a bully rebel line of battle wilt in ten minutes. The mail is to leave soon. Nothing but "short rations" came up. Some new commissions, among them that of Lt. Col. Hunsdon; though Col. Warner now says privately that if he knew as much of him as he now does, he should have promoted Fleming. Hunsdon is falling into discredit.

With love,

Aldace F. Walker

Middletown, Va.
Sunday Morning, Oct. 16th, 1864

Dear Father:

Here we are again on our old position on the hither side of Cedar Creek with the Johnnies beyond Strasburg on Fisher's Hill. I think I last wrote you from Front Royal. Thursday morning at six we started for Alexandria via Ashby's Gap. We marched some fifteen miles and were just going to ford the Shenandoah, Wright and Getty were crossing, when we were stopped by orders from Sheridan; so we turned back a little and went into camp. At 2 p.m. four scouts - our scouts dress in rebel uniform and are a dashing set of fellows - came through, stopped four times on the way, and ordered us immediately to this point. So we pushed back, making a remarkably rapid march for even the 6th corps. We were five hours actually marching and accomplished nearly twenty miles, and went into our present camp, where we are waiting. Reconnoisances from the 8th and 19th Corps find the enemy in force in their old position, but I don't expect to attack them just at present; because if Sheridan had wanted to keep them from that position he would have stayed on the other side; and they certainly can't subsist themselves long in that part of the country, with nothing but corn and no mills. Besides Sheridan went to Washington last night leaving Wright in command. So we look for a little quiet at any rate, and only wish that the rebs may attack us, which they won't. Lee must place a great deal of importance on holding a force in the valley. I suppose because it threatens the North, and so is of some political force, and also covers Lynchburg and Danville, his only route of supplies. But we can't go there from here with no railroads, for so big an army can scarcely be rationed by the transportation of this Department. I wonder why the papers insist on calling Crook a cavalry general. He is in command of part of the 8th Corps, united with the Army of the Kanawha, called the Army of Western Virginia. Everything remains much as usual here. I have seen a Herald of the 6th with the list of casualties in the 11th. That Sherman family is very unlucky - the Lieut. killed, one brother with a leg amputated, another in hospital with rheumatism, very severe for months. Among these promotions that came at Front Royal was Austin's as Capt. Co. A. We have a good many vacancies now, but Hunsdon is very slow about filling them, and in fact about doing anything any way. The 6th left for home today, what few there were to go.

I hope to hear from you tonight.

Aldace F. Walker

On Picquet
Oct. 20th, 1864

Dear Father:

The 19th of Sept. we fought the battle of Winchester, the 19th of Oct. that of Middletown - and a hard day's work we had of it yesterday too. Sheridan had gone to Washington - the 6th Corps was reported off for Petersburg - the Johnnies said they "knew they could whip the 8th Corps, thought they could the 19th, but expected to be brought up with a round turn when they struck the 6th." Kershaw's Div. had joined them.[14]

Ramseur led the attack, a classmate of Col. Warner, and was mortally wounded. They got in rear of Crook by a night march, got a good thing on him, and drove him off from his entrenchments almost without firing a gun, capturing all his camp and artillery. The 19th Corps followed suit. These were entrenched. We lay on the right, and at right angles to the line of the rest - were ordered up - went in at the double quick, but weren't big enough alone, or didn't get into shape quick enough or something. I was sent with my Battalion to "clear the rebel skirmishers out of a piece of woods," and I did. There weren't many there, as I said; but when they did come they cleared me out in a hurry. They sent on a skirmish line which didn't drive us much, and a line of battle which did. We had a mile to run, and I was immensely tired when I got back to the Brigade. (I was dismounted all day, in part because it's safer, and in part because my horse won't stand fire.) Then I took off my overcoat and went at it.

We formed our Division simply, on a crest. I don't know where any of the rest of the folks were, but our 2d Division at exactly this part of the day, about 8 a.m., saved the army. The Johnnies charged right at us, but we wouldn't stir. They got us back a little, only three or four rods apart, and we under a terrible artillery fire, so that we were at the bottom of the hill and the rebs at the top; but we made a little run at them, the best we could, and back they went. We had defeated the Southern Army.

Sheridan later in the day sent word to Getty that he (or his Division) had "outdone himself" that morning. (Grant was commanding the Division at this time, Getty the corps, Wright the army.) Then after fifteen or twenty minutes' rest they flanked us and we fell back, in remarkably good order, and found that we had gained time to get the wagons off and to rally the skedaddlers. We fell back about two miles - the enemy pressing our skirmishers hard - and reformed our line back of Middletown. 6th Corps on the right of the road, 19th on their right, and 8th Corps back at Newtown all over the country in a disgraceful rout.

Just as we were getting into shape, we saw a black horse coming at a dead run down the pike, with staff and escort a mile behind, and didn't we cheer and throw up our hats and holler and scream when little Phil. dashed off the road and ploughed down in front of our line of battle. "Turn your faces the other way, boys, we'll whip 'em before night." And every one felt that reinforcements had come and the scale was turned. It is strange what a new confidence everyone felt.

Wright is either "thick" or unfortunate, or both. Still Sheridan could only complete what Wright had begun - re-form the lines - put in the cavalry and artillery; and at 3 p.m. the army charged. It wasn't any fooling of Brigade or Division, but the Line went in - and went back again a few minutes, all but the Vermont Brigade, which got behind a stone wall (the country is full of them) and wouldn't run. Soon the rest came up again, and we got up to another wall, the Vermont Brigade in advance as usual. And then it was half an hour before we could make them budge an inch. We went in with fifty rounds of cartridges, and my men were complaining of a lack long before the (the Johnnies) concluded to run.

I was the only field officer of the Brigade in the extreme advance; was some afraid of being flanked, but I kept my eyes open and my guns hot, and finally they dusted, and the 6th Corps was after them with a yell. Another skedaddle and pell mell pursuit. We could not stop the active ones to form a line and the tired ones couldn't keep up. The colors all got in the advance, and we didn't want to stop either, but to give them no chance to form. They turned and fired a volley or two at us at different places in the race, but at last I put my colors in the rifle pit the 19th Corps had left, overlooking Cedar Creek; and how we hustled the bullets into them as they crowded across the narrow bridge. (We had replenished our cartridge boxes with the Johnnies' ammunition that they had abandoned as they ran.) Then the artillery came up, and the cavalry, and Custer charged through the Creek, up the high hill, into a line of fire that played out directly. And it was dark; and we marched back to our old camp, and built fires and told stories - while the cavalry hustled the enemy through Strasburg and over Fisher's Hill and got back all the material and ever so much more - till a Vermonter rode through the lines bringing a captured battle flag and the news, and with cheers and music and general joy we were ready for bed.

It was my ill luck to have the Division picquet line to establish, which took me till 10 o'clock, and then I slept out in the field - a dark, mean job of duty as ever I saw or performed. The camp is just moving off. I got some letters this morning - the first for eight days. And I shall have my line to break up soon. Our losses were heavy - don't know the number. We lost some prisoners on picquet that morning, whom Nicholson will know, was in the hands of the enemy all day, quite badly wounded, but was recovered at night. I don't think of any whom you will know. Lt. Lee,[15] brother of Capt. Lee, and soon to be

Capt. of "M," a 2d Lt. too, and a splendid fellow, was killed by a shell. Capt. Lee, Lts. Baxter,[16] Nichols and French[17] were wounded. Our dead were stripped of clothing in a most inhuman manner, and this morning has seen burial parties all through our camp. Please send me those clothes as soon as possible. I am getting in extremis.

I have never got a scratch yet.

Aldace F. Walker

I attach a little sketch of the last battle. Crook was flanked on extreme left and his works taken in house. He was driven to the northwest, rebs pressing from south east till they crossed the pike into position of "First enemy I saw." As we broke camp and bore to the east, the 8th and 19th Corps were breaking through our lines toward the northwest in a grand stampede. After a good deal of maneuvering the 2d Div. got into posish for its stand, which it kept till 8 a.m., on a little rise. I was out on a skirmish line. A skirmish line of the enemy halting near the house, and the line of battle coming up drove me back on the Division. Patch (1st Serg't of C.) was wounded - left at the barn during the day - found at night when we marched to our old camp. We fell back to where our artillery finally rested, then went up and took position in the old road, resting from about 10 to 3:15, when we advanced.

Troops both sides fell back, leaving the Vt. Brigade behind the first wall, then the right came up and we drove the rebs back to the other walls, where they made repeated stands, the Vt. Brigade getting a little to the front of the line for cover. The left now came up, the right advanced and flanked the enemy who fell back. We charged, going up to and striking the pike just beyond the town, then advancing along the pike, getting some artillery and other fire in their confused retreat, and finally halting in the extreme left of the 19th Corps pit. The cavalry charged down through our old camp, crossed Cedar Creek, formed and charged on over a line of battle to Strasburg, &c., even over Fisher's Hill. The hills east side of Cedar Creek are very steep and high. We poured a fire into the last of the rebs as they crossed the bridge. It was so dark when the cavalry charged that I could hardly see them, and so foggy in the morning I could not tell whether the force in front were rebs or not. Their cavalry had their horses faced south.

Strasburg, Va.
Oct. 23d, 1864

Dear Father:

I wrote you from our picquet station the day after the battle of the 19th. I was relieved the next afternoon and marched over here, where our Brigade is doing provost duty, and outpost too, being the farthest advance of the army. Our Division is all that there is on this side of Cedar Creek, except some cavalry. If the enemy should come up again, we should retire of course to the main army; but they won't do so just at present, for our victory the other day was the most thorough of the campaign. I disliked very much that tour of picquet duty the night after the fight, principally because it was not my turn but Hunsdon's, and though he begged off on account of ailment, I thought he was better able to go than I. And in fact, I was quite hard up. I had no breakfast the day of the fight, nothing any ways but hardtack and a few doughnuts at night, and no appetite either. I was too proud to back out of the detail, and so put it through, eating nothing, and have no appetite yet. When I got over here it was just at dusk. I slept quite comfortably in a barn, and the next day took up my quarters in a private house, where I stayed last night. I have quite a diarrhea, but am feeling better now. Did not go out of the house yesterday, but have been over to see Col. Warner today, and shall be well when I get my appetite.

Our regiment lost pretty heavily in the fight, 114, 28 of them, however, were prisoners, taken on picquet. Some taken at that time have since got away, and I presume more will succeed in doing so. The Brigade I think lost more than at Winchester. The 8th Vt. belongs to the only Brigade of the 19th Corps that did any fighting, and they lost very severely. I understand the 10th lost heavily also, but I have not been able to inquire for the Wallingford boys. "Luty," "Charley Morris," is all right. They lost their Col. and badly in other respects; distinguished themselves by bringing off a battery with drag ropes that would otherwise have been abandoned.

But our Division carried off the honor of the day. When Getty formed as the other troops came rushing through, Crook told him that it was "madness to undertake to make a stand there." But Getty did undertake it, and held the position for an hour, withdrawing at last in good order, and fairly saving the day; for we drove the whole rebel army back once, saving our transportation and when we marched away were ready to stop anywhere. We have come to the conclusion that they can't drive us by a direct attack. Getty is proud, I tell you, and I hope it will get him another star. We are anxious to see Sheridan's story.

We have heard from Bedell. He is all right, and going to be able to get home before long. He is in excellent hands. A woman had him moved to her house, got a daily visit from a doctor, and furnishes him with everything he needs. She came to Middletown the day before the fight, and I saw her and found out fully the Lieutenant's condition. She says she is going north with him when he is able to travel. I think it very providential, as from all accounts he would have died if he had remained where we were forced to leave him.

His recovery reflects great credit on our surgeon, who we all think can't be beat, for skillfulness, and for kindness and attention to the men. I think that Serg't Patch will not recover, as his spine is injured, and the lower part of his body paralyzed. Baxter was slightly wounded, but has reported again. Lt. Nichols, a brother of W. T., the Col., got quite a severe hit in the forearm, but Park expects to save it. It seems pleasant to have a cover in a house and a stove this cold weather, and I hope to be allowed to stay here till I get rid of this nausea that hangs on to me now.

How we did fight the 19th. We never got a tenth part as near the Johnnies as they got to us, and we put them back, though they clung on well. I will probably write more before the mail goes out again. We are so far to the front we can get no papers or news any way. Our advanced guard is on Fisher's Hill. You may believe any story you hear about captured artillery, for I counted forty-eight, besides those recaptured and returned, and I heard of fourteen more.

Monday Eve. - I am much better. All right. No news. Getty is breveted, for which we are all proud.

Strasburg, Va.
Oct. 26th, 1864

Dear Father:

Our Division has occupied this rickety old village for about a week now, and if Early does not interfere from his fortifications on Fisher's Hill we may await cold weather here. We have heard nothing of Early since his signal discomfiture of last week. There has been cannonading a little yesterday and today in the Luray Valley, toward Front Royal. But our advance picquet is far above us on this side the Massanutten, and we sleep secure, though only two hundred yards from the "front." We are occupying the houses of this tumble down locality as we choose. It is the rustiest place in the valley. I have my abode in the sitting room of a motherly widow. Sit by the fire and sleep on the lounge. She was good to me when I felt sick, and gave me a good dinner today, when I felt a big appetite and used it. Not entirely disinterested, however, for I protect her property, though I can't get her to talk for the Union. She is on the fence most persistently, like all the wiser inhabitants of this war ravaged valley. An open Unionist, even in Union ascendancy, is marked, and ruined when the Confederates return; and an avowed secessionist receives no mercy at our hands; while those that while we are here think "the war ought not to have been begun," and when the Johnnies are around think that "it ought to be carried through now it has been commenced," get some little sympathy from each, and like this family here, have a cow left to live on through the winter.

This portion of Virginia did not vote for either Breckenridge of Secession, but has since been persuaded that the South would succeed, and most of the citizens have applied their shoulders to the wheel, and all the able bodied men have been forced into the Southern army. What a population there is left - old men and cripples, widows and children, pale fellows that have been hiding, only showing themselves when our army is here, bearded and grimed ruffians that leave the Southern cause from fear of utter pecuniary ruin, and apply for and receive transportation North only to save their plunder and vent their spleen in the congenial counties of Maryland. Such we see in the Valley. Many of the refugees are the old men, who have been plundered of all, and deserve to be moved North, if only to reach a decent alms-house. It is terrible, and I am glad of it. I only wish that the leaders and not the victims might suffer in this sort, and so reap their traitor's doom in lingering poverty.

Since I have left Washington I have seen too many brave men die. My ideas are changed - I have no remorse. I want to see their punishment. Not a jot of sympathy can these people get from me, for when they ask if I think of Cold Harbor and Winchester and Cedar Creek, and shot and shell, and death. Still, I want to guard this property .. to save this house and cow; but rather to keep our soldiers in healthy discipline, which an army of pillagers cannot possess, than to keep the people from suffering. How my pen has run on. I don't know what I have said, but I do know that the screech of shell and the zip of bullet knocks overboard a man's compassion for the scoundrels. I have written to the Herald of our last fight. How wonderful it is that I don't get my clothes hit or something. I am rather ashamed of it, for I believe I am the only one in the army that has been in so many fights without a clip. It isn't because I don't go where lead flies, any way; for I do just what I see needs doing in battle, and let the bullets go. Luty is all right, did I tell you? I have not even seen a list of casualties in our own regiment yet. We are quite a way from head quarters and the other battalions. I hope that if we remain hereabouts for a season that we shall stay just here. When we started for Ashby's Gap a few weeks ago, we were ordered to Wilmington, North Carolina. Had rather go there than to Petersburg. But that is countermanded now, till we find out whether Lee gives up the Valley.

Evening - Our paymaster has come. Tomorrow I shall be in funds again. It is a big thing, though rather late in the day. Mail is just going out. The regiment is happy.

Aldace F. Walker

Strasburg, Va.
Oct. 28th, 1864

Dear Father:

We were paid off yesterday, just three days before muster - but it is not very probable that this two months' pay will come before January. I got $753, six months' pay, with a little out for that furlough last spring. There is no deduction now for officers absent on leave, and I hope to see Vermont for a few days some time this winter. It is so cold weather that it seems as if winter was close at hand, but there are two months yet for military operations, and there is no telling what that time may bring forth. I don't think, as you seem to, that Grant intends to take Petehrsburg and Richmond this winter. It seems to me as though he means to gripe 'em and hang on. Well, I sent you by express a 7.30 $100, which with the $5.20 interest you retained will, I suppose, nearly cancel my indebtedness to you. Just tell me how much the balance is, and I will settle it, as I may get plundered in this land of guerrillas. I think I shall need pretty much all the rest, as it will take about $450 or $500 to settle my debts. I had some due me, however. I have paid for my horses; the two cost $215. If we get quiet ever I shall get a new saddle and a double breasted dress coat, which I do not own yet; and running expenses will probably absorb the rest by another pay day. My rubber coat I got trusted for at a sutler's and it will cost $20 - a good one though, and a great comfort. I lost one, you know, at Spotsylvania. We think of furnishing stuff and let this good lady where we lodge cook for us while we stay here. She is a nice woman, though on the fence as I told you. I have seen the veritable snuff dippers in all their glory. How they look - ugh. I can contrive to get that bundle on from Washington before a great while I think. You were most unreasonably sanguine about our railroad. When the rails are up and bridges burnt and culverts knocked to pieces, it is a big job to build a railroad. Still, I think if we stay here a week or two longer we shall have a base to the east of us instead of at Martinsburg. Our train with paymaster came along the road just as Moseby was gobbling Gen. Duffie, going the other way. The escort drove him off. We heard the cannonading. Early is reported at New Market. In the November Harper there is a piece, "My Refugees," of extra excellence. I never cried over a magazine article before, - and I can appreciate it, as I have seen so much of trouble of late among these poor people. I will try and add more some time before I send this out.

Saturday P. M. - Mail goes soon, but none received. I am well and very comfortable. Still at Strasburg. Rode over Fisher's Hill today. Early is not within a dozen miles of us any way. I like being under a roof better than canvas.

With love,

Aldace F. Walker

----

1 Sergt. Charles Carroll Wilson (1839-1864), Sullivan, NH. Co. A, 14th N.H., killed at Opequan , VA, 9/19/1864. Augustus D. Ayling, Adjt. Gen., Revised Register of the Soldiers and Sailors of New Hampshire in the War of the Rebellion 1861-1866, (Ira C. Evans, Concord, N.H., 1895); KUACat, 61.

2 USA Maj. Gen. Henry Warner Slocum, commanded Twentieth Corps, also known as the Army of Georgia. Boatner, 765.

3 Lieut. John A. Hicks, Jr., Rutland., Co. B, 10th Vt. Infantry; wounded 9/22/1864. RR.

4 Lieut. Daniel Gilbert Hill, Wallingford. Co. G, 10th Vt. Infantry; mwia 9/19/1864, died 10/26/1864. RR.

5 Andrew Cowan's 1st N.Y. Independent Battery; Jeffrey D. Wert, Gettysburg Day Three, (Simon & Schuster, New York, 2001), p 142.

6 Bedell's wounding and subsequent recovery is probably the most heart-warming incident to come out of Vermont's participation in the Civil War.

7 Capt., later Maj., Henry M. Pollard, Ludlow, Co. I, 8th Vt. Infantry. RR.

8 USA Brig. Gen. William Woods Averell, commanded 2nd Division, Cavalry Corps. Boatner, 35.

9 USA Brig. Gen. Frank Wheaton. Boatner, 910.

10 Col. George Perkins Foster, Walden. RR.

11 USA Brig. Gen. James Shields, born in Ireland. Boatner, 752.

12 USA Brig. Gen. Alfred Thomas Archimedes Torbert, commanded cavalry in Army of the Shenandoah. Boatner, 842.

13 CSA Brig. Gen. Thomas Lafayette Rosser, commanded Early's cavalry at Cedar Creek. Boatner, 709.

14 CSA Brig. Gen. Joseph Brevard Kershaw's division.

15 Lieut. Oscar R. Lee, Waterford. His commission as Capt., to date from 10/16/1864, didn't arrive until 11/17/1864, weeks after he was killed in action at Cedar Creek, 10/19/1864. RR.

16 Lieut. Henry C. Baxter, Derby, Co. I. RR.

17 Lieut. George O. French, Castleton, Co. C. RR.

16.
The Shenandoah Valley Campaign Winding Down
November and December, 1864

Martinsburg, Va.
Friday P. M.
Nov. 11th, 1864

Dear Father:

I got on full as fast as I expected in my journey southward. I made connections at Troy and New York, reaching Philadelphia at five the next morning. There I missed a train. Left at eight and reached Baltimore at one. Visited the city all I wanted to, going up on to the big monument. Left in a sleeping car at nine, reaching Martinsburg at three, and got a bed for the rest of the night. It was said that no train would go to the front till Sunday. I have worked today on my returns and got nearly up and square. I hear tonight that a train goes up in the morning, and shall try and get off if so. The army has fallen back to the vicinity of Winchester, to be nearer supplies, I suppose. No enemy any where near, as I can understand. I am all right. Well and hearty. Hope we shall get a good location till cold weather, and then put up for the winter.

In haste,

Aldace F. Walker

Kernstown, Va.
Monday

I came up here yesterday, getting through in a day. Find Hunsdon a little unwell, and I am in command of the regiment. It won't last long of course, as Hunsdon is getting better. There was a little scare here when Lomax[1] felt of us, but it is all over and no enemy near. I am very well and have comfortable quarters, as a tent in the woods can well be. I got a letter from Em complaining that I didn't come and see her. Shall tell her Mother wouldn't let me. No particular news. All my things are O. K., and I had a good time at home.

In haste,

Aldace F. Walker

I might have told you at home that H—— said he resigned on account of his mother's health, that she is better and expects to come back.

Kernstown, Va.
Nov. 18th, 1864

Dear Father:

Our four day mail is just in with a letter from you, and I will send a little answer, though it is very dull here now. We are trying to get up the various ceremonies and shows and displays of military etiquette, but it rains so continually that it is rather hard. We have Guard Mounting for the Division and Dress Parade by Brigade, and various reviews, &c., that keep us busy some. This field service in time of peace is pleasant enough. We get boards and floor or tents, (the old barns suffer) and bricks to build fire-places, and it is very comfortable, especially the idea that the Johnnies are out of reach. We know they are not this side of Fisher's Hill, and I don't see how they can supply themselves there, and think they are still further up the valley. Early failed to be in Pennsylvania on election day, and has retired in disgust. I will send the October Atlantic. The boys lost the November one while I was gone, much to my disgust. I called on a family near here the other day; found an old man who pretends to be Union - said he opposed secession to save slavery; and two young women with husbands in the rebel army, who were very secesh. I don't blame a woman for holding Southern sentiments though, any more than a child. A woman who didn't believe in political matters with her husband would be too strong minded for me. Still it was rather amusing to hear them talk. I did not take cold by coming to the exposure again - am very well indeed - and hope Sherman and Grant will finish the war and let us rest here in the valley.

With love to all,

Aldace F. Walker

I have seen Pollard and Charley Hilliard. All well.

Camp Russell, Va.
Sunday, Nov. 20th, 1864

Dear Father:

Gen. Sheridan has issued an order, naming our present camp near Kernstown "Camp Russell" and giving his army the proud title of "Army of the Shenandoah." The 6th Corps belongs to the Army of the Potomac no longer, though doubtless it would have saved life if we had remained near Petersburg. Still, those of us that remain are well satisfied and more. We still expect to move back across the Opequon, but perhaps not until it is sure that the rebels will trouble us no more this season. Meanwhile we are very well off here. My tent is floored, I have a good bed, and could live nine months in this way quite comfortably. I got yours of last Monday today, with the Chronicle and Congregationalist.

So Duncan and Miss Abbie are married. I should like to see them at their Strafford home some time. He is at the copperas works you may not know. Little has not got back yet, though expected all the time. Presume he will be up on the train that brought this mail. It rains today, and very likely he stopped in Winchester. Dodge has gone home for fifteen days, and I am very glad of it. Surgeon Park has applied for a leave. He is very much of a man, as I told you. No case of amputation in this brigade that he performed has failed to recover. One boy lost a leg and arm. Bedell lost a leg at the point where 86 of 100 die, and the next day a finger was exsected, and is nearly well. We are getting quite short of officers now. A good many are getting out of the service by resignation or dismissal. Our prisoners are all away, though some are paroled, - Macomber among this number. Five are detailed as staff officers. Dr. Meigs, a fine young man in his profession, has been promoted to surgeon of the 3d. Our hospital steward, Bourne, will probably take his place.

I have commanded the regiment the past week, but Hunsdon has gone on duty today as Div. Officer of the Day, and will probably call himself well tomorrow. I find my slippers very handy, and have bought a knit jacket to wear outside my vest, and under my coat when I choose, that is very comfortable indeed. I left my new blouse at Martinsburg. I think the cloth is not very stout, as it has torn in a place or two. Don't know what to do with my dresses and indigo. Will save the delaine for Mother if she wants it. My horse has so much life on account of the little she has to do that she is a nuisance on parade. She prances so that I can hardly sheath my sword when "The Parade is Dismissed." I don't care much about the pocket handkerchief, but I think I left a pair of buckskin gloves there that I may need in the course of the winter. I have another pair now that will do for the present. We haven't had any snow, though last Sunday was bitter cold towards night. It has rained much more than half the time the past week.

Love to Mary, Belle and all.

Aldace F. Walker

Camp Russell
Nov. 22d, 1864

Dear Father:

A mail has just come in and leaves directly. I have forgotten to say in my other letters that Sergt. Patch is dead - died before I returned, and was buried of course at Winchester. Little has returned. Has been at Martinsburg some time. Had no means of coming up on the last train.

I am all right. No more time.

Aldace F. Walker

Camp Russell
Tuesday

Dear Father:

Another mail goes out today - none in. I have just time to say that I am well and all right. Hunsdon is on duty again. Little is at Martinsburg waiting to come on to the regiment. We had a review of the Corps, the fighting 6th, yesterday by Gen. Sheridan. It rained all the time - a cold storm that was very disagreeable as we could not wear overcoatand got wet through. It went off well, however. Our regiment marched the best in the Corps, and was a big sight to see too. Sheridan looked very pleasant, and his black horse was a hard one for the rest to keep up with. On our parades and reviews our regiment is formed in two battalions, so I have the same as the command of a regiment. We have now about 700 men in the Regt. still expect to move back a piece before long. It is quite cold. Very stormy weather all the time. Snow on the hills this morning. We are speculating on Sherman, of course. Early has left us, and I would not wonder if he went South. His men wouldn't fight sure if they only saw a Greek cross.

With much love to all, in haste,

Aldace F. Walker

Head Quarters 1st Vermont Art.
Sunday, Nov. 27th, 1864

Dear Father:

We are in a bad way as to mail matters these days. Four days' extra rations were accumulated at Winchester; so as, it is said in the Herald, to give the employees of the Quartermaster's Department as opportunity to rest on Thanksgiving Day. So we got a mail about last Tuesday, I believe, and have heard nothing since. We expect daily mail facilities soon, for the railroad from Harper's Ferry to Winchester is nearly completed; in fact a body of convalescents reached us over that route today, and I presume the depot will be moved during the ensuing week.

We get daily papers quite regularly now, though a little late of course - for instance, those of Friday today and consider ourselves quite comfortably well posted up. Two great questions now agitate our camps - What is Sherman doing with his army? - and, What will Sheridan do with the 6th Corps? The first we expect to know by waiting awhile - the second we have waited some time to discover, and know nothing about yet. I hope Sherman will bring up eventually at Beaufort; but my advice was not requested on the subject.

I wish the 6th Corps might winter in the Valley, but I presume I shall have as little to say in this matter as in the other. Several things look like remaining. For instance, continued orders to the men to make themselves comfortable in huts, &c., which may be a mere blind of course. The turning over of batteries, ambulances and other Corps property left at City Point last July, and the return of the men in charge to their commands. Then the Cavalry have found that Early has yet a heavy force on Roods Hill - though Kershaw may have gone, I doubt his going to Richmond. And in fact, the general opinion is that we shall stay in the Valley, though possibly we may re-cross the Opequon. But I incline to the opposite view, principally to be contrary, I suppose. Early very likely will be hustled down to meet Sherman in South Carolina, though Davis said he could not be spared to go to Georgia in the summer.

There seems to be a shutting down on the granting of furloughs and leaves of absence just now; none have come for a week, and if none are to be granted it means work. Templeton, Park, Warner and others have applications in, which are pigeon - holed at Army Head Quarters. It is said too that Phil's brother, on his staff, said to Maj. Whittier, our A. A. G., the other day that the 6th Corps was to leave the Department soon, &c., &c., on both sides, ad infinitum. What's the use of bothering?

I have been quite sick for two or three days. On Thanksgiving Day I got my allowance of turkey with potatoes and onions and jelly and peaches, &c. these last from the sutlers; but I could not eat much, and soon cast aside what I had eaten. Was quite bilious and down at the mouth. The next day ate nothing, and am about well now. Live on fresh oysters. Hunsdon was taken quite sick yesterday morning. Is some easier today. But I am well enough now for all practical purposes. We have been having a vast amount of rain of late, and if we had not a very good camp it would be quite muddy. To - day has been pleasant. We had our inspection at 10 and a meeting at 11. The Chaplain got off a kind of a Thanksgiving lecture, but he is rather out of his element in conducting a meeting. He has done a heap of good writing letters and saving property and mementos for wounded men, and that is where he can do the most, and any Chaplain can do the most in a campaign. I have been scratching this for want of employment rather. Don't know when it will go. A daily mail will be a great luxury to us. What shall we do with it?

Love to all,

Aldace F. Walker

Wednesday
Nov. 30th, 1864

Dear Father:

A mail came in today, eight days contents. Two letters from you. It is strange that you don't hear from me, as I have written several times. We expect a more frequent mail now, as Martinsburg is abandoned and the railroad is to be used. We got our first earnest of it last night in an installment of hay for our horses, which is pleasant of course. The end of the road is now about five miles from here. I was over to the 19th Corps yesterday, and had a visit with Capt. Pollard. All well. We have lots of business now in the way of drills, brigade and regimental. Hunsdon is still poorly, and I have all the work to do. I am quite well now. Expect a tour of picquet duty tomorrow. We thought a day or two ago that we were certain to move before long. Now we don't think much about it. Still, the Gov., Washburn, Baxter, &c., are hard at work to get us stationed at Washington this winter. I don't care much about that, unless we are disconnected from the brigade. If we are to take the field in the spring we had as lief pass the winter here, for there is nothing very bad about it any way. Every tent has a fire place, and expenses are comparatively small. Monotonous though. Well, I wrote you a letter a few days ago.

Will insert this and say Good bye.

Aldace F. Walker

Camp Russell
Dec. 1st, 1864

Dear Father:

This is probably the last letter I shall have a chance to write from our present posish, and when I can mail it I don't know. Yesterday we were quite getting confirmed to the idea that we were to remain in our present camp for the season, and acted accordingly, getting boards and trying to fit up comfortable winter quarters. At midnight we had to turn out 125 for picquet to relieve the picquets of the 1st Division, which marched at day break. Wright went with them, and we understand that the rest of the Corps is to follow; if so, we probably move in the morning. Getty is in command of the rest of the Corps now left here. He has sent orders to send sick men away to Gen. Hos., to turn over surplus property, &c., and I think that there is no doubt but that we travel somewhere. Where? I don't know. Petersburg? I think not, principally because I hope not. The lower Atlantic_Coast? Very possibly. Tennessee? Some say so, or Kentucky. So little we know of what is before us. I am on picquet today. Have a long line, - our old line and the line of the

1st Division, which we relieved last night. Am in camp for a few minutes while I scratch off this. Am very well. Expect a nightly job of relieving picquets.

With much love to all,

Aldace F. Walker

Camp Russell
Saturday P. M., Dec. 3d, 1864

Dear Father:

We did not leave as we expected to the other morning. Are still in our old camp, but expect only a day or two more here. The 3d Division has followed the 1st, starting this morning. These troops have marched to Stevenson's Depot, a little beyond Winchester, and taken cars for Washington. It seems to take about two days to transport a Division, so that we expect to start on Monday morning, though we may move tomorrow. Wright went on with the 1st Division. Getty went this morning, as I suppose to embark the troops at Washington. Grant commands what is left of the Corps here now, namely the 2d Division. We understand, or think most probable, that our destination is Petersburg. Sheridan and the War Dept. urged, it is said, that the 19th Corps should go, but Grant insisted on the 6th. So much for a reputation - you have the work to do. It is rather too bad, but "such is life." as Rollin said.

Col. Warner is Breveted Brigadier, and will probably be soon assigned to duty in accordance with his brevet rank immediately. I don't know as this removes him from our regiment; think not, and suppose that he could be reassigned to his old rank by a like order of the President. Still, he will doubtless be confirmed as Brig. Gen. during the winter. Everyone is pleased, as he is very popular in this Brigade and in the 1st, which he has commanded for some time. In case this vacancy occurs there will be an effort made to give me the command of the regiment.

This is all sub rosa of course. I shall do nothing myself, but think that it will be done. I would not accept it, but Hunsdon is notoriously unfit, and Fleming's only military feat was the sacrifice of his command, besides he formerly was my junior. The officers of the regiment all desire my promotion almost without exception, also Col. Warner and Gen. Grant. This is quite premature I suppose, but it has been talked of for some time. I shall let the hen set and wait orders. I have forwarded to Tichnor & Fields an Atlantic subscription and the other magazine for Mary.

We have a daily mail now. A letter from you last night of the 28th, five days. Presume you get mine quicker now. That unfinished letter in the Atlantic as probably written by Capt. Lewis, as he corresponds with a "Mary," though hardly a cousin. "Rood's Hill" is about twenty miles beyond Fisher's Hill. Very likely when we leave Early will make a break in this direction. About bank stock - I suppose that the 7.30's can be used to a little advantage, at lest the interest now due. If you think there is anything to be gained, as there probably is put them in.

I am very well, and ready for anything that may turn up. Wish we could put down the rebellion this winter; would be willing to fight all winter if it could be done, but something has got to turn up first, and perhaps there will - something providential.

With love to all,

Aldace F. Walker

Camp Russell
Monday Eve.
Dec. 5th, 1864

Dear Father:

I write just a line to let you know that we haven't gone from our old line yet, and no orders to move. The 1st and 3d Divisions have gone - the 2d remaining with Aunt Lydia in command. It is said that Sheridan is making strong efforts to have us retained in the Department. Perhaps he will succeed. At any rate, we don't feel as sure of going as we did and perhaps may remain here for the winter. No idea where the others have gone. I don't think Sheridan knows where the rest of the Corps has gone.

With much love,

Aldace F. Walker

Camp Russell, Va.
Wednesday Eve., Dec. 8th, 1864

Dear Father:

I am writing to you quite often nowadays; but you will be quite anxious to hear of our whereabouts, and we have a daily mail, or rather we send a daily mail and get just nothing in that line - the Corps being understood to be at Washington or elsewhere, I suppose, and the mail detained. It is a most provoking arrangement. Other troops get their regular mail. The newsboys expect us to leave every day and don't order papers enough to supply us. And on the whole we are neither fish nor fowl, and don't know what we shall be. I still am inclined to think we shall leave for Wilmington or elsewhere, though it is probably true that Sheridan is trying hard to retain our Division. Meanwhile we are quite well off generally, save in the matter of communications, and getting used to the state of uncertainty under which we live. I had a little sick turn yesterday, but some mercury and epsom have fixed me up again. Pollard was here a day or so ago. It is lovely weather now. If it would only keep so, the Valley would be a splendid place for a winter residence, but mud will come next month of course, and probably a more southern climate will be more agreeable. No news of any sort as I know of. I use my last postage stamp on this letter, but probably can hunt some more up.

With much love to all,

Aldace F. Walker

Camp Russell, Va.
Thursday Eve., Dec. 8th

Dear Father:

I scratch another little line because we understand that orders are on hand for us to march in the morning to Stevenson's Depot, and take the cars to follow the rest of the Corps. We have not received them yet, but presume the news is correct, and that we shall be in Washington some time tomorrow night. It is also rumored that the other two Divisions are at City Point, which rumor we fail to take any stock in, principally because we don't wish to. Another rumor places them on transports in the Potomac waiting for us to come on, with anywhere from eight to twenty-three days rations on board. A week will decide it, I reckon; so what's the use of guessing? It is terribly cold tonight, but we are comfortable enough, with our fire places and blankets. It will be a cold job traveling, but my overcoat is a grand institution. All our speculations may be at fault, and no orders up. Hope so, for I rather like this country. Still, when we get to Washington, we shall expect to get a mail, and a big one.

With much love,

Aldace F. Walker

National Hotel, D.C., Washington

Saturday Noon

We broke camp and marched at daylight yesterday. Had the advance of the Division. Were on the cars at Stevenson's Depot at noon. Have had a most miserable time. It was very cold - the worst day of the season by far. We were all in box cars, except some of the men who did not have even that, but were on top or on platform cars. A heavy snow storm, some six inches, fell in the night, and the train is not in yet. I jumped on to a passenger train at the Relay House about nine this morning and got ahead so. Got a good breakfast, and now feel first rate; but am absent without leave; expect to head them off when they come in. In the car where I was were all the officers of the regiment and the band and some dozen others, crowded tight. We stole a stove and pipe, and burned up the lining of the car trying to keep warm, and so got considerable comfort and some sleep. The other two Divisions are at Petersburg - have relieved the 5th Corps. We expect to embark this afternoon. I don't know whether we shall get a mail here or after we get to City Point. Dodge is here to join the regiment from furlough. Quite unwell. No news afloat as I know of.

In great haste,

Aldace F. Walker

On Board Steamer C. Vanderbilt
Near Fortress Monroe, Va.
Dec. 11th, 1864

Dear Father:

We are having rather a comfortable time this Sunday, though not the most agreeable imaginable either. It is not as cold as it has been, and we don't suffer as we did on the cars, but still it is too cold for pleasure and sloppy generally. The officers are well enough off, having the parlor and staterooms, with meals served up below. The men are crowded where they can stow themselves - all under shelter, however. As I wrote you from Washington, I came on ahead from the Relay House. Got a good meal and some articles which I much needed. The train came on about two p.m., and I scrambled aboard and rode down to the wharf. Hunsdon left for the Avenue to take his turn of shopping, and I had the job of embarking the troops, as I should any way. We got the men and horses aboard, and then the baggage, and the rations for men and horses, and no Hunsdon. So we set sail, and I am in command. I got three companies transferred to another boat we were so crowded; and got pretty tired, but had the best bed by virtue of my rank, and am rested this morning. We have about 700 men with the regiment now. Several other officers got left as Hunsdon did. We expect to reach City Point about seven tonight. Shall probably sleep on board - don't know what will become of us if we don't - and then take cars for Weldon R. R., where the 5th Corps was encamped. I am quite reconciled to the job now - have no other way. The trains, artillery and pack horses come from Winchester by the overland route. Warner's Brigade guards them. It is rather unfortunate, as it will be a week and more too before we see our cooking utensils again. But means are more at Petersburg than in the Valley, and we shall get along some way, I'll warrant. No mail. That'll come too. This boat is the one I rode up the Hudson in when I had sore eyes, but is rather the worse for wear. Among other things I bought a buffalo robe, and though especially designed to sleep on, I have passed nights very comfortable under them.

Must go out and see the Fortress, &c.

Aldace F. Walker

Petersburg, Va.
Dec. 15th, 1864

Dear Father:

Way round on the left, and pretty well off on the whole. I would have written sooner, but I have had two nights on picquet, and did not know that a mail was to leave yesterday. Am off today and a mail goes out at 3 p.m., so I will describe my journey and my new whereabouts. We made a quick passage, didn't we? Friday at Winchester, Tuesday morning at City Point, yes, clear round to the Weldon road. I wrote you a letter from the boat, which I dropped in the P. O. at City Point. We passed Fortress Monroe about noon Sunday. Found a big fleet of transports laden with troops from and Butler's army, and reported as waiting for fair weather, en route for Newbern, perhaps 6000 of them there. We hated to see others going South, and us to Petersburg; but we are better off than we expected, as I will develop presently. We might have come up to the Point Sunday night, but I hated to land in the cold, and persuaded the Captain to anchor in the river near the mouth of the Chickahominy. Monday morning we came up and went ashore, and at noon took cars for the front, getting up ahead of the Division. We got off at Parke Station near Army Head Quarters and right on the battle field of last June. Sergt. Donnelly of Co. C was buried right by our bivouac. And by the way, if Mr. Sherman wishes to obtain the body of the Lieutenant we can find the spot for him with no trouble at all - about five miles back of our present position.

We moved on Tuesday morning right through where our prisoners were taken, across the Weldon road to the left of the line. The 9th Corps extends from the Appomattox to somewhere, and from there the 6th corps continues the line to the end - very much extended, of course, but the works are strong. The 2d Corps joins us on the left, filling the western front and rear. We moved into some camps where other regiments have been living and had built huts. So all we had to do was simply to stretch our tents and have a good cover, chimneys, &c. - my house is built of logs, five feet high, and tent set over it - a floor of hewn timber, a bunk, table, &c. - and are well off, better than in the Valley. I had the picquet detail and went out, staying on the line two night's as I said.

I have seen no acquaintances in the Army of the Potomac as yet. If we are just put here to hold this line and to merely occupy, as it looks now, we are all right. We certainly can't move at present, for we have no transportation as yet - no ambulances, ammunition, wagons, or anything; so we shall sit still for awhile. The 2d and 5th Corps are loose and may operate. We are a little afloat in our mess arrangements, as our dishes &c. have not arrived, though they are now expected. Since I have been writing I have had a call from Maj. Knapp of the 17th. He is well. Conway has not returned to the regiment as yet. I enclose the result of my picquet duty - palpable, I mean. We got a mail yesterday, and a daily one now; I have your letter of Dec. 8th. I wish you would write to Mr. Sherman if you cannot see him right away, as we understand he intends to recover the body when he can be sure of finding it. I had also a letter from Bedell, who is in Vermont and doing well.. I will send Mother the dresses. The indigo I threw away, as I had no room in my valise.

Love to all,

Aldace F. Walker

Petersburg, Va.
Dec. 18th, 1864

Dear Father:

As I am now in the country of a daily mail I propose to resort to my old habit of two letters per week, and commence this Sunday morning. Our mail gets in at 7 p.m., goes out at 3 p.m. Last night I received yours of the 14th with postage stamps. That seems very like being in the world again. We get New York dailies, for instance, of Friday morning on Saturday evening, which is pretty quick. But we find here that we get the news way ahead of the papers, and I suppose ahead of the citizens of New York, for everything of importance is at once communicated to the army by Col. Rawlings in General Orders. We got the unofficial news from Thomas[2] as it came. Yesterday we received three closely written pages giving extracts from Richmond papers about the Saltville raid, Fort McAllister, Hood's official report of Franklin, with his dozen generals put one side, and last night we got Thomas' report of his last fight, and heard Meade's guns at sunrise. There was an unusual amount of picquet firing on the right last night - don't know what for, but the 9th Corps and Johnnies opposite have orders to fire all night, always cautioning one another when abut to commence, which is very considerate.

There has not been a gun fired on our front, though there is continual conversation going on. The Johnnies were greatly exercised to know the meaning of the cheering of the past few days, and when it began our picquets didn't know, and told them all manner of fish stories. But it must be a blue time in Richmond. I don't know as I care for anymore of the Journals, but the other papers I like to see very much, especially the Heralds. I have been bathing this morning. Find a good deal of comfort here on the whole. The great blessing of the cold weather is that we can live without the "creepers." The army isn't as big as I gathered from A———'s story. I'll give a few figures that are probably contraband, and you can add at your leisure. Will give the number of guns in each Corps as near as I can estimate: 5th Corps, 18,000; 2d, 14,000; 6th, 8,000; 9th, 10,000; Griggs' Cav., 2,000. This is Meade's army - about 50,000 men, and the Artillery, lots of it. and Butler has the 24th, a big Corps of perhaps 20,000 and Weitzel's niggers, the 25th. Our 6th Corps Artillery that we had in the Valley is not to come on; two batteries were left with Sheridan, and three at Washington to recruit; we have six here, however, that didn't go North with us - but we wish we had the others, for we are proud of them. This military railroad is the biggest thing entirely - runs clear around to where we are - trains ever two hours - scarcely any grading at all, but the trains go up hill and down quite heterogeneously. Warner's Brigade has got along, but our mess kit has not come up yet. We expect the wagons and pack animals every day. I want you to get up a bundle or box or something, and send it on right away. Principally for a tub of butter, which I will pay for of course. We get butter of the sutlers at 80 cents, which hardly pays, seeing that it is scarcely fit to eat. Put in about four codfish and my boots, which I hope Valiquette has stretched ad libitum. My new coat is a sham, half cotton or half rotten or something. There is no firmness to it any way.

Love to all,

Aldace F. Walker

Camp 1st Vt. Art.
Thursday Noon

Dear Father:

I sent either yesterday or Sunday for a tub of butter, &c. If they have not started yet, I want a box made big enough so that you can enclose my little mattress; it will be a great blessing if we spend the winter here, as I now think we may. Lieut. Parker of our regt. is dead - from Middlebury. I know the family. He was taken prisoner June 23d - was sent to Charleston, S.C. - from there to Columbia - made his escape - was recaptured by blood hounds set on by the rebels, and very badly bitten - after which he was taken to the hospital, and there took the yellow fever, and died in consequence of one or both. It's a pretty rough story, and I have got it to write to his father. Shall enclose the letter which came to me from Annapolis. Nothing new here, save that it is a terribly cold day after yesterday's rain, and I am on picquet, though the line is so near I take a few liberties.

In haste,

Aldace F. Walker

Wednesday, Dec. 21st, 1864
Near Petersburg, Va.
Patrick Station, U. S. M. R. R.

Dear Father:

This is the first rainy day we have had in our new camp. We are in the short days now, and the rainy weather must come before long. I know that people at the North are feeling as though this army ought to be "at work" while the good weather lasts - Why don't the army move? I was very much vexed when I was at home to hear the stay-at-homes talk in that manner. If they were here they wouldn't talk so. The army wants the war to close full as much as the people at the North do, but still we feel as though the past season, since May 6th, had seen enough of fighting for one year. Perfectly willing of course for Sherman and Thomas to fight, but don't want to here. And I have no idea that there will be any more fighting in this vicinity at present - 12,000 men sent away under and Butler to Wilmington, perhaps, don't look much like it. And even the reserves of Meade's army are going into winter quarters. Everything is very quiet just where we are.

There has been no firing at all on our front; but just a the left where the 2d Corps joins us the Johnnies made a break the other night, and gobbled three of the 2d Corps picquet posts. Considerable firing for a few minutes, and some of the bullets whistled over our camp, so they say - I didn't wake up. Down on the right we can hear the 9th Corps videttes ever night. They have orders to fire. I am glad Thomas has done a clean thing out West. He has disappointed ever body; or I, at least, supposed he would do well if he held his own. Savannah is not taken yet, but we have Sherman's word that it soon will be. And then I hope for rain, and want to wait for spring. I got your letter of the 16th last night. We had no mail on Monday, as none leaves Washington Sunday; but letters come through to us very quickly, and I hope that they go North with like dispatch. I don't want any sheets here. A to dress coat, I have none, nor shan't at present. I have written twice to the Frederick tailor, but get no answer. I had a letter from Ellena the other day. She is well off apparently, and seems unusually contented. Our tent is so dark in cloudy weather that it is hard work to see to write, especially with Arnold's fluid on blue paper, but I guess this letter is as distinct as the average. There is some trouble in getting our Commissary dept. to running. The men are well supplied, but the officers' sales are minus, and we live on short commons just now. Our pack mule has not got up. Then we miss the nice dry rails we had to burn in the Valley. Green pine is our fuel here, and we shall get the country bare of wood before the season is out. The next pleasant day I am going off to hunt up Sheldon. He is in the 9th Corps now I understand.

Much love to all,

Aldace F. Walker

Patrick Station, U. S. M. R. R.
Dec. 25th, 1864

Dear Father:

This Christmas Day is most lovely here - a little cold, but no fault to find with that. We see by the papers that you have been having a big snow storm up North. We have not seen a bit in this latitude. There has been very little rain and no mud as yet. The splendid news that keeps coming in makes the Johnnies quake in their shoes. When our picquets taunt them concerning Savannah or Wilmington or Hood, they open fire in the most spiteful manner, but have nothing to say. A big squad of them came in last night, of the size of which we have all manner of rumors. We got Ord's[3] telegraph operator's story yesterday morning, or Friday night. It is probably correct in the main, or it would not be published to the army. How hopeful the whole affair of the war appears just now. But we shall soon have to suspend operations for the season. I am in command of the regt. just now, and Hunsdon the Brigade. Grant has the Division, and Foster of the 4th the 1st Brigade, Getty and Warner having each gone home for twenty days. I rather wish you could see Warner in Vermont, but you probably will not meet him. He was very anxious to see his little girl, and has been disappointed two or three times about getting away.[4]

I have received your letter of last Sunday. It is strange that you did not hear from me sooner after reaching this locality, though I believe I did not write immediately. But letters ought to go as quickly one way as the other. Our mails are delayed now by ice on the Potomac, so that they are usually about six hours late these days. We get no news from this vicinity. The 8th Corps, or Crook's command, is understood to be across the James, and it is rumored that the 19th Corps is on its way hither. These movements of troops have delayed our wagons and they are not on yet. I went over to the 9th Corps and visited the 17th yesterday. They are in Fort Davis, next this side of Fort Hill, and about a mile from Petersburg. Are quite well off, though occasionally a man is struck in the foot by a stray bullet. Conway has not got on yet, though he is at City Point, and I suppose is at Bermuda Hundred visiting John and Harley, who are over there supplying a nigger Brigade. There have been several executions near here lately. I keep out of sight very persistently. Men who deserted to the enemy, took up arms and fought against us. We captured a batch of them in the Valley. New Hampshire furnishes quite a lot of them, filling its quota with B——paupers and kenuck substitutes. I rejoice in the new call. But the grand slump is coming some time, and soon I hope, and with some show of reason. No army left but Lee's, and if that holds out till spring we can finish it then. Well, a Merry Christmas, nearly a happy New Year when this reaches you.

Love to all,

Aldace F. Walker

Petersburg, Va.
Dec. 28, 1864

Dear Father:

I don't know as I have anything at all to write this time. I am still commanding the regiment, and it is a time of year when we are full of returns and papers - business on hand all the time in the Adjutancy office, and that is all there is going on. We get our daily mail and our regular papers. Savannah, we are informed, has gone up. We had the news several days old before it reached us from Washington. It is a pity, and will cause disappointment through the country, that Hardee and his 15,000 escaped. Still I do not see how it could be helped, and rather expected it. It's a big thing, any way. Capt. Lee has returned - recovered from his wound - one of our best officers. Our band is improving fast under the instructions of a Vermont teacher.

I really find nothing more to say today, save that I am well and contented, and send love to all.

Aldace F. Walker

----

1 CSA Maj. Gen. Lunsford Lindsay Lomax; joined Early in the Shenandoah Valley in August; Boatner, 489.

2 USA Maj. Gen. George Henry Thomas, the "Rock of Chickamauga," commanding the Army of the Cumberland. Boatner, 836.

3 USA Maj. Gen. Edward Otho Cresap Ord, commanding the Twenty-Fourth Corps and Department of Virginia. Boatner, p 609.

4 According to the "Organization of the Army of the Potomac, commanded by Maj. Gen. George G. Meade, U.S. Army, December 31, 1864," Getty had departed on leave December 22, and Col. Warner on December 23, leaving Grant, Foster, Hunsdon and Walker in temporary command of the division, brigades and regiment, respectively. OR, 42, (3):1120.

17.
Siege at Petersburg
January and February, 1865

Headquarters 1st Vt. Art.
Jan. 1, 1865

Dear Father and Mother:

What a frigid morning ushers in this New Year. We had a stormy day yesterday, turning to snow towards night, and this morning the ground is frosted, and so frozen - pretty rough on the soldiers that happen to be on picket or guard. The rest of us are will enough off. When we were in the Valley we made our fire places of stone with mud for mortar, and they answered a fine purpose. When we came to this country of dirt and clay, where not a stone is to be found, I was rather at a loss to know how a fire was to be obtained; but the soil is of a great consistency. Wells need no stoning, and never cave in; and by the way, the old-fashioned well sweeps make a camp look curious enough.

When we build our pen to put the tents over, we put up a double semi-circular set of upright stockades, thus, fill in between them with mud, and make a fire. By the time the inside is burnt out, the mud is baked, and no danger of setting fire to the wooden chimney. I am very busy latterly. Am on a permanent fatigue, building a double row of abatis in front of our division line. As we cover about a mile and a half, it is no fool of a job. I have 500 men daily. Think I shall do to boss a marble quarry when I get home.

We had our muster at 9 a.m. yesterday, details ordered out at 11. I mustered the regiment - took the detail and marched out to work, but it stormed so I just sent the men back to camp; don't know but I shall get into trouble for it - hope so. Today part of the detail reported, but we did nothing. Tomorrow we must go at it again. It was quite a job I had yesterday. Took nearly all day. And now I have the rolls to examine, sign and forward. Want to get them off as soon as possible, to increase our chance of getting paid. We expect the money sometime this month, if Fessenden can get it. There is not much chance to spend money in this country - about five dollars a week for board is the total. The January Atlantic is a very good number - will forward it soon.

I received Hugh Miller's Essays last night, and judge by the address that it comes from you as a New Year's present. Much obliged. I have long wanted some such reading. We lost a mail last week, or at least the boys got the wrong tags on them and we got a New York mail, and ours has not turned up yet - will sometime - meanwhile I suppose I lost a letter from you.

Porter is rather rough on and Butler and Weitzel - blunt and sharp too. I am very much of the opinion that if he could have kept the rebels down till the 6th Corps were within 20 yards of the work that we should not have asked nay more. Pretty rough. Eaton is Lt. Col. of the 17th and reported killed; may be a prisoner. Knapp is Major. It is very cold, and my fingers are numb so long away from the fire. Goodbye. Love to all. Happy New Year.

Aldace F. Walker

Patrick Station
Jan'y 4th, 1865

Dear Father:

Our weather now-a-days seems like a Vermont winter some; it is cold and a little snow on the ground. I still have to keep my big detail at work, and to ride out over the Division these cold mornings is not a very pleasant job. Still I can stand that well enough. I am very healthy now; have enough to do to keep awake, and not enough to hurt me. We sent off our muster rolls on Tuesday morning by the Adjutant who has gone to Washington on business for the regiment. Whether Fessenden can get any money or not is a very dubious question in my mind. I have enough for the present, however. There is no formal order for "leaves" now, but special applications are continually going through. There are several now pending from officers of this regiment - Hunsdon, Templeton, Park and others, and I doubt very much if they all get away.

Dinner. We get enough to eat now, and that which is good - potatoes and onions, beef and pork, soft bread and johnny cake - but we are still destitute of our conveniences; expect them every day, and know now that they are on the way. We don't get the least bit of news. Everything is quiet on our line, though we can hear continual firing to the right and left, and once in a while a little dash is made on the picquets here. Still we sleep quiet and have not formed for a fight as yet - a very customary thing when no fight comes off. Stories are told of a big plan in Lee's brain to astonish the natives, but we can afford to wait for its development. I must ride out on my fatigue again, so goodbye.

With much love,

Aldace F. Walker

Headquarters 1st Vt. Art.
Jan. 8th, 1865

Dear Father:

We have had rain of late, but it froze hard last night and is quite frigid today. I have finished my work on the abatis - have two lines all through the Division front now. The amount of it is, as the situation looks to me, Grant merely wants to hold Lee where he is for the present, while combinations are being worked out elsewhere. The 24th A. C. has gone down the river to Wilmington again, it is said; the 8th relieved them. and Butler's canal is open, and recruits are coming in. Sherman will move soon without doubt, and everything looks favorable. When Congress passes the clause abolishing slavery, or perhaps when the States ratify it, the South will soon be subjugated; that's my idea of the progress of the war and the "coming event." I applied the other day for leave to visit Bermuda Hundred and Capt. Sheldon; received very unexpectedly leave of absence for three days, and started yesterday morning. Went to the Point and over to Bermuda, but found no John. He had been relieved and was, some said, with the Army of the James, some, out

West with Thomas. So I came back to the Point again, made a few purchases and came home. O, yes; I had your letter with the Sherman enclosure, and I waded two miles or more through six inch mud and rain, to an embalmer's office, and made arrangements with him to take up and deliver the body disinfected and in a tight coffin at Castleton, Vt.," on receipt of the pay from Mr. Sherman, $109.00 Have written to him this morning. There will be no difficulty in finding the grave.[1]

When I got home I found the box with everything in good shape. I ripped it open and had some of the butter for supper, and the sausage is a big thing for breakfast. "Res magna est," as the Herald says Lincoln quotes from Terence. I have not tried on the boots yet. Our Quartermaster's train is up at last, and we are on a civilized footing again. That mattress did see comfortable last night. It is not only softer, but warmer than a stratum of boards, and vastly more comfortable in every way. Capt. Templeton has gone home for twenty days, also Park; Hunsdon has not got away, and some other applications have been negatived. Capt. Lee is living with me now - a very fine fellow he is, too. Lieut. Macomber has got back. He got sore eyes while in Libby,[2] and is not well yet, though in good bodily health. We have not had any picquet firing in our Division at all; still it is quite frequent on the right and left. Executions occur occasionally in the 2d Corps, for desertion to the enemy. The 19th Corps is rumored to have gone to Wilmington. Porter is rumored to have taken Fort Fisher. I hardly believe either. I have got my new boots on now. They fit very well, and I am all right for foot covering now. I am still very well, and feeling quite comfortable. Hope to stay here all winter; but we shall have the wood all burnt up, and really that will be a serious question presently.

With much love to all,

Aldace F. Walker

Camp 1st Vt. Art.
Wednesday, Jan. 11, 1865

Dear Father:

After a 24 hour's rain we have a beautiful day. Quite lucky for me, as I have the Division picquet line again. All is quiet so far, but the Johnnies have a provoking way around here of making dashes on to the line in dark nights, crawling up on the sly and a hundred or so rushing on to half a dozen posts, capturing what men don't get out of the way, and then picking up the blankets and haversacks, which seem to be the principal things that they are after. They made such a dash on our front Monday morning, routing up the whole camp, but of course getting back before any force could get out to trouble them. Our picquets are in a chain of posts of six men each, some three rods apart, each post with a vidette a little advanced, and propose to keep as good a lookout as possible. They opened on the 1st Division this morning, who were laying abatis in front of the picquet line to stop such dashes. No news here as usual. Getty has returned which brings Hunsdon in command of the regiment again. He is trying hard to get home, but don't make out yet. We are getting to be very comfortable. My mattress is a great comfort, though I doubt some if I ever get it home again. I have got those earthen dishes which I bought last summer, and we are living like white folks at last. Lt. Dunham was charged with desertion through the over officiousness of somebody at Washington; has made satisfactory explanation, and is all right again. I suppose in your arrangement abut the bank stock you include the whole 16 shares. I am certainly very much obliged for the six shares you have assigned to me. I have money enough for the present, and hope for a pay day some time this month. There will be about $300 due me then. I suppose Col. Warner's nomination as Brig. Gen. Vols. was included among the thousand recently sent to the Senate for confirmation. He will return on the 12th, and I presume will have the unconditional star soon.

With much love,

Aldace F. Walker

Camp 1st Vt. Arty.
Jan. 15, 1865

Dear Father:

Since I wrote you last we have had lovely weather and the roads are hard again - and the roads in this part of the country include pretty much the whole territory. Another month has half passed away, and quite pleasantly too on the whole; and the more the time goes off, the more I think of its going and am anxious to have it away. Still I am in very great hopes of seeing our way out of the Wilderness before next September. There are all sorts of stories rife about rebel destitution and general caving in. Two days last week the Johnnies had no rations, and deserters were generally blue. It is said that Lee's army is under marching orders - to evacuate Richmond, of course - though that is what we do not want. Blair will do what he can, and he is an honest man with the good of the country at heart. Still I haven't much faith in his diplomacy, or that of any other man; but a good deal in Sherman, and a good deal in the internal dissension's that are arising, as manifested in the Examiner and Inquirer, &c. That article on the blind mice in the clock running to the devil, and on Jeff Davis' "V," is pretty rough, and a convention in Virginia would be a turbulent affair.

Even if another campaign is to come off, its commencement will see great changes in the location of our armies, and I hope great additions to their strength; and a great many high officials here say there won't be much more fighting, but I am hardly as confident as that. The "Inquirer" contains the list of recommendations laid before the Senate for promotions by brevet or otherwise - I suppose rather surreptitiously obtained, as it appears in no other paper. Meanwhile, we are a good deal interested in it, as below general officers it principally belongs to the 6th Corps. Among the generals are Getty, who is already assigned to duty and wears the straps of a Major General - Grant, who we most earnestly hope will be assigned to duty, in some nigger division if possible, but any way to get him out of here. Warner is breveted Brigadier; and though I have not seen him yet, we understand that he has been informed by Senator Foot that his name is on the table for the full appointment. Other Vermonters - Foster of the 4th, and Henry[3] of the 10th regiment, to be Brig. Gens. Then in our Brigade, Lt. Col. Floyd[4] of the 3d is breveted Col., Majors Johnson and myself as Lt. Col., Capt. Eldridge as Major, and Baxter as Capt. Baxter is aid to Grant, and proves to be a very gallant fellow. Of course all this don't amount to much even if the confirmations are made by the Senate, as neither rank, nor pay, nor strap, follow, unless formally assigned to duty by the President and this won't happen without a vacancy; still the honorable mention is worth something. There is some mistake or miscarriage about Hunsdon's nominations to the vacancies now existing in this regiment; either the Gov. don't see fit to comply, or they are lost in the mail, or there is some other slip up. I presume Warner will know something about it, and perhaps he came last night. Hunsdon is on picquet today. The rebel Col. Young is on their side of the line - the one who has such a fancy for dashes on our picquet line, and perhaps Hunsdon will have a row. Our abatis is not in front of the picquet line, as you seem to suppose, but directly in front of our breastworks. We have a complete double line now, and the picquets are about a quarter of a mile in front. We are putting up a stockade on which to set a chapel tent, which has been procured by the Chaplain from the Chris. Com. It will be ready by next Sunday.

With much love to all,

Aldace F. Walker

Sunday Morning

Dear Father:

We got orders at four this morning to be ready to move very early with four day's rations - the old picquet being left on post, and a number, minimum, to hold the posish. So we routed, and are now waiting orders to march. Don't know anything about what's up; but probably shall have no other chance to write today. I visited the 17th and the Cavalry yesterday. Saw Henry Chellis, who is very well. Went over our old fighting grounds of last summer; but could not recognize much, the country has changed so much.

Love to all.

Aldace F. Walker

Sunday 2 P. M.

And not gone yet. We made all due preparations for a move, of course, this morning; but have not had the orders yet to fall in. We drew and issued four day's rations and forage, and were ready to haul out at daylight, but no orders came, and we are still ready and waiting; begin to think we shan't go. Suppose that part of the "reserves" are off on a reconnaissance, and we may be needed to support them; but his is pretty much guess work. There hasn't been much firing of late - a little last night, and none at all today. It is not cold at all; yesterday was quite sultry. I reckon we don't want to let the enemy slip off without our knowing it. At any rate, they haven't gone yet, for they are in plain sight. We are building a new watch tower 150 ft. high, near here. I have been up 104 ft., all that is up now, and obtained a fine view of the rebel position and defenses and camps. Our Chaplain has his tent ready, but has held no services as yet; expects to today, if we don't leave before he gets round to it. As I said, I took quite a trip yesterday. Found Henry's regiment camped close to where we lay last July. Found also Lt. Sherman's grave. I engaged an embalmer to disinter the body and wrote to Mr. Sherman the terms, suggesting that he forward the money directly to the embalmer who agreed to send on the remains. But just then embalmers were ordered from the army, and whether they have Sherman's money or not I don't know. As a class they are scamps. I wrote to Mr. S. last night.

PEACE. - Are Lincoln and Seward at Monroe on a Fool's Errand? I can't think it. I want Peace, or Reconstruction, Abolition, Extension of Amnesty to all, and Repeal of Confiscation. Of course if they reenter, or renew their fealty to the United States, they assume their proportion of the obligations, and their debt must take care of itself. It is almost too good to hope for. But many indications look that way. The passage of the amendment was a glorious thing.

May peace follow.

Aldace F. Walker

Camp in Field
Tuesday Eve., Jan. 17th, 1865

Dear Father:

I had nothing in particular to do this evening, and have transcribed for your edification and delectation a song which though expressing a somewhat questionable sentiment in every point of view, and not couched in the most elegant or polished phrase, is still just now a great favorite with the boys, who think, and correctly, that it aptly and forcibly expresses their sentiments. It goes to the celebrated camp tune of "Louisiana Lowlands," with which I hardly expect you or Mary to be familiar. The "cross" referred to is, of course, our 6th Corps badge. And the words some one in the Corps of course got up, had them printed on a slip, and very promiscuously distributed among the hotels and bars of Washington, so that they have quite a circulation; decidedly ephemeral, however. We had quite a stir here last night. The Johnnies in our front began to move at 2 a.m. yesterday, and it was reported were massing on our left. But they made no attack, though both that and a general evacuation were spoken of as probable. Nothing seemed to come of it. Probably troops were sent South - to Wilmington, or Charleston, or both.

We have the Fort Fisher news today, and are cheering for Gen. and Butler most sarcastically. He is no favorite with the army, not even his "Army of the James," of which he speaks so proudly; and Gen. Terry's success[5] on the heels of his castigation by Grant for going at all, and for coming back when he did go, ought to squelch him. I suppose he forced himself on to the command Smith was to have last spring, just as Weitzel had been especially designated this time, but he was in command of the "Department of Virginia and North Carolina," and if there was any glory lying around loose he meant to have it. "Good riddance," everybody says. Grant's dispatches in the matter of the failure read splendidly. Porter is blamed severely, and Butler appears most ridiculously. It is pretty strongly rumored that the 6th Corps is going to Wilmington. This winter will see great changes in the position of our armies. Even one division of the 19th Corps has taken transports at Baltimore for somewhere - so said, and believed - probably not Pollard's. How grandly Grant is handling this thing. And the come out will be not long postponed, I think. Eldridge is discharged on account of his Winchester wound. Porter (asst. surgeon) has resigned. Warner has returned; wears his eagles yet; will have the star soon no doubt.

We still have beautiful weather; very like spring, though once in a while an uncomfortable wind blows around and through us. We had a Brigade review yesterday, and the wind made it quite unpleasant. Our picquets had a great time last night telling the

Johnnies of the fall of Fort Fisher; and everybody here is disposed to rather rejoice that it wasn't taken the first attempt, though probably it could have been with little loss comparatively. But the army feels better over and Butler's downfall than over anything else that has happened for a long while - and everybody else, save the New York Tribune. The rebels in our front are on decidedly short commons. They get nothing now but a pint of meal per day - so deserters say. Two days last week they got nothing. The conversation last night took somewhat of this form. "Halloo Johnny." "Hey, Yank." "We've got Fort Fisher." "Is that so?" "Well 'tis." "Got anything to eat?" South Carolina boys don't desert much, but those in our front are beginning to come over a little. Can't get away very well unless put on as videttes, however.

Col. Hunsdon's "leave" I understand is at Brigade headquarters, and I presume he will start for Vermont tomorrow. Leaves of absence are granted quite freely now; whether it gets round to be my turn again this winter or not, depends much on the opening of the next campaign. Still I rather expect to be able to do so. Edward Everett's death came very suddenly, and must have created a great shock all over the country. He was older than I had thought, and an eminently shining light in the country. On account of his stand for the Union in spite of all his Southern friends and connections, it seems almost too bad that he could not be spared to see peace again over the land. Perhaps he can see clearer now. I am still very well. Have a tent by myself, and a good, warm, nice bed o'nights, which is a great luxury. John Sheldon and Harley called round here the other day. John has recently been assigned to a new brigade, now at Wilmington.

With much love to all,

Aldace F. Walker

Headquarters 1st Vt. Art.
Jan. 22d, 1865

Dear Father:

What a terrible storm we had on yesterday. When w rose the ground was covered with an inch or more of ice, and the bushes and buildings were in like manner coated with frozen rain, and the rain fell and froze all day long, and rained very hard at times. It was a most severe day for anyone who had outdoor duty to perform - for guards or picquets, for instance. The rest of us laid still, of course. I suppose it is a kind of an earnest of what we are to expect in days and months to come, but it was very much more uncomfortable than a common rain storm. Our mail got in a little late last night. The Baltimore boat, with the papers, has not come up yet. "Will be her at noon." Meanwhile, we don't expect much news in last Friday's papers, as we have had the Examiner of the same date, which without saying just so, implied that Wilmington was occupied by our forces. Said that "Branchville and Charleston would soon follow Fort Fisher and Wilmington," which seemed a very sensible view to take of the case.

There are rumors of a great transfer of forces from here to South Carolina, on both sides, and the 6th Corps is of course quite definitely involved. I don't take much stock in the stories, however, as leaves of absence are given with so much freedom that a long stay here seems to be contemplated. Still sutlers are not shipping any goods to the 6th A. C., and they usually know pretty well the straws that tell the direction of the wind. Gen. Wright went away on leave last week, and Getty commands the Corps in his absence. There are now eight of our of our officers away on leave, so I reckon my turn will come again sometime. Hunsdon has got away at last, and is probably in Vermont now. Hope he will settle the question in regard to the new commissions for our regiment that have been so long pending. He made about sixteen recommendations at the time he recommended for the vacant Majority, but as there was some question about that - some "pressure" - the whole lot hung fire till that should be decided. Capt. Templeton and Capt. Sowles,[6] the rival contestants, are both in Vermont, and I presume it will soon be decided in some manner. I hope Sowles will get it. Meanwhile, a recommendation that I made only a fortnight ago, when Hunsdon was in command of the Brigade, has been filled already - for the vacancy in "B" caused by the death of Parker - filled by Cyrus Thomas, who has shown himself a brave fellow and a good soldier. On Friday I went to work and enlarged my house. Have a shanty now about 16 x 10 and quite comfortable, though only one thickness of canvas on instead of two, as my tent and fly made before. I am living alone, and have comfort enough for the circumstances and place. I am used to being a bachelor - lucky for me. The bad weather has interfered rather with the building of our chapel, and it is not completed yet, though a few days more will finish it. Perhaps if I get home the latter part of February, you will want to come back with me and see the big army. I will see if I could get you through. I am glad your "visit" came off so pleasantly and so successfully. I sent for a volume for you as my contribution, but it won't be along for some days yet - too late for the fair. I am very well and quite contented, and sanguine too of our ultimate and perhaps speedy success. Am in command of the regiment of course, but don't find much more to do than before.

With love to all,

Aldace F. Walker

Wednesday P. M.,
Jan. 25th, 1865

Dear Father:

I had utterly forgotten the day of the week and that it was my letter day till now, and I have just time for a little and in haste. I am still well, but quite sleepy today, as I was on picquet again last night - about once in two days, I believe. We have had some terrible storms of late, and they are producing quite an effect on military operations around here, as the rebel papers show - washing away dams, obstructions, etc. At any rate, they make us some trouble in that line, as well as by interfering with our mail arrangements, &c. We have had no papers since Friday - except Petersburg papers, which we get occasionally; exchanges of that sort being permitted on our side, but rather objected to by the Johnnies, who seem to be restrained by their officers, probably on account of a way we have of inserting one of Grant's orders to stimulate deserters into every paper we pass over the border. But it is quite amusing to see the confidence the picquets put in each other. One of the Johnnies was peddling tobacco to our men yesterday - cheap too. We had quite an exciting time the other night wondering what the gunboat fight was. How the guns thundered. We could see the flash against the sky and estimate the distance by the watch. But we concluded we weren't engaged, and went to bed as usual, though the firing kept up till after daybreak. This morning it was rumored again. Said to be smashing up of the Southern gunboats. But our news is very indefinite and unreliable. We shall get it from the North some day.

With much love,

Aldace F. Walker

Camp, Sunday Afternoon
Jan. 28th, 1865

Dear Father:

It has been very cold of late, and communications have been again interrupted by ice on the Potomac. First storms and fogs, and then ice. And so we shall blunder along till the opening of spring. Our mails get in twelve or twenty-four hours behind time, but papers have not come this week. I suppose because there is so much uncertainty about their getting through, and so much danger of their becoming dead-wood in case the next day's edition should get along at the same time. The last paper I have seen was the Examiner of the 24th, which contains absolutely nothing of interest, except the customary diatribe against Jeff Davis, etc., but no leaning of favor to Blair. I wish he might be the means of making peace, but I can't believe that he will. We have had no newspaper accounts of the fights on the James, but from what we can learn it was a most lucky or providential escape.

There is no doubt but that it was the springing of Lee's "big thing" he had been so long preparing, which was to "astonish the world." We had only one Monitor on the river, the rest having gone to Wilmington. The enemy came down with six, expecting to scatter our merchant fleet at City Point, burn and destroy all valuable property at the base, and so create a panic in our army and a reduction of force at certain points, and then pitch in. There is no doubt, or little, but that their preparations were made to attack that morning, if the gunboats had performed their part of the service. And it opened well for them. Our monitor turned tail and ran; didn't know as his turrets would revolve, and I suppose went back to City Point to inquire. The shore batteries did what they could, which was not much. But to the confusion of the Johnnies, the channel had changed, and Mr. Ram Fleet was stuck in the mud in his impetuous charge down the river. Grant found a man who wasn't afraid to fight the Monitor, and sent it back. Told Ingalls he might wait awhile before he sank the sutlers' schooners in the channel, and the end of the matter was that the best ram didn't go back to Richmond. That's the way we understand the story. I am very anxious to see the stories of the correspondents. What a satisfaction the removal of and Butler has given the army. And what an unfortunate man Seymour is. He commands now Ricketts' 3d Div. And you may remember his letter to the Times apologizing for Butler and Weitzel - printed at an unfortunate time, too. He talks too much with his mouth. Grant relieved him from command, but he was reinstated at Meade's urgent request. Brave enough, but always making himself ridiculous.

They persist in sending "Our Young Folks" to me, though I asked them to change the address; because I suppose in the terms under which I subscribed, "to one address" is a condition. I'll give three cents a month for the reading of it, though. The Atlantic is also on hand, and will be forwarded soon. Those dresses I have yet, and mean to bring them myself by and by. Still, I may not be able to get away, as they are getting a little more particular on the subject of "leaves." Everything is quiet in the regiment. I have changed my mess to the head quarter crowd. Have better cooks just now, and like it rather better. Had an inspection at 1 p.m. today. The Chaplain has been continually disappointed about getting his chapel tent, and has not received it yet; expects to now, tomorrow. Gen. Getty surmises that Charleston is to be merely threatened and left out in the cold, while Sherman's army is transferred to Wilmington. One corps is said to be there now. Still, Gen. Getty don't know anything about it, if he does command the 6th Corps. Wright's horse threw him. He is a very poor rider. Sent him home on leave. Macomber wishes to be mentioned. Lee was wounded in the left arm, and his brother killed at Cedar Creek. The health of the army is quite good now, and mine very. We have an astonishing amount of comfort to one uninitiated, and quietly wait for the army to move, which I hope it won't at present.

Love to all,

Aldace F. Walker

Camp of the 1st Vt. Art.
Feb. 1st, 1865

Dear Father:

We have been very much stirred up today. Very busy all the week, but especially weary today, for I was aroused at daylight to red a circular to the effect that we must be ready to march at very short notice, with six day's rations. Of course we have been soldiering long enough not to mind particularly about such an order as that, being simply marching orders, not orders to march. Still we are a good deal exercised about the chance of a move somewhere, the more so as there have been preparations making all day for a start; such as sending off the sick, all who can't march, etc., and rumors have been thick enough. The most plausible one being that the rebels in our front are either evacuating or greatly reducing their force, and a reconnaissance or an attack is expected. Then there is the Wilmington story and the Savannah story and the Welden story, and rumors enough. Alex, Stevens, &c. went North today. Hope they will accomplish something. Don't care much what, if it looks towards reconciliation.

Dr. Park came in this morning. Says the 23d Corps is passing through Washington en route for somewhere. Rumor says, and speaks loudly, that Phil. Sheridan is going to command this army, which is devoutly to be wished for. I have been playing lawyer a little. Don't know with what result, for the sentence isn't published yet - defending a fellow tried by Court martial. We had an Inspection by Division Inspector yesterday; sprung upon us suddenly without notice, through the fault of Brig. Hd. Qr., and we made a very poor appearance. I don't take any particular discredit, however, because I have not been long in command, and Hunsdon has not ordered an inspection in all winter. It is beautiful weather now; no mud, and warm. If we are to move tomorrow, I hope this fine weather will continue. No other news as I know of. I have been writing in great haste, as I expected the mail boy all the time. Can write no longer.

With love,

Aldace F. Walker

Thursday Eve., Feb. 9th, 1865

Dear Father:

We have just received a circular from Army Hd. Qrs. Directing the construction of an entrenched line through the new position our troops have taken up, and assigning the army to various positions on the line, without moving us at all. Also directing the Chief Quartermaster to extend the military railroad to conform to the new disposition of troops, etc. So the movement has ended for the present, and we are not at all affected by it - a very satisfactory arrangement to us. Our lines are much extended and straightened, bringing us in the middle instead of the end. Also the enemy are probably cautioned against sending away any forces to the South, and will require more men to hold their lines now. I thought I would write a line to say that we were all right and expect to remain so for the present. The 3d Vermont Battery has gone into Fort Fisher on our left.

Love to all.

Aldace F. Walker

Sunday Forenoon,
Feb. 12th, 1865

Dear Father:

I don't seem to have much to do today, which has not been my experience by any means for the past week. A few days after Col. H. went away, we were ordered out on Inspection by Maj. Stevens, the Div. Inspector. We had no notice at all of the Inspection, while other regiments had twenty-four hours; and besides under Col. Hunsdon's lazy management things had come to be in a very loose and slack condition, and shameful generally. He had held no Inspection for months; had done nothing towards putting the camp in shape; and in fact, I have done all the work except signing my name to papers, for a long while; and when he is around I won't do more than I can help, or more than is necessary to keep things from being positively unfit to be seen.

Well, the result was that we got a first rate notice from the Inspector as being the poorest regiment in the Division save one. A special Inspection was ordered for yesterday, and all furloughs and passes were cut off until the result of that should be made known. I have been hard at work since to get the guns and the clothing and the camp and grounds in as good a shape as possible; and succeeded, for our men used to be remarkable for their excellence in these respects, and a little pains was all that was needed to set things right again. Col. Hunsdon is expected back tonight. We have received a lot of new commissions at last - Hunsdon's recommendations filled. Capt. Sowles is Major - and I don't think of any others that would interest you especially. I presume that when Sowles comes on he will share my quarters, though I have been alone for the past fortnight, and very much prefer that way of living.

Our new mess is very pleasant, and we live well enough for any body. I went out to ride with Park yesterday. Went over towards Hatcher's run, but couldn't see much, for the further I went the more it was woods and thickets and swamps, and nothing is to be seen at all. But the lines are very much extended, and if one could understand the wheel I presume it is a big thing. It is a big thing to run any way. Many miles of corduroy have been built out through there already, and in a fortnight the railroad will be running to Hatcher's run.

Lee's account gives quite a good look to the affair for us. But I doubt if the new line is any nearer the Southside than we are at this point. It may be. Nothing can be seen any way. Early's corps sustained their old reputation by getting licked. Mahone's is the best rebel division. Deserters come in here quite abundantly. A Whole picket post came over last night, Captain and all. They hoped for "peace," but the bubble burst. How the Richmond papers try to fire the Southern heart with their war revival. Sherman will give them an eye opener soon, I reckon.

Part of the 5th corps is going on transports now. The 23d Corps is represented as being at the White House, which I hardly believe. But Sherman will have a job in the spring. I mean to try and get home before long, though I may not succeed, and it may be some time before I succeed if I make out to go. It was a beautiful day yesterday. The wind is rising today and it is getting colder; but the moon is full and our picket duty is pleasanter, though by the extension of the Corps line we have a much larger ground to go over.

The Chaplain's tent is in full blast. He opened last Sunday with a crowded house, has had evening meetings through the week, and is to have two today. He gets a good deal of reading from the Commissions and distributes, and on the whole is doing a good deal. He is a very good man in time of war, taking care of mementos and writing letters, and did a great deal of good by his correspondence while we were in the "Valley." I very much hope that this promised general exchange will come off.

All the names you see mentioned as breveted are merely recommended. When the confirmations are made, if they are made, I suppose the list will be published. I may not be able to recall all; meant to have sent you the paper, but lost it, in which they were published. Cols. Warner, Foster (4th) and Henry (10th) to be Brig. Gens., Lt. Col. Floyd (3d) to be Col., Majs. Johnson (2d) and Walker to be Lt. Cols., Capt. Wales (2d), Ballou (2d), Damon (10th), Salisbury (10th), Barber (10th) (and A. A. Adjt. Genl. of our brigade), Eldridge (11th) to be Majors, Lt. Baxter (11th) to be Captain. He is on Grant's staff. If I get away, I think some of going via Binghamton and calling a day on the Prof. Don't know how I shall ever get another chance.

With much love to all, I remain, as ever, your son,

Aldace F. Walker

Head Quarters 1st Vt. Art.

3 P. M., Feb. 19th, 1865

Dear Father:

I am just out of meeting, which we have at half past one on the Sabbath, and at half past six in the evening. The morning service is an Inspection and reading of the Articles of War. These are highly conducive to morality, though hardly founded on texts, and as they are required to be statedly read, by common consent they are read on Sundays, once a month. But the chapel is a great institution, and it seems good to go to a stated place at a stated time and attend meeting. There is always a good attendance, as Sunday is a long day with its freedom from drill, and the tabooing of certain amusements common on other days, by the common consent of the regiment. All is still very quiet here. Our new tower is finished, and I have clambered up its 150 ft. and obtained a view of the Johnnies and their works. That does not have a very consoling impression of weakness - but the coming summer will tell a great story. We have now, as the papers say, one army ahead; and if Sherman comes up to Raleigh or thereabouts and locates, it will make bad work with the dismembered Confederacy. The 23d Corps has gone to Newbern, I think for a rear attack on Wilmington, as Schofield is now at Fort Fisher.

A large construction corps is in the same vicinity - all the officers from this army (engineers) that can be spared - and locomotives and railroad iron in abundance, to give Sherman a good water base with an inland location. Then Mr. Lee will have to come out and fight somebody, and if the North will rush in the conscripts or recruits will grind 'em hard this season. A Johnny came in this morning who didn't look especially starved, and said that they had enough to eat since Lee's appeal for bread. He was trading tobacco and soap and coffee, &c., and concluded to stay - a very intelligent looking chap, too. I've been considerably interested of late in reading about the Portland church squabble. Don't know anything about the real merits of the case, but certainly the common sense of the affair seems all with the Congregationalist, and it appears to me that George L. would have done a vastly more sensible thing than he did by taking his hat and withdrawing if he saw fit. It is rather too bad the thing occurred; but if Congregationalism means anything, I go in for the whole hog. How does the matter look to you? Rather as a matter of appeal, as I've been chaffing with Little a good deal on the thing, who is inclined to favor Bishop's doctrine.

In the irregularities of our last week's mails and express, I haven't been able to see more than 2 or 300 of the said to be 1300 confirmations, and none of the Field officers at all; so I don't know what has been done with my case - perhaps you have. We missed the New York paper, and the Washington paper of the day before, and so lost the grist. Of the brev. Brig. Gens. which we have seen, we find the name of Stephen Thomas[7] and not of Warner. If that is to be the disposition of the thing, it is a shame, as Thomas is merely an old blowhard and no soldier, Vermont papers to the contrary notwithstanding.

Sunday P. M.

Well, we didn't leave last night because the Johnnies didn't. I don't know who was fooled, but the rebs certainly are in sight this morning. So we are still quiet. Deserters report a big movement of the enemy about to take place any way, it if didn't come off last night. Also they report that Lee has gone to North Carolina to visit and advise Beauregard - leaving, probably, Longstreet in command here. It is certain that they have made preparations to leave Petersburg by removing heavy ordnance, piling the tobacco and cotton ready for burning, etc. Mr. Pease, who has been a beneficiary of your Fairbanks board, is with me now, recommended by a mutual friend. His present place of residence is in Nevada. Says he has corresponded with you recently on the subject of aid. I have visited our hospitals this p.m. Find them in much better shape than I had dared to think. It is said we have the best in the army. I saw Col. Warner, who is pleased with his brevet, but feels rather sore over Thomas' appointment - with reason, too.

Goodbye. With much love,

Aldace F. Walker

Head Quarters 1st Vt. Art.
Feb. 15, 1865

Dear Father:

After a long season of pleasant weather, we have another rain storm today, and our rain storms are so cold that I suppose they correspond to Northern snow storms. It is very tedious out, and hard again on the outposts. There is no especial news to chronicle here. Expect the return of some of our officers from leave of absence - Col. Hunsdon, Capt. Templeton, &c. Hunsdon reports a good deal of snow North, and hard traveling by rail-road. I put in an application for a leave last night, and was politely informed that "only two field officers could be absent at one time from the Brigade." Lt. Col. Lincoln and Maj. Johnson being now absent of course I have got to wait until one of them returns, which will be soon; but I think that Col. Foster expects a leave next, and in that case I shall have to wait longer. Shall get round about the middle of March if the army doesn't move, and the gate isn't shut down on absences. I am not at all sanguine about getting leave at all, but shall do it if possible. I don't think that there is much show for a paymaster this month. Fessenden seems to be amazingly short of funds. Still I have a ten dollar bill left, and a 14 dollar draft, and a 15 dollar debt that I can call in at any time, and as I don't have to advance any money toward the mess, other members having been recently paid off, I am well enough off for several weeks to come - and if I get a leave, I can draw my pay of course. Our mails and papers are late again. Nothing since Saturday in the way of news, but can get papers now I suppose. Well, there is a great dearth of items this rainy day, and I will close. Much love to all. When does Belle's school close for the winter?

Aldace F. Walker

Head Quarters 1st Vt. Art.
Feb. 21st, 1865

Dear Father:

I am up late tonight, and expect to be up later, and intend to be sleepy tomorrow, and so will get my letter ready a little in anticipation. I am Division Officer of the Day again, and every man on picquet is supposed to be awake through the night. Still I am in my quarters, as being nearer the middle of the line than either end is, and mean to catch a nap or two presently, previous to making my "grand rounds." Three has been a thing or two today to very the usual monotony of picquet duty. Deserters come in quite frequently, and a conversation with them is always amusing if not instructive. In fact so many shots are fired at the deserting Johnnies that an almost continual alarm is kept up. They never fire to hit one another though, and abut twenty a day get into our Corps. Eight South Carolinians came into our Division last night. Night before last, Co. I of the N. C. Vols. Was on picquet. The captain went to sleep, and the orderly sent over an avant courier, got together his men, and marched them in guns and all, thirty-four strong. Rather a blue time, I reckon, when the captain woke up. Gen. Getty told me that 150 daily come into the 9th Corps lines.

We have Mahone in front of us - the crack division; but they are all sick of fighting and admit the confederacy to be played out. At one point on our lines there is an old rail fence midway, very tempting, as fuel is scarce. Two of my men undertook to visit it and get some fire wood, but the Johnnies gave them a volley and they broke for the rear. One of them brought in his rail though; and I guess they meant to fire high, as the bullets whistled over where I was. They are very strict on their lines - allow no one front of their posts without a guard; can't even send out videttes, for they are sure to desert; and the principal business of their officers is to watch the men. Today there has been a chopping party (rebel) of a lieutenant, 10 men and 5 guards, very near our videttes, and our men have mingled with their party, cutting on the same log. We got today's Petersburg and yesterday's Richmond papers, which admit the fall of Charleston and Columbia, but say nothing further. (We have Gilmore's[8] dispatch, by the way.) And the lieutenant allowed one of his guards to come with us, instead of going back with him. Later in the day he asked our men what we had done with that fellow "he sent over," and professed his intention to come in himself; don't know whether he did or not. But enough of the picquet line. It is a beautiful day and a clear night, and I am feeling well and contented. Things are coming to a focus in the Carolinas, and something must turn up, at the hands of R. E. Lee, and that right early. I can't get away at present, so don't watch for me. It would not be at all surprising if I failed to get away at all before leaves were shut off. A letter from Henry F. tonight says that he is going to Brooklyn soon to complete his studies. I am amazingly pleased at the way Fry and Lincoln complete the quotas. It will give the men, and no humbug, though it grinds in places. If we had a big army here today, I should feel better than I do about our present position. Still I think it is good, and the prospect certainly is glorious. Grant, as Sheridan says, has "got a twist on 'em."

Love to all,

Aldace F. Walker

Head Quarters 1st Vt. Art.
Saturday Night, [February 25, 1865]

Dear Father:

We have just received orders to be in readiness to march at a moment's notice. The enemy, it is supposed, are evacuating Petersburg, and we are to follow at once in such an event. "The Maj. Gen. Comdg. hopes that this Corps will not be behind the others of the Army," &c., making a pretty sure thing of it. The 9th Corps batteries have been all at work, but have now ceased. Speculation is rife, but on the whole useless. If Lee moves en masse South towards Sherman, we have a hard march before us. If he hopes to contract on to a shorter line around Richmond, expecting to relieve a portion of his troops, we probably have a hard battle on hand across the Appomattox. Our paymaster was expected tomorrow, but his operations will doubtless be somewhat delayed. Lt. Col. Hunsdon is in arrest, with charges preferred for outstaying his leave of absence six days. It probably will amount to little. Wish if he is to be court martialed, that charges were put in big enough to break him - which could easily be done, but it is neither my business nor my place. Meanwhile I am in command, of course. Capt. Templeton is in the same fix as Hunsdon. Sowles has reported and been mustered as Major, and the Adjutant has also returned.

I may not have a chance to write tomorrow. If not, accept this, with love from Your affectionate son,

Aldace F. Walker

Head Quarters 1st Vt. Art.
Tuesday Eve., [February 28, 1865]

Dear Father:

I meant to have got a letter off today, as I know you will be very anxious on account of the fighting that has been going on in this region of late, but I did not succeed. We have not moved at all as yet. But have been listening to the sound of the cannon all the week, and tonight about dark a heavy infantry fight came off near our left. Of the actual condition of affairs we have only the wildest rumors and speculations, but we have seen nothing as yet to make us think that anything of a serious reverse had taken place, but rather the contrary. It looks to me as though the Peace movement must have been a failure, as the army moved so suddenly Sunday morning. Sunday and Monday were beautiful days, but today has been a terrible storm - rain which froze as it fell, and wind most furious. I don't see how operations could have been conducted at all on such a day, but they evidently have been by the noise we have heard. I'll try and give you a general outline of our lines here, though of course you understand it somewhat. The Vermont brigade is on the extreme left of the 6th Corps. The present movement evidently commenced as a right wheel of the 5th and part of the 2d Corps, with the Cavalry on the flank. Then as more troops were needed, part of the 9th corps lying in reserve, and the 1st Div. of the 6th have gone in - the policy being of course to weaken the right rather than the left, which is nearest the fighting. The 3d Div. has not moved yet, and is on our right. As to what has been done we have, as I said, a great variety of stories - all agreeing, however, that a new line of works has been thrown up.

The movement was evidently a surprise to the enemy, who made very great efforts to get troops up, by the railroad, &c., and the first day's operations seem to be comparatively successful. The second day, also, it is reported that we drove the enemy, or rather that they retired to their works and we did not find them. Some say we hold the railroad, which I very much doubt. Tonight, judging by the sound, an attack was made by the enemy near where I have written the word "guess," and apparently unsuccessful; but still, the whole line may have been driven back or withdrawn, and this be the finishing up of the dance for all that we know. So little do we know about matters only two or three miles off. Nobody comes to tell us anything, and we can't leave camp, we are so liable to move.

The last papers we have had were of Saturday morning, the boats being out of time again, and the mail a day or more late. Letters are a day longer on the way now, having to go through Annapolis. I am very well now still, but rather dread pulling up and moving this weather. Wish if we have got to fight that the enemy would come here - as they were expected to do this morning, and didn't. All we know about the fight is that it may be a big thing - a move of meaning - and it may be only a reconnaissance. Shall have to wait several days and find out from New York, for all that I see; and by the way, as to the Times, our Adjutant's clerk takes the Semi-Weekly, which comes quite promptly and contains the editorials and principal matter of the Daily. It is rumored that the 23d Corps has arrived - hope so - and that the Norfolk railroad is being repaired - for what purpose, I can't conceive.

Well, that is enough about the fighting - seeing I know absolutely nothing about it, only from some deserters who came in last night, and said they had been hurried off at double quick, fought all day, lost the battle and the railroad, marched back and put on picquet, and couldn't see it, so came in. There are also foolish stories afloat of prisoners being retaken in a train of cars going South - two depots burned - a little wagon train gobbled, which I guess is true - and greys subsequently licked, which I am also inclined to believe. Our lookout here has been of great use, as the country is all level.

The death of Dea. Chatterton was certainly very unexpected. And Dea. Humphrey's family is now completely broken up. I suppose that Brainerd and Rawson will keep things along, but they can either of them or both hardly sustain the position of the father; and Emily is the head of the house hold, in every sense. I am very glad Mother has had her face cleaned out. How long will it be before she can have the use of the new set.[9] She must be in rather a curious predicament now any way.

I didn't send that Sheridan song home to be criticized, and I don't feel at all flattered by your supposition that I wrote it, for I didn't, and can write better doggerel even, as doggerel, than that is. But Phil. Sheridan would be received, if he should visit our lines, as no other man in the world could be; and that song just reflects a little of the army feeling toward him, though in a very rude way indeed. Well, this must do for tonight. If I have a chance, I'll write the rumors of tomorrow.

Wednesday P. M. It is pleasant today, though somewhat windy. Still no authentic news from the fighting; but the last report is that batteries are in a position commanding the road, and that our lines can't be driven away from their present location. That we nearly took it at one time, but failed for want of ammunition. This always makes trouble in a fight, as each man carries but 40 rounds and men are very wasteful of their cartridges. I don't regard anything we have heard as yet reliable, however, and wait for news from the North. No signs of movement on our part. I saw the 10th in camp this morning.

I have got to wait for my leave until Maj. Johnson returns. He is due now, but I don't expect him this week. Lt. Col. Tracy of the 2d, and of Middlebury, is out of the service on account of a wound received at Cedar Creek. There has been a flag of truce in front today - don't know what for. I find it a good deal easier since Hunsdon came back. Still I had rather work hard and run the mill myself than see it managed so slackly as I have to now. I had got affairs into a pretty wholesome state when he returned. Don't mean to brag - but simply state what anyone can see. I rather envy Mary in her fun over the surprise parties, and the fine sleighing that makes them possible. The weather and traveling is generally good enough her, but the comforts of society are rather limited in their manifestations. Still I think I can get along for my six months, and I hope to come home to stay next September. I had something else to tell you, but I can't think what; perhaps I shall before mail time.

With much love,

Aldace F. Walker

Oh yes - it was that we have had notice that the paymaster was coming this month. It seems as though I had said this before, however.

Head Quarters 1st Vt. Art.
March 1st, 1865

Dear Father:

Everything is calm again, and the Army of the Potomac folks are still vigorously waiting for something to turn up. Just now our great fear is that some ill luck will happen to Sherman. The rebels insist upon it that there will. In fact, last night they were sure that he had been defeated; and perhaps it is true, though I cannot think that it is so. In case nothing happens, I still hope to get a leave the middle of the month; but my chance is blocked for the present by the prolonged absence of other officers now sick at home.

I have been on Court martial duty all the week; as a witness in the cases of Hunsdon, Templeton and Sowles; and as counsel in the case of a Captain of the 5th, whom I rather think I succeeded in clearing from a serious charge. Of course we don't know any of the sentences as yet; but as Hunsdon has been released from arrest, I don't think anything serious will befall them. And tonight a lieutenant from the 2d applied to me to defend his case; but I told him I was neither a lawyer nor the son of a lawyer, and incontinently declined the honor. It's a reputation I don't hanker after - this defending scape graces - and I am going to quit it. That 5th captain I honestly believed to have been unjustly accused, and think I convinced the Court of it too. My other fellow that I "counseled" awhile ago was dismissed, as he ought to have been. The paymaster is here at work, paying to Dec. 31st.

I send Mary her Young Folks tonight, and will send the Atlantic presently. I wonder if she has as much fun getting out the rebuses as I do. The one at the top of page 219 is tip-top - the old "Honi soit," as you will see by deciphering it. Our chaplain keeps up his frequent meeting, and has awakened considerable interest in them. There are not as many desertions just now as there were last week - when 79 came in to our division in one day - among them one driving a mule team with five in the wagon. Still at the present rates, will use up the rebellion in time - and not a very long time either. About those brevets - I don't know much, and care less, for the confirmation; for it amounts to nothing at all. I presume my name was acted on with the rest, but omitted from the published list, as were Warner and Foster at first. In fact, I have not seen any list of the confirmations that pretended to be complete. The nomination is a pleasant thing. It was made at Warner's suggestion, who is quite a friend of mine.

With much love to all, Goodbye.

Aldace F. Walker

Army of the Potomac
March 5th, 1865

Dear Father:

Our rains of the past week have ceased, and today is pleasant. The ground is rapidly drying and our camp is comfortable. We are fortunate in being encamped on comparatively elevated ground. A few of the regiments to the right of us are near swamps, and in situations which certainly look unhealthy; though the health of the army is wonderfully good for so long an encampment in the rainy season. We have had but one death from our regiment since we came here - three winter months - and but little serious sickness. Our hospital, though in the field, has had a great deal of labor expended on it to make it comfortable and pleasant; and the 6th Corps hospital is one of the sights of the army, with its exterior and interior decorations. There is nothing equal to it in any of the other Corps. Still, our medical director saw fit last summer to exclude the Sanitary and Christian Commissions from the Corps, and we do not get any of the benefits of them, except what our surgeons and chaplains can get on the sly from other stations. Perhaps if this fact was generally known in Vermont she would not be so liberal in her contributions, though there are other Vermont regiments outside the Vt. Brigade. It is a mean arrangement of a mean man any way, and it always seemed to me that he overstepped his authority in sending off the distribution carts. I am very well - still trying to get home.

One of the absent Field Officers has returned, and I have now another application in, which left Brig. Head Qrs. this morning. If it succeeds, I shall get away in time to spend the Sabbath at Binghamton and reach home the first of next week. But it is very doubtful, as I should have to make the sixth in a fifth of twenty-nine, and I doubt if they give me the advantage of the fraction. Today being Sunday will retard the papers a day, as Gen. Getty does not forward papers on the Sabbath. Still, others will soon be back; and if the giving of leaves is not stopped, I am pretty sure of being with you next week.

The day does not seem to be an impediment to our paymaster, who is at work paying off the regiment. He began with the Brigade on Monday morning, and has just reached us. Is under orders to get through as soon as possible, as our last muster rolls are waiting until the payment is completed. He will be two days, at least, with our regiment. I received pay for November and December, $293.00.

We are feeling relieved about Sherman, for whom considerable anxiety has been felt for the past week; principally because R. E. Lee had gone that way - a man whom the Army of the Potomac thoroughly respect, and somewhat fear. But yesterday's Petersburg Express put the matter right, acknowledging a Confederate defeat. Still I suppose his position is an exposed one; though he has an immense army, and goes plowing along through the Carolinas like a big dog among a crowd of village curs. It's all humbug about Grant massing on the Vaughn road, &c. Trains coming from the Point are covered with returning soldiers and recruits, and the Johnnies think we are moving troops. Much obliged for your views on the Church question. It is very like my own ideas, - looking at it as it seems to be proper, and knowing nothing about the "Fathers."

Much obliged to Mary for her long letter. I read Virgil next after the Reader, but that was getting on a little too fast; perhaps Sallust would be better.

With much love to all,

Aldace F. Walker

Wednesday
March 8th, 1865

Dear Father:

I am not traveling Northward these days so much as I hoped to be, the application I made being disapproved at Corps Head Quarters on the ground that the full number allowed is now absent, as I suggested, 30 instead of 29 present being required to make up the number necessary to grant another leave. So I am waiting again. Some of the absent officers are due in a few days, however, and I shall try again then unless something turns up - which is liable to happen every day in this war time. Sheridan is on the war path again. I am thinking he'll take a long ride this trip. The President's Inaugural came to hand, and I like it much. It is unique, like everything else he writes, but none the worse on that account, and the last two sentences are eloquent. Andy Johnson seems to have been most disgustingly drunk. Col. Warner's brother Ezra,[10] a Meriden and college friend of mine, is here now on a short visit. It is rainy and disagreeable here. Rumors of depletion of the army in front, and an impending move by the Army of the James to stop it.

Love to all.

Aldace F. Walker

Head Qrs. 1st Vt. Art.
Sunday P. M., March (12), 1865

Dear Father:

We have most beautiful spring-like weather these days. I fear the ground is going to settle sooner than our comfort and ease, setting aside the national welfare, would demand. It is quite dry just around here, though some portions of the army are stuck in the mud. Another application for a leave for me goes up tonight. Four of our absent officers came back tonight, and I think that there is no doubt but that I shall get my leave if the gate is not shut down. If the papers come around right, I shall get home about the last of the week. We are busy rigging up for another inspection, and I hope to do a clean thing. Have worked all day at it so far. Our Court martial victims have all got their sentences. Hunsdon was sentenced to be reprimanded, Templeton the same, with a slight stoppage of pay. The way Getty administered the reprimand was by saying that the "sentences were inadequate and disapproved." Sowles was acquitted. He is now tenting with me, and probably finds less to do as a general thing than I do. That Captain of the 5th that I defended is also acquitted. I have got a new gold pen that I will bring home if I come. It runs so easy that I can neither write slow or plain. Wouldn't wonder if it fitted your hand. Charley Sheldon spent the night with me last night. He is hoping to get a clerkship here for a couple of months or so, for his health. John is closing up his affairs and going home soon. There is absolutely nothing going on here now - no sign of a move at all, and we seem to be very decidedly waiting for something to turn up. Phil Sheridan is at it again, and from all accounts he has got a big thing this time. If Wilson comes through from Knoxville and joins them, Sheridan can't be stopped, and will absolutely ruin Lee's arrangements for spring subsistence. Everything is concentrating on Richmond, and the time is coming. Gold seems to be tumbling, and considerable interest and confidence seems to be manifested in our new Secretary of the Treasury. The sky is bright generally, and we hope for a speedy consummation. I hear that Mary Hascall is in Washington, having married her friend and my slight acquaintance, Hall of Portland. I shall try and find her when I go through. With love to all,

Aldace F. Walker

---

1. Lieut. Merritt H. Sherman, Clarendon. KIA at Weldon River, 23 June 1864. RR.

2. A prison for Union officers in Richmond, previously a ship chandler's warehouse. Boatner, 482.

3. Col. William Wirt Henry (1831-1915). RR.

4. Lieut. Col., later Col. and Bvt. Brig. Gen., Howard W. Floyd, Springfield. 3rd Vt. Infantry.

5. USA Brig. Gen., soon to be Maj. Gen., Alfred Howe Terry, received the Thanks of Congress for capturing Fort Fisher. Boatner, 831.

6. Capt., later Maj., George D. Sowles, Alburgh. Co. K. RR.

7. USA Brig. Gen. Stephen Thomas, who commanded the 8th Vt. Infantry. James Warner would not get his first star until 5/8/1865. Boatner, 837, 890.

8. USA Maj. Gen. Quincy Adams Gillmore, commanding the Department of the South and the Tenth Corps. Boatner, 343.

9. Although it is a strange way to describe it, I believe Walker is talking about his mother having her teeth removed.

10. Ezra Joseph Warner (1841-1910), KUA 1857. KUACat., 53.

18.
Aftermath of the War
April through June, 1865

On Board Str. T. Collyer
Near City Point, Va.
Wednesday A. M. [5 April][1]

Dear Father:

I have had a most favorable trip thus far, and will try and give you a little account of it, as well as I can. Our boat is fast, and trembles so that writing will be hard. We are like to reach the Point about two, and then I shall have the job of looking for the front. I shall try and find our Quartermaster with his train, and see what will turn up. These past few days have been full of great events, though my share of them has been very humble. I have not regretted my absence till I read on the bulletin in the St. Nicholas of the fall of Richmond, and then I was very much chagrined to be away. I reached New York a little earlier than I expected, and went at once to Hoboken via Barclay St. Henry came over in the morning, and I had a good visit with him all day, attending church with Uncle, with a very cream cheesy minister, not their own, to preach. Henry staid with me that night. Monday morning I went over to New York and spent the day. Visited Charley; saw his wife. Bought a carpet bag and a glass, gloves, &c., and enjoyed the telegrams. Left at 7 for Washington. Reached there at 5:30. Went to bed immediately and got a little sleep. Called on Mary Hascall Hall. Found her keeping house, and as pleasant as ever - two rooms in a third story. Made some other calls and some more purchases, and left at three in the boat. Don't find many aboard that I know, but make acquaintances fast enough. Did not succeed in getting a berth at first, but found a man who had a whole room and divided with me; so have had a good night's rest; got along finely. I can't see where the rest of my crew are; perhaps they went down yesterday. But where is the front these days? - that is the question. And when I find out, I'll let you know.

As ever,

Aldace F. Walker

Petersburg, Va.
Wednesday Eve. [5 April]

Dear Father:

I mailed a letter to you from City Point today, telling somewhat of my journey, and will now write a little further detailing my further progress. Firstly, I have got as far towards my regiment as I expect to be able to go at present. The whole army has gone, baggage wagons and all, with sixteen days rations. When a supply train goes out, I shall of course accompany it. I reached City Point about one - spent an hour or two in fruitless endeavors to find out where the "front" was - and came on in the three o'clock train. It didn't run direct to Petersburg, as trains will tomorrow, but to Meade Station near the old

Norfolk R. R. The rest of the army line has been abandoned and discontinued; that was three or four miles from the city, and I lugged my valise and overcoat, which I concluded to bring along, getting somewhat tired, as it is a hot day. I came right by Fort Steadman and Haskell and over the Johnny works; it seemed funny enough.

When I got into Petersburg, the first thing was to find a place to lodge. I rambled around in the endeavor. First found an empty house with no furniture but a shell, which a man said I might use. Locked my duds in a closet, and rambled on. Found a house abandoned below, but occupied by a lot of nigger wenches above, where I could have a lounge to sleep on and my victuals cooked. I can buy of the Post Commissary, of course. The old wench of all says she has a husband in our army, but don't like him, and is going to have another if she can get one. Then I wandered along and found a very nice (externally) hotel, where they were letting beds without grub at a dollar a night, with a bedfellow; but the last one was gone, so I did not patronize. And on my next tack, I saw a couple of pretty girls sitting on a door step. I had just pluck enough to go and enter into a conversation with them, and after exerting myself as much as possible to be entertaining, had the satisfaction of finding that I had struck ile.

I have a good bed, and a supper - not very nice, but it would do very well for the region - good company, though terribly secesh of course - and on the whole am in a good country. Don't know as I can stay another night though, as I heard something about someone's going to occupy the room then. Rich folks and live in style. Name is Hunt. Old lady, a widow, is very much exercised about a son in Pickett's Div., which is all either gone up or taken prisoners; but as he is an asst. surgeon, I reckon he is all right. She has another son here, blind in his right eye, and had another killed. I don't find the city very much damaged, though nearly every house has been hit once or twice by our shell. They usually go right through, with no particular damage done, and I think few of the inhabitants have been struck. Some big tobacco warehouses were burnt by the rebels on Saturday. Our folks are busy in repairing the southside road, down which Grant has moved. It is a 5 foot gauge, and all will have to be changed to the 4-8. Well, I am right tired and must go to bed.

With much love, as ever,

Aldace F. Walker

Thursday Morning [April 6]

I have reported to the Commanding Officer, and been assigned to duty in command of a Camp of Distribution to organize and take to the front soldiers and officers in the city. Have a big tobacco warehouse for quarters and barracks, and a capital office, and a big thing as long as it lasts. It all seems funny enough; but I am on my dignity now, and spread myself accordingly.

Head Qrs. 14th N. Y. Heavies
24 miles from Petersburg
Saturday, April 8, 1865

Dear Father:

I worked at my camp distribution all day Thursday, as I told you in my letter from there, and was relieved the next morning by an officer of the command there stationed,

Gen. Hartsuff[2] saying that he had no authority to retain me; and I was very glad of it, for it was a thankless job, and I was very anxious to get to the front. I should have got away as soon as possible any way; but as soon as I was fairly out of that scrape, I determined to push for the "forrards." Friday morning I came across a train going out on the South Side with several other officers on board in my predicament, and I determined to push on and see what would turn up at the other end of the route.

I rather expected to find the army trains, but I didn't. The Southside road is of 5 foot gauge, and has to be changed to 4 ft. 8 inches to allow our trains to run over it; and besides has to be rebuilt very extensively where Sheridan and the 6th Corps came on to it with destructive propensities. They are pressing the work very fast, however, and have got by now where it was torn up. Expect to build about 10 miles a day, through to Burkeville, 52 miles. I came out 16 miles on the cars, which was as far as they had completed yesterday, and then was all afloat - found a division of the 9th Corps guarding the road, and a Col. said that a supply train of the 2d and 6th corps had just left for the front. Said that it had been gone for about 15 minutes, and we knew that if we could overtake that we should be all right. So we pushed for it, about 15 or 20 of us.

I had my valise (quite heavy) and my big overcoat, but soon I found a team and pitched them into it. We traveled about eight miles, and the team went on to another road before I got that far, leaving me my duds to lug. It got to be night, and I hadn't had any dinner, and the train was further and further ahead; so I just hauled off the course at this camp - found a ready welcome, as I expected. I would treat anyone well that came to my camp in such a fix. Got a good supper, and a good bed in a house near by, and a breakfast, and I am just going to wait for another train.

I expect a 5th Corps train along towards night. Pretty good time I made yesterday - 24 miles. Reckon I can afford to wait awhile. But if I had succeeded in getting that train I should have been all right. If I can't do any better, I can hire a nigger to tote my duds and plow along. The road is well guarded by the 9th Corps. We have Sheridan's dispatch telling what he did with two Divisions of the 6th Corps, and I am crazy to get to my command. Shall crowd along the best I can, and don't know when I can write again.

Aldace F. Walker

Burkeville, Va.
Monday, April 10, 1865

Dear Father:

"Lee has surrendered with 30,000 men." That is the news we have just officially received, but have not had time to fairly believe it yet. Still from the cheering around, and the music of the bands, and general jubilation, it seems a little real - though its importance is not fairly comprehended. Well, I wasn't there, but they seem to have got along well enough without me, and maybe a bullet went where my carcass might have been - who knows. Still I am somewhat chagrined to have been absent. "When this cruel war is over," the band says now. I can hardly write of myself, or think of anything but the great news for the country, and the satisfaction I have lost in not being "in at the death."

I sent you a letter awhile ago from the 14th N. Y. I am now in the 17th Vermont, stopping pro tempore with Maj. Knapp, my old classmate. Soon after writing to you before the gang came along - a thousand men rebuilding the railroad. I put my duds on the construction train, and have been working along with them to this point; as rapid a way as I could come, as we have made about 15 miles a day, reaching here about noon. Have had a pleasant journey - sleeping with the farmers on feather beds, and living with them or with the hands - and got along very well indeed. When I can get to my command, I don't know. They must be running supply trains from here tomorrow, I think; and perhaps the Corps will move this way now. - Just received Grant's dispatch ending, "We leave immediately for Burkeville." Whether "we" means the army, or headquarters, I don't know - the army probably. If so, I am all right and shall see my regiment soon. I am so overwhelmed with the news and my wonder, that I won't undertake to write further just now. Hope to see you soon.

Aldace F. Walker

Johnston must follow suit as soon as he hears the news. Smith of Wallingford, a 1st Sergt. here, has spoken to me. Is said to be a very fine fellow.

Burkeville, Va.
Thursday, April 13, 1865

Dear Father:

I am inclined to think I am getting a pretty long twenty day leave, as I left the Heavies on the 15th ult. and have not reached them yet. I reached Burkeville Monday noon - as I told you from the camp of the 17th - stayed there two nights, having a very comfortable time and a pleasant visit with a good many friends, and yesterday the Corps wagon train got along, with my regimental quartermaster and his baggage wagons along. I stopped last night with him, and the troops are expected back today. When I found that the army was coming this way, I stopped making efforts to reach them, and am waiting patiently for them to come to me. They camped 12 miles out last night. Capt. Kingsley and Charley Sheldon are close by, and it seems good to see them around. And quartermasters take along their mess kits and stoves and mattresses and comforts generally.

Clark has two cows, so that we are living happy. My mattress is in his wagon, and I expect to get somewhere before long where I can use it to advantage again. I saw little Phil. yesterday, also Custer and 34 Johnny flags. Sheridan has shaved all but his mustache, and looks better. The great speculation now is, What will the army do? Probably go to various places of importance and do duty as garrison, now we have Virginia fairly subjugated at last. I understand Meade's headquarters are to be at Richmond for the present.

Some of the officers who got to Petersburg a day later than I have reached the regiment, not stopping there as I did, but shoving along directly. Still I have done the best I could, and don't worry at all. I find that our regiment suffered very little. In fact, the Brigade has not been engaged since the fight of the 2d at Petersburg, having been with the trains and doing duty at Farmville, 17 miles above here, as Provost, for the past few days. The fight of Thursday last was by the 1st and 3d Divisions. Getty for a wonder marching in rear and not up till all was over. I understand that Wright thought the men too tired to fight on that occasion; but Sheridan put himself at the head of the 3d Division and charged with them, going through Ewell's Corps "like a dose of salts." He is the man who has the credit for the gobble, and the 6th A. C. has the credit for forcing Lee to evacuate Petersburg, in the fight of Sunday week. Lt. French of Castleton was killed; Macomber wounded severely, but not dangerously; Thomas, slightly. In fact, the losses were very much less than anyone could have hoped. I think that our regiment lost more in the fight of the 25th than of the 2d, or nearly as many, at any rate.

Col. Warner distinguished himself very much on the 25th, taking the Brigade Colors himself, and leading his men in in great shape. Lt. Bailey[3] of our regiment took our colors into the rebel works, and was complimented by Getty and put on his staff, as also was Adjt. Anson.[4] Wright noticed our yellow flag, and spoke of it to Warner. On the whole I think the boys did well, and the Corps is full of glory - happy as kings.

Love to all,

Aldace F. Walker

Head Qrs. 1st Vt. Art.
Friday, April 14th, 1865

Dear Father:

I will try and write a little more particularly of our affairs - if I can, in the confusion of officers telling stories of their fights, and the general confusion of camp noises. The army feels huge; all are happy as clams, and now quite comfortably situated. After I wrote you yesterday from the Quartermaster's tent, I took his horse and rode out to meet the Corps, which we understood was coming in. It was terribly muddy, and our Brigade was in the rear of the Corps, so I went out about five miles and waited for them.

They came along at last, and I found myself in command of the regiment, Col. Hunsdon having been put in arrest for having failed to urge his men over a bad place in the march or something of that sort - nothing serious, or that will last long, I presume. We went into camp about two miles east of Burkeville, issued rations, and today have moved on a mile further into a better camping ground. Things look very like remaining here quite a little while; and the men need rest, as the last campaign has been very exhausting.

We are in a fine piece of woods, piney and soft, with room enough and to spare; and if we are allowed to remain here, we can have a nice time while Abe is pacifying the country. I find my duds and horses all right; and am in a fair way to have a pleasant time if we aren't sent to Sherman's assistance, a thing that is possible, and rumored in some circles. We have stories that Johnston has surrendered, but nothing authentic, and no papers later than the 8th.[5]

I am very well, and hope now to reach home perhaps before September. With love to all,

Aldace F. Walker

I saw Luty yesterday. He is all right and looking well. I have received yours of the 6th with Mary's enclosure, and am much obliged.

Head Qrs. 1st Vt. Art.,
Burkeville, Va.
Sunday, April 16th 1865

Dear Father:

What terrible news the country received yesterday. We know nothing of the particulars - nothing of the affair any way, except from a telegram which was published to the army and which reached us late last night, saying that the President was assassinated at Ford's theater at 10:30 of the 14th, the wound a pistol shot through the head and that he cannot recover, and that Secretary Seward and his son were assassinated at the same time and lie in a critical condition.

Who were the assassins - what party they belong to or what creed they hold is all a mystery - and what they attempted or expected to accomplish, a still greater mystery. Of course the first impression is that it was the work of rebel sympathizers; and if so, they have most surely slain their best friends, and destroyed all hope for future mercy. If a march was to be made now by the army, it would leave a most awful trail of desolation. Other suppositions are made as to the perpetrators of the deed, and we must wait for further explanations.

Meanwhile, in any event, or with any explanation, the country has suffered a most terrible blow - the man of all others the man of the times, and the man who from obscurity has risen to secure the love and admiration of the world in a most distinguished degree. It is the most atrocious deed on record - of not only unparalleled wickedness, but of no possible palliation – no excuse. And the South is doomed. I believed in Beecher's preaching, but I don't know - and Andy Johnson don't either. Well, I wish I knew more about the affair; but in two or three days we shall get the whole particulars. We have got regular communications established with the outer world - good supplies and plenty of them - and I received this morning your letter of last Monday. We have now the Herald of the 14th and the Richmond Whig of the 15th. I am still in command of the regiment, and likely to be for the present. We are fixing up our camp again, and things look as though we might remain here a week or so.

I saw Charley Hilliard last night. He is all right. Has been through all the fighting - no wounds and very well. We have a good many back reports on hand to make, that have accumulated during the move, and are quite busy these days at headquarters. The Monthly Inspection is also to come off this week. I am afraid this is all very illegible, but I can't find a pen I can write with at all. Austin got back the day before I did, though he reached Petersburg the day after. He did not stop. I do not know of any acquaintances of yours that have suffered in the late fights.

Love to all,

Aldace F. Walker

P. S. Grant has just relieved Hunsdon. Aunt Lydia is as much of a nuisance as ever, and his wound only kept him from the Brigade on Sunday's fight. Sherman, the brother of the Lt., who has been rheumatic so much and in hospital, was with the regiment last week, and died instantly of heart disease night before last. His body has been sent to City Point.

Head. Qrs. 1st Vt. Art., Burkeville, Va.
Wednesday, Apr. 19, 1865

Dear Father:

We have received at last the full particulars of the assassinations, and had the knowledge that today was the day of the funeral. We have had all flags at half mast, a funeral salute, and a general cessation from all labor; and had also a meeting this p.m., when our chaplain gave a little of a funeral discourse. We received, just after it was over, the papers of Monday, with full accounts of the affair, and of the grief of the nation over the great affliction. It is much to be hoped that Booth cannot escape. The crime was without a parallel. I have been reading Shakespeare to find a comparison in Julius Caesar; but for all of Anthony's eloquence, there was some reason for and some sense in the acts of those conspirators. But perhaps all will yet be well. His words will be preserved as wisest counsel, and Johnson will give traitors no peace. I hope and trust that he will do well, and am thankful that Seward is spared to counsel him. Portus Baxter is here on a visit of a few days. I saw Charley today, also Hilliard, and Adams,[6] the brother of the Capt., and Winn[7] of Wallingford. Ricketts has that Division, and Seymour that Brigade just now; though I don't know as you know anything of the circumstances of the case. We had an interesting ceremony here Monday, in the presentation of rebel battle flags taken by the 6th corps to Major General Meade. I presume the papers will tell the story. Any way Meade made a capital speech, and praised the 6th Corps very extensively. And they did, as he said, "strike the decisive blow," though I must confess that he said "decissive." The Atlantic for April is not here just now, but will turn up sometime. Meanwhile I have one which I am reading belonging to Capt. Austin, and two of Bulwer's novels are also in camp. We are busy just now fitting up for the Monthly Inspection. Grant thinks if we turn out a good report, he can get a soft thing for the summer. I am afraid I shan't be able to accommodate Uncle Joel in the saddle line; shan't put myself particularly out to do it any way; and am terribly afraid he will rejoice secretly is not openly over Lincoln's death. I found Hoboken folks all well, and had a capital visit. Henry spent the Sunday and Sunday night there. I have written to Aunt concerning Luty.

Love to all.

Aldace F. Walker

Head Qrs. 1st Vt. Art. On the March
Monday, April 24th, 1865

Dear Father:

I fear you will sadly miss my customary Sunday letter this week - with good reason too, as I did not send any, and don't know when I can. I presume the papers will say something of our movement, so that you will understand what is up. We were roused at four Sunday morning with orders to move at daylight, and we moved - not towards City Point and a base, but towards the Blue Ridge and Barbarism. It was a great surprise to us; but off we went, and astonished ourselves still further by making 23 miles the first day, to Keysville. Tonight we are encamped on the north side of the Staunton, and our destination is understood to be Danville - our Commander, Sheridan. What's in the wind we can't imagine. The rebs burnt a big railroad bridge here. The cars are running from the other side to Danville. We expect to cross on Pontoons. And it is supposed that the object of our visit is to occupy the land and open the railroad. We couldn't move our cars out this way, ass the gauge is wrong. But the president of the R. R. wants to go to work again from Danville to Richmond. We set out with eight day's rations, and are having a pretty good time on the whole, though the marching is hard and the weather warm. The difficulty has been increased by marching on the railroad a good deal, to let the teams have the road. Still we made 18 miles today, stopping at 4 p.m., though we led, and all are not up yet; our column being about six hours long, teams and all. Nothing her but the 6th Corps - Gen. Wright's. While the men are on the railroad of course mounted officers can't keep with the column, so we have a good chance to bum around and see the folks. The march of yesterday was through a most desolate region, but today it has been pleasanter and richer; though most of the citizens, as is usual in Virginia, live off the roads. And what is wonderful, all, to a man, woman and child, claim to have been for the Union from the commencement. If we believe them all, there were no rebels in the Confederacy. The country is full of deserters from Johnston's army, going home. It must be entirely going to pieces. Love to all,

Aldace F. Walker

Danville, Va.
Thursday, April 27, 1865

Dear Father:

We have reached our journey's end, at least for the present; though of course we are liable to move out tomorrow and go somewhere or any where else. We think we made quite a march - 86 miles by rail and 100 by the road. We came in five days, and we got into camp at three this afternoon, though the Corps is not all up yet. We have had most beautiful weather on the trip, and on the whole have rather enjoyed it; though there are a great many foot sore men. We have marched very slowly and easily, though steadily for the last three days - made about 18 miles or more a day, and 23 yesterday; and not nearly as tired as the fist part of the tramp, when we went bumming around the railroads. I don't know exactly what we are here for, but suppose now it has somewhat to do with Johnston's operations. At any rate we have fairly got possession of Danville, and are nearer North Carolina than I ever expected to be. It seemed strange enough to go marching through the country with no skirmishing, no flanking, no picquets at night; but I suppose there is no enemy any where near us. The people are generally glad to have us come, as a protection against the guerrillas that have been troubling them, and as a partial return towards civilization. I am rather disappointed in Danville. It is situated somewhat like Burlington - on such a slope from the river Dan on the south side, but is not nearly as large or as pretty a place. It was fortified somewhat, and a good deal more work laid out, but not finished; but - there was no garrison. The place surrendered very readily and properly to our advance Brigade, and the rest of us marched through with the customary colors and bands. The season seems very much advanced - roses and lilies in bloom, and I have seen wheat headed out already. I have received your letters quite promptly. We got a mail yesterday bringing the letter which Mary mailed. But our facilities for sending out letters are not as good;

presume communications will be open soon, however. There is quite a railroad bridge to build over the Staunton - but engines and cars enough to run the road. I am very well indeed.

Love to all,

Aldace F. Walker

Saturday Morning, 29th (April)

I have had no chance to send off any mail yet, and will add another scratch to my letter. We are lucky again in our camp. At Burkeville we were in a big pine wood and had the best camp in the army. Here we are in an oak grove, and shall have a pleasant place soon. Wouldn't wonder if it was to last quite a while, too. We have received the news of Johnston's surrender, and in connection, orders for the 6th Corps to remain here till further orders. And I don't well see where we could be of more use in pacifying the country than in our present position; and I had as lief be here as any where, if the railroad is opened and communications established. I presume, however, that before long we shall be scattered by Divisions or Brigades into various places, so as to generally occupy more territory.

Now that the war in this region is over I begin to be homesick. I don't think the army will any of it be disbanded at present; and in any event, those regiments that go out in '65 will be held their full term. There is some armed force left in the southwest; and for the present, there will be danger of trouble if the whole South is not kept thoroughly under military rule. Their civil government is not strong enough at present to protect their won citizens from the marauders left loose in the country; and the respectable portion of the citizens desire an armed force in their vicinity for a while at any rate. Meanwhile it is pretty dull business for me. I don't have anything to do, except to punch Hunsdon in regard to matters that must be attended to; and I can't always get him to do even that. For instance, there have been vacancies in officers for over two months that he has made no recommendations for as yet - and other things are managed as loosely. Well, I have no especial authority - there are officers enough - and I am now very anxious to get out of the army, and to resume my studies once more.

Time spent here now don't seem to amount to much, and seems to me to be wasted, almost. With these considerations, I would go to work and try at once to get out of the army, if it were not for some reasons on the other side. Firstly, there is the $200 a month that is certainly worth having next September; and the summer is not the best season of the year to begin study again either. Still it would be worth something, of course. And then I have served with the regiment nearly my three years, and it is soon to go home any way, comparatively; and of course it would be very pleasant to finish my time and go to Vermont with the organization - and this has really, although merely a matter of feeling, a good deal of weight with me. And, on the whole, I am in a good deal of doubt as to what I had better do. That $800 matter is no small consideration, either. But this military life, with all its checks and inconveniences, is a great nuisance in time of peace. I want your ideas about the matter. We are having beautiful weather, and are all nicely off. Saw Charley Sheldon last night, and I think all your acquaintances here are well enough off.

Love to Mother and Mary.

Aldace F. Walker

Sunday P. M., 30th

I have no chance yet to send out my letter, and so suppose I can keep writing. Don't know how long it will be before we get our bridge built and our railroad opened, but suppose some time yet - some days, I mean. We have no papers later than a week yesterday, except our Danville "Sixth Corps." We seem to be farther off from the world than ever before, and in point of miles we are. Still, at the upper end of the Shenandoah there was no chance for anything but a wagon train, that came with some regularity however. Now we have no communications until we get them made. Our chief amusement now is in talking with the original secessionists around here. This vicinity is one of the strongest secession districts in Virginia; but of course they acknowledge that game played out, and say for the future, "a burnt child dreads the firs." But the great question now is, "What are you all going to do with we all, now you've got we all whipped?" And it is a pretty serious question, too, and hard to answer. I rode out yesterday fifteen miles to the west of here in Virginia, where our troops or soldiers had never been before, and created great stir and anxiety among the population, who were immensely curious to see a live Yank, and had withal a great fear of what would be done with them. We didn't molest them, of course, but the visiting was amusing enough. And we have had a very intelligent man in camp today, talking for hours. They still believe in State Sovereignty - the original evil - profess that they opposed seceding at the out set, but couldn't assist in "coercing" South Carolina, and can't imagine what will become of them and their niggers when they are let loose among them - no more can I.

Danville, Va.
Wednesday Eve., May 3, 1865

Dear Mary:

We have got a road open to our far home at last, and we received a mail last night which brought your letter of the 24th, seemingly very recently from Vermont. We have had papers of the 25th - the latest, though another train is expected soon with a variety of things pleasant and necessary. In the arrangement of the troops for the permanent occupancy of Virginia, the 6th Corps is to guard the railroad from Richmond and Petersburg to Danville. The 1st Division has gone to take up its position along the lower portion of the line, and we expect to move last, and to be left near with our 3d Brigade, which "took" Danville in the town. We have already sent Maj. Sowles with a hundred men out 16 miles toward Burkeville, and presume that the location of the command will be in the neighborhood of that portion of it which has gone. Any way, we shall go somewhere by rail, and that soon, as we have been asked how many horses we shall require transportation for. Where it is we don't much care, only the sooner we get quiet the better we shall like it. I have been down town this p.m. with Charley Sheldon, and learnt from him of Wallace Slason's sickness. He expects it will call him home. It has been quite cold here of late - much like a Northern May Day. I presume you are having frosts these days.

There is a rumor around now that the '62 men are to be mustered out first, and soon; perhaps so, but I hardly think it. I have received the May Atlantic and Young Folks. The April Atlantic I have not got hold of yet; it is at City Point. I have been requested to deliver the Master's Oration next Commencement. Shan't answer at present, and may be there, though I doubt very much my speaking; I am rather out of that line of business. Still, if I get home, perhaps I could tell a war story, and give them a little variety on the occasion. "Les Miserables" is very fine, but I presume you will enjoy it better a few years hence than you would if you read it now. I was expecting of course to go "over the mountain" when I got home, and that family party you speak of will be very pleasant indeed. I heard Katie play the Slumber Song, and like it very much. Give my love to her and Cornelia. What is the report from Harvey these days? That performance of Gen. Sherman's was certainly most remarkable, but it seems to be all right now. To think of recognizing the present State governments, and State Sovereignty, which is the back bone of the struggle. I continue very well. Had another swim today in the Dan. Hope Miss Merrifield is posted. When I get home I will read Cicero with you.

Love,

Aldace F. Walker

Danville, Va.
May 7th, 1865

Dear Father:

We have got our railroad in capital running order, I should think now; any way our mails come through with punctuality. I received on Friday yours of the 27th, and last night the one mailed the 1st; so I don't look for any more at present. Meanwhile, our mails at least go out with regularity, and I hope get through promptly. We have not moved since we came into camp here about two days ago. The only marked event has been an Inspection by Gen. Grant in propria persona, which was as much of a nuisance as inspections generally are - and all the other schemes for maintaining discipline in an army in time of peace. It has been quite hot some of the time, and quite cold some of the time - has rained once or twice - and still we lay here in the woods. At present the hot element in the atmosphere seems to predominate, and at the present writing I have for vest and coat my linen duster. The fact is, I have leaned how to make myself comparatively comfortable under nearly all changes and inconveniences, and can make a very pleasant thing of a hard campaign. Our bread box is a little short - no lack for quantity, but the usual variety is not apparent. Butter, the Danville ites profess to sell for a dollar a pound - with faint recollections of Confederate currency at its time of first depreciation - and vivid remembrances of losses to make up on "money" that has evaporated with their Jefferson D.

As near as I can make out, our Corps is gradually working off to the north along the line of railroad. We hear vague rumors of the position of other troops - 9th Corps at Alexandria, 2d and 5th to march to Washington from Richmond, 19th corps at Fort Stevens, Sherman's army at Burkeville, Nottaway, Dinwiddie - anywhere in the country, moving north in three or four lines of battle. Our 1st Division has certainly gone back as railroad guard somewhere, and I am beginning to fear that the 6th Corps is to constitute the force necessary for the proper police of Virginia after the rest are mustered out. We have received orders to discharge all sick men, and don't expect to see our paroled prisoners again. Fleming is on leave to May 17th any way, and they are all ordered to be mustered out. I see Eugene Mead frequently. He is in the 4th Vt. The 10th is a couple of miles off now. When I said "Grant relieved Hunsdon," I either meant "released" or might have added, "from arrest." I think your advice to the Prof. is wise for him, but rather rough on U. V. M. Still, the best possible, I presume, and I very much hope he will be Pres. of Midd[lebury College] next fall. Well, the great question hereabouts is, When shall we go home? It seems that a good share of the army is to leave; they may leave by corps, and they may by years. Meanwhile, we watch and wait, sure of getting home in September any way.[8]

Love to all,

Aldace F. Walker

Head Qrs. 1st Vt. Art.
Danville, Va.
May 10th, 1865

Dear Father:

We are still here and are beginning to think we are booked for quite a stay in these regions. It is rumored that Halleck has applied for the 6th Corps to remain here for six or eight weeks and that the request will probably be granted, and per contra, that the Army of the James is to do all this guard duty when they get around to it. Meanwhile all the Army of the Potomac except our Corps, are en route for Alexandria. If we are to lay around any length of time before being sent home, I would much prefer to do it here rather than in the neighborhood of Washington, because it is so much easier to control the men - no chance to get much rum or to bother us with their sprees. Still it seems rather ridiculous to keep so large a force down in here, as the people thoroughly humbled, and ready to keep the peace and subside quietly. The country is quiet and safe in these parts. This week I have made a horseback ride of eighteen miles and back with no side arms - stopped at almost every house - treated civilly, and given all I wanted for self and beast by those that had it to give. Still the people are in a wretched plight. They have their acres, and that is all. Men tell of bushels of "money" good for nothing; and a man with fifteen hundred acres, no animals, no laborers, no implements, no see, no money, is a very poor man. Such men bring their two pounds of butter to camp to exchange for sugar, and their wives have no shoes to their feet.

I think the people generally will take the amnesty oath and try to be good citizens. But one thick headed Methodist minister I saw is still rabid enough; wants to sell out and emigrate rather than "perjure" himself. I consoled him with the statement that he could not even give away his property legally without taking the oath, and left him to chew the cud. He wanted to be regarded as an alien. I insisted that he was a felon. Like to talk to 'em flat, for they can't get mad - no use kicking against the pricks; and we have the might, which is bound to make right, even if our cause wasn't just, which they are beginning to generally admit. But when the old sinner in answer to my count against the South of mob law and no freedom of speech against Slavery prior to the war, he instanced men North who had been imprisoned for approving the murder of Lincoln, my blood was up, and he was gently advised not to make that comparison again or he would get poked over. Such people are very rare, however, and speech is free - at least when backed by bayonets. I am very much surprised that you speak of Jeff. & Co.'s complicity with Booth and arraignment by the President as a "joke." It is very sober earnest to me, and much more so to Jeff's supporters, who are loath to believe it, and yet hardly dare to doubt Johnson's assurance concerning the testimony in his possession. That is the last thing needed to make them disgusted with their recent leaders, and to make them loyal, as they see they have been befooled by villains and cutthroats.

Our prisoners are all exchanged - just before Order 77 which discharged such - and are returning. They all tell of having seen this week Dick Turner in his own Libby, and in his underground dungeon too, living on hardtack and water, and a very short allowance at that, and his former victims gibing at him through the grating. Lt. Richards, a steady, quiet old fellow, says he asked him if he remembered him. "No." If he hadn't taken his money away from him last June. "Very likely." If he had ever returned it. "Probably not, but he was acting under orders." If that was a good place for repentance. "Yes." "Well, you'd better be about it, for you'll stretch hemp before many days." And that is a sample of his conversation - quite a case of retributive justice, I think. Lt. Chase has returned - now Capt. Chase. He was with Parker at the time he was bitten, and tells the horrible story - worse than I ever thought of. He was with Adams also, but retaken again. We are full of Inspections now, and that's all we have to do. Great nuisances, anyway, and I hope most devoutly that that grand Washington review will be a myth of newspaper correspondents, for soldiers hate 'em. Got your letter of the 4th last night. I remember that tomorrow is my birthday - begin to feel old. Have letters from Ellena, Alice, and Aunt Minerva. Beautiful weather.

Much love to all,

Aldace F. Walker

Danville, Va.
Sunday, May 13th, 1865

Dear Father:

We are still engaged very diligently in devising ways and means to pass the time, and with moderate success. When a change is to come over the spirit of our business I can't say. It seemed a few days ago to be agreed upon by a kind of general consent that we were to start for the North on next Wednesday, but this seems to have blown over in the same indefinite way as that is which the story started - and we may go any time, or no time. Gen. Wright has gone to Richmond, and it is likely that we may have orders on his return. The story was that the niggers were to relieve us; and still I partially believe in it, for the Army of the James is certainly big enough to garrison Virginia - now the Army of the Potomac have got it conquered. And I am very much in hopes to be in Vermont by the 4th of July. In fact, I think that it is Gen. Grant's intention - "I ask no prouder fame" - to have the Brigade on exhibition at Burlington or elsewhere on that day - which scheme I profoundly hope will be frustrated. It will be a matter of time of course to disband this big army, and if we have any heavy sitting around to do I am very willing to do it here rather than further north - seeing that strawberries are ripe and green peas beginning to be plenty, and no rum for the men.

I get letters very promptly now; have yours of last Thursday concerning my staying or going. I think the advice very good, and will hold on awhile. An officer resigning here would not get a shake at that "three month's pay proper." This day has passed away very quickly so far. We generally have a Battalion Drill at 7 a.m., but as it is Sunday I laid abed till 8. After breakfast, went down to the Dan, washed and changed my clothes, and found a mail and newspapers on my return. Then I rode into town and attended service at the Presbyterian church - the best in town, but not as good as yours - with an organ, however, very well played by a Johnny. Plain sort of a minister, and a discourse about the evil power of Satan. No allusions at all to the state of the country or anything of the kind. He announced that this was the Sabbath for an afternoon service for the colored population, which would occur at 3 p.m. I think I shall go in again and attend one of the other churches. The Methodist is said to have the smartest minister and the best singing.

If it was not for my horse I don't know what I should do, for riding around constitutes my principal employment, and loafing, wherever I go. Spent the forenoon with Charley yesterday. It seems quite pleasant to have him in the vicinity. I've been broke on postage stamps for three weeks - forgot to say so before. We are now twenty four hours from City Point, over this old rickety railroad, and seem to be quite within the pale of civilization. Have plenty of supplies of all sorts. It is said Warner has his full "star." He has worn it lately on his Brevet. Is on leave of absence now.

Danville, Va.
Wednesday Morning

Dear Father:

We are still in Danville - three weeks tomorrow, but the time of our sojourn here is nearly over. We are under orders to Manchester as fast as the cars can take us there. The 1st Division has been distributed along the railroad for some time and "will join the command at Manchester on the 20th." The 3d Division went yesterday - the last of it this morning - with two regiments of our Brigade. We expect to get away tonight or tomorrow morning. The wagons went yesterday, an wheels. Of course we are to wait at Richmond until they get around, and then it is the general and well founded understanding that we are to hoof it to Alexandria via Spotsylvania and Fredericksburg - as the others have done. We don't expect a very pleasant time on the cars, as we shall be badly crowded, and the engines are very poor and the road in bad order. Still, anything will be readily endured in preference to going over the ground again on foot. About our getting home when we get to Washington, I can't say. There is a good deal of rebellion in some parts of the South yet. Still, it may be the plan to discharge the Army of the Potomac and Sherman's troops, which have done the most of the work. Gen. Wright thinks that it is, and that the troops now assembling at Washington will be discharged en masse. Still, many think that we can't make so great a reduction of our forces at present.

Gen. Grant suggests that the Cavalry system be adopted in the Infantry as well; and that would please us of course, as it would discharge us at once, and furthermore relieve us of the necessity of going home with the rest of the Vermont Brigade, and helping to constitute a portion of Gen. Grant's "fame," than which he asks "no prouder." Mails come this way with great promptness now. I have yours of the 12th. On the whole am very glad we made this trip. We had the time to spend somewhere, and I had very much rather spend it in this vicinity than in Alexandria, as I believe I mentioned on a former occasion or two. I sincerely hope that review will blow over, and we understand that Grant has disapproved it. Don't care especially because I am ragged, but don't like such performances any way. We got a yellow paper, probably the last of the series, announcing the capture of Jeff. Hope he won't have to wait long before he takes his turn looking up a rope. Will write again from Richmond. Hope to see my Petersburg friends once more.

Love to all.

Aldace F. Walker

Head Qrs. 1st Vt. Art.
Manchester, Va., May 21st, 1865

Dear Sister:

I propose to devote a little time this Sunday morning to telling you about my journey and what I saw in Richmond. I also mean to enclose, if I don't forget it, for your especial consideration, a $500 bond, signed, sealed and delivered, the present market value of which is exactly 50 cents, and dear at that. Rough on C. S. A. and the unprotected female. And, by the way, they have a story in Richmond that we didn't catch Jeff D. after all, but only somebody who "favored him" and allowed the mistake so as to help the fugitive off. Wish them joy in the supposition, but I reckon they'll believe it when he hangs. We didn't get away from Danville till Friday morning. Left camp at five and the city at seven. Found the Richmond & Danville railroad in rather a shaky, blundering condition, and got to Burkeville about dark. The engines rattle and wheeze, and just manage to get over the ground in some way. From Burkeville we took Northern engines, and came along faster, getting to Manchester about 2 a.m.; not a very promising time to unload our men and horses and baggage, but we went at it, and after an hour or so of work, we camped down in a road near the cars to wait for morning. I spread out my blankets in somebody's clean front yard, and got up when the boys had some fresh fish and boiled eggs ready for us.

We found the brigade encamped about three miles from the river, right on the Petersburg railroad; in fact, the railroad runs about two rods in front of my tent; the regiment is on the other side. After I got my share of the work done toward making the camp, setting up the tents, etc., a party of us started for Richmond. Crossed the James on pontoons because the bridges were all burned, and turned up to the Libby. I suppose we saw about what everyone goes to see when they visit the place, and such things as one wants to see after four year's fighting to get a chance. Rather a pleasant entrance we had of it, too. Much more so than the thousands of our boys who promenaded the streets under guard, and seen the sights through a grating. We saw some Johnnies in Castle Thunder,[9] but did not stop to ask them how they liked it. Libby is empty now, and we wandered around. Found it much as I expected, only bigger, and it must have been able to hold a large number when all the rooms were crowded - not much chance for comfort either. Dick Turner has got away., Then we rode up through Main St., stopping at the Spottswood and elsewhere, rummaged over the capital thoroughly - carpeted with very poor homemade carpet, rather an affectation. Saw Lee's house and Davis's, &c. Got a good dinner with green peas, &c., at the Gen. Grant restaurant and got back before dark. But it is a much nicer place than I expected - pleasanter streets, better houses, &c. The stores are poor, but the best business portion of the city was burned in that big fire, and the burnt district looks barren enough. I want to get to Petersburg again, but don't know as I shall make out. We leave for Washington Tuesday or Wednesday, I suppose, via Spotsylvania. Presume I shall have no chance to get a letter off again till I reach Alexandria. Will write as usual if I can, of course; but expect we shall be without a base again for seven or eight or ten days. Hope to get to Vermont next month sometime.

Love to all.

Aldace F. Walker

Manchester, Va.
Wednesday, May 24, 5 A. M.

I write a line this morning to say what I suppose you will see in the papers - that our Corps starts this morning for Washington, passing through Richmond in grand style. The 24th Corps is moving down now to look at us, and we are to start directly. It is a most beautiful morning, and bids fair for a pleasant march. We have had heavy rains the last few days, and I presume will have pleasant weather now. I was in Richmond again yesterday, and have a pretty good idea of the place. Have also visited Fort Darling and the famous vicinity on Drury's Bluff. Warner is full Brigadier now, and Fleming is out of the service. If any more commissions are to be issued I shall have one, but I shall take care not to get mustered. We have had to send in a report of the number whose time expires before Oct. 1st. Still, it is the general opinion around here that the Vermont troops will go home together - which I most sincerely hope not.

Love to all.

Aldace F. Walker

Head Qrs. 1st Vt. Art.
Sunday, May 28, 1865

Dear Father:

My date is not at all distinct as to geographical locality - in fact I have a very indefinite idea as to where we are, save that it is about twenty miles south of Fredericksburg and stuck in the mud. We aren't making a particularly rapid journey this trip. Started off fast enough, but got brought up standing presently. I tried to mail a letter from Richmond giving the date of our starting, but don't know whether I succeeded or not. We left on Wednesday, breaking camp early, and passing in review before Gen. Halleck about 10 o'clock. Nothing very noticeable about that operation anyway, except that everybody didn't seem to know what was up or where to find it. The principal part of the population, to be sure, were the niggers, as usual. The white secesh keep very close there as yet - naturally feeling very sore, and still retaining a good deal of their chivalrous pride. After we got out of Richmond - presume the papers will chronicle our passage there - we pushed on twenty miles to Hanover Court House, striking for about a mile the scene of our journey last summer, when we destroyed the Va. Central R. R. on the 29th of May. Camped after dark, and moved on at five the next - Thursday morning. Crossed the Pamunkey on pontoons, and marched to Chesterfield, about fifteen miles. The march might have been easy, but we took a short cut, and lost about four miles, and in hurrying to catch up tired our men all out, so that the march was one of the hardest we have ever had.

We passed Chesterfield last year in our movement from the North Anna, and our breakfast there on Friday morning was just a year to an hour from our former meal in the same field. Well, to proceed - on Friday it rained; in fact it rained all Thursday night and Friday and Friday night and Saturday and Saturday night; and haven't we had a sweet time? And it don't rain now, but the wind is in the northeast. Friday we waited for the rain to stop till 8 a.m., when we came on, our Division leading the Corps. We got two miles and stopped in the mud, and the wagons have not all got up yet. A good many of the troops couldn't get through on Friday but got over the streams the next day. Folks North don't have any idea of such storms as this. It rains harder, the ground in two hours becomes porridge a foot deep, the streams and brooks rise in half a day so that horses can scarcely get through them. There are several streams between here and Alexandria that we shall have to pontoon. Five days out, and we have made 40 miles. Hope for better luck when we start again - tomorrow, I suppose. We have smuggled a wagon into the Head Qr. Train, and have our tents and dry clothing with us; if it wasn't for this, I don't know what we should do. Existing orders have reached us that will send us to Vermont from Washington just as soon as we can complete our records and make our rolls. This will probably take a fortnight. I still hope to be home by the 4th of July. I think the rest of the Brigade will have to stay. We muster out 696 officers and men, including about 50 one year men, and leave about 700 behind, many of whom will be mustered out from hospital. Love to all.

Will send this when I can.

Aldace F. Walker

Hd. Qrs. 1st Vt. Art.
June 3d, 1865

Dear Father:

We got round from Richmond to our present camp in ten days, with no delay save two days in the mud. And rather a pleasant march on the whole, that is as pleasant as such a march could well be; immensely fatiguing; the marches were not excessively long after the first day, and on the whole the trip was well managed. We did not have an opportunity to see any of our old fighting grounds. We went west of Cold Harbor and east of Spotsylvania. Noticed various places where we crossed the track of our former marches, but saw none of the battlefields. We stopped one night at Fredericksburg, a place of great interest to a good many in the Corps, but of very little to me. I met Joseph Smith while there on his way to Richmond looking over the ground. Shouldn't wonder if he was thinking of investing a little in Southern land. We got into camp here yesterday afternoon. Have received a mail since with letters from you quite late, and we got another mail the day before at Fairfax. Still there are some back days that we have not received. We are in camp near the rest of the Army of the Potomac, at Bailey's Cross Roads nominally, and really somewhere in the slashing south of the Potomac. We are, I suppose, about six miles from Long Bridge, and about three miles from Aqueduct Bridge and Georgetown. Col. Hunsdon has gone to town this p.m. I shall try and go the first of next week. Need some summer clothing very much, and hope to be able to square my government accounts. We are in a passable camp, and can easily and comfortably spend the few weeks remaining for us in Virginia. We have received a certificate from Gov. Smith, who is now in Washington, that he has issued commissions to our regiment. His certificate is as good as the document to obtain muster on, or to put on the strap. But the commissions can't come till he goes home and signs them - as follows: Hunsdon, Colonel; myself, Lieut. Col.; Templeton and Safford, Majors. I think we will all be mustered, as the organization is ordered to be discharged as soon as it can be got ready, and there will be no show to keep us. Still there is, of course, a little chance that I should have to resign in order to get away, and so lose the three month's pay proper, if I accept muster on the new commission; very little indeed, however, and I presume I can fix it all right with the mustering officer who runs the wheel. There is a little doubt, however, as to whether musters can be made into these regiments who go out under the Oct. 1st order. The question has been referred and awaits decision. Any way, I shall be Lieut. Col. on the State Records. Thwing is out of the service, also Capt. Lewis, and several others - discharged in hospitals. It will take us from two to four weeks to get ready to get away, and the chances are now that we shall go home alone, much to our satisfaction. The 9th, 10th and 11th Vt. Regiments go out now, and no others, according to the existing orders.

Aldace F. Walker

Hope that Mother will have a good time with her teeth, and that Mary will survive her experiment of playing in church.

Head Qrs. 1st Vt. Art.
June 7th, 1865

Dear Father:

We are not at all likely to perish of ennui these days while waiting for our discharge, that is if they keep us as busy hereafter as they have for the last few days. We don't get to work at all yet on our muster out papers, because we have had no chance, and tomorrow will be the tiresomest day of all the year, we anticipate. After that is over we think we shall settle down to our work, and are quite sure of being in Vermont by the 1st of July. I was in the city on Monday and Tuesday. Had a good deal of business of one kind and another. Expect to be able to settle my accounts next week some time, so as to avoid a journey hitherward to get my pay after I have been to Vermont. I took tea at Mr. Blagden's Monday eve., and found the same family there which I used to visit when at Brightwood. I rode up to Fort Stevens in the night and looked the country over, natural enough it looked too. But it was a terribly hot day. I got a linen coat and a thin trouser and a straw hat and cloth shoes, and took considerable pleasure in my citizen's attire - so much so that I keep it on in camp in view of my expected promotion to that sphere where one can wear any clothing he chooses.

And, by the way, I introduce here as a parenthesis the most important part of my letter. I am played out of money, besides having borrowed a good deal. If I could get mustered in on my new commission, for which I now wear the straps, I could draw my pay; but he prospect of our speedy exit from the service of Uncle Sam blocks that business, and so I am in the lurch. I shall have about $1000 coming to me when I leave the service; and with my present liabilities, it will cost me about $200 as near as I can calculate, to get out. If you can raise the money, I wish you would send me a check for that amount. We have not leaned where in the State we shall rendezvous - probably at Burlington or Montpelier - the former, I hope. The 9th and 10th go home about the same time, I suppose, and we may have a consolidated celebration; though as to that I presume we feel less interested than the good people of the State. We were reviewed today about four miles from here by Gov. Smith and staff. We comprising this Brigade, the 10th and the Cavalry. The 8th is now in the Brigade and camped near us. Pollard is all right as far as visible. Tomorrow is the grand 6th corps thingumbob in Washington, of which I presume the papers will make some mention. We have to leave camp at four a.m., and shall hope to get back by four p.m., though it is somewhat to be doubted. It will make a march of about twenty miles, and will be immensely tedious. Our place is just in the middle of the column. We fixed up in a new camp on Monday, and have now a very pleasant place; are ready to see our friends if any happen along.

Hoping to see you all at home soon, I remain, as ever,

Aldace F. Walker

Ball's Cross Roads
June 11th, 1865

Dear Father:

We are making very slow progress in our endeavors to get out of the service; everything seems to combine against us; the chief trouble being that the mustering officers of the Corps and Division are both new men in their posts, and know very little of their business, besides having very little original brightness whereon to build any future knowledge. We have not even got hold of the blanks yet, because the above excellent officials have not become able to give directions as to how they should be made out. We have got our books, however, about ready for examination, and have nearly made one copy of the descriptive roll of men who are to remain in the service. Three more copies of this remain, and six copies of a muster out roll, embracing the names and history of every man who has ever been connected with the regiment. I still hope, however, to be in Vermont by the first of July. I have been mustered as Lt. Col. Don't know whether I can draw pay or not, but hope so. The officers all go out when the organization is discontinued. There is, however, an effort being made to retain four companies with a Battalion organization of heavy artillery. In that case I thought my chances to be disbanded would be better as Lt. Col. than as Major.

We had our 6th Corps review on Thursday, and a terrible time it was too - by far the hottest day of the season. We left camp at 4 a.m., marched six miles, crossed long bridge, and massed in Maryland Avenue. We were about the center of the column, and when we started we had about a mile to march in a terrible dust before we reached Pennsylvania Avenue, which had been well sprinkled. The men worked hard, and kept up well till we had passed the reviewing officer, and the review was called successful. But then when we commenced to move off by the flank, through Georgetown and across Aqueduct Bridge, before halting, it was too much, and the men were all the afternoon getting to camp, pretty much everyone on his own hook. I got the colors and a few men here by 2 o'clock, and just then a terrible thunder storm came off, which cooled the roads and the air so much that no especial damage was done. But I never suffered more from the heat than that afternoon while mounting Arlington Heights. The review of Wednesday by the Gov. was quite a success, everything being comparatively comfortable, and passing off well. I have received your letter of Thursday.

Our regiment is getting pretty well demoralized, now that the term of service is so near out. I am getting very impatient at the delay in going home, and at the inefficiency displayed in doing the business. Still time will bring it all about, and I presume it is as well after all. It is more for the sake of the men than my own that I am anxious to get off, for most of them can earn more money elsewhere, and I can't. Besides, I have a great antipathy to seeing business drag as this appears to. I presume the 10th will get away this week. The Cavalry I understand has gone, the portions which remain in service being detailed for "frontier duty" whatever that is.[10] With love to all,

Aldace F. Walker

Head Qrs. 1st Vt. Art.
June 14th, 1865

Dear Father:

Our mail facilities are very good now. I have already received yours of the 12th, and wonder that you don't receive my letters more regularly. I haven't much to say as I know of, except that we have got fairly at work on our muster out rolls and are getting along as well as could be expected. I hope to start for Vermont in about two weeks. After we get through with these immense rolls we have discharges for every man to make out, additional transfer rolls of men that remain, &c., and then we shall have to wait some days for the mustering officer to do his part of the work on the papers, then send up to Army Head Qrs. for an order for our muster out, then do that job, then send again for transportation, and wait until we can get it.

I think all this will take a fortnight, and my old expectation to get to Vermont about the first of July will be correct. We are hurrying all we can to get away. We are having some rain these days and the weather is not very comfortable.

With much love to all, I remain,

Aldace F. Walker

Saw Charley Hilliard yesterday. Presume they will get home before we do, as the regiment is smaller.

Union Hotel, Georgetown.
June 18th, 1865

Dear Father:

I have had rather a busy Sunday of it today. I hope that the time for such extra work is nearly by. We are getting our rolls nearly done, and, as I think I told you before, I have the supervision of it to do. Today we have been comparing them - proof reading - and studying them over. Have got half through the regiment, and mean to get our documents into the mustering officer's hands by Tuesday. I think it will take about two days more to get through this end of the rope. After that though it may not take so long, as he says he is ready to go right to work on our papers - a thing I did not expect.

I applied for a pass for Monday, and got it this evening for today, good for twenty four hours. So I came in, and shall try and draw my pay and settle my accounts tomorrow. I went across the street, and went into a church where services were just commencing, and found an ordination ceremony - heard a sermon by Dr. Gurley. I hope and expect that one Sunday more will finish up my Southern Sabbaths. See by the papers that our regiment was expected in Burlington on the 12th inst. Hope they will have a pleasant time waiting for us. I have fixed on the 1st of July all the time, you know.

Love to all,

Aldace F. Walker

Wednesday Evening- our mustering officer has received instructions to muster us in. If he does so, we can draw back pay. At any rate, you need not send the check at present. We are to be discharged at Burlington.

Head Qrs. 1st Vt. Art.
June 21st, 1865

Dear Father:

I expect a letter from you this p.m., but as I have a little leisure now just before dinner, I am disposed to write my letter now. I sent a line from Georgetown on Monday morning - rather hastily written and under rather difficult circumstances. I was in Georgetown Sunday and Monday nights, coming out to camp before breakfast Tuesday. And the fact is, I had rather sleep under canvas on a bed of poles than in any bed there is in Washington, or any where else, this time of year. We have had some very heavy thunder storms yesterday, but my tent is perfectly dry, and always cool and comfortable. I think when I get home I shall spread my buffalo in the front yard o'nights. When I was in the city in bed I couldn't sleep after 5 a.m. Here I have no trouble in sleeping till eight, save that the flies bother a little. While in Washington Monday I settled my accounts, or rather settled at them. Got through with the Ordnance Department all straight and clear, and got a sight at my papers in the W. M. Dept. It takes an application ten days old to do that. Found that they had lost four months of my returns - from January to April, 1864. So I had to go to work and make "approximate" returns for the lacking months, which took all day; but I approximated near enough to dispose of all the accountability which appeared, and got the documents in again, flanked by powerful affidavits, which will puzzle them to read. They promised to send them at once to the examiners, and that I could hear the answer on Thursday. I propose to go down on Friday and find out about it. I drew my pay as Major to June 1st, the time when I was promoted, and so have money enough now. We sent up our papers to the mustering officer this morning, and if we don't have any of them to make out over again, we shall be able to get away next week sometime. I am somewhat afraid that part of them will have to be duplicated. In that case, of course we shall be delayed. I still expect to reach Vermont by the 1st prox., the day I have always stuck to. It is the understanding now that the remnant of our regiment are to be consolidated into an artillery battalion and sent to the defenses again; nothing official, however, is known now. I send a few photographs; want to look up one or two more. The 9th we understand have gone home. The 10th can't get away much before we do, if we are not delayed by a repetition of papers.

Love to Mary and all.

Aldace F. Walker

----

1. Aldace missed the break-out at Petersburg on April 2, 1865; he had been on furlough since March 15; among other things, he carried the "shot-torn colors of the regiment, under which two color-sergeants and fifteen corporals had been killed or wounded in the campaigns between Spottsylvania and Cedar Creek." Benedict, 2:385.

2. USA Maj. Gen. George Lucas Hartsuff, commanded the defenses of Bermuda Hundred, Dept. of Va. and N.C. (Boatner 382).

3. Lieut., later Capt., George A. Bailey, Woodstock, Co. M. RR.

4. Adjutant Charles H. Anson, Montpelier. RR.

5. CSA Gen. Joseph Eggleston Johnston, commanding the Army of Tennessee, did not sign an armistice with Sherman until April 18, and did not surrender until April 26. Boatner, 441.

6. Qm. Sergt., later Lieut., Henry H. Adams, Wallingford, 10th Vt. Infantry. RR.

7. Private Joseph H. Winn, Wallingford. Co. C, 10th Vt. Infantry. RR.

8. The regiment mustered in for three years U.S. service on September 1, 1862. RR.

9. A converted tobacco warehouse in Richmond, used by the Confederates for political prisoners during the war. Boatner, 131.

10. "Frontier duty" turned out to be duty in St. Albans, Vt. and different points in northern New York until August 9, 1865, a continuing reaction to the St. Albans Raid, October 19, 1864. RR.

Aldace Freeman WALKER
In Later Years
(Walker Family Collection)

19.
Aldace Freeman Walker
A Biographical Sketch
by Roberts Walker.[1]

TO THE HONORED MEMORY OF

ALDACE FREEMAN WALKER

LT-COL. 11TH VT. INF. U.S. VOLS.

AN UPRIGHT LAWYER

AND LEGISLATOR.

A FAITHFUL SOLDIER

AND PUBLIC OFFICER.

AN ABLE ADMINISTRATOR

OF IMPORTANT RAILWAY

INTERESTS.[2]

Vermont has produced many men who have attained eminence within her boundaries. Many more, and, we believe, a greater number than can be claimed as native by any but the most populous states, have achieved success and distinction in wider fields of activity in the country at large. They had gone out to work under conditions often more exacting than such as prevail at home. Their success, however, has been the result of the same qualities, — vigor, devotion to duty and a high sense of honor — that have characterized our resident men of mark. A transplanted Vermonter who illustrated these qualities in a preeminent degree is the subject of this obituary.

Aldace Freeman Walker was born in West Rutland on May 11th 1842. His father was the pastor of the Congregational Church of the parish then comprising the western portion of the town of Rutland. Mr. Walker's ancestry was entirely of the English strain that has made the bone and sinew of New England.

Aldace F. Walker's boyhood was passed in West Rutland. The local schools and Kimball Union Academy at Meriden, New Hampshire, gave him his preparation for college. He entered Middlebury College, graduating in the class of 1862. Always a quick and thorough student, he stood at the head of his class. For almost a year before graduation, he had been trying to enter the army. The last months of his college course were spent in enlisting and drilling recruits for the Eleventh Vermont Infantry, of which regiment he was commissioned First Lieutenant on August 13, 1862. By reason of his military duties, he was almost too late for the commencement exercises, and delivered his valedictory address amid great enthusiasm in the uniform of his rank.

The Eleventh Regiment was assigned to duty in the defences of Washington. For a year and eight months, it was kept employed in constructing and garrisoning Forts Slocum, Stevens and Totten. The regiment's work was good; its discipline was thorough. Lieutenant Walker was made a Captain in December 1862. The regiment began its field service in the spring of 1864 and was engaged for eleven months in hard fighting. It was attached to the Old Vermont Brigade on May 15th 1864, near Spotsylvania Court House, Virginia, and was in every battle fought by the Sixth Corps from May 1864 to April 1865. Its engagements included the battle of Cold Harbor; the repulse of General Early's attack on Fort Stevens, the battles of the Opequon, Fisher's Hill, and Cedar Creek, in Sheridan's brilliant Shenandoah campaign; and the winter's siege of Petersburg. Captain Walker commanded the Second Battalion of his regiment at the beginning of its field service. In July 1864, he became a major. On April 20, 1865, he was breveted Lieutenant-Colonel "for distinguished gallantry in the several engagements in the Shenandoah Valley." He was commissioned Lieutenant Colonel in June 1865, and was mustered out holding that grade during the same month.

Colonel Walker was a gallant soldier. His heart was thoroughly in all his work, — in the humdrum duties of the camp with its daily drudgery and drill as well as in the stress of active campaigning. His men admired and trusted him. His superior officers relied upon him. He never lost sight of the true purpose of the War nor ceased to hope for an ultimate happy outcome of the bloody struggle between the States.

Colonel Walker made it his pleasant task, soon after the close of the war, to write a brief history entitled: "The Vermont Brigade in the Shenandoah Valley." Simple, soldierly and straightforward, it is an absorbing narrative of the magnificent service of that unique Brigade, which suffered a greater loss of life than any other brigade in the Civil War.

At the close of the War, Colonel Walker re-entered civil life and took up the study of his profession. He read law in offices in Wallingford and Manchester and in the office of the Hon. George F. Edmunds at Burlington. He completed his studies under the inspiring tuition of Professor Dwight of Columbia College, and for seven years practiced in the office of Strong & Shepard in New York City. Upon the death of the head of the firm, he was offered a partnership with a surviving member, Elliot F. Shepard, but at that time, he was weary of the city and felt drawn toward his native town. In 1873, he removed to Rutland, having accepted a partnership with Ex-Judge John Prout, who had need of a vigorous young man competent to relieve him of the burden of a large docket of important causes. The court work fell principally to him, in the firm that was successively known as Prout, Simons & Walker, Prout & Walker, and Walker & Swinington. His practice was general, but toward the end of his Vermont career, he was chiefly engaged in equity causes involving patents and railroads. He was one of the leading counsels on the side of the Vermont and Canada Railroad Company in its prolonged litigation with the Vermont Central Railroad Company and the various holders of the securities of the two corporations. That he was fully occupied is indicated by the record in volumes 46 to 59 of our reports, in which he or his firm are mentioned as counsel in ninety-four cases. As a lawyer, he was quick to comprehend and marshal related facts, resourceful in choosing the methods of attack or defence, and was a sound, logical debater. He was President of the Vermont Bar Association in 1884-1885, and during his term of office read to us his capital paper on the Dartmouth College case, entitled "A Legal Mummy."

In these years at Rutland, he was at the same time observing the traditions of his ancestry. He was often moderator at town meetings. For several years, he was an energetic school commissioner. His management of the Rutland Musical Festivals made them events of artistic importance for northern New England. An engaging and forceful orator, he made addresses on Decoration Day and other public occasions. He was a helpful member of the Congregational Church. In 1882, he served his county as State Senator. He was a faithful and influential member of an unusually able Senate, and, as chairman of the Judiciary committee, was leader and spokesman in the consideration of many measures of unusual importance at this Session.

Upon the creation of the Interstate Commerce Commission, President Cleveland appointed Colonel Walker in April 1887, one of the five commissioners. He served for two years. The commission's work required organization under and interpretation of a statute unlike any previously enacted by the Congress. Commissioner Walker speedily mastered the difficulties of this new work, and was known as one of the strongest members of the Commission. His opinions, of which he wrote his full quota, are well reasoned and clear. His strong qualities came out no less distinctly in the administrative work of the Commission, and his services in connection with the auditing and statistical bureaus were noteworthy.

In 1889, he resigned his public office to become the Chairman of the Interstate Commerce Railway Association, a rate-maintaining organization composed of most of the railroads operating from Chicago to the West and Southwest. This Association was succeeded by another called the Western Traffic Association, of which also Colonel Walker was the Chairman. During the life of these two organizations, he lived in Chicago, always growing in reputation for character and ability and increasing his wide circle of friends and admirers. Among other activities, the Chicago Literary Club and the Military Order of the Loyal Legion were gainers by his efforts. He was one of Vermont's Commissioners to the world's Columbian Exposition in 1893.

At the dissolution of the Western Traffic Association, he was for a time one of the commissioners of the Joint Committee of the Central Traffic and Trunk Line Association, comprising railroads between Chicago and the Atlantic seaboard. As in the other two associations, his duties were mainly to sit in arbitration upon rates made by the various lines running between the same points or between the so-called "common points." It was work that constantly called for nice balancing of complicated facts and for the equitable application of the principles underlying the Interstate Commerce Law. It was in the nature of things that these organizations should successively disintegrate by strifes between their members, as the desire to obtain the most business by competitive methods seemed always to raise superior to the desire to maintain rates at a fair and identical level. But that Colonel Walker was chose to preside over the western organizations and later over their eastern counterpart needs only to be stated to demonstrate the high confidence place in him by the railroad managers.

For a few months in 1894, he practiced law again in Chicago and New York, chiefly in connection with the Interstate Commerce Law and corporation problems, matters in which he was becoming a widely recognized authority. On September 1, 1894, he was appointed one of the receivers of the Atchison, Topeka & Santa Fe Railroad Company and its allied lines, then consisting of over ten thousand miles of road. Of the three receivers, one died soon after and the other was forced to remain much of his time in the east, so that Colonel Walker was the active head of the Atchison system during the receivership. His record was brilliant. The rehabilitated and greatly improved system was reorganized toward the end of 1895, and Colonel Walker was made the Chairman of its Board of Directors and of its Executive Committee, with offices in New York. This position he held until his death, on April 12, 1901. As a mark of respect, no successor to him has ever been chosen to fill the office of Chairman of the Board. The resolutions adopted by his fellow directors are fitting here, for they illustrate with emphasis that even mere business relations with him could not long continue without inspiring affection for his sympathetic and lovable qualities as well as respect for his conspicuous abilities:

Throughout his whole honorable career, in his early practice as a lawyer in his native State of Vermont, during his meritorious service in the Union army through the civil war, and later in the various responsible positions that he filled, Colonel Walker was distinguished for uprightness and honor in all his dealings and for faithfulness to duty. He was a man of unusually large information, and his mind was notable for the rare qualities of fairness, tolerance and sound judgment. In all the important positions which he held, as a lawyer of high rank, as a member of the Interstate Commerce Commission, as chairman of the Western Traffic Association and of the joint committee of the Trunk Line and Central Traffic Association, as receiver of the Atchison, Topeka & Santa Fe Railroad Company, and as chairman of this board he performed all his duties with credit to himself and to the satisfaction of all. The wide range of his official duties and his cordial human sympathies brought him into personal relations with a very large number of people, and he was always so courteous in manner and so kind in feeling that everybody who knew him became his friend. Sorrow for his death will be felt widely and with unusual sincerity, and by none more keenly than by his associates on this board.

Turning from practical affairs Colonel Walker occasionally contributed to magazines and professional journals articles upon public questions the tenor of which is indicated by the following titles to his contributions published in the "Forum":

Operation of the Interstate Commerce Law

Unregulated Competition Self-destructive

The Western Traffic Association

Recent Labor Rulings by Federal Courts

Has the Interstate Commerce Law been Beneficial?

Anti-trust Legislation

The Preliminary Report of the Isthmian Canal Commission.

Colonel Walker was married to Katherine Shaw of Wallingford, Vermont, who survives him. The remaining members of his immediate family are two sons; Roberts, a lawyer in New York, Harold, a lawyer now residing in the City of Mexico; a daughter, Ruth Elsa, and a sister, Miss Mary Walker of Northampton, Massachusetts.

To rise rapidly in fortune is not unusual in this country. It seems to be a typical American characteristic to shift easily from one department of business activity to another without special training for any. But in trade and commerce, a young man, once launched, is receiving through his daily task a training to take further steps in the same general direction.

The case with Colonel Walker is different. His stride from a country law office to become arbitrator and prosecutor in matters of interstate commerce was a long one into a new field, and he not simply occupied the new position — he filled it. His next employment as umpire between warring interests of great railway systems as represented by their managers, — men of large technical experience and marked general ability, the service requiring from him a growing expert skill in traffic problems and knowledge of the conditions of railway competition, was indeed an abrupt transition from the professional life for which he was educated and equipped. And yet, again, to assume the managing directorship of a trans-continental railroad, including its finances, was an unusual experience for a lawyer who, in his own behalf, probably had never engaged in any financial operations whatever beyond the investment of his savings. No one but a man of remarkable intellectual grip and comprehensive ability could have successfully met, within the limit of a few years, such ever changing an increasing responsibilities. On the surface, it would seem that he had no special training for the public transportation service in which he distinguished himself. Fundamentally, it may be that he had some such preparatory discipline through the general practice of the law, in which there is a daily demand for the application of the principles of justice and common sense to facts and conditions as varied as the changing colors of the kaleidoscope.

The moral qualities of Colonel Walker also counted for much. His position in the railway association was made for him because he was known to be fair and just as well as able, and he was honored by a place at the head of the Atchison system because he was honest and so was relied upon to give to the stockholders a business administration and not a speculative one.

In person and manner, he carried weight. From the beginning of his active life, the first as well as the continuing impression made by him was that of a man of force and character. He was not called upon to prove himself but was at once accepted at a high valuation. His admirable self-confidence, far removed from petty conceit, carried him easily through large undertakings, and, as he felt himself equal to any task that came to his hand, no one doubted him or feared for him.

As seems appropriate to the occasion, emphasis has been placed in this sketch upon the serious side of Colonel Walker's character as expressed in his strenuous life and as understood and appreciated by the public. But his friends of the inner circle must here miss an adequate portrayal of the human of him - his big heart, his loyalty in friendship, his quiet constant unselfishness, his abounding hospitality, and his highmindedness. His short life was a full one. A rapid worker, he seemed always to have time for the amenities and had intellectual interests in many directions. Hearty and often jovial he enjoyed the society of friends. He had knowledge as well as taste in literature and music. The picture of him, so often seen by his intimates, that will remain most vividly in the memory of many of them, is of the busy many of affairs, the center of the life of his home, surrounded by books, newspapers and periodicals, both grave and gay, and sharing the laughter, music, and merry din of the young people of the household.

----

[1] This is the transcript of an annotated final draft of a biography of his father, by Roberts Walker, for the National Cyclopedia of American Biography on February 20, 1916.

[2] Epitaph on Aldace Freeman Walker's tombstone, Evergreen cemetery, Rutland, Vt.

Appendix A
The Forts Surrounding Washington.

The First Artillery, Eleventh Regiment Vermont Volunteers were stationed in the northeast quadrant of the Defenses of Washington, north of the Potomac River, from September 1862 until mid-May 1864. From east to west, Forts Lincoln and Thayer straddled the Bladensburg to Baltimore Turnpike and the Baltimore and Ohio Railroad, south-southwest of Bladensburg, Maryland. Forts Thayer and Saratoga straddled the Old Bladensburg Road, followed by Forts Bunker Hill, Slemmer, Totten, Slocum and Stevens, which guarded the Seventh Street Road between Washington, D.C. and Silver Spring, Maryland. Between, behind and before these forts were a series of armed and unarmed batteries, part of a total of 163 installations that surrounded Washington.

Fort Lincoln, ¼ mile east of the Bladensburg Road and 4 miles from the Capitol., was named for the President.

Fort Thayer, ¾ mile west of Fort Lincoln and on the west side of the B&O Railroad track, was named for Colonel Sylvanus Thayer, of Massachusetts, the "father" of the United States Military Academy.

Forts Saratoga, 2 miles southeast of the Military Asylum, and Bunker Hill, 1 3/8 miles southeast of the Military Asylum, were named for Revolutionary War battlefields.

Fort Slemmer was named for Lieutenant Adam Slemmer, a Pennsylvanian.

Fort Totten, ½ mile northwest of the Military Asylum, provided protection for the Military Asylum area, including the President's summer house. It was named for Brigadier General Joseph Totten,[1] Chief of Engineers, U.S. Army.

Fort Slocum, 1 ¼ miles north of the Military Asylum, was named for Colonel John S. Slocum, 2d R.I. Infantry, who was killed at First Bull Run.

Fort Massachusetts, named by a Massachusetts brigade, was later expanded and renamed in honor of Brigadier General Isaac I. Stevens, who was killed at Chantilly, Virginia, on September 1, 1862, was 1 ¾ miles northwest of the Military Asylum.

Source: Benjamin Franklin Cooling III and Walton H. Owen II, Mr. Lincoln's Forts: A Guide to the Civil War Defenses of Washington, (White Mane Publishing, Shippensburg, Pa., 1988), pp. vii, xi-xii, 156-185, 241.)

----

[1] USA Brig. Gen. and Bvt. Maj. Gen. Joseph G. Totten. He died on active duty April 22, 1864. Boatner, 843-4.

Appendix B.
Glossary.

The following abbreviations and terms have been used either in Walker's letters or in endnotes and occasionally benefit from expansion or explanation.

A.A. A.G.	Acting Assistant Adjutant General
A.A.G.	Assistant Adjutant General
A.C.	Army Corps
Adjt.	Adjutant
Ag.	Agricultural
Art'y	Artillery
ATS	Andover Theological Seminary
Aub.TS	Auburn Theological Seminary
Bat./Btry	Battery
Brig. Gen.	Brigadier General
BTS	Bangor Theological Seminary
Bvt.	Brevet
Capt.	Captain
Cav.	Cavalry
Col.	Colonel
Corp.	Corporal
D.C.	District of Columbia
DC	Dartmouth College
Dea.	Deacon
Dept.	Department
Dutchmen	Germans
G.C.M.	General Court martial
Gen.	General
Hon.	Honorable
KIA	Killed in Action

KUA	Kimball Union Academy
Lieut.	Lieutenant
Lieut. Col.	Lieutenant Colonel
Lieut. Gen.	Lieutenant General
Lt. Col.	Lieutenant Colonel
Maj.	Major
Maj. Gen.	Major General
MC	Middlebury College
MWIA	Mortally wounded in action
N.C.O.	Non-commissioned officer
NTS	Newton Theological Seminary
NU	Norwich University
Orderly	Orderly (1st) Sergeant
Prof.	Professor
P.V.	Pennsylvania Volunteers
Regt./Rgt.	Regiment
Sergt., Sgt.	Sergeant
Wdd	Wounded

Bibliography

Ayling, Augustus D., Adjutant General. Revised Register of the Soldiers and Sailors of New Hampshire in the War of the Rebellion 1861-1866. Concord, N.H.: Ira C. Evans, Public Printer, 1895.

Barr, John L., compiler, The Genealogy of Ethan Allen and his Brothers and Sisters. Burlington, Vt.: Ethan Allen Homestead Trust, 1991.

Bedell, Henry E. Diary, January 1 to September 12 1864. Original manuscript from the Collection of Ed Italo. Available from http://vermontcivilwar.org/1bgd/11/bedell-diary.shtml; Internet.

Benedict, George Grenville. Vermont in the Civil War, A History of the Part Taken by the Vermont Soldiers and Sailors in the War for the Union, 1861-5. Burlington, Vt.: The Free Press Association, 1886.

Boatner, Mark Mayo. The Civil War Dictionary. New York: Vintage Books, 1988.

Brainerd, Dr. Ezra. "Dr. Brainerd's Tribute." Fine Tributes Paid Late Ex-Gov. Mead. Clipping from an unidentified, probably Rutland, Vermont area newspaper, dtd January 16, 1920.

"Col. Walker's Funeral," Rutland Herald, Tuesday morning, 16 April 1901.

Cooling, Benjamin Franklin III. Symbol, Sword and Shield: Defending Washington During the Civil War. Shippensburg, Pa.: White Mane Publishing Company, 1991.

—. Jubal Early's Raid on Washington 1864. Baltimore, Md.: The Nautical & Aviation Publishing Company of America, 1989.

— and Walton H. Owen II. Mr. Lincoln's Forts: A Guide to the Civil War Defenses of Washington. Shippensburg, Pa.: White Mane Publishing Company, 1988.

Crockett, Walter Hill. Vermont, the Green Mountain State. New York: The Century History Company, 1921

Dyer, Frederick H. A Compendium of the War of Rebellion, 1861-1865. Des Moine, Iowa: The Dyer Publishing Company, 1908. CD-ROM edition, Guild Press of Indiana, 1996.

Fox, Lt. Colonel William F. Regimental Losses in the American Civil War 1861-1865: A Treatise on the Extent and Nature of the Mortuary Losses in the Union Regiments, with Full and Exhaustive Statistics Compiles from the Official Records on file in the State Military Bureaus and at Washington. Albany, N.Y.: Albany Publishing Company, 1889. CD-ROM edition, Guild Press of Indiana, 1996.

Glazier, Nelson Newton. Biography and Correspondence. Available from http://vermontcivilwar.org/1bgd/11/nng1.shtml; Internet.

Haynes, E.M. A History of the Tenth Regiment, Vt. Vols. With Biographical Sketches. Rutland, Vt.: The Tuttle Company, 1894.

Hearn, Chester G. Six Years of Hell: Harper's Ferry During the Civil War. Baton Rouge: Louisiana State University Press, Baton Rouge, 1996.

Hoffman, Elliott W. History of the First Vermont Cavalry Volunteers in the War of the Great Rebellion. Baltimore: Butternut & Blue, 2000.

Kimball Union Academy, Meriden, N. H. General Catalogue 1813-1930. Hanover, N.H.: Dartmouth Press, c1930.

Jenkins, Mark F. "The Iron Captains," Ironclads and Blockade Runners of the American Civil War, available from http://www.ameritech.net/users/maxdemon/ironcapt.htm; Internet.

Laas, Virginia Jeans, ed. The Civil War Letters of Elizabeth Blair Lee. Urbana, University of Illinois Press, Urbana, 1991.

Leech, Margaret. Reveille in Washington. New York: Harper & Brothers, 1941.

Onions, C. T. The Shorter Oxford English Dictionary. London: Book Club Associates, 19863.

Peck, Theodore S. Revised Roster of Vermont Volunteers and Lists of Vermonters Who Served in the Army and Navy of the United States During the War of the Rebellion, 1861-66. Montpelier, Vt.: Press of the Watchman Publishing Co., 1892.

Picerno, Nicholas P. "Courageous and Faithful: Kimball Union in the Civil War." Kimball Union Magazine. Meriden, N.H.: Kimball Union Academy, 1997.

Poirier, Robert G. By the Blood of our Alumni: Norwich University Citizen-Soldiers in the Army of the Potomac. Mason City, IA: Savas Publishing Co. 1999.

Ripley, Edward H., "Memories of the Ninth Vermont at the Tragedy of Harper's Ferry, Sept. 15, 1862," Personal Recollections of the War of the Rebellion. New York: G. P. Putnam's Sons, 1912.

Reunion Society of Vermont Officers. Proceedings, 1864-1884. Burlington, Vt.: Free Press Association, 1885.

Robinson, Duane L. General Catalogue of Middlebury College. Middlebury, Vt.: Middlebury College Publications. 1950.

Sifakis, Stewart. Who Was Who in the Union: A Biographical Encyclopedia of more than 1500 Union participants. New York: Facts on File, 1988.

Toomey, Daniel Carroll. The Civil War in Maryland. Baltimore: Toomey Press, 1983.

United States Congress. Biographical Directory of the United States Congress, 1774-Present. Accessed several times between 1/8/2002 and 1/20/2002, available from http://bioguide.congress.gov/biosearch/biosearch.asp; Internet.

United States War Department. The War of the Rebellion: A Compilation of the

Official Records of the Union and Confederate Armies. Washington, D.C.: Government Printing Office, 1880-1901. CD-ROM edition, Guild Press of Indiana, 1996.

Walker, Aldace Freeman. "The Old Vermont Brigade." Military Essays and Recollections, Military Order of the Loyal Legion of the United States. Illinois Commandery, Volume 2. Chicago: McClurg, 1894

—. "A Rebel Heroine." Military Essays and Recollections, Military Order of the Loyal Legion of the United States. Illinois Commandery, Volume 4. Chicago: 1907.

—. The Vermont Brigade in the Shenandoah Valley, 1864. Burlington, Vt.: Free Press Association, 1869.

Washburn, Peter T. Report of the Adjutant & Inspector General of the State of Vermont, from October 1, 1863, to October 1, 1864. Montpelier, Vt.: Walton's Steam Press, 1864.

—. Report of the Adjutant & Inspector General of the State of Vermont, From Oct. 1, 1864, to Oct. 1, 1865. Montpelier, Vt.: Walton's Steam Printing Establishment, 1865.

—. Report of the Adjutant & Inspector General of the State of Vermont, From Oct. 1, 1865, to Oct. 1, 1866. Montpelier, Vt.: Walton's Steam Printing Establishment, 1866.

Wert, Jeffrey D., Gettysburg Day Three. New York: Simon & Schuster, 2001.

Index

A

B

C

D

E

F

G

H

I

J

K

L

M

N

O

P

R

S

T

U

V

W

Y

ISBN 1-55369-394-9

9 781553 693949